Financial Management for Public, Health, and Not-for-Profit Organizations

THIRD EDITION

FINANCIAL MANAGEMENT FOR PUBLIC, HEALTH, AND NOT-FOR-PROFIT ORGANIZATIONS

Steven A. Finkler, Ph.D., CPA

Professor Emeritus of Public and Health Administration,
Accounting, and Financial Management
The Robert F. Wagner Graduate School of Public Service
New York University

Prentice Hall

Boston   Columbus   Indianapolis   New York   San Francisco   Upper Saddle River
Amsterdam   Cape Town   Dubai   London   Madrid   Milan   Munich   Paris   Montreal   Toronto
Delhi   Mexico City   Sao Paulo   Sydney   Hong Kong   Seoul   Singapore   Taipei   Tokyo

Library of Congress Cataloging-in-Publication Data

Finkler, Steven A.
  Financial management for public, health, and not-for-profit organizations / Steven A. Finkler.—3rd ed.
    p. cm.
  Includes bibliographical references and index.
  ISBN-13: 978-0-13-607073-3 (casebound)
  ISBN-10: 0-13-607073-6 (casebound)
    1. Finance, Public—United States.   2. Finance, Public—United States—Accounting.   3. Health facilities—
United States—Business management.   4. Nonprofit organizations—Finance.   I. Title.
HJ257.2.F555 2009
658.15—dc22

                                                                                    2008054706

Editor: Julie Broich
Editorial Director: Sally Yagan
Editor in Chief: Eric Svendsen
Product Development Manager:
  Ashley Santora
Editorial Project Manager: Kierra Kashickey
Marketing Assistant: Ian Gold
Permissions Project Manager: Charles Morris
Senior Managing Editor: Judy Leale
Production Project Manager: Kerri Tomasso
Senior Operations Specialist: Arnold Vila
Operations Specialist: Carol O'Rourke

Art Director: Jayne Conte
Cover Designer: Lisbeth Axell
Cover Illustration/Photo: VisionsofAmerica/
  Joe Sohm
Manager, Cover Visual Research & Permissions:
  Karen Sanatar
Composition: Integra Software Services, Ltd.
Full-Service Project Management: Thistle Hill
  Publishing Services, LLC
Printer/Binder: Hamilton Printing Co.
Typeface: 10/12 Garamond

Credits and acknowledgments borrowed from other sources and reproduced, with permission, in this textbook appear on appropriate page within text.

Pearson Education Ltd., London
Pearson Education Singapore, Pte. Ltd
Pearson Education, Canada, Inc.
Pearson Education–Japan
Pearson Education Australia PTY, Limited

Pearson Education North Asia, Ltd., Hong Kong
Pearson Educación de Mexico, S.A. de C.V.
Pearson Education Malaysia, Pte. Ltd
Pearson Education Upper Saddle River,
  New Jersey

Prentice Hall
is an imprint of

PEARSON

www.pearsonhighered.com

10 9 8 7 6 5
ISBN-13: 978-0-13-607073-3
ISBN-10:   0-13-0607073-6

BRIEF CONTENTS

CONTENTS

PREFACE

Today, perhaps more than at any time in the past, managers and policy makers of public service organizations must have a working knowledge of financial management. This does not mean that all managers and policy makers of government, not-for-profit, and health care organizations must be financial managers. However, they cannot simply rely on others to be aware of the financial issues that involve the organization. All managers must be able to understand and make use of financial information.

This book provides a foundation in financial management to allow people to understand and use financial information. The intent of the book is not to make the reader into an accountant. Rather, its goal is to provide enough of the language and tools of financial management to make the reader conversant in the field. The primary goal is to provide the skills necessary to use financial information rather than the more technical skills needed to generate that information. However, one must have some sense of where numbers are coming from to be able to beneficially interpret and use those numbers. The book strives to provide that conceptual foundation.

One of the skills that all users of financial information must have is a strong financial vocabulary. The fields of accounting, finance, and public finance are heavily laden with jargon. Any accountant can bury a nonaccountant in debits and credits, journals, and reversing entries. A major emphasis of this book is on providing a working vocabulary for communication, so that the reader can develop the ability to ask the right questions and interpret the answers.

In addition to vocabulary, this book describes a wide variety of methods, processes, and tools of accounting and finance. They are not described in sufficient detail for the reader to fire the treasurer and controller and take over their jobs. (How many of you really want to do that?) Instead, there is sufficient detail so that the reader can comfortably use the wide variety of financial reports that are generated in the typical organization. Also, the user of this book will have an awareness of the techniques available that can provide information to help improve decision making.

What are the typical types of organizations with which this text is concerned? The focus of the book is on the financial management of government, health, and not-for-profit organizations. Most financial books are oriented toward the for-profit corporate sector. Historically, they have had a heavy emphasis on manufacturing or financial markets. Recently, as the service sector of society has grown, there has been some shift in financial management toward service industries. However, government, health, and not-for-profit organizations are not typical service industries. The public sector that these organizations represent has developed its own financial management style and rules. Unusual public sector accounting approaches, such as fund accounting, heighten the challenge of studying financial management. As a result, it is vitally important to have a targeted book, such as this one.

Some users of this book will indeed want to go further in the field of financial management and gain a specialized knowledge. Those persons will need to be able to not only use but also generate financial information. Some of the more technical aspects needed by those individuals are contained in the appendixes to a number of the chapters in the book.

It is the author's hope and belief that this book fills a void in a number of ways. First, a substantial effort has been made to present all the material the target audience needs, while not including excess material that would obfuscate more than it would clarify. The balance of being sufficiently inclusive to adequately cover the topic and yet not so inclusive as to overwhelm the reader is a difficult one. It is one that the author has devoted substantial efforts to achieve.

Second, the book has been written with an awareness that there is substantial movement of managers among the three sectors covered in this book. For example, Stanley Brezenoff moved from being executive director of the Port Authority of New York and New Jersey to become the president of Maimonides Medical Center in New York. Dr. Jo Boufford, the past dean of New York University's Robert F. Wagner Graduate School of Public Service, has not only worked in not-for-profit education but also as the president of New York City's Health and Hospitals Corporation; as the director of The King's Fund, a not-for-profit foundation; and as the principal deputy assistant secretary for Health in the U.S. Department of Health and Human Services. Public service is a broad concept. Often people who enter public service find that their careers take unexpected twists and turns, moving from one part of the public sector to another. By providing information on government, health, and not-for-profit organizations, this book provides the user with the background needed for future opportunities in public service careers that may as yet be beyond the reader's imagination.

Third, this book presents the order of material in a revolutionary way. It is believed that the order of presentation of material used in this text will substantially improve the learning process. Historically, accounting education has predominantly been targeted to those going into public accounting with the primary goal of becoming Certified Public Accountants. As such, the elements of accounting most necessary for public accountants are taught first. Financial accounting, an area primarily involving the generation of information to be reported to people outside of the organization, is generally taught before any of the elements of managerial accounting. However, most readers of this text will be managers, rather than auditors. Their needs are oriented toward getting and using financial information to make decisions and manage effectively. Most managers will be exposed to budgets long before they ever see their organization's audited financial statements. Therefore, the book reverses the normal order of most financial management texts, providing the foundation of managerial accounting before the discussion of financial accounting.

The order in which the material is presented in this book is unique yet logical. The process of developing a plan for the future, implementing the plan, controlling operations to keep to the plan, reporting results, analyzing results, and using that information to improve future plans is the normal flow of financial information within an organization. It is the way that most managers deal with financial information. In testing this book in the classroom, it has become apparent that this flow also helps readers get a better grasp of the entire financial management process.

The book is organized as follows. Chapter 1 provides an introduction and overview of financial management. The chapter also provides background information on the primary sources and uses of money in the public sector. The text then moves on to the organization's mission and the planning process in Chapters 2 through 6. A variety of budgeting techniques are discussed, as well as cost behavior. Managers must create a plan for the coming time period. Once made, plans must be implemented, with an effort to run the organization efficiently and to achieve its goals. Implementation and control issues are discussed in Chapters 7 and 8. These chapters focus on the management of short-term resources and obligations, and on issues of accountability and control. Managers need feedback to measure whether actual results are varying from the plan, so that midstream corrections can be implemented. This feedback, in the form of variance reports, is also discussed in Chapter 8. At year-end the organization needs to aggregate the events of the year and prepare a report of what has transpired. This report contains a set of financial statements, which are discussed in Chapters 9 and 10. Special reporting concerns of health, not-for-profit, and governmental organizations are addressed in Chapters 11, 12, and 13. Finally, managers must analyze these results to understand the organization's financial position and how well it has done. Financial statement analysis and financial condition analysis are covered in Chapters 14 and 15.

This new edition is accompanied by materials on the Web. Both Instructor and Student Resources are available at: www.pearsonhighered.com/finkler. If there are problems with the link, please contact me directly at steven.finkler@nyu.edu. The online materials include:

- Student Resources

  Glossary
  Homework-related material

- Faculty Resources (available to instructors only)

  Word document solutions to all assignment material
  Excel templates for selected homework problems. These may be made available to students at faculty discretion.
  Excel solutions to selected homework problems
  A test bank
  Updated and expanded PowerPoint class notes

Many excellent suggestions were received from colleagues around the country for this third edition. I have tried to incorporate material related to as many of the suggestions as possible. I regret that due to space limitations, I was not able to include discussions related to all of the fine ideas that were received.

The new edition has been updated throughout, and many additional homework problems and cases have been added. In addition to the greater range and number of homework problems and cases, the most important change in this edition has been the separation of each of the old Chapters 5 and 12 into two chapters. Chapter 5 was divided into two parts to allow for a clearer focus on the capital budgeting decision separate from the long-term financing decision. The discussion of cost-benefit analysis, which is primarily a capital budget technique, has been moved from Chapter 3 to Chapter 5. Chapter 12 was divided in order to allow a separate focus on recording government financial information in contrast to reporting financial results.

Other key additions include the addition of or expansion of discussion related to:

- Behavioral Aspects of the Budget Process [Chapter 2];
- Expanded cash budgeting discussion and example [Chapter 2];
- Expanded break-even analysis discussion applying the technique to solving for fixed cost, price, and variable cost [Chapter 4];
- Sarbanes-Oxley [Chapter 8];
- Balanced Scorecards [Chapter 8];
- Controlling Quality including Total Quality Management, Six Sigma, and Quality Control Charts [Chapter 8];
- Triple Bottom Line Performance Measurement [Chapter 8];
- The Form 990 [Chapter 8];
- Integrating Case Studies [Chapter 8];
- International Financial Reporting Standards [Chapter 9]; and
- The Accounting Cycle [Appendix 10-E].

For the most part, however, I have taken an approach of "if it isn't broken, don't fix it." I have received many favorable comments about the current structure and content of the book, and I tried to make only those changes that would enhance the book's usefulness for the largest number of users.

This book was a major undertaking. The results were substantially improved by the valuable comments and suggestions made by my colleagues and students. I offer my thanks to my many colleagues at the Wagner School and around the country who reviewed the manuscript and made important suggestions, including Thad Calabrese, Bob Purtell, Khaled

Amin, Emily Crawford, Tim Ettenheim, Santa Falcone, Francesca Frosini, Patrice Iatarola, Dick Netzer, Pam Ouellette, Yousuf Rahman, Mark Robbins, Amy Schwartz, Bill Voorhees, Shanna Rose, Dall Forsythe, and Robert Winthrop. I am grateful to Laura Hoguet who reviewed all of the assignment material for the second edition. Special thanks go to Dwight Denison, Marty Ives, Bernard Jump Jr., Ken Kriz, Dean Mead, William Moore, Robert Purtell, Ross Rubenstein, and Leanna Stiefel, whose efforts went beyond the call of duty. I would also like to thank the publisher's reviewers, whose comments led to a number of improvements: First Edition—Tom Courtney, U.C. Berkeley and University of San Francisco; Stan Davis, St. Joseph's University (Phila., PA); Rev. Albert J. DiUlio, Santa Clara University (CA); William Zelman, University of North Carolina; Second Edition—Harwell Herring III, Utica College; Ken Milani, University of Notre Dame; and Laura Peck, Arizona State University; Third Edition—Chaman L. Jain, Indiana University School of Public and Environmental Affairs; Robert Bartolacci, Carnegie Mellon Heinz School of Finance; Ken Milani, University of Notre Dame, and an anonymous reviewer. Ken Milani has been particulary generous in allowing me to include some of his material on budgeting and also on the unrelated business tax.

Bernard Jump Jr. of the Maxwell School gets the medal of valor for having used the earliest drafts of the first edition of this book with his classes before even the most obvious and significant errors were removed. His tenacity in going through a number of different drafts of the book and his conceptual and technical comments throughout the process were invaluable.

My thanks also go to Dwight Denison, Robert Purtell, Ed Roche, Louis Stewart, and Drew Franklin for specific valuable contributions to the book. Dwight Denison authored a number of homework problems that appear at the end of chapters throughout the book, as well as the Ponderosa case study at the end of Chapter 15. Robert Purtell prepared the first version of most of the PowerPoint class notes as well as many of the case studies that are used in the text. Special thanks to Khaled Amin for compiling the problem bank in the second edition.

I would like to thank the entire Prentice Hall team for their remarkable job in getting this book to the reader. I thank my editors, Eric Svendsen and Julie Broich, and Project Manager Kierra Kashickey for overseeing the entire project. Production Project Manager Kerri Tomasso managed the production process and Angela Urquhart and her team at Thistle Hill Publishing did a fantastic job copyediting and paging the manuscript. I would also like to thank Charles Morris, Permissions Coordinator.

Any errors that remain are my responsibility. I welcome all comments and suggestions. Please feel free to contact me by email at: steven.finkler@nyu.edu

Steven A. Finkler, Ph.D., CPA
Professor Emeritus of Public and Health Administration, Accounting, and Financial
   Management
The Robert F. Wagner Graduate School of Public Service
New York University
New York, NY

ACKNOWLEDGMENT

Portions of *What You Should Know About Your Local Government's Finances: A Guide to Financial Statements*, copyright by the Governmental Accounting Standards Board, 401 Merritt 7, P.O. Box 5116, Norwalk, Connecticut 06856-5116, are reproduced with permission. Complete copies of this document are available from the GASB.

CASE EXAMPLES

Throughout this text there are running case examples regarding the Town of Millbridge, the Hospital for Ordinary Surgery, and Meals for the Homeless. These organizations and their managers are fictitious, and any similarity to any real organization or person is strictly coincidental.

ABOUT THE AUTHOR

Dr. Steven A. Finkler is Professor Emeritus of Public and Health Administration, Accounting, and Financial Management at New York University's (NYU) Robert F. Wagner Graduate School of Public Service (NYU/Wagner). At NYU/Wagner he headed the specialization in health services financial management for over twenty years. An award-winning teacher and author, Dr. Finkler is engaged in a variety of research topics in the areas of economics and accounting.

Among his publications are nineteen books, several of which are *Accounting Fundamentals for Health Care Management* (with David Ward, 2006), *Finance and Accounting for Nonfinancial Managers*, 3rd ed. (2003), and *Cost Accounting for Health Care Organizations*, 3rd ed. (with David Ward and Judith Baker, 2007). He has also published more than 200 articles in many journals, including *Health Services Research*, the *Journal of Public Policy and Management*, and *Healthcare Financial Management*.

He received a Bachelor of Science degree in economics (dual major in accounting and finance) and Master of Science degree in accounting from the Wharton School at the University of Pennsylvania. His master's degree in economics and doctorate in business administration were awarded by Stanford University.

Dr. Finkler, who is also a Certified Public Accountant, worked for several years as an auditor with Ernst and Young and was on the faculty of the Wharton School before joining NYU. He is a member of the Executive Board of the International Society for Research in Healthcare Financial Management, former member of the Editorial Board of *Health Care Management Review*, and is currently treasurer and a member of the Board of Governors of Daughters of Israel Geriatric Center. He served as editor of *Hospital Cost Management & Accounting* for 12 years, and is a past member of the National Advisory Council for Nursing Research at the National Institutes of Health (NIH). He consults extensively, both around the country and abroad.

1

Introduction to Financial Management

The learning objectives of this chapter are to:

- define *financial management*;
- define *accounting* and *finance*;
- discuss the sources and uses of resources in the public sector, including the federal government, state and local governments, health care organizations, and not-for-profit organizations;
- explain why public service organizations should be concerned with financial management;
- explain why public service organizations should earn profits; and
- introduce a hypothetical ongoing example to be used throughout the text.

INTRODUCTION

This book is written for current and future public service managers and policy makers. Each person working in such a capacity will need to generate and/or use financial information. This includes persons working for governments, health care organizations, and not-for-profit organizations. Some of these individuals will become financial specialists and will use this book as their introduction to the field. For many readers, however, this book may be their only formal exposure to the concepts of financial management.

By the end of this book, the reader should be comfortable with the basics of financial management. That means that the reader should be able to read and interpret financial information, and perform straightforward financial analyses. The reader should also have an appreciation for some of the things that financial management can do and know when to call upon a financial expert. Most importantly, the reader should have an improved ability to use financial information in making decisions.

Even those individuals who do not expect their careers to focus primarily on financial issues will find that an understanding of basic financial concepts is essential. Today, nearly all organizations are dependent on having adequate financial resources. Economic theory teaches the need to allocate scarce resources among competing uses. Financial management provides information about how scarce those resources will be and how they will be or have been used. It gives managers tools that will aid them in achieving the broad and specific goals of the organization.

1

This chapter begins with an overview of financial management and public finance; they are defined and discussed. The chapter next moves on to examine public sector resource flows. Where do each of the major public service sectors get their resources from, and what do they spend those resources on? The chapter then addresses the question of why government, health care, and not-for-profit organizations are all included in this one text. The discussion next turns to whether such organizations should earn a profit from their activities. This gives rise to consideration of the tax implications if a public sector organization does earn a profit. The chapter concludes with the introduction of a hypothetical example that will be used throughout the text.

In this and every chapter a great deal of new vocabulary is introduced. The first time a new term appears in the text, it is shown in italics. Words in italics are defined within the context of the chapter in the "Key Terms" section at the end of each chapter. These words are also defined, sometimes from a broader perspective, in the glossary located with the book's online resources at: www.pearsonhighered.com/finkler.

WHAT IS FINANCIAL MANAGEMENT?

Financial management is the subset of management that focuses on generating financial information that can be used to improve decision making. In *proprietary*, or for-profit, organizations, an underlying goal of those decisions is to maximize the wealth of the owners of the organization. In public service organizations, the decisions are oriented toward achieving the various goals of the organization while maintaining a satisfactory financial situation. Financial management encompasses the broad areas of *accounting* and *finance*.

Accounting is a system for keeping track of the financial status of an organization and the financial results of its activities. It has often been referred to as the language of business. The vocabulary used by accounting is the language of nonbusiness organizations as well. Governmental bodies, health care organizations, and not-for-profit organizations often do not see themselves as being businesses. Yet they must deal with many of the same financial issues as other types of organizations or risk "going out of business." Receivables, payables, inventory, net assets, depreciation, and debt are just a few of the accounting terms that managers of public service organizations encounter in their interactions with the organization's financial managers. These terms, and many others, will be introduced and explained throughout the book.

Accounting is subdivided into two major areas: *managerial accounting* and *financial accounting*. Managerial accounting relates to generating any financial information that managers can use to improve the future results of the organization. This includes techniques designed to generate any financial data that might help managers make more effective decisions. Major aspects of managerial accounting relate to making financial plans for the organization, implementing those plans, and then working to ensure that the plans are achieved. Some examples of managerial accounting include preparing annual operating budgets, generating information for use in making major investment decisions, and providing the data needed to decide whether to buy or lease a major piece of equipment.

Financial accounting provides retrospective information. As events that have financial implications occur they are recorded by the financial accounting system. From time to time (usually monthly, quarterly, or annually), the recorded data are summarized and reported to interested users. The users include both internal managers and people outside the organization. Those outsiders include those who have lent or might lend money to the organization (*creditors*), those who might sell things to the organization (called suppliers or *vendors*), and other interested parties. These interested parties may include those with a particular interest in public service organizations, such as regulators, legislators, and citizens. Financial reports provide information on the financial status of the organization at a specific point in time, as well as reporting the past results of the organization's operations (i.e., how well it has done from a financial viewpoint).

Finance focuses on the alternative sources and uses of the organization's financial resources. Obtaining funds when needed from appropriate sources and the deployment of resources within the organization fall under this heading. In addition, finance involves the financial markets (such as stock and bond markets) that provide a means to generating funds for organizations.

WHAT IS PUBLIC FINANCE?

Public finance, often referred to as *public economics*, focuses on governmental policies related to spending, taxing, and borrowing decisions. What kinds of goods and services, and at what level, should governments finance or produce? How should resources be drawn from the private sector for government use? Are some services properly the domain of government and others not? Should governments charge directly for the services they provide, or should they impose broad-based taxes to pay for them? What types of taxes or borrowing should governments implement? Who should bear the brunt of taxes? What are the effects of different types of taxes on peoples' decisions to work, save, or consume? What other sources of funds are available to governments, such as municipal bonds, and what rules should govern such borrowing?

In studying the effects of governmental spending, taxing, and borrowing on efficiency and equity there is both a positive and normative focus. We are interested in how government finances are structured (positive approach), and on how people believe they ought to be structured (normative approach).

From a public economics perspective, governments have a role in allocating resources, distributing resources, and stabililizing the economy.[1] If certain goods and services cannot be provided efficiently by the private market, then the government may improve overall results by taking on an allocation role. If there is an accepted belief that the free market does not appropriately distribute income and wealth across all members of society, the government may decide to redistribute either income or wealth. If the economy tends to fall into recessions, or even depressions, the government may decide to act in an affirmative action to minimize the depth and duration of those economic downswings by stabilizing the economy. All three elements—allocation, distribution, and stabilization—are therefore critical parts of public finance.

The economic system in the United States (U.S.) is well known as a free-market system, where we allow the forces of supply and demand to dictate which goods and services are produced, the quantity of production, and the prices that are paid for the goods. However, that is somewhat of a simplification. Actually, the U.S. economy is a mixed economy with free-market elements, but also with government as well as not-for-profit production and provision of goods and services. In fact, the government sector accounts for approximately one-third of the U.S. gross domestic product (GDP).[2] The justification of such a large role for government is based on economic analysis of market failures and society's desire for a redistribution of resources.

---

[1] John E. Anderson. *Public Finance.* Houghton Mifflin, Boston, Mass. 2003, p. 10.
[2] Derived from the *Economic Report of the President, 2008*, Tables B-78 and B-82.

Market Failure

Free markets do not always achieve outcomes that are considered to be acceptable to society. Because of unacceptable free-market outcomes, governments intervene in four key areas: public goods, externalities, inadequate competition, and imperfect information.

Public goods are those where the consumption by one person does not impact on the ability of the good to be consumed by another. For example, suppose that a local government converts an unsightly swamp into a beautiful park. Every person passing the swamp may have found it unpleasant. And each person who uses the park may find it very enjoyable. Yet, no one person might enjoy the park enough to have been willing to personally pay the entire cost of converting the swamp into a park. Nevertheless, if the combined total enjoyment of the park has a value that exceeds the cost of the reclamation of the swamp, then the government intervention has increased the total welfare of society.

In contrast, some goods are produced excessively. The classic example is pollution. If a manufacturer, in the process of making its products, generates substantial air pollution, that pollution is referred to as an *externality*. It has a negative impact on many individuals, but the manufacturer may not consider that negative impact as a cost of production. However, since the negative effects of pollution do pose a cost to society, the government may step in and raise the manufacturer's production cost (for example, by taxing production that creates pollution). This should ensure that the manufacturer considers not only its own internal costs, but also its external costs when it makes its decisions regarding production.

Another role of government is to deal with cases where, for some reason, competition in the provision of goods and services doesn't exist. A classic case would be the electric industry. When the industry first developed, it was too expensive to run electric wires throughout all streets unless a company knew that all potential customers would buy the service from them. Putting up multiple sets of telephone poles and wires would be unduly duplicative, and therefore wasteful of society's resources. To encourage the provision of the service, governments granted monopolies, preventing other companies from competing. Once this is done, the government then intervenes in ways (such as price controls) to avoid potential ills related to monopolistic behavior, which unchecked could lead to overpricing and underproduction.

Another market failure relates to consumers who lack full and complete information. Sellers often know more about the products they are selling than buyers, and government will at times step in and create laws to protect buyers.

Redistribution

Another element of public finance relates to redistribution. Society may chose to redistribute income or wealth from one group to another. Governments might carry out such redistribution, for example, by taxing those with large incomes at a high rate, and using some of the money collected through that income tax to pay for food or health care for those with little or no income. That effectively takes money from the rich and gives it to the poor. As one might expect, determining the "appropriate" level of redistribution is one of the most politically difficult aspects of public finance.

Taxes and Expenditures: Efficiency and Equity

Governments employ many different types of taxes to accomplish the goals related to allocation, distribution, and stabilization as previously discussed. Most readers are familiar with sales and income taxes, from personal experience. Sales taxes apply to the items one purchases. Income tax is based on the amount one earns from either work or investments. Property taxes are assessed on the value of property you own, most typically on buildings or land you own, such as your home. Payroll taxes are designed to provide for Social Security retirement payments, for Medicare health care coverage for the elderly and disabled, and for unemployment insurance. These are just a few examples of different taxes that exist. Each tax has its own peculiar characteristics. Governments select each type of tax with careful consideration of the efficiency and equity implications of the tax.

Taxes tend to cause individuals to change their behavior. As such, the government may be intefering with the free market in ways that it doesn't intend. For example, a government decides to build a new bridge as a public good. A politician promises that, if elected, he will pay for the proposed bridge by enacting a 100 percent tax on the earned income of those individuals in the top 1 percent of all wage earners. Clearly, he might think that 99 percent of the population will favor that political position. The problem is that if a worker will be taxed at a rate of 100 percent on all earned income, then why work?

This creates a significant problem. The workers who earn in the top 1 percent of all wage earners may well be highly productive. If we provide an incentive that causes them to stop working, or even to simply cut back their efforts so they drop out of the top 1 percent, we will be impacting the production of goods and services that have nothing to do with the bridge. This is obviously an extreme example. However, even at lower tax rates, we must be concerned about whether the tax will influence the individual's behavior. This issue has been of great concern to those studying the impacts of welfare programs. On the one hand, the government wants to help the neediest members of society. On the other hand, we don't want to create a situation where individuals find that they are financially better off if they don't work than if they do because of the way that taxes and subsidies have been structured.

Another example relates to taxing savings. Economic theory holds that it is good for individuals to save part of their income. Those savings become available to be lent to companies who invest them in new factories, increasing the overall amount of goods produced by society. If people save less, it hurts the economy. So, should interest on savings be taxed? If it is, then it makes saving money less appealing. Some people who would have saved money will decide just to spend it currently instead. The impact will be less overall economic activity in the long run. Governments must be cautious to minimize the impact of their taxes on the efficiency of the private sector.

We are also concerned about the equity effects of government actions. Many would argue that those who have more can afford to pay more. Suppose that we enacted a flat 10 percent income tax with no exceptions, exemptions, or loopholes. A person earning $20,000 would pay $2,000 and one earning $2,000,000 would pay $200,000. Clearly, the person earning more is paying more. However, one could argue that the $200,000 paid by the latter individual is much less of a burden to him than the $2,000 is to a person earning only $20,000. The high wage earner will certainly have plenty of food and shelter after paying the $200,000 income tax. That might not be the case for someone who earned only $20,000 to begin with.

As a result, many argue in favor of the current system of progressive income taxation, under which those with higher incomes not only pay more, but actually pay tax at a higher rate. Thus high wage earners might pay 30 percent of their income in tax, while lower earners might only pay 15 percent. The goal of such a progressive tax is to create a greater level of fairness or equity. Of course, what is considered fair by one might be considered unfair by another. At a minimum, however, we would strive for taxing individuals in similar situations in the same way. If one taxpayer earning $2,000,000 is taxed at a 30 percent rate, we would strive for other taxpayers with the same income and other circumstances to also be taxed at that 30 percent rate.

This section has served as just a brief introduction to public finance or public economics. This text has a primary focus on financial management. However, in thinking about the financial management of public sector organizations, keep these public finance concepts in mind because they help to both provide the justification for the public sector, and explain many of the activities that we see government do. Interested readers should pursue this topic further, either with coursework in public finance or by reading one of the public finance texts suggested at the end of this chapter.

PUBLIC SECTOR RESOURCE FLOWS

The public sector in the United States is large. Federal government receipts were nearly $2.6 trillion in 2007.[3] State and local government receipts exceed $2 trillion annually.[4] Spending on health care exceeds $2 trillion each year and is expected to pass $4 trillion by 2016.[5] Spending by not-for-profit organizations in 2003 was $945 billion.[6] Public sector organizations obtain their financing from a variety of sources. The focus here will be on the major sources and uses of money in the public sector.

Governments

THE FEDERAL GOVERNMENT   The federal government represents a major component of the entire American economy. Where does the federal government get all of its money, and how does it spend it? Table 1-1 provides a summary of the inflows to the federal government. Many organizations choose a year-end for accounting purposes that differs from the

TABLE 1-1 Federal Receipts for the Year Ending September 30, 2007 (in Billions, on and off Budget)

Receipts	Amount
Individual Income Taxes	$1,164
Social Insurance Taxes	870
Corporation Income Taxes	370
Other	165
Total	$2,568

Totals do not add exactly due to rounding. Projected total for year ending September 30, 2009, is $2,700 billion.

Source: Abstracted from "Table B-80, Federal Receipts and Outlays, by Major Category, and Surplus or Deficit, Fiscal Years 1940–2009," *The Economic Report of the President, 2008* (Washington, D.C.: United States Government Printing Office, 2008), 321.

---

[3] *The Economic Report of the President, 2008*, Table B-80, Federal Receipts and Outlays, by Major Category, and Surplus or Deficit, Fiscal Years 1940–2009, p. 321.

[4] Ibid, Table B-86, State and Local Government Revenues and Expenditures, Selected Fiscal Years, 1938–2005, p. 327.

[5] Centers for Medicare & Medicaid Services, Office of the Actuary. National Health Expenditure (NHE) Projections 2007–2017. Amounts by Type of Expenditure and Source of Funds: Calendar Years 1965–2017. First projected year is 2007. http://www.cms.hhs.gov/NationalHealthExpendData/03_NationalHealthAccountsProjected.asp

[6] National Council of Nonprofit Associations, "The United States Nonprofit Sector." http://www.ncna.org/_uploads/documents/live//us_sector_report_2003.pdf

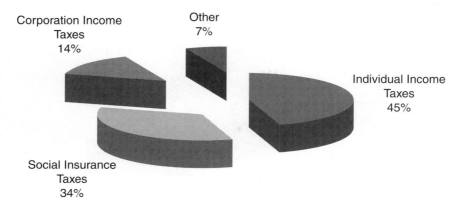

FIGURE 1-1   Federal Receipts by Source (in Percentages) for the Year Ending September 30, 2007

Source: Derived from "Table B-80, Federal Receipts and Outlays, by Major Category, and Surplus or Deficit, Fiscal Years 1940–2009," *The Economic Report of the President, 2008* (Washington, D.C.: United States Government Printing Office, 2008), 321.

calendar year. The reasons for such a choice are discussed later in this book. Such years are referred to as *fiscal* years. The federal 2010 fiscal year begins on October 1, 2009, and ends on September 30, 2010.

The federal government has several types of receipts, which make up the bulk of government collections. These are individual income taxes, social insurance taxes (the majority of which are Social Security taxes), and corporation income taxes. Their relative proportions of total federal receipts can be seen in Figure 1-1. The "Other" category in Figure 1-1 includes things such as taxes on cigarettes and liquor, estate (inheritance) and gift taxes, and customs duties (charges on imports).

Social Security has become the largest federal outlay (see Table 1-2), now accounting for over 20 percent of all federal spending, as can be seen in Figure 1-2. National defense, Medicare, income security, health, and net interest are other large parts of federal spending. Total spending on defense increased substantially in the years following the 9/11 attack and then even more during the Iraq War. Income security includes welfare and the food stamp

TABLE 1-2 Federal Outlays for the Year Ending September 30, 2007 (in Billions, on and off Budget)

Outlays	Amount
Social Security	$ 586
National Defense	553
Medicare	375
Income Security	366
Health	266
Net Interest	237
Other	347
Total	$2,730

Projected total for year ending September 30, 2009, is $2,400 billion.

Source: Abstracted from "Table B-80, Federal Receipts and Outlays, by Major Category, and Surplus or Deficit, Fiscal Years 1940–2009," *The Economic Report of the President, 2008* (Washington, D.C.: United States Government Printing Office, 2008), 321.

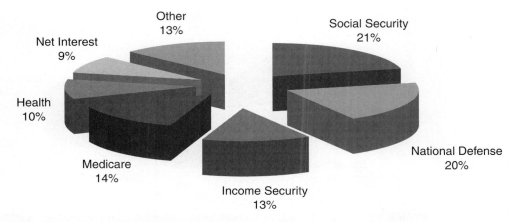

FIGURE 1-2   Federal Outlays by Category (in Percentages) for the Year Ending September 30, 2007

Source: Derived from "Table B-80, Federal Receipts and Outlays, by Major Category, and Surplus or Deficit, Fiscal Years 1940–2009," *The Economic Report of the President, 2008* (Washington, D.C.: United States Government Printing Office, 2008), 321.

program. Medicare is a program of health benefits for the elderly and permanently disabled. The "Health" category includes Medicaid and all other federal government spending on health care and health research, aside from Medicare. Net Interest represents the amount that the federal government spends on interest annually, primarily on the federal debt. The "Other" category in Figure 1-2 includes a wide variety of areas, such as education, international affairs, the space program, agriculture, commerce, housing, transportation, and general government administration.

The total receipts in Table 1-1 are less than the outlays shown in Table 1-2. In 2007, the federal government received less than it spent. An excess of receipts over spending is referred to as a *surplus*. An excess of spending over receipts is referred to as a *deficit*. Table 1-3 provides information about federal receipts, outlays, surplus or deficit, and debt for selected years from 1990 through 2009.

The receipts and outlays in Table 1-3 represent the total of *on-budget* and *off-budget* items. A large portion of the Social Security receipts and payments are considered to be off-budget. Off-budget items are not included in the normal federal government budget

TABLE 1-3 Federal Receipts, Outlays, Surplus or Deficit, and Debt (in Billions)

	Year Ending September 30							
	1990	**1995**	**2000**	**2005**	**2006**	**2007**	**2008***	**2009***
Total Receipts	$1,032	$1,352	$2,026	$2,154	$2,407	$2,568	$2,521	$ 2,700
Total Outlays	1,253	1,516	1,789	2,472	2,655	2,730	2,931	3,107
Surplus or Deficit	($221)	($164)	$237	($318)	($248)	($162)	($410)	($ 407)
Federal Debt	$3,206	$4,920	$5,629	$7,905	$8,451	$8,951	$9,654	$10,413

* Estimates. It should be noted that these estimates were prepared by the government before the subprime mortgage and credit crisis of 2008. As a result of that crisis, receipts are likely to be lower than projected for 2008 and 2009, and the outlays and federal debt are likely to higher than projected in this table.

Source: Abstracted from "Table B-78, Federal Receipts and Outlays, Surplus or Deficit, and Debt, Selected Fiscal Years, 1939–2009," *The Economic Report of the President, 2008* (Washington, D.C.: United States Government Printing Office, 2008), 319.

process. For example, Social Security taxes and payments are an off-budget item. Which number better represents the surplus or deficit for the federal government? That is difficult to say.[7] Based on receipts and disbursements, one could argue that the total receipts and total outlays reported in Table 1-3 are reasonable. Others would argue that Social Security collections in excess of Social Security payments should not be used to offset general spending of the government. Those monies are collected with the expectation that they will be used for Social Security payments.

Another concern is that the federal debt has grown large. The federal government's *national debt* represents the total cumulative amount that the federal government has borrowed and not repaid. Thus, a deficit shows the amount spent in one year in excess of receipts. The debt shows the accumulated amount that the government owes because spending over time has exceeded receipts.

If the government incurs deficits year after year (as it did for several decades near the end of the twentieth century), then the size of the debt will grow. However, note in Table 1-3 that even during the period around 2000 when the federal government had surpluses, the total debt continued to grow! This is a result of the on-budget, off-budget accounting of the federal government. The surplus and deficits shown in Table 1-3 are on-budget and off-budget items combined. Off-budget surpluses are being used to offset on-budget spending. This allows the government to report a lower deficit or a higher surplus. However, when the federal government uses social insurance trust funds (off-budget money) to offset the deficit, it must borrow them from the Social Security trust fund, increasing the overall level of the national debt. In other words, the overall amount of federal debt does recognize that taxes raised currently for future Social Security payments create obligations to make future payments. However, the calculation of the annual federal surplus or deficit is based more on a cash in and cash out perspective. If the cash is available to the government and is spent, that doesn't create a deficit for the year, even if the cash was supposed to be used for some future purpose such as making Social Security payments down the road.

In Table 1-4, it can be seen that the total national debt was expected to reach $10.4 trillion by the end of 2009. That is before taking into account the impact of the subprime mortgage and credit crisis of 2008. Given the government actions during that crisis, the federal debt is likely to be even higher by the end of 2009. Clearly, the national debt

TABLE 1-4 Federal Debt and Gross Domestic Product—Selected Years (Billions of Dollars)

	Year Ending September 30						
	1955	1965	1975	1985	1995	2005	2009*
Federal Debt	274	322	542	1,817	4,921	7,905	10,413
Gross Domestic Product	395	687	1,561	4,142	7,326	12,238	15,027

* Estimate. It should be noted that these estimates were prepared by the government before the subprime mortgage and credit crisis of 2008. As a result of that crisis, the 2009 federal debt is likely to be higher and the gross domestic product is likely to lower than projected in this table.

Source: Abstracted from "Table B-78, Federal Receipts and Outlays, Surplus or Deficit, and Debt, Selected Fiscal Years, 1939–2009," *The Economic Report of the President, 2008* (Washington, D.C.: United States Government Printing Office, 2008), 319.

[7] See James Howard. "Government Economic Projections: A Comparison Between CBO and OMB Forecasts," *Public Budgeting and Finance*, Vol. 7 (1987), pp. 14–25.

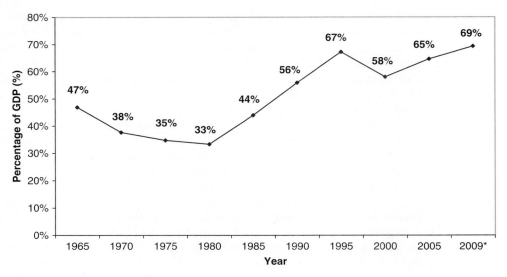

FIGURE 1-3 Federal Debt as Percent of GDP

* Year 2009 percent is an estimate.

Source: Derived from "Table B-79, Federal Receipts, Outlays, Surplus or Deficit, and Debt, as a Percent of Gross Domestic Product, Fiscal Years 1934–2009," *The Economic Report of the President, 2008* (Washington, D.C.: United States Government Printing Office, 2008), 320.

is a large number of dollars. Figure 1-3, however, provides additional information—the debt as a percent of the gross domestic product (GDP). Although the debt has been growing as a percent of the GDP in recent decades, it is not at an all-time high as a percent of GDP. The debt was nearly 120 percent of GDP in 1945.

For several years before the 9/11 attack, the debt-to-GDP ratio had been falling and it was projected to fall further. Following the attack, Homeland Security, the Iraq war, and a weak economy quickly reversed the decline. Many would argue that a growing debt allows the government to provide services to taxpayers today, at the expense of their children, who will have to repay the debt. Others contend, however, that the debt will never actually be repaid and that all generations have borne the burden of the interest on the debt of their predecessors.

Another argument involves whether the debt is really a burden. Some would argue that as the overall economy grows, it is reasonable for the debt of the government to grow proportionately. This is similar to the concept that the higher your salary, the larger the mortgage you can afford on a home. Also, to a great extent, the money that the federal government owes has been borrowed from U.S. citizens. Therefore, one could contend that we simply owe ourselves the money and will pay interest to ourselves. In that case, the interest would simply be a transfer from some members of our society to others. This argument ignores the equity questions involved in the transfer that taxes some members of society to pay interest on the debt to other members, and it also ignores foreign ownership of the debt.

Another issue concerning the debt is that it may "crowd out" private capital. That is, since the federal government is borrowing large amounts of money, money is not available to be lent to the private sector. This may inhibit economic growth in the private sector.

STATE AND LOCAL GOVERNMENTS   What are the sources and uses of money at the state and local government level? Sales, property, and income taxes are the major forms of taxation used by state and local governments to raise money, as is seen in Table 1-5 and Figure 1-4.

TABLE 1-5 State and Local Government Receipts for the Year Ending 2005 (in Billions)

Receipts	Amount
Federal Government	$ 438
Sales and Gross Receipts Taxes	383
Property Taxes	336
Individual Income Taxes	241
Corporation Net Income Taxes	43
Other	580
Total	$2,021

Source: Abstracted from "Table B-86, State and Local Government Revenues and Expenditures, Selected Fiscal Years, 1938–2005," *The Economic Report of the President, 2008* (Washington, D.C.: United States Government Printing Office, 2008), 327.

Clearly, however, another significant source of funds for state and local governments is the federal government. Other receipts include taxes on motor vehicles, various fees, other taxes, and miscellaneous revenues.

Different state and local governments rely to a different extent on each of these sources, and not all state and local governments have the same mix. For example, local governments tend to rely heavily on property taxes, whereas state governments do not. Also, not all states have income taxes on individuals.

Table 1-6 and Figure 1-5 show how state and local governments use their resources. The single largest cost is education, representing 28% of state and local outlays. Public welfare and highways are other significant items for state and local governments. Note that 48 percent of spending is in the "Other" category. This is a reflection of the tremendous diversity in the states and localities of the country. Some have high costs for snow removal

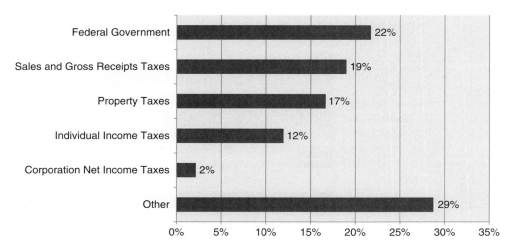

FIGURE 1-4 State and Local Government Receipts in Percent: 2005

Source: Derived from "Table B-86, State and Local Government Revenues and Expenditures, Selected Fiscal Years 1938–2005," *The Economic Report of the President, 2008* (Washington, D.C.: United States Government Printing Office, 2008), 327.

TABLE 1-6 State and Local Government Outlays for the Year Ending 2005 (in Billions)

Outlays	Amount
Education	$ 689
Public Welfare	367
Highways	124
Other	834
Total	$2,014

Source: Abstracted from "Table B-86, State and Local Government Revenues and Expenditures, Selected Fiscal Years, 1938–2005," *The Economic Report of the President, 2008* (Washington, D.C.: United States Government Printing Office, 2008), 327.

and subway systems. Others have no snow and little public transit. Common types of costs included in the "Other" category are libraries, police and fire protection, and parks.

The Health Care Services Industry

Since 1965, spending on health care has risen at a rapid rate. Total spending increased from $42 billion in 1965 to $2,106 billion in 2006. During that time, there was a dramatic shift in the relative sources of financing the health care sector. Consider a comparison of the private and public roles in paying for national health expenditures over time, as shown in Table 1-7. The public funding is projected to increase from just less than one-quarter in 1965 to nearly half of all health care expenditures by 2017. Thus, the public is now paying for a larger share of much larger total spending. The rate of increase in total spending on health care has far exceeded the growth in the GDP.

The state and local government funding of health care over the period from 1965 to 2000 and through the projections for 2017 grew in absolute amount but remained a fairly constant percentage of national health expenditures, dropping from 14 percent to 13 percent, as is seen in Table 1-8. In contrast, the federal role in financing the health care sector changed dramatically. Federal outlays went from 11 percent of overall

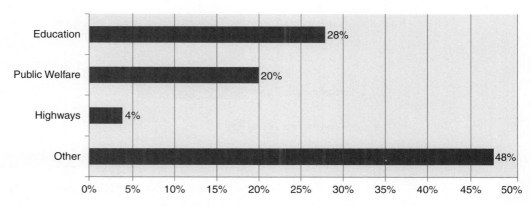

FIGURE 1-5   State and Local Government Outlays in Percent: 2005

Source: Derived from "Table B-86, State and Local Government Revenues and Expenditures, Selected Fiscal Years 1938–2005," *The Economic Report of the President, 2008* (Washington, D.C.: United States Government Printing Office, 2008), 327.

TABLE 1-7 National Health Expenditures, Private Versus Public, 1965, 2000, and 2017

	1965		2000		2017*	
	$ in Billions	(Percent)	$ in Billions	(Percent)	$ in Billions	(Percent)
Private	32	76	757	56	2,198	51
Public (Federal, State, and Local)	10	24	597	44	2,079	49
Total	42	100	1,354	100	4,277	100

* Projected

Source: Abstracted from "National Health Expenditure (NHE) Amounts by Type of Expenditure and Source of Funds: Calendar Years 1965–2017 in PROJECTIONS Format," Center for Medicare & Medicaid Services, Office of the Actuary, http://www.cms.hhs.gov/ NationalHealthExpendData/03_NationalHealthAccountsProjected.asp.

health spending to 31 percent in 2000 and are projected to rise to 36 percent by 2017 (see Table 1-8).

One can get a better sense of the sources of health care financing from Figure 1-6. Medicare is a federal program; Medicaid and the State Children's Health Insurance Program (SCHIP), and other public programs are paid for by federal, state, and local governments. As can be seen, those three items make up almost half of the health care pie. Private health insurance, including managed care programs, is the single largest source of funding. The "Out-of-Pocket" category represents direct payments by individual persons for care. The "Other Private" category includes payments by those other than patients. For example, it includes health services provided for employees at the employer's site.

What is this money spent on? Figure 1-7 provides a breakdown of the total spending. Hospital care, at 31 percent, is the largest single cost. Physician services, nursing home care, prescription drugs, and administration are also large individual items. Other spending includes dental, home care, vision, research, construction, and other medical and nonmedical costs.

The Not-for-Profit Sector

The not-for-profit sector in the United States is extremely large, with 1.5 million different tax-exempt organizations. The largest single grouping is that of charitable and religious organizations, which number more than 900,000. Next comes social welfare organizations such as civic leagues, fraternal societies, social clubs, business leagues, and war veterans groups, totalling approximately a half million organizations. Finally, there are over 100,000

TABLE 1-8 National Health Expenditures, Private, Federal, and State and Local, 1965, 2000, and 2017

	1965		2000		2017*	
	$ in Billions	(Percent)	$ in Billions	(Percent)	$ in Billions	(Percent)
Private	32	75	757	56	2,198	51
Federal	5	11	418	31	1,536	36
State and Local	6	14	179	13	543	13
Total	42	100	1,354	100	4,277	100

Totals do not add up exactly due to rounding.

* Projected

Source: Abstracted from "National Health Expenditure (NHE) Amounts by Type of Expenditure and Source of Funds: Calendar Years 1965–2017 in PROJECTIONS format," Center for Medicare & Medicaid Services, Office of the Actuary, http://www.cms.hhs.gov/ NationalHealthExpendData/03_NationalHealthAccountsProjected.asp.

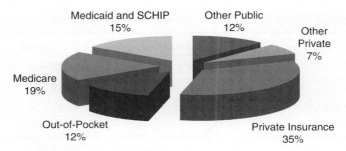

FIGURE 1-6   The Nation's Health Dollar: Where It Came From, 2006

Source: The Nation's Health Dollar, Calender Year 2006: Where It Came From. Center for Medicare & Medicaid Services, Office of the Actuary, National Health Statistics Group, http://www.cms.hhs.gov/NationalHealthExpendData/downloads/PieChartSourcesExpenditures2006.pdf

private foundations.[8] There is a tremendous range of charitable organizations, including but not limited to the arts, culture and humanities, education, environment, health, human services, international, religion, and foundations.[9]

Although corporations and foundations make substantial contributions to the not-for-profit sector, the largest component of contributions, 76 percent, comes from individuals (see Figure 1-8). $295 billion was contributed in 2006.[10] Most American households contribute to not-for-profit organizations. In 2000, 89 percent of all households made contributions, which averaged a total of $1,620 per household. This represents 3.1 percent of average household income for those making contributions.[11] Contributions are spread across a wide variety of organizations, as can be seen in Figure 1-9. The greatest share of

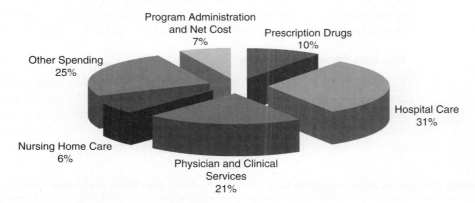

FIGURE 1-7   The Nation's Health Dollar: Where It Went, 2006

Source: The Nation's Health Dollar, Calendar Year 2006: Where It Went. Center for Medicare & Medicaid Services, Office of the Actuary, National Health Statistics Group, http://www.cms.hhs.gov/NationalHealthExpendData/downloads/PieChartSourcesExpenditures2006.pdf.

---

[8] The Urban Institute, National Center for Charitable Statistics, Number of Nonprofit Organizations in the United States, 1996–2006, http://nccsdataweb.urban.org/PubApps/profile1.php?state=US

[9] A good source for additional descriptions of and information about various types of not-for-profit organizations is the National Center for Charitable Statistics, at http://nccs.urban.org.

[10] Amy Blackwood, Kennard T. Wing, and Thomas H. Pollak, The Nonprofit Sector in Brief—Facts and Figures from the Nonprofit Almanac 2008: Public Charities, Giving, and Volunteering, The Urban Institute, 2008, http://nccsdataweb.urban.org/kbfiles/797/Almanac2008publicCharities.pdf.

[11] The Independent Sector. "Giving and Volunteering in the United States—Key Findings," Washington, D.C.: Independent Sector, 2001. www.Independentsector.org.

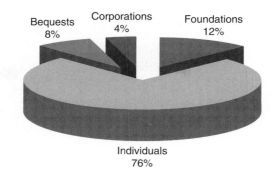

FIGURE 1-8   Contributions: $295 Billion by Source of Contribution: 2006

Source: Giving USA Foundation. AAFRC Trust for Philanthropy. (2007). *Giving USA 2007.* Indianapolis, Ind. http://www.aafrc.org/press_releases/gusa/20070625.pdf.

dollars contributed, 33 percent, went to religious organizations. Education, with 14 percent of the contributions, was a distant second.

The not-for-profit sector is not totally reliant on contributions. Although the latest available data are dated, they are still informative. In 1996 private donations made up only 19 percent of not-for-profit sources of funds, as is seen in Table 1-9. By far, the largest source of money for the not-for-profit sector comes from payments for services. The health care sector generates approximately half of all money in the not-for-profit sector and receives the vast majority of that money from payments, rather than donations.[12] In contrast, donations make up the bulk of funds for religious organizations. Education and research and social and legal services receive substantial amounts of money from donations as well as from private and government payments, and other sources. "Other" includes endowment and investment income and a variety of other sources. These relationships seem to be fairly stable. In 2002 the percentage of each source of revenue for not-for-profits was reported as being 20 percent private donations, 38 percent private payments, 31 percent government payments, and 11 percent other. That is very similar to the 1996 data reported in Table 1–9.[13]

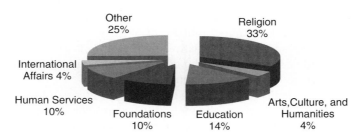

FIGURE 1-9   Contributions: $295 Billion by Type of Recipient Organization: 2006

Source: Giving USA Foundation. AAFRC Trust for Philanthropy. (2007). *Giving USA 2007.* Indianapolis, Ind http://www.aafrc.org/press_releases/gusa/20070625.pdf.

---

[12] Any reviewer of the not-for-profit sector statistics should bear in mind that not-for-profit health care providers are included in the not-for-profit sector. One cannot determine the size of the public sector by adding the government, health, and not-for-profit sectors without first excluding the health element from not-for-profit to avoid double-counting. One should also be careful not to inappropriately double-count government payments to health organizations and to non-health-related not-for-profit organizations.

[13] Weitzman, Murray S., *The New Nonprofit Almanac & Desk Reference, 2002* (Washington, D.C.: Independent Sector, 2002), p. 91.

TABLE 1-9 Not-for-Profit Organization Sources of Funds, 1996 (in Billions)

Sector	Private Donations	Payments		Other	Total
		Private	Government		
Health	$ 11	$148	$127	$23	$310
Education/Research	15	67	23	13	118
Religious	66	5	0	(3)	69
Social and Legal Services	15	13	40	7	75
Other	11	7	7	27	49
Total	$118	$240	$197	$67	$621
Percent	19%	39%	32%	11%	100%

Totals do not add up exactly due to rounding. Note that numbers in the "Other" column may be negative for reasons such as losses on investments.

Source: Abstracted from Independent Sector, "Table 4-2, Sources and Disposition of Annual Funds by Sub-sector: 1977, 1982, 1987, 1992, and 1996" (Washington, D.C.: The Independent Sector), http://www.independentsector.org/programs/research/table4_2.html.

How do not-for-profit organizations obtain donations and grants? Fund-raising has become an important part of the job of managers of not-for-profit organizations. There are two major types of fund-raising: contributions or donations, and contracts or grants. The funds that not-for-profit organizations receive from these sources are either unrestricted or restricted. The organization may use unrestricted funds for any valid organizational purpose. If the funds are restricted, the organization must comply with specific limitations on how the funds may be used.

For example, the *New York Times* reported that when Joan Kroc died she left $1.5 billion of the McDonald's restaurant fortune to the Salvation Army. However, the charity had to contemplate whether or not to accept the gift, because the donation was restricted. If accepted, half of the money had to be used to build 25 to 30 community centers and the other half placed in permanent endowment, with the income from the endowment used to pay for the costs to operate the centers. Based on the Salvation Army's past experience, it is likely that the endowment income will only be enough to pay approximately half the total operating cost of the centers. By accepting the gift with its restrictions, the Salvation Army essentially committed itself to raising an additional $70 million a year from other sources, after the construction of the centers has been completed.[14] Sometimes gifts create burdens for charities.

Fund-raising has become a sophisticated area of management, and many not-for-profit organizations employ full-time staffs that specialize in fund-raising, often called development. A brief introduction to fund-raising is provided in Appendix 1-A.

How do not-for-profit organizations use their funds? Table 1-10 provides a summary. The largest share of funds, 85 percent, are used to finance current operations. A 5 percent share goes to construction and capital improvements. However, this pattern varies substantially among subsectors. For example, religious organizations spend more than 10 percent of their receipts on construction and capital improvements, whereas social and legal services spend a very low percentage of their funds on construction and capital.

---

[14] Stephanie Strom. "Salvation Army Receives a Gift of $1.5 Billion," *New York Times*, January 21, 2004, http://www.nytimes.com/2004/01/21/national/21GIFT.html?th.

TABLE 1-10 Not-for-Profit Organization Uses of Funds, 1996 (in Billions)

Sector	Current Operations	Construction and Capital Improvements	Other	Total
Health	$287	$12	$11	$310
Education/Research	96	8	14	118
Religious	48	7	13	68
Social and Legal Services	65	1	9	75
Other	30	1	19	50
Total	$526	$29	$66	$621
Percent	85%	5%	11%	100%

Totals do not add up exactly due to rounding.

Source: Abstracted from Independent Sector, "Table 4-2, Sources and Disposition of Annual Funds by Sub-sector: 1977, 1982, 1987, 1992, and 1996" (Washington, D.C.: Independent Sector), http://www.independentsector.org/programs/research/table4_2.html.

The International NGO Sector

The World Bank had defined non-governmental organizations (NGOs) as "private organizations that pursue activities to relieve suffering, promote the interests of the poor, protect the environment, provide basic social services, or undertake community development" (World Bank Operational Directive 14.70). NGOs are similar to the not-for-profit organizations described in the previous section. They are primarily mission-focused rather than profit-focused. Essentially, any not-for-profit organization, independent from the government, can be considered an NGO.

We can think of NGOs as falling into three main categories: community-based, national, and international. Community-based organizations (CBOs) are membership groups that advance the interests of the members. They may be anything from farmers or trade associations, to clubs or even lending organizations. National NGOs are larger organizations, more likely to have full-time staff, that operate solely within a country. International NGOs have a presence in more than one country.

The NGO sector grew at a rapid rate in the last quarter of the 20th century. It has been estimated that there are over 2,500 international NGOs in the northern industrial countries, and more than 150,000 NGOs, including CBOs, in the developing world.[15] Each year the revenues and spending of NGOs amount to billions of dollars. A good source for additional information about the international NGO sector is the *Yearbook of International Organizations*, published annually.[16] It provides profiles of over 30,000 NGOs.

WHY PUBLIC, HEALTH CARE, AND NOT-FOR-PROFIT IN ONE BOOK?

The reader might wonder why public or government, health care, and not-for-profit financial management are all discussed in one text. One argument for this grouping is that these organizations, for the most part, are exempt from taxes.[17] Although that is something that

---

[15] Peace Corps Master's International, The Evans School, University of Washington, http://www.evansuw.org/mpa/program/Peace_Corps/why_pcmi.html.

[16] *Yearbook of International Organizations* 2007–08, 44th Edition, Union of International Associations, K.G. Saur, 2007.

[17] Although it is generally true that the public and not-for-profit sectors are exempt from taxation, this is less true for the health care services sector. This book will address issues related to both not-for-profit and also for-profit, or proprietary, health care organizations.

many of these organizations have in common, it is not the primary issue. The common thread that binds these organizations is their "raison d'être"—their reason for existence. All of these organizations are in the public service. As such, their major focus is to provide benefits to the community.

The underlying public service motivation creates a large number of special circumstances in the area of financial management. Since not-for-profit organizations do not have owners watching to make sure their profits are maximized, there must be other mechanisms put in place to ensure that managers achieve their organization's goals.

Measurement of profit does not adequately provide the bottom line for public service organizations. Since they operate with a goal of providing a public benefit, there must be ways to ensure that the level of public service achieved is measured and reported. Tools must be provided that allow managers to work toward achieving the specific goals of their organizations. This book will serve to help explain those tools and mechanisms, with a special focus on these three vital areas: public, health, and not-for-profit.

WHY SHOULD PUBLIC SERVICE ORGANIZATIONS WORRY ABOUT FINANCIAL MANAGEMENT?

If the primary mission of public service organizations is not to make a profit, should they even be concerned with issues of financial management? Should organizations such as governments, hospitals, churches, and museums spend time on financial management? The answer is a strong yes.

In for-profit organizations, profits are the goal. They represent the end result that the organization is trying to achieve. In public service organizations, financial resources are a means to an end. The profits themselves may not be the ultimate goal. However, without adequate financial resources, an organization generally cannot achieve its mission.

For example, suppose that an organization's mission is to provide food to homeless individuals. The goal is to keep people from being hungry. To achieve that goal, the organization needs a physical location. It must pay rent, heat, and electric bills. Any needed food that is not donated must be purchased. The organization's managers could spend all of their time and efforts planning meals, cooking meals, and getting the meals to the homeless. But if they do that, there is a significant possibility that the organization will run out of money and will have to close its doors.

Achieving the goals of the organization requires financial planning. How much will it cost to provide the meals? How much money can the organization expect to receive? From what sources? Are there adequate resources, or will there be a shortfall?

By focusing on financial issues, managers can determine whether to increase fund-raising efforts. They can decide if survival requires cutting back from serving three meals per person per day to just breakfast and dinner, or even just dinner. The desire to accomplish the goal of feeding the hungry can work against accomplishment of that goal. Managers can ignore the organization's finances and keep serving three meals a day—finances be damned. But bankruptcy and closure may be worse than cutting back to two meals a day. An understanding of the current financial status of the organization—how well it is doing financially and what it can or cannot afford to do—is essential for all organizations.

The field of financial management involves attempting to generate useful financial information that is free of value judgments. It is not the role of financial managers to say what the organization should do. Financial management can provide information about how many meals a day the organization can afford to provide to how many people, given expected financial circumstances. General managers often must use the information to make decisions. Suppose that the only choices available that will allow the organization to continue to provide meals for the hungry are to limit the number of people served or to change the menu to one with less nutritious food. Should the organization turn some people away, or should it reduce the quality of the food served? Such value judgments are outside of the domain of financial management.

Financial management focuses not only on questions of survival, but also issues of *effectiveness* and *efficiency*. Effectiveness relates to whether an organization is accomplishing its mission. If there is a goal to feed 1,000 people per month, financial management can assess how effective the organization is in achieving that goal. How many people are in fact being fed? Efficiency relates to whether the organization uses the minimum needed resources to produce its outcomes or outputs. To avoid wasting resources, organizations need to understand their productivity. How much did it cost per person fed? Is the organization maximizing the use of resources by finding the lowest-cost approach for achieving each of its results?

SHOULD PUBLIC SERVICE ORGANIZATIONS EARN A PROFIT?

Okay, so not-for-profit organizations need to be aware of their finances. But should they earn a profit? Again, the answer is yes. The term *not-for-profit* is meant to convey the fact that earning a profit is not the mission of the organization. However, organizations clearly would not want to lose money, because then they might be forced to cease operation. Even further, not-for-profit organizations should not be content to just break even. Earning a profit is essential to almost all organizations.

Although earning profits is not why public service organizations exist, profits enhance that existence. Earning profits allows organizations to better accomplish their goals. This is true for several reasons. First, profits provide an organization with a safety margin. Things do not always go according to plan. If for some reason financial results are poorer than expected, a profit earned in a prior period can make up the shortfall.

Second, organizations must be able to replace their equipment and facilities over time as they wear out. If there is inflation, it will cost more to replace these items than they originally cost. For example, if inflation is 3 percent per year, a piece of equipment that lasts five years will cost 15 percent more to replace than it originally cost.[18] So a profit will be needed to allow for replacement of facilities.

Third, organizations often want to be able to expand their services over time. This may be to reach out to more potential clients. Similarly, organizations want to be able to improve their services over time, perhaps taking advantage of new technologies. Some reasonable level of profits is necessary to allow for such expansions and adoptions of technologies.

What about governments? Should they earn a profit as well? Governments' profits are more commonly called surpluses. And one can make a good argument that governments also should attempt to earn at least limited surpluses. Cycles in the general economy tend to cause tax receipts to vary upward and downward from year to year. Often, in the years when tax receipts are low because of a recession, the demand on the government to provide public services, such as unemployment insurance payments and welfare payments, rises. Because the demands of government may be higher at times when tax revenues are lower, many governments will plan to have a surplus in good years. This provides available resources to cover needs in bad years. It can also protect the government from unexpected events, such as unusually severe winters requiring extra snow removal or overtime related to cleanup after a rare flood. Governments may have laws governing whether they may incur a surplus or deficit.

---

[18] Actually, the cost will increase by more than 15 percent, since the impact of inflation compounds over time. Issues related to compounding are discussed in Chapter 5.

Corporate Income Taxes

If a not-for-profit organization earns a profit (surplus), will it be subject to corporate income taxes? No. Organizations that are exempt from federal income taxes, referred to as *tax-exempt* organizations, will not be subject to income tax simply because they earn profits. However, the profits earned must be used for the benefit of the organization and its clients, rather than being used to benefit any select group that might be perceived as receiving the benefits of ownership.

For example, if a hospital gives free office space to physicians for their private practices, the Internal Revenue Service (IRS) would likely consider that free space to be a distribution of profits to a group of physicians, placing the organization's tax-exempt status at risk.

In some cases, tax-exempt organizations are subject to income tax on profits they earn that come from sources not related to their primary tax-exempt mission. For example, if a museum operates a restaurant that is open to the general public (beyond just those people visiting the museum), the profits from that restaurant might be subject to income tax. See Appendix 11-A.

Even most organizations that are fully tax-exempt are required to file an annual income tax return with the IRS, called Form 990. This document is available to the public either over the Internet or directly from the organization. Tax returns of for-profit corporations are private.

Issues related to income taxes can be extremely complex. Although many public service organizations are tax-exempt, all organizations should seek out the advice of competent tax experts to ensure that they are in compliance with the various tax laws.

ONGOING CASE STUDY

This book uses a fictional example to help the reader learn about financial management in not-for-profit, government, and health care organizations. This case study introduces a wide range of financial management material in a realistic yet simplified setting. The case study will run throughout the entire book, with many chapters adding information to it.

The Setting

The Robert F. Wagner Graduate School of Public Service at New York University was having an alumni reunion. The reunion culminated with a formal dinner in the luxurious Bobst Penthouse faculty dining facility. Sitting next to each other at one particular table on this evening were three persons. Each had known the other two nearly a decade earlier when they had been working on their Master of Public Administration degrees at the Wagner School. They had gone their separate ways, but on this evening they found themselves in similar positions.

Leanna Schwartz had left the Wagner School and worked in a variety of positions in the not-for-profit field. Having performed in an excellent manner in each position, she had received a series of increasingly more important positions. The culmination was that she had just been appointed the Executive Director of Meals for the Homeless.

Sitting a few seats from Schwartz was Steve Netzer. He had worked in just one organization since leaving Wagner, the Hospital for Ordinary Surgery. Working his way up through the ranks, from night administrator to assistant admitting department head to director of medical records, he had recently been promoted to the position of Chief Operating Officer of the hospital.

In between Netzer and Schwartz was Dwight Ives. He had gone directly into government management upon leaving the Wagner School. After a stint in Washington as a White House fellow, he worked for a number of years in various roles in management in New York

City. In a bit of a dramatic change, he had now taken on the job of Town Manager for the suburban town of Millbridge.

As the three alumni chatted, they realized that not only had they taken on the most challenging position of their careers to date, but also they now had substantially more financial responsibility than ever before. None of them were financial managers per se. In fact, none of them had even specialized in financial management while at the Wagner School. However, each of them would now have financial managers working for them, and each of them would need to have a good working understanding of many basic aspects of financial management to be successful in their positions.

What financial skills will each of these managers need? How will those skills help them oversee their organizations? These are some of the questions that will be addressed throughout this book. Often students in not-for-profit, government, and health care management and policy programs have difficulty understanding exactly what value financial management has to them. It is hoped that this continuing case study will help the reader understand more easily why financial information is important. That in turn should make it substantially easier to try to absorb the general and even some of the more technical aspects of financial management.

Summary

The primary focus of the book is on providing current and future managers with an understanding of financial information. The goal of the book is not to provide a highly technical grounding in accounting and finance. Rather, by the end of this book, the reader should be comfortable with the basics of financial management.

Financial management is the subset of management that focuses on generating financial information that can be used to improve decision making. It includes both accounting and finance. Accounting is a system for keeping track of the financial status of an organization and the financial results of its activities. It is subdivided into two major areas: Managerial accounting relates to generating any financial information that managers can use to improve the future results of the organization; and financial accounting provides retrospective information about the results of operations and the financial position of the organization. Finance focuses on the alternative sources and uses of the organization's financial resources.

Public sector organizations obtain their financing from a variety of sources and use them for a wide variety of purposes. Federal government outlays are approximately $3 trillion annually. State and local government spending exceeds $2 trillion. Spending on health care also exceeds $2 trillion each year. Spending by not-for-profit organizations is more than $600 billion annually. Combined, the federal, state and local, health, and not-for-profit sectors' spending equals roughly half of the U.S. GDP.

In public service organizations, financial resources are a means to an end. The profits themselves may not be the ultimate goal. However, without adequate financial resources, one generally cannot achieve the organization's mission. So it is essential for public service organizations to be concerned with financial management. The field of financial management attempts to generate useful financial information that is free of value judgments. It is not the role of financial managers to say what the organization should do. Financial management provides financial information that can help managers make decisions.

Public service organizations should not be content to just break even. Earning a profit is essential to almost all organizations. First, profits provide an organization with a safety margin. Second, organizations must be able to replace their equipment and facilities over time as they wear out. Third, organizations often want to be able to expand their services over time and adopt new technologies. Some reasonable level of profits is necessary to allow for safety, replacement, and expansion. Because the demands of government may be higher at times when tax revenues are lower, many governments will plan to have a surplus in good years. This provides available resources to cover needs in bad years or for unexpected costs.

Preview

This chapter represents all of Part I of this book, "Introduction: Setting the Stage." The remainder of this book is divided into four sections. Part II focuses on planning—to be successful, organizations must plan for the future. Part III emphasizes implementation and control. Once a plan has been developed, it must be implemented, and then actions must be taken to control operations so that the planned results can be achieved. Part IV focuses on reporting results. Once a plan has been devised and implemented, and actions have been taken to control results, we must determine what has actually transpired and report those outcomes. We do this through a financial reporting process. Part V of the book is concerned with financial analysis. Many individuals, both within an organization and external to it,

have an interest in knowing the results of the organization's activities and its financial condition. Part V considers how one can use the reported results to assess the financial status of an organization.

As the reader now turns to Part II of the book, the focus, as noted previously, is on planning. Part II consists of five chapters. Chapter 2 introduces planning and budgeting. Chapter 3 provides additional information and techniques for budgeting. Chapter 4 provides a focus on what it costs the organization to provide its services, with a focus on how cost information can be used for decision making. Chapters 5 and 6 provide critical financial management tools for making decisions related to the long-term resources and obligations of the organization.

Key Terms from This Chapter

accounting.   A system for keeping track of the financial status of an organization and the financial results of its activities.

capital campaign.   A fund-raising effort aimed at attracting donations to be used to acquire long-term resources such as buildings and equipment.

charitable remainder trust.   A trust from which a donor gets income that is earned on the resources in the trust, but at the donor's death, the charity gets the money remaining in the trust.

creditors.   Individuals or other organizations to whom the organization owes money.

deficit.   The excess of spending over receipts.

effectiveness.   A measure of the degree to which the organization accomplishes its desired goals.

efficiency.   A measure of how close an organization comes to minimizing the amount of resources used to accomplish a result.

externality.   An impact (either negative or positive) that one individual or organization's actions have on others. A product or service may be over- or under-produced because of failure of the free market to consider such impacts in the absence of government intervention.

finance.   A field that focuses on the alternative sources and uses of an organization's resources.

financial accounting.   A system that records historical financial information, summarizes it, and provides reports of what financial events have occurred and of the financial impact of those events.

financial management.   The subset of management that focuses on generating financial information that can be used to improve decision making.

fiscal.   Financial. Often used to refer to a financial year that differs from a calendar year.

managerial accounting.   A subset of accounting related to generating financial information that managers can use to improve the future results of the organization.

national debt.   The total cumulative amount that the federal government has borrowed and not repaid.

not-for-profit.   An organization that has a primary mission related to providing a public service rather than maximizing profit.

off-budget.   Items that are not included in the normal federal government budget process.

on-budget.   Items that are included in the normal federal government budget process.

proprietary.   For-profit.

public economics.   See public finance.

public finance.   Government policies related to spending, taxing, and borrowing decisions, and the study and implementation of those policies.

public goods.   Goods or services that the free market fails to produce or underproduces, which if provided by the government will create aggregate benefits that exceed their cost.

surplus. An excess of receipts over spending.

tax-exempt. Exempt from federal income taxes. Tax-exempt organizations are often also exempt from state and local property, sales, and income taxes.

vendor. Supplier who sells things to the organization.

Questions for Discussion

1-1. What is financial management?

1-2. What is the goal of proprietary, for-profit organizations?

1-3. What is the focus of decisions in public service organizations?

1-4. What is accounting?

1-5. What are the two major subdivisions of accounting? Explain.

1-6. What is finance?

1-7. Is financial management important for public service organizations? If so, why?

1-8. Is it appropriate for public service organizations to earn profits?

1-9. What are the major sources of financing for the federal government, state and local governments, the health sector, and the not-for-profit sector?

1-10. What is public finance?

1-11. What are public goods?

1-12. What is an externality?

1-13. Are monopolies illegal, or does the government sometimes intentionally aid in the establishment of a monopoly?

1-14. How large is total federal and state and local government spending, compared to the U.S. GDP?

1-15. How is it possible for the federal debt to increase in a year when the federal government has a surplus?

1-16. Is there any reason that a not-for-profit organization might decide to decline a gift?

1-17. What is an NGO?

1-18. What is the difference between effectiveness and efficiency?

Suggested Readings

Abramson, Alan J., and Lester M. Salamon. *The Federal Budget and the Nonprofit Sector: FY 1996 and FY 1997*, report prepared for Independent Sector, July 1996.

Anderson, John E. *Public Finance—Principles and Policy*. New York, N.Y.: Houghton Mifflin Company, 2003.

Anthony, Robert N., and Leslie Pearlman Breitner. *Core Concepts of Accounting*, 8th ed. Upper Saddle River, N.J.: Prentice Hall, 2003.

Choi, Frederick D.S., Carol A. Frost, and Gary K. Meek. *International Accounting*, 5th ed. Upper Saddle River, N.J.: Prentice Hall, 2005.

Cleverley, William O., and Andrew Cameron. *Essentials of Health Care Finance*, 6th ed. Sudbury, Mass.: Jones and Bartlett Publishers, 2007.

Emery, Douglas R., John D. Finnerty, and John D. Stowe. *Corporate Financial Management*, 3rd ed. Upper Saddle River, N.J.: Prentice Hall, 2007.

Executive Office of the President, *Economic Report of the President, 2008*. Washington, DC: Government Printing Office, 2008.

Freeman, Robert J., Craig D. Shoulders., Gregory S. Allison, Terry Patton, and G. Robert Smith, Jr. *Governmental and Nonprofit Accounting*, 9th ed. Upper Saddle River, N.J.: Prentice Hall, 2009.

Horngren, Charles T., Gary L. Sundem, William O. Stratton, et al. *Introduction to Management Accounting*, 4th ed. Upper Saddle River, N.J.: Prentice Hall, 2008.

Howard, James. "Government Economic Projections: A Comparison Between CBO and OMB Forecasts." *Public Budgeting and Finance*, Vol. 7 (1987), 14–25.

Hyde, Albert C. *Government Budgeting: Theory, Process, Politics*, 3rd ed. Belmont, Ca.: Wadsworth/Thomson Learning, 2002.

McLaughlin, Thomas A. *Streetsmart Financial Basics for Nonprofit Managers*, 2nd ed. New York, N.Y.: John Wiley & Sons, 2002.

Mikesell, John L. *Fiscal Administration—Analysis and Applications for the Public Sector,* 7th ed. Belmont, Ca.: Thomson Wadsworth, 2006.

Nobes, Chris, and Robert Parker. *Comparative International Accounting*, 9th ed. Upper Saddle River, N.J.: Prentice Hall, 2006.

Pope, Thomas R., Kenneth E. Anderson, and John L. Kramer. *Prentice Hall's Federal Taxation 2009: Comprehensive*. Upper Saddle River, N.J.: Prentice Hall, 2009.

Quarter, Jack, Laurie Mook, and Betty Jane Richmond. *What Counts: Social Accounting for NonProfits and Cooperatives*. Upper Saddle River, N.J.: Prentice Hall, 2003.

Van Horne, James C. *Financial Management & Policy*, 12th ed. Upper Saddle River, N.J.: Prentice Hall, 2002.

Weitzman, Murray S. *The New Nonprofit Almanac and Desk Reference*. San Francisco, Ca.: Jossey-Bass, 2002.

Wilson, Earl R., and Susan C. Kattelus. *Accounting for Governmental and Nonprofit Entities*, 13th ed. Boston, Mass.: McGraw Hill Irwin, 2004.

Wing, Kennard T., Thomas H. Pollak, and Amy Blackwood. *Nonprofit Almanac 2008*. Washington, DC: Urban Institute Press, 2008.

APPENDIX 1-A

Fund-Raising

Not-for-profit organizations have three primary sources of funds. One source is simply borrowing money. Often banks and other lenders will provide loans to not-for-profit organizations. A second source is from the sale of goods or services. This is the primary source of funds for many not-for-profit organizations—e.g., hospitals. The third source is from fund-raising. This appendix provides a brief introduction to fund-raising.

Fund-raising is critical to the financial survival of many not-for-profit organizations. It is a broad field with many dichotomies. Funds are raised from either private or public sources. They come from donations or grants/contracts. They may be restricted or unrestricted. They focus on either operating or capital needs. They may come while donors are alive or after they have died. This appendix will briefly explain some of the dichotomies, and also discuss some essential issues of fund-raising. However, this is just a brief introduction to this topic—the interested reader should explore fund-raising further by reading some of the books listed at the end of this appendix.

Many not-for-profit organizations receive unsolicited donations. However, some statistics should be kept in mind:

- Fifty-seven percent of households were asked to contribute in 2000. Of these households, 61 percent actually contributed, compared with 39 percent of the households that were not asked.
- The average donation from contributing households asked to contribute was $1,945, significantly more than the $1,114 average contribution from non-asked households.[19]

As these statistics demonstrate, there is little doubt that a well-planned campaign, requesting donations, has the potential to increase the flow of resources into a not-for-profit organization.

We often think of fund-raising as the process of getting individuals to donate money to a not-for-profit organization. And that is clearly a key element of fund-raising. However, it is significantly more complicated than that. Fund-raising refers not only to raising money from private sources by generating donations, but also to receiving funds from grants and contracts. Many not-for-profits raise their money from public rather than private sources. For example, many private not-for-profit universities receive a substantial amount of money from governments.

Contributions

Contributions are the most basic form of support for not-for-profit organizations. Contributions may be received from individuals, but are often also received from foundations, corporations, or the government. Contributions may be unrestricted. In that case, the not-for-profit organization can use them for any reasonable purpose related to the mission of the organization. Alternatively, donors may place restrictions on the use of the contribution. The restriction may be related to time or purpose. A time restriction would indicate that the donation cannot be used before a certain date, or must be used by a specific date. A purpose restriction would limit what the organization does with the donation. For example, it is common to restrict donations to pay for construction of a new building, rather than being used for routine operating activities. Endowment gifts are restricted in a way that prohibits them from ever being spent. Instead, such gifts are invested and the organization can use the income from the endowment in accordance with the instructions of the donor.

Donations come in many forms. Donations in cash or by check are easy for the organization. However, for convenience or for tax advantages, many donors give items such as stocks and bonds, real estate, computers, clothing, or services. Organizations receiving various types of donations should become aware of tax rules governing the donations.

---

[19] The Independent Sector, "Giving & Volunteering in the United States: Key Findings," Washington, D.C.: Independent Sector, 2001; www.IndependentSector.org.

Operating Versus Capital

Capital contributions are used to acquire resources that will last for more than one year. Operating contributions are used for the routine day-to-day costs of running the organization throughout the year. Frequently, a not-for-profit organization will hold a *capital campaign*, a fund-raising drive to raise money to acquire long-term resources. Typically such a campaign is used to build and equip a new building or to renovate an existing building. Money raised through a capital campaign is usually restricted for use for capital (long-term) acquisitions, and may not be diverted to pay for the routine current operating expenses of the organization. Many charities also hold operating-fund drives to generate donations that can be used to pay for current operating costs.

Planned Giving

Often not-for-profit organizations benefit from being creative in their fund-raising efforts. Two of the most obvious ways to donate are to just give a gift currently, or to leave money to the organization in a person's will. However, a number of planned giving approaches that are more complicated but have certain advantages have been developed. These approaches often allow donors to get the psychic benefit of donating money while they are alive, while still being able to enjoy the earnings on the money donated during their lifetime. Generally, these arrangements require the establishment of some form of charitable trust.

Once money is placed in an irrevocable charitable trust, donors cannot change their mind and get the money back. Nevertheless, such planned giving has advantages. A *charitable remainder trust* is one in which the donor gets income that is earned on the resources in the trust. When the donor dies, the charity gets the money remaining in the trust, hence its name. One type of remainder trust pays the donor a fixed payment each year. If the income on the trust is not enough to make the payment, some of the principal will be distributed to the donor. The charity may therefore wind up receiving less than the amount originally placed in the trust. Another form distributes a percentage of the trust's assets to the donor each year. If the trust goes up in value due to successful investments, the donor will receive increased annual payments. Alternatively, sometimes trusts are set up where the charity gets annual income from the trusts, but the

principal amount passes to the donor's heirs upon the donor's death. Other arrangements are possible as well.

An individual's specific circumstances dictate which approach may be preferable. Most of the approaches have tax implications. Fund-raisers should acquaint themselves with the tax law in the area of charitable donations, so that they can explain to potential donors the advantages of each approach to planned giving.

Contracts and Grants

Contracts generally involve a quid pro quo. Unlike a donation, which is a gift with nothing expected in exchange, contracts usually provide something to each party. For example, if a corporation signs a research contract with a university, the university will receive funding and the corporation will receive the results of the research study. Grants are often similar to contracts. A foundation might award a grant to a researcher at a university to fund that individual's research. However, a grantor does not receive something in return for the grant in the same way that a contractor does.

This is a fine line of distinction. If a city contracts with Meals for the Homeless to provide meals to homeless people in the city, the city only pays if meals are provided. There might be a contractual arrangement requiring a payment of $8 for each dinner meal provided. On the other hand, a foundation might give Meals for the Homeless a grant of $1,000,000 restricted to providing meals to homeless in the city. Given the mission of Meals for the Homeless, which is to provide meals to homeless in the city, it will be anxious to obtain both contracts and grants like those described. Often grants and contracts may create a more stable source of funding than relying solely on contributions from individuals.

Governments and foundations frequently have programs that provide funds to not-for-profit organizations. Often they will solicit requests for that funding by issuing a request for proposal (RFP). It is helpful for a not-for-profit organization to place itself on the mailing list of potential funders, so that it is aware of any relevant RFPs. Although not-for-profit managers are often familiar with local foundations, exploring new potential grant makers may be a worthwhile activity. The organization Foundations On-Line provides lists of foundations as well as other resources for charities at http://www.foundations.org.

Once an award is received, either as a grant or contract, the not-for-profit organization must inquire about its specific rules and policies before spending begins. That way the organization can ensure that it only spends money on allowable items, and that it gathers all financial information needed to be in compliance with any reporting requirements related to the grant or contract.

Raising Money

Most not-for-profit organizations find that, although they receive some unsolicited donations, they must ask for contributions or grants to have adequate financial resources to achieve their mission. Fund-raising can be very time consuming, and it is common for not-for-profit organizations to employ a development officer who directs their fund-raising efforts.

The role of the development officer is to prioritize, prospect, cultivate, and solicit.[20] First, there is a need to determine the highest priorities for funding. Is the organization most desperate for funds for routine operations, a new building, or a new program? Prospecting refers to researching potential donors to determine what is important to them, and what would be the largest gift that they could afford. This includes not only researching individuals, but also finding the best mailing lists to use for direct mail campaigns, etc. Cultivating refers to the process of educating the potential donors about the organization, its needs, and the difference it makes. Again, this is a broad topic. It may call for a personal visit by the development officer and the CEO of the organization or for direct mail of a carefully designed brochure that educates about the organization, without directly asking for donations. Solicitation is the final step where the donor is actually asked for a gift.

Although the development officer will visit some potential donors, not all donations are solicited in a one-on-one process. There are many approaches to fund-raising. The Girl Scouts sell cookies. Jerry Lewis holds an annual television telethon for the Muscular Dystrophy Association. Public television stations run begathons, where they offer premiums (tote bags, CDs, etc.) for donations. There are $1,000-a-plate dinners, charity balls, golf tournaments, picnics, car washes, and bake sales. There is direct mail and telephone solicitation. Not-for-profit managers should try to be creative in determining approaches that will be sensible and successful for their organization.

Fund-Raising Readings

Anonymous. *Funding Sources for K-12 Education 2005*, 7th ed. Westport, Conn.: Oryx Press, 2005.

Anonymous. *Operating Grants for Nonprofit Organizations 2005*. Westport, Conn.: Oryx Press, 2005.

Bancel, Marilyn. *Preparing Your Capital Campaign: An Excellence in Fund Raising Workbook Series Publication*. The Fund Raising School. San Francisco, Ca.: Jossey Bass, 2000.

Bauer, David G. *The "How To" Grants Manual—Successful Grantseeking Techniques for Obtaining Public and Private Grants*, 6th ed. Westport, Conn.: Praeger Publishers, 2008.

Brown, Larissa Golden, and Martin John Brown. *Demystifying Grant Seeking: What You Really Need to Do to Get Grants*. Hoboken, N.J.: Pfeiffer Wiley, 2nd rev. ed., 2009.

Browning, Beverly A. *Grant Writing for Dummies*, 2nd ed. New York, N.Y.: IDG Books Worldwide, 2005.

Browning, Beverley A. *Perfect Phrases for Writing Grant Proposals*. New York, N.Y.: McGraw Hill, 2008.

Burnett, Ken, *Relationship Fundraising: A Donor-Based Approach to the Business of Raising Money*, 2nd ed. San Francisco, Ca.: Jossey-Bass, 2002.

Ciconte, Barbara L., and Jeanne G. Jacob. *Fundraising Basics: A Complete Guide*, 3rd ed. Boston, Mass.: Jones and Bartlett Publishers, 2009.

Dove, Kent E., Alan M. Spears, and Thomas W. Herbert. *Conducting a Successful Major Gifts and Planned Giving Program: A Comprehensive Guide and Resource*. San Francisco, Ca.: Jossey-Bass, 2002.

Fitzpatrick, Joyce J., and Sandra S. Deller. *Fundraising Skills for Health Care Executives*. New York, N.Y.: Springer Pub., 2000.

Fredricks, Laura. *Developing Major Gifts*. Boston, Mass.: Jones and Bartlett Publishers, 2001.

Graham, Christine. *Keep the Money Coming: A Step-by-Step Strategic Guide to Annual Fundraising*, rev. ed. Sarasota, Fla.: Pineapple Press, 2001.

Greenfield, James M. *Fundraising Fundamentals: A Guide to Annual Giving for Professionals and Volunteers*, 2nd ed. New York, N.Y.: John Wiley & Sons, Inc., 2002.

Grobman, Gary M. and Gary B. Grant, *Fundraising Online: Using the Internet to Raise Serious Money for Your Nonprofit Organization*. Harrisburg, Penn.: White Hat Communications, 2007.

Hart, Ted, James M. Greenfield, and Sheeraz D. Haji, People to People Fundraising: Social Networking and Web 2.0 for Charities, Wiley, 2008.

Hogan, Cecilia. *Prospect Research: A Primer for Growing Nonprofits*, 2nd ed. Boston, Mass.: Jones and Bartlett Publishers, 2008.

---

[20] Jo Ann Hankin, Alan Seidner, and John Zietlow. *Financial Management for Nonprofit Organizations*, New York, N.Y.: John Wiley & Sons, 1998, p. 276.

Karsh, Ellen, and Arlen Sue Fox. *The Only Grant Writing Book You'll Ever Need*, rev. ed. New York, N.Y.: Basic Books, 2006.

Knowles, Cynthia R. *The First-Time Grantwriter's Guide to Success*. Thousand Oaks, Ca.: Corwin Press, Inc., 2002.

Mutz, John, and Katherine Murray. *Fundraising for Dummies*, 2nd ed. New York, N.Y.: IDG Books Worldwide, 2006.

Rosso, Henry A. *Hank Rosso's Achieving Excellence in Fund Raising*, 2nd ed. San Francisco, Ca.: Jossey-Bass, 2003.

Seltzer, Michael. *Securing Your Organization's Future: A Complete Guide to Fundraising Strategies*, rev. and expanded ed. New York, N.Y.: Foundation Center, 2001.

Thompson, Waddy. *The Complete Idiot's Guide to Grant Writing*, 2nd ed. New York, N.Y.: Alpha, 2007.

Warwick, Mal. *How to Write Successful Fundraising Letters: Sample Letters, Style Tips, Useful Hints, Real-World Examples*. San Francisco, Ca.: Jossey-Bass, 2001.

Weinstein, Stanley. *The Complete Guide to Fundraising Management*, 2nd ed. New York, N.Y.: John Wiley & Sons, 2002.

2

Planning for Success: Budgeting

The learning objectives of this chapter are to:

■ define *mission* and describe the role of mission for public service organizations;

■ define *strategic plan* and discuss the importance of selecting a strategy and identifying goals for the organization;

■ explain the role of the long-range or operating plan in setting the organization's specific objectives to aid in achieving its goals;

■ define *budget* and explain how the budget provides the detailed plan for accomplishing the objectives defined in the long-range plan;

■ define and discuss different types of budgets, including *special purpose, operating, capital,* and *cash budgets*;

■ explain the budgeting process, including budget preparation, review and adoption, implementation, and evaluation of results; and

■ acknowledge the political aspects of the budget process.

INTRODUCTION

Organizations are not successful by accident. It takes careful thought and planning to excel. What is the organization trying to achieve? Why does it want to achieve that goal? How does it intend to translate that goal into results? The most successful organizations are the ones that specifically address these questions, rather than simply letting things happen. The budget is the organization's plan.

In the sphere of public service, budgeting is complicated by the fact that not all activities are directly related to maximizing the organization's profit. Although earning a surplus is a healthy financial result, governments, health care organizations, and not-for-profit organizations often undertake activities that will not earn an immediate financial return. What is the benefit from spending additional resources for teaching math in public schools? In the long run, society is likely to benefit. In the budget for the coming year, however, this will simply be an additional expenditure. Planning is accomplished by establishing the mission for the organization, defining a strategy to accomplish the mission, developing a long-range plan that defines the organization's financial and nonfinancial objectives, and preparing specific detailed budgets that define the resources needed to accomplish its goals and objectives.

The budget describes where resources will come from and how they will be used. As part of the budgeting process, it is essential to communicate goals to the people who must achieve them, forecast future events, develop alternatives, select from among alternatives, and coordinate activities.

The budget process includes the preparation of budgets; their review, revision, and ultimate adoption; their implementation; and after-the-fact evaluation of results. A primary responsibility of management is to control results. Control represents a process of trying to keep to the plan. This is done by motivating people to want to achieve the plan, evaluating performance of both organizational units and individual persons, and taking corrective action when things are not going according to plan.

These issues are discussed in this chapter; Chapter 3 picks up where this chapter leaves off, looking at a variety of additional budgeting issues for governmental, health, and not-for-profit organizations. It examines a number of different types of budget presentations and ways to organize budgets, and also discusses a variety of budgeting techniques. That chapter finishes with a discussion of some unique aspects of budgeting for governmental organizations.

MISSION

The organization's *mission* represents its raison d'être. Public, health care, and not-for-profit organizations have missions that relate to providing a public service. Their mission may be to improve society through providing wide access to culture—through museums, opera, ballet, or symphony. Or the mission may relate primarily to healing the ill of society or feeding and sheltering the poor. For government, the mission may be to provide essential common services such as police, education, sewers, and fire protection.

For public, health, and not-for-profit organizations, then, money is a means to an end rather than the end itself. To some extent, the health care industry is becoming more and more a part of the for-profit sector. Similarly, the for-profit education sector has grown. For such proprietary public service organizations, profits do play an important role in the organization's mission. However, that profit focus must be balanced with the public service elements of the organization's mission.

In Chapter 1, Meals for the Homeless, a hypothetical organization, is introduced. One of the first activities for Leanna Schwartz, the new executive director of Meals for the Homeless, would be to examine the *mission statement*. To lead the organization, she must be thoroughly familiar with what the organization hopes to achieve. The mission statement of Meals for the Homeless might be:

> Meals for the Homeless recognizes the plight of the many poor, disenfranchised citizens of Middle City. Whether the problems of these individuals are caused by our society or brought on by their own personal misfortune, we hold that society must provide at least some minimal level of services for these individuals. First and foremost among those services is an adequate supply of nutritional food. It is the mission of Meals for the Homeless to meet that need, whenever it is not being met by other sources.

Like all good mission statements, the mission of Meals for the Homeless includes both breadth and limitations. A mission should be targeted. If the goal is to do everything for everyone, the mission is unlikely to be achieved and the organization will lack clear direction. If the mission is too narrow, it may not provide the organization with sufficient challenge to sustain itself over time.

In the mission statement for Meals for the Homeless, breadth is represented by the fact that the goal of the organization is to meet the nutritional needs of everyone who cannot get food from other sources. The limitations are that the organization is geographically limiting its efforts to Middle City, and to supplying food. It is not providing jobs, shelter, medical care, or other services.

STRATEGIC PLAN

Once the organization has a clearly defined mission, it can develop its *strategy* for accomplishing that mission. The *strategic plan* defines the primary approaches that the organization will take to achieve its mission. Generally, strategic plans do not have specific financial targets. However, they set the stage for specific, detailed budgets.

The mission of Meals for the Homeless (Meals) is to ensure an adequate supply of nutritious food for the homeless. It could attempt to achieve that mission by a large number of approaches. Meals could be a lobbying organization, raising money and using it to lobby for legislation requiring the government to provide nutritious food for the homeless. Another strategy would be to start a "take a homeless person to dinner" campaign. This approach would consist primarily of an advertising blitz, trying to get the general public to buy meals and give them directly to homeless people. The general strategy that Meals has taken is to solicit donations of food and money, and to use those resources to prepare and serve meals directly to the homeless. Meals uses two delivery trucks and one soup kitchen to carry out this strategy. This was pretty much the way things had been for the past 10 years, despite an unfortunately growing number of homeless in the city.

When Leanna Schwartz became executive director of Meals for the Homeless, she decided that Meals had a clear mission. It also had an overall strategy or approach for accomplishing that mission. However, it had no broad goals. As a result, as the needs of the homeless had grown, Meals had not responded. Therefore, as one of her first priorities, she decided to form a subcommittee from her Board of Trustees to establish a more formal strategic plan, including a set of goals for the organization. The strategic plan would serve as a link between the mission and activities that the organization would undertake to achieve that mission.

As part of the new strategic plan, Meals developed the following goals:

- Directly provide nutritional meals for the homeless of Middle City.
- Directly provide nutritional meals for indigent individuals in public housing.
- Increase the percentage of the target population served from 20 percent to 60 percent within five years.
- Expand funding sources to cover the increase in services. Include corporate sponsorship and direct fund-raising activities.

Schwartz was pleased with this set of goals. She believed that it pointed the organization in the direction its mission dictated. She also believed that it gave her some tangible targets to work toward. The next step would be to translate the goals of the strategic plan into attainable objectives.

LONG-RANGE PLAN

While the strategic plan establishes goals and broad strategies, the *long-range plan* (sometimes referred to as the operating plan) considers how to achieve those goals. Long-range plans establish the major activities that will have to be carried out in the coming three to five years. This process provides a link between the strategic plan and the day-to-day activities of the organization. Organizations that do not prepare a long-range plan are often condemned to just sustain current activities, at best. Many managers simply try to replicate the current year's results when they plan for the coming year. They take whatever has happened, add a few percentage points for inflation, and assume that they have an adequate plan for the future.

The problem with that approach is that after five years the organization will likely be exactly where it is today. It will be providing the same quantity and quality of services. It will not be able to look back at where it was five years ago, compare that to where it is today, and find that a satisfying amount of progress has been made. Most public service managers believe that they are trying to achieve something. They do not work in the field just to collect a paycheck, but rather to provide some service to society. Given that, it does not make sense to try to sustain operations without any significant gains over time.

Management needs vision. Great managers are those individuals under whose steward-ship organizations make great strides forward. In some cases, vision may come from inspiration that only a few people ever have. In many cases, however, vision is a result of hard work and careful planning. It is the result of taking the time to think about the organization's mission, form a strategic plan with goals, and then establish the tactics to carry out that plan and achieve the goals.

For example, one element of the strategic plan for Meals for the Homeless is expansion of meals provided from 20 percent to 60 percent of the target population. This cannot be achieved by simply carrying out the existing daily routine, day after day, year after year. Nor can it happen overnight. A long-range plan must be developed that will specify how the organization expects to achieve that goal.

The managers of Meals will have to determine what must happen to attain its goals. Schwartz would likely start by having conversations with many interested parties about how best to get meals to the poor of the city. Next a variety of approaches or tactics might be considered. Finally, a long-range plan will be formulated.

The long-range plan should focus on both financial and nonfinancial issues. For example, there are many dimensions to quality in providing a service. How long do the homeless have to wait in line for the meal? Do the homeless like the way the food tastes? What is the relationship between each soup kitchen and its community? Organizations, especially public service organizations, need to be concerned with more than just the number of units of service provided (*output*). The number of meals served is important. But Meals' long-range plan should more broadly help it to achieve its desired *outcomes*. Outcomes are the results that the organization is trying to achieve. These objectives are not all easily quantified in financial terms.

For example, Meals' mission calls for providing the homeless with an adequate amount of nutritional food. Therefore, a desired outcome is providing the homeless with nutritional meals. To achieve its mission, Meals might adopt a strategy of having its meals meet all federal government daily recommended levels for a balanced diet. The long-range plan needs to include specific tactics for that strategy. Meal's long-range plan may indicate that every meal must contain some protein, fat, carbohydrates, vegetables, and fruit. The organization will only deem itself to be effective if it not only provides meals to enough homeless, but also provides meals that meet its nutritional targets.

Some objectives are more directly tied to financial issues. After gathering input and considering choices, Schwartz might decide that the most efficient way to expand from 20 percent to 60 percent coverage (the goal) would be to add three new locations, strategically located to be readily accessible to the largest number of homeless, and to add four more vehicles to its current fleet of two (specific tactics to achieve the goal). These changes will require specific financial resources.

All of these tactics could probably be carried out within three months, except that the organization does not have the money for the expansion. Money will be needed to buy equipment and vehicles, pay rent, buy food, and hire staff. The long-range plan will also have to address how to raise the money and when to spend it (more tactics). A reasonable long-range plan for Meals for the Homeless might include the following objectives:

Year 1: Establish fund-raising campaign and begin fund-raising. Raise enough money to open one new site.

Year 2: Add a food distribution/soup kitchen location. Raise additional money to acquire and operate a vehicle and open another location. Solicit more restaurants for leftover food donations.

Year 3: Add another food distribution/soup kitchen location and a new vehicle. Raise additional money to acquire and operate a vehicle and open another location. Solicit more restaurants for leftover food donations.

Year 4: Add another food distribution/soup kitchen location and a new vehicle. Raise additional money to acquire and operate two vehicles. Solicit more restaurants for leftover food donations.

Year 5: Add two new vehicles. Raise additional money to begin replacement of old kitchen equipment and old vehicles. Get enough contributions to at least reach a steady state in which replacements take place as needed.

As can be seen from the preceding objectives, unless planning is done in year 1 to raise money, the organization will never be able to undertake the acquisition and expansion in years 2 through 5. The organization cannot be satisfied with raising enough to get through the coming year. For it to thrive, rather than merely survive, it must think ahead. The long-range plan provides the opportunity to think ahead prior to making budgets for the coming year.

The objectives included in the long-range plan can be thought of as quantified targets. These targets can relate to both inputs and outputs. For example, we can think in terms of specific fund-raising objectives, specifying the total dollar amount of donations we plan to receive each year over the coming five years. We can also think in terms of the specific number of delivery trucks to be purchased. These targets or objectives make it possible to create specific detailed budgets for the organization in financial terms.

BUDGETS

What is a *budget*? It is simply a plan. The plan indicates management's objectives and shows how it expects to obtain and use resources to achieve those objectives. In some cases the plan may be the result of enacted legislation. The budget indicates the amount of money that the organization expects to receive from all sources for the time period it covers, often a year. It also indicates the amount of money that the organization will have available to spend to provide services. Thus, it provides managers with a detailed action plan. Based on the information in the budget, managers make decisions that they believe will help them to carry out the plan and therefore accomplish the organization's objectives.

Budgets must be developed to plan for the accomplishment of goals and objectives. The process requires that a number of predictions and decisions be made. How many homeless will there be next year? What percentage of the homeless will be children? How many workers should the organization assign to fund-raising? How many restaurants should be solicited for food? What vehicles will be purchased, and at what price? How much will kitchen employees be paid per hour and in total for the coming year? How much money will Meals receive in donations each month of the year? All of these questions and many more must be answered in the process of developing the budgets for the organization.

Virtually all managers become involved in creating and using budgets. Budgeting is not the sole domain of financial managers. Budgets establish the amount of resources that are available for specific activities. As we learn from economics, resources are not unlimited. They must be used wisely. Organizations attempt to do this by planning the activities they will undertake and how much they will spend on them. However, budgets do not merely limit the resources that can be spent. They help the organization achieve its goals and objectives.

Budgets help the manager to understand whether the organization expects that receipts will exceed disbursements and a surplus (profit) will occur, or if spending is expected to exceed receipts, resulting in a deficit (loss). If the latter is the case, the budget may indicate how the organization plans to cover that deficit without having to cease operations.

Budgeting for governments as compared with budgeting for other types of public service organizations is significantly different. It is common for decisions by the Board of Trustees of a not-for-profit organization to require that the budget for the organization not show a deficit. In carrying out the plan, however, many times a not-for-profit organization will actually spend more than the amount in the approved budget, sometimes resulting in a deficit. For governments, however, the amount that is actually spent generally cannot exceed the budgeted amount, by law. As a result, governments tend to place more controls on spending, and the options available to government managers are often more limited than those available to managers of other types of organizations.

Often, balancing the budget results in limiting services provided. This is true for all kinds of public service organizations. It is frustrating to managers to have to limit the amount of services provided to the organization's clients. However, it is worse to run out of money and to have to stop providing any services at all. Failure to plan carefully can result in a level of spending that exceeds an organization's resources and leads to a financial crisis; in some instances the organization will even be forced to cease operations.

Special Purpose Budget

Although most organizations prepare broad annual budgets that are intended to include all of their activities for the year, at times a special opportunity may arise. An organization may wish to consider undertaking an activity, but there is no money set aside for it in the annual budget. This does not necessarily create an insurmountable roadblock. At any time during the year, a *special purpose budget* can be developed for a specific project, program, or activity. The organization can then decide whether it wishes to undertake the activity based on the proposed special purpose budget.

For example, suppose that Steve Netzer, the new chief operating officer (COO) of the Hospital for Ordinary Surgery (HOS), has an idea for a program that could help the public and might generate additional patients for the hospital. He would like to send nurses to local supermarkets to do free blood pressure screenings. The hospital would pay for the nurses and the supplies. The costs of the nurses and supplies are referred to as *expenses*. Expenses are the resources consumed in the process of providing goods and services. The hospital expects to earn *revenues* from supermarket customers that become patients as a result of medical problems uncovered by the screening. Revenues are the resources the organization receives in exchange for providing goods or services.

Will the extra revenues from these new patients be enough to cover the expenses of care provided to them as well as the expenses related to the screening? A special budget comparing all of the expenses and revenues can be developed. If the revenues exceed the expenses as a result of the program, then a *profit* will be earned. Profit is simply the excess of revenues over expenses. A profit is sometimes referred to as a surplus or as net income. If the expenses exceed the revenues, the excess of expenses over revenues is referred to as a loss or deficit. Once the expected profit or loss is known, the organization can decide if it would like to implement the plan. It is not necessary to wait until the next annual budget cycle to consider and implement special budgets.

Depending on the financial magnitude of the special activity, the organization's management may be able to approve the activity, or it may have to be approved by the board of directors, governors, or trustees. In the case of governmental bodies, the additional activity may constitute a change in the overall budget, and it is essential to ensure that such a change is legal.

CASE STUDY
Special Purpose Budget

To develop a more detailed special purpose budget example, assume that Dwight Ives, town manager of Millbridge, received a call from one of the churches in town. The church had a very rudimentary accounting system, recording cash receipts when received and cash payments when made. As long as the church had money in the bank, its governing body assumed that everything was okay. When it ran out of money, the church made special appeals to its congregants. Over the years, this had created several financial crises, such as the winter when the boiler died and the church had no heat for weeks. In that instance, as now, the parish priest, Father Purtell, had asked his friend the town manager for advice on financial planning.

Father Purtell's current problem involved a proposal by some congregants to send a group of teenagers to the Holy Land for about two weeks during the coming summer. The concept called for the families of the students to pay part of the cost, the students to hold fund raisers, and the church to provide a subsidy. The church elders felt that the church could afford to contribute $5,000 to the program, but that was all. Father Purtell had no idea how to decide how much to charge the families and whether the trip could be arranged within the limits of the subsidy. He did know that a decision must be made soon, so that there would be time to enroll teenagers in the program and make all the necessary airline and hotel reservations. He called on Dwight for some advice. What did he think? Could the church run the program? He was worried about the consequences if it turned out that the church had to provide a subsidy above the $5,000.

Dwight's first questions involved whether Father Purtell felt comfortable with the basic concept: Was the church in the business of setting up trips to Israel? Did such a trip make sense, given the mission of the church? Father Purtell explained that he strongly believed that the concept of the trip was an appropriate church activity. First of all, the church was always struggling with developing programs to keep teenagers active with supervised activities during the summer months. Second, the visit to the Holy Land would include stops at Bethlehem and Jerusalem. The potential positive religious experience for young impressionable minds could not be surpassed by any other program he could imagine. Since the program did fit nicely with the overall mission of the church, Dwight indicated that the next step was to develop a plan to determine if the program could work. Only by developing a plan could one have an idea of how much to charge families and whether the program would likely be financially feasible.

Dwight suggested that they start the plan by calculating the profit or loss from the program. "How many participants are you expecting, and what will you charge them?" asked

Dwight. "That's the problem," Father Purtell replied. "I want to have enough participants and charge them the right amount so that the program can work. Can't we calculate that? Maybe we should start with the costs and then determine the necessary price."

Dwight explained that he felt the father was starting the process without gathering enough background information. The first element of the plan should be an environmental scan. What other trips to the Holy Land are available? How are they similar and dissimilar from what the church had in mind? What do other organizations charge for the trip? Why might some people prefer what the church was offering? Even if the trip fit with the church mission, was there really a need for the church to get into this new venture? Dwight cautioned that one must look around outside the organization to see what others are or are not doing before developing a reasonable plan for the organization's proposed activity. Father Purtell agreed, and they scheduled a meeting for one week later.

At the next meeting, Dwight Ives and Father Purtell discussed the results of the environmental scan. The priest was grateful for having taken the approach. In his mind, he relayed to Dwight, he had assumed that at least half of the teenagers in his parish would jump at the opportunity to go on the church-sponsored trip. Having talked to travel agents, school authorities, a group of interested parents, and others, he had learned a lot. In fact, there were few if any formalized programs that would compete with the church for a trip to the Holy Land. However, a number of travel agents had attractive family packages, and some families had already purchased airline tickets and made hotel reservations for family trips to the Holy Land. The travel agents also had pointed out that many families make travel plans early, with a variety of destinations, and he should consider that. In fact, based on conversations with parishioners, he found that to be the case. He also found out that many of the teenagers already had plans to return to summer camps they had gone to in the past.

Based on his environmental review, he now felt that he could attract a group of thirty to fifty teenagers if the price was right. Travel agents were charging about $2,500 per person for a similar trip. His trip had the added advantage of church chaperones and the benefit of the youngsters being able to spend a lot of time with other children their age.

Dwight felt that using this, they could start to develop a specific plan. He explained that a budget was needed to decide if the project was feasible. He sat down with the father near his computer and turned on a spreadsheet program, Excel.[1] Dwight suggested that they set up the budget in terms of anticipated receipts and payments related to the program. He typed in headings, resulting in Table 2-1.

TABLE 2-1 Holy Land Trip—Special Budget

	A	B	C
1	*CHURCH OF MILLBRIDGE*		
2	*Budget*		
3	*Holy Land Trip*		
4			
5	PROJECTED RECEIPTS		
6	Charges		
7	Less Uncollectibles		
8	Net charges		
9	Fund-raising		
10	Total Receipts		
11			

---

[1] Excel is a registered trademark of Microsoft Corp. There are a number of other spreadsheet programs, such as LOTUS 1-2-3® from Lotus Development and Quattro Pro® from Corel.

"Whoa!" Father Purtell said. "What is that line for *Uncollectibles?*" Dwight explained that it was certainly likely that some people would make a deposit but would never fully pay for the trip. It would be very risky to assume that everyone would pay the full amount charged. They then discussed the fact that to estimate the revenues, they would need to project both an anticipated number of participants, as well as a projected price. They would also need to know what types of expenses would be incurred. They gave this some thought, trying to anticipate all the different things on which money would have to be spent. Working together, they generated Table 2-2.

The priest decided that 30 teens would be an easily obtainable goal, and he wanted to start out seeing if the church could afford the program making conservative assumptions. Line 6 in Table 2-2 shows the 30 teens. The value in line 6, column B, was then multiplied by an assumed charge of $2,000 (line 6, column C) to get the total charges of $60,000. After discussion, Dwight and the priest decided to use 3 percent of total charges as an estimate for uncollectibles. Assuming that each student not only paid $2,000, but also raised $250 through fund-raising activities (e.g., bake sales, car washes), there would be an additional $7,500 in receipts. Dwight felt this was a bit ambitious, but the father felt it was an attainable goal. He felt that if each teen committed to raising those funds, they would value the trip more and get more out of it. Dwight remained skeptical.

Based on his discussions with travel agents, Father Purtell was sure he could get airfare for $1,000 or less. With a guarantee of 30 or more teens, probably substantially less. To be conservative, however, they used the $1,000 airfare. The father felt that there would have to be one chaperone for every 15 teens. With 30 teens anticipated, there would be two chaperones, and their airfare was included.

They would need hotels for 15 nights. Hotels were calculated based on what the travel agents said they could get, assuming double occupancy. The hotels were calculated, therefore, at $80 per person per night. For $160 per night per room, they should be able to get something reasonable. The room cost was therefore $1,200 per teen ($160 per room ÷ 2

TABLE 2-2 Holy Land Trip—Special Budget: Draft

	A	B	C	D
1	**CHURCH OF MILLBRIDGE**			
2	*Budget*	*Projected*	*Per*	
3	*Holy Land Trip*	*# of People*	*Person*	*Total*
4				
5	**PROJECTED RECEIPTS**			
6	Charges	30	$2,000	$60,000
7	Less Uncollectibles			1,800
8	Net charges			$58,200
9	Fund-raising	30	250	7,500
10	Total Receipts			$65,700
11				
12	**PROJECTED PAYMENTS**			
13	Airfare	32	$1,000	$32,000
14	Hotels	30	1,200	36,000
15	Chaperone Salaries	2	3,000	6,000
16	Food	32	600	19,200
17	Admisssion fees	32	250	8,000
18	Guide	1	3,000	3,000
19	Local transport (bus)		2,500	2,500
20	Entertainment	32	300	9,600
21	Other	32	200	6,400
22	Continency fund			2,500
23	Total Payments			$125,200
24				
25	Projected Surplus / (Deficit)			($59,500)

teens per room × 15 nights). The travel agents assured him that hotels would provide free rooms for the chaperones if he booked rooms for the rest of the group.

The rest of the payment or expense budget was generated based on similar discussions, through line 21. When they got to line 22 Dwight suggested a contingency fund. "What for?" asked Purtell, "What will that money be used for?" Dwight explained that he had absolutely no idea. "That's why it's called a contingency fund. If we could identify something we need to spend money on, we'd list it specifically. This is to protect the church against costs it doesn't anticipate. Remember, you have no experience running trips of this sort." They finally agreed on a lump sum $2,500 contingency fund.

When the projected deficit was calculated, Father Purtell was devastated. "We only set aside $5,000 for a subsidy, not $60,000!"

Dwight was less dejected. "A budget is a plan," he pointed out, "but we can work some more on the plan. Things don't always work out the way you first plan them. That's why we go through the planning process rather than just going full steam ahead." He suggested that the father spend a week working on each revenue and expense category, getting more information, and making some choices about the existing plan.

The next week they met again. "I've made some decisions," the father explained. "Let's put them in the computer and see what happens." He then relayed the following details to Dwight.

1. Raise the price to $2,500.
2. Raise the number of teens to 50.
3. Lower the airfare to $600.
4. Lower the hotel cost to $40 per person per night.
5. Change the chaperone salaries to zero.
6. Cut the admission fees per person in half.

Dwight started to protest about several of the changes, but he changed the numbers in the spreadsheet, which automatically recomputed all of the math, resulting in Table 2-3. The priest was elated when he saw the result.

TABLE 2-3 Holy Land Trip—Special Budget: Final

	A	B	C	D
1	CHURCH OF MILLBRIDGE			
2	Budget	Projected	Per	
3	Holy Land Trip	# of People	Person	Total
4				
5	PROJECTED RECEIPTS			
6	Charges	50	$2,500	$125,000
7	Less Uncollectibles			3,750
8	Net charges			$121,250
9	Fund-raising	50	250	12,500
10	Total Receipts			$133,750
11				
12	PROJECTED PAYMENTS			
13	Airfare	54	$600	$32,400
14	Hotels	50	600	30,000
15	Chaperone Salaries	4	0	0
16	Food	54	600	32,400
17	Admisssion fees	54	125	6,750
18	Guide	1	3,000	3,000
19	Local transport (bus)		2,500	2,500
20	Entertainment	54	300	16,200
21	Other	54	200	10,800
22	Continency fund			2,500
23	Total Payments			$136,550
24				
25	Projected Surplus / (Deficit)			($2,800)

"But how do you justify all of these changes?" Dwight gasped.

"Aha!" responded Father Purtell, "As you said, I just had to examine the plan and see what could be done about it."

"But you can't expect to raise the price and raise the number of participants," Dwight argued. "That flies in the face of the laws of supply and demand."

"No," said the priest. "It doesn't. You see, I could tell that I would have to raise the price, and I know that I will probably only get 25, or perhaps even 20 at the higher price. So I went over to my colleague, Father Stewart, in West Oak and proposed that some of the teens from his parish come on the trip. Between the two parishes, we will be able to get 40 to 50 teens at the higher price. I'm sure of it. And if I'm wrong, we can cancel the trip with no lost money."

"Well, that explains the price and the number of teens," Dwight responded. "What about the other changes?" Father Purtell answered, "First, I realized that with the additional teens we would need at least one more chaperone. I started thinking about whom we could hire and came up with the most wonderful idea. Several of our adult parishioners would love to take a trip to the Holy Land but cannot afford it. If I can pay the airfare, hotel, and all expenses, they would be more than happy to go as chaperones and not charge any salary. Father Stewart and I decided that two parent chaperones would come from each parish.

"When I went to the travel agent and mentioned 54 people, we were able to get a substantial group discount on the flight and on all admission charges as well. The hotel cost is more of a problem; we will have to have four teens to a room. The rooms all have two double beds. They can double up or they can bring sleeping bags and take turns sleeping on the floor. I got our parish teen council involved, and it was their suggestion as a way to lower the cost per person. I found that getting more input in the budgeting process can open your eyes to things that you wouldn't think of on your own. The four chaperones will share two rooms, which the travel agent will get for free when we book the rooms for the teens. We still have to rent only one bus for the whole group."

"Well, this seems good, but what if you only get 40 teens instead of 50?"

"Oh, I don't see that as a problem. The only reason that would occur is because of the price. Now, however, as you can see, we are only projecting a $2,800 deficit. And the deficit will only be that high if we need to use the entire $2,500 contingency fund. Our church is still willing to put up a $5,000 subsidy. I convinced Father Stewart to come up with a similar $5,000 subsidy from his parish. Even with the $2,800 deficit, we still have over $7,000 available for financial aid for those teens who cannot afford the full amount. We will give scholarships.

"I must say, this has worked out splendidly. If I hadn't come to you, we might have just done the program without really planning the finances. We probably would have lost nearly $60,000. It would have been a disaster. And I'm glad you told me not to be discouraged by our first plan. When I saw the $59,500 deficit, my first reaction was just to assume we couldn't do this wonderful program. But by having the budget, I had a plan to work with. You were so right to encourage me to reexamine each element of the plan to see what changes could be made. I was able to make changes and still accomplish the overall goal of getting teens over to the religious sites in the Holy Land. And the way the revised budget has come out, we will be able to send 50 teens instead of just 30!"

LESSONS FROM THE CASE This special purpose budget case study raises a number of important points. First, there is no magic to budgeting. Budgeting requires thought. Does the planned project fit with the organization's mission? Does it make sense to undertake this, given what other organizations are already doing? Can the organization afford to undertake the project? Budgeting requires estimating all the likely receipts and all the likely payments. The more facts that are available, the better. Knowing the airline fares, the hotel prices, the willingness of teens to live four to a room, and the admission rates at various attractions leads to a more accurate budget. Inevitably, some assumptions must be made, such as the number of participants. The assumptions should be reasonable. A contingency plan should exist in case the assumptions do not all come out as anticipated. And the process is very likely to require a number of preliminary drafts and revisions before a feasible plan is developed and accepted by all parties. Even so, things may not occur according to the budget. Once approved, efforts must be made to try to keep as closely to the plan as possible.

The Master Budget

Although some budgeting is done on an ad hoc basis, as in the case study discussed previously, most budgeting is done on a regular basis. The *master budget* incorporates and summarizes all of the budget elements for the coming year. These elements provide the specific detail to accomplish both the routine ongoing activities of the organization, as well as the coming year's portion of the long-range plan. By incorporating the service volume, prices, costs, cash flow, and capital spending, the master budget becomes the plan for everything the organization will be doing during the coming year. It is prepared each year.

The main elements of the master budget, sometimes called the comprehensive budget, are the *operating budget* and the *financial budget*. The operating budget presents a plan for revenues and expenses for the fiscal year. The financial budget includes a *cash budget* and a *capital budget*. While the cash budget focuses primarily on the coming year, the capital budget considers outlays for resources that will provide service for a number of years into the future.

Operating and cash budgets provide estimates for the organization's various types of revenues and expenses or *expenditures*.[2] For example, for the Hospital for Ordinary Surgery (HOS), the major types of revenue in the operating budget might be patient revenue, donations, investment income, gift shop, and cafeteria. For the town of Millbridge, revenues would be more likely to consist of real estate taxes, state aid, sewer taxes, and user fees. Meals for the Homeless is likely to have items such as donations, grants, and government aid. For all three types of organizations, typical expenses would include salaries, supplies, and rent.

Capital budgets focus on the acquisition of long-term resources. Expenses such as salaries, supplies, and rent would not appear in a capital budget. Instead, one might see a listing of specific pieces of equipment and/or a building. Revenues are often not included in the capital budget, which focuses on the cost of and justification for the acquisition. However, revenue flows that result from acquiring the items in the capital budget are considered in the capital budgeting process. Also, if old equipment or buildings are sold as they are replaced by new equipment and buildings, the revenues from the proceeds of those sales may be included in the capital budget.

THE OPERATING BUDGET   The operating budget is a plan for expected revenues and expenses. For-profit organizations generally receive resources, such as money, in exchange for goods and services. Such exchanges generate revenues for the organization. Not-for-profit organizations

---

[2] Health care providers typically use the word *expense*, whereas governments refer to *expenditures*. Some not-for-profits use *expense*, whereas others use the term *expenditure* more frequently. There are some subtle differences in meaning, which are discussed in Chapter 12.

may earn revenues in a similar fashion and may also receive revenue from contributions or grants. Governments may earn revenues from the sale of goods and services, but they also are entitled by law to receive tax revenues to be used to provide services. Expenses represent the resources that the organization uses in carrying on its activities.

Revenues and Other Support. When patients are treated at HOS, they receive bills for the care provided. Suppose that a patient pays $5,000 for the care received. HOS receives the $5,000 in cash. The organization is said to have earned revenue of $5,000. The revenue measures the amount of resources that have been received in exchange for the services that HOS provided.

The basic approach to developing an operating budget is not substantially different from the approach taken in preparing the special purpose budget. One must consider all possible sources of revenue or other *support*. Revenues can be calculated by predicting the volume of goods or services to be provided and their unit price. Multiplying the price per unit by the volume of units provides the organization with an estimate of its revenues.

In the case of governments, revenues are often calculated by multiplying tax rates by the tax base. For example, assume that in Millbridge, the real estate has a total assessed value of $200,000,000. That amount is referred to as the town's tax base. The town's tax rate might be stated as $5 per hundred dollars of assessed value. This means that the taxpayer would have to pay $5 for every $100 of assessed property value. Therefore, if the taxpayer's house is assessed at $300,000, the taxes would be $15,000. For the town as a whole, the taxes would be $10,000,000 ($200,000,000 tax base × [$5 ÷ $100]).

When revenues are listed in the operating budget, they are generally separated by type. Suppose that the state gives the town of Millbridge $2,000,000 in aid for use in the school system. The town charges a sewer tax, which is $80 per year for each residential property. There are 10,000 homes in the town, yielding a total sewer tax of $800,000. Finally the town charges users of the town pool, golf course, and tennis courts varying fees. Based on the number of users of each facility and the prices charged, the town expects to bring in a total of $500,000 in user fees. In preparing its budget for the coming year, the town would likely have a listing such as the following:

Town of Millbridge
Operating Budget
Projected Revenues

Real Estate Taxes	$10,000,000
State Aid	2,000,000
Sewer Tax	800,000
Recreation User Fees	500,000
Total Revenues	$13,300,000

There is often great latitude in the budgeting process. Except in governmental situations, where laws may dictate the format and content of budgets, organizations can develop their budgets in any way that the managers believe will be most useful. Therefore, unless prohibited by law, Millbridge's revenue budget might be grouped as taxes and other sources, as follows:

Taxes	$10,800,000
Other Revenues	2,500,000
Total Revenues	$13,300,000

In this format, real estate and sewer taxes have been grouped together. Other groupings are possible as well.

In addition to having a revenue budget that shows the revenues by each major source, there should be detailed supporting schedules backing up each line on a budget. This is true for an expense budget as well. These schedules provide the information that explains the derivation of each number that appears on the budget. For example, each piece of property and the assessed value of that property should be listed. These supporting schedules are not a part of the finished budget. However, they provide important backup information, especially if questions arise before the budget is adopted.

In preparing the revenue budget, it is extremely important to consider all possible sources of revenue or support. In addition to taxes or charges for services, these sources might include ancillary activities such as gift shops or restaurants, endowment income, gifts, or grants.

In predicting revenue for the coming year, managers should consider many issues. Managers need to be concerned not only with what they might want to do, but also other factors such as the economy, inflation, growth, employment, interest rates, and so on. In some cases, formalized forecasting of variables is needed to arrive at a sound budget. For example, Millbridge's town manager, Dwight Ives, would likely realize that he has to undertake a commonsense review of the likely impact of the economic environment on the organization. He would plan to use a variety of forecasting approaches to predict variables that would affect the revenues of the town. (Forecasting is discussed in Chapter 3.)

Some variables are uncontrollable. However, not everything is outside of the control of the manager. For example, managers often have to make investment decisions. If the organization has money that it will not be using right away, it must decide how to invest that money. Managers can decide to invest in safe investments with low rates of return or can seek out somewhat more risky investments that have higher possible returns.

Also, things like user fees are subject to some degree of control. Suppose that last year the town sold 3,000 pool passes at $100 per pass for the season. Since the town's population is fairly stable, the forecast is for similar results in the coming year. However, that represents a forecast of what will happen rather than a budget. Before the budget can be finalized, it is necessary to consider factors such as the impact of raising or lowering the price, competition from new county facilities, the potential impact of making improvements at the town's pool, and so on.

Although it is true that not everything is out of the manager's control, neither can managers do whatever they want. In preparing the previously mentioned revenue budget, Ives made assumptions of modest increases in taxes and user fees. He knows, however, that if the expense budget is higher than the revenue budget, he will need larger increases in taxes. Such increases will be politically difficult to attain. At that point, there will be difficult negotiations with the mayor and town council over whether to increase taxes or cut services.

Expenses. Some organizations budget revenues first and then expenses, and some do the reverse. The order is not critical, since it is likely to be necessary to make revisions to arrive at an acceptable budget in any case. In many situations, the revenue and expense budgets will be prepared simultaneously. For example, government agencies may be preparing their expenditure budgets individually, while the central government administration is estimating total revenues that will be available.

Dwight Ives's first attempt at developing a budget for expenses considered all of the costs currently incurred as well as additional expenditures required to incorporate elements of the town's long-range plan. Aggregating all of the individual costs required to operate the town resulted in the following budget for expenditures:

Town of Millbridge
Operating Budget
Projected Expenditures

Salaries	$ 10,800,000
Utilities	1,800,000
Supplies	1,500,000
Total Expenditures	$ 14,100,000

Surplus or Deficit. The budgeted expenses of the organization are subtracted from the budgeted revenues to determine whether the plan projects a surplus or deficit for the coming year. In some instances, a loss may be acceptable. Organizations with large amounts of accumulated profits from earlier years may be willing to lose money in other years. In other cases, losses may be inevitable. In no case should an organization be indifferent. Unfortunately, Millbridge does not have a balanced operating budget, as can be seen:

Town of Millbridge
Operating Budget
Projected Revenues and Expenditures

Revenues	
Real Estate Taxes	$ 10,000,000
State Aid	2,000,000
Sewer Tax	800,000
Recreation User Fees	500,000
Total Revenues	$ 13,300,000
Expenses	
Salaries	$ 10,800,000
Utilities	1,800,000
Supplies	1,500,000
Total Expenditures	$ 14,100,000
Deficit	$ (800,000)

In general, the town council would not legally be allowed to adopt a budget containing a deficit. Ives would have to go back to each element of the operating budget, finding additional revenues and reducing expenditures. This would be similar to the process that Ives required Father Purtell to undertake to revise the Holy Land trip budget. It would be very helpful if Ives could look at the budgeted results for each main activity of the town. For example, is the town swimming pool expected to make money or lose money? Such breakdowns of budget information into more useful formats are discussed in Chapter 3.

The surplus or deficit reported in the operating budget relates just to the time period covered by that budget. Each period's surplus or deficit is determined based just on the revenues and expenses of that period. The budgets presented in this chapter are highly simplified. Table 2-4 presents a somewhat more realistic budget for one department in the hypothetical HOS.

Cash versus Accrual Accounting. In some organizations, revenues are only acknowledged, or *recognized*, by the organization when they are received in cash. In those cases, expenses are only recognized when they have been paid in cash. They are said to use a *cash basis* of

TABLE 2-4 Department Budget

Hospital for Ordinary Surgery
Laboratory Department
Operating Budget

Account	Budget
311. Revenue	
010 Routine	$31,244,410
020 Other	27,590
Total Operating Revenue	$31,272,000
411. Salary Expense	
010 Salaries—Regular	$24,230,881
020 Salaries—Per Diem	112,845
030 Salaries—Overtime	140,128
050 FICA	1,575,007
060 Health Insurance	862,125
070 Pension	1,211,544
090 Other	217,228
Total Salary Expense	$28,349,758
611. Supply Expense	
010 Laboratory Supplies	$ 1,841,692
020 Office Supplies	10,097
030 Forms	32,111
050 Equipment	91,553
060 Seminars/Meetings	4,163
070 Books	1,145
080 Equipment Rental	8,385
090 Miscellaneous	2,388
Total Supply Expense	$ 1,991,534
911. Interdepartment Expense	
010 Central Supply	$ 77,828
020 Pharmacy	9,527
030 Laundry	16,046
040 Maintenance	28,977
060 Telephone	15,962
070 Photocopy	2,124
090 Miscellaneous	4,165
Total Interdepartment Expense	$ 154,629
Excess of Revenues Over Expenses	$ 776,079

accounting. For example, suppose that the HOS treats a patient in December 2011 and issues a bill to the patient upon discharge on December 12, 2011. HOS receives payment for the care from the patient's insurance company on January 18, 2012. Assuming that HOS ends their *fiscal*, or accounting, year on December 31 of each year, when should it recognize the revenue from the patient? Under a cash basis of accounting, the revenue is considered to occur in 2012.

Many would argue that preparation of an operating budget based on cash inflows and outflows may give a misleading idea of what happened. The cost of caring for the patient would be treated as an expense in 2011, if those costs were paid in 2011. Thus, the nurses, technicians, and supplies used in 2011 will all be recognized as expenses in 2011, if they were paid for during that year. However, the related revenues are recorded in the year 2012, if they are not received in cash until 2012. Across a large number of patients, it might seem that the organization had a deficit in 2011, even if the revenues that will ultimately be collected for those patients in 2012 will exceed the expenses. The operating budget for 2011 would provide an unduly pessimistic view of the expected financial results from treating patients.

It is important for organizations to have a *matching* of revenues and expenses. A matching means that for a given unit of service provided, the revenues arising from providing that service and the expenses incurred in providing that service are both recorded in the same fiscal period. In that way, the organization will be able to determine if the provision of specific services results in a profit or loss.

Should the money that HOS is entitled to receive for providing care be considered revenue in the year care is provided or the year payment is received? If the revenue is recorded in the year the service is provided, the organization is said to be using an *accrual basis* of accounting. As noted earlier, if revenue is recognized in the year the cash is received, the organization is using a cash basis of accounting.

The choice of whether to use a cash or accrual accounting system is an often debated topic. Cash accounting is easier. But it does not do a good job of letting managers understand whether the organization has a surplus or deficit from the services provided during a specific time period, or how large a surplus or deficit. Accrual accounting is more difficult, but it provides a matching of revenues and expenses. When operating budgets are prepared using the accrual basis of accounting, the organization accrues, or anticipates, the eventual receipt of money once the service has been provided. When the organization provides its goods or services, it is said to have earned its revenue. Thus, in the 2011 operating budget, HOS will include all amounts that are earned in 2011 and are expected to be received eventually, even if they will not be received by the end of 2011.[3]

This accrual approach applies to not only the sale of goods or services, but charitable support as well. Suppose that the director of the Millbridge Ballet Company convinces the Millbridge town council to provide the not-for-profit organization with an annual subsidy of $10,000 as long as it gives at least 20 performances a year. If it uses the accrual basis of accounting, Millbridge Ballet would be able to record the town support in the current year if it has 20 performances in the year, even if the town does not make the payment by the end of the year.

By the same token, under an accrual approach to preparing an operating budget, expenses are recorded in the year in which resources are consumed. If supplies are bought and used this year, they are considered to be a cost, or expense, in the operating budget, even if the supplier is not paid until the following year.

The accounting profession strongly endorses accrual accounting. Accrual allows the organization to compare the money that it is entitled to receive for this year's activities to the cost of resources used up carrying out those activities. There is less room for manipulation than in a system based on cash. Imagine an operating budget that used cash receipts and disbursements. If one wanted to look especially poor, it is possible to accelerate payments and postpone collections. If one wanted to look like the year was especially

---

[3] Most organizations do not actually collect all of the money that is owed to them for goods or services that they have provided. The amounts that are never collected are referred to as uncollectible accounts or *bad debts*. Under accrual accounting, the operating budget would show the full amount earned less the portion that it expects it will not be able to collect.

good, the reverse could be done. In contrast, with accrual accounting revenues and expenses are associated with a year based on actual activity, and are much less subject to manipulation.

To better understand the implications of cash versus accrual, consider the following example. Tricky Hospital provides $100 million of care each year and always eventually collects all of that money. Tricky consumes $100 million of resources each year. In 2009 Tricky's board of directors wished to look especially needy so that they could encourage a donor to make a large gift. They paid for all their current consumption and even prepaid for supplies that would not be received and used until sometime in 2010. They also made no efforts to encourage rapid payment by their patients or their patients' insurers for the care provided in 2009. As a result, they only collected $90 million in cash, and they made payments of $110 million.

In 2011, however, Tricky wanted to convince a bank that they were particularly financially solid so that the bank would lend them $300 million for a major expansion program. Tricky again provided services for $100 million that consumed $100 million of resources. However, in 2011 Tricky worked hard to collect as much cash as possible from patients and insurers. Meanwhile it kept its employees and suppliers waiting for their payments until early in 2012. It wound up collecting $110 million (partly from care provided in 2010 and the rest from care provided in 2011) and paying $90 million in cash during 2011.

In both years the amount charged for services provided was the same, and the cost of resources consumed was the same. However, consider the financial results that would be reported on a cash basis in contrast to an accrual basis:

	Cash Basis		Accrual Basis	
	2009	2011	2009	2011
Revenues	$ 90,000,000	$110,000,000	$100,000,000	$100,000,000
Expenses	110,000,000	90,000,000	100,000,000	100,000,000
Profit or (Loss)	$ (20,000,000)	$ 20,000,000	$ 0	$ 0

Note that the accrual system is clearly not as subject to manipulation as the cash basis approach. When accrual accounting is used, the operating budget gives a good idea of how profitable the organization is expected to be based on its activities for a particular period of time. However, it does not give an accurate idea of how much cash it will have. Tricky Hospital really does use more cash in 2009 than it collects. Since cash may be received at different times than the revenues and expenses are reported on an accrual basis, it is necessary to have a cash budget as well as an operating budget to be sure enough cash is available to meet obligations as they come due.

THE FINANCIAL BUDGET The financial budget has two primary components: the cash budget and the capital budget. The cash budget plans for the cash receipts and disbursements of the organization. The capital budget plans for the acquisition of long-term resources, such as buildings and equipment.

The Cash Budget. The *cash budget* is a plan for expected cash receipts and payments. It is identical to the operating budget for organizations that use a cash basis of accounting. For organizations using an accrual basis of accounting, the cash budget provides vital additional information. It helps managers know when there will be cash available for investment and when a shortage of cash is expected. This information allows the organization either to arrange for sources of cash (such as a loan from the bank) to alleviate an expected shortage or to change the organization's planned revenues and expenses to avoid the shortage.

In the case of HOS, the cash budget estimates the amount that will be paid during the year for expenses and the amount that will be collected during the year for patient treatment. Any other sources and uses of cash would also be included in the cash budget. The general format for cash budgets is as follows:

Beginning cash
+ Cash receipts
Total Available Cash
− Less cash payments
Total Cash Payments
Cash before Borrowing, Repaying or Investing
+ borrowing or − repaying or investing
Ending Cash Balance

Note that the amount of cash we have at the end of a period of time is still available at the beginning of the next period. So the beginning cash balance for any cash budget is identical to the ending cash balance from the previous time period.

This budget is generally prepared for the coming year. However, it is also important to have more frequent cash projections. For example, within the annual cash budget, there may be monthly cash budgets. Just knowing that cash receipts are sufficient to cover cash payments for the year may be inadequate. It is helpful to know if the organization expects to have enough cash to pay its bills each month.

For example, the Town of Millbridge has variable cash flows. The town issues bills for its real estate taxes on a quarterly basis, its user fees mostly during the spring and early summer, its sewer taxes once a year near the beginning of the year, and its state aid once a year near the middle of the year. Even if annual cash receipts are enough to cover payments, Millbridge might need to borrow money to get through certain times of the year when cash receipts are low.

The cash flow is complicated by the fact that not only are billings not constant throughout the year, but different sources of money arrive with differing payment lags. Most people pay their taxes promptly, since the town charges a high interest rate on late payments. In contrast, the state does not make its payments until near the very end of the year. This allows the state to have the political advantage of being able to show aid to the municipalities and also keep the money in the state account earning interest until the very last possible day.

Let's consider an example of how a cash budget might work. For this example, assume that Meals for the Homeless has a fiscal year of January through December. They had $15,000 of cash at the end of last year, and had no investments and outstanding loans. If you finish a year with $15,000 of cash, that cash will still be available at the beginning of the following year. Meals expects to receive $10,000 a month from the city next year. However, this is a new contract and the city pays each month with a one-month delay, so the payment for January won't be received until February, and so on. Meals expects to receive $60,000 of contributions for the coming year. However, most of them will come in during December. They expect to receive $3,000 every month from January through November, and the remaining $27,000 in December. They also expect to receive $5,000 every month from other sources. Despite the fairly wide fluctuations in the receipt of contributions, Meals provides its services evenly throughout the year. They pay $1,000 for rent every month. They expect to pay their staff $11,000 every month. Their supplies are increasing in cost due to inflation. In the last month of last year they used $4,500 of supplies, but they expect that cost to rise $100 a month. They pay their suppliers with a one-month lag, so the $4,500 for December will be paid in the first month of the coming year. Other expenses that are paid in cash every month total $3,000. Meals wants to be sure to begin every month after January with $4,000 of cash available. If they have less than that amount at the end of a month they borrow money. If they have more they invest it. Their plan is to pay back any outstanding loan balance in December when they receive the bulk of their contributions. The monthly cash budget for the first quarter of the coming year would be:

**Meals for the Homeless
Cash Budget**

	For the First Three Months of Next Year			
	January	**February**	**March**	**Total**
Beginning Balance	$15,000	$ 4,000	$ 4,000	$15,000
Cash Receipts				
City		10,000	10,000	20,000
Donations	3,000	3,000	3,000	9,000
Other	5,000	5,000	5,000	15,000
Total Available Cash	$23,000	$ 22,000	$22,000	$59,000
Less Cash Payments				
Labor	$11,000	$ 11,000	$11,000	$33,000
Rent	1,000	1,000	1,000	3,000
Supplies	4,500	4,600	4,700	13,800
Other	3,000	3,000	3,000	9,000
Total Cash Payments	$19,500	$ 19,600	$19,700	$58,800
Subtotal Before Borrowing, Repaying or Investing	$ 3,500	$ 2,400	$ 2,300	$ 200
Borrowing/(Repaying or Investing)	500	1,600	1,700	3,800
Ending Cash Balance	$ 4,000	$ 4,000	$ 4,000	$ 4,000

Notice that in the January column we start with $15,000. There is no cash received from the city in January so the only receipts that month are from donations and other sources. The starting cash balance plus cash receipts in January provide available cash of $23,000 for that month. Payments are made for labor, rent, supplies, and other. Note that the payment for supplies is the $4,500 for the previous month. All four of these cash payment items total to $19,500 in January. That total of cash payments is subtracted from the $23,000 of available cash to arrive at a $3,500 subtotal before borrowing or investing. Since Meals wants to start February with $4,000 of cash on hand, it will have to borrow $500 at the end of January.

The ending cash balance for January becomes the beginning balance in the February column. During February Meals expects to receive $10,000 from the city as well as the donation and other cash inflows. Cash payments are the same as January except for the increasing supply payments. Despite the cash receipt from the city, payments once again exceed receipts, and Meals expects to have to borrow $1,600 in order to end February and begin March with $4,000 of cash.

Notice, in the total column for the three months, that the first and last rows are not added across the page. That is, the starting cash balance in the total column is the $15,000 we begin the year with. This represents the starting balance at the beginning of the year. And the ending cash balance in the total column is the $4,000 that we have at the end of March. But we can add all of the cash receipts, cash payments, and borrowing values across the page to get the total for the three-month period. The starting cash balance of $15,000 plus all of the cash receipts in total for the three months, less all of the cash payments in total for the three months equals a $200 subtotal for the three months (note that this subtotal is arrived by adding down the total column, not across the subtotal row). Combined with the $3,800 total amount that has been borrowed over the three months, we get the $4,000 cash value at the end of the quarter. Notice that Meals had to borrow money every month in the quarter, but it would appear that if things keep going as they are, the $27,000 of expected cash receipts from donations in December should be enough to allow for repayment of the total outstanding loan by the end of the year. Being able to demonstrate in a cash budget that you know when you will be able to repay a loan increases the likelihood of being able to obtain a loan.

The Capital Budget.   Another type of budget is a *capital budget*. A capital budget is a plan for acquisitions of *capital assets*. Capital assets are resources that will have lifetimes that extend beyond the year in which they are acquired. This typically includes buildings and equipment.

One reason the capital budget is used relates to the issue of accrual accounting. If Meals for the Homeless buys a delivery truck with a five-year life, it would be inappropriate to charge the entire cost of the truck to the coming year. Suppose that a delivery truck costs $40,000. Even if Meals will pay $40,000 cash for the truck next year, and therefore it will be a $40,000 reduction in the cash budget, it will not fully use up the truck in the one year. Part of the truck will be used in future periods. It would not be reasonable to charge the entire $40,000 cost of the truck as an expense in its first year. Organizations that use accrual accounting would spread the $40,000 cost of the truck out over the years it is used, charging a portion as an expense each year. Thus, the full cost of the truck will be included in the capital budget, but only a one-year portion of the cost of the truck will be included as an expense, called *depreciation expense,* in the operating budget each year.

For example, we expect the $40,000 delivery truck to last for five years. At the end of five years assume that we will just dispose of it. It will have no value at that point and cannot be sold for anything. We simply divide the $40,000 cost by the five-year expected lifetime. The resulting $8,000 ($40,000 ÷ 5 years = $8,000 per year) is the amount of expense that we will record each year as we use the truck. That expense is depreciation expense. Depreciation can become complicated. There are issues concerning how we determine the lifetime, the amount the asset can be sold for at the end of its lifetime, and whether it is reasonable to assume that an equal amount of the asset is used up each year. Depreciation is discussed further in Chapter 10 and Appendix 10-A.

Most organizations that do not use accrual accounting do not use a true cash basis. Rather, they use a *modified cash basis.* Under such a modified cash approach, routine revenues and expenses are recorded on a cash basis, but capital assets, such as buildings and equipment, are recorded as expenses gradually over the years they are used rather than all in the year the organization pays for them.

Capital budgets are closely coordinated with the long-range plan. Often, in order to carry out that long-range plan, it is necessary to make major investments in buildings and equipment that will have relatively little initial benefit. However, the long-range plan looks far enough into the future to recognize the long-term benefit that may come from that current investment. Chapter 5 examines financial management methods used to evaluate the financial impact on the organization of capital asset acquisitions.

Capital acquisitions are evaluated in a separate budget from the operating budget for a number of reasons. First, as noted, it does not make sense to include the full cost of the capital asset in the operating budget for one year, since it is not fully used up in that year.

A second reason for having a separate capital budget is that capital assets often represent large costs for major pieces of equipment and buildings. A poor decision could be costly, so it is worthwhile to give the decision focused attention. Since capital items will last for a number of years, the organization is making a long-term commitment. If it makes an error in selection, it will be committed to that error for a long time. In the case of governments, capital budgets are often mandated by law or regulation.

A third reason that capital assets receive special attention is related to their financing. Since capital items are often expensive, the organization often has to make special arrangements to acquire the financing necessary to buy them. For example, suppose that HOS plans on building a $100 million new wing that will generate $40 million dollars a year in revenue. The revenue over the life of the wing may be sufficient to pay for its construction. However, the cash receipts from the wing in the first year will certainly not pay the full construction costs. That money may have to be borrowed. The revenue earned in the future has to be great enough to repay both the amount borrowed and the interest on that loan. This requires careful calculations related to the timing of the cash receipts and payments related to the project, including the interest costs. Capital budgeting, as noted previously, is discussed further in Chapter 5.

The Budget Process

Although a budget is a plan, budgeting is a process of planning and control. In the budget process, resources are allocated, efforts are made to keep as close to the plan as possible, and then the results are evaluated. "Properly applied, budgeting can contribute significantly to greater efficiency, effectiveness, and accountability in the overall management of an organization's financial resources."[4]

The budgeting process is one of exploring possibilities. Organizations determine what things they can do and what they cannot. They examine alternatives and choose those that will likely yield the best results. They become attuned to possible problems and can work to find solutions. Ideally, budgeting causes managers, policy makers, and legislators to think ahead, have clear expectations against which to measure performance, and coordinate the activities of the organization so that everyone is working toward a common purpose.

In larger organizations, coordination is inherently more difficult, and the budget process can become cumbersome. Such organizations will often have budget departments that devote substantial efforts to aid managers and policy makers in developing budgets. Governmental budgeting is often subject to a variety of laws, making the need for assistance even greater.

The budget preparation process includes developing revenue and spending projections. In modern government management, approaches for making projections vary from simple guesses to projections based on the current year plus inflation to use of sophisticated econometric forecasting. Forecasting is discussed further in Chapter 3.

THE BUDGET CYCLE   In most organizations, the budget process consists of a cycle of activities. We can summarize this cycle as follows:

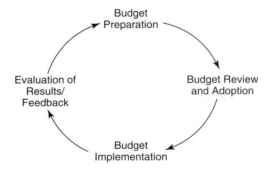

The budget is first prepared. After review by the body with the authority to adopt the budget (often the board of trustees or the legislature), it is adopted, with or without changes. It is not uncommon for the decision-making body to request or make changes prior to approval. Once approved, the budget is implemented. It is the responsibility of the management of the organization or the executive branch of the government to ensure that the

---

[4] Alan Walter Steis. *Financial Management in Public Organizations.* Pacific Grove, Ca.: Brooks/Cole Publishing Company, 1989, p. 146.

adopted budget is carried out. Finally, the results must be evaluated. Often, actual results will vary from the adopted budget. This may be because of inefficiency, or it may be due to noncontrollable factors. All significant variations should be analyzed. This evaluation in turn will provide information to be used for feedback in preparing the next budget.

Budget Preparation.   Initially, a draft budget must be prepared. Generally, top executives will prepare a set of assumptions and guidelines that department or agency managers should use as they develop detailed budgets for their areas. In government, the chief executive will generally provide a *budget guidance memorandum,* which provides policies, goals, and performance expectations.[5] The managers in the organization (unit and department heads or bureau chiefs and agency directors) then prepare draft budgets, considering their *responsibility center's* needs and the guidelines they have received. A responsibility center approach divides the budget into units for which individual managers are held accountable, called responsibility centers.

Organizations quantify their budgets, often assigning measures in dollars or units or both. For example, during the budget preparation process, Meals for the Homeless will need estimates of not only the dollar cost of meals, but also the number of pounds of food needed and the number of meals expected to be served. This requires plans to become specific, so they can be summarized in a document that can be shared across the organization.

Budgets are prepared using forms that are generally unique to each organization. The forms help guide the manager to assess the need for resources to carry out the objectives of the responsibility center. The budget process will generally require the manager to justify the need for the requested resources. Chapter 3 provides additional discussion about the elements of a budget and some of the techniques that can be used in preparing budgets. Chapter 4 addresses issues related to planning for costs. Chapter 5 addresses special issues related to the capital budget.

It is common for budget requests to be "supported by detailed *objects of expenditure—* tabulations of the myriad items required to operate each program, including salaries and wages, rent, office supplies, travel, equipment and other inputs."[6]

Budget Review and Adoption.   Budget requests are reviewed to ensure that the forms have been completed fully and without error. The various budget requests from all responsibility units are aggregated to determine the total resources that have been requested. There is also a review to ensure that the department budgets all follow the same assumptions about salary increases, expected workload, and other factors that need to be consistent across departments.

It is common for the total of all spending requests to exceed projected revenues. In most cases, this requires the organization to go through a process of negotiation. The first goal of this process should be to eliminate any inefficiency in the budget. If this still leaves the budget unbalanced, it is necessary to find additional sources of revenue or to reduce spending. Spending reductions should be selected so as to minimize the impact on the accomplishment of the organization's goals and objectives. In many instances, this requires the organization to establish priorities. Managers should be given the opportunity in this process to provide their rationale for why their budget requests are high priorities and should not be among the first items cut.

Once the top management of an organization is comfortable with the budget, it submits it to the decision-making body for review and approval. In the case of the government, the executive branch submits the budget to the legislative branch for review. In many cases, the legislative process includes an opportunity for public scrutiny and comment. In some

---

[5] Ibid, p. 151.
[6] Ibid, p. 146.

cases, the public actually votes on the budget, but this is less common and occurs primarily with respect to school budgets. If the executive is unhappy with changes made by the legislature, the budget can be vetoed. In many cases the veto can be for the entire budget; in some cases it may be line-item by line-item. Generally, there is some provision for the legislature to override a veto.

The body that must approve the budget should receive not only the budget, but also an executive summary. This summary should focus on the policy implications of the proposed budget. One should try to avoid letting the trees get in the way of seeing the forest. Often the extreme detail provided with budgets causes managers to lose sight of the goals that should be accomplished as the budget is implemented.

Finally, after discussing and perhaps requiring changes in the budget, it is accepted by the board or, in the case of government, passed by a legislative vote in favor of an *appropriation*. When a legislative body—be it a senate or an assembly, a town committee or a council—approves spending for a specific line-item, that is called an appropriation. Appropriations create the authorization for spending the amount in the budget.

Budget Implementation. Once adopted, the budget must be implemented or executed. Steis describes this part of the process:

> Budget execution is both a financial process and a substantive operational process. This stage of the budget cycle involves the initiation of authorized projects and programs within an established time schedule, within monetary limits, and ideally, within standard cost limits. Budget execution is the longest stage in the budget cycle, covering the full fiscal year and overlapping both the formulation and review stages of the budget for the succeeding and prior years, respectively.[7]

Budgets authorize and limit the amount of spending for each responsibility center in an organization. Appropriations tend to be specific in terms of the amount that can be spent and what it can be spent on. Governments next make *allocations,* subdividing the appropriation into more detailed categories, such as responsibility centers, programs, or objects of expenditure. Sometimes, spending is further broken down into *allotments.* Allotments refer to a system that allocates budget resources to specific time periods or for use only after a certain event occurs. This allotment process serves "(1) to avoid premature exhaustion of appropriations, necessitating supplemental appropriations; (2) to keep the rate of expenditures in line with the flow of revenue; and (3) to provide the funds agencies actually need in the course of budget implementation and no more."[8] While the process is not quite as formalized in other public service organizations, the same elements apply.

Part of the budget implementation process focuses on expenditure control. A widely used technique in governments and some not-for-profit organizations is a system of *encumbrances.* When the organization places an order for a resource, an encumbrance is created. The encumbrance identifies the portion of the budget for a specific line-item that has already been "spoken for" by purchase commitments that have been made.

For example, suppose that the Millbridge Town Council has adopted a budget that includes an appropriation of $20,000 for computer equipment. On the first day of the government's fiscal year, October 1, an order is placed for $15,000 worth of equipment. The equipment arrives two months later. The government pays for the equipment a month after that. In the interim between the placing of the order and the payment for the computers, Dwight Ives, the town manager, would like to know how much money is available

---

[7] Ibid, p. 153.
[8] Donald Axelrod. *Budgeting for Modern Government.* New York, N.Y.: St. Martin's Press, 1988, p. 12.

for computer purchases. He knows that the budget was $20,000, but he suspects that some purchases may have already been made. As soon as an order is placed, the government accounting system records an encumbrance in the dollar amount of the order. If Ives looks at the town budget report on November 1, he will see that the budget is $20,000, but that there is a $15,000 encumbrance. The available, or unencumbered, balance is $5,000. Special approvals are generally required to place additional orders that would exceed the unencumbered balance.

When the computers that were ordered have been received, the encumbrance will be removed. At that point the financial records would show a budget for computers of $20,000, an expenditure of $15,000, an encumbered balance of $0, and an unencumbered balance of $5,000.

Other aspects related to managing the organization within the limits of the adopted budget are discussed in Chapter 7, which looks at management of the short-term resources and obligations of the organization, and Chapter 8, which focuses on issues of accountability and control.

Evaluation of Results. The last element in the budget cycle is the evaluation of results. Budgets not only create plans, but can be used to help accomplish those plans. One way that this is done is by comparing actual results to the budget. This is sometimes referred to as performance evaluation. This is especially helpful if done on an interim basis, during the year. That allows problems to be corrected midstream, helping the organization to accomplish its budget.

Things do not always go as planned. It is important to attempt to assess why. In some cases, money is being wasted through inefficiency. If so, the inefficiency should be determined, and corrective action should be taken. In other cases, events have occurred (e.g., price increases in supplies that are essential) that are beyond the control of the organization or its managers. In any case, there should be a thorough investigation of why variations occur.

Looking at its results, the organization can assess what needs to be corrected. How good a job did the organization's management do? How well did the organization itself do? Ideally, the organization's performance should be evaluated in a number of different ways. Meals wants to know if it served as many meals as expected and whether they cost more or less than expected. However, it also wants to know if the meals met its standards for nutrition. It wants to know if the homeless felt that the meals tasted good. The measurement of performance is discussed in Chapter 3.

To evaluate performance, one must have a standard or benchmark to use for comparison with actual results. The budget establishes the organization's expectations. When actual results vary from those expectations, the organization can use feedback to investigate the cause of the variations. The results of such investigation can provide the information needed to improve the management of the organization in the future. The difference between a budgeted amount and an actual result is called a variance. Variance analysis is discussed in detail in Chapter 8.

Governments often have a formal midyear review. This serves a critical function. Since state and local governments must have a balanced budget, it is critical to examine whether the organization is on track for spending no more than the appropriated amount. If it turns out that spending is above the budget level, or that revenues are less than budgeted, then actions must be taken to avoid a deficit. Often this requires cutting expenditures for the remainder of the year to a lower level than had been expected when the budget was passed. Many health and not-for-profit organizations undertake similar reviews for the same purpose.

Another purpose of performance evaluation is to enhance accountability. All organizations want to ensure that their resources are used efficiently and effectively. This is enhanced if the organization can hold managers and responsibility centers accountable for their activities and results. Accountability is partly ensured by frequent comparison of the budget with actual results and analysis of the causes of variances. Another element critical to accountability is the audit process.

An audit is an examination of records or procedures. Operating or performance audits seek to identify inefficiencies in the way the organization operates so that they can be avoided in the future. Financial audits examine whether financial reports are presented in a fair manner[9] and whether all resource use has complied with relevant laws, rules, or regulations. Although not all audits are intended to dig deeply enough to discover all fraud and embezzlements, some audits are conducted specifically to determine if resources have been used for their intended purposes.

Mikesell uses the example of a state's purchase of salt for its roads to distinguish between a financial audit and an operations (or efficiency and economy) audit:

> A financial audit would consider whether the agency had an appropriation for salt purchased, whether salt purchased was actually delivered, whether approved practices were followed in selecting a supplier, and whether agency reports showed the correct expenditure on salt. An efficiency and economy audit would consider whether the salt inventory is adequately protected from the environment, whether the inventory is adequate or excessive, and whether other methods of selecting a supplier would lower the cost.[10]

Clearly, audits serve an important role in ensuring accountability in the use of resources.

BUDGET PRESENTATION   Another element in accountability is the presentation of the budget. Organizations formalize their budgets by recording them in written form. This allows the budget to be used to communicate to all of its managers. Human resource managers can do their job better by knowing the staffing plans of other departments. The managers of the recovery room in a hospital can manage their department better if they know the number of surgeries that are expected by the operating room department.

The choice of revenue and expense groupings and the level of detail of information shown in the budget can have a dramatic impact on the amount of information that is communicated by the budget. In the case of government, budgets become public documents. An effective presentation can give the public a tool to keep government accountable for its actions. The specific contents and presentation of budgets are discussed further in Chapter 3.

A BUDGET TIMELINE   The budget process can be quite complicated and time-consuming. The process may take one to three months in small organizations, and four to six months or even longer in larger ones. In order to ensure that the budget is ready for adoption sufficiently early to be implemented at the start of the coming year, many organizations prepare a budget calendar or budget timeline. Government timelines are often set by law or regulation. Examples of timelines are provided in Exhibits 2-1 and 2-2. These timelines indicate the deadline by which each major activity must be completed in order to ensure the possibility of timely adoption of the budget.

Note the word "possibility" in the previous sentence. Even if every deadline in the timeline is met, except for approval, the budget may not be adopted on time. The body that must approve the budget may decide that the budget is not acceptable. The process of revising the budget until it is acceptable may extend into the next fiscal year. In the case of not-for-profit organizations, the board generally will authorize that operations continue pending adoption of the budget, but often at a reduced level of activity or on an austerity basis. This can be quite deleterious to the organization. At times, the final budget adopted

---

[9] Often audits seek to determine if financial statements have been prepared in accordance with rules that are referred to as Generally Accepted Accounting Principles (GAAP). See Chapter 9 for further discussion of GAAP.
[10] John L. Mikesell. *Fiscal Administration—Analysis and Applications for the Public Sector*, 6th ed. Belmont, Ca.; Thomson/Wadsworth, 2003, p. 54.

EXHIBIT 2-1 Hospital Budget Timeline

Activity	Responsibility	Deadlines
1. Appointment of the budget committee	CEO	June
2. First meeting of budget committee	Committee chair	July
3. Complete assumptions and guidelines and communicate to department heads	Budget committee	August 31
4. Complete long-range budget	Budget committee	September 30
5. Unit capital and operating budgets	Unit managers	October 15
6. Negotiation between units and their department heads	Department heads	October 22
7. Compilation of all unit budgets into department budgets	Department heads	October 30
8. Development of cash budget	Chief financial officer	November 15
9. Negotiation and revision process	All managers	December 15
10. Approval	Board of trustees	December 16
11. Implementation	All managers	January

EXHIBIT 2-2 Simplified Example of State Budget Timeline

(a) Agency Budget Planning — *April to Mid-September*
- Governor policy letter issued — Governor's office — April
- Bureau chiefs prepare budget requests — Bureau chiefs — April–June
- Agencies review bureau requests — Agency directors — July–August
- Agency budgets prepared — Agency directors — August–first half Sept.

(b) State Budget Review
- Agencies submit requests to Department of Budget (DoB) — Agency directors — One week after Labor Day
- Analysis by DoB — DoB — Sept.–Nov.
- Informal hearings — Budget examiners — Sept.–Nov.
- Formal hearings—comparative data — Budget director — Sept.–Nov.
- Final recommendations — Budget examiners — Mid-December
- Preparation of alternative plans — Fiscal analysts — Mid-December

(c) Final Review
- Budget director recommendations on policy — Budget director — Mid-Dec. to Mid.-Jan.
- Governor's decisions on policy — Governor — Mid-Dec. to Mid.-Jan.
- Fiscal analyst plan recommendations — Fiscal analysts — Mid-Dec. to Mid.-Jan.
- Governor and budget director formulate plan — Gov./Budg. director — Mid-Dec. to Mid.-Jan.
- Budget message prepared — Governor — Mid-Dec. to Mid.-Jan.

(d) Passage of Budget Bill
- Governor submits budget bill to legislature — Governor — Mid-Jan. to February 1
- Analysis, hearings, passage — Legislature — Mid-Jan. to April
- Passage of special appropriation bills — Legislature — Mid-Jan. to April
- Fiscal year begins—implementation of budget — Agency directors — April 1

Source: Adapted from New York State Division of the Budget. *Budget Request Manual.* Albany, N.Y.: 1983. This simplified timeline is not meant to indicate the current specific process of New York State.

calls for less spending than occurred during the period the organization operated without an approved budget. This results in even harsher cuts in spending for the remainder of the year. In rare cases, the organization will actually come to a halt, with only the most essential activities continuing. This happened to the federal government several times in the latter half of the 20th century.

The budget timelines in Exhibits 2-1 and 2-2 both stop at the point of implementation. However, the process of auditing results, analyzing variances, and providing feedback for the next budget cycle is critical; this is shown in some organizations' timelines.

Political Realities in the Budget Process

The process of developing budgets is highly politicized. This is true in most public service organizations. To the extent possible, managers should try to establish and use an objective budget process that best leads to the accomplishment of the organization's mission, goals, and objectives. In reality, it is inevitable that politics will play at least some role in almost all organizations.

Politics may take on a variety of forms. The politics may be personal. A department manager may be a relative of a member of the board and may get, or be perceived as getting, special breaks at budget time. More broadly, however, politics often revolves around agendas. Proponents of a particular service or program will lobby for resources for that program. This is true in most organizations.

Politics is of special concern in the government, which is, after all, a political arena. It is at least partly through the political process and voting that the public makes its desires known. Politics serves a major role in resource allocation in governments. Although budgets should be objective in trying to accomplish the goals and objectives of the organization, politics has an appropriate role in setting those goals and objectives.

Politics in the public sector takes many different shapes. It takes the form of special interest groups lobbying for their cause. It takes on the perspective of competing policies to accomplish similar or different objectives. Sometimes politics in budgeting is manifested as a power struggle between the branches of government, or between political parties.

Managers should be aware of the political nature of budgets within their organization. This can help them to better define their role in the budget process.

BEHAVIORAL ASPECTS OF THE BUDGET PROCESS

Although it sometimes seems that budgets are all about numbers, that is not the case. Once a budget has been adopted, it is up to the employees of the organization to come as close as possible to achieving the budget. People are the key to successful budgeting. It is critical to understand that the actions of people within an organization have a tremendous impact on how well the organization does. If people work to accomplish the goals of the budget we are likely to have much better outcomes than if they are indifferent about accomplishing those goals, or even worse, work in opposition to accomplishment of the organization's goals. The numbers on paper are just that. People—their attitudes, needs, and desires—are the key to budgeting. If we don't specifically focus on why people would want to accomplish the organization's goals as defined by the budget, we are not likely to achieve the best possible actual outcomes.

Therefore, an essential part of the budget process is understanding what motivates the organization's employees. We need to understand why employees would make their best effort to accomplish the organization's goals, and why they wouldn't. And we need to understand how incentives can be used to motivate employees to work at their highest level to accomplish the organization's goals.

The more input employees have in making plans, the more likely it is that they will strive to achieve them. People working in a unit or department of an organization know a great deal about how that unit or department functions. They are in a good position to be able to propose changes that will improve efficiency. If we solicit input from managers and staff members in preparing budgets, and develop budgets based on that input, employees are likely to become vested in showing that the approaches they have proposed are sound. If budgets are prepared without staff input, staff will likely feel much less motivated to meet the budgets that have been handed down to them.

Budgets and Motivation

Motivation is the critical underlying key to budget success. One of the best features of budgets is that they present a measurable goal. When there is a clearly stated goal, managers and staff can work toward that goal. Most people are inherently motivated to do a good job. They want to gain a sense of accomplishment from their job, and a budget goal can help them do that. Setting demanding but realistic budget goals, combined with public praise and rewards when goals are met or exceeded, can enhance motivation and resulting performance.

Compare the likely progress of a dieter with specific weight-loss goals to one who simply wants to lose a lot of weight, or compare an athlete with measurable objectives to one who just wants to be strong or run fast. Setting specific goals and working toward them is a tremendous self-motivator. Most employees want to have a sense of pride in their organization and want their organization to do well. Nevertheless, a goal of "spending as little as possible" is no better than the dieter's hope to "lose weight." A more specific goal, such as "Let's reduce electric consumption by 10 percent as compared to the prior year" is likely to be a better motivator.

Control is complicated by the fact that even when the primary goal is clearly stated, it is the basic nature of individuals that their own personal goals will often be different from the goals of their employer. This does not mean that human nature is bad—just that there is such a thing as human nature and it is foolish to ignore it. For example, most employees would prefer a salary that is substantially larger than the salary they are currently receiving. There is nothing wrong with employees wanting more money. In fact, ambition is probably a desirable trait. On the other hand, employers generally will not provide employees with more money because they lack the revenues to pay those higher wages. While the employees are not wrong to desire large raises, the employer is not wrong to deny such raises. Inherently, a tension or conflict exists as a result.

Nor is it just an issue of salaries. Often employees would like larger offices with new furniture and remodeled facilities. They would certainly like more staff to enable them to carry out their department's mission more effectively. However, organizations have limited resources and must make choices concerning how to spend those limited resources.

As a result, even when morale is generally excellent and is not considered to be a problem, an underlying tension naturally exists. Even though the employees may want to achieve the mission of the organization, their personal desires will be for things the organization cannot or will choose not to provide. This is referred to as *goal divergence*. For example, employees might prefer to take long breaks frequently throughout the day. That might well impair their ability to efficiently get their work done.

To best achieve its goals, the organization must bring together the interests of the individual with its own interests so they can work together. In the budgeting process, the organization wants to control spending. But it is not the "organization" that controls costs; it is the human beings involved in the process. There must be some motivation for the human beings to want to control costs. We need to find a way for the employees to feel that it is in their interests not to take frequent, long breaks. Bringing the individuals' desires and the organization's needs together is referred to as *goal congruence*.

Since congruent goals are not inherently the norm, it is necessary to address formally how convergence is to be obtained. Organizations generally achieve such convergence or congruence by setting up a system of incentives that makes it serve the best interests of the employees to serve the best interests of the organization.

Incentives

Although employees serving in government, health, and not-for-profit organizations are motivated by factors other than money, it would be foolish to ignore the potential of monetary rewards to influence behavior. Public service organizations must search for the proper mix of incentives that will motivate managers and staff to control costs. Financial incentives are frequently employed. The most basic financial incentives are the ability to retain one's job and to get a good raise. We can use a carrot or a stick to motivate. The stick: If you constantly take long breaks frequently throughout the year, you may be fired.

Another common motivating tool that incentivizes employees is a bonus system. This is a carrot approach. For example, one could tell a manager that her department budget for the year is $3,000,000. However, if her department spends less than $3,000,000, she and her staff can keep 20 percent of the savings. If the department spends only $2,900,000, the manager and the staff will get a bonus of $20,000 (i.e., $3,000,000 less $2,900,000, multiplied by 20%) to share. The total cost to the organization is $2,920,000 including the bonus, as opposed to the $3,000,000 budget, so it has saved $80,000 after paying the bonus. The staff benefits and the organization benefits. In this case, goal congruence is likely to be achieved. Workers will not take frequent, long breaks, because they are trying to work more efficiently so they will earn the available bonus.

Many public service organizations have in fact added bonus systems. The use of bonus systems has both positive and negative aspects. The positives relate primarily to the strong motivation employees have to reduce costs. The negatives relate to the fact that bonuses sometimes create unintended incentives. For example, bonuses give employees a strong incentive to lower quality of services provided in order to reduce costs and earn a bonus. Careful metrics must be put in place to ensure that the bonus is not being earned at the expense of the quality of products and services provided. Managers must try to anticipate unintended consequences when developing incentive systems. Also, the bonus must be adequately large to achieve the desired congruence. If you can get away with taking frequent long breaks, and you are inclined to do so, a bonus that only adds up to $10 a week for each employee might not provide sufficient motivation to change that behavior. Would $50 a week per employee be sufficient? $100? Each organization must give careful thought to developing a motivation system that provides sufficient incentives to achieve an appropriate level of goal congruence.

Another potential problem with bonuses relates to changes in volume of services provided. A bonus should not reward employees for lower spending that results simply from lower volume. Nor should employees fail to get a bonus simply because costs increased as a result of higher volume. We don't want to provide an incentive that results in employees being motivated to reduce the volume of service provided. This can be avoided by making the bonus system adjust automatically for changes in volume.

Bonuses are not the solution to all motivational problems. Bonus systems have a variety of other problems. Some bonus systems reward all employees equally if overall spending is reduced. But if everyone gets a bonus, no one feels that her or his individual actions have much impact. Individuals may feel that they do not have to work particularly hard to reap the benefits of the bonus. They will let everyone else do the hard work, and they will share in the bonus distributed. That can lead to a situation in which no one makes any effort to control costs. There won't be a bonus to be shared, and the organization won't keep costs under control. In that case, the bonus system will not be providing the incentives we need. On the other hand, bonuses given only to some employees based on their individual performance may create jealousy and discontent.

There are incentive alternatives to bonuses. For example, one underused managerial tool is a letter from supervisor to subordinate. All individuals responsible for controlling costs should be evaluated explicitly with respect to how well they control costs. That evaluation should be communicated in writing. This approach costs little to implement but can have a dramatic impact. Most people respond well to praise and other forms of positive feedback about their personal performance and their department's performance. Framed certificates of achievement along with a moderate monetary reward for an outstanding achievement can be a strong motivator. Employee of the month and other similar programs can be strong motivational tools as well.

Telling individuals they've done a good job and that their boss and their boss's boss know that they've done a good job can be an effective way to get people to continue trying to do a good job in the future. We tend to take a biased approach, complaining to employees when there is a problem without correspondingly praising them for a job well done when there are no problems. In the real world, praise is both cheap and, in many cases, effective. On the other hand, fair criticism, especially in writing, can have a stinging effect that managers and staff will work hard to avoid in the future. Ultimately, however, people tend to respond better to praise than to criticism.

Unrealistic Expectations

There is no question that many people do attempt to satisfice—to do just enough to get by. One thing incentives are used to accomplish is to motivate those individuals to work harder. A target that requires hard work and stretching, but that is achievable, can be a useful motivating tool. If the target is reached, there might be a bonus, or there should be at least some formal recognition of the achievement, such as a letter. At a minimum, the worker will have the self-satisfaction of having worked hard and reached the target.

However, it is important to recognize that budget targets should be achievable. Some organizations have adopted the philosophy that if a high target makes people work hard, a higher target will make them work harder. This may not be the case. If targets are placed out of reach, they will probably not result in people reaching to their utmost limits to come as close to the target as possible. In fact, that approach may lead to cynicism and hostility toward a management that promises to make bonuses available and then places them out of reach. It may seem that the organization is short-changing itself whenever someone achieves a target. One may think, "We set the target too low. Perhaps if the target were higher, the higher target would have been achieved." The problem with that logic is that there are risks associated with it. If an employee fails to meet a target because of incompetence or because of insufficient hard work, the signal of failure that is sent is warranted. In fact, repeated failure may be grounds for replacing that individual in that job. But if an employee is both competent and hard working, failure is not a message that should be sent. Even if it is desirable to encourage the individual to achieve even more, the signal of failure will be discouraging.

When people work extremely hard and fail, they often question why they bothered to work so hard. If hard work results in failure to achieve the target, then why not ease off? If they are going to fail anyway, why try very hard? And when people get discouraged, they may become angry. This situation can lead to turnover and even sabotage by angry persons who feel their supervisors are against them and that they are being set up to fail. Thus managers at every level of the organization must be extremely careful to ensure that all goals assigned are reasonable, or results may be less favorable than they otherwise would be.

CASE STUDY

Developing a Government Budget

To gain a better sense of the budget development process, we will now discuss the development of a hypothetical budget for Millbridge. According to Ives, Razek, and Hosch, some of the specific steps that must be taken are to:

- prepare budgetary policy guidelines.
- prepare a budget calendar.
- prepare and distribute budget instructions.
- prepare revenue estimates.
- prepare departmental (or program) expenditure requests.
- consolidate departmental expenditure requests . . . and revenue estimates.
- prepare the budget document.
- present the budget document to the legislative body.
- determine the property tax (millage) rate.[11]

We will consider each of these steps in turn.

Prepare Budgetary Policy Guidelines

As noted, the first step in budget preparation is for the top management to prepare a budget guidance memorandum, which provides assumptions and guidelines about policies, goals, and performance expectations that managers should use as they develop detailed budgets for their areas. The Millbridge guidelines indicate that, given current economic conditions, an average increase in all taxes and fees of 3 percent would be considered acceptable. Due to a housing boom in the town, population growth of 5 percent is expected and this will translate into increased property values and sales tax. Inflation in the cost of supplies is expected to be 4 percent and, if possible, employees will be given 5 percent salary increases.

Prepare a Budget Calendar

The budget process can take from three to six months, or even longer. To ensure that everything is done efficiently, Millbridge prepares a budget calendar (see Exhibit 2-3).

Prepare and Distribute Budget Instructions

As we can see from Exhibit 2-3, the budget committee meets to set guidelines from July 1 to 5. These guidelines are distributed to department heads on July 10, along with specific instructions for completing the budget. The materials provided should give each department head information about their current year budget, their actual expenditures to date, and projected expenditures through the end of the year. Additionally, it should provide guidance regarding anything that would impact the departments, but of which the department heads might be unaware. For example, the school superintendant should be informed if new housing construction will likely affect the number of students in the school system. The same housing construction and resulting expansion of the town population might also impact the service demands on police, fire, ambulance, and public works. Each department must be informed for their budgets to reflect the resources needed to maintain the desired level of services.

---

[11] Martin Ives, Joseph R. Razek, and Gordon A. Hosch. *Introduction to Governmental and Not-for-Profit Accounting,* 5th ed. Upper Saddle River, N.J.: Pearson Education, 2004, p. 71.

EXHIBIT 2-3 Millbridge Budget Calendar

July 1–5	Mayor, town manager, and other key officials meet to develop budget guidelines.
July 10	Department heads receive budget guidelines and forms.
August 31	Department budget requests must be submitted to town manager.
September 10–15	Meetings between mayor, town manager, and department heads to discuss individual department budget requests.
September 16–30	Department heads revise and resubmit budget requests.
October 15	Town budget is presented to Town Council.
October 15–31	Town Council holds meetings to discuss budget.
October 31	Town Council proposes adjustments to the budget.
November 1–15	Budget is revised and printed.
November 15	Budget is mailed to residents.
December 1–15	Public hearings on the budget are held.
December 16	Town Council votes on budget.
January 1	New budget year begins.

Prepare Revenue Estimates

The money available to the town for the coming year will consist of its revenues generated for the year, as well as any surplus carried over from the previous year. Therefore, the finance department of the town, working with each department manager, should estimate any surpluses that will likely exist at the end of the current year. In Exhibit 2-4 we can see that total projected 2011 revenues of $14,757,133 are about $53,000 above budgeted revenues of $14,704,151. However, any changes in expenses from the budget would also have to be considered before knowing if Millbridge expects to have a surplus at the end of the current year.

EXHIBIT 2-4 Millbridge Revenue Budget, Fiscal Year 2112

Department	2010 Actual	2011 Budget	Jan.–June 2011 Actual	July–Dec. 2011 Projected	Total 2011 Projected	2012 Budget
General government						
Property taxes	$ 6,344,928	$ 6,747,196	$ 3,373,598	$ 3,373,598	$ 6,747,196	$ 7,297,093
Sales tax	253,797	269,888	127,387	173,920	301,307	325,864
Education	4,856,028	5,163,900	2,581,950	2,581,950	5,163,900	5,318,817
Public safety	1,198,855	1,274,862	601,735	702,351	1,304,086	1,343,209
Public works	0	0	0	0	0	0
Health and sanitation	355,920	378,485	178,645	193,028	371,673	382,823
Recreation	529,541	405,344	148,523	264,333	412,856	589,834
Water	294,305	312,964	147,719	159,612	307,331	316,551
Sewer	142,478	151,511	71,513	77,271	148,784	153,247
Total	$ 13,975,852	$ 14,704,151	$ 7,231,071	$ 7,526,062	$ 14,757,133	$ 15,727,437

Note: Some totals are incorrect due to rounding error.

The next step is to determine revenues for the coming year. For each department we first attempt to determine what current year results will be. Typically, a budget worksheet would provide the information shown in Exhibit 2-4. The first numerical column in this exhibit shows the actual results for the entire year prior to the current year. Next, the budget for the current fiscal year 2011 is shown. From the first two columns we can see the expected changes from last year to the current year. That information may be helpful in planning the changes from the current year to the coming year. Next, we see the actual revenues for the current year-to-date. Assume that Millbridge's fiscal year is identical to the calendar year. Since this information is provided to Millbridge department managers in July, only six months' worth of actual data are provided. A projection must then be shown for the remaining months of the current year, as well as for the entire current year.

This projection requires care. One cannot just assume that the second half of the year will be like the first half. In Exhibit 2-4, we see that property tax revenues for general government and education revenues are expected to split evenly between the two halves of the year. In contrast, sales tax does not. The total projected sales tax for 2011 is above the budget for the year, possibly indicating that by the time the 2012 budget was being prepared, the expectations were that the 2011 Christmas sales season was going to be stronger than had been anticipated a year earlier.

The managers should employ forecasting approaches (see Chapter 3 for a discussion of forecasting) to estimate their likely revenues for the coming year. The budget guidelines for Millbridge have also provided the town's managers with some information. Specifically, tax rates are expected to increase by 3 percent, and population to grow by 5 percent. That population growth is expected to impact both property and sales taxes. Managers considered those factors when preparing the 2012 budget (Exhibit 2-4).

Additionally, individual managers may be aware of specific reasons why their revenues might differ for the coming year. For example, suppose that the town's pool was closed during the current year for major renovations. This would adversely impact the revenues of the recreation department. Notice that the 2011 budget for Recreation revenues was down from the 2010 actual result in anticipation of the renovations. Next year the pool will be open, and with the improvements will likely attract more members than ever before. The head of Millbridge's Recreation Department has taken that revenue growth into account in preparing the budget for the coming year.

Some departments may not have any direct revenue. For example, the public works department may be funded by the general revenues of the town. In such instances its budget will not include a revenue component.

In Exhibit 2-4, the revenue increases that are projected are largely the result of an increasing tax base due to construction, and an assumption that all tax rates will be increased by 3 percent. At this point the budget has not been approved, and tax rate increases that are ultimately approved may be greater or smaller than that amount, requiring adjustments to the revenue budget. According to the timetable in Exhibit 2-3, the revenue budgets would have to be submitted by August 31.

Prepare Departmental (or Program) Expenditure Requests

Each department must prepare a detailed listing of the items that it believes it needs to fund for the coming year. Often the requests of all departments, when combined, will exceed revenues. At that point either revenues will have to be raised (by actions such as tax increases), or negotiations will take place with departments to reduce their expenditure levels. Ives, Razek, and Hosch suggest that to prepare the expenditure budget one should:

1. Determine the level of the expenditure for the past year and project the level of the expenditure for the current year.
2. Apply inflation and cost-of-living factors and other allowances for "uncontrollable" factors to each current-year expenditure. This will result in a "stand-still" expenditure request.

3. Determine what activities should be expanded, contracted, or discontinued. Identify any new activities that, if funded, will commence the following year.
4. Adjust each proposed expenditure for the changes in the type and level of activities determined and identified in step 3.
5. Prepare a justification for each new activity or each increase in the level of an existing activity. Include in this justification the effect that not adopting, or increasing the level of, the activity will have on the organization.
6. Prepare a budgetary work sheet for each type of expenditure. The formats of the work sheets will vary with the type of expenditure being projected, although each work sheet should show the prior-year, current-year, and projected budget-year level of expenditures for each line-item (object-of-expenditure).
7. Summarize the information from each work sheet on the expenditure request.[12]

Generally, departmental expenditure budgets are divided into personnel budgets, other than personnel services (OTPS), and capital budgets. Based on the timetable in Exhibit 2-3, all of the expenditure budget requests would have to be submitted by August 31.

Personnel Services

The personnel budget lists all of the categories of employees, the number of paid hours expected for the category, the pay rate, and the total pay. Frequently, the document will include not only the budget request for the coming year, but also the actual value for the prior year, and the projected spending for the current year. See Exhibit 2-5 for an example for the Millbridge Recreation Department personnel budget for the 2012 year. A similar budget would be required for each department. Millbridge assumes that a full-time worker will be paid for 40 hours a week for 52 weeks a year. Therefore, the Director of the Recreation Department, who is a full-time year-round employee, will be paid for 2,080 hours. The three manager positions only cover the four summer months, so they are budgeted for 693 paid hours each year. The lifeguard and maintenance hours dropped during 2011 when the town pool was being renovated. Both figures are expected to increase in 2012 once the renovation is complete.

EXHIBIT 2-5 Millbridge Recreation Expenditure Budget, Personnel Services, Fiscal Year 2012

Position Code	Position Title	2010 Actual			2011 Estimated			2012 Budget		
		Hours	Rate	Amount	Hours	Rate	Amount	Hours	Rate	Amount
1001	Director	2,080	$40.10	$ 83,408.00	2,080	$41.30	$ 85,904.00	2,080	$43.37	$ 90,209.60
1002	Pool Manager	693	20.50	14,206.50	693	21.12	14,636.16	693	22.17	15,363.81
1003	Golf Course Manager	693	18.40	12,751.20	693	18.95	13,132.35	693	19.90	13,790.70
1004	Tennis Club Manager	693	18.40	12,751.20	693	18.95	13,132.35	693	19.90	13,790.70
1010	Lifeguards	6,240	12.00	74,880.00	4,160	12.36	51,417.60	6,411	12.98	83,214.78
1020	Maintenance Workers	10,400	10.25	106,600.00	9,360	10.56	98,841.60	10,574	11.09	117,265.66
1030	Clerical	4,160	14.75	61,360.00	4,160	15.19	63,190.40	4,160	15.95	66,352.00
	Total	24,959		$365,956.90	21,839		$340,254.46	25,304		$399,987.25

---

[12] Ibid, p. 81.

The budget for 2012 includes raises of 5 percent, in accordance with the budget guidelines provided to each manager, but does not include fringe benefit costs, which would often be added directly by the government's finance department when the individual department budgets are combined to get the overall costs of the governmental body. Fringe benefits are usually calculated as a percentage of wages. Fringes include payments into the Social Security system (FICA), health care benefits, retirement plan payments, and a variety of other costs. The fringes are not determined employee by employee. Rather, an average rate is used for a large segment of employees. A typical rate might be around 30 percent of wages. Fringes can have a dramatic impact on any organization's spending. For example, one of the largest components of the overall fringe rate is the cost of employee health insurance. If health insurance costs increase more than expected, the fringe benefit rate can easily increase at least several percent, creating a large budget imbalance for the organization.

Many government bodies adopt personnel classification systems that list the various types of positions that exist and establish a pay grade for each. Individual pay grades often have "steps," allowing employees to move up in pay over time, even if they are not promoted to a new position. In a given year an employee may move up a step to reflect experience and longevity, and also receive a general salary increase that is applied across the board to all grades and steps. Once individuals have reached the top step for their grade, they must change to a different position at a higher grade, or else only receive general salary increases each year.

Some of the benefits of a classification system are a greater degree of uniformity in pay for positions requiring similar skills. They also allow for systematic and consistent consideration of employee experience and longevity. Also, if budgeted positions are vacant when the budget is prepared, or new positions are being added in the coming year's budget, the budget can still be prepared with some degree of certainty about expenditures, because the classification system dictates the wages that will be earned when the positions are filled. Some critics are concerned, however, that when the public is told that raises are going to be 5 percent for government employees for the coming year, they may not be aware that many employees receive substantially bigger raises than 5 percent, when their step increases are considered.

Other Than Personnel Services

The other major part of the operating budget for departments is referred to as the other than personnel services (OTPS) budget. This would include a variety of different types of expenses such as office supplies, subscriptions, and copying costs. Again the actual budget form would typically include information about the prior and current years, as well as the projected budget request for the coming year. In making their budget projections for the coming year, managers must carefully determine what most influences the amount that must be spent on each item. For example, office supply costs might vary based solely on inflation. However, the amount spent on the supply items to test the composition and safety of the pool water might vary most with the number of hours the pool will be open (assuming that the water is tested once an hour during all hours of operation). If the renovated pool will be open more hours, then we must anticipate the cost of additional supplies to test the water.

Some organizations budget for OTPS costs using a formula to simplify budget calculations. For example, a government may have found that historically, the amount spent on supplies can be related to the number of workers. To budget supply costs for the future, one would first determine the increase or decrease in the number of workers. Then one could estimate the change in supply cost due to inflation. Suppose that an agency spent $80,000 on supplies last year, expects a 2 percent increase in manpower, and a 3 percent increase in the price of supplies. The budget for the coming year would increase to $81,600 to cover the manpower increase ($80,000 + [2% × $80,000] = $81,600) and then to $84,048 to cover the price increase ($81,600 + [3% × $81,600] = $84,048). This is a much easier approach then trying to figure out exactly how many pens, pads, and paper clips will be needed.

Similar "rules of thumb" can be used in budgeting for other OTPS costs. For example, when planning on the purchase of blacktop for pothole repair, the department of transportation might develop a formula based on tons of blacktop needed in a typical year per mile of two-lane road that must be maintained. That could be adjusted for roads that have more than two lanes.

Capital Acquisitions

Earlier in the chapter capital budgets were discussed, and it was explained that a separate capital budget is generally prepared. We will assume that Millbridge is not planning any capital expenditures for the coming year. Capital budget issues are discussed further in Chapter 5.

Consolidate Departmental Expenditure Requests and Revenue Estimates

Once the revenue estimates and expenditure requests have been prepared, all of the elements from all of the departments can be consolidated so that the initial projected surplus or deficit can be calculated. Based on the timetable presented in Exhibit 2-3, this consolidation would take place during the first 10 days of September. We can see in Exhibit 2-6 that the general revenues of Millbridge are expected to be substantially more than the amount needed to cover general administrative costs. Also, the school system is budgeted to just cover its costs. However, a number of departments are projecting deficits. Public works, which has no revenues of its own, is projecting the largest deficit amount. Public safety is another department that requires large amounts of support from the general revenues of the town. On the other hand, the Recreation, Water, and Sewer departments have all submitted budget requests that project surpluses.

The mayor, town manager, and other key top level executives of Millbridge would review the consolidated budget from September 10 to September 15. Overall the consolidated budget requests result in a projected deficit of over $1 million. If the town has a requirement to show a break-even or surplus budget, then the draft budget in Exhibit 2-6 will be unacceptable. It will be necessary to either increase tax rates further, find other revenues, or trim expenditures. According to the budget timetable in Exhibit 2-3, department heads will revise budgets during the last half of September, so that the finalized budget can be submitted to the town council on October 15.

Prepare the Budget Document

Once the budget has been changed (which may take a number of rounds back and forth), and the chief executive officer (in the case of Millbridge, the mayor and the town manager) has decided that the budget is acceptable, a formal budget document is prepared. This document will include a message to the reader addressing the financial situation of the government, and discussing what the budget tries to accomplish. New programs will be discussed, as will significant changes in revenues or expenditures. The budgeted revenues and expenditures are shown along with detailed supporting schedules allowing the reader to better understand what the summary numbers represent. Justifications will typically also be provided so that the reader understands the negative consequences of eliminating any of the elements of the budget. This does not mean that the budget must be adopted as submitted, but rather that the reader should understand the implications of various types of changes.

Present the Budget Document to the Legislative Body

Once prepared the budget document is sent to the legislative body for review and adoption. In the case of Millbridge, the budget is presented to the town council on October 15. For the next two weeks, the council holds meetings to discuss the budget. The council members may

EXHIBIT 2-6 Town of Millbridge, Draft Fiscal Year 2012 Budget

	Projected Revenues	Projected Expenditures	Projected Net
General Revenues			
Property Taxes	$7,297,093		
Sales Tax	325,864		$ 7,622,957
General Administration			
Personnel		3,104,095	
OTPS		1,076,523	(4,180,618)
Education			
School Taxes	5,318,817		
Personnel		4,295,403	
OTPS		1,023,414	0
Public Safety			
Fines and License Revenue	1,343,209		
Personnel		2,357,349	
OTPS		423,520	(1,437,660)
Public Works			
Revenue	0		
Personnel		2,139,542	
OTPS		924,008	(3,063,550)
Health and Sanitation			
Fee Revenue	382,823		
Personnel		295,468	
OTPS		98,463	(11,108)
Recreation			
Fee Revenues	589,834		
Personnel		399,987	
OTPS		180,549	9,298
Water			
Usage Charges	316,551		
Personnel		228,435	
OTPS		73,058	15,058
Sewer			
Usage Charges	153,247		
Personnel		84,375	
OTPS		42,058	26,814
Total			$(1,018,809)

accept the budget as proposed or they may adjust it. If adjustments are made, the budget must be modified and then printed, and in the case of Millbridge, mailed to all residents for their review. This is followed by public hearings on the budget before the final vote by the Town Council. Public hearings are common practice by governments, although not universal. The timing of the public hearings will vary as well. They may come at an earlier point than they do in this example. The budget is adopted by passage of an appropriation ordinance or act, which establishes the maximum spending by the government body for the coming year. The approved Millbridge budget, as revised by department managers and by the Town Council, appears in Exhibit 2-7.

EXHIBIT 2-7 Town of Millbridge, Approved Fiscal Year 2012 Budget

	Budgeted Revenues	Budgeted Expenditures	Net
General Revenues			
Property Taxes	$7,671,435		
Sales Tax	325,864		$ 7,997,299
General Administration			
Personnel		3,001,435	
OTPS		983,564	(3,984,999)
Education			
School Taxes	5,318,817		
Personnel		4,295,403	
OTPS		1,023,414	0
Public Safety			
Fines and License Revenue	1,343,209		
Personnel		2,139,743	
OTPS		388,426	(1,184,960)
Public Works			
Revenue	0		
Personnel		1,983,045	
OTPS		884,356	(2,867,401)
Health and Sanitation			
Fee Revenue	382,823		
Personnel		295,468	
OTPS		98,463	(11,108)
Recreation			
Fee Revenues	589,834		
Personnel		399,987	
OTPS		180,549	9,298
Water			
Usage Charges	316,551		
Personnel		228,435	
OTPS		73,058	15,058
Sewer			
Usage Charges	153,247		
Personnel		84,375	
OTPS		42,058	26,814
Total			$ 0

Determine the Property Tax (Millage) Rate

Once the budget has been passed, the legislative body must enact legislation to provide revenues in support of the budget. Some revenues are recurring and do not require any annual action of the part of the government. For example, Millbridge might have a sales tax that continues at a set rate unless specifically changed by the government. Similarly, rates are established for parking tickets, licenses, and other sources of revenue. However, for many local governments, one of the primary sources of revenue, the property tax, is adjusted each year.

This approach is not universal. In some localities, the property tax is a flat percentage of assessed property value, and that percentage does not change from year to year. As assessed values change, the revenues from the tax will change correspondingly. That does not require any action on the part of the legislature each year. However, it also substantially limits the ability of the local government to control its revenues. As a result, expenditures must be matched to available revenues. In localities where the property tax rate is adjusted each year, the government has a greater ability to adjust revenues to meet expenditure needs.

Millbridge is assumed to have a property tax rate that is adjusted annually. Usually such rates go up from year to year, but that is not necessarily the case. For example, in an older community with a falling number of school-age children, the costs of the educational system may drop enough to actually allow property tax rates to decline. Also, if property values are rising rapidly, then the assessed property tax base may rise enough to offset the need for a tax increase. In the case of Millbridge, additional housing construction is increasing the tax base. Also, with the opening of a new direct rail connection to the nearby large city, house prices in the town have risen dramatically. The overall increase in the assessed value therefore offsets some of the additional costs of services that will be incurred due to the larger town population.

From Exhibit 2-7, we see that the property taxes for general revenues will be $7,671,435 and school taxes will be $5,318,817 for Millbridge for the coming year. In the case of Millbridge, both of these property taxes are collected by the town, but the tax rates are stated separately. Due to exemptions from tax for not-for-profit organizations, veterans, and the elderly, not all property in Millbridge is taxed. Also, based on past experience, Millbridge has found that a portion of billed taxes is never collected from property owners. They have found that adding 1 percent to the amount needed for the budget provides an appropriate cushion to cover those uncollectible amounts. Millbridge would take the following approach to set its tax rates:

Total Assessed Value of Property in Township	$1,423,540,000
Property Exempt from Tax	(180,243,000)
Net Assessed Value of Property	$1,243,297,000
Amount Needed for General Revenues (see Exhibit 2-7)	$ 7,671,435
Allowance for Uncollectible Taxes (1%)	76,714
Required Tax Levy for General Revenues	$ 7,748,149
Amount Needed for Schools	$ 5,318,817
Allowance for Uncollectible Taxes (1%)	53,188
Required Tax Levy for Schools	$ 5,372,005

Calculation of Tax Rate:

$$\text{Tax or Millage Rate:} = \frac{\text{Required Tax Levy}}{\text{Net Assessed Property Value}}$$

$$\text{Town General Revenues Property Tax} = \frac{\$7,748,149}{\$1,243,297,000} = 0.00623$$

$$\text{School Property Tax} = \frac{\$5,372,005}{\$1,243,297,000} = 0.00432$$

$$\text{Combined Property Tax Rate} = 0.00623 + 0.00432 = 0.01055$$

For a homeowner with a house appraised at $300,000, the taxes would be calculated by multiplying the rate by the appraised value:

$$\$300,000 \times 0.00623 = \$1,869.00 \text{ Town Tax}$$
$$\$300,000 \times 0.00432 = \$1,296.00 \text{ School Tax}$$
$$\$300,000 \times 0.01055 = \$3,165.00 \text{ Total Property Tax}$$

These rates would normally be multiplied by $100 to get the tax rate per $100 of assessed value. For example, the overall property tax rate would be $1.055 per $100 of assessed value (.01055 × $100). New tax bills should be mailed out as early as possible, to ensure that the government collects its property taxes on time.

Summary

Having a plan is essential for getting the most out of any organization. Planning is accomplished by establishing the mission for the organization, defining a strategy to accomplish the mission, developing a long-range plan that defines the organization's objectives, and preparing specific detailed budgets that define the resources needed to accomplish its goals and objectives.

A budget is simply a plan. The plan shows how management expects to obtain and use resources to achieve the organization's objectives. It provides a detailed action plan. There is no magic to budgeting. It requires thought. Budgeting requires estimating all the likely receipts and all the likely payments. The process usually requires a number of preliminary drafts and revisions before a feasible plan is developed and accepted by all parties. Once approved, efforts must be made to try to keep as close to the plan as possible.

Although some budgeting is done on an ad hoc basis (special purpose budgets), most budgeting is done at regular intervals. The master budget incorporates and summarizes all of the budget elements for the coming year. The main elements of the master budget, sometimes called the comprehensive budget, are the operating budget and the financial budget. The operating budget presents a plan for revenues and expenses for the fiscal year. The financial budget includes a cash budget and a capital budget. While the cash budget focuses on cash flows for the fiscal year, the capital budget considers outlays for resources that will provide service for a number of years into the future.

In some organizations, support and revenues are only acknowledged, or recognized, by the organization when they are received in cash. In those cases, expenses are only recognized when they have been paid in cash. They are said to use a cash basis of accounting. In contrast, if revenue is recorded in the year service is provided, the organization is said to be using an accrual basis of accounting. Accrual accounting is more difficult than cash accounting, but it provides a matching of revenues and expenses, allowing the manager to get a better sense of the profitability of the organization's activities.

The process of developing budgets is highly politicized. To the extent possible, managers should try to use an objective budget process that best leads to the accomplishment of the organization's mission, goals, and objectives. All organizations seek to accomplish some end. Hospitals exist to provide health care services to their communities. Museums exist to provide the public with access to fine art. Governments exist to provide essential services. The budget becomes the tool to facilitate the accomplishment of these missions.

Preview

This chapter has introduced the basic elements of budgeting. Chapter 3 focuses on some additional elements of budgeting for governmental, health, and not-for-profit organizations. It begins with a discussion of budget development contrasting a line-item approach with a responsibility center approach. A line-item expense is a specific class or category of resource used by an organization, such as rent or salaries. In contrast, a responsibility center approach divides the budget into units for which individual managers are held accountable.

Chapter 3 also considers the issue of centralization versus decentralization in the budget process and program versus functional budgets. Different organizations have different philosophies as to how centralized the budgeting process should be. Budgets can also be displayed in different ways, providing different types of information. Program budgets focus on the costs and revenues of specific programs as opposed to responsibility centers. Functional budgets represent another way to look at an organization, focusing on the main purpose or objective of spending.

After having focused on the different ways that budgets can be organized, the chapter discusses a variety of budgeting techniques. These techniques include flexible budgeting, performance budgeting, cost-benefit analysis, zero-based budgeting, and forecasting. The chapter finishes with a discussion of some unique aspects of budgeting for governmental organizations.

Key Terms from This Chapter

accrual basis. An accounting system that matches *revenues* and related *expenses* in the same *fiscal year* by recording revenues in the year in which they become earned (whether received or not) and the expenses related to generating those revenues in the same year.

allocation. Subdivision of an *appropriation* into more detailed categories, such as *responsibility centers* or programs or *objects of expenditure.* Sometimes, spending is further broken down into *allotments.*

allotments. A system that allocates budget resources to specific time periods or for use only after a certain event occurs.

appropriation. Approval by the legislative body—be it a senate or an assembly, a town committee or a council—of spending for a specific line-item. Appropriations create the authorization for spending the amount in the budget.

bad debts. The amount of money that is owed to an organization for goods or services provided, but which the organization is never able to collect. See also *uncollectibles.*

budget. Plan.

budget guidance memorandum. Document that provides policies, goals, and performance expectations.

capital assets. Resources that will have lifetimes that extend beyond the year in which they are acquired.

capital budget. Plan for the acquisition of buildings and equipment that will be used by the organization in one or more years beyond the year of acquisition.

cash basis. Accounting system under which revenues are recorded when cash is received and expenses are recorded when cash is paid.

cash budget. Plan for the cash receipts and cash disbursements of the organization.

depreciation expense. Amount of the original cost of a capital asset allocated as an expense each year.

encumbrance. Identification of a portion of the budget for a specific line-item that has already been "spoken for" by purchase commitments.

expenditure. Another term for *expense,* often used by governments.

expenses. The resources consumed in the process of providing goods and services.

financial budget. The *cash budget* and the *capital budget* together.

fiscal. Financial.

fiscal year. One-year period defined for financial purposes. A fiscal year may start at any point during the calendar year and finish one year later. For example, "fiscal year 2012 with a June 30 year end" refers to the period from July 1, 2011, through June 30, 2012.

goal congruence. Bringing the goals, desires, and needs of the organization together with those of its employees.

goal divergence. The natural differences between the goals, desires, and needs of the organization and those of its employees.

long-range budget. See *long-range plan.*

long-range plan. Plan that covers a period of time longer than one year, typically three, five, or ten years.

long-range planning. Planning process that provides a link between the *strategic plan* and the day-to-day activities of the organization.

master budget. Set of all the major budgets in the organization; generally includes the *operating budget, long-range budget, capital budget,* and *cash budget.*

matching. For a given unit of service provided, the revenues arising from providing that service and the expenses incurred in providing that service are both recorded in the same *fiscal* period.

mission. Organization's set of primary goals that justify its existence, such as providing high-quality hospital care to the surrounding community or providing research and education.

mission statement. Statement of the purpose or reason for existence of an organization, department, or unit.

modified cash basis. A basis for accounting under which routine revenues and expenses are recorded on a cash basis but capital assets are recorded as expenses gradually over the years they are used rather than all in the year the organization pays for them.

objects of expenditure. Specific individual types of items consumed in the operations of the organization, such as wages, rent, office supplies, travel, equipment, and other resources.

operating budget. Plan for the day-in and day-out operating revenues and expenses of the organization. It is generally prepared for one year.

outcomes. The results that the organization is trying to achieve.

output. The number of units of service provided (e.g., the number of meals served).

profit. The excess of revenues over expenses.

recognition. The point at which a financial event is considered to have occurred and can be recorded in the financial records of the entity.

responsibility center. Part of the organization, such as a department or a unit, for which a manager is assigned responsibility.

revenues. The resources the organization receives in exchange for providing goods or services.

special purpose budget. A plan for a specific project, program, or activity not covered by another budget.

strategic plan. Defines a broad set of goals for the organization and selects the primary approaches that the organization will take to achieve those goals.

strategy. Broad plan for the attainment of goals and mission.

support. Revenue that consists of either contributions or grants.

uncollectibles. Estimated amounts that are not expected to be collected because the organization is not paid amounts that are owed to it; also called bad debts.

Questions for Discussion

2-1. How does planning help an organization?

2-2. What is the organization's "mission" and why is it important?

2-3. What is the purpose of the strategic plan?

2-4. What is the role of the long-range plan?

2-5. Why are budgets used?

2-6. Why would a special purpose budget be used?

2-7. What are the different types of budgets?

2-8. How are budgets useful for motivation?

2-9. How do individual goals differ from organizational goals?

2-10. Discuss the concept of goal congruence.

2-11. What are several incentive approaches? Are there weaknesses in any of the approaches?

2-12. What are some negative consequences of unrealistic budget expectations?

2-13. What are the elements of the budget cycle?

2-14. Distinguish between cash basis and accrual basis accounting.

2-15. What is a modified cash basis of accounting?

2-16. What is the purpose of a budget timeline?

Problems

2-17. Calabrese Cares is a new charity that reconditions used cell phones for use by victims of domestic violence. Calabrese Cares has arranged to get the phones for free from churches in the area. The churches collect the old phones from their congregations. The first year Calabrese is in operation, shelters for victims of domestic violence buy phones from the organization for $20,000. They paid $15,000 during the year, and owe $5,000. Calabrese uses donated labor, and their only cost is a fee paid to the phone company to activate the phones. Total phone company fees were $18,000 for the year. During that first year Calabrese paid the phone companies $16,000. It owes the balance.

  i. What is the profit or loss to Calabrese Cares on a cash basis?

  ii. What is the profit or loss to Calabrese Cares on an accrual basis?

  iii. Which basis reflects the long-term stability of the organization?

2-18. Accrual budgets plan for expenses for supplies when _____ while cash budgets plan for the expense when _____. (choose from below)
   a. they are ordered
   b. they are delivered to the organization
   c. they are paid for
   d. they are consumed
   e. It depends of the type of expense.

2-19. Monroe Outpatient Surgery Center (MOSC) is developing an operating budget for the month ending June 30, 2012. The Center expects to perform 80 surgical procedures during the month. MOSC's average charge (price) per surgical procedure is $2,500. The cost of disposable surgical supplies is $300 per surgical procedure. MOSC also contracts with orthopedic surgeons at a fee of $1,500 per surgical procedure. The monthly salaries for the Center's receptionist, bookkeeper, and two surgical nurses total $10,500. The Center's occupancy costs, which include space rental, insurance, and all utilities, are $8,200 per month. Average monthly communication costs are $1,200. Office and operating room equipment was installed at a cost of $240,000. The equipment is expected to have a five-year life and has no salvage value. Prepare MOSC's operating budget for the month of June 2012.

2-20. Westchester City is constructing a new city hall. The building will cost $40,000,000 and is estimated to have a useful life of 40 years. Based on the experience of other similar cities, and the best estimates of the city's engineers, Westchester's planners expect that at the end of 40 years the building will have to be torn down and rebuilt, so it is not expected to have any value at the end of 40 years. It will cost $6,000,000 to acquire equipment for the new center. Equipment is assumed to last for 10 years. The city estimates that the equipment can be sold for 20 percent of its cost at the end of its useful life. If the city undertakes this project, what will the building and equipment expense be in the first year after the center is opened?

2-21. Children's Best Hope (CBH) provides day care services to low income families. CBH bills the state for its services under a service contract. Billings for the first four months of 2011 are anticipated to be as follows:

January	February	March	April
$220,000	$200,000	$240,000	$230,000

CBH finds that it collects 25 percent of the amounts billed in the month of service with the balance collected in the month following service.

CBH is planning to acquire a new building as an additional site for its services in March 2011. The full $250,000 purchase cost of the building will be financed with a mortgage loan.

CBH anticipates a February 28, 2011, cash balance of $26,000.

CBH anticipates the following expenses and disbursements for the month of March 2011:

Payroll payments	$170,000
Personnel expenses	$160,000
Payments to suppliers	$ 45,000
Supplies expense	$ 48,000
Depreciation expense	$ 12,000
Interest expense	$ 6,000

Prepare an operating budget, cash budget, and capital budget for CBH for the month of March 2011.

2-22. Middleboro Township plans to order supplies every quarter of the year. It expects to receive the supplies in the quarter after they are ordered. It expects to use them the quarter after that and pay for them the quarter after that. For example, if it orders supplies in the first quarter of the year, it will receive them in the second quarter, use them in the third quarter, and pay for them in the fourth quarter. The township pays salaries in the quarter that the employees work.

The township earns its income tax revenues equally throughout the year. However, it receives substantially more cash in April, when tax returns are filed. It plans to borrow $35,000 on a 20-year, 8 percent annual interest note, on the first day of the fourth quarter. Interest will be paid once each year at the end of the third quarter.

The town prepares its operating budget following the unique rules of modified accrual accounting employed by governments. Under these rules expenses are recorded when the town receives goods or services and becomes legally obligated to pay for them. It does not matter if they have been used or not. Also, cash inflows or proceeds from long-term loans are treated as if they were revenues. Using the information from the table below, prepare an operating budget and a cash budget for Middleboro Township for the fourth quarter only. Assume the town has $300,000 in cash when the fourth quarter starts.

	Jan.–March	April–June	July–Sept.	Oct.–Dec.	Total
Supply Orders	$300,000	$360,000	$ 390,000	$330,000	$1,380,000
Salaries	600,000	750,000	825,000	720,000	2,895,000
Income Tax Cash Receipts	600,000	600,000	1,200,000	600,000	3,000,000

2-23. Local Hospital (LH) has decided that it would like to send nurses to a local supermarket to provide a free health screening for interested supermarket customers. The screening will consist of measuring the individual's blood pressure and taking a drop of blood, which will immediately be tested for several critical indicators. The director of public relations at the hospital believes that 100 people will take advantage of the screening each day. The plan is to provide the screening every day for one week; thus a total of 700 screenings are expected. LH expects the supermarket to provide a $1,000 grant to help defray the costs of the program (since it will likely draw more customers to the store). LH anticipates the following expenses:

Test equipment rental	$500	For 1 week
Nurses	$50/hr	A total of 10 nurse hours/day for 7 days
Blood tests	$1	Per individual tested

Determine the special purpose budget for the program. Show revenues and expenses by line item, and show the expected profit or loss. If there is an expected loss, should LH necessarily abandon the project or are there other factors that must be considered?[13]

2-24. Roche City has two major sources of revenues, property tax and sales tax, which are billed according to the schedule at the bottom of the page.
Traditionally, property tax revenues have been received in cash according to the following schedule:

40 percent one month following the billing date
20 percent in second month
10 percent in third month
10 percent in fourth month
8 percent in fifth month
5 percent in sixth month
7 percent are not collected

The state collects the sales tax revenues and will transfer cash to the city on March 1, 2012, for the sales tax revenues earned in the last quarter of 2011.
Roche City is not planning any capital asset purchases during the next three months. Monthly cash disbursements for general operations are $3,700,000.

Beginning cash balance for January 1, 2012, is $500,000. Roche City will borrow to ensure that the ending cash balance each month is at least $100,000.
Use this information to prepare a monthly cash budget for Roche City for January, February, and March of 2012.

2-25. In the chapter, a special purpose budget was developed for a youth trip to the Holy Land. The chapter also referred to Steve Netzer's idea for the HOS to provide blood pressure screening in supermarkets. Prepare a hypothetical special purpose budget for the blood pressure screening program.

2-26. River County is planning several capital acquisitions for the coming year. These include the purchase of two new garbage trucks at $150,000 each, one new bulldozer at $240,000, three new riding lawn mowers at $16,000 each, and construction of an activity center in the park for $650,000. The expected lifetime of the various capital items is 10 years for garbage trucks, 8 years for the bulldozer, 5 years for the lawn mowers, and 40 years for the activity center. Prepare a capital budget for the items to be acquired, showing their estimated lifetimes, and their per unit and total costs.

2-27. Zoo Extravaganza is a not-for-profit organization. Zoo Extravaganza took over the county zoo, with the provision that the county would provide a subsidy for its operations. The county provides $7,000 per month. The rest of the zoo's revenues comes from admission charges, which are as follows: $20 for a family admission (the average family has four people), $3 per child in school groups, $5 per child ticket when not in a school group, and $8 per adult ticket.
Each ticket entitles the visitor to ride on the "Train Around the Zoo." However, only one-third of all visitors actually ride the train.
The zoo expects the following number of visitors per month:

Visitor Type	Monthly Number of Admission Tickets
Adult	800
Child	950
Schoolchild	1,000
Families	300

2011 ($)	July	August	Sept.	Oct.	Nov.	Dec.
Property Tax	—	—	45,000,000	—	—	—
Sales Tax	50,000	55,000	62,000	50,000	68,000	112,000

[13] This problem and problems 2–24, 2–27, and 2–28 are adapted from problems written by Dwight Denison.

The zoo has the following monthly expenses in four general areas:

Administration	$ 12,000
Zoo staff	$ 10,000
Train rides	$ 1 per person who rides the train
Maintenance	$ 1 per visitor

Determine the operating budget per month. Show revenues and expenses by line-item, and show the expected profit or loss.

2-28. Draft a quarterly cash budget for the Zoo Extravaganza (ZE) for the first two quarters of the coming year. Use just the information in this problem.

1. Interest is paid on the last day of the year and can be ignored in Quarters 1 and 2.
2. Annual expenses are $220,000 for administration and ZE staff (other than maintenance workers). Those costs are paid evenly throughout the year.
3. Assume the cash balance on January 1 is $5,000 and ZE policy is to have at least a $5,000 ending cash balance each quarter.
4. Train expenses are incurred in the same seasonal pattern as admissions and are paid with a one-quarter lag. The budgeted annual expense for this year is $20,000. Last year the annual cost for the train was $18,000.
5. The cost of the maintenance crew is 20 percent of admissions revenue each quarter. Maintenance workers are paid in the quarter in which they work.
6. The total annual county grant of $84,000 is received on the last day of the fourth quarter of the year.
7. ZE collects all admissions in cash at the time of admission. Total admissions revenues are $180,000 for the year. The seasonal pattern of admissions is shown in the following table.

	Quarter			
	1	2	3	4
Admissions by Quarter	30%	25%	15%	30%

2-29. Answer the following questions about methods of accounting.

1. Under accrual accounting, revenues and support are recognized when an organization _____ an amount that it is likely to collect, and it recognizes expenses when it _____ a resource.
2. Accrual-based expenses associated with capital assets are called _____.
3. Capital projects are analyzed on the basis of _____.

2-30. Prisons R Us (PRU) delivers counseling services to prison inmates for the state on a fee-for-service basis. It is preparing its cash budget for the month of March. Its operating budget reflects accrued fee-for-service revenues of $12,500, $13,000, and $14,000 respectively for the months of January, February, and March. PRU bills the state electronically at the end of each month for the services that it delivers to its fee-for-service clients. PRU collects 60% of its fee-for-service billings in the month following the delivery of service, with the remainder being collected in the second month after the delivery of services. What are PRU's total cash receipts from the state for the month of March?

2-31. You are the executive director of a community service agency in the inner city. Your operation is funded through a combination of cash contributions, federal government grants, and city contracts. Your revenue budget for the coming fiscal year is shown below.

You know from past experience that not all of your revenue and support is collected when you earn it. Cash contributions are collected in the quarter they are pledged. Federal government grants are collected one quarter after you send the granting agency a bill. The city pays 25 percent of what it owes you one quarter after you send in the bill. An additional 25 percent is collected from the city in two quarters and the remaining 50 percent takes three quarters to collect.

Starting with the revenue budget below, calculate the amount you can expect to collect in the fourth quarter of coming fiscal year.

Revenue Budget for Coming Fiscal Year

Source of Revenue	Q 1	Q 2	Q 3	Q 4
Contributions	$ 25,000	$ 35,000	$ 35,000	$ 50,000
Federal Grants	$250,000	$375,000	$350,000	$250,000
City Contracts	$240,000	$300,000	$320,000	$360,000
Total	$515,000	$710,000	$705,000	$660,000

2-32. The county has an initiative for students in underperforming schools. To get funding, schools provide each student with eight 2-hour-long group tutoring sessions each month. Also, parents must agree to pay $10 per month for each child they register for the program. The county will pay each school $200 per enrolled child, per month.

Schools must provide one tutor for every five students enrolled in the program, at a cost of $50 per hour at a teacher's home school, or $60 per hour if the teacher has to commute from another school in the system.

Schools that participate also need to acquire a site license for a self-study computer program, at a cost of $2,400 per year regardless of the number of students. The school also incurs a cost of $1.50 per child, per tutoring session, for workbooks that are tied to the self-study program.

Generally the county takes one month to pay bills submitted by schools. Parents pay all tuition bills at the beginning of each month. Participating teachers are paid for all after-school programs at the end of each month. The full cost of the software must be paid by the end of the first month of the program. Workbooks are paid for in the month they are used.

You are the budget manager for Typical County School (TCS). Five teachers in your school have agreed to be tutors. Since you expect to need 15 tutors by the end of the year, you will also use 10 teachers from other schools, as needed. Your calculations indicate an expected 25 students in the program during the first month it is offered, 41 in the second month and 52 in the third month. As budget manager:

1. Prepare operating budgets for each of the first three months of the program.
2. Summarize the three monthly budgets into a quarterly operating budget.
3. Starting from a zero cash-balance, prepare a cash budget for the first quarter (three months) of the program. You do not have to prepare monthly cash budgets.

2-33. Marquoya College[14]

Part I

Marquoya College (MC) is a medium-sized private school located in the Midwest. In the past, MC administrators established a budget for the next academic year by adding a specific percentage (e.g., 6%, 8%) to the tuition revenue and operating expenses. This year MC has asked for your assistance in developing its budget for the next academic year. You are supplied with the following data for the current year.

Enrollment	4,300 students
Tuition	$3,300/year
Full-time faculty	250 (72% tenured)
Fees	$280/year
Average faculty salary	$36,000/year
Full tuition only scholarships	400 students

For the next academic year, enrollment is expected to increase by 300 students with each student taking an average of 32 credit hours. Tuition will increase by $100/year.

Prepare a schedule computing the next academic year's tuition and fee revenue budget. Explicitly show the effect of scholarships.

Part II

The additional students will require MC to hire 20 adjunct faculty members. Each adjunct will teach 18 credit hours and will be paid at the rate of $750/credit hour. Full-time faculty members will receive a 5 percent pay increase. Additional merit increases to be awarded to individual faculty members will amount to $280,000.

Prepare a schedule computing the next academic year's budget for faculty salaries. The payroll budget should reflect payroll taxes using a rate of 10 percent.

Part III

The current budget is $1,200,000 for operation and maintenance of plant and equipment, including $190,000 for salaries and wages. Experience of the past three months suggests that the current budget is realistic. However, expected increases for next year are $10,000 in salaries and $50,000 in other expenditures for maintenance of plant and equipment.

The IRS has determined that MC has unrelated business income. In the year just past MC paid $48,000 of federal income taxes and a penalty of $2,000. MC's administrators feel that proper allocation of costs and timely payments to the IRS will result in a total tax liability of $36,000.

Estimates for other costs include:

Mortgage payments	$ 264,000	(Reducing principal by $100,000)
Administrative and general	1,440,000	(Including salaries of $1,200,000)
Library	1,800,000	(Including salaries of $1,000,000)
Health and recreation	750,000	(Including salaries of $300,000)
Athletics	320,000	(Including salaries of $60,000)
Insurance and retirement benefits	548,000	
Capital improvements	1,300,000	

---

[14] This problem was written by Ken Milani and Jim Gaertner. Used with permission.

Where applicable use a payroll tax rate of 10 percent.

Anticipated revenues, other than tuition for the next academic year, are:

Endowment receipts (e.g., interest, dividends)	$ 514,000
Net income from auxiliary services	$ 538,000
Athletics	$1,580,000

MC's remaining source of revenue is an annual alumni support campaign. Last year, the alums were very generous (MC's basketball team was ranked high throughout the cage campaign) and contributed over $600,000.

MC borrowed $200,000 from the Golden Dome Bank for summer operations on June 15. The principal plus interest (at an annual rate of 12%) is to be paid on September 15.

On the basis of the tuition and fee revenue budget and faculty salaries budget computed in parts I and II, prepare a schedule computing the amount which must be raised during the annual support campaign in order to cover the expenditures budgeted.

Part IV

Using anticipated alumni support of $750,000, prepare a cash budget for the first quarter (Sept., Oct., Nov.) of the MC fiscal year. (Round all calculations to the nearest hundred dollars.) The following patterns of cash flows are anticipated:

MC must maintain a cash balance of $3,000. Financing can be arranged at the Golden Dome Bank at a rate of 12 percent. Borrowing occurs in $1,000 increments. All loans are repaid as soon as possible, but a minimum of one month's interest is charged. Estimated cash on September 1 is $3,700.

	Sept.	Oct.	Nov.	Dec.	Jan.	Feb.	Mar.–Aug.
Tuition revenue	20%	-	15%	5%	30%	15%	15%
Fee revenue	50%	-	-	-	50%	-	-
Endowment income	25%	-	-	25%	-	-	50%
Net income from auxiliary services	10%	10%	10%	10%	10%	10%	40%
Athletic revenue	10%	-	50%	10%	10%	5%	15%
Alumni support	2%	2%	12%	25%	6%	3%	50%
Faculty salaries	10%	10%	10%	10%	10%	10%	40%
Operation and maintenance of plant and equipment	8%	8%	10%	10%	10%	8%	46%
Insurance and retirement	10%	10%	10%	10%	10%	10%	40%
Athletic expenditures	10%	5%	10%	10%	15%	10%	40%
Capital improvements	-	80%	-	10%	-	-	10%
Federal income tax	-	-	25%	-	-	25%	50%
All others	12 equal receipts/disbursements						

CASE STUDY
The DMV

The Division of Motor Vehicles (DMV) is part of the State Department of Transportation (DOT). The purpose of that department is to ensure the safety and free flow of people and goods throughout the State by ensuring that there is a reliable system of transportation and motor vehicle services. This mission is accomplished by funding the maintenance of the existing transportation infrastructure, by adding to and improving the infrastructure, and by otherwise operating a transportation system that minimizes congestion and promotes safety and the economic growth of the State.

Among the key functions served by the DOT are:

- driver licensing and insurance
- vehicle inspection
- bridge and highway construction and maintenance
- public transit

The current year budget for the DOT is $874 million. Of that amount, $96 million is budgeted to be spent on the DMV, which has the following objectives:

- to provide customer-friendly, efficient motor vehicle services;
- to regulate drivers and motor vehicles to deter unlawful acts and protect the public safety;
- to further protect public safety by identifying vehicle safety problems; and
- to further protect the public by ensuring that all drivers carry insurance.

The state is currently preparing its budget for the coming fiscal year, which runs from September 1, 2013, through August 31, 2014. As the Director of the DMV, you are responsible for three major areas:

- licensing, registration, and inspection of motor vehicles;
- driver licensing; and
- compulsory insurance.

A major issue for the coming year will be the overhaul of the driver's license program to include the latest enhanced digitized security technology. To cover this increased cost, the DMV is planning to charge $5 more for new drivers' licenses and license renewals. This charge is not enough to fully cover the cost of the new licenses, but raising fees was a political hot potato during the last session of the state assembly, and the Governor would be reluctant to propose any further increase to that fee.

Another major initiative being planned for the DMV for the coming year is a centralized computer system to verify that all registered vehicles are insured. Once the system is in place, the DMV will be able to check insurance coverage not only when a vehicle is registered, but also when law enforcement officers stop a vehicle, when the vehicle has its biannual safety inspection, and at other times. The system will require an initial capital investment of $3 million, and operating costs of $1.30 per inquiry. It is expected that there will be 1 million uses of the system spread evenly during the coming year. None of the capital investment cost appears as part of the operating budget for the coming year.

To comply with the state's 2011 *Clean Air Act,* the auto inspection program must be modified. The DMV has estimated that it will cost $7.2 million to equip the state vehicle testing centers with the necessary equipment for the new, stricter test. None of this cost will be part of the operating budget for the DMV.

During the coming year, the DMV expects to issue more licenses per month early in the year, as drivers try to avoid the extra cost and documentation requirements associated with the new higher security licenses. The DMV expects to issue 923,456 licenses using the old technology spread evenly throughout the first four months of the year, and 843,023 licenses using the new digitized technology spread evenly throughout the last eight months of the year.

There are expected to be 342,587 vision tests, 847,129 written driving tests, and 429,222 road tests in total for the year. These tests are expected to occur in the same proportion as the number of licenses issued each month. It is expected that there will be 962,135 vehicle registrations and 1,106,455 annual vehicle inspections, and these will occur evenly throughout the year. Note that the vehicle inspection number includes re-inspections for vehicles that fail their initial inspection.

The sources of revenue for the DMV are as follows:

- auto license fees: $25 for the old style license and $30 for the new improved digitized license with all security features;
- vehicle registration fees: $53 per vehicle registered, on average;
- vehicle inspection fees: $35 for failing the inspection—otherwise no fee. It is expected that 15 percent of the total number of vehicle registrations will result in inspection failures and re-inspections;
- state appropriation—for any balance not funded by fees; and
- transportation trust fund—for capital acquisitions.

The costs of running your department consist of personnel expenses, materials and supplies, and a variety of purchased services. Personnel costs have a fixed administrative component of $6.5 million per year that is not affected by the DMV's service volume. Administrators are paid evenly throughout the year. Other personnel costs average $2 per transaction, regardless of transaction type, including issuance of an auto license, vehicle registration, vehicle inspection, or administration of any type of test. Materials and supplies cost $.30 per transaction. These costs are incurred each month in direct relation to the number of transactions for the month. The $2 personnel and $.30 materials and supplies cost per transaction are not required for insurance inquiries. Other departmental overhead costs include heat, electricity, and rent. Those costs are fixed at $8 million, and are paid evenly throughout the year.

Additionally, the DMV pays outside contractors on the following fee schedule:

- $17 per vehicle inspected
- $2 per vision test
- $15 per road test
- $5 per written test
- $25 per license plate (30 percent of all vehicle registrations require new license plates)
- $10 per driver's license (old style) and $37 per license (new digitized licenses)

The Director of the DOT is hoping the DOT's financial situation will allow for expanded subsidies of public transportation. As such, she is hoping that each division of the DOT will at least break even, if not show a profit. Although you realize that the DMV will receive a State subsidy to operate if needed, you know that your boss would be unhappy if such a subsidy is needed for your division.

Using a computer spreadsheet, prepare a budget for the DMV for the coming year, based on the information you currently have. If the budget shows a deficit, you may need to make some adjustments, so use formulas for your calculations. That way you will be able to make changes in your worksheet and easily calculate updated results. Specifically,

1. Prepare a monthly operating budget for the DMV for the fiscal year ending August 31, 2014. Determine the operating surplus and deficit for each month and for the year as a whole. Use one page or worksheet in your spreadsheet to list all of the base information, and another for the operating budget. [Hint: It may be easier to prepare the budget if you add a third page or worksheet to calculate the number of transactions each month.]
2. To what do you attribute the changing surplus/deficit pattern during the year?
3. What would happen to the overall deficit or surplus if the number of vehicles failing inspections increased from 15 percent to 30 percent? Keep in mind that vehicles must be re-inspected, so this would also increase the total number of inspections. Does this give the DMV a reason to make its standards tougher? Is this good policy?
4. Suppose the DMV can choose when to implement the new digitized licensing system.
   a. What would happen to the finances of the DMV if the new licenses are implemented at the beginning of the year and issued throughout the year?

b. What would happen if the new licenses are not implemented at all during the coming year? In either case, assume the total number of licenses issued for any month does not change. Is that assumption realistic? How does it affect your results?

5. What other changes would you suggest that might help the DMV's situation? What are the advantages and disadvantages of the various suggested changes? Select the approach that you believe is best, create a worksheet showing the resulting budget, and provide an explanation defending your choice of changes.

CASE STUDY
Denison Specialty Hospital—Part I

Denison Specialty Hospital is planning its master budget for the coming year. The budget will include operating, capital, cash, and flexible budgets. The hospital is noted for its three fine programs: Oncology (cancer), Cardiac (heart), and Rhinoplasty (nose jobs).

Part I. Section A

The managers at Denison have been busy working. They have reviewed past records, considered changes in competition, the general economy, and overall medical trends. Using past charges and anticipated rates of medical inflation, they have also made a first attempt at setting their prices.

Based on a thorough review and discussion of these data, they have projected that next year they will have 240 patients. They expect 120 oncology patients, 80 cardiac patients, and 40 rhinoplasty patients.

The charge, or list price, for Oncology patients will average $50,000. Cardiac patients will be charged an average of $40,000, and Rhinoplasty, $25,000 per patient. However, those charges often are not the actual amount ultimately received.

The amount the hospital receives depends on whether patients pay their own hospital bills or have health care insurance. Assume that private insurance companies pay the full charge or list price. However, Medicare and Medicaid have announced rates they will pay for the coming year as follows: Oncology patients $40,000, Cardiac patients $30,000, Rhinoplasty $10,000. Self-pay patients are supposed to pay the full charge, but generally 25 percent of self-pay charges becomes a bad debt. Note that *bad debts are treated as an expense* in health care. They may not be shown as a reduction lowering revenues. The full charge for self-pay patients is shown as revenue, and then the uncollectible amount is shown as an expense. No payment for charity care is ever received, and *charity care is not shown as a revenue or expense.*

The payer mix is as follows:

	Private Insurance	Medicare/Medicaid	Self-Pay	Charity
Oncology	30%	50%	10%	10%
Cardiac	20%	60%	10%	10%
Rhinoplasty	10%	20%	60%	10%

Gift shop revenue is projected to be $120,000 for the current year and is expected to remain the same. However, this revenue will increase or decline in proportion to changes in patient volume.

Denison Hospital has an endowment of $1,000,000. It is invested as follows:

- $500,000 in 6 percent U.S. Government Bonds that pay interest annually,
- $250,000 in AT&T stock, which pays a dividend of 8 percent annually, and
- $250,000 in growth stocks that pay no dividend.

Section A requirements:

1. Calculate patient revenue on an accrual basis for the coming year. Subdivide revenue by program, and within each program subdivide it by type of payer.
2. Calculate endowment revenue on an accrual basis for the coming year.
3. Prepare a revenue budget on an accrual basis, including all sources of revenue discussed previously. The revenue budget does not have to show all of the detail from requirements 1 and 2, but should show each major source of revenue, such as patient services and endowment.

Section B

The hospital expects to employ workers in the following departments:

	Radiology	Nursing	Administration	Total
Managers	$ 100,000	$ 200,000	$200,000	$ 500,000
Staff	1,900,000	4,200,000	300,000	6,400,000
Total	$2,000,000	$4,400,000	$500,000	$6,900,000

Supplies are expected to be purchased throughout the year for the departments, as follows:

	Total
Radiology	$360,000
Nursing	160,000
Administration	20,000
Total	$540,000

Assume that *all* supply use varies with the number of patients.

Denison Hospital currently pays rent on its buildings and equipment of $300,000 per year. Rent is expected to be unchanged next year. The rent is paid $75,000 each quarter.

To better serve its patients, Denison would like to buy $500,000 of new oncology equipment at the start of next year. It would be paid for immediately upon purchase. The equipment has a five-year life and would be expected to be used up evenly over that lifetime. Although the capital budget would normally include justification for why the equipment is needed, it is sufficient for our purposes to know that the capital budget for Denison is $500,000 and the equipment to be purchased has a five-year useful life. It will have no value left at the end of the five years. Denison charges the cost of its capital acquisitions on a straight-line depreciation basis. That means that the cost is spread out over the useful life, with an equal share being charged as an expense, called depreciation expense, each year.

Section B requirements:

1. Calculate expected bad debt expenses on an accrual basis for the coming year.
2. Calculate an expense budget on an accrual basis for the coming year. The expense budget does not require detailed information by program or department, but should

show each type of expense such as salaries and supplies. Be sure to consider the impact of capital acquisitions on the expense budget.

3. Combine the revenue (Section A) and expense budgets to present an operating budget for the coming year.

Note: Part II of this case study appears at the end of Chapter 3.

Suggested Readings

Anthony, Robert N., and Leslie Pearlman Breitner. *Essentials of Accounting*, 9th ed. Upper Saddle River, N.J.: Prentice Hall, 2006.

Atkinson, Anthony A., Robert S. Kaplan, and Mark S. Young. *Management Accounting*, 4th ed. Upper Saddle River, N.J.: Prentice Hall, 2004.

Finkler, Steven A., and Mary L. McHugh. *Budgeting Concepts for Nurse Managers*, 4th ed. St. Louis, Mo.: Saunders Elsevier, 2008.

Hyde, Albert C. *Government Budgeting: Theory, Process, Politics*, 3rd ed. Belmont, Ca.: Wadsworth/Thomson Learning, 2002.

Lee Jr., Robert D., Ronald W. Johnson, and Philip G. Joyce. *Public Budgeting Systems*, 8th ed. Sudbury, Mass.: Jones and Bartlett Publishers, 2007.

Mikesell, John L. *Fiscal Administration—Analysis and Applications for the Public Sector*, 7th ed. Belmont, Ca.: Thomson Wadsworth, 2006.

Nice, David. *Public Budgeting*. Belmont, Ca.: Wadsworth/ Thomson Learning, 2002.

Rosen, Harvey S. *The Fiscal Behavior of State and Local Governments*, Studies in Fiscal Federalism and State-Local Finance Series. Northampton, Mass.: Edward Elgar Publishing, 1997.

Rubin, Irene S. *The Politics of Public Budgeting: Getting and Spending, Borrowing and Balancing*, 5th ed. Chatham, N.J.: Chatham House Publishers, 2006.

Wheelen, Thomas L., and David J. Hunger. *Strategic Management*, 11th ed. Upper Saddle River, N.J.: Prentice Hall, 2007.

3

Additional Budgeting Concepts

The learning objectives of this chapter are to:

- define *line-items* and *responsibility centers*, and distinguish between line-item and responsibility center budgeting;
- explore the issue of centralization versus decentralization in the budget process;
- examine the presentation of budget information categorized by program or function;
- define and discuss *flexible budgeting*;
- define and discuss *performance budgeting*;
- define and discuss *zero-based budgeting*;
- introduce forecasting and explain which forecasting techniques are useful when historical data are available and which are useful when such data are not available; and
- address additional budgeting issues related particularly to governments, specifically focusing on limitations on management actions, the role of budget reserves, and communicating the budget to the public.

INTRODUCTION

The basic elements of budgeting are discussed in Chapter 2. This chapter focuses on some additional elements of budgeting for governmental, health care, and not-for-profit organizations.

This chapter begins with a discussion of budget development using a line-item approach, as contrasted with a responsibility center approach. A *line-item* expense is a specific class or category of resource used by an organization. For example, salaries are a line-item. In contrast, a *responsibility center* approach divides the budget into units for which individual managers are held accountable. A government might have a parks department with a manager who is responsible for the total amount spent on parks. The total budget for the government could be divided into line-items that would indicate the total amount being spent on salaries, the total amount being spent on supplies, and so on. Alternatively, it could be divided by responsibility center, indicating the total amount budgeted for parks, the amount for police, and so on. Or it could be divided by line-item and responsibility center.

The chapter then considers the issue of centralization versus decentralization in the budget process. Different organizations have different philosophies as to how centralized budgeting should be.

Following that, the chapter moves on to a discussion of different ways of organizing and presenting budget information. In addition to reporting budget information by line-item or responsibility unit, another alternative is to organize the budget by program. Program budgets focus on the costs and revenues of specific programs. For example, we could evaluate the town's new safety awareness program, which draws resources from both the police and fire departments. That program budget would include some elements from each of those two responsibility centers. Functional budgets represent yet another way to look at an organization, this time focusing on the main functions of the organization. For example, the police and fire department budgets could be combined in total to report on the public safety function of a government.

The chapter then moves to a discussion of a variety of budgeting techniques:

- Flexible budgeting takes into consideration the fact that the actual output level often differs from expectations. Managers must have some way of controlling operations in light of varying levels of activity.
- Performance budgeting is an approach designed to improve the focus on outcomes in the budget process.
- Zero-based budgeting is a technique that requires annual budget justification of all items in a budget, rather than just the incremental change.
- Forecasting focuses on how managers make predictions of expenses, revenues, and other items in the budget.

The chapter finishes with a discussion of some unique aspects of budgeting for governmental organizations.

LINE-ITEM AND RESPONSIBILITY CENTER BUDGETS

Budgets are most often created to provide information by line-item and/or by responsibility center. *Line-item* expenses represent specific individual types of expenses, such as wages or supplies. *Responsibility centers* are organizational subdivisions that a specific person is responsible for supervising.

For example, suppose that the Hospital for Ordinary Surgery (HOS) expects to spend $100 million in the coming year. One way that the expense budget might be organized would be by line-item, as follows:

Hospital for Ordinary Surgery
Expense Budget
for the Coming Fiscal Year

Salaries	$ 60,000,000
Supplies	25,000,000
Utilities	4,300,000
Rent	7,700,000
Interest	3,000,000
Total	$100,000,000

This is referred to as a line-item budget. Managers need to know the amounts of money budgeted for salaries versus supplies, two of the line-items in the budget. However, this budget is limited in its ability to help managers implement and control the plan. There are many managers in a hospital, each responsible for a different part of the organization. If the organization is to hold individual managers accountable for what happens in their areas, the managers must have specific budgets for their parts of the organization. Those parts of the organization are called responsibility centers.

For example, HOS might have a responsibility center expense budget that would appear as follows:

Hospital for Ordinary Surgery
Expense Budget
for the Coming Fiscal Year

Radiology	$ 13,000,000
Nursing	10,000,000
Pharmacy	5,000,000
Laboratory	7,000,000
Operating Room	50,000,000
Administration	15,000,000
Total	$100,000,000

By preparing a budget for each responsibility center (department or cost center), managers know the amount they are authorized to spend. Then the organization can track how well the managers and units do in keeping to that spending level. However, providing a manager with only a total amount for a responsibility center makes it difficult to control spending. Combining line-item and responsibility center information provides managers with more information and a better ability to control spending (for example, see Table 3-1).

Notice how the budget format in Table 3-1 provides information on the budgeted spending for each responsibility unit and also provides detailed breakdowns of how much each responsibility unit will be spending on each line-item.

CENTRALIZATION VERSUS DECENTRALIZATION

An organization's budget process is often characterized by its degree of centralization or decentralization. When one imagines the development of a budget for an entire organization, the process may seem overwhelming. Developing detailed line-item budgets for individual responsibility centers breaks the budgeting process down into more manageable pieces. The individual responsibility center line-item budgets may be prepared primarily by the manager of the responsibility center or by higher levels of management.

TABLE 3-1 Line-Item and Responsibility Center Budget

Hospital for Ordinary Surgery
Expense Budget
for the Coming Fiscal Year

	Radiology	Nursing	Pharmacy	Laboratory	Operating Room	Administration	Total
Salaries	$ 3,700,000	$ 8,000,000	$1,300,000	$4,000,000	$32,000,000	$11,000,000	$ 60,000,000
Supplies	3,600,000	1,200,000	3,500,000	2,500,000	13,700,000	500,000	25,000,000
Utilities	3,400,000	100,000	100,000	200,000	400,000	100,000	4,300,000
Rent	2,300,000	700,000	100,000	300,000	3,900,000	400,000	7,700,000
Interest						3,000,000	3,000,000
Total	$13,000,000	$10,000,000	$5,000,000	$7,000,000	$50,000,000	$15,000,000	$100,000,000

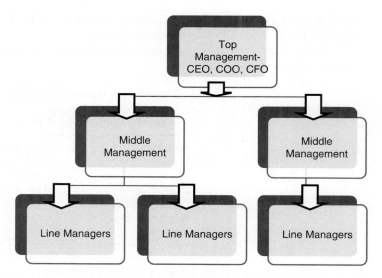

FIGURE 3-1 Top-Down: Budgets are developed by top management and then disseminated to middle managers and line (first-level) managers for implementation.

Responsibility center budgets can be prepared in a centralized fashion by the organization's top management. In such an instance, the responsibility center managers are told the budgeted amount and are expected to achieve the budgeted result. This is sometimes referred to as a *top-down budget* (see Figure 3-1). It is often hard for responsibility center managers to achieve such top-down budget expectations because it is very difficult for top managers to be aware of all of the factors affecting spending in each responsibility unit. At the other extreme, responsibility center managers would create the budgets for their own centers and inform the top management of their spending plans for the coming year. This could be described as a *bottom-up budget* approach (see Figure 3-2). However, responsibility center managers are rarely knowledgeable about the overall limitations on financial resources available to the organization. Their bottom-up budgets may exceed such limitations.

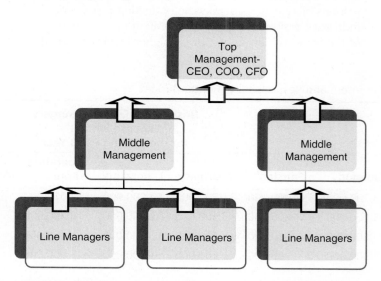

FIGURE 3-2 Bottom-Up: Budgets are developed by the lowest level of management, and passed up for review, negotiation, modification and approval.

Some organizations tend to be more centralized in the budgeting process, and some are less centralized. Rarely, however, would one see either of the extreme situations described in the preceding paragraph. In fact, one can think of the process of top-down budget management and bottom-up budget development as being complementary.

In general, all budgets will start with some input from top management. Broad policy goals are formulated by top executives, policy makers, and, in the case of government, political representatives. These goals should reflect public needs and preferences, and the mission and strategy of the organization. Most organizations then incorporate their responsibility center managers into the process by asking unit or department heads to prepare detailed budgets, incorporating the broad objectives that top management has provided.

A bottom-up approach allows the individuals who are most involved with the day-to-day activities and specific aspects of the organization's operations to be involved in the planning process. This empowerment of employees often leads to better morale and better results. However, it requires top managers who are willing to accept some degree of decentralization. In very autocratic, centralized organizations, where top managers desire to retain high levels of control, a top-down budget is more likely to be employed.

In some cases, organizations have multiple goals that cut across departments. In such cases, top management may need to make resource *allocation* decisions. At other times, unit managers may initiate new proposals. They may see a need for something new that the organization does not currently do at all. For example, a mid-level manager at the HOS might suggest conducting a blood-pressure screening of shoppers at local supermarkets. After proposing the concept, the manager may be given the responsibility of developing the special-purpose budget for the program.

Centralized budgeting and *decentralized budgeting* each have advantages and disadvantages. Top-down has a speed advantage. Decisions can be proposed, adopted, and implemented with a minimum of delay. In times of crisis, speed may be a critical element. The primary disadvantage is that it is much harder to get cooperation and commitment from the people at all levels of the organization to carry out the budget. Bottom-up budgeting is better for gaining consensus and support for the budget. However, it is not only time-consuming but also creates the need for negotiation and compromise. It works better when times are stable than in times of crisis or significant change.

As noted, most organizations use neither top-down nor bottom-up budgeting exclusively. Hybrid approaches are much more common. Such approaches combine direction from above with input from below. Ideally, the result is a budget that takes into account the overall organizational needs and expectations, and also incorporates the creativity and superior detailed knowledge that may exist at lower levels of the organization.

PROGRAM AND FUNCTIONAL BUDGETS

Line-item and responsibility center are two common ways to classify budget costs, but they are not the only approaches. Budgeted costs can be divided by type of program or by functional area.

Program Budgets

Suppose that HOS specializes in three programs: Oncology (cancer care), Rhinoplasty (nose jobs), and Cardiac Surgery (heart operations). Budgets can be prepared that would show expected revenues and costs of each major program. This could be done for regular programs or for special projects or specific services. If HOS made budgets for different programs, it could prepare *program budgets* to evaluate each program's profitability and decide whether it can afford each program. For example, if rhinoplasty is mostly elective surgery, and the program loses money, as shown in the following budgets, the hospital might use that budget information to decide to eliminate the program:

Hospital for Ordinary Surgery
Program Budgets
for the Coming Fiscal Year

	Oncology	Rhinoplasty	Cardiac	Total
Revenues	$40,000,000	$ 12,000,000	$50,000,000	$102,000,000
Expenses	37,000,000	17,000,000	46,000,000	100,000,000
Profit	$ 3,000,000	$ (5,000,000)	$ 4,000,000	$ 2,000,000

Governments, in contrast, often have a weak ability to match revenues and expenses by program. In many cases, the government uses its general tax revenues to support a wide range of programs. In other cases, governments do have the ability to create specific budgets such as the preceding HOS budget. For example, revenues and expenses for education are often matched against each other, especially for local governments.

The preceding numerical example is highly summarized. However, a budget could be prepared for each program that also shows line-item and responsibility center details that make up the total revenues and expenses.

Note in the preceding example that the total cost of the three programs is $100,000,000, the same as the total expenses for HOS in the earlier examples. This means that all costs from the responsibility center budgets in Table 3-1 have been allocated to these three programs. Some allocations may be fairly arbitrary. For example, it is hard to determine how much of the administration cost of the hospital rightfully should go to each program. HOS must be careful in its decisions. If it closes the Rhinoplasty program, it may not be able to eliminate some of those allocated costs.[1]

Functional Budgets

When not-for-profit organizations report their annual results to outsiders, they often prepare *functional* financial statements. These statements separate activities into their major functions. Consider Meals for the Homeless, for example. The organization's primary mission is to provide meals. However, suppose that it also provides counseling to some of its clients. The role of the counseling is to direct the homeless to various government agencies and other charities that can provide them with assistance. Also, there are fund-raising and administrative departments. A budget for Meals for the Homeless might be categorized as shown on the top of the next page.

Notice in this budget, Meals is using a functional segregation of its primary *program services*, separated from its *supporting activities*. However, it is also providing information by line-item. It would also be possible for there to be a subdivision of this budget by responsibility centers. For example, the program service Meals might be provided by a Kitchen department that cooks the meals, a Distribution department that delivers meals to soup kitchens and other locations, and a Serving department that serves the meals to the homeless. Each department might have its own manager, responsible for the costs of that department. Thus, the "Meals" column under Program Services might be subdivided into three

---

[1] Often some costs of running an organization do not relate to individual services. For example, suppose that HOS's building must be heated in the winter. The heating cost is not specifically a cost of Oncology, Rhinoplasty, or Cardiac Surgery. However, it is a cost of the organization. Such costs are often referred to as indirect, *overhead,* or joint costs and are frequently *allocated* to specific programs or services. That means that a portion of the total overhead cost is assigned or charged to each program or service. There are a wide variety of possible allocation approaches, from a simple division (one-third each to Oncology, Rhinoplasty, and Cardiac) to more sophisticated alternatives. See Chapter 4 for additional discussion of cost allocation.

Meals for the Homeless
Expense Budget
for the Coming Fiscal Year

	Program Services		Supporting Activities		
	Meals	**Counseling**	**Management and General**	**Fund-Raising**	**Total**
Salaries	$ 500,000	$25,000	$60,000	$40,000	$ 625,000
Supplies	900,000	1,000	6,000	20,000	927,000
Rent	100,000	5,000	15,000	5,000	125,000
Other	50,000	2,000	8,000	4,000	64,000
Total	$1,550,000	$33,000	$89,000	$69,000	$1,741,000

individual responsibility center budgets by line-item that total to the amount shown in the preceding budget.

BUDGETING TECHNIQUES

The budget process is described in Chapter 2. At this point, the chapter addresses several specific budgeting techniques: *flexible budgeting, performance budgeting, zero-based budgeting,* and *forecasting.*

Flexible Budgeting

Preparing a budget requires many assumptions and predictions. One of the most prominent of these involves the *workload* level. *Workload* refers to the volume of goods or services that the organization will provide. If the volume of services, cost of services, and revenues related to services all rose and fell in equal proportions, this might not create a significant problem. However, that is generally not the case. Revenues may change in a sharply different proportion than costs. Managers need to be able to anticipate such variations. A *flexible budget* is a tool to aid managers in this area.

A flexible budget is an operating budget for varying workload levels. For example, suppose that Leanna Schwartz, executive director of Meals for the Homeless, expects to provide 40,000 meals and has the following operating budget for the coming month:

Meals for the Homeless
Operating Budget
for Next Month

Revenues	
Donations	$105,000
City	60,000
Total Revenue	$165,000
Expenses	
Salaries	$ 46,000
Supplies	100,000
Rent	12,000
Other	6,000
Total Expense	$164,000
Surplus	$ 1,000

This budget provides Meals with confidence that they will have a good month. A surplus of $1,000 is projected. But what will happen if the number of meals provided is greater or less than expected?

Assume that donations do not change if the number of meals provided changes. However, Middle City is paying Meals $1.50 for each meal provided. If the number of meals increases or decreases, revenue will change. Also, some of the expenses are *fixed costs*; that is, they will not change as the volume of work changes. For example, rent on the kitchen location is a flat monthly amount, regardless of the number of meals served. If the volume of meals goes up or down, rent will remain the same. For most organizations, however, some costs are *variable*; they vary as the volume of goods or services provided goes up or down. Meals will have to buy more food if it gets very busy. Or it can buy less food if it gets slow.

A flexible budget takes the basic operating budget and adjusts it for the impact of possible workload changes. Assume that payments from the city and purchases of supplies (food) are the only items that vary with the number of meals served. Consider a flexible budget for Meals, assuming that 35,000 or 45,000 meals are served next month:

Meals for the Homeless
Flexible Operating Budget
for Next Month

	Volume of Meals Provided		
	35,000	**40,000**	**45,000**
Revenues			
Donations	$105,000	$105,000	$105,000
City	52,500	60,000	67,500
Total Revenue	$157,500	$165,000	$172,500
Expenses			
Salaries	$ 46,000	$ 46,000	$ 46,000
Supplies	87,500	100,000	112,500
Rent	12,000	12,000	12,000
Other	6,000	6,000	6,000
Total Expense	$151,500	$164,000	$176,500
Surplus/(Deficit)	$ 6,000	$ 1,000	$ (4,000)

This flexible budget shows that if the number of meals provided increases, a loss is likely to occur. This information can serve as a warning to the managers at Meals. If they start seeing demand and the number of meals served increase, they can anticipate the likely financial shortfall without waiting until the end of the month or later to find out. Actions can be taken to increase fund-raising efforts or to try to find ways to cut costs. Decisions can be made regarding whether Meals can financially sustain a loss. If it cannot, managers may have to choose among cutting the cost of the food used per meal, limiting the number of meals served, or finding other places to cut costs.

Flexible budgets focus on an output measure. Hospitals treat patients. Soup kitchens serve meals. Government agencies may build miles of roads or carry passengers in public transit vehicles or educate students in schools. In each case, some measure of volume is needed to prepare a flexible budget.

The key to preparing a flexible budget is determining which numbers in the budget are likely to change and which are likely to remain the same. Will the costs that vary change in direct proportion to volume changes, or will their change be more or less than proportional? Management must work to understand revenue and cost structures enough to be able to anticipate the changes caused by volume variations.

Performance Budgeting

Operating budgets are an attempt to plan the resources needed to accomplish desired *outcomes*. The outcomes are the results that the organization hopes to achieve. However, the process tends to focus more on the budgeted level of resources (the *inputs*) and less on the various outcomes to be achieved. To the extent that outcomes are taken into account, they are usually summarized by one limited measure, such as the number of meals served. *Performance budgeting* is an approach designed to improve the budget process by focusing more on what the organization hopes to accomplish.

A hospital's goal is for its patients to get well. A soup kitchen's goal is to reduce levels of hunger and malnutrition. A parks department's goal is to provide rest and recreation. However, these outcomes are extremely difficult to measure. Often organizations are forced to rely on simpler *output* measures, such as the number of patient treatments, meals served, or park users. More sophisticated performance measurement approaches are discussed in Chapter 8.

Performance budgeting is a useful approach in situations that do not have a clear relationship between resources and outcomes. The method calls upon the manager and organization to define goals, plan the amount of resources needed to accomplish those goals, and then assess how well the goals have been achieved. This may not result in measurement of outcomes, but it is a step in that direction.

Consider, for example, the Parks and Recreation Department of the Town of Millbridge. One of the primary reasons Millbridge has the Parks and Recreation Department is to maintain the town's parks for the pleasure of its residents. There are 10 parks in Millbridge. Dwight Ives, town manager for Millbridge, was concerned that the town had no way to evaluate the budget of the Parks and Recreation Department. How much money should it receive to maintain the parks? There are baseball diamonds to be groomed, tennis courts to be cleaned and repaired, lawns to be mowed, and snow to be removed. Litter must be picked up and trash cans emptied. Paths must be paved and trees pruned.

A typical operating budget for a parks and recreation department would show the money available for salaries, supplies, equipment, and so on. It would tend to be a line-item budget for a responsibility center. Such a budget focuses on inputs such as salaries and supplies. If the town is looking to save money, there might be support for cutting the spending of the parks and recreation department. Spending cuts often translate into reductions in service. However, one could argue that the parks and recreation budget could be cut by 10 percent, and all 10 parks would still be available for the citizens of Millbridge. Therefore, there will be no reduction in service.

That argument is unlikely to be completely correct. If the budget is cut by 10 percent, then the reduced spending may well cause a decrease in the maintenance of each park. Lawns may not be mowed as often. Paths may not be repaved when needed. There will be difficulty in evaluating what has happened. Ten parks will still be maintained, but not as well. The cost per park maintained has decreased. However, that might not translate into higher efficiency. It can translate into lower performance.

Clearly, a simple quantity or output measure, such as the number of parks maintained, does not tell the whole story. To improve the budgeting process, it is necessary to get a better sense of the goals of a department or organization. What is it really trying to achieve, and how can achievement of that goal be measured? Public, health, and not-for-profit organizations tend to have this problem more than most private, for-profit industries. For a proprietary organization making a specific product, if the amount of inputs can be reduced, keeping outcomes the same, it would be more productive. The problem, however, is whether outcomes can be adequately measured in the public service sector to see if they are the same. A key element is whether the organization can readily define what it does. If it cannot, then it will have trouble planning how much it will do and, after the fact, measuring how much has been done.

If HOS reduces the number of clinical care hours per patient per day, does that represent improved efficiency or decreased quality and quantity of patient care? The performance budgeting approach can help managers answer these questions by defining the outcomes of a department in a way that allows measurement.

For the Millbridge Parks and Recreation Department, how could the goals be thought of, rather than simply maintaining 10 parks? Millbridge could consider the following as goals: the number of trash cans to be emptied, the number of miles of pathway to be repaved, the number of acres of lawn to be mowed, or the level of satisfaction of park users. In the government sector, it is common to use specific performance measures such as these to keep pressure on agencies or departments to be productive. Rather than just providing a budgeted spending level and requiring that parks be maintained, the agency or department will be held accountable for achieving certain levels of performance based on a number of different criteria.

The first step is to define objectives clearly. What is the organization trying to accomplish? Are these the appropriate objectives? The objectives are considered performance areas. Next, one must identify the operating budget. How much money has the organization budgeted for the department or cost center? The percentage of operating budget resources that will be devoted to each objective must be determined. The operating budget resources can then be allocated to the performance areas. Measures of performance for each objective or performance area must be established. For each performance area, a specific outcomes level should be budgeted. Then a performance budget can be developed.

EXAMPLE   An example of performance budgeting for a hospital cardiac laboratory is provided in Appendix 3-A. The key performance areas for the lab were determined to be: perform diagnostic catheterizations, perform interventions, improve quality of care, improve throughput (the time from the beginning of one procedure to the beginning of the next), control the supply cost per patient, improve patient satisfaction, improve physician satisfaction, and improve staff satisfaction. The performance budget developed in that example is shown in Table 3-2.

This budget provides a summary of each performance area, the type of activity required to achieve the desired results, the primary measure for each output or outcome, the level of budgeted output or outcome for each performance area, the cost of resources devoted to each area, and the average cost per unit for each output or outcome. See Appendix 3-A for a discussion of the derivation of this budget.

RETURN ON INVESTMENT ANALYSIS   Once the performance budget has been developed, it is possible to perform a return on investment analysis for each performance area. The reason for such analysis is to assess whether it is worthwhile, from a financial perspective, to allocate the budgeted amount of resources to each of the performance areas.

For example, suppose the supplies budget is $1,520,000. Each 1 percent difference in the cost of supplies will cost the hospital $15,200 (i.e., $1,520,000 × 1 percent = $15,200). From Table 3-2, we see that the performance budget calls for spending $34,000 to keep supply costs 3 percent below the industry average, or $11,333 for each 1 percent savings. On a savings-to-cost basis, the return on investment calculation would be as follows:

$$\text{Savings/Cost} = \$15,200/\$11,333 = \$1.34 \text{ savings per dollar spent}$$

For every dollar the department spends to control supply costs, it saves $1.34 in the cost of supplies. Since it is saving more than it is spending, it is appropriate to devote $34,000 of resources to control supply costs.

This is a very limited form of cost-benefit analysis, a technique discussed in Chapter 5. A further discussion of performance budgeting return on investment calculations is provided in Appendix 3-A.

TABLE 3-2 Performance Budget

Performance Area	Type of Activity	Output Measure	Budgeted Output	Total Cost	Average Cost
Perform diagnostic catheterizations	Catheterizations	Number of caths	1,200	$777,000	$648/cath
Perform interventions	Interventions	Number of interventions	1,200	$890,000	$742 per intervention
Improve quality	Change in specific procedures	Number of complications	10% reduction in complication rate	$ 59,000	$5,900 per 1% reduction
Improve throughput	Develop new coordination procedures with OR and MDs	Turnaround time	5% reduction in turnaround time	$ 64,400	$12,880 per 1% reduction in turnaround time
Control supply cost/patient	Work on vendor contracts, work with clinical staff	Supply dollars per patient	Constrain increase to 3% versus expected industry 6% increase	$ 34,000	$11,333 per 1% below industry expectations
Improve patient satisfaction	Improve staff communication with patients	Number of complaints	Reduce number from 60 to 40	$ 53,900	$2,695 per eliminated complaint
Improve physician satisfaction	Redesign work scheduling to meet MD demands	Cases/MD	2% increase per MD	$103,000	$51,500 per 1% increase
Improve staff satisfaction	Allow longer breaks and free coffee/donuts	Turnover rate	Reduce turnover by 50% from 4/year to 2/year	$ 18,700	$9,350 per staff member retained

The performance budgeting concept can be helpful to most public service organizations. For example, what does the executive director of Meals for the Homeless do? The budgeted costs for the director could be divided into performance areas for fund-raising, public relations, cost control, increased meal volume, managerial supervision, and long-range planning. How can one measure these performance areas? One way to get started is by focusing on the activities that will occur. Perhaps Leanna Schwartz, executive director of Meals, intends to make 25 personal visits to philanthropists. And suppose that although many philanthropists will turn her down, it is anticipated that a total of $500,000 will be raised. The organization can determine the percentage of her effort that goes to this objective, the cost of her time for this, and the budgeted goal. This can be translated into a return on investment analysis. In this way, even the many areas that have seemed to defy measurement can in fact be evaluated.

Zero-Based Budgeting

Conceptually any expense budget should call for consumption of only those resources that are needed to accomplish the organization's goals. Excessive resource use is wasteful and detracts from the organization's financial stability and its ability to achieve its mission. In reality, as organizations get larger, the budget process becomes complex. It is not unusual for an organization to try to simplify its budgeting process by authorizing across-the-board incremental increases in budgets from one year to the next. For example, Dwight Ives, the town manager of Millbridge, might authorize a 4 percent increase for all departments that are part of the town government. The 4 percent increase represents an increment over the amount authorized for the previous year. This approach is therefore often called *incremental budgeting.*

Although this may be easier than careful item-by-item, department-by-department evaluation, it does not ensure that only the minimum resources necessary are used. Further, it does not ensure that scarce resources are allocated to the highest priorities. One department might have a very strong need for a 10 percent increase, while another might not need any increase at all. As technology, unemployment levels, and social needs change, some departments have growing financial needs, while other departments could get by with decreasing resources.

Some organizations examine all requested increases in budgets carefully. That is, no across-the-board increase is automatically authorized. Every increase must be justified. Although this is better than a flat equal percentage across the board, it assumes that the previous year's budget is an acceptable starting point. There is no critical examination of the base, only of the increase. *Zero-based budgeting* (ZBB) is an approach that argues that each year every item in every budget should be closely examined for the value it adds.

Any items that do not add value or do not add sufficient value to justify their cost should be eliminated from the budget. ZBB gets its name from the fact that each department or program starts with a zero base of justified costs. All spending from zero on up must be explained and justified. ZBB helps to keep budgets from developing "fat." No expenditure is automatically accepted without some explanation of why the organization is better off with that expenditure.

The evaluation of every item in each budget is a very time-consuming process. Rather than make such a large investment in budgeting, some organizations use ZBB only to evaluate new programs. As such, ZBB has become a leading program budgeting technique. Some other organizations use ZBB for their operating budgets but rotate agencies or departments, with each receiving a thorough ZBB review every three (or four or five) years, and incremental budgets in the intervening years.

Whether it is used to evaluate annual operating budgets, or budgets for new or existing programs, ZBB focuses on alternatives. Information is collected into a *decision package.* This package provides the analysis of the program or department being evaluated. It contains broad information about the program being evaluated, including why the program has been proposed, the negative effects of not doing the program, and the costs and benefits of the program. One of the key elements is a statement of alternatives.

ZBB requires evaluation of alternatives in a variety of ways. Different programs aimed at the same goal should be compared. Different ways of performing each given program should be compared. Different quality and quantities of each program should be compared. For example, if Meals for the Homeless decides to start a new suburban program, it may have to choose whether to use a fixed location (soup kitchen) or use a truck to deliver meals. The truck alternative must consider different sized trucks. There must be consideration of not only whether to serve one, two, or three meals a day, but also the nutritional value (and therefore cost) of the meals provided. By examining alternative approaches and the costs and benefits of each approach, managers are placed in a better position to make informed choices when allocating limited resources. Each alternative is ranked, with the manager giving consideration to the costs and benefits of the differing approaches.

ZBB can also be used for *decremental* budgeting. Decremental refers to a reduction. In such a use, decision packages become the source of information needed for reducing the overall budget rather than for evaluating budgets from a zero base. For example, suppose that due to a downturn in the economy and a rise in unemployment rates, Millbridge municipal tax revenues are expected to fall. The town, in an effort to reduce expenditures and avoid a deficit, can use the ZBB technique as an evaluative approach for making the budget cuts that will have the least negative impact on the town and its residents.

Forecasting

Budgets are plans for the organization for a future period of time. Budgets are based on estimates of expected revenues and expenses. Lee and Johnson note that

> Little imagination is required to appreciate the importance of revenue estimating. If a government is required to have a balanced budget, as state and local governments are, then accurate revenue forecasts become critical. Estimates that are too high can create major crises during the execution phase, at which time expenditures must be cut in order not to exceed revenues. Low estimates also cause problems, because programs may be needlessly reduced at the beginning of the fiscal year.[2]

Estimates of expenses are equally important. Consider, for example, a school budget. The budget will depend on the number of students. Part of the school budget is the cost to heat the school building. That cost will depend on the average temperature throughout the winter. Part of the school budget may depend on the average price of textbooks. These are just a few of the many expense expectations in a school budget. The future depends on many unknown factors and events. When managers develop budgets, they must make predictions called *forecasts*. Forecasts are little more than guesses about what the future will be. However, there are statistical approaches to forecasting that can improve accuracy of the predictions and give you a sense of how variable the actual results may be.

The manager preparing a school budget will forecast the number of students, the average temperature, and the price of textbooks. The more accurate the forecast, the easier it will be to manage the budget. If the winter is colder than expected, the school system will have to spend more on heating. Within the closely regulated budget systems of governments, this may require spending reductions in another area.

There are many approaches to making forecasts. Forecasts often are the result of a combination of the output from an analytical model and the judgment of the forecaster. Most forecasts are accomplished by using historical information and projecting that information into the future. There are a wide variety of approaches for doing this, ranging from very simple to very complex. However, all of these approaches have the benefit of being based on a firm, historical foundation. Predictions are even more difficult to make in the absence of any experience or history. However, organizations in the public service at times have to make such predictions.

FORECASTING WITHOUT THE BENEFIT OF HISTORICAL DATA   Every time a new service or program is suggested, the financial evaluation is performed without any history. How can estimates be made in the absence of such data? To some extent, one can rely on engineering calculations. A determination can be made of exactly what resources should be required for each unit of the service provided. However, even such an objective analysis cannot tell the organization how much of the service will be demanded. In such cases, individual managers can use their own judgment. However, it is often better to base such forecasts on the collective opinion of groups of individuals.

Two common techniques are designed specifically to help improve the accuracy of estimates when no specific historical information is available: the nominal group and Delphi techniques. In both approaches, a team or panel must be selected that consists of individuals

---

[2] Robert D. Lee Jr. and Ronald E. Johnson. *Public Budgeting Systems,* 6th ed. Gaithersburg, Md.: Aspen Publishers, 1998, p. 26.

who are likely to have reasoned insights with respect to the item being forecast. Industrial experience has shown that by arriving at a consensus among a team of experts, subjective forecasts can be reasonably accurate. The experts do not have to be expert in the specific project, but they should come from areas as closely related as possible.

The nominal group technique is one in which the group members are brought together in a structured meeting. Each member writes down a forecast. Then all of the written forecasts are presented to the group by a group leader without discussion. Once all of the forecasts have been revealed, the reasoning behind each one is discussed. After the discussions, each member again makes a forecast in writing. Through a repetitive process, eventually a group decision is made.

By using a group approach, a number of individuals focus their attention on the same problem. Each person has a somewhat different perspective that influences his or her subjective forecast. Being exposed to competing forecasts and explanations of the reasoning behind them can be extremely helpful in providing the central planner with insights that had not already been considered. The underlying concept is that both the additional ideas and the discussion of the ideas by all members of the group will result in an improved forecast.

Obviously, the nominal group technique has weaknesses. One problem involves lack of information. If different individuals base their forecasts on different assumptions, it may be impossible to reach consensus. A more serious problem involves politics and personalities. As members of the group defend their forecasts, extraneous issues having to do with whose idea it is may bias the group decision. Some individuals may be reluctant to share their ideas in public for a variety of reasons. The Delphi technique overcomes that weakness.

In the Delphi approach, the group never meets. All forecasts are presented in writing to a group leader, who provides summaries to all group members. After several rounds, a decision is made based on the collective responses. The weakness of the Delphi method is that it takes more time and is more cumbersome than the nominal group method. Nevertheless, Delphi has several particular advantages. By avoiding a face-to-face meeting, the technique avoids confrontation. Decisions are based more on logic than on personality or position.

These two methods recognize that individual managers cannot be expected to think of everything. Different individuals, bringing different expertise and different points of view to the same problem, can create an outcome that is superior to that which any one of them could create individually.

FORECASTS BASED ON HISTORICAL DATA   In cases where historical data do exist, forecasting is somewhat easier. Knowledge about the past is often an excellent starting point for predicting the future. Forecasts based on historical data fall into the categories of *causal models* and *time-series models*. The simplest approaches to forecasting are informal. For example, next year can be assumed to be just like the current year. More effort and sophistication in the forecasting method can result in more accurate forecasts—but simple models often provide the most reliable results.

In causal models, changes in one variable are used to predict changes in another. For example, Meals for the Homeless can examine the amount of food it used in past years as the number of meals served has varied. Based on that relationship, it can predict how much food will be needed in the coming year if it has an expectation of the number of meals that will be served in the coming year. Changes in the number of meals causes a change in the amount of food needed.

In time-series models there is assumed to be a relationship between the item we wish to forecast and the passage of time. For example, Meals may believe that the best indicator of the number of meals to be served in the future is simply the underlying trends that occur over time.

Consider property tax revenues. Will next year's revenues be the same as this year's? That is unlikely. However, the manager has much of the information available to make the forecast. Property tax revenues are the tax rate multiplied by the tax base. Over time there are additions of new or remodeled properties increasing the base, and property values in general may rise or fall.

Over time, trends may exist that would make it unlikely that the value of a variable will be the same next year as it was this year. Trends make forecasting more complicated. The linear regression statistical technique can be used to take a series of historical points and provide a projection in such situations.

However, what if there is an intra-year seasonal pattern or a long-term cyclical pattern? Perhaps certain times of the year are always busy and other times are always slow. Or perhaps the economy cycles through years of economic expansion alternating with recessions. Linear regression is inadequate when there are underlying nonlinear patterns. A variety of more sophisticated statistical time-series techniques, such as exponential smoothing, can smooth out fluctuations in a historical series.

In some cases, governments and other organizations will rely on sophisticated econometric forecasting models. These causal models use multiple variables (e.g., multiple regression) or in some cases multiple equations (solved simultaneously) to provide improved forecasts. In multiple regression models, several independent variables are used to create the forecast. In the case of multiple equations models, the predictor variables need not be assumed to be independent of each other. This is perhaps more realistic.[3]

In the case of governments, and many other public sector organizations as well, it is critical to consider general economic and other regional factors when making forecasts. Many elements of a budget (e.g., sales tax receipts and income tax receipts) will vary with the general economic conditions. Similarly, demographics can have a significant influence. The closing down of a major employer and the emigration of former employees of that employer can have dramatic impacts on both revenues and expenses of a government.[4]

One would think that sophisticated statistical techniques would make forecasting a fairly straightforward and well-defined science. In fact, it remains largely an art. Lee and Johnson note that

> Despite the availability of a wide range of indicators and extensive historical series, forecasting remains a risky business. It is common to find two or more major federal organizations in substantial disagreement over expected economic trends. . . . Not surprisingly, during major economic changes both businesses and government are sometimes criticized for not having anticipated the degree of change or sometimes even the direction of change.[5]

Before using a forecasting model, it is always beneficial to test it out. This can be done by running the model parallel to the current forecasting approach to see if it does better than existing techniques. Another way to verify the accuracy of a model is to use it to predict the past few most recent periods and see how accurately it would have predicted what actually happened.

Even in periods of relative stability, with a model that seems to forecast well, the judgment of the manager is critical in the forecasting process. Only the manager of a specific responsibility center can be aware of the many reasons that history may not be a good

---

[3] Ibid, p. 87.
[4] Ibid, p. 88.
[5] Ibid, pp. 493–94.

predictor of the future. For example, in the health sector, clinical technology changes rapidly. Forecasting models are limited when discontinuous changes occur. A new machine or technique can have a dramatic impact on the costs of procedures or even the number of procedures performed, and therefore on revenues. One should never rely totally on statistical techniques alone. Careful thought about the subject of the forecast, and managerial knowledge, intuition, and judgment are essential to the forecasting process. Forecasting is discussed further in Appendix 3-B.

Using Budgeting Techniques

An organization would rarely use just one budgeting technique. It is not expected that a manager will always choose to use flexible budgeting or zero-based budgeting. Rather, the specific situation determines the appropriate budget technique. The decision of whether to build a new baseball stadium to prevent a team from leaving a city might best be evaluated using a cost-benefit analysis (see Chapter 5). Efforts to reduce the growing administrative costs of an organization might be dealt with using ZBB. Concerns about what will happen to Meals for the Homeless if the demand for services increases might be addressed using flexible budgeting. Thus, managers must use a combination of techniques to address the many resource allocation issues that they confront in their organizations.

ADDITIONAL GOVERNMENTAL BUDGETING ISSUES

Many of the issues discussed in this chapter and Chapter 2 relate generally to government management as well as to health care and not-for-profit management. Governments, however, have a number of unique budgeting concerns. Governments tend to have much less flexibility in structuring budgets than other organizations do. Government budgets often have mandated forms and content. Government budgets are public and are often used by individuals outside of the government for a variety of purposes. For example, the budget of a government may be used by lenders to decide whether to make a loan to the government or to determine what interest rate to charge.

One of the reasons that governmental budgeting is different is that governments have taxing authority. This creates an ability to generate revenue that many organizations do not have. At the same time, however, it places a greater responsibility on the organization to be accountable to the public in its spending.

When the government decides on taxes, they are often based on achieving some policy objective. Taxes on cigarettes may be partly a method of raising revenue and partly a way for the government to discourage cigarette smoking. The social policy role in governmental budgeting has wide implications. Policy decisions will affect who or what to tax and at what rate. Decisions to help those with less money may require tax increases for those with more money. Policy decisions also affect transfers of revenue between governmental units. For example, in an effort to provide more self-determination, Medicaid money can be given from the federal government to state governments with few strings attached, allowing the states to decide what health care services to provide to Medicaid beneficiaries. States in turn may pass on block grants and authority to local governments.

This decentralization process, shifting money and authority to lower levels of government, is referred to as *devolution*. It serves a policy of allowing each state and locality greater control over spending. Devolution takes place on a selected basis. For example, the federal government may decide that it wants to retain control over the health care treatment of the elderly. Therefore, all Medicare decisions might be made at the federal rather than local levels, even though Medicaid decisions are not made by the federal government.

Suppose that an approved budget turns out to be inaccurate due to poor forecasts, and that it becomes apparent during the year that spending will exceed receipts. Service cuts may be required to keep spending within legal limits. The government does this by making a *rescission*. The term *rescission* refers to the fact that the authorization to spend the money is rescinded. Service cuts are often immediately apparent to the public and often receive unfavorable response.

One might think the solution is simply to increase taxes and revenues to ensure that service cuts will not be required. However, if taxes are deemed to be unacceptably high, people may find legal ways to avoid those taxes. These approaches may be detrimental to the community. For example, suppose that Millbridge, in its effort to have the cleanest streets in the nation, institutes a local sales tax to pay for it. The town managers expect this tax to bring in extra revenue. However, to get around the sales tax, many buyers may choose to shop in the towns surrounding Millbridge that have no such sales taxes.

With fewer customers, local merchants go out of business. With rows of unoccupied stores, urban decay begins. Unoccupied buildings are likely to attract rodents and squatters; fires and physical deterioration of the buildings may occur. With the unappealing look of the downtown area, people start to sell their houses and leave town. Property values fall and property tax receipts decline. Faced with falling property tax revenues, the property tax rate rises to cover lost money needed by the town. This tax increase accelerates the decline in property values and the flight of homeowners to other communities. Eventually, most government services are cut because there is not enough money to pay for them. Millbridge soon earns the distinction of having the dirtiest streets in the country.

This extreme example of a downward spiral is meant to show that the power to tax is not absolute. Governments have limited resources, just as other organizations do. High taxes in themselves are often politically undesirable. (Voters like to throw those who vote for higher taxes out of office.) Furthermore, they do not always generate higher revenues, as the preceding example demonstrates. It requires a skillful balancing act to provide all necessary services without creating an excessively high tax structure.

Tying Managers' Hands

The political and professional management sides of government should work together. Unfortunately, the nature of laws enacted through the political process often ties the hands of professional government managers in the financial management process. For example, both *mandates* and *entitlements* create required spending patterns that must be built into budgets. Managers must also deal with the fact that there are legal limits on changes in budgets.

The federal and state governments often create mandates that require local governments to provide services at their own expense. A state may have a teachers' pension system. To keep the administration cost per participant low, the state may require that all local school districts participate in the system. For some local governments, the pension may be more generous than they would otherwise negotiate with the local teachers' union. However, if mandated by the state, they must participate and pay the higher costs.

Entitlements tend to create burdens on the federal and state budgets. These represent benefits that must be given to any individuals who meet eligibility criteria specified in the law creating the entitlement. For example, Medicare provides health care for not only the elderly, but also the permanently disabled. If the number of disabled individuals rises, total Medicare benefits will increase, and resources must be provided to pay for those benefits, unless the law creating the entitlement is changed. Politicians have found that eliminating or reducing some entitlements is extremely unpopular and politically difficult to do.

Governmental budgets have the force of law. Managers are generally restricted from spending more than the total amount budgeted for their department. They also tend to have a limited ability to move funds from one account to another within their department. For example, it is often the case that money budgeted by governments for salaries cannot legally be used for supplies. This reduces managers' flexibility when dealing with unexpected events. On the other hand, it also prevents managers from using more funds than intended, or using funds for a different purpose than their intended use.

In proprietary organizations, the owners have a personal financial interest in watching over the actions of the organization's managers. In public service organizations, the members of the public are the owners. However, the public's ability to act as watchdogs over government management is very limited. Therefore, controls are put in place to safeguard the use of the public's money. These tend to limit the flexibility of management. Some would argue that they keep governments from being as responsive and efficient as possible and are wasteful. However, it is a price that is paid to prevent misappropriations and potentially much greater waste.

Budget Reserves

As noted earlier, if revenues fall short, it may be necessary to cut spending to avoid an illegal budget deficit. Another alternative to risking the need for sudden painful spending cuts is to establish *budget reserves* at the time the budget is created. These reserves are sometimes called *rainy day funds*.

No matter how carefully one budgets, it is rare for actual results to exactly match the plan. It is not possible to know for sure when and how much cash will be received from taxes. It is not possible to know if there will be unusually heavy snowfalls requiring unexpected overtime and salt use. Nor can one know exactly what equipment will break down and how much the repairs will cost. It is sensible to have reserves for unexpected events.

When reserves are established, the government must decide how large they should be, who can authorize use of the reserve, and what happens if all of the reserve is not used. Presumably, if some reserves are left, the government as a whole will have a surplus. That money can be used toward balancing the next year's budget, or it can be accumulated. By accumulating reserves, the annual reserves can be smaller. For example, suppose that Millbridge expects to spend $200,000 per year on snow removal. In a really bad winter, this could rise as high as $500,000. A winter that bad would only occur once in 10 years. One solution is to have a reserve of $300,000 each year to protect against a really bad winter. An alternate solution would be to have a reserve of $30,000 each year and allow that reserve to accumulate until it reaches a level of $300,000.

Communicating with the Public

Very few organizations share their plans with the public. Governments are fairly unique in that they must communicate budget information to the public. Although each budget document will be unique, there are some elements that are common to most government budgets reported to the public: a budget message from the manager or chief executive, a table of contents, summary tables of revenues and expenditures, and other supporting information.[6]

The presentation of the information, use of graphics and exhibits, and other general elements should be aimed at informing the public about the government's plans for the collection and expenditure of resources. The budget should present the goals and objectives of the government as well as information about how it expects to measure its performance. Performance budgets can be particularly useful in this respect. The budget document should be readable and should avoid complexity whenever possible.

---

[6] Robert L. Bland and Irene Rubin. *Budgeting: A Guide for Local Government.* Washington, D.C.: International City/County Management Association, 1997, p. 54.

Summary

This chapter builds on the basic budgeting concepts of Chapter 2. Budgets may be organized to provide information in many different ways. They can be line-item budgets, focusing on the amounts spent on various types of resources, such as labor or supplies. Or they can be organized to present the budget for responsibility centers, programs, or functions. Often there is a combination of approaches used within the same budget. Most responsibility center, program, or functional budgets will generally show line-item information.

Note that often the organization will present information about the same total spending in different formats. For example, Meals for the Homeless can show its total spending divided by responsibility centers such as the kitchen, delivery, serving, fundraising, and administration departments. The same total spending can also be divided up and reported in terms of the meals, counseling, and support services functions of the organization.

The budgeting process at some organizations is highly centralized. Other organizations take less of a top-down approach, giving managers throughout the organization more say in the development of budgets for their responsibility centers. There are advantages and disadvantages to both top-down and bottom-up budgeting. As a result, most organizations use an approach that incorporates both direction from above and detailed input from below.

A number of specialized budgeting techniques can be very helpful for managers: flexible budgeting, performance budgeting, zero-based budgeting, and forecasting are some of the more prominent techniques. Flexible budgeting is an approach that provides budgets at different volume levels. This helps managers plan actions that will be necessary if actual volume exceeds or falls short of expectations. Performance budgeting is an approach that helps organize budget information so that managers can see the cost of achieving different outcomes, instead of focusing primarily on inputs. Zero-based budgeting is a technique that requires budget justification of all costs in a budget, rather than just justification of the increase in costs from one budget year to the next. Forecasting focuses on how managers make predictions of expenses, revenues, and other items in the budget.

Government managers have some special budgeting concerns. These result from the structure provided to protect the public's resources and hold governments accountable. Governments tend to have much less flexibility in developing budgets than other organizations do. Their budgets often have mandated forms and content, and must be disclosed to the public. It is much more difficult to change spending from the authorized amount in total or to use funds intended for one purpose for another. Often decisions of how much to spend are out of the control of managers because of mandates or entitlements. Nevertheless, government managers must actively work on developing and managing the budget to ensure that the public receives the services it needs when it needs them, to the extent possible.

Preview

Chapters 2 and 3 focus on the planning process and the development of budgets. As managers work on the preparation of budgets, a critical requirement is a good understanding of costs. The better managers understand costs, the more accurate their plans will be. Chapter 4 focuses on providing an understanding of costs.

Many cost terms are widely used but are not well understood. Direct costs, indirect costs, average costs, fixed costs, variable costs, and marginal costs are concepts that managers should understand. Chapter 4 provides definitions of these, and other key terms.

The chapter also considers how costs change as volume changes. The relationship between costs and volume has a dramatic impact on the profits or losses incurred by an organization. As part of the planning process, organizations must decide whether it makes sense to expand volume or contract volume, or whether to add services or to eliminate services. Issues such as these require sophisticated analysis in order to optimize the results for both the organization and its clientele.

Chapter 4 also examines a decision method called break-even analysis. Break-even analysis is a technique that assists the manager in determining what volume of activity is required for a program or service to become financially self-sufficient. The chapter concludes with a discussion of cost measurement, including coverage of cost allocation and activity-based costing.

Key Terms from This Chapter

allocation. The process of taking costs from one area or cost objective and allocating them to others.

bottom-up budget. Budget prepared by *responsibility center* managers, who inform the top management of their spending plans.

budget reserves. Amounts in a budget that are to be used for unanticipated expenses.

causal analysis. One in which we theorize that the variations in the *independent variable(s)* cause the changes in the *dependent variable*.

causal models. Forecasting approach based on the relationship between two or more variables. Changes in one or more variables, called independent variables, are used as predictors of the likely change in another variable, called the dependent variable.

centralized budgeting. See *top-down budgeting*.

coefficient of determination. A measure of the goodness of fit of a regression, generally referred to as the *R-squared*.

constant variance. Uniformity in the scatter of actual historical data points around an estimated line.

curvilinear. A curved line.

decentralized budgeting. See *bottom-up budget*.

decision package. The information related to and analysis of a program or department being evaluated in a zero-based budgeting review.

decremental budgeting. Refers to a budget reduction.

dependent variable. The item the value of which is being predicted.

devolution. The decentralization process of shifting money and authority to lower levels of government.

entitlements. Benefits that must be given to any individuals who meet eligibility criteria specified in the law creating the entitlement to the benefit.

fixed costs. Costs that do not change in total as volume changes.

flexible budget. An operating budget for varying workload levels.

flexible budgeting. Process of developing a budget based on different *workload* levels.

forecast. Prediction of some future value such as unemployment claims, police arrests, or the number of children enrolled in the school system.

functional. Referring to the primary functions of the organization, such as providing meals, counseling, fund-raising, and administrative activities.

goodness of fit. The ability of one variable to explain the variations in another.

heteroscedasticity. A situation in which the scatter of historical points around the estimated line is consistently near the regression line in some areas and systematically further away in other areas.

homoscedasticity A situation in which the scatter of historical points around the estimated line is fairly uniform.

incremental budgeting A budget approach in which the approved budget consists of the amount spent the prior year, plus an additional amount.

independence. With respect to specification analysis, a condition where each of the residuals is not related to the value of any of the others. The residuals are a measure of the distance from the regression line to each of the actual historical points.

independent variable. The variable used to predict the dependent variable. The causal variable that is responsible for changes in the dependent variable.

inputs. Resources used for producing the organization's output. Examples include labor and supplies.

linearity. A straight-line relationship.

line-item expense. Specific individual types of expenses such as labor or materials.

mandates. Federal or state laws that require state or local governments to provide services, often at their own expense.

normality. An element of specification analysis that requires that there be a normal distribution of historical points around the regression line.

outcomes. The results that the organization is trying to achieve.

output. The number of units of service provided. For example, the number of meals served.

overhead. Indirect costs; costs other than direct labor and supplies.

p-value. The likelihood that there is really no relationship among the dependent and independent variables.

performance budget. Plan that relates the various objectives of a cost center with the planned costs of accomplishing those activities.

program budget. A plan for a specific portion of the organization's operations, such as a type of service offered or a special project.

program services. The programs of the organization that provide services to its clients—for example, a heart surgery program or a meals on wheels program. Any program may consume resources from a number of different *line-items* or *responsibility centers*.

R-squared (R^2). A regression analysis statistic that can range from a low of zero to a high of 1.0. The closer it is to 1.0, the more of the variability in the dependent variable that has been explained by the independent variable.

rainy day funds. See *budget reserves*.

rescission. A rescinding or reversal of the authorization to spend the money.

responsibility centers. Organizational subdivisions that a specific person is responsible for supervising.

serial correlation. A situation in which the residuals in a regression line are not independent of each other. The residuals are a measure of the distance from the regression line to each of the actual historical points.

supporting activities. Those activities an organization carries out in order to allow it to provide its program services.

t-test. A statistical test performed to ascertain that the value for the slope is indeed significantly different from zero. If the t-value is greater than 2.00, then the slope is assumed to be statistically different from zero.

time-series analysis. See time-series model.

time-series model. Forecasting approach that uses past trends and seasonal patterns for a variable to predict the future values of that variable.

top-down budget. Budget prepared in a central fashion by the organization's top management. *Responsibility center* managers are told the budgeted amount and are expected to achieve the budgeted result.

variable costs. Costs that vary in direct proportion with volume.

workload. The volume of goods or services that the organization or a subdivision of the organization provides.

zero-based budgeting (ZBB). Budgeting approach that requires an examination and justification of all costs rather than just the incremental costs and that requires examination of alternatives rather than just one approach.

Questions for Discussion

3-1. Are there any limits on government taxation or spending? Explain.

3-2. Distinguish among line-item, responsibility center, and program budgets.

3-3. The Museum of New Art traditionally offers a new exhibit each month, in addition to its permanent collection. Mary Moser, the new museum director, has found that the number of exhibits must be reduced because of financial constraints. The museum has always used a line-item budget, but Mary has asked for a program budget for each of the proposed exhibits for the coming year. Explain the difference between the line-item and program budget, and why Mary wants the latter.

3-4. Distinguish between a top-down and bottom-up budget process.

3-5. The advantage of a centralized approach to budgeting is that staff has more involvement in setting organizational priorities. True or false?[7]

3-6. In the past year, a major factory closed in Parsons City. Following the closure, a number of residents moved from the town. Property values are falling, and the mayor believes that a tax cut is necessary to avoid further exodus. He believes that the high unemployment rate will place a substantially increased demand for some public services. On the other hand, the declining population may reduce demand for other services. What budget

[7] This question, and questions 3-10 and 3-12, were written by Dwight Denison.

approach would make the most sense for the city for the coming year? Why?

3-7. What are the two main categories of functional budgets? Why do you think this might be a useful way to budget?

3-8. Distinguish between a mandate and an entitlement.

3-9. What is performance budgeting? What does it try to accomplish? How does the method work?

3-10. Performance budgeting is concerned more with reducing costs than monitoring outcomes. True or false?

3-11. Describe zero-based budgeting.

3-12. Which of the following is *not true* about zero-based budgeting?

 a. generally more costly to prepare

 b. reevaluates all program activities every year

 c. most commonly used budget method

 d. reduces "slack" in budgets

3-13. What is a flexible budget?

3-14. Many managers simply average historical data to get a forecast of future results. Is that approach adequate?

3-15. What is the principal advantage of curvilinear forecasting?

3-16. A carefully done computerized analysis should be sufficient for most forecasts. True or false? Why?

3-17. What are two forecasting techniques that can be used if no historical data are available?

3-18. What do functional financial statements do?

Problems

3-19. Select from the following to answer questions 1 and 2.[8]

 i. Zero-Based
 ii. Formula
 iii. Incremental
 iv. Accrual
 v. Capital
 vi. Flexible

 1. If your boss, the town's chief financial officer, told you that the town expected tax revenues to be 22 percent lower than last year and asked you to prepare decision packages to justify all of the town's discretionary programs, you would use a(n) _____ budget.

 2. To test the sensitivity of your operating expenses to changes in the number of campers coming to Camp Summertime Fun this summer, you would use a(n) _____ budget.

3-20. Performance budgets focus on _____ rather than solely on outputs.

3-21. The executive director of Dogs Need Help (DNH) animal shelter has asked you to prepare an annual budget for the coming fiscal year as well as a flexible budget based on a 10 percent increase in the number of dogs taken into DNH's shelter during the year. She has given you the following guidelines.

 Number of dogs rescued and placed by DNH: 600
 Average length of stay for a dog in the shelter: 10 days
 Daily cost of feeding one dog: $.90
 Number of veterinary visits per dog on average: 1.2
 Cost per veterinary visit: $35

 Cost of spay/neuter and transportation per dog rescued: $45
 Cost of the kennel and related equipment: $300,000
 Useful life of the kennel and related equipment: 20 years
 DNH uses straight-line depreciation
 Salvage value of the kennel and related equipment: $0

 DNH has three full-time employees. An executive director, who earns $40,000 per year, an evaluator/trainer, who earns $30,000 per year, and a kennel manager, who earns $25,000. Fringe benefits are equal to 25 percent of each employee's annual salary.

 DNH expects to place all of the dogs that it takes into the program by the last day of the fiscal year. It charges an adoption fee of $225 per dog. Experience has shown that 15 percent of the people elect to make an additional donation to DNH at the time of adoption. Historically, these extra donations have averaged $200. In addition, DNH has an active fund-raising program and expects to raise $40,000 in donations during the fiscal year.

3-22. Big C is adding a band program that will be open to college students and also to the community. The music department chair has asked you to prepare a special purpose budget for the program for the next two semesters. Prepare the budget for the full academic year using an *accrual basis* using the following information:

 The band will derive revenue from three sources. Students enrolled in band classes will pay $500 per semester. Big C has two semesters each year. Community members will pay $25 per semester to play in the band, but will not receive course credit. The only other revenue will come from the sale of tickets to the four concerts that the band intends to give each academic year.

The faculty expects to have thirty students enrolled in band classes each semester, and also expects another thirty people from the community to play in the band each semester. Based on discussions with other universities, Big C expects their concerts to attract 200 people on average, and expects to charge $3.00 per ticket.

To run the band program, Big C will have to hire a graduate assistant at a cost of $15,000 per academic year (two semesters). They will also have to rent an average of 10 brass and 15 woodwind instruments per semester. Brass instrument rentals will average $90 per semester per instrument and woodwinds will cost $50 per instrument per semester.

The band will rent rehearsal space from the local high school at a cost of $250 per night. The band will meet one night each week for fifteen weeks in each semester.

The department will also pay $100 to clean the hall after each concert and $50 per concert for student ushers. They will also spend $200 on promotion for each concert and $75 per concert for insurance. Ticket and program costs will average $.75 per attendee.

Finally, the school needs to buy a tuba at a cost of $4,000, a baritone saxophone for $2,500 and a full set of percussion instruments at a cost of $7,500. The department figures that the instruments will only last five years, and will not be able to be sold for anything after five years. The department will also need to buy 30 sets of band music pages at an average cost of $150 per set. The music pages often get lost, so the department wants to treat the sets as an expense in the year they are acquired.

3-23. Refer to Problem 2-27 in Chapter 2. Assuming that the mix of visitors does not change, provide a budget assuming admissions are 10 percent lower and 10 percent higher than expected.

3-24. The Free Health Care Center (FH) charges each patient $5 (not quite free after all, but pretty close). Due to rising costs, the center has been forced to consider raising this charge to $6 or $7. If the price goes up, fewer people will come to the center for care. At a price of $6 only 18,000 patients are expected, and at a price of $7 there will likely be only 16,000 patient visits. Prepare a flexible budget for the FH at prices of $5, $6, and $7. The variable cost per patient is $4, and the

fixed costs of operating the center are $32,000. They currently expect to have about 20,000 patient visits. What do you recommend the clinic do? Why?

3-25. The Georgeville city government provides a wide variety of services to the community. Among them is the protection provided by the police force. In order to provide that force they spend $2.7 million on salaries, $100,000 on vehicle costs, and $200,000 on supplies.

The police force expects to have 6,000 measurable actions, consisting of 1,000 arrests, 4,000 traffic citations, and 1,000 responses to emergency calls. They have noted that the average cost for each one of these actions is $500 if you simply divide the $3,000,000 department cost by the 6,000 specific individual actions. Some have argued that it is not cost-effective to give out traffic tickets, since the $500 cost per ticket exceeds the fine collected. The Georgeville Police Department is considering adopting a performance budget. The performance areas would be Arrests, Citations, and Emergency Responses.

They believe that activities related to making arrests consume 20 percent of salaries and 70 percent of supplies. Traffic citations consume 30 percent of salaries and 10 percent of supplies. Emergency response takes up 15 percent of salaries and 5 percent of supplies. Additionally, they perform many other activities that collectively take up 35 percent of salaries and 15 percent of supplies. They also estimate that their vehicles are used 25 percent for arrests, 30 percent for citations, and 5 percent for emergency responses. How much money is budgeted for each arrest, citation, and emergency response? Regardless of your answer, assume that the cost per traffic citation exceeds the average fine collected. Should the police cease issuing citations? Why?

3-26. Eger Township is preparing their budget for their fiscal year ending March 31, 2013. The township has a Management Department, a Public Works Department, a Recreation Department, and a Public Safety Department. The proposed budget calls for them to spend money on the items listed in Exhibit 3-1 on the next page. Based on the information in that exhibit, prepare a line-item budget for the township. Group all types of supplies together as one line-item.

3-27. Eger Township is preparing their budget for their fiscal year ending March 31, 2013. The township has a Management Department, a Public Works Department, a Recreation Department, and a Public Safety Department. The proposed budget calls for them to spend money on the items listed in Exhibit 3-1. Based on the information in that exhibit, prepare a responsibility center budget for the township, just showing departmental totals.

3-28. Eger Township is preparing their budget for their fiscal year ending March 31, 2013. The township has a Management Department, a Public Works Department, a Recreation Department, and a Public Safety Department. The proposed budget calls for them to spend money on the items listed in Exhibit 3-1. Based on the information in that

exhibit, prepare a budget that shows both line-item and responsibility center information. Group all types of supplies together as one line-item for each responsibility center.

3-29. Eger township is preparing their budget for their fiscal year ending March 31, 2013. The township government has a Management Department, a Public Works Department, a Recreation Department, and a Public Safety Department. The Management Department provides support to the other departments. The Public Works Department

EXHIBIT 3-1 Eger Township Budget Data

Line-Item Type	Department	Function	Amount
Salaries	Management	Management	$1,248,720.00
Supplies: Office	Management	Management	23,984.23
Rent	Management	Management	128,349.00
Gas & Electric	Management	Management	32,550.00
Telephone	Management	Management	14,201.00
Fringe Benefits	Management	Management	262,231.20
Interest	Management	Management	42,410.00
Depreciation Exp.	Management	Management	14,200.00
Salaries	Public Works	Garbage	241,089.00
Supplies: Office	Public Works	Garbage	1,832.00
Gas & Electric	Public Works	Garbage	2,385.00
Telephone	Public Works	Garbage	1,832.00
Fringe Benefits	Public Works	Garbage	50,628.69
Depreciation Exp.	Public Works	Garbage	40,000.00
Salaries	Public Works	Snow	84,736.00
Supplies: Office	Public Works	Snow	831.59
Supplies: Salt	Public Works	Snow	36,748.00
Gas & Electric	Public Works	Snow	18,236.00
Telephone	Public Works	Snow	1,272.77
Fringe Benefits	Public Works	Snow	17,794.56
Depreciation Exp.	Public Works	Snow	20,128.00
Salaries	Public Works	Road Repair	61,632.00
Supplies: Office	Public Works	Road Repair	3,163.00
Supplies: Blacktop	Public Works	Road Repair	42,979.00
Gas & Electric	Public Works	Road Repair	2,016.34
Telephone	Public Works	Road Repair	1,025.37
Fringe Benefits	Public Works	Road Repair	12,942.72
Depreciation Exp.	Public Works	Road Repair	28,944.00
Salaries	Recreation	Parks	31,555.00

EXHIBIT 3-1 Continued

Line-Item Type	Department	Function	Amount
Supplies: Office	Recreation	Parks	427.00
Supplies: Parks	Recreation	Parks	4,278.00
Gas & Electric	Recreation	Parks	524.00
Telephone	Recreation	Parks	617.00
Fringe Benefits	Recreation	Parks	6,626.55
Depreciation Exp.	Recreation	Parks	8,293.00
Salaries	Recreation	Concerts	14,315.00
Supplies: Office	Recreation	Concerts	624.00
Supplies: Concerts	Recreation	Concerts	2,941.00
Gas & Electric	Recreation	Concerts	262.00
Telephone	Recreation	Concerts	619.00
Fringe Benefits	Recreation	Concerts	3,006.15
Depreciation Exp.	Recreation	Concerts	2,744.00
Salaries	Recreation	Athletics	61,201.00
Supplies: Office	Recreation	Athletics	3,890.00
Supplies: Athletic Facilities	Recreation	Athletics	27,443.00
Gas & Electric	Recreation	Athletics	8,079.34
Telephone	Recreation	Athletics	3,178.38
Fringe Benefits	Recreation	Athletics	12,852.21
Depreciation Exp.	Recreation	Athletics	118,742.00
Salaries	Public Safety	Police	310,432.00
Supplies: Office	Public Safety	Police	7,957.00
Supplies: Uniform Allowance	Public Safety	Police	2,856.00
Gas & Electric	Public Safety	Police	3,890.00
Telephone	Public Safety	Police	4,755.00
Fringe Benefits	Public Safety	Police	65,190.72
Depreciation Exp.	Public Safety	Police	52,888.00
Salaries	Public Safety	Fire	150,771.50
Supplies: Office	Public Safety	Fire	4,426.00
Supplies: Fire Truck	Public Safety	Fire	22,856.00
Gas & Electric	Public Safety	Fire	3,890.00
Telephone	Public Safety	Fire	4,755.00
Fringe Benefits	Public Safety	Fire	31,662.02
Depreciation Exp.	Public Safety	Fire	152,888.00
Total			$3,568,296.34

Note: Many of the above line-items, such as salaries, are summaries of detailed information listing individual employees and their salaries.

This Exhibit is available as an Excel Worksheet file at: www.pearsonhighered.com/finkler. Open the folder for Student Resources. Then open the folder for Excel Templates. Then open the Excel file for Exhibit 3-1. Use of that file will aid in solving Problems 3-26 to 3-29.

has three functions: garbage collection, snow removal, and road repair. The Recreation Department has three functions: park maintenance, concerts, and athletics (including tennis courts, golf course, and swimming pool). The Public Safety Department has two functions: police protection and fire protection. The proposed budget calls for them to spend money on the items listed in Exhibit 3-1. Based on the information in that exhibit, prepare a functional, line-item budget for the township. Show each type of supply item separately.

3-30. The State Department of Labor is working on its revenue budget for the year ending June 30, 2014. The State uses a system of account numbers to simplify its bookkeeping processes. The system uses four digits to the left and four digits to the right of the decimal point. The basic structure for an account would appear as: 0000.0000. The first digit in the number (on the extreme left) represents whether the account is describing an asset (resource owned by the state), a liability (obligation owed by the state), revenue, or expense. The code would be:

1 Asset
2 Liability
3 Revenue
4 Expense

The second and third digits signify the department. Several examples for the State are as follows:

01 Legislature
02 Governor's Office
03 Judiciary
04 Agriculture
05 Transportation
12 Labor

The fourth digit represents the subdivisions within each department. For the Department of Labor these are:

1 Economic Planning and Development
2 Economic Assistance and Security
3 Manpower and Employment Services

The first two digits to the right of the decimal point represent specific line-item revenue sources and expense codes:

01 Direct State Appropriations
02 Grants-in-Aid
11 Salaries and Wages
12 Materials and Supplies
13 Maintenance

The third and fourth digits to the right of the decimal point represent programs. For the Department of Labor the programs are:

01 Administration and Support Services
02 Unemployment Insurance
03 State Disability Insurance
04 Vocational Rehabilitation Services
05 Workplace Standards
06 Employment Services

For example, account 3122.0104 represents revenue for the Department of Labor intended for the Economic Assistance and Security subdivision of the department. The revenue comes directly from state appropriations and is intended for use in the Vocational Rehabilitation Services program. This can be seen as follows:

3122.0104	The 3 in the first digit location on the far left indicates that this is a revenue account.
3**12**2.0104	The 12 in the next two digits indicates that the account is related to the Department of Labor.
312**2**.0104	The 2 in the next digit indicates that the account is related to the Economic Assistance and Security subdivision of the department.
3122.**01**04	The 01 in the first two digits to the right of the decimal point indicates that the source of the revenue is direct state appropriations.
3122.01**04**	Finally, the 04 in the last two digits indicates that this money is earmarked for the Vocational Rehabilitation Services program.

Using this account code system, and the information in Exhibit 3-2, prepare the following budget reports for the year ending June 30, 2014:

a. Prepare a line-item revenue budget for Department of Labor. Note that the only two line-items are Direct State Appropriations and Grants-in-Aid.

b. Prepare a responsibility center revenue budget for the Department of Labor showing just the three main subdivision totals without line-item information.

c. Prepare a responsibility center revenue budget for the Department of Labor showing the three main subdivisions and line-items.

d. Prepare a functional revenue budget with line-item information for the Department of Labor. Treat each of the programs as a separate function of the Department.

EXHIBIT 3-2 State Department of Labor Budget Information

Account Code	Budget Amount
3 1 2 1 . 0 1 0 1	$ 143,063
3 1 2 1 . 0 1 0 2	634,623
3 1 2 1 . 0 1 0 3	334,444
3 1 2 1 . 0 1 0 4	734,683
3 1 2 1 . 0 1 0 5	6,743,323
3 1 2 1 . 0 1 0 6	4,565,344
3 1 2 2 . 0 1 0 1	346,678
3 1 2 2 . 0 1 0 2	2,456,787
3 1 2 2 . 0 1 0 3	234,111
3 1 2 2 . 0 1 0 4	123,378
3 1 2 2 . 0 1 0 5	453,337
3 1 2 2 . 0 1 0 6	357,982
3 1 2 3 . 0 1 0 1	813,416
3 1 2 3 . 0 1 0 2	334,587
3 1 2 3 . 0 1 0 3	2,457,845
3 1 2 3 . 0 1 0 4	353,467
3 1 2 3 . 0 1 0 5	1,118,238
3 1 2 3 . 0 1 0 6	530,213
3 1 2 1 . 0 2 0 1	45,488
3 1 2 1 . 0 2 0 2	543,543
3 1 2 1 . 0 2 0 3	564,577
3 1 2 1 . 0 2 0 4	745,764
3 1 2 1 . 0 2 0 5	363,466
3 1 2 1 . 0 2 0 6	553,888
3 1 2 2 . 0 2 0 1	546,346
3 1 2 2 . 0 2 0 2	2,122,547
3 1 2 2 . 0 2 0 3	276,453
3 1 2 2 . 0 2 0 4	8,634,678
3 1 2 2 . 0 2 0 5	8,745,666
3 1 2 2 . 0 2 0 6	353,353
3 1 2 3 . 0 2 0 1	513,254
3 1 2 3 . 0 2 0 2	1,342,424
3 1 2 3 . 0 2 0 3	462,342
3 1 2 3 . 0 2 0 4	342,342
3 1 2 3 . 0 2 0 5	325,623
3 1 2 3 . 0 2 0 6	476,476
Total	$49,693,749

This Exhibit is available as an Excel Worksheet file at: www.pearsonhighered.com/finkler. Open the folder for Student Resources. Then open the folder for Excel Templates. Then open the Excel file for Exhibit 3-2.
Use of that file will aid in solving Problem 3-30.

3-31. (Appendix 3-B) The Billings Multi-Specialty Physician Group Practice is trying to forecast the number of patient visits they will have for the coming year. They have data from the previous three years to use for the forecast.

a. Create a graph of the historical data that demonstrates whether their volume contains a trend, a seasonal component, or both.

b. Develop a forecast for the next four quarters. Use whatever approach is appropriate given the pattern identified in the data.

Year	Qt	Patient Visits
1	1	20,000
	2	23,000
	3	27,000
	4	20,000
2	1	21,000
	2	25,000
	3	29,000
	4	20,000
3	1	19,000
	2	24,000
	3	26,000
	4	21,000

3-32. Give an example of a *line-item* or an *object of expense*.

3-33. Select from the following to answer questions 1 through 4:

a. Zero-Based
b. Formula
c. Incremental
d. Accrual
e. Capital
f. Flexible

1. If your boss told you to test this year's budget for the impact of changes in expected client volume on your budgeted revenue and expenses, you would use a(n) _____ budget.
2. _____ budgets focus on proposed investments in valuable, long-lived resources.
3. Decision packages are normally associated with a(n) _____ budget.
4. Operating budgets are normally done on a(n) _____ basis.

3-34. Senior Ride Access (SRA) provides a van service for senior citizens. SRA receives a $100,000 grant each year from a local foundation for the aged. SRA expects to spend $2,500 each year to pay for copying and supplies to operate the service. Insurance will cost the SRA $1,750 per year for each of the two vans that it operates. SRA employs a supervisor, earning $36,000 a year to run the van service. There are also six part-time coordinators that organize the routing of the vans and provide outreach to the senior community. Each coordinator works an average of 17 hours per week for 50 weeks in the year. Coordinators earn $10 per hour. All drivers are volunteers. The costs associated with carrying each passenger are $0.35 per mile. The average ride for each passenger is 5 miles. Seniors are asked to donate $0.75 for each ride, but only 80 percent of the riders are able to afford the donation.

Prepare an operating budget for the upcoming year, assuming 5,000 seniors use the van service during the year. In the past, there have been fluctuations in ridership so SRA would also like to see what would happen should there be a 10 percent increase or decrease in the number of rides.

3-35. You are the manager of the Corn is Not Just for Ethanol (CNJE) relief organization, which works with a coalition of countries to help provide corn, wheat, and other food staples to countries where food is in short supply. CNJE's Board has asked you to prepare a monthly operating budget based on feeding 15,000 people per day as well as a flexible budget based on a 30 percent increase in the number of people you will have to feed each day.

Your operation has three full-time employees: a manager who earns $48,000 per year, a security chief, earning $30,000 per year, and a field manager, who earns $24,000 per year. CNJE spends an additional 25 percent of each employee's annual salary to pay for the cost of health insurance and retirement benefits.

You use trucks to deliver food and cooking fuel to the remote feeding sites. You estimate it takes one truck to service every 500 people you feed each month. It costs you $2,600 to pay for the fuel, drivers, and maintenance it takes to operate one truck for one month. Truck depreciation adds an additional $14,000 to your monthly expenses.

Direct costs for food are $3.95 per person per day. The coalition of countries has agreed to pay CNJE $4.10 per day for each person you feed. For budgeting purposes, assume there are 30 days in a month. Finally, the World Nutrition Society has pledged $50,000 per month to support the CNJE effort for the coming year.

CASE STUDY

Denison Specialty Hospital—Part II[9]

To complete the requirements in this section, use the information from both Parts I (see Chapter 2) and II.

Section C

The programs at Denison consume the services of departments as follows:

	Radiology	Nursing	Administration
Oncology	80%	50%	50%
Cardiac	15%	40%	35%
Rhinoplasty	5%	10%	15%

That is, oncology patients consume 80 percent of the services of the radiology department but only 50 percent of the nursing services provided.

Note that Denison classifies rent, depreciation, and bad debts expenses as "General Expenses" rather than assigning them to any specific department. However, if equipment can be specifically traced to a program, the depreciation on that equipment is charged to that program.

Section C Requirements:

1. In Part I, Section B, number 2, you prepared a line-item expense budget on an accrual basis. Prepare the expense budget again as a responsibility center budget, showing the projected costs for each department (Radiology, Nursing, and Administration).
2. Prepare an expense budget with expenses shown by program (Oncology, Cardiac, Rhinoplasty). For simplicity, assume that bad debts are not assigned to specific programs.

Section D

The hospital usually prepares a flexible budget as part of its annual master budget to assess the likely impact of patient volume variations on revenues and expenses.

The salaries of managers are all fixed costs. That type of expense does not change as patient volume changes. The staff salaries are variable costs (expenses) in all areas except in the administration department, where they are fixed. All salaries are paid in equal amounts each month. Variable salaries vary in direct proportion to patient volume. Supplies vary in direct proportion to patient volume.

Section D Requirement:

1. Prepare a flexible budget assuming patient volumes are 10 percent and 20 percent higher and 10 percent and 20 percent lower than expected. Also include the expected patient volume level in the flexible budget. Prepare the flexible budget before doing the cash flow budget in Section E.

Section E

Patients are expected to be treated and discharged throughout the year as follows:

Quarter 1 Jan.–March	Quarter 2 April–June	Quarter 3 July–Sept.	Quarter 4 Oct.–Dec.	Total
30%	25%	20%	25%	100%

---

[9] Part I of this case appears at the end of Chapter 2.

Historically, Denison has found that private insurance pays in the quarter after patient discharge. Medicare/Medicaid pays half in the quarter after discharge and half in the following quarter. Twenty-five percent of all self-pay revenue is collected each quarter for three quarters following discharge. Twenty-five percent is never collected. Also, charity care is never collected.

For simplicity, assume that the current year's patient flow, payment rates, staffing, and supplies purchases are the same as those projected in the budget for the coming year. Supplies are expected to be purchased in the following months:

Quarter 1 Jan.–March	Quarter 2 April–June	Quarter 3 July–Sept.	Quarter 4 Oct.–Dec.	Total
$150,000	$124,000	$138,000	$128,000	$540,000

The supplies are paid for in the quarter after purchase.

Assume that all interest and dividends on endowment investments are received on the first day of the seventh month of the year. Assume that gift shop revenue is received equally each quarter. (This may be an unrealistic assumption.) Assume that salaries are paid equally each quarter.

Denison plans to start next year with $50,000 of cash and likes to end every quarter with at least $50,000 in their cash account. If necessary, it will borrow from the bank at a rate of 12 percent per year. Each quarter it must pay interest on any outstanding loan balance from the end of the previous quarter. When it has extra cash, it repays its outstanding bank loan. If it has extra cash beyond that, it simply leaves it in its non-interest-bearing cash account.

Denison prepares its operating budget (revenues and expenses) on an accrual basis. The hospital expects to buy the oncology equipment as described in Part I of the case.

Section E Requirements:

1. Prepare a cash budget for the coming year. It will help if you prepare it in the following order:
   a. Determine patient revenues by quarter by type of payer for the coming year. That is, determine private insurance revenues for each quarter, Medicare/Medicaid revenues by quarter, etc.
   b. Determine patient revenues by quarter for the current year. Since many payers pay with a lag, some of the coming year's cash receipts come from current year's revenues.
   c. Determine patient cash collections by quarter for the coming year, using revenue information from parts a and b, and payment lag information provided in the narrative of the problem.
   d. Develop the cash budget by quarter.
      Start with the beginning cash, add cash receipts shown by source (e.g., patient revenue by payer, endowment). Calculate the available cash. (Note that it will be necessary to determine other cash receipts and payments by quarter. For example, determine how much is received from endowment each quarter and how much is paid for supplies.)
      Deduct cash payments by line-item (e.g., salaries). Be sure to include interest payments. Assume Denison does not owe any money at the beginning of the year. Subtract cash payments (called disbursements) from available amount to get a subtotal.
      Based on the subtotal calculate the amount to be borrowed or repaid. Combine the amount borrowed or repaid with the subtotal to get ending cash balance for quarter.
      Show loan payable amount on cash budget below the ending cash balance.
      It is easier to develop a correct cash budget if you work one quarter at a time.

2. Based on your cash budget, prepare a revised operating budget. That is, take the operating budget Part I, Section B, number 3, and incorporate the interest expense from the cash budget. Do not prepare a revised flexible budget.

3. As an advisor to the Denison Hospital, you are certain of one thing: the Board of Trustees of the hospital will not approve a budget that projects an operating deficit. If the operating budget projects a deficit, what do you suggest that Denison do about it?

Suggested Readings

Bamber, Linda S., Karen Braun, and Walter T. Harrison. *Managerial Accounting*, Upper Saddle River, N.J.: Prentice Hall, 2008.

Bland, Robert L., and Irene Rubin. *Budgeting: A Guide for Local Government*. Washington, D.C.: International City/County Management Association, 1997.

Finkler, Steven A., and Mary L. McHugh. *Budgeting Concepts for Nurse Managers,* 4th ed. St. Louis, Mo.: Saunders Elsevier, 2008.

Hyde, Albert C. *Government Budgeting: Theory, Process, Politics,* 3rd ed. Belmont, Ca.: Wadsworth/Thomson Learning, 2002.

Lee Jr., Robert D., Ronald W. Johnson, and Philip G. Joyce. *Public Budgeting Systems,* 8th ed. Sudbury, Mass.: Jones and Bartlett Publishers, 2007.

Mikesell, John L. *Fiscal Administration—Analysis and Applications for the Public Sector,* 7th ed. Belmont, Ca.: Wadsworth, 2006.

Nice, David. *Public Budgeting*. Belmont, Ca.: Wadsworth/ Thomson Learning, 2002.

Rosen, Harvey S. *The Fiscal Behavior of State and Local Governments,* Studies in Fiscal Federalism and State-Local Finance Series. Northampton, Mass.: Edward Elgar Publishing, 1997.

Rubin, Irene S. *Class, Tax, and Power: Municipal Budgeting in the United States*. Chatham, N.J.: Chatham House Publishers, 1998.

———. *The Politics of Public Budgeting: Getting and Spending, Borrowing and Balancing,* 5th ed. Chatham, N.J.: Chatham House Publishers, 2006.

APPENDIX 3-A

A Performance Budget Example

Assume that the Laboratory Department at the Hospital for Ordinary Surgery consists of several specialized labs. One of them, the Cardiac Lab, decided to move its activities from a traditional budget, which provides resources based simply on the number of lab procedures, to a performance budget. After careful consideration, the manager decided that there were eight main objectives for the department: perform diagnostic catheterizations, perform therapeutic interventions, improve quality of care, improve throughput (the time from the beginning of one procedure to the beginning of the next), control the supply cost per patient day, improve patient satisfaction, improve physician satisfaction, and improve staff satisfaction.

There is no question that development of a good set of performance measures for any department requires some thought and reflection. However, that in itself is a worthwhile exercise. Departments should have to consider what they are really trying to accomplish. That will allow them to more easily eliminate activities that are done just because they always have been done, whether they add value or not.

Assume that the regular operating budget for the responsibility unit in this example is as follows:

Manager	$ 70,000
Staff Salaries	400,000
Education	10,000
Supplies	1,520,000
Total	$2,000,000

One of the main things that must be determined to establish a performance budget is the percentage of resources that should be devoted to each performance area. There are several ways to do this. The manager could simply make allocations based on what seems appropriate. Alternatively, the allocations could be based on current actual practice. This information could be obtained by asking employees for their best guess or by having employees keep a log for a period of time to see how they actually spend their time. In this hypothetical example, assume that the allocations below are based on the manager's judgment about how time and resources should be used:

Manager's Time	Percent
Perform Diagnostic Catheterizations	10
Perform Interventions	10
Improve Quality of Care	20
Improve Throughput	20
Control Supply Cost per Patient	20
Improve Patient Satisfaction	5
Improve Physician Satisfaction	10
Improve Staff Satisfaction	5
Total	100

Staff Time	Percent
Perform Diagnostic Catheterizations	40
Perform Interventions	30
Improve Quality of Care	10
Improve Throughput	5
Control Supply Cost per Patient	5
Improve Patient Satisfaction	5
Improve Physician Satisfaction	5
Improve Staff Satisfaction	0
Total	100

Education Resources	Percent
Perform Diagnostic Catheterizations	20
Perform Interventions	30
Improve Quality of Care	50
Improve Throughput	0
Control Supply Cost per Patient	0
Improve Patient Satisfaction	0
Improve Physician Satisfaction	0
Improve Staff Satisfaction	0
Total	100

Supplies	Percent
Perform Diagnostic Catheterizations	40
Perform Interventions	50
Improve Quality of Care	0
Improve Throughput	2
Control Supply Cost per Patient	0
Improve Patient Satisfaction	2
Improve Physician Satisfaction	5
Improve Staff Satisfaction	1
Total	100

In this example, the manager spends relatively little time performing clinical procedures. Other managerial activities include efforts to improve the quality of care, improve throughput, control the supply cost per patient, and improve satisfaction of patients, physicians, and staff. In contrast, the staff are budgeted to spend 70 percent of their time in clinical procedures (diagnostic catheterizations and therapeutic interventions). They also will devote some of their efforts to the other performance areas, but not the same amount of their time as the manager.

The money to be spent on education is divided fairly equally between education to learn how to do clinical procedures and education to learn how to improve quality of care. This represents a choice in the use of resources. Another department or hospital might choose to devote all of its education dollars to learning ways to better control supply costs.

As one might expect, the vast majority of supplies in this department is used for clinical procedures.

As an intermediate step in arriving at a performance budget, it is necessary to assign operating budget costs to performance areas. The information about how each budget item is expected to be used, taken from the previous information, is summarized in Table 3-A-1.

Using this summary, the costs in the operating budget can be allocated to the different performance areas, as shown in Table 3-A-2. The bottom row in Table 3-A-2 is the operating budget for the lab, shown earlier. The table takes that bottom row and multiplies it by the percentages shown in Table 3-A-1 to determine the budgeted cost for each performance area. In other words, the rows in Table 3-A-2 are calculated using a combination of the percentages shown in Table 3-A-1 and the operating budget, which is shown in the last row of Table 3-A-2. For example, from the operating budget, for the lab, the manager's salary is $70,000. As seen in Table 3-A-1, 10 percent of the manager's efforts go to diagnostic catheterizations. Therefore $7,000 (10 percent × $70,000) of the manager's salary is in the Diagnostic Catheterization row of Table 3-A-2.

Consider another example: 5 percent of staff costs are for improving patient satisfaction. From the operating budget, $400,000 is being spent on staff salaries. Five percent of $400,000 is $20,000. In Table 3-A-2 in the column for staff salaries and row for "Improve Patient Satisfaction," the cost is therefore $20,000.

Looking at Table 3-A-2, consider the allocation of department resources. The total budget for the department is $2,000,000. Of that amount, the largest amounts are spent on diagnostic catheterization procedures and interventions, as one might expect. Interestingly however, the department is spending $103,000, or just over 5 percent of its total budget, to improve physician satisfaction. Is this an appropriate allocation of resources?

The information provided in a budget often tends to raise more questions than it answers. In some environments it might make sense to use resources to keep physicians happy. If they are not satisfied, they may take profitable procedures to other hospitals instead of this hospital. In other situations, it may be a managed care organization rather than the physician that determines the hospital that patients use. In that case, it might not make sense to allocate so much of the department's budget to physician satisfaction. In either case, it is valuable to be able to highlight the

TABLE 3-A-1

Performance Area	Expense Item			
	Manager	Staff	Education	Supplies
Diagnostic Catheterizations	10%	40%	20%	40%
Interventions	10	30	30	50
Improve Quality	20	10	50	0
Improve Throughput	20	5	0	2
Control Supply Cost	20	5	0	0
Improve Patient Satisfaction	5	5	0	2
Improve Physician Satisfaction	10	5	0	5
Improve Staff Satisfaction	5	0	0	1
Total	100%	100%	100%	100%

TABLE 3-A-2 Allocation of Operating Budget to Performance Areas

Performance Area	Expense Item				Total	Percent
	Manager	Staff	Education	Supplies		
Diagnostic Catheterizations	$ 7,000	$160,000	$ 2,000	$ 608,000	$ 777,000	38.9%
Interventions	7,000	120,000	3,000	760,000	890,000	44.5%
Improve Quality	14,000	40,000	5,000	0	59,000	3.0%
Improve Throughput	14,000	20,000	0	30,400	64,400	3.2%
Control Supply Cost	14,000	20,000	0	0	34,000	1.7%
Improve Patient Satisfaction	3,500	20,000	0	30,400	53,900	2.7%
Improve Physician Satisfaction	7,000	20,000	0	76,000	103,000	5.2%
Improve Staff Satisfaction	3,500	0	0	15,200	18,700	0.9%
Total	$70,000	$400,000	$10,000	$1,520,000	$2,000,000	100.0%

fact that $103,000, or approximately 5 percent of department resources, are going toward this goal.

Table 3-A-2 does not represent a performance budget, because it does not specify budgeted expectations for each of the performance areas. First, it is necessary to define measures that can be used for each area, and then a certain level of attainment can be budgeted. This is one of the most difficult aspects of developing a performance budget.

The diagnostic catheterizations and the interventions can be measured the way they traditionally have been, using the number of procedures performed. Improvement in quality of care could be measured by the number of medical complications, the patient length of stay (adjusted for patient mix), and mortality rates. None of those measures are completely satisfactory outcome measures. They are proxies to get as close as possible to the underlying issue of quality. Throughput improvement could be measured by the turnaround time from one patient to the next. Controlling the supply cost per patient could be measured in dollars per patient.

Satisfaction is difficult to measure. For patients the number of complaints can be used. If that declines, it is likely that overall satisfaction is improving. For physicians, one could use the number of cases per doctor. If they are more satisfied, they will treat more of their patients at this hospital. For staff, the turnover rate is a possible proxy for satisfaction. More satisfied staff are less likely to quit. None of these are outcome measures. If we are interested in satisfied patients, physicians, and staff, these are just substitutes for satisfaction. A more accurate measure could be obtained if we used a survey instrument designed to measure satisfaction. It could be prepared and administered by outsiders to better ensure objectivity. However, that is

a costly approach. It might be done on rare occasions by organizations, but is unlikely to be done monthly, or even annually, for every department.

Organizations need ways to get better assessments of performance than can be yielded by a single output measure, such as the number of patients treated. But they need methods that are not overly costly or time-consuming. Performance budgeting seeks that middle ground. Each department of each organization should give careful thought to trying to develop the best possible measures of performance that are available, at a reasonable data collection cost.

Table 3-A-3 presents the performance budget. The first column on the left lists the performance areas. The second column highlights the type of activity to be undertaken to accomplish each of the major objectives of the department. The third column tells how attainment of the objective will be measured. The fourth column sets a specific measurable target for accomplishment. The fifth column tells how much it is expected to cost to attain that target. That number comes directly from the "Total" column on Table 3-A-2. The last column divides the total cost for the objective by the target, to find the cost per unit.

For example, consider the Control Supply Cost/Patient performance area row in Table 3-A-3. The organization expects to work with its suppliers (vendors) to get contracts with lower prices for supplies and to work with clinical staff to use fewer, or less expensive, supplies. This area will be measured based on the supply cost per patient in dollars. The target is to have the supply cost per patient rise only 3 percent. It is expected that without specific work in this area, supply costs would be likely to rise by 6 percent per patient. The goal here is to constrain the rate of increase, rather than actually lowering

TABLE 3-A-3 Performance Budget

Performance Area	Type of Activity	Output Measure	Budgeted Output	Total Cost	Average Cost
Perform diagnostic catheterizations	Catheterizations	Number of caths	1,200	$777,000	$648/cath
Perform interventions	Interventions	Number of interventions	1,200	$890,000	$742 per intervention
Improve quality	Change in specific procedures	Number of complications	10% Reduction in complication rate	$ 59,000	$5,900 per 1% reduction
Improve throughput	Develop new coordination procedures with OR and MDs	Turnaround time	5% Reduction in turnaround time	$ 64,400	$12,880 per 1% reduction in turnaround time
Control supply cost/patient	Work on vendor contracts, work with clinical staff	Supply dollars per patient	Constrain increase to 3% versus expected industry 6% increase	$ 34,000	$11,333 per 1% below industry expectations
Improve patient satisfaction	Improve staff communication with patients	Number of complaints	Reduce number from 60 to 40	$ 53,900	$2,695 per eliminated complaint
Improve physician satisfaction	Redesign work scheduling to meet MD demands	Cases/MD	2% increase per MD	$103,000	$51,500 per 1% increase
Improve staff satisfaction	Allow longer breaks and free coffee/donuts	Turnover rate	Reduce turnover by 50% from 4/year to 2/year	$ 18,700	$9,350 per staff member retained

cost per patient. A total of $34,000 has been budgeted for this effort to constrain the rate of increase in supply costs per patient.

The $34,000 amount shown in the total cost column of Table 3-A-3 came from Table 3-A-2. The average cost column in Table 3-A-3 shows that the organization expects to spend $11,333 for each percent that costs are kept below the expected industrywide increase (i.e., the $34,000 cost of controlling supply costs divided by the 3 percent expected benefit = $11,333 for each percent savings below the industry average). Is the savings worth the investment?

Performance budgeting allows the manager to calculate the return on investment for various activities undertaken by the department. For example, the supplies budget for this department, shown earlier, is $1,520,000. Each 1 percent difference in the cost of supplies will cost the hospital $15,200 (i.e., $1,520,000 × 1 percent = $15,200). On a savings to cost basis the calculation would be

$$\text{Savings/Cost} = \$15,200/\$11,333$$
$$= \$1.34 \text{ savings per dollar spent}$$

For every dollar the department spends to control supply costs, it saves $1.34 in the cost of supplies.

The return on investment would be the profit from the activity divided by the cost of the activity ($15,200 − $11,333 = $3,867):

$$\text{Return on investment} = \$3,867/\$11,333 = 34\%$$

Note, however, that if the department only consumed $500,000 of supplies per year, the effort would not be worthwhile. Each percent reduction in supply cost would only yield a savings of $5,000 ($500,000 cost × 1 percent = $5,000):

$$\text{Savings/Cost} = \$5,000/\$11,333$$
$$= \$.44 \text{ savings per dollar spent}$$

In other words, the organization would only get back 44 cents for each dollar invested. This would indicate that it would be better off not using resources for this effort. The savings/cost ratio must exceed 1.0 for the action to result in a positive financial benefit. On the other hand, the organization may choose to allocate resources to outcomes that are desirable for other qualitative reasons, even if they do not yield positive financial results. Public service organizations must always consider whether there are other reasons to do things beyond strictly financial ones.

APPENDIX 3-B

Forecasting Using Historical Data[10]

INTRODUCTION

Forecasting future volumes, revenues, and costs is a problem commonly grappled with in public sector organizations. Most often forecasts project historical information into the future. The simplest approaches to forecasting are informal "seat of the pants" type approaches. For example, we may assume that next year will be like the current year. However, underlying trends may exist that would make it unlikely that next year will simply reflect this year.

This Appendix gives the reader a more detailed introduction to the complex field of forecasting than the one in Chapter 3. However, readers should either study forecasting techniques in more depth, or consult an expert when making forecasts.

FORECASTING BASED ON AVERAGES

One approach to forecasting is to take an average value for a set of historical data points. Such an approach assumes that the data have neither seasonality nor trend. If the ups and downs over time are caused by random events, such an approach is reasonable. However, the result is just a prediction for the year as a whole. Forecasting can be much more useful if the forecasts are broken down by month. The user can then benefit from the knowledge of anticipated variations within the year. When an averaging approach is used for monthly data, a problem arises because it does not allow for longer and shorter months. The variation in the number of days in a month from 28 days to 31 days can create a problem. Also, if one is forecasting for a department that is only open weekdays, there is a variation from 20 to 23 possible weekdays per month. Thus, a forecast based on the average value of data for a number of months might be inaccurate. One would have to find an average forecast value per day (or per weekday) and apply that value to the number of days in each month in the

coming year. Such an averaging approach, however, assumes that there is neither trend nor seasonality—an unlikely situation for many organizations.

This appendix uses an example to consider forecasting techniques. For simplicity, an example with quarterly data for three years is used. Generally, the more historical data points you use, the more reliable the resulting forecast. Some analysts consider five years of monthly data to be the minimum data set for good forecasts. However, if any major change has taken place that would make data before the change a poor predictor of the future, then such data should be used cautiously, if at all.

Suppose that a state agency needed to project volume for the coming year to prepare its budgets. The data for this hypothetical example is shown in a Microsoft Excel worksheet: Table 3-B-1.[11] A critical first step after collecting the data is to graph it. The data from Table 3-B-1 is shown in an Excel chart in Figure 3-B-1.[12] The graph or chart can help the user to get a quick sense of any trends or patterns in the data. Figure 3-B-1 clearly shows an upward trend. Suppose one were to simply average the values of all of the data points from Table 3-B-1, and use that average as a forecast for each quarter going into the future. That means we would be predicting the value for each quarter of the coming year to be identical, at the average value of the prior three years. That forecast makes little sense given the upward trend observed in Figure 3-B-1.

USING LINEAR REGRESSION FOR FORECASTING

To improve on forecasts generated by using a simple average, linear regression is often used for forecasting. Regression is a technique that can plot a single line that will provide a reasonably good predictor,

---

[10] Abstracted and adapted from Chapter 7 in Steven A. Finkler and David M. Ward. *Essentials of Cost Accounting for Health Care Organizations,* 2nd ed. Boston, Mass.: Jones and Bartlett, 1999. Used with permission.

[11] Microsoft Excel 2002 Version (10.4524.4219) SP-2 was used for the examples in this appendix. Other versions of Excel may differ somewhat from the descriptions used here.
[12] This appendix assumes that the reader is familiar with the basic functions of Excel, such as creating a chart and using pull-down menus. Readers new to Excel should refer to a basic guide such as Faithe Wempen. *Microsoft Excel 2002 Fast & Easy.* Roseville, Ca.: Prima Tech, 2001.

TABLE 3-B-1 Data with Trend

	Quarter	Data Point	Permits
Year 1	July–September	1	20,000
	October–December	2	25,000
	January–March	3	22,000
	April–June	4	26,000
Year 2	July–September	5	24,000
	October–December	6	28,000
	January–March	7	29,000
	April–June	8	33,000
Year 3	July–September	9	30,000
	October–December	10	34,000
	January–March	11	32,000
	April–June	12	36,000

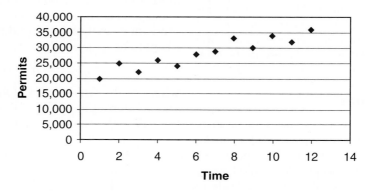

FIGURE 3-B-1 Graph of Data from Table 3-B-1

based on existing data, for a trend. Regression is used for both causal and time-series analyses.

Causal and Time-Series Analyses

A *causal analysis* is one in which we theorize that the variations in the *independent* variable (or variables) cause or result in changes in the *dependent* variable. For example, suppose that one department in a state agency issues hunting permits. Based on past experience the department manager believes that the more permits issued, the more costly it is to run the department. That is, the cost depends on the volume. If we know the cost and the volume of permits from each past period, we can use that information to predict future costs for any given volume. However, to predict those costs, we would also have to have some idea of future volume.

In *time-series* analysis, time becomes the independent variable used in the regression model. The manager might believe that there is a trend in the number of permits issued over time. Thus, we might review how many permits have been issued in past periods, and use a time-series approach to estimate the number that will be issued in the future. Then we could use a causal analysis to predict the department's cost, using the predicted future volumes.

This appendix gives an introductory look at relatively simple forms of time-series analysis. More sophisticated techniques can handle more complex sequences of data, such as a situation in which a single event or series of events have created shifts in the trends. However, those advanced approaches, such as the Box-Jenkins model, are beyond the scope of this appendix.

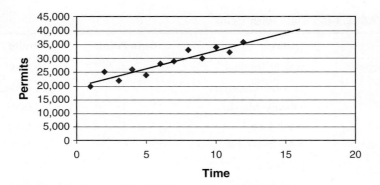

FIGURE 3-B-2   Regression Analysis Forecast

Example

For example, consider the data in Table 3-B-1. We would like to know the number of permits we are likely to issue for each of the four quarters of the coming Year 4. The volumes from Table 3-B-1 have been plotted on the graph in Figure 3-B-1. The vertical axis represents the number of permits (the *dependent variable*), and the horizontal axis represents time, (the *independent variable*). Figure 3-B-2 presents the forecast for the coming year using a regression line.

Ordinary Least Squares

Linear regression, using a technique called the ordinary least squares (OLS) method, attempts to find a straight line that comes as close as possible to all of the historical points. The underlying concept is that if the line we find comes close to the historical points, it is likely to come close to the actual future values for the variable we are predicting as well. The OLS model is derived from the equation used to define a straight line:

$$y = mx + b$$

Where y is the dependent variable, m is the slope of the line, x is the independent variable, and b is the point at which the line crosses the vertical axis, called the y intercept (see Figure 3-B-3).

Suppose that we were interested in forecasting permits for the first quarter of Year 4. The x value would be data point 13 (following the 12 data points in Table 3-B-1). Assume that the slope (m) of the line was 1,400, and that the intercept (b) was 19,000 permits. Then we could solve for y as follows:

$$y = mx + b$$
$$y = (1,400 \times 13) + 19,000$$
$$y = 37,200$$

Clearly, if we know the slope m and intercept b we can predict the future value y (in this case the volume of permits) for any particular time period x. The key is that we generally do not know the values for the slope m and intercept b, and we have to find those values. Linear regression uses a set of paired x and y values to estimate the slope and intercept. In regression analysis, the traditional equation for a straight line is generally shown as:

$$y = \alpha + \beta x$$

where α, the Greek letter alpha, is equivalent to b, and is referred to as the *constant*. The Greek letter beta, β, is the same as m, and is referred to as the

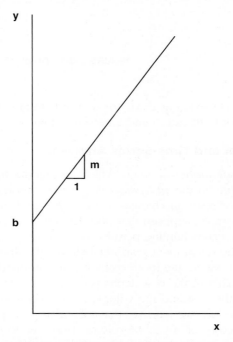

FIGURE 3-B-3   Graph of a Straight Line

x coefficient because it is multiplied by *x*. Often this equation would be shown with an additional variable on the right side to represent the fact that it is likely that there will be some variation, or error, not accounted for by the independent variable.

Historical points probably will not all lie along a straight line. Therefore, the goal of the linear regression process is to estimate a line that is as close as possible to the given data points. Any line other than the regression line would be further from the historical data points, and therefore likely to be further from the actual points in the future as well. Most statistical forecasting software programs provide not only a forecast, but also a confidence interval for the forecast, which indicates the likelihood that the future result will fall within a given range of values. The mathematics of regression

analysis will not be discussed here. The reader who is unfamiliar with linear regression is referred to any statistics text that covers regression analysis.

Regression analysis can be performed using either specialized statistical computer software such as the SPSS software program, or more general programs such as Excel. Using the Data Analysis choice from the Tools menu in Excel, regression analysis can be performed on the data in Table 3-B-1.[13] The resulting values are:

$$\text{Intercept} = 19{,}818$$
$$x\text{ coefficient} = 1{,}297$$

Using that information we can forecast the number of permits for each quarter of Year 4:

Year 4	Time Period	$y = mx + b$
July–September	13	$y = (1{,}297 \times 13) + 19{,}818 = 36{,}679$
October–December	14	$y = (1{,}297 \times 14) + 19{,}818 = 37{,}976$
January–March	15	$y = (1{,}297 \times 15) + 19{,}818 = 39{,}273$
April–June	16	$y = (1{,}297 \times 16) + 19{,}818 = 40{,}570$

Similarly, we could do a causal regression analysis using historical values for departmental costs and volumes. The regression would generate an intercept and slope (*x* coefficient) as indicated. The four volumes shown for Year 4 can then be used to predict the Year 4 department costs. Assume that historical data for costs and volume were used in a

regression analysis, and the resulting intercept and slope were:

$$\text{Intercept} = \$142{,}100$$
$$x\text{ coefficient} = \$10$$

Using that information we can forecast the department cost for each quarter of Year 4:

Year 4	Volume	$y = mx + b$
July–September	36,679	$y = (\$10 \times 36{,}679) + \$142{,}100 = \$508{,}890$
October–December	37,976	$y = (\$10 \times 37{,}976) + \$142{,}100 = \$521{,}860$
January–March	39,273	$y = (\$10 \times 39{,}273) + \$142{,}100 = \$534{,}830$
April–June	40,570	$y = (\$10 \times 40{,}570) + \$142{,}100 = \$547{,}800$

Regression Analysis Cautions Regression analysis is often used without being given adequate thought. Managers or policy makers must use this tool cautiously. It is generally sensible to try to keep forecasting models as simple as possible. Simpler models have been shown to generate more reliable results

than complex ones, unless the complexity is addressing a particular problem. A number of factors must be considered when using regression. First, always ensure that the relationship between the variables makes sense. Second, the results should indicate that the independent variable is responsible for the variations in the dependent variable. Third, assess the significance of the independent variable(s). Fourth, also consider the reasonableness of the assumptions made in the analysis. Finally, consider the potential problem caused by outliers. Each of these five areas will be discussed briefly. Although a more detailed examination of these technical statistical issues will

---

[13] Instructions for using Microsoft Excel to perform regression analysis are included in the web page for *Essentials of Cost Accounting for Health Care Organizations*, 3rd ed., at http://www.jbpub.com/samples/0763738131/ExcelInstructions_7.pdf Note: If Data Analysis is not available on the Tools menu in your Excel software, follow the directions in Excel help to load the Analysis Toolpack.

not be presented, the forecaster should be aware of their existence and should try to ensure that there are not serious problems related to any of them.

Plausibility Regression analysis uses a relationship between two variables as a basis for prediction. However, it is important to assess whether it makes sense that one variable would be predictive of another. For example, we could do a regression analysis using the population in China and a United States town government's budget as the two variables. However, just because the population in China is growing and the government's budget is growing does not mean that the number of people living in China is actually having any impact on the town government's costs.

This issue is referred to as plausibility—the relationship between the variables must make reasonable sense. There should be some reason that we believe that the independent variable is *causal*—it causes the dependent variable to vary. Similarly, if we are using time as the independent variable, and predicting the behavior of some variable over time, we need to have some reason to believe that the relationship makes sense.

Goodness of Fit The ability of one variable to explain the variations in another is referred to as the *goodness of fit*. If the independent variable rises and falls in direct proportion with the dependent variable, the goodness of fit will be excellent. Goodness of fit is usually not perfect because it is rare for one variable to be influenced only by one or several other variables. Usually, some variables that impact the dependent variable are not taken into account in a forecasting model. For example, the weather, changes in social values, and the animal population affect the number of permits issued, but would not be considered in a time-series forecast of permits.

Goodness of fit is measured by the *coefficient of determination*, referred to as the *R-squared*. Most calculators or computer software programs with linear regression capability will calculate the R-squared, which can range from 0 to 1. The closer the value to 1, the better the equation is as a predictor. A value close to 0 would indicate that our independent variable is not a good basis for predicting the dependent variable.

Independent Variable's Statistical Significance For the independent variable to be responsible for changes in the dependent variable, the cause-and-effect relationship must be clear. The regression analysis will indicate the slope of the estimated line. If the slope of the line is 0, the dependent variable will not vary as the independent variable changes. For example, there would be no change in permit volume over time. To ensure that this is not the case, a *t-test* is performed to ascertain that the value for the slope is indeed significantly different from 0. The *t* value of the slope measures significance. If the *t* value is sufficiently high, then the slope is assumed to be statistically different from 0. This doesn't ensure that there is a cause and effect relationship—it only indicates a correlation between the variables. But unless that correlation exists there is no cause and effect relation.

The *t* value, or *t* statistic, and a corresponding *p-value* are automatically calculated by most statistical computer programs. The *t* statistic consists of the value estimated for the slope divided by its standard error. For any given *t* statistic, we can determine the likelihood that there really is no relationship among the variables. That likelihood is indicated by the *p*-value. If the *p*-value is .01, that would imply that the result is significant at the .01 or 1 percent level of significance. This would imply that there is less than a 1 percent chance that there is not really a relationship between the variables. The *p*-value levels of .05 and .01 are commonly used. The .05 level is probably the most common cut-off that is cited in determining whether results are considered to be statistically significant and reliable.

Reasonableness of Assumptions Whether or not the assumptions made in preparing the linear regression forecast are reasonable is referred to as specification analysis. Specification analysis has four elements: (1) *linearity*, (2) *constant variance*, (3) *independence*, and (4) *normality*. If the requirements of all four of these factors are met, then the resulting estimates are considered to be the best linear, unbiased estimates.

Linearity refers to a straight-line relationship. We are concerned with whether regression analysis, which projects a straight line, can reasonably estimate the relationship between the variables. It only makes sense to use a linear estimator if the relationship between the variables is linear. If one looked at the points on a scatter diagram, it should be reasonable to believe that a straight line could be an approximation. This is one of the reasons that it is critical to graph the data and examine it before beginning the forecast analysis.

Constant variance refers to the fact that the scatter of actual historical data points around the estimated line should be fairly uniform. This is referred to as *homoscedasticity*. If for some reason the scatter of points are consistently near the regression line in some areas, and systematically further away in other areas (*heteroscedasticity*) it would indicate that the results are less reliable.

The third element of specification analysis relates to the independence of the residuals. The residuals are a measure of the distance from the regression line to each of the actual historical points. Each of these should be independent. If the residuals are not independent of each other, a problem called *serial correlation* arises. This problem can also be identified by looking at the scatter and the regression line, or by using a test called the Durbin-Watson statistic. If there is serial correlation, the reliability of the results decreases.

The fourth element of specification analysis is that a normal distribution of historical points occurs around the regression line.

Outliers Outlier data points are not representative of typical results and can throw off the results.[14] Regression can only predict the future based on information it has about the past. The intelligence and judgment of a manager are called for to interpret the results. If there is reason to believe that the future will not be like the past, then the results must be adjusted. Outlier points represent unusual conditions that often are not expected to reoccur in the future.

CURVILINEAR FORECASTING

The most significant limitation of regression is that it is based on a straight line. Seasonal patterns cannot be estimated well with straight lines. Trends and seasonal patterns occurring at the same time increase the complexity further. *Curvilinear* forecasting uses curved lines for making its estimates of the future. Because the forecast line can curve, it can more closely match a seasonal historical pattern. This results in a much more accurate forecast.

Sometimes, to deal with the non-linear patterns that we observe in data, simple mathematical transformations are made. Log or exponential transformations may make it possible to observe trends that one could not see before the transformation was made. As Moore notes,

For data that is not "smooth," that is, the data pattern is very jagged with sharp

spikes up and down, the data must be "smoothed" to see the actual trend. . . . In the case where you have smooth data but it has hills or valleys, that is, it is nonlinear or curvilinear, you will have to transform the original X variable. The two most common transformations are squaring the X variable and taking the logarithm of the X variable. Either approach requires the user to create a new transformed X variable that will be included along with the original X variable. So now you will have two X variables, the original and the transformed. Again, you may wish to consult with an expert or refer to materials on the issue of non-linearity and misspecification. A good source of information for both issues noted above, and forecasting in general, is Gupta, Dipak K. (2001), *Analyzing Public Policy: Concepts, Tools and Techniques,* CQ Press. (William S. Moore, Appendix from *Evaluating Financial Condition: A Handbook for Local Government,* International City/Country Management Association, 2003, p. 217.)

In addition to transforming data, some forecasting approaches are specifically designed to deal with non-linear data. A number of specialized forecasting programs, such as SmartForecasts,[15] perform curvilinear forecasting. Spreadsheet programs, such as Excel, can also develop curvilinear forecasts, although they are not as sophisticated. Excel allows the user to develop a variety of types of trend lines. For example, the data in Table 3-B-1 was graphed in Figure 3-B-1. Once the graph or Excel chart has been created from the data, the user can click on the chart, and then right click and select the "Add Trendline" choice. An Add Trendline window opens (see Figure 3-B-4). As you can see linear regression is only one of six types of trend lines that Excel can calculate.

To arrive at the regression trend line such as the one shown in Figure 3-B-2, the second choice, Linear, would be selected. Then near the bottom of Figure 3-B-4, we need to indicate how far forward we want the trend line to project. In our example, we wanted to know the number of permits that are likely to be issued for the coming year. Since the data

---

[14] For a discussion of the treatment of outliers, see Steven A. Finkler. "Regression-Based Cost Estimation and Variance: Resolving the Impact of Outliers," in *Issues in Cost Accounting for Health Care Organizations,* 2nd ed. Boston, Mass.: Jones and Bartlett, 1999.

[15] SmartForecasts. Belmont, Mass: SmartSoftware, Inc., http://www.smartcorp.com.

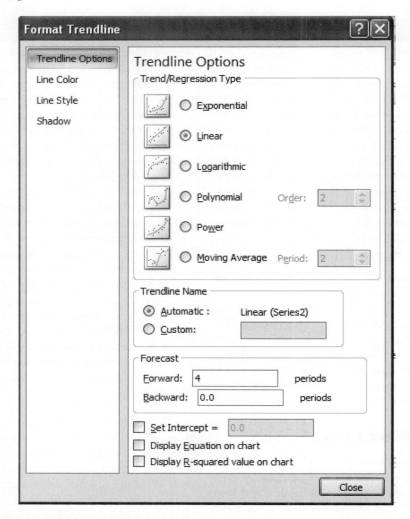

FIGURE 3-B-4 Trendlines

were quarterly, we would indicate that we want the forecast Forward 4 units. Clicking okay results in the trend line similar to the one we saw in Figure 3-B-2.

Linear regression is just one of our choices. It may be that upon examining the graph of our data, the forecaster feels that another equation form (other than the equation for a straight line) will generate a trend line that is a better fit for the data. Figure 3-B-4 indicates that six trend line approaches are available in Excel:

- *Exponential:* If the underlying pattern shows that the data points are rising or falling at progressively faster rates, then an exponential equation would fit the data well. This approach cannot be used if any of the data points are zero or negative.
- *Linear:* A linear equation will provide the best fit, if the data on the graph present a pattern that

looks very much like a straight line. Typically linear data will increase or decrease at a steady rate.

- *Logarithmic:* If we observe data where the rate of change increases or decreases rapidly, and then tapers off to become fairly horizontal, a logarithmic trend line may yield the best result.
- *Polynomial:* A polynomial trend line tends to work well if the data vary up and down. For example, if the length of the hunting seasons were to vary drastically up or down from year to year this might be helpful. The specific polynomial equation that provides the best fit will be influenced by the number of up and down variations in the data.
- *Power:* If we observe that the data are increasing at a specific rate, then a trend line based on the equation of a power may make sense. Note

that such a trend line cannot have data points that are zero or negative values.

- *Moving Average:* The approach taken by a moving average is to smooth out the variations in the data to reveal the underlying pattern. For example, we can take an average of the first two months of a year to get the first predicted value on the trend line. Then the actual values for the second and third month can be used to predict the next month, and so on. In Excel you must indicate the specific number of data points to be averaged (using the Period option that can be seen in Figure 3-B-4). For example, if Period is set to 4, then the average of the first four data points is used as the first point in the moving average trend line.

Even though these curvilinear approaches are available, sometimes it is necessary to use data transformations, as discussed briefly at the beginning of this section. For example, Moore points out that:

> The use of techniques such as moving average or exponential smoothing is available in Excel. Note however that for example when using the moving average method, you will "lose" one or more data points depending on the interval you choose to smooth the data. Thus . . . you may lose valuable information that will make forecasting more difficult and care should be taken prior to using this technique. You may wish to consult with an expert or refer to materials on the issue of degrees of freedom and prediction. (William S. Moore, Appendix from *Evaluating Financial Condition: A Handbook for Local Government,* International City/County Management Association, 2003, p. 217.)

How do you select the trend line type from among the six alternatives discussed above? Your data should dictate your choice. Keep in mind that you desire a reliable forecast. As was discussed above, the higher a trend line's R-squared value, the more reliable it is. Fortunately, for each type of trend line it calculates, Excel automatically calculates the R-squared value. Notice near the bottom of Figure 3-B-4 that the R-squared may be displayed on the chart. Therefore, if you are unsure of which approach is likely to give the most reliable result, you can forecast using several or all of the methods, and select the one that yields the highest R-squared.

HOW FAR INTO THE FUTURE CAN YOU FORECAST?

Forecasting models allow you to select the number of periods into the future that you wish to forecast. However, the accuracy of forecasts tends to decline the further into the future you go. A forecast for the coming month is likely to be far more accurate than a forecast for the same month five years in the future. Therefore forecasts should be updated frequently (at least annually), incorporating the latest historical information available to assure the greatest possible degree of accuracy.

THE ROLE OF HUMAN JUDGMENT

Forecasting is often viewed as being a mechanical process. However, an underlying assumption is that the results of the past are a good indication of what will happen in the future. To the extent that the future differs from the past, the ability of regression to provide accurate information is limited. The human role in forecasting should not be understated. Forecasts must be tempered by an understanding of circumstances that might cause the future to be something other than merely a reflection of the past.

Furthermore, despite the sophisticated analytical models employed in forecasting, the user should be aware that the process is part science, but also part art. The person preparing the forecast should consider the use of the forecast results. For example, earlier we discussed adjusting for the number of days in different months. Some months have as few as 20 weekdays while others have as many as 23. Suppose you are forecasting labor costs, and staff is paid by the day. The number of weekdays may be a critical factor. However, what if staff is paid by the month rather than by the day? In that case the difference in weekdays per month might have no impact on costs. The person preparing the forecast model must consider the context and ultimate use of the forecast. Based on that context and use, choices can be made such as whether a forecast based on a simple average would suffice, whether a more sophisticated regression or curvilinear model is needed, or whether someone with particular expertise in forecasting should be brought in to assist with the forecast.

4

Understanding Costs

The learning objectives of this chapter are to:

- define cost terms, including *direct costs, indirect costs, average costs, fixed costs, variable costs, marginal costs, relevant range, mixed costs,* and *step-fixed costs;*
- discuss the behavior of costs, with a focus on the impact of changes in the volume of services provided;
- introduce the use of graphs for cost analysis;
- discuss outsourcing decisions using marginal cost analysis;
- explain the break-even analysis technique and provide an example of the technique;
- extend the use of break-even analysis to situations with multiple products or services;
- discuss the managerial implications of break-even analysis;
- define and discuss the *margin of safety* concept;
- introduce the concept of cost measurement;
- discuss cost allocation, including the selection of the base for allocation, approaches for allocation from mission centers to service centers, and allocation to units of service; and
- introduce and explain *activity-based costing.*

INTRODUCTION

As managers work on the preparation of plans, one of the critical requirements is a good understanding of costs. The better managers understand costs, the more accurate their plans will be. Further, a solid understanding of costs will improve the manager's ability to make effective decisions.

Costs, however, are complicated. Many cost terms are widely used but are not well understood. Direct costs, indirect costs, average costs, fixed costs, variable costs, and marginal costs are concepts that managers should understand. This chapter provides definitions of these and other key terms.

After defining costs, this chapter considers how costs change as volume changes. The relationship between costs and volume has a dramatic impact on the profits or losses incurred by an organization. An understanding of this relationship can be instrumental in decision making. As part of the planning process, organizations must decide whether it makes sense to expand or contract volume, or whether to add or eliminate services. Issues such as these require sophisticated thinking in order to optimize the results for both the organization and its clientele. Managers must learn which costs are relevant for evaluating these decisions.

The chapter next examines a decision method called break-even analysis, a technique that assists the manager in determining what volume of activity is required for a program or service to become financially self-sufficient. Although many not-for-profit organizations are willing to undertake projects that lose money, the organization's survival depends on managers knowing when that will happen and how much money projects will probably make or lose. An awareness of likely losses will give managers critical information. They can then respond by finding other profitable activities that will make up for the losses or by trying to obtain grants or donations to subsidize specific services.

The chapter concludes with a discussion of cost measurement. The measurement of costs is complicated by the fact that some responsibility centers provide services to other centers. To determine the costs of products or services provided by the organization, it is necessary to allocate all of the costs of the organization to the centers that produce the organization's products or services. In addition to addressing cost allocation, this section also discusses activity-based costing, a technique designed to improve the accuracy of cost measurements.

BASIC CONCEPTS AND DEFINITIONS

Cost measurement is more complex than one might expect. When someone asks what something costs, accountants usually respond that "it depends." The reason for this apparently evasive answer is that the appropriate measure of cost depends substantially on the intended use for the cost information. For Steve Netzer, chief operating officer of the Hospital for Ordinary Surgery (HOS), to find out what it cost to treat each patient in the hospital the previous year is very different from calculating what it might cost to treat one more patient the following year. The cost per patient when 100 patients are treated may be very different from the cost per patient when 500 patients are treated.

The purest definition of cost stems from the economist's concept of *opportunity cost*. Economics focuses on the allocation of scarce resources among alternative uses. The cost, or opportunity cost, to the organization when it chooses to use resources for a specific purpose is that it cannot use those same resources for other alternatives or opportunities. It is necessary to forgo doing some things when a choice is made to do something else. The cost of doing anything can be viewed as the value of the forgone alternatives.

The opportunity cost concept makes it easier to understand the nature of costs at a conceptual level. To make it easier to measure costs for practical purposes, cost is measured based on the amount that must be paid to obtain resources for the organization's desired use. Specific measurement of that amount is sometimes difficult. To make sense in this complicated area, managers rely upon a set of definitions. These definitions provide the basis of a common language so that when the Millbridge town controller and Dwight Ives, the town manager, have a discussion, both managers can interpret that information in the same way and effectively communicate with each other. Communication about costs should begin by identifying the *cost objective:*

Cost objective: anything in particular for which a measurement of cost is desired.
This could be a unit of service, a program, department, or organization.

For example, one might be interested in the cost of plowing snow from the roads of the Town of Millbridge.

The cost objective must be defined clearly. Suppose that Dwight Ives asks the Public Works manager how much the latest snowfall cost the town. In Ives's mind, he may be wondering about the cost of plowing the snow. In the mind of the Public Works manager, the cost of the snowfall includes both plowing and subsequently filling the potholes caused by the snow and plows. If the Public Works Department reports a cost to Ives that includes pothole repair, there will be a miscommunication. Ives may compare the cost with that reported by other towns and wonder why Millbridge's costs are so high. It may turn out the other towns are only reporting the cost to plow the roads, whereas Millbridge also includes the cost of road repair. The most basic point in costing is to clearly define and communicate the cost objective. Communication is critical, and data only become useful information if they are communicated in a way that everyone understands.

Costs are often measured both in total and per unit. Millbridge might want to know the total cost of plowing snow and also the cost per unit. However, the unit could be miles plowed, inches of snow, or labor hours. The town might want to know the cost per mile, cost per inch of snow, or cost per labor hour. The total cost is often referred to as the *full cost:*

Full cost: the total of all costs associated with a cost objective. This includes direct and indirect costs.

The terms direct and indirect often cause some confusion. They are defined here as follows:

Direct costs:
a. the costs incurred within the organizational unit for which the manager has responsibility, or
b. the costs of resources for direct production of a good or service.

Indirect costs:
a. costs that are assigned to an organizational unit from elsewhere in the organization, or
b. costs of resources that are not used for direct production of a good or service.

Direct and indirect costs are particularly difficult to understand because their definitions relate to the object of the analysis. If one is interested in the direct cost of the Public Works Department, it is appropriate to include department supervisory personnel in that cost. In contrast, if one is interested in the direct cost per mile of road plowed, that would include the plow, the driver, and the cost of the salt spread on the road, but not the cost of supervisory personnel. In that example, the supervisors are direct costs of the Public Works Department (i.e., what it costs to operate the Public Works Department) but indirect costs of plowing the road (i.e., what it costs to plow the roads). The various scheduling and other administrative activities carried out by supervisory personnel are essential to running the *department*, but they are not a direct cost of *plowing snow*. If part of the cost of the town manager's salary is allocated to each department, including the roads department, that cost would be an indirect cost of both the department and each mile of road plowed. Direct and indirect costs, when added together, make up the full costs of the cost objective.

Thus, the full cost of plowing the road includes all of the costs that the organization incurs, including a fair share of indirect costs. Indirect costs are often referred to as *overhead*. In general, the terms *indirect cost* and *overhead* are used interchangeably. However, one should always determine the meaning of technical terms in specific situations. The Public Works manager may consider the plow driver to be a direct cost of plowing roads, his administrative assistant to be an indirect cost, and a share of Dwight Ives's salary to be a wasted, oops, overhead cost. In such a view, the department manager considers indirect costs within the department to be different than overhead costs.

Think of this distinction another way. A department has the direct costs of providing some specific service (e.g., the plow driver). There may also be indirect costs incurred within the department that are needed to run the department but are not directly related to the service (e.g., an administrative assistant). Indirect costs that are needed to run the organization may also be incurred outside of the department (e.g., the town manager's salary or the costs of the Payroll Department).

In some instances, the indirect costs outside of the department are called overhead, but those inside the department are not referred to by that term. In other cases, all indirect costs may be referred to as overhead. This is often the result of different people defining the cost objective differently. If one person believes that determining the direct cost of plowing the road is the cost objective, the administrative assistant and Payroll Department may both be viewed as being indirect costs and, therefore, overhead. If another person views the costs of running the Public Works Department as being the cost objective, then both the plow driver and administrative assistant are considered to be direct costs, and only the Payroll Department is an indirect cost, or overhead.

There is no question that this haziness in the use of terms can cause confusion. The confusion generally is the result of miscommunication. Managers should explicitly define the cost objective, the types of costs being treated as direct, and those being treated as indirect.

Suppose that all town workers, including snowplow drivers, wear a uniform that is cleaned by the town in its own laundry. What type of cost is the worker who does the laundry? Well, it is an indirect cost of plowing the roads. It is also an indirect cost of the Public Works Department, so it is an indirect cost.

To the Laundry Department, however, the worker doing the laundry is a direct cost. So a specific cost can be measured as both a direct cost and an indirect cost for the same organization! The classification depends on the cost objective. If one is interested in the cost of doing laundry for the town, it is a direct cost. If one is is interested in the cost of plowing snow off roads, it is an indirect cost.

> *Average cost*: the full cost of any cost objective divided by the number of units of service provided.

If all of the costs of plowing snow, both direct and indirect, are added and the total is divided by the number of units, the result is the cost per unit or the *average cost*. The total cost could be divided by the number of miles to find the cost per mile plowed. Often managers require information on the cost per mile, cost per patient, cost per meal, and so on.

> *Fixed costs*: those costs that do not change in total as the volume of service units changes over a relevant range of activity.
>
> *Variable costs*: those costs that vary directly with changes in the volume of service units over a relevant range of activity.

Once Meals for the Homeless (Meals) rents space for a soup kitchen, the rent will not change from day to day, even if the number of meals provided varies by a substantial amount. Perhaps Meals is serving 300 people a day at a given soup kitchen. If Meals were to feed another person, the rent would stay the same. Therefore, it is a *fixed cost*. In contrast, the amount of food that Meals must purchase represents a *variable cost*. If more people are served, Meals will need more food. Activity represents the volume of services provided.

> *Relevant range*: the normal range of expected activity for the cost center or organization.

Fixed costs are fixed over the *relevant range* of activity. Suppose that Meals expects that each of its soup kitchens will serve between 250 and 500 people. Within that normal expected range, costs that are fixed will remain fixed. Rent would not change regardless of whether 250, 300, or 500 are people served. However, what if the demand suddenly jumped to 1,200 people? That might be more than could physically be handled at one location. It might be necessary to rent additional space. The rental cost would increase. Thus, fixed costs are only fixed within the relevant range for an activity. However, most managers can accurately predict the likely range of activity for a coming year and plan their fixed and variable resources accordingly.

Fixed costs are also only fixed over a relevant period of time. Rent that is a fixed cost currently can change when the lease expires. Salary costs for a manager may be fixed for a period of one year. After that, the manager may receive a change in salary. Thus, fixed costs remain fixed only within the relevant range of activity and within a relevant period of time. Different fixed costs will have different periods of time over which they remain fixed: Rent may be fixed over a five-year lease period; managers' salaries might change once a year.

> *Marginal costs*: the additional costs incurred as a result of providing one more service unit (such as one more meal).

At first, *marginal costs* would appear to be identical to variable costs. In both cases, if there is one more unit of activity, there will be an increase only in variable costs. Marginal costs, however, more broadly look at all costs that might change as a result of a decision. Suppose that HOS has an x-ray machine that can take 5,000 x-rays per year. Assuming that HOS expects to have 3,000 x-rays, the cost of the x-ray machine is a fixed cost. However, what if HOS is already doing 5,000 x-rays? What is the cost of doing one more x-ray?

If HOS has to buy another machine to do the 5,001st x-ray, then on the margin, the cost of the additional patient is the variable cost of one more patient plus the cost of acquiring another machine. It would be reasonable to argue that instead of buying another machine, HOS should try to push the existing machine a little further. And that might be done. But at some point, whether it is 5,001 or 5,002 or 5,500 or 6,000, the hospital will have to acquire another machine. The cost for that marginal patient would include both the variable costs for that patient and the increase in the fixed costs.

> *Mixed costs*: costs that contain both fixed and variable cost elements.

Some costs are both fixed and variable. For example, electricity is a mixed cost. Meals for the Homeless uses electricity to provide general lighting for its soup kitchens and offices, and also to run its ovens. Since the lights are on every day, the electricity consumed for that purpose is a fixed cost. But the more meals it cooks, the longer the ovens are on and the more electricity it uses.

Mixed costs create some problems for managers. If the number of meals served by Meals for the Homeless is expected to increase by 20 percent next year, how much should Leanna Schwartz, the executive director, budget for electricity? Electricity will clearly rise as a result of cooking the extra meals. But lighting costs will probably not change. So costs will rise, but by less than 20 percent. Regression analysis can be used to separate the mixed cost into its fixed and variable cost components. That approach is described in advanced financial management texts and is beyond the scope of the discussion here.

> *Step-fixed or step-variable costs*: costs that are fixed over ranges of activity that are less than the relevant range.

Often organizations require a fixed number of employees for a range of activity. Within that range, the personnel costs will remain fixed. However, if the volume increases by a large enough number, additional personnel will be needed. That personnel level will then be fixed for a new, higher range of activity. The key to understanding step costs is that they are fixed over volume intervals but do vary within the relevant range.

COST BEHAVIOR

One of the most critical cost issues relates to *cost behavior*. Cost behavior is the way that costs change in reaction to changes in volume. If the volume of activity rises by 5 percent, what do costs do? What if volume falls? How can one predict whether total costs will exceed revenues or remain at a level less than revenues?

Cost behavior depends on the specific elements of cost in any organization and its cost centers. A *cost center* is any unit or department in an organization for which a manager is assigned responsibility for costs. Some types of costs are stable, changing little, if at all, even in response to significant changes in the volume of services provided. Other costs are highly changeable, reacting directly to changes in volume. The goal of this section is to lay out a framework for understanding cost behavior.

Fixed versus Variable Costs

The total costs of running an organization, program, or department are generally divided into those costs that are fixed and those costs that are variable. Graphs help clarify the concepts of cost behavior. In the following example, the service unit measure is assumed to be patient days at HOS. Figure 4-1 provides an example of fixed costs. Specifically, the graph shows the $80,000 annual salary for a gastrointestinal (GI) endoscopy lab manager for the coming year.

That salary is a fixed cost for HOS. The salary paid to a lab manager is not dependent on any patient-volume statistic. In Figure 4-1 the vertical axis shows the cost to the institution. As one moves up this axis, costs increase. On the horizontal axis are the number of lab procedures. The farther to the right one moves, the more procedures the lab does. Regardless of the volume, the $80,000 salary for the lab manager will remain the same. Therefore, the cost is the same for 400, 700, or 1,000 procedures.

Variable costs, as noted earlier, vary with the volume of service units. Suppose that each procedure in the GI Lab at HOS uses a disposable set of supplies. The cost of those supplies would be expected to increase in proportion with the number of procedures. Assuming that each set of supplies costs $500, the expected supply cost would be $500 multiplied by the number of procedures.

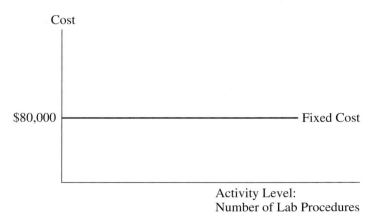

FIGURE 4-1 Graph of Fixed Cost

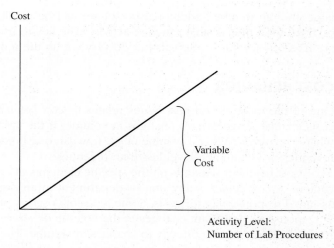

FIGURE 4-2   Graph of Variable Costs

Consider Figure 4-2. This graph plots the cost for disposable supplies as they vary with patient volume. As in Figure 4-1, the vertical axis represents the cost, and the horizontal axis represents the procedure volume. Unlike Figure 4-1, which showed some positive cost even at a volume of zero, this graph shows zero cost at a volume of zero, since zero procedures implies that none of this particular supply will be used.

In Figure 4-3, dashed lines have been inserted to show the total cost when there are 500 and 800 procedures. As can be seen, there is $80,000 of fixed cost regardless of volume. At 500 procedures, the total cost is the $80,000 fixed cost plus $500 variable cost per procedure for 500 procedures ($500 × 500 = $250,000). The total cost is $330,000. At 800 procedures, the variable cost is $400,000 ($500 × 800) and the total is $480,000. Note that the total costs start at $80,000, even at a volume of zero, because of the fixed costs of the manager's salary.

Cost Graphs and the Relevant Range

In Figures 4-1 and 4-2, it is assumed that fixed costs are fixed throughout the entire range of the graph and that variable costs vary in direct proportion throughout the entire range of the graph. This is likely to be a simplification.

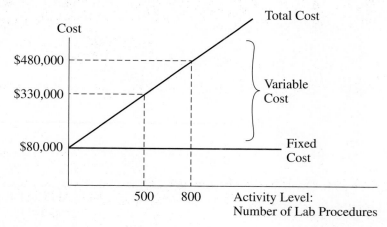

FIGURE 4-3   Graph of the Total Cost

If volumes were extremely low, it would be unlikely that the lab would be kept open. The manager would be let go, and the fixed cost would be eliminated. If volume were extremely high, an assistant manager might have to be hired, thus causing a jump in fixed costs. For many analyses done by managers, however, the true expected range of changes in volume is relatively small. If the organization currently does 500 procedures a year, next year it might do 400 or 600, but it is unlikely that volume would fall to 50 or rise to 2,000. Within typical volume swings, fixed costs are generally likely to remain fixed.

Variable costs increase proportionately over the relevant range. However, if the volume of a lab fell from 500 to 50, the organization might have to pay more per unit for supplies because it is no longer purchasing a reasonably high volume. In contrast, if volume rose to 5,000, it might get a lower price for each unit of supplies. So the cost of supplies does not vary exactly proportionately (doubling the cost with each doubling of volume) over any range of activity.

Again, however, such wide swings in activity are unusual, and it is reasonable for most managerial analyses to assume that within the relevant range, variable costs will vary proportionately. But it is important to be aware that fixed costs are fixed and variable costs are directly variable only over a reasonable relevant range of activity.

Many costs are *step-fixed* and vary within the relevant range but not smoothly. This is quite common with labor. The GI Lab in the example might need the following staff in addition to the managers:

Staff	Activity Level
One technologist	Up to 250 procedures per year
Two technologists	251–500 procedures
Three technologists	501–750 procedures per year
Four technologists	751–1,000 procedures per year

If somewhere between 400 and 600 procedures are expected, then there will be a need for at least two technologists, and perhaps three. The cost behavior pattern for these step-fixed costs are shown in Figure 4-4.

The Impact of Volume on Cost per Unit of Activity

If a GI Lab manager were to ask what it costs to do each procedure in the lab, accountants would probably answer that it depends, as noted earlier. Costs are not always the same. The cost to treat a patient depends on several critical factors. One of these is the volume of

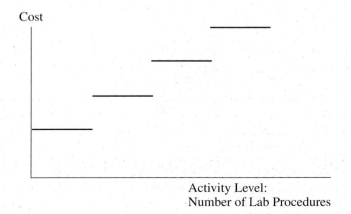

FIGURE 4-4 Graph of Step-Fixed Costs

procedures or, more generally for any organization, the overall volume of activity. The cost per meal at Meals for the Homeless depends on how many meals are served. The cost per person arrested by the Millbridge Police Department depends on the total number arrested. The cost per patient procedure at HOS depends on the number of procedures.

Suppose that the Town of Millbridge School System has annual fixed costs of $15,000,000 and variable costs of $3,000 per student.[1] Using these hypothetical data, what is the average cost per student per year? If there are 3,000 students for the year, the total costs will be the fixed cost of $15,000,000 plus $3,000 per student for each of the 3,000 students. The variable costs would be $9,000,000 (i.e., $3,000 per student × 3,000 students). The total cost would be $24,000,000 (i.e., $15,000,000 fixed cost + $9,000,000 of variable cost). The cost per student would be $8,000 (i.e., $24,000,000 total cost ÷ 3,000 students).

However, what if there were only 2,500 students? Then the variable costs, at $3,000 per student, would be $7,500,000 and the total cost would be $22,500,000. In that case, the cost per student would be $9,000. The cost is higher because there are fewer students sharing the fixed costs. Each student causes the Millbridge Department of Education to spend another $3,000 of variable costs. The $15,000,000 fixed cost remains the same regardless of the number of students. If there are more students, each one shares less of the $15,000,000 fixed cost. If there are fewer students, the fixed cost assigned to each rises. Table 4-1 calculates the fixed, variable, total, and average cost per student at a variety of student volumes.

Figure 4-5 shows the average cost at different student volumes. The cost declines as the volume of students increases because more students are sharing the fixed costs. The impact of sharing fixed costs over increasing levels of volume is referred to in economics as "short-run economies of scale." Suppose there are only 1,500 students. The total variable costs of $3,000 per student would be $4,500,000, and the total cost would be $19,500,000. The cost per student would be $13,000—substantially more than the cost per student with 2,500 or 3,000 students.

In trying to understand costs, it is essential to grasp the concept that because fixed costs do not change in total, the cost per student does change as volume changes. The school superintendent receives a set salary, it costs a fixed set amount to maintain the school buildings and athletic facilities, and so on. The greater the number of students that share those fixed costs, the lower the cost per student. There is no unique answer to the question, "What is the cost per student?" That question can only be answered by giving the cost per student assuming a specific volume of students. The volume is critical.

One implication of this result is that most organizations generally are better off with higher rather than lower volume. As volume increases, the average cost per unit of service

TABLE 4-1 Fixed, Variable, Total, and Average Costs

Volume (A)	Fixed Cost (B)	Variable Cost (C = $3,000 × A)	Total Cost (D = B + C)	Average Cost (E = D ÷ A)
1,500	$15,000,000	$4,500,000	$19,500,000	$13,000
2,500	15,000,000	7,500,000	22,500,000	9,000
3,000	15,000,000	9,000,000	24,000,000	8,000

[1] The existence of high fixed costs, relative to variable costs, is not uncommon. For example, a school system may be required to make large annual payments each year to repay money borrowed to build a new school building. Those payments will not relate to the number of students each year. The school system may have many tenured faculty members. Salary requirements for those faculty also will not vary with the number of pupils. Similarly, administrative costs (e.g., principals, vice principals, administrative assistants) and maintenance costs (e.g., electric, heat, custodial services) may not vary substantially with volume changes.

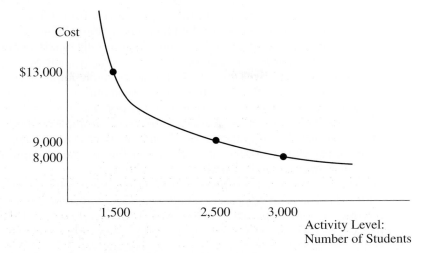

FIGURE 4-5   Average Cost per Student

declines. If prices can be maintained at the original level for an organization that charges for its services, the declining cost will result in lower losses or higher profits.

Outsourcing and Marginal Cost Analysis

Often public service organizations have to decide whether to provide services themselves or to purchase them from an outside consultant or other provider. When an organization decides to have activities performed by an outside provider rather than doing them itself, it is said to be *outsourcing* that service or activity. An example is a government's decision to collect garbage itself or to outsource that activity to a private company. This is sometimes referred to as a *make or buy* decision. In recent years, outsourcing has become much more popular. The range of activities being outsourced has increased and the use of offshore companies to provide services has soared.

One form of outsourcing is the use of workers from a temp agency on a long-term basis instead of hiring full-time employees. The workers do the same work as if they had been hired full-time, but the organization receives two major benefits. First, even though there is an agency fee and typically a higher hourly wage for the temp worker than for a full-time employee, the organization does not have to pay as much for benefits such as health care and retirement for temp workers. Second, the organization retains flexibility. It is much easier to reduce staff by simply discontinuing an employee from a temp agency rather than firing an employee.

The other major form of outsourcing is one in which an activity is taken over by an outside firm that specializes in that activity. For example, we have long seen private laundry companies that provide laundry services to a number of hospitals. But in recent years the range of activities being outsourced has grown dramatically. Information systems (program-ming), training, payroll, billing, receivables, public relations, insurance claims processing, technical assistance, and customer service are some examples of outsourcing activities.

A laundry service that provides laundry to 10 hospitals in a large city may be much more efficient than having each hospital run its own laundry department. That efficiency can result in a profit for the laundry company and reduced costs for each of the 10 hospitals. However, in recent years a great deal of outsourcing has resulted in activities being done in other countries (referred to as offshore), where labor earns lower wages. It is not uncommon for a customer to call an organization with a question, and find that the person providing the answer is in India, Argentina, or the Philippines. More and more often organizations are scanning documents, and then sending them electronically to other countries where data from the documents are entered in databases for processing or analysis.

A full discussion of the political and economic implications of outsourcing is beyond the scope of this text. In short, the trend toward outsourcing has grown over the last decade, but more recently opposition because of the potential job loss that it creates has also grown. The organization first needs to assess the financial implications of a make or buy decision. Once an organization understands whether a specific outsourcing proposal makes financial sense, it can then consider the various social and political implications of the decision and take them into account as well.

From a financial perspective, the decision of whether to outsource is one that is best addressed using an approach called *marginal cost analysis*. This approach is sometimes referred to as *incremental analysis* or *out-of-pocket analysis*. The essence of the approach is that decisions such as whether to provide a service or to change the volume of a service should be based on marginal rather than average costs.

As the previous section shows, the cost per pupil will depend on the number of pupils in the school system. The measurement of cost also depends on what the measurement will be used for. If the question is just one of historical curiosity, the average cost is an adequate response. However, if the information will be used for decision making, that response may well be incorrect.

Suppose that the town has recently had a large influx of families with young children. Dwight Ives realizes that in a few years the population in the school system will start to grow dramatically. The town can hire additional staff and accommodate the additional students with the existing buildings. Alternatively, an adjacent town has offered to educate Millbridge students for $7,000 per student. Although this would be somewhat unusual, it is not unheard of. And if the neighboring town has excess capacity, why should Millbridge add more classes? This represents an example of a *make or buy* or *outsourcing* decision: educate the students in the township or purchase the services.

Suppose that the township currently has 2,500 students and believes that the new influx will cause the size of the town's student body to rise to 3,000. Looking at Table 4-1, the immediate reaction would be to accept the offer. The $7,000 price that has been offered would be less than the $8,000 average cost per pupil within the town, at a volume of 3,000 students. It looks like a good deal. However, Table 4-1 shows the average cost, rather than the marginal cost.

The marginal cost represents the additional costs that result from a decision. If one more student is added, the marginal cost would be the cost of that one additional student. If 500 more students are added, the marginal cost would be the costs incurred because of those additional 500 additional students. Clearly, this involves the variable costs. If new schools must be built for the additional students, the cost of those schools would also be included in the marginal costs. But if the fixed costs can remain the same, then they would not be included.

Assuming that the fixed costs would not change going from 2,500 to 3,000 students, what is the marginal cost? It is the amount that costs increase as a result of the additional students. In this example, the marginal costs would be $3,000 per student. That is substantially less than the offer from the other town.

If the decision is made to purchase the services, the town will pay $7,000 additional for each of the extra students, in addition to what it is paying currently for its students. If the additional students are educated within the town, the cost will be $3,000 per student in addition to current costs.

Another way to view this is to consider the total costs of the school system. From Table 4-1, it can be seen that with the current student population of 2,500, the total cost of the system is $22,500,000. If 3,000 students are educated within the town, the total cost rises by $1,500,000 to $24,000,000. However, if Millbridge were to pay the adjoining town $7,000 for each of 500 students, the total costs would rise $3,500,000 ($7,000 × 500 students) to $26,000,000 ($22,500,000 + $3,500,000). It clearly is less expensive for the town to educate the students itself.

These same principles apply any time an organization must decide whether to add or eliminate a service, or expand or contract volume of an existing service. The decision always requires the organization to consider how much additional cost it will incur if it makes one choice versus another. In some cases, revenues will also change, and the change in revenue must be considered as well. It is, however, the change in revenues and costs that is the key measurement when one is considering making a change.

In recent years, many government, not-for-profit, and health care organizations have focused on the issues of outsourcing and privatization. However, if an organization is considering elimination of a current service, caution is necessary. Often, an outside vendor can offer a price that is less than the average cost. The organization, however, must assess the marginal costs and marginal revenues. If a hospital can eliminate many fixed costs of running its laundry, there may be a cost savings from outsourcing. However, what if most of the fixed costs of running the laundry will be incurred anyway? In that case, it may not pay to shift to the outside supplier. The organization must consider its likely reduction in internal spending versus the price that it will be charged by the outside provider.

Marginal cost analysis is sometimes referred to as *relevant costing.* This is because all decisions should be made based on those costs that are relevant to the decision. The simplest way to think about this concept is to consider costs before and after a change. The relevant costs are those that change as a result of the decision. The approach applies equally to revenues.

In the Millbridge School District example, the many fixed costs of the school district were not relevant. This is because they would not have to change as a result of adding the extra students. If the town would have had to build an additional school, the new fixed costs of that school would have been relevant costs. It would have had to consider those fixed costs in determining whether the total costs to the town would be higher or lower if it kept the students versus sending them to the next town for their classes.

BREAK-EVEN ANALYSIS

Many health, not-for-profit, and public organizations are moving toward adding new projects and ventures as a way of improving the financial stability and results of the organization. Profitable new ventures are seen as a way to subsidize other activities of the organization that lose money. However, managers must be able to determine whether a new venture will indeed be profitable. The *break-even analysis* technique is a useful tool for making such determinations in situations in which there is a specific price associated with the service. The price may result from a specific charge made for the service, or perhaps from some system of cost reimbursement.

At first blush, this would seem to be a fairly transparent exercise. First, find out the likely price or reimbursement that can be received for each unit of the new service. Then determine the cost per unit for the service. If the price is greater than the cost, a profit will be made. If the price is less than the cost, the new activity will lose money. The only problem is that when one tries to determine the cost per unit, the result is "it depends."

The cost per unit depends on volume, as discussed earlier in this chapter. At low volumes, the cost per unit will be higher than it is at high volumes. It is possible that at low volumes the cost per unit will exceed the average price that can be earned for the service. At higher volumes, the service may become profitable. The goal of break-even analysis is to determine the volume at which the activity moves from losing money to making money. Understanding whether a particular unit or service will lose money, make money, or just break even is useful for the evaluation of both new and continuing projects or services.

The profitability of an activity is determined by whether its revenues are greater than its costs or expenses. If revenues exceed expenses, the organization earns a profit. If revenues are less than expenses, a loss is incurred. *Only when revenues are exactly equal to expenses does the venture break even.* The revenues of an organization will be the average price collected multiplied by the number of units of service. This can be shown in equation form as follows:

$$\text{Total Revenues} = P \times Q \qquad \textbf{(4-1)}$$

where P is the price and Q represents the volume. The price, P, is not the amount we charge, but rather the average amount that we can expect to collect. There are situations in which we will collect less than our official price. Therefore the revenue per unit of service is sometimes shown as variable revenue or VR. The expenses of the organization are the fixed and variable costs, shown in equation form as follows:

$$\text{Total Expenses} = (VC \times Q) + FC \qquad \textbf{(4-2)}$$

where VC is the variable cost per unit, Q is the volume, and FC is the total fixed cost. At the volume at which we just break even, we refer to Q as the BEQ. Since the organization will only break even when the total revenues equal the total expenses, the volume needed to just break even can be found by solving the following equation for BEQ:

$$(P \times \text{BEQ}) = (VC \times \text{BEQ}) + FC \qquad \textbf{(4-3)}$$

Next subtract $(VC \times \text{BEQ})$ from both sides of the equation (see Equation 4-4), factor out the BEQ from all items on the left side of the equation (see Equation 4-5), and divide both sides of the equation by $(P - VC)$ (see Equation 4-6), as follows:

$$(P \times \text{BEQ}) - (VC \times \text{BEQ}) = FC \qquad \textbf{(4-4)}$$

$$\text{BEQ} \times (P - VC) = FC \qquad \textbf{(4-5)}$$

$$\text{BEQ} = \frac{FC}{P - VC} \qquad \textbf{(4-6)}$$

This results in a formula for the quantity, BEQ, that is needed to break even.

Break-Even Analysis Example

Suppose that the hypothetical Feed-a-Child Foundation is contemplating starting a new program in South America. It does not currently have any operations on that continent and does not have sufficient funds to provide a subsidy to a new program. The program would have to be completely self-sufficient.

The proposal is to generate donations of $50 to feed each child. There would be new fixed costs of $10,000 for a special mailing (postage and printing) to solicit funds for the program and also new variable costs of $30 per child. In the unlikely event that there are no donors, then no children would be fed because there would be no revenue, but there would still be fixed costs of $10,000, resulting in a $10,000 loss. If there are 100 donors at $50 each, there would be $5,000 of revenue ($50 × 100 donors), $10,000 of fixed costs, and $3,000 of variable costs ($30 × 100 children). Total costs would be $13,000 ($10,000 of fixed cost + $3,000 of variable cost), revenues would be $5,000, and the loss $8,000.

How many donors would the Feed-a-Child Foundation need for the program to be expected to break even? Each additional donor contributes $50 of support but causes the foundation to spend an additional $30. The difference between the $50 donation and the

$30 variable cost is called the *contribution margin*. That is because it is the amount available to contribute to paying fixed costs, and, if all fixed costs are covered, to contribute to profits.

If the contribution margin is negative, the more donations the organization receives and children it feeds, the more money it will lose. When the contribution margin is negative, the organization can never expect to break even. If the contribution margin is positive, it means that each extra unit of activity makes the organization better off by the amount of the contribution. In that case, the organization will break even if the volume is high enough that the contribution margins from all donors will add up to enough to cover the fixed costs.

For the Feed-a-Child Foundation, when there are 100 donors, there is $20 of contribution margin for each of the 100 donors, or a total contribution margin of $2,000. Note that the loss with zero donors is shown previously to be $10,000; it is only $8,000 when there are 100 donors. The loss decreased by $2,000, exactly the amount of the total contribution margin for those 100 donors.

How many donors at $50 each would the foundation need for the new program to break even? The answer is 500. If each additional donor generates $20 of contribution margin, then 500 donors would generate $10,000 of contribution margin (500 donors $\times$ $20 = $10,000), exactly enough to cover the fixed costs of $10,000.

This can be calculated directly using the formula from Equation 4-6, derived earlier:

$$BEQ = \frac{FC}{P - VC}$$

BEQ is the break-even quantity. It is the quantity at which the organization, program, or service just breaks even. In the Feed-a-Child Foundation example,

$$BEQ = \frac{\$10,000}{\$50 - \$30}$$

$$= \frac{\$10,000}{\$20}$$

$$= 500$$

Note that the price less the variable cost, $P - VC$, is the contribution margin.

The concept of break-even analysis is illustrated using graphs such as Figure 4-6. The total cost line starts at a level of $10,000 because of the fixed costs. The total support or revenue line starts at zero because there is no money coming in if there are no donors.

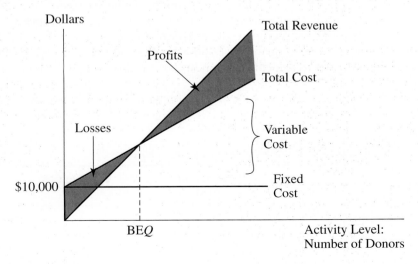

FIGURE 4-6   Break-Even Graph

Where the revenue line and the cost line intersect, they are equal and the foundation just breaks even. Note that at quantities of donors below the break-even point (i.e., to the left of BEQ on the graph), the total cost line is higher than the total revenue line. The program is then losing money, or operating in the red. At a number of donors higher than the break-even point (to the right of the intersection), the organization is making money, or operating in the black. At the intersection point, it just breaks even.

Break-Even with Multiple Products

When there are different types of services or products, break-even analysis becomes somewhat more complicated. The formula for break-even involves assuming that there is only one price and one variable cost, and therefore one contribution margin. If there are different prices and different variable costs for differing services, which price or variable cost should be used? It is necessary to use all of them, and in order to get the correct result, it is necessary to find a weighted average contribution margin. That weighted average can be divided into the fixed costs to find the break-even volume in total.

For example, suppose that the Feed-a-Child Foundation is interested in knowing the total number of donors needed for the entire foundation to break even for the coming year. The foundation has current programs for feeding children in Africa and Asia. The African program solicits $36, under a campaign that 10 cents will feed an African child for a day (10 cents × 365 days per year is approximately $36). Its variable costs are $32. Although the contribution margin is much lower than the proposed South America program, there are many donors for this long-standing program. The Asia program solicits donations of $40. The variable costs for this program are $29. The contribution margin for each program can be calculated by subtracting the variable cost from the price, as shown in Table 4-2.

The crucial piece of information for calculating the break-even point is the relative proportion of donors to each program. Management of the foundation expects that 70 percent of all donations will be to the African program, 25 percent will be to the Asian program, and 5 percent will be to the new South American program. This information can be used to determine a weighted average contribution margin. This is done by multiplying each program's contribution margin from Table 4-2 by the percentage of donations that program is of the total. The results are added together to get an overall weighted contribution margin, as shown in Table 4-3.

This $6.55 weighted contribution margin represents the average contribution margin for all types of donations. It can be used to calculate the break-even quantity. Assume that fixed costs for the entire organization, including all three programs, are $100,000 per year. The break-even quantity of donors can be calculated using the basic formula, but using the weighted average contribution margin instead of the individual contribution margins:

$$BEQ = \frac{FC}{P - VC}$$

TABLE 4-2 Contribution Margin by Program

	Donation (A)	Variable Cost (B)	Contribution Margin (C = A − B)
Africa	$36	$32	$ 4
Asia	40	29	11
South America	50	30	20

TABLE 4-3 Calculation of Weighted Average Contribution Margin

Program	Percentage of Donations		Contribution Margin		Weighted Average Contribution Margin
Africa	70%	×	$ 4	=	$2.80
Asia	25	×	11	=	2.75
South America	5	×	20	=	1.00
Total	100%				$6.55

or

$$BEQ = \frac{FC}{CM}$$

where CM is the contribution margin.

$$BEQ = \frac{\$100,000}{\$6.55}$$

$$= 15,267$$

The Feed-a-Child Foundation will need to receive 15,267 donations over the next year to cover all of its costs. Of that total, 70 percent would be $36 donations to the Africa program, 25 percent would be $40 donations to the Asia program, and 5 percent would be $50 donations to the South America program.

This method works for three different programs. What if there are more than three kinds? The same weighted average approach can be used to find the break-even volume whether there are three different types of programs or hundreds of programs. It would simply make the arithmetic more time-consuming. That is a good reason to use computer spreadsheets for financial management calculations.

Additional Break-Even Applications

Break-even analysis is a powerful method to help managers make decisions. In addition to determining the volume of services that are required to achieve a financial break-even situation, it can answer other questions as well.

For example, organizations are not always able to provide an unlimited amount of service. An ambulance service may be limited in the amount of trips it can make because it has a limited number of vehicles. A soup kitchen may have a limited capacity for cooking meals. A city golf course may have a limited number of tee-off times. Break-even analysis can be used to determine the price that would have to be charged in situations in which capacity is constrained so that the organization could still break even. The manager would then have to assess whether there would be sufficient demand at that price to reach the capacity constraint.

Sometimes, the total revenue is constrained. For example, a charity may have received a donation to be used to provide a specific service. The donation represents the total amount of revenue available. Break-even analysis can be used to determine the maximum number of units of service that could be provided without losing money.

In some cases, an organization may know both its price and number of units of service. Break-even analysis can be used to determine the maximum costs that can be incurred without losing money.

Another use of break-even analysis would be if the organization receives a grant allowing it to lower the charge for a particular service. The analysis can be used to determine how much the price can be lowered without losing money.

In each of these situations one must consider the elements of Equation 4-6:

$$BEQ = \frac{FC}{P - VC}$$

As the various elements of this equation are varied, the equation can be solved for any one missing element.

SOLVING FOR FIXED COST, PRICE, AND VARIABLE COST   The break-even formula can be used to find the fixed cost, price, or variable cost that will allow us to break even at a particular volume level. For example, suppose that we know that the HOS clinic has fixed costs of $250,000, average collected revenue of $95 per patient, variable costs of $80, and operates at its maximum capacity of 12,000 patient visits per year. Unfortunately, the clinic is losing money. How much would it have to collect per patient, on average, to just break even at its 12,000 maximum capacity volume?

$$BEQ = \frac{FC}{P - VC}$$

$$12,000 = \frac{\$250,000}{P - \$80}$$

$$12,000 \times (P - \$80) = \$250,000$$

$$12,000\, P - \$960,000 = \$250,000$$

$$12,000\, P = \$250,000 + \$960,000$$

$$12,000\, P = \$1,210,000$$

$$P = \$100.83$$

If we could collect $100.83 per patient visit, we would break even. However, suppose that studies have shown the clinic that if it were to raise prices to a point where it collects more than $95 per visit, that would dramatically lower demand. There would be far fewer than 12,000 visits, and the loss to be even greater. Suppose they keep the average collection per patient at $95, keep their variable costs at $80 per visit, and retain their volume of 12,000 visits; what is the most that they could spend on fixed costs and still break even?

$$BEQ = \frac{FC}{P - VC}$$

$$12,000 = \frac{FC}{\$95 - \$80}$$

$$12,000 \times (\$95 - \$80) = FC$$

$$FC = 12,000 \times (\$95 - \$80)$$

$$FC = 12,000 \times \$15$$

$$FC = \$180,000$$

The clinic would break even if it lowered its fixed costs to $180,000. After further study, the clinic determines that it can cut its fixed costs to $200,000, but no lower. If the clinic keeps the average revenue collected per patient at $95, patient volume at 12,000 visits, and lowers fixed costs to $200,000, what is the most it could spend per visit on variable costs and still break even?

$$BEQ = \frac{FC}{P - V}$$

$$12,000 = \frac{\$200,000}{\$95 - VC}$$

$$12,000 \times (\$95 - VC) = \$200,000$$

$$12,000 \times \$95 - 12,000\ VC = \$200,000$$

$$\$1,140,000 - 12,000\ VC = \$200,000$$

$$\$1,140,000 - \$200,000 = 12,000\ VC$$

$$\$940,000 = 12,000\ VC$$

$$VC = \$940,000/12,000$$

$$VC = \$78.33$$

At a variable cost of $78.33, the clinic would break even.

BREAK-EVEN AND FIXED REVENUES Sometimes organizations have both variable and fixed revenues. For example, not-for-profit Eye Care Services receives an average of $100 per patient visit, and also receives an annual donation of $50,000 from a health care foundation. If Eye Care Services has fixed costs of $250,000 and variable costs of $80 per visit, what is the break-even quantity of visits? Fixed revenues (*FR*) serve to offset some of the fixed costs of the organization. We can restate the break-even formula as:

$$BEQ = \frac{FC - FR}{P - VC}$$

Solving for the BEQ, taking the *FR* into account:

$$BEQ = \frac{\$250,000 - \$50,000}{\$100 - \$80} = 10,000 \text{ visits}$$

MARGIN OF SAFETY The *margin of safety* is a useful managerial tool related to break-even analysis. The margin of safety is the amount by which expected volume or revenues exceed the volume level or revenues required to break even. For example, suppose that HOS is considering a new outpatient mental health clinic. Its managers believe that the clinic will have 12,000 visits per year and will collect an average of $100 per visit, generating total revenue of $1,200,000 (12,000 visits × $100 per visit). However, what if they are wrong? What if the number of visits falls short of expectations?

The margin of safety compares the expectations with the break-even point. Assume that HOS expects to collect $100 per patient on average, have variable costs of $70 per patient, and fixed costs per year of $300,000. The break-even volume is 10,000 patient visits per year, as follows:

$$BEQ = \frac{FC}{P - VC}$$

$$BEQ = \frac{300,000}{\$100 - \$70} = 10,000 \text{ patient visits}$$

At that level the revenue would be $1,000,000 per year (10,000 visits × $100 per patient). Since HOS expects 12,000 visits and the break-even point is 10,000, there is a margin of safety of 2,000 visits. In their planning, HOS managers know that even if the number of visits falls as much as 2,000 visits below expectations, there will not be a loss on the new clinic. Alternatively, if they are focusing on the total revenues, if a decline in the number of visits causes revenues to fall by $200,000, HOS will still break even.

Managerial Implications of Break-Even Analysis

If a particular program, service, or activity is expected to have a volume of activity well in excess of the break-even point, managers have a clear-cut decision to start or continue the service. If the volume is too low to break even, the activity may not be feasible. However, sometimes changes in the activity can be made to achieve a break-even status.

One approach is to lower the volume needed to break even. The required break-even level can be reduced in three ways. One can lower the fixed costs by getting by with less expensive or fewer fixed resources. That may or may not be possible, depending on the specific circumstances. A second way to lower the break-even point is to increase prices. Price increases would increase the contribution margin per unit. That would have the effect of lowering the break-even point. However, price increases might reduce the expected volume for many activities or services.[2] In that case, the price increases may be defeating their purpose. Also, prices are sometimes regulated and beyond the control of the organization. Finally, one could try to reduce the variable cost per unit. This might be accomplished by increased efforts toward improved efficiency.

If it is not feasible to change the fixed costs, price, or variable costs, an organization can try to increase the number of units of activity. In the Feed-a-Child Foundation example presented, what type of donor would be desirable? The most desirable type is the one with the highest contribution margin. Every donation to the South America program provides a contribution margin (CM) of $20 (Table 4-2). Although this type of donation provides the highest support or revenue, it is not the revenue, but rather the CM that is important. If an organization has a service with very high revenue, but also very high variable cost and low CM, it would not be as financially attractive as another with a higher CM.

Break-Even Analysis Cautions

A few words of caution are advisable when working with break-even analysis. First, once a break-even point is calculated, one must decide whether it is likely that the actual volume will be sufficient to meet or exceed that point. That will require managers to predict the volume that will occur. If the forecast of volume is incorrect, the decision to go ahead with a new service may turn out to be a bad one, even if the break-even analysis is otherwise done correctly. Also, correct classification of costs as being either fixed or variable is critical to the analysis.

Another potential problem is that break-even analysis assumes that prices and costs are constant. If it can be reasonably expected that prices will fall over time, then a higher volume would be needed to keep a service viable, unless variable or fixed costs would be falling as well. When a new service is first offered, the price may be high because only one organization provides that service. It has the ability to set prices based on a temporary monopoly situation. If competitors start offering the product, prices may fall. In contrast, if prices are expected to rise faster than costs, then a marginal service today may become profitable over time, even without an increase in volume.

---

[2] Based on economic theory, price and quantity are related. Price increases are likely to reduce quantity. However, the extent to which this occurs depends on the shape of the demand curve and the elasticity of demand. In some cases, minor price changes can have dramatic impacts on quantity (high elasticity), but in other cases it is possible that substantial price changes have only minor impacts on quantity.

As with all budgeting tools, judgment is essential. Based on experience, insight, and thought, the manager must examine the assumptions of any modeling technique and consider the reasonableness of the results. If a result does not seem to make sense, often that is because it does not make sense. Break-even analysis is a tool that can help give a manager a firm starting point in understanding whether a project or service is likely to be financially viable.

COST MEASUREMENT

Up to this point, the focus of the chapter has been on understanding costs for planning. Another important concern is the measurement of costs that have been incurred. One might expect that cost measurement would be a relatively straightforward process of tracking the amount spent. How much did Meals for the Homeless spend on labor? How much was spent to acquire food? In practice, cost measurement is more complicated.

For example, suppose that a government agency agrees to reimburse Meals for the Homeless for all of its costs related to providing meals in its soup kitchens. However, the agency has made clear that it is against its policy to pay any of the costs for the counseling services that Meals provides. Suppose that Meals is organized into departments, two of which are Soup Kitchens and Counseling. The government agency is willing to reimburse all of the costs incurred by the Soup Kitchens Department but none of the costs of the Counseling Department.

Some of the costs that Meals for the Homeless incurs are clearly direct costs of the Soup Kitchens Department. For example, the amount paid to buy food and the wages of the workers who place the food onto each person's plate would be direct costs. Those direct costs would be included in the calculation of cost for reimbursement by the agency. However, Meals also incurs a number of indirect costs.

Indirect costs are more difficult to deal with. Suppose that one manager supervises both the Soup Kitchens and Counseling Departments. How much of that manager's salary should be treated as part of the cost of the Soup Kitchens Department? The part of the manager's salary that is assigned to the soup kitchen operations will be reimbursed by the agency. So the decision concerning how to assign the manager's salary is an important one. The process of assigning indirect costs is generally referred to as *cost allocation*.

Cost Allocation

Cost allocation refers to taking costs from one area or cost objective and allocating them to other areas or cost objectives. Indirect costs must be allocated to arrive at an accurate measurement of the cost of running a department or providing products or services. For example, a portion of the cost of heating and lighting the Soup Kitchens Department should be included in that department's costs.

Often this involves allocating indirect costs from some departments or cost centers to other departments or cost centers. For example, suppose that Meals has a Purchasing Department that is responsible for everything that Meals buys. This includes not only food and kitchen equipment, but also administrative and counseling equipment and supplies. The Soup Kitchens Department could not function without the services provided by Purchasing. Meals would want to allocate part of the cost of Purchasing to the Soup Kitchens Department.

To assign costs from one area to another, it is necessary that there be a *cost pool* and a *cost base*. A cost pool is any grouping of costs to be allocated. A cost base is the criterion upon which the allocation is to be made. For example, costs could be allocated based on the number of purchase orders processed. The cost pool in this example would be the costs of operating the Purchasing Department, and the cost base would be the number of purchase orders (POs) processed.

If the base is divided into the cost pool, an *overhead rate* can be calculated. For example, suppose that it costs Meals $25,000 in direct costs to run the Purchasing Department for the year and the department processes 5,000 purchase orders for the year. The $25,000 cost of the Purchasing Department is the cost pool. The 5,000 POs processed is the base.

$$\frac{\$25,000}{5,000 \text{ orders}} = \$5 \text{ per PO processed}$$

The overhead rate is therefore $5 per PO processed. Suppose that 3,000 of the purchase orders were to acquire items for the Soup Kitchens Department. Then Meals would allocate $15,000 ($5 per order × 3,000 orders) to the Soup Kitchens Department. That would become part of the cost of providing meals by the soup kitchen. From the perspective of the Soup Kitchens Department, this $15,000 is an indirect cost, but it is part of the total cost of the department.

SELECTING THE BASE FOR OVERHEAD RATES   Selecting the base to use for the allocation is an important issue. It is critical to use a base that makes sense. If a department or cost center can affect the amount of services it consumes from other departments or cost centers, then the base should relate to use.

Suppose that the Soup Kitchens Department could request that canned food be ordered daily, weekly, or monthly. The more frequently the orders are made, the more Purchasing spends to process the orders. In that case the number of purchase orders processed is a good base. The Soup Kitchens Department will be charged more if it causes Purchasing to spend more money processing orders. The Soup Kitchens Department knows that by ordering something once a month it will be assigned $5 of cost ($5 per PO × 1 order per month), whereas if it ordered that item daily it would be charged approximately $150 of cost ($5 per PO × 30 orders per month). This causes the department to act in a responsible manner in deciding how frequently to order.

In contrast, some organizations select arbitrary bases, such as the number of square feet that a cost center occupies. Suppose that the Soup Kitchen occupied half of Meals' space and the Counseling service occupied the other half. Suppose that Counseling orders almost nothing each year, whereas the Soup Kitchens Department processes many, many orders. In this simple scenario, Counseling would be charged for half of the Purchasing costs even though it did not cause much of those costs to be incurred. The result is inequitable to the Counseling Department and also does not cause the Soup Kitchens to realize the impact of placing frequent orders on the costs of running the Purchasing Department.

However, it is simpler to track how many square feet are in each cost center than it is to track which cost center was responsible for each purchase order processed. Managers must always consider whether the benefits of improved information justify the cost incurred to obtain that information.

ALLOCATION FROM SUPPORT CENTERS TO MISSION CENTERS   If Meals consisted only of Soup Kitchens, Counseling, and Purchasing Departments, the preceding discussion of cost allocation might suffice. However, most organizations have more than one cost center or department providing direct services to clients and also have more than one cost center generating indirect costs. For example, a hospital might charge patients for services from the pharmacy, the lab, radiology, operating room, and so on. And indirect or overhead costs would likely be incurred in housekeeping, maintenance, security, purchasing, and many other areas. The existence of many different departments complicates the cost allocation process.

The first thing that must be done is to classify each cost center as being either a *mission center* or a *support center*. A mission center is simply one that produces the final product or service provided by the organization. For some organizations such as health care providers, mission centers are referred to as *revenue centers*. Revenue centers often charge customers for the services they provide. Support centers are those departments or cost centers that are not mission centers. Health care providers frequently refer to support centers as *nonrevenue centers*.

All support center costs must be allocated to mission centers. That way, when the costs of providing all of the organization's products or services are tallied up, the full costs of running the organization will be measured. Consider a highly simplified example: Assume that Meals for the Homeless has just four cost centers. Two of these cost centers are mission centers: Soup Kitchens and Counseling. Two of these cost centers are support centers: Purchasing and Administration. Further assume that the government has agreed to reimburse Meals for all costs of providing meals but not for counseling. Meals must determine which of their costs appropriately belong in each mission center. Once the total costs (direct and indirect) of running the Soup Kitchens Department are determined, Meals will know how much reimbursement it can request.

To make that determination, Meals must allocate all of the costs of Purchasing and Administration to the Soup Kitchens and Counseling Departments. Figure 4-7 provides a simplified image of what this allocation attempts to do. As the arrows indicate, all of the costs of the support centers must be transferred to the mission centers.

Table 4-4 provides a simplified numerical example. As in Figure 4-7, Purchasing and Administration Departments are support centers, and the Soup Kitchens and Counseling Departments are mission centers. The "Direct Cost" column in the table shows the direct costs that were incurred in each of the four centers. The next two columns show the allocation base chosen and the proportion of the base related to each department.

Purchasing will be allocated on the basis of the number of purchase orders, and Administration will be allocated based on the number of personnel. The use of purchase

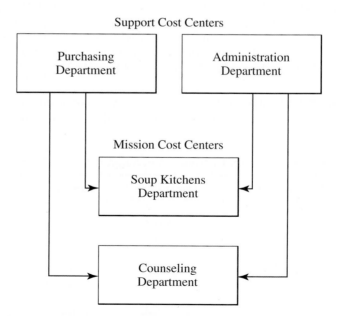

FIGURE 4-7 Direct Distribution Allocation of Support Centers

TABLE 4-4 Direct Cost and Allocation Bases

Cost Centers	Direct Cost ($)	Allocation Statistics	
		Purchasing: Purchase Orders (%)	Administration: Personnel (%)
Support			
Purchasing	25,000	—	2
Administration	280,000	95	—
Mission			
Soup Kitchens	500,000	1	92
Counseling	50,000	4	6
Total Cost	855,000	100	100

orders as a base was discussed earlier. Meals considers the primary role of administration to be supervision of employees. Therefore, the number of personnel in each department is the basis used for allocating administrative costs. Other organizations might choose a different base for allocating administrative costs.

Table 4-4 shows the percentage of all purchase orders originating from each cost center and the percentage of all employees working in each cost center. The purchase orders originating from the Purchasing Department and the number of people working in the Administrative Department cost center are excluded because no support cost center allocates its own costs to itself. If it did, it would not achieve the goal of allocating all support center costs to the mission centers because each support center would be allocating some of its costs back to its own cost center.

Table 4-4 shows that 95 percent of all purchase orders originate in Administration, 1 percent come from the Soup Kitchens, and 4 percent from Counseling. It would appear in this scenario that Administration is probably handling most of the ordering of food and other supplies used in the soup kitchens. The table also shows that 2 percent, 92 percent, and 6 percent of the Administrative cost is to be allocated to Purchasing, Soup Kitchens, and Counseling, respectively, based on the number of personnel they employ.

Several approaches can be used to allocate the costs of the support centers to the mission centers: the *direct distribution* approach, the *step-down* method, and a group of more sophisticated *multiple distribution* techniques.

DIRECT DISTRIBUTION   Table 4-5 shows an allocation of the direct costs to the mission centers. The allocation in this table is called a direct distribution. In the direct distribution

TABLE 4-5 Direct Distribution of Support Center Costs

Cost Centers	Direct Cost	Purchasing	Administration	Total
Support				
Purchasing	$ 25,000	$(25,000)	$ 0	$ 0
Administration	280,000	0	(280,000)	0
Mission				
Soup Kitchens	500,000	5,000	262,857	767,857
Counseling	50,000	20,000	17,143	87,143
Total Cost	$855,000	$ 0	$ 0	$855,000

Purchasing column: $5,000 = $25,000 × [1/(1+4)]; $20,000 = $25,000 × [4/(1+4)]
Administration column: $262,857 = $280,000 × [92/(92+6)]; $17,143 = $280,000 × [6/(92+6)]

method, support center costs are allocated only to mission centers since that is where all of the costs must ultimately wind up. However, a problem arises in trying to make the allocation. Table 4-4 shows 95 percent of all purchase orders being done for Administration, which is a support center. That leaves only 5 percent of POs done directly for mission centers (1 percent of purchase orders for the Soup Kitchens + 4 percent for Counseling). If only 5 percent of Purchasing costs are allocated, most of the costs of that cost center will not wind up in the mission centers.

This problem is resolved by allocating to the mission centers based on the relative proportion of POs processed for each mission center. Since 5 percent of the purchase orders are in all of the mission centers combined (1 percent Soup Kitchens + 4 percent Counseling), the 1 percent in the Soup Kitchens divided by the 5 percent total for the mission centers gives the proportion of the Purchasing cost allocated to the Soup Kitchens. Similarly, the 4 percent in Counseling divided by 5 percent gives the portion of the Purchasing cost allocated to Counseling; 1 percent divided by 5 percent (1/5 or 20 percent) is multiplied by the $25,000 direct Purchasing Department cost. This results in $5,000 of cost being allocated to Soup Kitchens.

Note in Table 4-5 that the Purchasing cost is reduced by $25,000 on the Purchasing line and the allocation to the mission centers increases by $5,000 and $20,000 on the mission center lines in the Purchasing column. Administration costs are allocated to mission centers in a similar fashion. Also notice that when the allocation is done, there is no cost remaining in the Purchasing or Administration cost center lines (see the "Total" column), and the total cost in the Soup Kitchens and Counseling cost centers ($767,857 and $87,143, respectively) equals the $855,000 that was the original direct cost for all four cost centers. In other words, after the cost allocation has been completed, we would say that the full costs of operating the Soup Kitchens Department is $767,857, and the full cost of operating the counseling service is $87,143. These full costs include an allocation of overhead.

The direct distribution approach fails to take into account that some support cost centers provide service to other support centers. Purchasing has primarily processed purchase orders requested by Administration. If all Purchasing costs are allocated directly to mission centers, none would be allocated to Administration and a distortion in costs might occur.

For example, note that Purchasing is primarily processing purchase orders for Administration (95 percent of POs, from Table 4-4). Suppose that most of the purchases by Administration are for food used by the Soup Kitchens Department. It would be logical for most of the Purchasing cost to be allocated to Administration and then most of Administration cost to the Soup Kitchens. However, because direct distribution does not allocate costs from some support centers to other support centers, Purchasing did not allocate to Administration, and only $5,000 of Purchasing cost was allocated to the Soup Kitchens. The bulk of the Purchasing costs, $20,000, was allocated to Counseling, which used only 4 percent of Purchasing's services. This is not a reasonable result. The potential distortions of direct distribution are so great that the method is not generally used.

THE STEP-DOWN METHOD   Instead of direct distribution, a cost allocation approach called the *step-down method* is commonly used. This approach is shown in Figure 4-8. The step-down method requires the organization to allocate all of the cost of a support cost center to all other cost centers (both mission and support). First, one support center's costs are allocated to every other cost center. Then another support center is allocated. As each center is allocated, its cost balance becomes zero, and it is no longer part of the process. In other words, no costs can be allocated to a support center once it has allocated its costs.

Note in Figure 4-8 that Purchasing would allocate costs to Administration, Soup Kitchens, and Counseling in the first step of the allocation (solid lines). In the second step, Administration allocates costs to Soup Kitchens and Counseling only (dashed lines). Therefore, some amount of distortion still remains in the allocation process, because

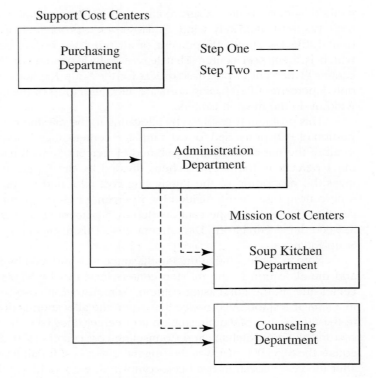

FIGURE 4-8 Step-Down Allocation of Support Centers

Administration does not allocate any of its costs to Purchasing even though Purchasing probably uses some services provided by the Administration department. If Administration and Purchasing provide services to the mission centers in different proportions, this creates a somewhat inaccurate allocation of costs.

Table 4-6 provides the results of the allocation using the step-down method. First, the $25,000 of purchasing costs are removed from Purchasing and placed in the other cost centers using the allocation statistics from Table 4-4; that is, 95 percent of the $25,000 goes into Administration, 1 percent into Soup Kitchens, and 4 percent into Counseling (all in the "Purchasing" column). The total in the "Purchasing" column is now zero, as all of the Purchasing costs have been allocated to the other three cost centers.

Next, a subtotal column is added, showing the remaining cost in each cost center. Note that the Administration costs in this subtotal column are higher than when they started because they include both the $280,000 direct costs of Administration as well as $23,750 of

TABLE 4-6 Step-Down Distribution of Support Center Costs

Cost Centers	Direct Cost	Purchasing	Subtotal	Administration	Total
Support					
Purchasing	$ 25,000	$ (25,000)	$ 0		
Administration	280,000	23,750	303,750	$(303,750)	$ 0
Mission					
Soup Kitchens	500,000	250	500,250	285,153	785,403
Counseling	50,000	1,000	51,000	18,597	69,597
Total Cost	$855,000	$ 0	$855,000	$ 0	$855,000

the Purchasing costs. This makes sense since Administration requested most of the POs. The total of the subtotal column is the full $855,000 of cost that was incurred originally as direct costs in the four cost centers combined.

The next step in the step-down is to allocate the $303,750 of Administration costs to the remaining cost centers. None of the cost will be allocated to Purchasing, since that support center has already allocated its costs. The $303,750 must therefore be allocated in a manner similar to that used in the direct distribution method. From Table 4-4, it can be seen that 92 percent of all Administration costs should be assigned to the Soup Kitchens and 6 percent to the Counseling cost center. A proportion is used, with 92 out of a total of 98 going to Soup Kitchens ($303,750 × 92/98 = $285,153) and 6 out of a total of 98 going to Counseling ($303,750 × 6/98 = $18,597). After this allocation, the total in the Administration column is zero. No costs are left in that cost center.

By adding the subtotal column together with the values in the Administration column, the total costs for each cost center can be determined. The total costs in the Soup Kitchens and Counseling rows ($785,403 and $69,597, respectively) equal the full $855,000 that Meals has spent. Notice that the result differs substantially from the direct distribution results in Table 4-5. For example, the Soup Kitchens cost found in the step-down allocation is $785,403, whereas Table 4-5 showed it as $767,857. If Meals is being reimbursed the cost for the Soup Kitchens and is not being reimbursed the cost of Counseling, the total reimbursement to be received will be approximately $17,500 higher under the more accurate step-down cost allocation.

The use of step-down does create another problem: Should Purchasing Department costs be allocated before or after Administration Department costs? The order of the allocation may affect the ultimate outcome. Table 4-7 changes the order of allocation. Administration is allocated in that table before Purchasing.

The results from Table 4-7 differ substantially from Table 4-6. For example, in Table 4-7 the costs of the Counseling Department are $91,280; they were only $69,597 in Table 4-6. Suppose that Meals did not have an arrangement to get the costs of meals reimbursed but did have an arrangement to get reimbursement from a foundation for all costs related to providing counseling services. It would be in Meals' interest to use the allocation in Table 4-7 rather than the allocation in Table 4-6 because the Counseling Department costs are calculated as being more than $20,000 higher. Therefore Meals would receive a much higher reimbursement from the foundation if it used the step-down order shown in Table 4-7 rather than the order shown in Table 4-6.

However, Table 4-6 gives a more accurate result. Recall that most of the purchase orders were processed for Administration and that Administration's efforts go largely to the Soup Kitchens cost center. In Table 4-6 it can be seen that $23,750 of the Purchasing costs are allocated to Administration in the first step. Those costs later are allocated primarily to the Soup Kitchens in the second step. However in Table 4-7, only $6,120 is being allocated

TABLE 4-7 Step-Down Distribution with Changed Order of Allocation

Cost Centers	Direct Cost	Administration	Subtotal	Purchasing	Total
Support					
Administration	$280,000	$(280,000)	$ 0		
Purchasing	25,000	5,600	30,600	$(30,600)	$ 0
Mission					
Soup Kitchens	500,000	257,600	757,600	6,120	763,720
Counseling	50,000	16,800	66,800	24,480	91,280
Total Cost	$855,000	$ 0	$855,000	$ 0	$855,000

from Purchasing to the Soup Kitchens. The resulting Soup Kitchens total cost of $763,720 is not as accurate as the cost measured in Table 4-6.

OTHER ALLOCATION APPROACHES   Other allocation approaches eliminate most or all of the cost distortion. The methods are referred to as multiple distribution techniques. Most common are the double distribution and the algebraic approaches. The latter is sometimes referred to as the reciprocal or matrix distribution approach. These rely on each support center distributing its costs to *all* centers, including both mission and support centers. These approaches greatly reduce not only distortion but also the ability to manipulate the resulting costs.

If every support center distributes costs to every other cost center, at the end of the allocation, there will still be some costs remaining in the support centers. For example, suppose that Purchasing allocated its costs to Administration, Soup Kitchens, and Counseling. At that point there is no cost in the Purchasing Department. Then Administration allocates its costs to Purchasing, Soup Kitchens, and Counseling. Now all support centers have allocated their costs, but Purchasing now has some costs that were allocated to it from Administration. This process did not achieve the goal of getting all support center costs into mission centers. Therefore, at least one more distribution must take place. The distribution process must be repeated until no costs remain in the support centers—hence the name *multiple distribution*. The double distribution method distributes all support center costs to all other cost centers in the first allocation. It then uses the step-down approach for its second and final allocation of costs. There is less distortion, but using the step-down method in the second pass still leaves some distortion and some room for manipulation of the results.

The algebraic or reciprocal approach is based on solving a set of simultaneous equations. This generates the same result as an infinite number of distributions. Under this method the percentage relationships are set up as equations. The equations can be solved simultaneously using matrix algebra and inverting the matrix of the equations. Although the allocation that results from this method is more accurate, it is more complicated to understand and implement. Step-down allocation is generally considered to be sufficient, despite its inherent limitations.

ALLOCATING COSTS TO UNITS OF SERVICE   Up to this point, the discussion has focused on allocating all costs of the organization into the cost centers that are mission centers. The next part of the cost measurement process is to assign each mission center's costs to the units of service that it provides. For example, Meals could take the total costs of the Soup Kitchens Department and divide it by the number of meals served to find the cost per meal. Counseling could take its total costs and divide them by the number of persons counseled to find the cost per person.

Activity-Based Costing and Activity-Based Management

Activity-based costing (ABC) is a process-based approach for allocating indirect or overhead costs to determine the cost of products or services. It attempts to model the production process in an effort to measure costs more accurately. ABC attempts to determine the underlying activities that cause an organization to incur costs, and then to assign costs based on the amount of each activity undertaken, rather than using an arbitrary allocation base. Activity-based management refers to using ABC information when making decisions.

To measure the costs of a product or service, we must know the direct and indirect costs of providing that product or service. Direct costs are generally considered to be easy to assign. For example, if we consume identifiable supplies to produce a specific product or service, we would directly assign the cost of those supplies to that product or service. We try to trace or track the various costs of the organization to the output it is producing.

For example, suppose that the Millbridge school system is interested in knowing the distinct costs of elementary, middle, and high school education. A third-grade classroom teacher is clearly a direct cost of the elementary school. So are the textbooks used by students in that teacher's class. In the school system's accounting records, we would track those costs directly to the category of elementary school education.

In contrast, indirect costs are generally not product or service specific, and cannot easily be directly assigned to products or services. A school system superintendent is an indirect cost of elementary school education. What part of the superintendent is devoted to elementary versus middle versus high school education? That is a difficult question to answer. Without an ABC system, indirect costs are allocated based on some general measure such as units or labor hours. For example, we might find the total number of students in the Millbridge school system at all levels, and allocate the superintendent to the various school levels based on the number of students in each level. If 30 percent of the students are in the elementary school, then 30 percent of the superintendent's salary would be assigned to the elementary school.

Whether a cost is direct or indirect often depends on the unit of analysis. Consider all government costs, and assume that school costs are part of overall government costs. Even though the superintendent is an indirect cost of elementary school education, she is a direct cost of the school system as a whole.

Consider another example. The Hospital for Ordinary Surgery has a housekeeping staff to empty wastebaskets, wash floors, etc. Is the cost of a housekeeper a direct or an indirect cost? From the perpective of the housekeeping department, a housekeeping staff member is a direct cost of providing housekeeping services, just as the third grade teacher is a direct cost of elementary school education. On the other hand, if we are trying to find out the cost of providing patient care, housekeeping staff costs are indirect. The housekeeping cost might be allocated to each patient-care department based on the number of square feet that the department occupies. If there are 100,000 square feet in total and the radiology department occupied 10,000 square feet, then it would be allocated 10 percent of the cost of housekeeping (10,000/100,000 = .10 or 10 percent). In turn, if the radiology department performed 1,000 x-rays, a patient receiving 10 x-rays would be assigned a cost that would include 1 percent of the housekeeping costs that had been charged to radiology (10 x-rays/1,000 x-rays = .01 or 1 percent).

In recent years it has become apparent that the traditional approach used to allocate indirect costs may cause distortions in determining the cost of specific products or services. Suppose that the superintendent spends 90 percent of her time dealing with problems related to the high school. The simplistic allocation based on the number of students may not generate useful information. The ABC approach aims at improving the overhead allocation process so that product and service costs are measured more accurately.

The problem with the traditional approaches to cost allocation is that many indirect costs do not vary in direct proportion with the allocation base used. For example, as noted earlier, square feet would be a poor allocation base for Purchasing Department costs. The number of purchase orders would be a better base. ABC takes this one step further. ABC questions whether the costs of the Purchasing Department really vary based on the number of purchase orders. Perhaps the costs of the Purchasing cost center vary as the result of some specific types of activities that are carried out by that cost center. The things that cause us to undertake those activities are referred to as *cost drivers*.

From the ABC perspective, the production of goods and services requires a set of activities. If we focus on the activities, we can seek to minimize the cost of, and even completely eliminate, activities that do not enhance the final product or service.

Consider an example. Suppose that a Purchasing Department spends $25,000 to process 5,000 purchase orders. The simple way to allocate the cost of the Purchasing

Department to other areas of the organization is to divide the $25,000 cost by the 5,000 purchase order volume, and assign the resulting overhead rate of $5 for each purchase order. For example, suppose that Millbridge's Purchasing Department issued 200 purchase orders to acquire supplies and equipment for the Public Works Department. Public Works would receive an overhead allocation of $1,000 as follows:

$$200 \text{ purchase orders} \times \$5 \text{ per purchase order} = \$1,000.$$

However, ABC argues that it is not simply the volume of purchase orders that accounts for the costs of running the Purchasing Department, but rather the activities involved in issuing purchase orders. Perhaps routine orders require a certain simple process of taking the purchase request, filling out a form, and mailing it. We can refer to that process as Activity A. Rush orders require Activity A, but they are also disruptive as the Purchasing Department has to drop everything to process them. After processing the rush order, purchasing clerks lose time as they find the place where they were when the rush order arrived and resume normal processing. We can call the activities related to dropping everything and then picking up where you left off, Activity B. So a rush order requires one unit of Activity A and one unit of Activity B.

Rush orders also require that items be shipped by an overnight express service. In the pre-ABC approach, these express costs might be lumped in with all other costs, and in this example would be included in the $5 per purchase order for all purchase orders. However, the amount paid for express shipping can be treated as a direct cost, and charged directly to each order that is shipped overnight, in the exact amount that it cost for that order to be shipped.

Orders over a certain dollar amount might require competitive bids. Soliciting and processing competitive bids is extremely time-consuming and costly. Those activities can be referred to as Activity C. All orders over the dollar limit for competitive bids would require one unit of Activity A and one unit of Activity C.

ABC would advocate undertaking a special study to determine the costs related to each activity. Suppose we found that Activity A consumes resources that cost $2. Assume that 4,000 purchase orders are routine. The study found that Activity B imposes $1 of cost each time it occurs. Assume that 800 purchase orders require Activity B. The study finds that Activity C, soliciting competitive bids, costs $56 because of the extensive process involved in getting competitive bids. Assume this occurs 200 times. In addition, the study might find that $3,000 of freight costs are incurred specifically for overnight shipment of rush orders, charged to Millbridge at the rate of $8 per pound. Purchasing cost center costs would then consist of the following:

Activity A	5,000	×	$ 2.00	=	$10,000
Activity B	800	×	$ 1.00	=	800
Activity C	200	×	$ 56.00	=	11,200
Express Shipping					3,000
Total					$25,000

Recall that without an ABC system, the Purchasing Department would allocate $5 per purchase order. Public Works would be charged $1,000 for their 200 purchase orders. Under ABC, however, we would examine the activities generated by Public Works a bit more closely. Suppose that the purchase orders generated as a result of Public Works Department activity consisted of 100 routine orders, 60 rush orders, and 40 orders that had to go out for competitive bidding. The Public Works rush orders had a total weight of 100 pounds. Under ABC, Public Works would be assigned $3,500 of purchasing cost as follows:

**Purchasing Department Costs Allocated
to the Public Works Department**

Activity	Cost Driver	Cost Driver Volume		Cost per Unit of Activity ($)		Public Works Purchasing Cost ($)
A	All Orders	200	×	2.00	=	400
B	Rush Orders	60	×	1.00	=	60
C	Competitive bids	40	×	56.00	=	2,240
FedEx	Weight	100	×	8.00	=	800
Total						3,500

Each of the 200 purchase orders generated for Public Works requires the normal processing that makes up Activity A. Additionally there are 60 rush orders, so we must include the extra Activity B cost related to a rush purchase. Further, 40 of the orders require the extra Activity C for orders requiring a competitive bid. Finally, Public Works is being charged for the cost of express shipment on their rush orders, at a rate of $8 per pound.

The resulting $3,500 charge is much more than the $1,000 charge under the pre-ABC system. This would indicate that Public Works orders are more likely to be rush orders or to require competitive bids than the average purchase processed for all departments. This more accurate costing creates greater equity across departments. Until now, other departments were being assigned some of the costs resulting from Public Works orders. Additionally the $3,500 allocation allows the Public Works manager to better understand the impact the Public Works Department has on overall spending. This is where activity-based management comes into play. Perhaps upon seeing the extra $60 of Activity B costs and $800 of FedEx costs, Public Works will try to reduce the number of rush orders it requests. If managers perceive that a rush order costs the same $5 as any other order, there doesn't seem to be much need to plan in advance. If the same managers find out that the 60 rush orders added an extra $860 to the costs of running the department, they might plan more carefully so that fewer rush orders are needed. In other words, not only does ABC improve the accuracy of cost measurement, which is useful for decision making and external reporting, it also provides information to help managers manage better.

Public Works can now assign all of its costs, including the Purchasing Department allocation, to its own services to generate a more accurate measure of the cost of each of its services, such as snow removal, pothole repair, and garbage collection. In turn, activity-based management uses that improved information from the ABC measurement process to make improved decisions for the organization.

REFLECTIONS ON ABC ABC is primarily viewed as a superior method for allocating overhead or indirect costs. However, it is worth examining this view a bit closer. When a product or service is produced, direct and indirect costs are incurred. Direct costs have a cause and effect relationship with the product or service we are trying to find the cost of. In other words, generating a product or service causes us to incur certain costs. If we didn't offer the product we wouldn't incur the cost. Those are direct costs. The organization also incurs other costs that are not due to producing the specific product or service. Those are indirect costs.

Consider a simple example. When Millbridge's Public Works Department plows snow, it pays the plow driver. Assume the driver is paid on an hourly basis, and would not have been paid anything if it hadn't snowed. Clearly, the driver is a cost of plowing the streets. We can assign the cost of the driver directly to snow removal on a cause and effect basis.

Even though the Public Works Department plows snow, fills potholes, and collects garbage, we don't have to use a cost allocation approach to determine the portion of the driver that related to snow removal. It is really a direct cost.

On the other hand, the mayor is an indirect cost. The salary of the mayor does not change in any way if it snows. If we wanted to allocate the mayor's salary to the various functions of the city, we could allocate some of it to plowing the streets. However, the allocation of the mayor's salary is not really the key focus of ABC because it is a true indirect cost. The mayor works for the general good of the town, and there may be no way to identify activities that will allow us to assign the mayor's time in any but an arbitrary manner to Public Works or other departments, because there is no discernible cause and effect relationship.

The key focus of ABC should be less on true indirect costs, and more on direct costs that are treated as if they were indirect. Many organizations, in their attempt to become more efficient, have streamlined their accounting systems. Rather than measuring every direct cost as a direct cost, they take shortcuts that wind up treating direct costs as if they were indirect.

For example, suppose that City Hall orders 10 boxes of paper clips for $2. The cost is 20 cents per box. The paper clips are then consumed by the mayor's office, the tax assessor's office, the city engineer's office, and so on. Does it make sense to try to measure exactly how many paper clips were used by each office? No. That measurement would cost a lot more than the paper clips. Often, we allow costs that are directly associated with a department or product or service to be allocated *as if* they were indirect costs. A pro rata share of the paper clip cost can be assigned to each department without examining how many clips were used by each department. Will this accurately assign the costs to the departments that use them? Probably not. Probably some departments use more paper clips and others use fewer. But what if we counted every single paper clip used by each department and assigned the cost directly based on the exact number of paper clips used? It would cost a lot to do that, and would probably only improve accuracy by a little bit.

However, that is not always the case. The salt that the city spreads on the streets to melt snow and ice is a direct cost of the Public Works Department. It is also a direct cost of clearing the streets of snow and ice. But it has nothing to do with garbage collection. Many governments, not-for-profit, and health care organizations extend the paper clip philosophy to a variety of direct costs. It is a type of slippery slope. Once you justify treating a very low cost direct item such as paper clips as if they were an indirect cost, the next step is to treat more and more costly direct costs as if they were overhead items.

Why would anyone do this? Because it is easier. Millbridge's Public Works Department may not bother tracking any of their supplies to any of their services. They use salt to melt snow and ice. They use blacktop to fill potholes. They use trash bags in city garbage cans. All of these supplies may be lumped together as if they were paper clips. Rather than trying to track the salt to the function of clearing the streets of snow and ice, it is easier to simply allocate the cost of Public Works supplies on some arbitrary basis—for example, one-third to snow, one-third to potholes, and one-third to garbage removal.

Is this any worse than paper clip allocations? It depends. How much is Public Works spending on supplies? Suppose that it spends $5,000,000 a year on salt, $2,000,000 on pothole filler, and $500,000 on garbage bags. The total spending on supplies is therefore $7,500,000. If those costs are treated as if they were indirect, the department would allocate $2,500,000 of cost to each area, simply by dividing supply costs by three. However, the salt is really a direct cost of snow removal. Snow removal should be charged $5,000,000 rather than $2,500,000 if we are concerned about accuracy. In contrast, the supply costs for garbage collection are allocated as $2,500,000, even though the trash bags cost only $500,000. Treating direct costs as if they were indirect, and then allocating those costs, results in inaccurate measurement of cost. The Town might decide to privatize garbage collection to save money because it thinks that it costs $2,000,000 more to collect garbage each year than it really does. This might well be the wrong decision. More accurate cost information would help the organization avoid making costly errors.

The problem is created by treating direct costs as if they were indirect, because it is easier to collect cost information if we treat the costs as if they were indirect. However, cost measurement will be most accurate if we assign direct costs directly on a cause and effect basis. But that is costly. ABC provides a middle ground. It says, "If you are not willing to assign all direct costs on a direct assignment basis, at least allocate these so-called indirect costs based on the activities that cause them to be incurred." This approach may be less costly than treating all direct costs on a direct basis. However, you should not be fooled into thinking that ABC is easy. Determination of activities that drive costs, then measurement of the amount of the activity, and ultimately allocation of costs based on activities are also time-consuming, and expensive.

The Theory of Constraints

Sometimes organizations have bottlenecks that impact on the efficiency with which they produce products or services. The theory of constraints has been developed to minimize the financial impact of such bottlenecks. Organizations employ costly resources, and bottlenecks can result in use of more resources than are necessary.

For example, suppose that a blood bank collects blood by sending a crew to various locations, such as a large employer's factory. Assume that the crew includes two people who interview potential donors to ensure their suitability for donation (e.g., they are not currently sick or on medications that would disqualify them), and six people who collect blood from donors. Over the last decade the interview process has become more detailed and time-consuming to better protect our blood supply. However, assume that the ratio of one interviewer for three technicians (techs) has not changed over time. It is possible that the techs may be waiting for donors, while donors are waiting to be interviewed. In that case, there is a bottleneck at the point where donors are interviewed. Since the techs that collect the blood are being paid an hourly wage while they are waiting for donors, clearly resources are being wasted.

The theory of constraints (TOC) focuses our attention on how to best address this bottleneck issue. Three main factors are taken into account: *throughput contribution, investment,* and *operating costs.* Throughput contribution represents the revenues less the costs of direct materials related to output. Investment represents the costs of buildings, equipment, and materials. Operating costs are the costs other than materials, (e.g., labor, rent, and utilities). The TOC attempts to increase throughput contribution while decreasing investment and operating costs. Unlike ABC, which takes a long-term perspective on cost management, TOC assumes that most operating costs are fixed, and therefore is more focused on short-term solutions.

In the blood bank example, the throughput contribution depends on the amount the blood bank charges for blood and the cost of the materials used to draw and store the blood. The investment includes not only the materials to draw and store the blood, but also the tables that donors lie on while blood is drawn and the mobile blood center van. The operating costs would include the salaries of both the interviewers and the techs.

TOC requires that the organization first be aware that bottlenecks can cost money. Then it must investigate to determine bottlenecks that exist. Finally, everything possible must be done to ensure that the production at the bottleneck is continuous, since delays at that point are costly in other areas of production. Finally, it must implement changes to improve the efficiency or the capacity at the point of the bottleneck.

Applying TOC in the blood bank example would require a thorough review of the process of blood donation. If a line of donors is waiting to donate, but the techs are standing around without donors, it is quickly apparent that a bottleneck exists. There are many possible ways to improve results. First, we want to be assured that there is no idle time at the point of the bottleneck itself. If donors are waiting in line, the donors should be efficiently moved into the interview area as soon as the interviewer is free. Interviewers should not be waiting for donors if donors are available to be interviewed.

Next, we should find ways to reduce processing time at the bottleneck. For example, we might find that donors ask a lot of questions during the interview, slowing things down. A frequently-asked-questions sheet could be distributed to donors when they first get in line, so that they have the answers to most questions by the time they reach the interview.

If possible the bottleneck should be bypassed, or only the elements at the bottleneck that are essential should be processed. For example, suppose that new donors have to answer far more questions than those who have donated blood frequently in the past. As a result, an interviewer can process a new donor in 10 minutes, but a repeat donor in 4 minutes. Perhaps whenever techs are idle, an express line can be formed for frequent donors. Another approach would be to cross-train one of the techs to perform interviews. When the bottleneck causes blood techs to wait for their next donor, the cross-trained tech can become a third interviewer until enough donors have been interviewed so that all technicians are operating at capacity. If all else fails, the interview crew could be expanded from two individuals to three.

What would be the ultimate benefit of these bottleneck changes? As a result of improved efficiency, the same number of donors can be processed with the entire team at the site for a shorter time. Or it may be that fewer potential donors will see a long line and decide not to donate. So there may be more donations of blood. Horngren et al. summarize the TOC, by noting that, "The theory of constraints emphasizes management of bottleneck operations as the key to improving the performance of production operations as a whole. It focuses on the short-run maximization of throughput contribution-revenues minus direct materials costs. . . . The short-run TOC emphasis on maximizing throughput contribution by managing bottlenecks complements the long-run strategic cost management focus of ABC."[3]

Summary

For public service organizations, an understanding of costs is essential. The better managers understand costs, the more accurate their plans will be, and the better they will be able to control spending. A solid understanding of costs improves the manager's ability to make effective decisions.

As the reader has seen in this chapter, however, costs are complicated. One focus of this chapter is on providing the reader with a solid grasp of the definitions of widely used terms such as direct costs, indirect costs, average costs, fixed costs, variable costs, and marginal costs. Another focus is on understanding how costs change as volume changes. The relationship between costs and volume has a dramatic impact on the profits or losses incurred by an organization and is critical to effective decision making.

Managers who understand the relationship between costs and volume can apply the break-even analysis technique, a tool that assists in determining the required volume level for a program or service to be financially self-sufficient.

The chapter concludes with a discussion of cost measurement. To determine the costs of products or services provided by the organization, it is necessary to allocate costs. Some responsibility center costs are allocated to other centers, and the costs of a specific responsibility center are allocated to units of service or products within that center. Methods of cost allocation, including step-down allocation and activity-based costing, are discussed.

---

[3] Charles T. Horngren, Srikant M. Datar, and George Foster. *Cost Accounting: A Managerial Emphasis,* 11th ed. Upper Saddle River, N.J.: Prentice Hall, 2003, p. 671. For further discussion on the topic, also see E. Goldratt. *The Theory of Constraints.* New York, N.Y.: North River Press, 1990; and E. Noreen, D. Smith, and J. Mackey. *The Theory of Constraints and Its Implications for Management Accounting.* New York, N.Y.: North River Press, 1995.

Preview

Chapter 5 examines issues related to capital budgeting. When organizations contemplate major, long-term acquisitions, special attention is often paid to the appropriateness of the decision. Assets with lifetimes of more than one year are often referred to as capital assets, and planning for their purchase is often referred to as capital budgeting.

Capital budgeting is an important part of the organization's planning process. Often large amounts of money are involved, mistakes can be costly, and the organization may be locked into its decision for a long period of time. In addition, it is necessary to consider the fact that money is not equally valuable when paid at different points of time. Other things being equal, money is worth more today than it is in the future. If given the choice of receiving $100 today or receiving $100 in five years, it would be financially sensible to take the $100 today. At a minimum the $100 received today could be invested for five years in a very safe investment. At the end of five years you would have $100 plus the earnings on that investment. When large amounts of money are involved, as is often the case with capital asset purchases, it is particularly important to take this time value of money into consideration. Chapter 5 addresses this issue in detail.

Key Terms from This Chapter

activity-based costing (ABC).   Cost measurement system that focuses on the activities of the organization that drive its costs.

average costs.   The *full cost* of any *cost objective* divided by the number of units of service provided.

break-even analysis.   Technique for determining the minimum volume of services or goods that a program or service must provide to be financially self-sufficient.

contribution margin.   Amount by which the price exceeds the *variable cost*. If the contribution margin is a positive number, it means that each extra unit of activity makes the organization better off by that amount.

cost allocation.   The process of taking costs from one area or *cost objective* and allocating them to others.

cost base.   The statistic used as a basis for allocation of *overhead;* for example, patient days or labor hours.

cost behavior.   The way that costs change in reaction to events within the organization.

cost center.   Unit or department in an organization for which a manager is assigned responsibility for costs.

cost driver.   An activity that causes costs to be incurred.

cost objective.   Anything in particular for which a measurement of cost is desired—for example, a unit of service, a program, department, or organization.

cost pool.   Any grouping of costs to be allocated.

direct costs.   The costs incurred within the organizational unit for which the manager has responsibility; the costs of resources for direct production of a good or service.

direct distribution.   Approach to allocating *support center* costs to *mission centers* in which costs are only allocated to mission centers.

fixed costs.   Those costs that do not change in total as the volume of service units changes over a relevant range of activity.

full cost.   The total of all costs associated with a *cost objective*. This includes *direct* and *indirect costs*.

incremental analysis.   See *marginal cost analysis*.

indirect costs.   Costs that are assigned to an organizational unit from elsewhere in the organization; costs of resources that are not used for direct production of a good or service.

investment.   As used in the theory of constraints, represents the costs of buildings, equipment, and materials.

make or buy.   The decision to produce goods or services versus purchasing them from an outside provider.

margin of safety.   The amount by which expected volume or revenues exceed the volume level or revenues required to break even.

marginal cost analysis.   Use of *marginal costs* for assessing the impact of a decision on the organization.

marginal costs.   The extra costs incurred as a result of providing one more service unit (such as one more meal).

mission center.   A cost center that produces the final product or service provided by the organization.

mixed costs.   Costs that contain both *fixed* and *variable cost* elements.

multiple distribution.   *Cost allocation* approach in which all *support centers* are allocated to all other support and *mission centers* in a first distribution and then the remaining costs in the support centers are allocated through one or more additional distributions.

nonrevenue center.   See *support center.*

operating costs.   As used in the theory of constraints, represents costs other than materials (e.g., labor, rent, and utilities).

opportunity cost.   A measure of cost based on the value of the alternatives that are given up in order to use the resource for the specified purpose.

out-of-pocket analysis.   See *marginal cost analysis.*

outsourcing.   Purchasing goods or services from an outsider provider rather than producing them within the organization.

overhead.   *Indirect costs.*

overhead rate.   The *cost base* divided into the *cost pool.*

relevant costing.   See *marginal cost analysis.*

relevant range.   The normal range of expected activity for the *cost center* or organization.

revenue center.   See *mission center.*

step-down method.   Approach to allocating *support center* costs in which each support center is allocated to every other center (both support and mission) that has not yet allocated its costs.

step-fixed costs.   Costs that are fixed over ranges of activity that are less than the *relevant range.*

step-variable costs.   See *step-fixed cost.*

support center.   *Cost centers* that are not *mission centers.*

throughput contribution.   Revenues less the costs of direct materials related to output.

variable costs.   Those costs that vary directly with changes in the volume of service units over a *relevant range* of activity.

Questions for Discussion

4-1. What is a "cost objective"?

4-2. Distinguish among full, direct, and indirect costs.

4-3. Distinguish among average, fixed, and variable costs.

4-4. What are marginal costs?

4-5. What are several reasons that a financial manager says "it depends" rather than directly answering a question about how much something costs?

4-6. What are some direct and indirect costs of elementary school education? Clearly specify your cost objective.

4-7. Why is the relevant range the key to the difference between variable and marginal costs?

4-8. What is an allocation base, and how is it used in setting allocation rates?

4-9. What is the focus of ABC (activity-based costing)?

4-10. What approach should be taken in evaluating make-or-buy decisions? That is, should an organization provide a service itself, or outsource it to another organization?

4-11. What can a manager do if a break-even analysis indicates that a venture will lose money?

Problems

4-12. Camp Hole-in-the-Wall provides children with chronic medical conditions with one-week summer vacations. The Camp owns a 500-acre facility in the Berkshire Mountains where it brings the kids. The annual depreciation expense for the camp is $100,000. The Camp hires one counselor for every ten campers. It also employs a full-time doctor, nurse, two cooks and a camp director. It costs $75 per week to feed each camper and an additional $30 round trip to transport them to and from the camp. Which of the camp's expenses are:

a. fixed

b. step-fixed or semi-variable costs

c. variable

d. not included in the camp's cash budget

4-13. Relevant costs are those that change because of the action being considered or undertaken by an organization. Which of the following factors should be considered when determining which costs are relevant in a decision to expand an after-school reading program for neighborhood children?
a. the mission of the organization
b. the number of children that will be added to the program
c. the impact of adding the children on the quality of the program
d. the impact of adding the children to the existing facility
e. all of the above

4-14. Marginal costs are not equal to variable costs when: (indicate all that apply)
a. the time frame for a decision is more than one year
b. there is a change in fixed costs
c. there is excess capacity
d. some costs are outside an organizational unit making the decision

4-15. Answer the following questions about the break-even analysis.

1. New City Day Care Center operates from Monday to Friday. It has fixed expenses of $5,000 per week and charges each child that attends the program $15 per day. It costs the center $5 per day for supplies and snacks for each child. How many children have to come to the center each day for it to break even?
2. If the center gets a contribution of $1,000 per week, its break-even point (choose the correct answer)
   a. increases
   b. decreases
   c. stays the same

4-16. Doctors Without Borders (DWB) operates health programs around the world. It has a central staff of 100 people who administer its worldwide programs. DWB's central operation buys and distributes all of the supplies used in its various country operations. DWB's country director for Afghanistan and her staff run 20 clinics around the country. At the clinic level, doctors and nurses hired under two-year fixed contracts administer medical treatment free of charge to the local population using supplies shipped to them by DWB's central staff.

1. From the perspective of the program director for Afghanistan, which of the program's expenses are: (Write the general category of the expenses next to the categories below.)
   a. direct
   b. indirect
   c. fixed
   d. variable

2. Which of the direct expenses for Afghanistan would be classified as indirect from the perspective of a clinic director?

4-17. When determining costs, which of the following factors will not be taken into account?
a. The cost objective
b. The relevant time period
c. The relevant range of volume
d. Who is measuring the cost
e. Whether the person asking the question is inside or outside the organization

4-18. You are the finance director for faculty research at Big and Prestigious University (BPU). The research division has an administrative staff that is responsible for managing the administrative aspects of all of BPU's research grants. Faculty research is carried out in a dedicated research building that is divided into twenty specialized laboratories. Grants are expected to pay for a share of the building expenses as well as the cost of the portion of the laboratory they use. When a grant is awarded, a faculty researcher is paid to manage the project and she hires graduate assistants to work on the grant. Faculty researchers and research assistants are paid fixed amounts for their work on a grant. In general, carrying out the research funded by a grant also requires the use of supplies.

1. If you are trying to measure the costs associated with one specific grant, which of the grant expenses would be considered to be:
   a. direct
   b. indirect
   c. fixed
   d. variable
2. The thing we are trying to find the cost of is referred to as the _____.

4-19. When determining costs, which of the following factors will be taken into account?
a. The relevant time period
b. The relevant range of volume
c. Who is measuring the cost
d. Whether the person asking the question is inside or outside the organization

4-20. Consider the cost of service delivery for a public service organization. Match the correct term with its definition below:
a. Average Cost
b. Full Cost
c. Marginal Cost

1. The direct cost and the indirect cost of service delivery equals its:
2. The total cost of service delivery divided by the total units of service delivered equals its:
3. The cost of the last unit of service delivered equals its:

4-21. Select the best available answer to fill the blank.

1. The We Give Gifts Foundation's accounting manager prepares reports about the Foundation's grant making, investments, and general administrative activities. The cost of her salary and fringe benefits would be included as part of the _____ of its investment management activity.

   a. direct cost
   b. indirect cost
   c. variable cost

2. The We Give Gifts Foundation pays Beta Capital Management a fee for managing a portion of its $83 million investment in stocks and bonds. The cost of this fee would be included as part of the _____ of its investment management activity.
   a. direct cost
   b. indirect cost
   c. variable cost

4-22. Select the best choice from the following to answer questions 1 and 2:

1. An increase in the level of service volume will have the following effects:
   a. Increase unit variable cost and decrease unit fixed cost
   b. Unit variable cost remains constant and unit fixed cost remains constant
   c. Decrease unit variable cost and unit fixed cost remains constant
   d. Unit variable cost remains constant and unit fixed costs decrease

2. Which one of the following is a name for the range of service volume over which an organization expects to operate?
   a. Mixed range
   b. Fixed range
   c. Variable range
   d. Relevant range

4-23. Select from the following to answer questions 1 through 3:
   a. zero-based
   b. formula
   c. operating
   d. accrual
   e. capital
   f. flexible

1. To test a budget for the impact of changes in forecasted service volume on revenue and expenses, you would use a(n) _____ budget.

2. A(n) _____ budget represents forecasts of revenue and support earned and resources used during a fiscal year.

3. Decision packages are normally associated with a(n) _____ budget.

4-24. If the contribution margin for Independent Lab stays constant and their fixed costs increase from $8,000 to $12,000, then the Lab's break-even quantity _____?
   a. increases
   b. decreases
   c. stays the same

4-25. To break even, an organization's _____ must equal its _____.
   a. total revenues, fixed costs
   b. total revenues, variable costs
   c. total revenues, total costs
   d. total revenues, total support

4-26. Answer the following questions about break-even analysis.

1. Break-even is defined as the point at which _____ equals _____.

2. The contribution margin is equal to _____ minus _____.

3. The Local Town Concert Band has fixed costs of $500 per concert and variable costs of $2.00 per person who attends the concert. If they raise their ticket price from $2.25 to $2.50, their break-even level:
   a. increases
   b. decreases
   c. stays the same

4-27. Answer the following questions regarding break-even analysis:

1. The marginal contribution or contribution margin is the difference between _____ and _____.

2. The Campaign for Better Politicians expects to have $5,000 in fixed costs. If their fixed costs do not change but the amount of money each marcher raises through pledges (price/unit) declines from $75 to $60 and their variable cost/unit increases from $40 to $50, their break-even quantity will:
   a. increase
   b. decrease
   c. stay the same

4-28. If all other factors remain unchanged, an increase in the variable cost per unit of service will:
   a. reduce the break-even volume of service.
   b. reduce the contribution margin per unit of service.
   c. increase total fixed costs.

4-29. Answer the following questions regarding break-even analysis:

1. The difference between marginal revenue and marginal cost is called the _____.

2. If an organization sells ten fewer tickets to its annual gala than are needed to break even, the gala will produce:

a. a loss or deficit
b. break-even results
c. a profit or surplus

4-30. Keepingyourhealth Clinic had annual total costs of $2,000,000 at a volume of 10,000. The fixed costs for the year were $1,600,000.

1. What are the total variable costs for the year?
2. What would the total costs be if the volume increased by 10 percent?

4-31. Millbridge Family Services (MFS) currently operates a foster care program that is fully funded by the state. Changing government priorities are expected to result in a 20 percent reduction in its state foster care funding for the upcoming fiscal year. MFS's management is considering eliminating the foster care program in the next fiscal year in light of these anticipated funding cuts. The total foster care program expenses for the upcoming fiscal year is $120,000. The foster care program's budgeted expenses include $25,000 of salaries and occupancy costs that are allocated to its program budget from MFS central administration. These allocated expenses of $25,000 are unavoidable even if the foster care program is eliminated. What is the total relevant cost that should be considered in making this decision?

4-32. Hudson University has just received a proposal from Speak and Tell (S&T), a New York public relations firm. Under the terms of the proposal, S&T has offered to meet all of the university's external media relations needs at a fixed cost of $750,000 per year.

These activities are currently performed by Hudson staff. The expenses associated with the media relations department during the current year were as follows

Staff Salaries: $650,000 including a senior staff member who is paid $80,000 and who will remain on staff to oversee the university's interests in dealings with the public relations firm. All other staff would be let go. The university incurs additional costs for health care and other benefits at a rate of 30 percent of staff salaries.

Fixed Equipment: The computers and media equipment in the department were purchased four year ago. They cannot be used by any other department at Hudson and cannot be sold. Depreciation expenses from the equipment are $20,000 per year. The net book value of the equipment is $60,000.

Printing Costs: If the university contracts out it will no longer have to print external media documents, which cost $150,000 this year.

1. Which of the costs listed above should be included in Hudson's consideration of the proposal? Why should they be included?

2. Based solely on financial considerations, should Hudson accept the contract? Why?

4-33. The Center for Baseball Art (CPA) is thinking about bringing a new Johan Santana exhibit to the Center. It will cost the center $30,000 to bring the exhibit to town, an additional $13,000 to install it, and $5,000 for an insurance policy. The manager of the center thinks that she can charge $12 per person to see the exhibit; she estimates that 300 people per day will come to see the exhibit. If the total costs for security, extra power, and added custodial services are $1,600 per day, how many days will the exhibit need to be at the center in order to cover the costs?

4-34. Millbridge Memorial Hospital provides comprehensive physical exams. The charge per exam is $100, while the variable cost per exam is $65. Thirty percent of the patients that come in for exams are private pay. They must pay the full charge. Seventy percent of the patients are covered by an insurance company that has an agreement with the clinic that reduces the charge by 20 percent. The clinic has $210,000 in fixed costs per year. How many exams must the clinic provide in order to break even?

4-35. The fixed costs of running a fund-raising dinner for Meals for the Homeless are $10,000 and the variable costs are $75 per attendee. The facility where the event is being held can accommodate 500 people. Answer the following questions about the event:

1. If Meals charged $275 per ticket, how many people would have to attend the gala for the organization to break even on the event?
2. If Meals charged $300 per ticket, the contribution margin from each ticket sold would be:

_____.

3. If 500 people attend the event, how much does the organization have to charge each attendee to earn a profit of $100,000? (Assume costs from original problem are still in effect.)

4-36. Millbridge Animal Protective Services (MAPS) is planning its spring awards dinner as a fund-raising event. It is planning to charge each attendee $150. Feast Hall, the site of the dinner, will charge MAPS $5,000 for the use of its posh VIP Room and $50 per plate for food. The VIP Room has a capacity of 180 people. Rocky Mount and the Tar Heels (one band) will provide the entertainment for their standard performance fee of $1,000 per night.

1. How many people would need to attend in order for MAPS to break even?
2. If MAPS sells 100 tickets for the dinner, what is the average cost to MAPS for each person with a ticket?

4-37. The Children's Museum of Millbridge is considering catering birthday parties for members as a way to generate additional revenue.

The costs associated with each party are:

Staff	$90
Cake and Food	$60
Decorations	$30
In addition, party favors are $5 per child.	

1. Find the break-even price per child assuming that 12 children attend each party.
2. The Museum expects to make a profit of $300 on every party. Find the price per child to break even and produce the $300 profit on every party (again assume 12 children each party).

4-38. The Millbridge Fine Arts Museum (MFAM) is thinking about bringing a Van Gogh exhibit to Millbridge for 30 days. MFAM expects 2,000 people per day to visit the exhibit, each paying the $10 entrance fee. Daily costs for security, extra power, and added custodial services will be $1,000. What is the maximum amount that MFAM can afford to spend on fixed costs, such as organizing and bringing the exhibit to town, and still break even? Hint: "break-even quantity" in this problem is measured in days.

4-39. Answer the following questions about break-even analysis.

1. Millbridge Day Care Center operates from Monday to Friday. It has fixed expenses of $18,000 per week and charges each child that attends the program $300 per week. It costs the center $30 per week for supplies and snacks for each child. How many children have to come to the center each day for it to break even?
2. If the center gets a rent increase of $1,000 per week, its break-even point: (circle the correct answer)
   a. increases
   b. decreases
   c. stays the same

4-40. Kids Early Start (KES) operates from Monday to Friday. KES provides childcare and educational services for inner-city kids between the ages of three months and five years. It has fixed expenses of $36,000 per week and charges parents $10 per day for each child that attends the program. A city contract pays the center $30,000 per week. It costs KES $3 per day for supplies and snacks for each child. KES also offers an optional early-reading program for children over the age of three. Parents pay an additional $3 per day to enroll a child in the reading program. It costs the center an additional $5 per day for each child in

the program. Thirty percent of the children attending the center are enrolled in the reading program.

1. How many whole children have to come to KES each week for it to break even?
2. If the percentage of children in the reading program rises from 30 percent to 35 percent, the break-even level:
   a. increases
   b. decreases
   c. stays the same

4-41. The Walk for the Cure is an annual fund-raising event that raises money for research on children's blood disorders. The Walk costs $100,000 to stage even if nobody shows up. To encourage people to participate, each walker is given a T-shirt that costs the Walk $5.00 and refreshments that cost an average of $10 per person. This year, the organizers of the walk got a $25,000 grant from the City Foundation to offset part of the costs associated with staging the Walk. The Walk raises money by asking each walker to pay $5 to register and requires each walker to solicit sponsors who agree to pay $.50 (fifty cents) per mile for each of the ten miles that the walker completes. In the past, all of the walkers have completed the ten-mile course and have had an average of 15 sponsors.

1. How many whole walkers have to participate in the Walk for the event to at least break even?
2. If the cost of refreshments per walker increases from $10 to $11, the break-even number of walkers will:
   a. increase
   b. decrease
   c. stay the same

4-42. PPO of Millbridge Township (PPOMT) sells health benefit plans to local employers. The organization charges its clients (local employers) $50 for each office visit provided to a covered employee. PPOMT contracts with individual physicians to provide the office visits to its health plan beneficiaries. The organization pays its contracted physicians a fee of $40 for each new patient visit and $30 for each follow-up office visit. Twenty percent of all office visits are new patient visits. PPOMT maintains an office building where all routine office visits are conducted. The organization pays $6,000 in occupancy expenses each month for the building. PPOMT also incurs monthly staffing costs of $12,000 for maintenance and administrative staff at its facility.

1. How many office visits must PPOMT deliver to break even?
2. Assuming that PPOMT's facility is open 21 days in a typical month, how much profit will it earn if each of its five contracted physicians sees an average of 12 patients each day?

4-43. The Millbridge High School Student Association (MHSSA) is planning a fund-raising event for the spring semester. The MHSSA is planning to hire the Dizzy Gillespie Heritage Band as entertainment for a fee of $750. The Fine Arts Museum was selected as the site for the event. The museum will charge the MHSSA $600 for the use of its banquet room. Good Eats Restaurant was selected to cater the event. Good Eats will charge the MHSSA a flat fee of $400 and a $20 per meal charge.

1. The MHSSA expects 250 students and alumni to attend its spring fund-raising event. What is the minimum (break-even) ticket price for the event?
2. The MHSSA is considering two ticket prices, a $25 price for students and a $75 price for alumni. If three students are expected to attend the event for each alumni, how many students and alumni must attend the spring fund-raising event if it is to break even?

4-44. A Greener World expects to have $25,000 in fixed costs. If their fixed costs do not change but the amount each marcher raises through pledges declines from $75 to $65 and their variable cost/unit increases from $35 to $40, how much will their break-even quantity increase?

4-45. You are given the following information about We-Save-Um Animal Rescue (WSU):

Number of dogs rescued and placed by WSU—600
Average length of stay for a dog—10 days
Daily cost of feeding one dog—$.90
Number of veterinary visits per dog—1.2
Cost per veterinary visit—$35
Cost of spay/neuter and transportation per dog rescued—$45
Cost of the kennel and related equipment—$300,000
Useful life of the kennel and related equipment—20 years
WSU uses straight-line depreciation.
Salvage value of the kennel and related equipment—$0

WSU has three full time employees. An executive director, who earns $40,000 per year, an evaluator/trainer, who earns $30,000 per year, and a kennel manager, who earns $25,000. Fringe benefits are equal to 25 percent of each employee's annual salary.

WSU expects to place all of the dogs that it takes into the program by the last day of the fiscal year. It charges an adoption fee of $225 per dog. Experience has shown that 15 percent of the people elect to make an additional donation to WSU at the time of adoption. Historically, these extra donations have averaged $200. In addition, WSU has an active fund-raising program and expects to raise $40,000 in donations during the fiscal year.

The executive director wants to know how many dogs she has to place next year to break even. Calculate WSU's break-even.

4-46. The Stick-em-Quick Inoculations Center provides early childhood checkups and vaccinations for children in the South Bronx. It pays annual rent of $25,000 and has a permanent staff consisting of a nurse practitioner and an administrative assistant who are paid $125,000 per year. The center hires doctors on a per-diem basis to provide exams and uses $15.00 worth of supplies for each exam not including vaccines. Inoculation appointments are scheduled in advance and the Center needs one per-diem doctor for every 100 children they have scheduled on any given day. It also spends $7.50 per child for the vaccines used in its inoculations program. Which of Stick-em's expenses are:
a. fixed
b. step-fixed or semi-variable costs
c. variable

4-47. Answer the following questions about costs:

1. Whether a cost is considered to be a direct or indirect cost depends on: (select the best choice):
a. the cost objective
b. who is doing the analysis
c. the time frame for the analysis
d. whether costs are inside or outside an organizational unit
e. the expected range of volume
2. If you are trying to determine the cost of the third grade classes in an elementary school, the principal's salary is:
a. direct and fixed
b. indirect and fixed
c. direct and variable
d. indirect and variable

4-48. Answer the following questions about break-even analysis.

1. Break-even analysis for multiple products requires a _____ approach.
2. The contribution margin must be a positive number for the organization to have any chance of having a _____.
3. The NYU Concert Band has fixed costs of $200 per concert and variable costs of $1.00 per person who attends the concert. If they raise their ticket price from $1.25 to $1.50, their break-even level:
a. increases
b. decreases
c. stays the same

4-49. Jamestown Clinic had the fixed and variable costs shown on the top of the next page.
a. What are the fixed, variable, total, and average costs per patient for volumes of 100, 500, 1,500, 2,500, and 3,000?

Variable Costs (VC) per Patient		Fixed Costs per Year	
Personnel	$150	Rent	$100,000
Supplies	20	Administration	120,000
Laundry	30	Other	80,000
Other	50		
Total VC/Patient	$250	Total Fixed	$300,000

b. Draw a graph of the average cost per patient. Plot cost on the vertical axis, and the number of patients on the horizontal axis.

c. An outside organization, such as a health maintenance organization, offers to send Jamestown 500 patients per year but only offers to pay $300 for each one. Should the hospital agree to this arrangement? It currently has 2,500 patients per year and can easily handle 3,000.

4-50. The Helensville Symphony incurs $2,400,000 of fixed cost each year. The variable cost for each person attending one of the orchestra's performances is only $5. If the average charge for a ticket to attend a performance of the Helensville Symphony is $75, how many tickets must it sell each year to break even?

4-51. Millbridge Township provides a variety of summer recreation alternatives. You can belong to the town pool, play tennis, or play golf. Summer passes allowing residents to use these facilities are sold each year. One quarter of the season passes that are purchased are golf passes, 35 percent are for tennis, and the rest are for the pool. The golf passes are $30, the tennis passes are $50, and the pool passes are $70. The cost of providing these services is mostly fixed, with a $3 variable cost per pass, regardless of type. The fixed cost of operating the summer recreation program is $250,000. How many people must buy recreation passes for the town to break even? How many passes would be sold for the pool at that break-even volume?

4-52. Calabrese City allocates some indirect or overhead costs to each of its police stations. The city charges each station for common services such as the city food service and for administrative services such as payroll. For the coming year, the Washington Square Police Station will have a total budget allocation of $1,400,000. That will be its only revenue. All direct and indirect charges have to be paid from that budgeted amount.

Each police station must pay $100,000 for processing its payroll. In addition, once arrests are made, the prisoners spend a day or two in the local police station, where the city must feed them. On average, the City Food Service charges each police station $40 for meal service for each arrest.

The station would like to maximize its number of arrests to reduce the number of criminals on the street. However, more arrests require not only more food, but also more police officers.

The personnel employed by the Washington Square Station are supervisors, desk clerks, and police officers. The minimum staffing levels based on total budgeted arrests are as follows:

Annual Number of Arrests	Police Officers	Desk Clerks	Supervisors
0–1,000	11	6	2
1,001–2,000	12	6	2
2,001–3,000	12	7	2
3,001–4,000	13	8	3

Annual salaries for each class of employee follow: supervising officers, $68,500; desk clerks, $59,000; and police officers, $54,000. Note that this police station cannot process more than 4,000 arrests per year.

Calculate the maximum number of arrests that Washington Square can budget and still expect to break even for the coming year.

4-53. Review Father Purtell's Special Purpose Budget in Chapter 2. Determine which costs are fixed and which are variable. Assume that a $10,000 subsidy is available from the two parishes. How many teens are needed for the trip to break even? What is the contribution margin per teen above that break-even point? What complicating issues exist?

4-54. The New City Subway has 40,000 passengers every day. However, they are fairly price sensitive. If the current price of $2 were to increase to $2.50, it is likely that there would only be 30,000 passengers each day. On the other hand, if the price were to drop to $1.50, the ridership would increase to 50,000. The variable costs are only 8 cents per passenger. The fixed costs of operating the subway are $70,000 per day. How many passengers are needed each day to break even at the current $2 price?

Prepare a flexible budget for the subway system at prices of $1.50, $2.00, and $2.50. (Refer to Chapter 3 for a discussion of flexible budgets.)

Considering only the financial implications, what should be done? Why? How can you reconcile the results of the flexible budget with the results of the break-even calculation?

4-55. Millbridge Ambulance Service has been considering consolidating their three locations into just two locations. The location they are considering closing currently costs $155,000 to operate. If the location is closed, the ambulances from that location would be moved to the other two locations. The savings from the closure would be partially offset by increased expenses at the two remaining locations. Millbridge will lose $40,000 of state subsidy if they close the location. They only want to close the location if the closure results in an overall financial improvement. The current costs of the location are as follows:

Salaries of Staff	$80,000
Rent	20,000
Repairs and Maintenance	10,000
General and Administrative	20,000
Supplies	25,000
Total	$155,000

The general and administrative expenses of $20,000 are an allocation of costs from the central office. The costs of the central office are not affected by the existence of the specific locations. If the location is closed, the staff would be transferred to the other two locations, and the lease will be canceled, so there will be no rent or repairs and maintenance. While they won't purchase supplies for this location, the supply cost of the other two locations will rise by $20,000. What should Millbridge do?

4-56. The Millbridge tax collector's office spent $32,000 in the first quarter of the year, during which they processed 8,000 tax bills. It took a total of 1,000 hours of clerical time to process the tax bills. What are two possible allocation bases and rates?

4-57. Mr. Robbins's detailed medical records indicated that a total of 20 labor hours were directly used in providing his care. The cost of the labor was $380. It was expected before the beginning of the year that a total of 90,000 direct labor hours would be consumed by the health care organization's patients, at a cost of $1,350,000. The total overhead to be allocated to patients was expected to be $810,000.

Determine the overhead to be assigned to Mr. Robbins based on the data given above. Solve this problem two ways: First, assign overhead on a basis of direct labor hours; and second, assign overhead on the basis of direct labor cost. Why might your results differ?

4-58. Use the information in the table at the bottom of this page to allocate costs to the mission centers using the direct distribution method.

4-59. Using the information from Problem 4-58, allocate the costs using the step-down method. Compare the results with Problem 4-58. Do they differ?

4-60. Using the information from Problem 4-58, allocate the costs using the step-down method, but change the order of step-down from that used when you solved Problem 4-59. Do your results differ from those you found in Problem 4-59?

4-61. Jump Hospital currently allocates all maintenance department costs based on departmental square feet. However, the manager of the pharmacy department has suggested that an ABC approach be used for the portion of the maintenance department costs that relate to repairing equipment. Her contention is that the pharmacy has relatively little equipment that breaks. However, it must subsidize many high-tech departments that require expensive equipment repairs. Using the data at the top of the next page, calculate the maintenance cost assigned to the pharmacy using the existing method and using an ABC approach.

Allocation Statistics

Cost Centers	Direct Cost ($)	Purchasing: Purchase Orders (%)	Administration: Total Salaries (%)
Support			
Purchasing	80,000	—	5
Administration	40,000	15	—
Mission			
Soup Kitchens	900,000	40	90
Counseling	300,000	45	5
Total Cost	1,320,000	100	100

	Maintenance Costs		
	Routine Maintenance	**Repairs**	**Total**
Volume (Square Feet)	100,000	800	
Labor Hours	10,000	4,000	14,000
Labor Cost/Hour	$ 12.00	$ 18.00	$ 13.71
Supplies	$ 20,000	$ 80,000	$ 100,000
Administration			$ 15,000

	Department Information		
	Pharmacy	**All Other Departments**	**Total**
Square Feet	2,000	98,000	100,000
Volume of Repairs	3	797	800
Hours of Repairs	6	3,994	4,000
Supplies Used for Repairs	$ 200	$79,800	$80,000

CASE STUDY
Mead Meals on Wheels Center—Part I[4]

You may make whatever assumptions you think are necessary. Be sure to state every assumption *explicitly*.

Problem 1

The Mead Meals on Wheels Center (MMWC) provides two meals per day to the homebound elderly. The Town of Millbridge pays MMWC $32 per week for each person it services for the week. Each person receives 14 meals for the week. There is no shortage of demand for MMWC's services among the elderly citizens of Millbridge and MMWC can find qualified recipients for as many meals as it can deliver.

To service the contract, MMWC has a central kitchen which can produce a maximum of 9,600 meals per day. It costs MMWC an average of $36,000 per week to operate the kitchen and MMWC's other central facilities regardless of the number of meals that MMWC serves. This covers *all* of MMWC's fixed costs (i.e., rent, equipment costs, and its personnel including administrative staff) as well as its fixed contract costs (e.g., utilities, snow removal).

The first problem that MMWC faces is figuring out how much it can afford to spend per person, per week for food to supply the program. Food is MMWC's *only* variable expense. You are MMWC's only financial analyst and your boss has asked you to decide what to do.

Executive Director Marty Purtell has asked you to calculate how much MMWC can spend per week per person on food and still break even. What do you tell her?

Problem 2

Using your work to define MMWC's spending limit, the executive director prepared a request for bids and sent it to all of the food purveyors in and near Millbridge. The best bid came in at $.50 below the number that you have calculated as MMWC's break-even per person-week.

---

[4] Mead Meals on Wheels Center and its solution were written by Robert Purtell, Robert F. Wagner Graduate School of Public Service, New York University. Reprinted with permission. Part II appears at the end of Chapter 5.

Using this bid and the information given in the preceding problem, the director wants you to prepare a budget for MMWC in a format that will allow her to monitor MMWC's performance on a quarterly basis for the coming year.

For budgeting, the director has told you to assume that there are 13 weeks in each quarter. You know from your experience that the fixed expenses for the organization vary by season. Fixed costs average $38,000 per week in the winter (first quarter), $34,000 per week in the second quarter, $35,000 in the third quarter, and $37,000 in the fourth quarter.

Prepare an operating budget for the next four quarters of operation for the director and summarize it (provide totals) for the full year.

Suggested Readings

Atkinson, Anthony A., Robert S. Kaplan, Ella Mae Matsumura, and S. Mark Young. *Management Accounting,* 5th ed. Upper Saddle River, N.J.: Prentice Hall, 2007.

Bland, Robert L., and Irene Rubin. *Budgeting: A Guide for Local Government.* Washington, D.C.: International City/County Management Association, 1997.

Finkler, Steven A., and Mary L. McHugh. *Budgeting Concepts for Nurse Managers,* 4th ed. St. Louis, Mo.: Saunders/Elsevier, 2008.

Hyde, Albert C. *Government Budgeting: Theory, Process, Politics,* 3rd ed. Belmont, Ca.: Wadsworth/Thomson Learning, 2002.

Lee Jr., Robert D., Ronald W. Johnson, and Philip G. Joyce. *Public Budgeting Systems,* 8th ed. Sudbury, Mass.: Jones and Bartlett Publishers, 2007.

Mikesell, John L. *Fiscal Administration—Analysis and Applications for the Public Sector,* 7th ed. Belmont, Ca.: Thomson Wadsworth, 2006.

Nice, David. *Public Budgeting.* Belmont, Ca.: Wadsworth/ Thomson Learning, 2002.

Rosen, Harvey S. *The Fiscal Behavior of State and Local Governments,* Studies in Fiscal Federalism and State-Local Finance Series. Northampton, Mass.: Edward Elgar Publishing, 1997.

Rubin, Irene S. *Class, Tax, and Power: Municipal Budgeting in the United States.* Chatham, N.J.: Chatham House Publishers, 1998.

_____. *The Politics of Public Budgeting: Getting and Spending, Borrowing and Balancing,* 5th ed. Chatham, N.J.: Chatham House Publishers, 2006.

APPENDIX 4-A

Additional Break-Even Analysis Issues

This appendix addresses the issue of break-even for multiple products with multiple prices, raises the issue of target-profit analysis, and considers two-tier pricing models.

BREAK-EVEN WITH MULTIPLE PRODUCTS EXTENDED

In Chapter 4, the problem of break-even analysis for multiple products was considered. An example for the Feed-a-Child Foundation was given in which there were three different programs. It was necessary to calculate a weighted average contribution margin (see Table 4-3) and use that weighted average contribution margin when solving for the break-even point. In many cases there are not only multiple products, but also different prices and/or variable costs for each product. How can that problem be addressed?

Reconsider the problem of the Feed-a-Child Foundation. Still assume that there are three programs: Africa, Asia, and South America. However, now assume that there is more than one level of donation for each program. Although the program appeals are based on feeding one child for one year for a set amount, some people may make larger or smaller donations. The method would still work in the same way. It would be possible to list each donation amount for each program as a separate item, estimate the percent of donations in that amount, and calculate a weighted average.

For example, assume no change in the South America and Asia programs, but assume that half of all Africa program donations are in the amount of

$36, 30 percent in the amount of $50, and 20 percent in the amount of $100. The contribution margin by program and donation size would be as shown in Table 4-A-1. Note that there are five different classes of donation, shown in the table as a, b, c, d, and e.

To use the individual contribution margins from Table 4-A-1 to calculate an overall weighted average contribution margin, it is necessary to know the percentage of total contributions that each donation makes up. The Africa program is expected to receive 70 percent of all donations to the foundation. It is also known that 30 percent of the Africa donations are type b donations for $50. Then 21 percent of the donations to the foundation are to the Africa program in the amount of $50 (70% × 30% = 21%). Table 4-A-2 shows this calculation for each type of donation. The resulting percentages in the right-hand column can then be used in Table 4-A-3 to calculate the weighted average contribution margin.

The weighted average contribution margin of $18.45 (Table 4-A-3) can be used to determine the number of donations needed to break even:

$$BEQ = \frac{FC}{CM}$$

$$BEQ = \frac{\$100,000}{\$18.45}$$

$$= 5,420$$

If the revenues, expenses, and relative proportion of donations by type can be projected, it does not matter how many products, services, or programs

TABLE 4-A-1 Contribution Margin by Program and Donation Size			
	Donation (A)	Variable Cost (B)	Contribution Margin (C = A − B)
a. Africa	$ 36	$32	$ 4
b. Africa	50	32	18
c. Africa	100	32	68
d. Asia	40	29	11
e. South America	50	30	20

TABLE 4-A-2 Calculation of Percentage of Donations by Program and Contribution Size

Program and Donation Size		Program's Percentage of Foundation Donations		Portion of all Donations to This Program Based on Size		Percentage of All Donations to the Foundation
a. Africa	$36	70%	×	50%	=	35%
b. Africa	50	70	×	30	=	21
c. Africa	100	70	×	20	=	14
d. Asia	40	25	×	100	=	25
e. South America	50	5	×	100	=	5
						100%

an organization has, or the number of different prices for each program or service. The weighted average approach can be used to determine the activity level needed to break even.

TARGET PROFIT ANALYSIS

At times an organization will decide that it only wants to undertake a new program or project if it will earn some minimum amount of profit. This might be because there are losses in other parts of the organization that must be subsidized. Another reason is that organizations desire to have a safety cushion, in case everything does not work out as expected. To find the volume for the activity that is required to not only break even, but also earn some minimal required profit level, the required profit is treated as a fixed cost. Equation 4-6 then becomes

$$TPQ = \frac{FC + TP}{P - VC} \qquad \textbf{(4-A-1)}$$

where TP is the target profit and TPQ is the volume required to achieve the target profit. Target profits have the same effect as if fixed costs had increased.

TWO-TIER PRICING MODELS AND BREAK-EVEN ANALYSIS

Many not-for-profit and government organizations occasionally find themselves in a situation in which there is not one unique price for their services. Consider, for example, a charitable organization with an endowment. The income from the endowment is used to subsidize the services provided to its clients. This subsidy might take place in several ways. For example, the endowment income could be used to offset fixed costs. Alternatively, it could be used to provide a price subsidy.

Suppose that the Leetch Blood Bank normally charges $100 per pint of blood. The variable costs of

TABLE 4-A-3 Calculation of Weighted Average Contribution Margin

Program and Donation Size		(From Table 4-A-2) Percentage of Donations		(From Table 4-A-1) Contribution Margin		Weighted Average Contribution Margin
a. Africa	$ 36	35%	×	$ 4	=	$ 1.40
b. Africa	50	21	×	18	=	3.78
c. Africa	100	14	×	68	=	9.52
d. Asia	40	25	×	11	=	2.75
e. South America	50	5	×	20	=	1.00
Total		100%				$18.45

processing blood are $80, and the fixed costs of running the organization are $80,000. The break-even point would be as follows:

$$BEQ = \frac{FC}{P - VC}$$

$$= \frac{\$80,000}{\$100 - \$80}$$

$$= 4,000 \text{ units of blood}$$

Suppose further that Leetch generates $20,000 in endowment income. How would that affect the break-even point? That income could be treated as a source to offset part of the fixed costs of running the blood bank, as follows:

$$BEQ = \frac{FC - Endowment\ Income}{P - VC}$$

$$= \frac{\$80,000 - \$20,000}{\$100 - \$80}$$

$$= 3,000 \text{ units of blood}$$

Alternatively, the bank could decide that it will charge the regular price to those who can pay the full amount and will charge a subsidized price to those who are poor. Assuming that the bank believes it will provide 5,000 units of blood, and 40 percent of the units will have to be subsidized, what is the lowest subsidized price the blood bank can charge and still break even?

This can be solved in a fashion similar to break-even analysis with multiple products. The break-even formula can incorporate the endowment income as a reduction of fixed costs and then can be solved for the subsidized price. Here, 60 percent of the clients pay $100 and have variable costs of $80, for a contribution margin of $20. The remaining 40 percent pay the lower, unknown price. Since there is only one unknown variable in the equation, it can be solved for S, the subsidized price, as follows:

$$BEQ = \frac{FC - Endowment\ Income}{P - VC}$$

$$5,000 = \frac{\$80,000 - \$20,000}{[(60\% \times \$100) + (40\% \times \$S)] - \$80}$$

$$5,000 = \frac{\$60,000}{[\$60 + \$.4S] - \$80}$$

$$5,000 = \frac{\$60,000}{\$.4S - \$20}$$

$$5,000 \times (\$.4S - \$20) = \$60,000$$

$$\$2,000S - \$100,000 = \$60,000$$

$$\$2000S = \$160,000$$

$$S = \$80$$

If the blood bank charges $80 to the 40 percent of the clients that are subsidized, it will still be able to break even. Thus, break-even analysis can be helpful in determining prices that are needed in two-tier pricing systems.

5

Capital Budgeting

The learning objectives of this chapter are to:

- introduce capital budgeting and explain why a separate capital budget is needed;
- define *capital assets*, both in theory and practice;
- explain the *time value of money* (TVM) concept and discuss the basic tools of TVM, including compounding and discounting, present and future value, and annuities;
- present the tools of investment analysis, including net present cost, annualized cost, net present value, and internal rate of return;
- define and discuss *cost-benefit analysis;* and
- define and discuss *payback* and *accounting rate of return*.

INTRODUCTION

As discussed in Chapter 2, when an operating budget is prepared, it includes costs that the organization expects to incur for the coming year. Sometimes, however, the organization spends money on the acquisition of resources that will provide it with benefits beyond the coming year. A *capital asset* is anything the organization acquires that will help it to provide goods or services in more than one fiscal year.[1] When organizations contemplate the acquisition of capital assets, special attention is often paid to the appropriateness of the decision. The process of planning for the purchase of capital assets is often referred to as *capital budgeting*. A *capital budget* is prepared as a separate document, which becomes part of the organization's master budget.

In some organizations, all capital budgeting is done as part of the annual planning process. Specific items are identified, and their purchase is planned for the coming year.

---

[1] A fiscal year may be a calendar year, or it may be any 12-month period. December 31 is the most common fiscal year-end. However, many not-for-profit organizations and local governments begin their fiscal year on July 1, or September 1, rather than January 1. The federal government begins its year on October 1. Generally, the fiscal year is chosen so that the end of the year coincides with the slowest activity level of the year. This allows accountants to take the time needed to summarize the year's activity. Governments may choose a fiscal year that allows sufficient time for the body that approves the budget to review, revise, and adopt the budget by the beginning of the fiscal year. This requires coordination between the choice of the fiscal year-end and the time of the year that the legislative body is in session.

In other organizations, an overall dollar amount is approved for capital spending for the coming year. Then individual items are evaluated and approved for acquisition throughout the year as the need for those items becomes apparent.

One concern in the capital budget process is that adequate attention be paid to the timing of cash payments and receipts. Often large amounts of money are paid to acquire capital items well in advance of the collection of cash receipts earned from the use of those items. When an organization purchases a capital asset, it must recognize that by using cash today to acquire a capital asset, it is forgoing a variety of other potential uses for that money.

At a minimum, cash could be put in an interest-earning account, and in the future the organization would have the original amount plus interest. As a result, paying $1,000 today cannot be equated with receiving $1,000 several years from now. One would only give up $1,000 today if the benefit to be realized from doing so was worth at least the $1,000 plus the interest that could be earned. This gives rise to a concept referred to as the *time value of money* (TVM).

Based on the TVM concept, which is discussed in this chapter, the financial appropriateness of an investment can be calculated. The discussion in this chapter examines TVM techniques for investment analysis, including net present cost, annualized cost, net present value, and internal rate of return.

Governments often use an approach called cost-benefit analysis in evaluating capital budgeting decisions. That approach is discussed in this chapter.

The chapter concludes with a discussion of the payback and accounting rate of return approaches. These two methods both have limitations, but since the methods are sometimes used the reader should be aware of the methods and their drawbacks.

WHY DO WE NEED A SEPARATE CAPITAL BUDGET?

Assume that the Hospital for Ordinary Surgery (HOS) is considering adding a new wing. The hospital currently has annual revenues of $150 million and annual operating expenses of $148 million. The cost to construct the new wing is $360 million. Once opened, the new wing is expected to increase the annual revenues and operating costs of HOS by $70 million and $20 million, respectively, excluding the cost of constructing the building itself.

The operating budget for HOS would include $220 million in revenue (the original $150 million plus the new $70 million). If the entire cost of the new wing is charged to operating expenses, the total operating expenses would be $528 million (i.e., $148 million of expenses, the same as last year, plus $20 million in new operating expenses, plus the $360 million for the new building). This would result in a loss of $308 million for the year. This amount is so huge that the project might be rejected as being totally unfeasible.

However, the benefit of the $360 million investment in the new wing will be realized over many years, not just one. When large investments that provide benefits beyond the current year are included in an operating budget, they often look much too costly. However, if one considers their benefits over an extended period of time, they may not be too costly. The role of the capital budget is to pull the acquisition cost out of the operating budget and place it in a separate budget where its costs and benefits can be evaluated over its complete lifetime.

Suppose that the top management of HOS, after careful review and analysis, decides that the benefits of the new hospital wing over its full lifetime are worth its $360 million cost. Based on the recommendation of chief operating officer (COO) Steve Netzer, as well as the hospital's chief executive officer (CEO) and chief financial officer (CFO), the Board of Trustees of HOS approves the capital budget, including the cost of construction of the new wing. The cost of that capital asset will be spread out over its useful life, with a portion included in the operating budget each year.

The process of spreading out the cost of a capital asset over the years the asset is used is called *amortization,* a general term that refers to any allocation over a period of time. Amortization of the cost of a physical asset is referred to as *depreciation.* Each year a portion of the cost of the asset is treated as an expense called *depreciation expense.*[2] The aggregate amount of the cost of an asset that has been charged as an expense over the years the asset has been owned is referred to as *accumulated depreciation.*

For example, if HOS builds the new hospital wing for $360 million and expects it to have a useful lifetime of 40 years, the depreciation expense each year would be $9 million ($360 million ÷ 40 years).[3] Rather than showing the full building cost of $360 million as an expense in the first year, only $9 million is shown as an expense for the first year. After owning the building for three years, the accumulated depreciation will be $27 million ($9 million × 3 years).[4]

DEFINITION OF CAPITAL ASSETS: THEORY AND PRACTICE

In theory, a capital asset is any resource that will benefit the organization in more than one fiscal year. This means that, in theory, if we were to buy something that will last for just six months, it could be a capital item if part of the six months falls in one year and part falls in the next. In practice, however, organizations only treat items with a lifetime of more than one year as being capital assets. This is done to keep the bookkeeping simpler.

Similarly, most organizations only treat relatively costly acquisitions as capital assets. In theory, there should be no price limitation. A ballpoint pen purchased for 50 cents can be a capital asset if its life extends from one accounting year into the next. However, no organization would treat the pen as a capital asset. The pen would simply be included in the operating expenses in the year it is acquired. This is because its cost is so low. The cost of allocating 25 cents of depreciation in each of two years would exceed the value of the information generated by that allocation.

What about something more expensive like a $200 report-binding machine? In practice, most organizations would look at a $200 machine that is expected to last for 10 years and not treat it as a capital asset. The reason is that even though it will last for more than 12 months, it is relatively inexpensive. If we were to depreciate it, we could divide the $200 cost by 10 years and come out with a charge of $20 per year. For some very small organizations, the difference between charging $200 in 1 year and zero in the subsequent 9 years versus charging $20 per year for 10 years might be significant. However, that would generally not be the case.

Accounting information is rarely perfectly accurate. Compromises are made in the level of accuracy based on the cost of being more accurate and the value of more accurate information. Some estimates are unavoidable. Did we use half of the ink of the 50-cent pen in

---

[2] At times, an organization may own a capital asset that does not have physical form, such as a patent. The allocation of the cost of such an asset is simply referred to by the generic term amortization. Some assets literally empty out (e.g., oil wells, coal mines), and amortization of the cost of such assets is referred to as depletion.

[3] This example has been somewhat simplified. In most cases, we would expect the building to still have some value at the end of the useful lifetime. That residual, or salvage, value would be deducted from the cost before calculating the annual depreciation expense. For example, if we expect the building to be worth $40 million after 40 years, then only $320 million ($360 million cost less $40 million salvage) would be depreciated. The annual depreciation would be $8 million ($320 ÷ 40 years) instead of $9 million.

[4] From an economic perspective, true depreciation represents the amount of the capital asset that has been consumed in a given year. We could measure that by assessing the value of the asset at the beginning and end of the year. The depreciation expense would be the amount that the asset had declined in value. In practice, it is difficult to assess the value of each capital asset each year. Therefore, accounting uses simplifications such as an assumption that an equal portion of the value of the asset is used up each year. Alternatives, referred to as accelerated depreciation methods, are designed to better approximate true economic depreciation. They are discussed in Appendix 10-A at the end of Chapter 10.

each of two years? Perhaps we used 40 percent of the ink one year and 60 percent of the ink the next. A truly correct allocation would therefore require charging 40 percent of the cost of the 50-cent pen in one year and 60 percent of the cost the next year. Similarly, we do not know exactly how much of the binding machine is used each year. Will it really last 10 years, or will it last 11 years? Accounting records should be reasonable representations of what has occurred from a financial viewpoint and should allow the user of the information to make reasonable decisions.

It is true that charging the full $200 cost in the year of purchase will overstate the amount of resources that have been used up in that year. However, it is easier to do it that way. The organization must weigh whether the simplified treatment is likely to create so severe a distortion that it will affect decisions that must be made. For the 50-cent pen, that is never likely to happen. For a $360 million building addition, in contrast, treating the full cost as a current year expense would likely affect decisions. The hard part is determining where to draw the line.

Organizations must make a policy decision regarding what dollar level is so substantial that it is worth the extra effort of depreciating the asset (allocating a share of its cost to each year it is used) rather than charging it all as an expense in the year of acquisition. To most organizations, the difference between charging $200 in one year or $20 a year for 10 years will not be large enough to affect any decisions. In some organizations, the difference between charging $50,000 in one year versus $5,000 per year for 10 years would not be large enough to affect any decisions. A cutoff of $1,000, or $5,000, or even $10,000 would be considered to be reasonable by many public, health, and not-for-profit organizations. Many organizations use even higher levels.

WHY DO CAPITAL ASSETS WARRANT SPECIAL ATTENTION?

It seems reasonable to include just one year's worth of depreciation expense in an operating budget. However, that does not fully explain why a totally separate budget is prepared for capital assets, or why there should need to be special approaches for evaluating the appropriateness of individual capital asset acquisitions. Some additional reasons that capital assets warrant special attention:

- the initial cost is large,
- the items are generally kept a long time,
- we can only understand the financial impact if we evaluate the entire lifetime of the assets, and
- since we often pay for the asset early and receive payments as we use it later, the time value of money must be considered.

Since small capital expenditures (e.g., the ballpoint pen, the binding machine) are often not treated as capital assets, the items that are included in the capital budgeting process are generally expensive. When the cost of an item is high, a mistake can be costly. Long-term acquisitions often lock us in, and a mistake may have repercussions for many years.

For example, suppose that HOS unwittingly buys 10 inferior patient monitors for $50,000 each. As we use them, we learn of their shortcomings and hear of another type of monitor that we could have purchased that performs better. Although we may regret the purchase, we may not have the resources to be able to discard the monitors and replace them. We may have to use the inferior machines for a number of years. To avoid such situations, the capital budgeting process used by many organizations requires a thorough review of the proposed investment and a search for alternative options that might be superior.

The impact of capital acquisitions can only be understood if we consider their full life-time. Suppose that a donor offers to pay the full cost for a new, larger, wonderful building for the organization. Do we need to look any further? The building will be free! However, that is not quite correct. Perhaps the new building will cost money to operate (for heat, power, maintenance, security, and so on) but will not generate any additional revenue or support for the organization beyond the donation to acquire it. The operating costs of the building must be considered. Capital budgets should consider all revenue and expense implications of capital assets over their useful lifetime.

Governments face similar issues when they determine whether they should build a new school. Analysis of the feasibility of the new school building must consider whether we will be able to afford to run it once it is built. Governments must try to assess the likely impact of the added annual operating costs on the tax structure of the town, city, county, or state. Thus, capital budgeting takes a broad view, considering all the likely impacts of making a capital acquisition.

A last, and critical, issue relates to the timing of payments and receipts. Often capital assets are acquired by making a cash payment at the time of acquisition. However, the cash the organization will receive as it uses the asset comes later. In the meantime, there is a cost for the money invested in the project. Since cash is not available for free, we must consider the rent we pay for it.

When we use someone's office or apartment, we pay rent for it. When we use some-one's money, we also pay rent for that use. Rent paid for the use of someone's money is called interest. For capital assets, the rental cost for money used over a period of years can be substantial, and its effect must be considered when we decide whether it makes sense to acquire the item.

In fact, there is an *opportunity cost* for all resources used by an organization. Each resource could be used for some other purpose. We often refer to the opportunity cost of using resources in an organization as the *cost of capital.* Part of the cost of capital is reflected in the interest that the organization pays on its debt. However, there is also a cost of using the resources that the organization owns. If they are not used to buy a particular capital asset, they could be used for something else. Thus, whenever a capital asset is purchased, we must consider the cost of the money used for that purchase. Calculations related to the cost of capital or cost of money are referred to as time value of money computations.

THE TIME VALUE OF MONEY

A dollar today is not worth the same amount as a dollar at some future time. Imagine whether we would be willing to lend someone $10,000 today with the expectation that they would give us back $10,000 in five years. Would we consider that to be a reasonable investment? Probably not. If we had instead invested the money in a safe bank account or U.S. Treasury security that pays interest, at the end of five years we would have our $10,000 plus interest. Getting $10,000 in five years is not as good as having $10,000 today.

This gives rise to a concept referred to as the time value of money (TVM). Suppose that the Museum of Technology is considering buying computers for an exhibit for $50,000. The money would come from cash that the museum currently has. It will be able to charge $12,000 per year in special admissions fees for the exhibit each year for five years. At that point, the exhibit will be closed and the computers will be obsolete and will be thrown away.

If the museum uses a capital budget, the initial cash outlay will be $50,000, and the full five years of revenues will also be shown. The $12,000 of admission revenues per year for five years totals to $60,000. However, can we compare the $50,000 to acquire the exhibit with the $60,000 that we will receive and conclude that there will be a $10,000 profit from the exhibit? No. The two numbers appear to be comparable, but the cash is paid and received at different times. A dollar received at some point in the future is not worth as much as a dollar today. We will need some mechanism to help us make a reasoned comparison.

It is sometimes easier to understand TVM mechanics using a time line such as the following:

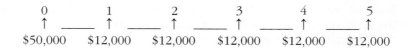

The $50,000 initial cost is spent at the very beginning of the project, or time 0. It is shown in parentheses to indicate that this amount is being paid out, rather than being received. Each year there is a total of $12,000 collected in admissions fees. In this example, we are assuming that $12,000 is collected at the end of each of the five years. For example, the $12,000 shown at time period 1 on the time line is received at the end of the first year.

Although a timeline as it appears above is a helpful conceptual tool, in practice managers tend to do their calculations in a spreadsheet, such as Excel. The same information in Excel might be shown as:

Time Period	0	1	2	3	4	5
Cash Flow	($50,000)	$12,000	$12,000	$12,000	$12,000	$12,000

To evaluate the investment, we use a methodology that is based on compound interest calculations. If the museum had borrowed the $50,000 for the exhibit, it would be clear that in addition to the cost of the exhibit, the admission fees would have to be enough to pay the interest that the museum would pay on the money it borrowed. In this example, however, the museum has not borrowed money. It is using money it already has.

However, TVM calculations are still required. Why? Because the museum could have put the money into some safe investment and earned a return if it did not open the proposed exhibit. In every case that a *capital acquisition* is considered, we must recognize that the acquisition is paid for either by borrowing money (and therefore paying interest) or by deciding not to invest the money elsewhere (and therefore failing to earn a return). There is a cost of capital opportunity cost for all capital asset purchases. If this were not the case, we would not mind lending our own money to someone at a zero interest rate.

Compounding and Discounting

TVM computations are based on the concepts of compounding and discounting. *Compound interest* simply refers to the fact that when money is invested going forward in time, at some point the interest earned on the money starts to earn interest itself. *Discounting* is just the reversal of this process as we go backward in time. Compounding and discounting can be applied to any returns for an investment, whether earned as interest on a bank account or profits on a venture.

For example, suppose that Meals for the Homeless invests $100 of cash in a certificate of deposit (CD) that offers to pay 6 percent per year for two years. What will the value be after two years? Six percent of $100 is $6. If we earned $6 a year for two years, we would have a total of $12 of interest and would end the two years with $112. That assumes that the CD pays *simple interest*. By simple interest, we mean the initial investment earns interest, but any interest earned does not in turn earn interest. We can see the simple interest process as follows:

$100.00 investment	$ 6.00 interest/year	$100.00 investment
×.06 interest rate	×2 years	+12.00 interest for 2 years
$ 6.00 interest/year	$12.00 interest for 2 years	$112.00 ending value

In contrast, what if the CD compounds interest annually? In that case, at the end of one year interest would be calculated on the $100 investment. That interest would be $6 (i.e., 6% of $100 = $6). At that point, the $6 of interest would be added to the initial investment. In the second year, we would earn 6 percent of $106. That comes to $6.36. The total investment at the end of two years would be $112.36. The difference between simple and compound interest seems to be a minor point, because it adds up to only $.36 in this example. We can see the compound interest process as follows:

$100.00	$100.00	$106.00	$106.00
×.06	+6.00	×.06	+6.36
$ 6.00	$106.00	$ 6.36	$112.36

However, suppose instead that we invested $10,000 this year for our retirement in an 8 percent investment. Assume that we plan to retire in 40 years. Eight percent of $10,000 is $800. If we earned $800 per year for 40 years, that would be $32,000. Together with the initial investment of $10,000, we would have $42,000 in the retirement account at simple interest.

In contrast, assume that the 8 percent interest was compounded annually. That is, every year the interest earned so far is added to the principal and begins earning interest itself. Then, the total investment at the end of 40 years would be worth $217,245. If the interest were compounded quarterly, the total would be $237,699 (see Table 5-1)—quite a difference from $42,000. The compounding of interest is a powerful force. Note that with simple interest, it does not matter how frequently the interest is calculated. The total is $42,000 with annual or quarterly calculations.

Compound interest is a valuable concept if we would like to know how much a certain amount of money received today is likely to be worth in the future, assuming that we could earn a certain rate of return. Often, however, our concern is figuring out how much an amount to be received in the future is worth today. For example, the Museum of Technology is trying to decide if it makes financial sense to invest $50,000 *today* to earn admission revenues of $12,000 per year for the next five years. We are concerned with taking those future payments of $12,000 each year and determining what they are worth today. The approach needed for this calculation is called discounting.

TABLE 5-1 $10,000 Invested at 8 Percent for 40 Years

	Simple Interest	Compound Interest
Annual Interest Calculations	$42,000	$217,245
Quarterly Interest Calculations	$42,000	$237,699

Discounting is the reverse of compounding. If we expect an investment to earn $60,000 five years from now, how much is that worth today? Is it worth $60,000 today? No, because if I had $60,000 today, I could earn interest and have more than $60,000 five years from now. It is worth less than $60,000. We need to remove the simple interest that has been earned on the original amount and also the compound interest that has been earned on the interest. Discounting is a process of unraveling or reversing all of the compound interest that would occur between now and the future payment.

Present Value versus Future Value

When interest computations are done for compounding and discounting, one often speaks of the *present value* (PV) and the *future value* (FV). The PV represents the beginning point for an investment. It is when the investment starts. The FV represents a time after the investment's start when an amount of money will be paid or received.

Time Value of Money Calculations

Although we could calculate interest by laboriously multiplying the interest rate by the amount of money invested over and over for the number of compounding periods, our life is made somewhat simpler by the mathematical development of formulas for interest calculations. For example, using the following notation:

$$PV = \text{present value}$$
$$FV = \text{future value}$$
$$i \text{ or rate} = \text{interest rate}$$
$$N \text{ or nper} = \text{number of periods}$$

the FV can be calculated from the following formula:

$$FV = PV(1+i)^N \tag{5.1}$$

This formula says that the amount that we will have in the future (FV) is equal to the amount we start with (PV) multiplied by the sum of one plus the interest rate (i) raised to a power equal to the number of compounding periods (N). For example, suppose that we want to calculate the amount of money we would have after two years if we invested $100 today (called time period 0) at 6 percent compounded annually. A time line for this problem would look like this:

```
        0              1              2
        ↑    6%        ↑    ____       ↑
     $(100)                           FV
```

We are investing (paying out) $100 at the start, time period 0, and expect to get an amount of money, FV, two years in the future. The 6 percent interest rate is shown on the time line between the start and the end of the first compounding period. We could use the formula from Equation 5.1 to solve this problem as follows:

$$FV = \$100 \times (1 + .06)^2$$
$$= \$100 \times [(1.06) \times (1.06)]$$
$$= \$100 \times (1.1236) = \$112.36$$

This simply formalizes the process that we followed earlier. Similarly, for the retirement investment calculated earlier with quarterly compounding, the time line would be as follows:

0		1	2			159		160
↑	2%	↑	↑		···	↑		↑
$(10,000)								FV

The number of compounding periods, N, is 160. This is because the investment is compounded quarterly for 40 years. There are four quarters in a year. Therefore, four compounding periods each year for 40 years results in a total of 160 periods ($4 \times 40 = 160$).

Note that time periods and interest rates must be adjusted for the compounding period. The annual interest rate must be divided by the number of compounding periods per year to get the interest rate per period. The number of compounding periods per year must be multiplied by the total number of years to get the total number of compounding periods.

Using the formula to solve for the FV, we find the following:

$$FV = \$10,000\,(1 + .02)^{160}$$
$$= \$10,000 \times (1.02)^{160}$$
$$= \$10,000 \times (23.7699) = \$237,699$$

This is the result seen in Table 5-1. The interest rate, i, is .02, or 2 percent. This is because of the quarterly compounding. The interest rate of 8 percent per year (as used earlier for this retirement example) must be divided by four to get the interest rate per quarter year. Rather than multiply 1.02 times itself 160 times, it would be simpler to use a handheld calculator or a computer spreadsheet program such as Excel.

For discounting, the process is just reversed. If we start with the same formula,

$$FV = PV(1 + i)^N \qquad \textbf{(5.1)}$$

we can rearrange the equation to find the PV:

$$PV = \frac{FV}{(1 + i)^N} \qquad \textbf{(5.2)}$$

If someone offered to pay us $237,699 in 40 years, how much would that be worth to us today if we anticipate that we could invest money at 8 percent per year, compounded quarterly? The time line would be as follows:

0		1	2			159		160
↑	2%	↑	↑		···	↑		↑
PV								$237,699

We could use the Equation 5.2 formula to solve for the PV, as follows:

$$PV = \frac{\$237,699}{(1+.02)^{160}}$$
$$PV = \frac{\$237,699}{23.7699}$$
$$= \$10,000$$

As we can see, discounting is merely a reversal of the compounding process. If we invest $10,000 today, it would grow to $237,699 forty years in the future at 8 percent interest with quarterly compounding. Making the same assumptions, then, $237,699 paid 40 years in the future is worth only $10,000 today.

A number of present and future value tables have been developed that can aid in solving TVM problems. However, the tables can only include a limited number of interest rates and time periods. Appendix 5-A at the end of this chapter discusses the use of PV and FV tables. More recently, calculators have become widely available to solve these types of problems.

Using Calculators for TVM Computations

It is now possible to buy inexpensive handheld calculators to do TVM computations. These calculators have the formulas built in and can rapidly produce accurate results. For example, given the following information,

$$FV = ?$$
$$PV = 100$$
$$i = 6\%$$
$$N = 2$$

one could simply input the three known pieces of information and have the calculator compute the missing piece of information.

Often calculators that can do TVM computations have a row of buttons that would appear something like this:

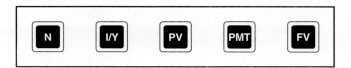

Sometimes the interest key is shown as an I/Y as above, or it might appear as r, %i, i. For the time being, we will ignore the PMT button. We will come back to that shortly. Generally, the way to use the calculator is to enter the appropriate information using the keys and then press a compute button followed by the desired variable. On many calculators the compute button appears as COMP or CPT. Each brand of calculator tends to have a different compute button and often a slightly different approach to entering data, so the instructions for the calculator should be carefully reviewed.

For our simple example of $100 invested for two years at 6 percent interest compounded annually, one would first clear the calculator and then enter the following keystrokes into the calculator:

- 100, then press +/-;
- press PV;
- 6, then press I/Y;
- 2, then press N;
- then press CPT;
- then press FV; and
- 112.36 would appear on the calculator display.

Some calculators require the initial present value to be entered as a negative number, since $100 is first paid out into the investment and then at the end, $112.36 is received from the investment. By pressing the +/- key on the calculator, you convert the initial 100 that you entered to a negative number.

Another way to show the calculator approach would be to treat the information that is available and relevant to the problem as the raw data and the desired information as the result in a form such as the following:

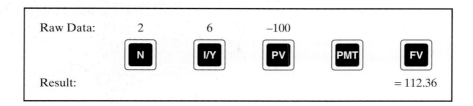

We will use the approach shown in the preceding box to indicate the calculator approach to solving TVM problems throughout this chapter.

Note that the calculator simply calculates the result using the formulas shown in Equations 5.1 and 5.2. They do the arithmetic for the user. The hard part of working with TVM is determining the data that are relevant to the problem and the variable that one needs to calculate. Once any three of the variables (N, %i, PV, FV) are known, the fourth can be calculated by using a calculator or computer.

Annuities

Although there are many times that we anticipate paying or receiving a single amount of money paid at one point in time, sometimes capital assets result in a number of payments over a number of different compounding periods. For example, one might wish to determine the maximum amount that should be paid for a piece of equipment to result in receipts of $3,000, $5,000, and $7,000 over the next three years.

```
    0          1          2          3
    ↑ _____   ↑ _____   ↑ _____   ↑
  (PV)      $3,000     $5,000     $7,000
```

To find out how much this is worth today, we would have to add up the present value of each of the three payments. Essentially, one could break the preceding time line down into three separate problems:

```
    0          1          2          3
    ↑ _____   ↑ _____   ↑ _____   ↑
  (PV)      $3,000
```

```
    0          1          2          3
    ↑ _____   ↑ _____   ↑ _____   ↑
  (PV)                 $5,000
```

```
    0          1          2          3
    ↑ _____   ↑ _____   ↑ _____   ↑
  (PV)                            $7,000
```

and add the PV solutions from the three problems together.

However, if all three payments are exactly the same and come at equally spaced periods of time, the payments are referred to as an *annuity*. Computations are somewhat easier for this special case.

Although we may think of annuities as being annual payments, that is not necessarily the case for TVM computations. An annuity payment is any amount of money paid at equal time intervals in the same amount each time. For example, $110 per week, $500 per month, and $1,250 per year each represent annuities.

In notation, an annuity is often referred to as PMT, an abbreviation for payment, and appears on calculators as a PMT button. Formulas have been developed that can be used to calculate the future value of a stream of annuity payments and the present value of a stream of annuity payments.[5] These formulas have been included in spreadsheet computer software programs and in handheld calculators that perform TVM computations. Note that annuities generally assume the first payment is made at time period 1, not time period 0. An annuity with the first payment at time period 1 is referred to as an *ordinary annuity* or an *annuity in arrears*. Some annuities, such as the rent one pays on an apartment, are called *annuities in advance*, and the first payment is made at the start, or time period 0. Many calculators assume annuities are ordinary (first payment at time period 1), unless the user indicates the type of annuity. With computer spreadsheet programs you can generally indicate the type of annuity as well.

Suppose that we expect to receive $100 per year for the next two years. We could normally invest money at an interest rate of 10 percent compounded annually. What is the present value of those payments? Using the time line and calculator, we can solve the problem as follows:

```
        0              1              2
        ↑    10%       ↑    _____    ↑
      (PV)           $100           $100
```

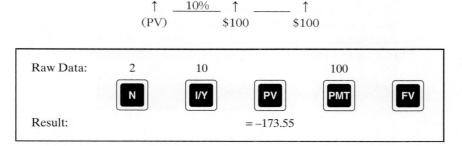

Remember, it is important to clear your calculator memory before each calculation. For example, with the Texas Instruments BAII Plus Professional calculator, you would press the second button and then CLR TVM. Check the calculator instruction manual for the proper way to clear the memory of your calculator. The result shown here indicates that receiving two annual payments of $100 each for the next two years is worth $173.55 today if the interest rate is 10 percent. The $173.55 is shown as a negative number because you would have to pay that amount today to receive $100 a year for two years. How much would those two payments of $100 each be worth at the end of the two years?

```
        0              1              2
        ↑    10%       ↑    _____    ↑
                     $100           $100
                                    (FV)
```

---

[5] The present value of an annuity of $1 equals $\{(1 - [1/(1 + i)^N])/i\}$ and the future value of an annuity of $1 equals $\{[(1 + i)^N - 1]/i\}$.

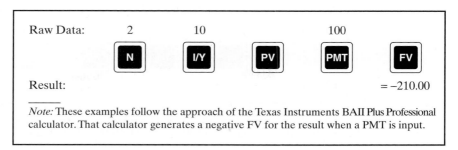

Result: = –210.00

Note: These examples follow the approach of the Texas Instruments BAII Plus Professional calculator. That calculator generates a negative FV for the result when a PMT is input.

Observe that there is a great deal of flexibility. If we know the periodic payment, interest rate, and number of compounding periods, we can find the FV. However, if we know how much we need to have in the future and know how many times we can make a specific periodic payment, we can calculate the interest rate that must be earned. Or we could find out how long we would have to keep making payments to reach a certain future value goal. Given three variables, we can find the fourth. For example, suppose that we are going to invest $100 a year for five years and we want it to be worth $700 at the end of the fifth year; what interest rate must we earn? Using the time line and calculator, we can solve the problem as follows:

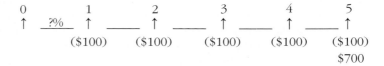

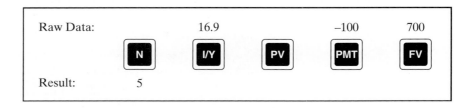

If we are investing $100 each year, we pay that money out into the investment, so it is shown as a negative amount. The $700 will be received at the end, so it shown as a positive amount. As you can see, we have calculated that if we pay out $100 a year for five years, in order to receive $700 at the end of the fifth year, we would have to earn a rate of 16.9% per year.

Similarly, we can solve for the number of periods. Suppose we know that we can invest $100 a year, we can earn a 16.9% annual rate of return, and we want to have $700 at the end of our investment. We can find the number of periods before we will accumulate the desired amount. Using the time line and calculator, we can solve the problem as follows:

```
0         1         2         N
↑  16.9%  ↑ _____ ↑  ...  ↑
        ($100)   ($100)    ($100)
                           $700
```

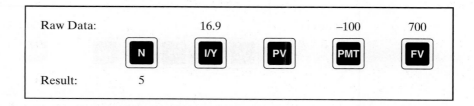

We see that if we invested $100 a year at 16.9%, it would take five years for it to grow to $700.

Cash Flow versus Revenue and Expense

Note that TVM computations are always done based on *cash flow* rather than accrual-based revenues and expenses. This is because we can only earn a return on resources that are actually invested. For example, interest on a bank account is calculated from the time that money is deposited. Therefore, one should remember that all TVM computations are based on the timing of cash receipts and payments rather than the recording of revenues and expenses. For this reason TVM calculations are often referred to as *discounted cash flow* analyses.

Using Computer Spreadsheets for TVM Computations

A number of different computer spreadsheet software programs can be used to solve TVM problems. They are particularly useful for the more complicated calculations. Some of the most popular are Microsoft Excel, Lotus 1-2-3, and Corel's Quattro Pro. This chapter gives examples of how to solve TVM problems with Excel.[6] The approach of other spreadsheets is similar.

Consider the problem discussed earlier, of finding the future value of $100 invested for two years at 6 percent. Using Excel, begin by entering the data that will be used to solve the problem. In this example, the problem could be set up as shown in Figure 5-1. This figure

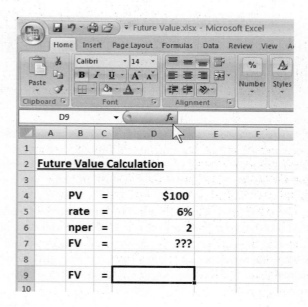

FIGURE 5-1 Initial Data Entry

[6] The Excel approach used in this chapter is based on Microsoft Excel 2007. Other versions of Excel may differ somewhat in the exact approach, steps, or formulas used, or in the exact appearance of the screen.

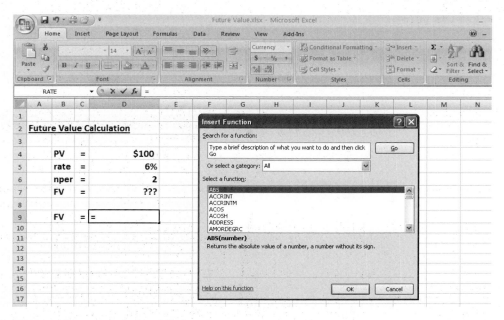

FIGURE 5-2 The Insert Function Window

shows the data you have, the variable (FV) that you are looking for, and indicates where the answer will be shown. Once data have been entered, move the cursor to the cell where you want the solution to appear (in this case, Cell D9). Then press the Function Wizard button "*fx*" which is located on the tool bar at the top of the figure. In Figure 5-1, the cursor arrow is pointing at the Function Wizard button.

After clicking on the Function Wizard a box headed "Insert Function" opens (see Figure 5-2). Within the box that has opened, users can search for a function by describing what they are trying to do, such as "find a future value," or can select a category and a function name. For TVM calculations, the category is always *Financial*. To solve the above problem, the function is *FV* (see Figure 5-3).

Note in Figure 5-3 that the *Financial* catgory and the *FV* function have been selected. Next, click on the *OK* button at the bottom of the Insert Function window. A new window called "Function Arguments" will open (see Figure 5-4). In this window insert the *Rate* (interest rate), *Nper* (number of compounding periods), and *Pv* (present value). There is no annuity payment in this problem so we can ignore *Pmt. Type* refers to whether the payments come at the beginning or end of each period. This pertains primarily to annuities. For now, we can ignore it as well. Each variable can be inserted as either a numeric value or a cell reference. For example, we could insert the *Rate* as 6%, *Nper* as 2, and *Pv* as (100).

Two things should be noted in Figure 5-4. First, the interest rate is shown in the spreadsheet as 6% (see Cell D5). For most handheld calculators we would simply need to enter 6 and the calculator automatically converts it to a percent. In Excel it is critical that the rate either be entered as a percent, such as 6% or as a fraction, such as .06. If you enter 6 rather than 6% the answer will be grossly incorrect. Second, the *Pv* in the Function Arguments window is shown as −*D4*. Excel follows the logic that if you pay out something today, you will get back something in the future. So if the *Fv* is to be a positive amount, representing a receipt of cash, the *Pv* must be a negative amount, representing a payment of cash. We could have accomplished the same thing by showing a negative initial present value ($100) in cell D4 instead of showing it as $100. Now the user can click on *OK* at the

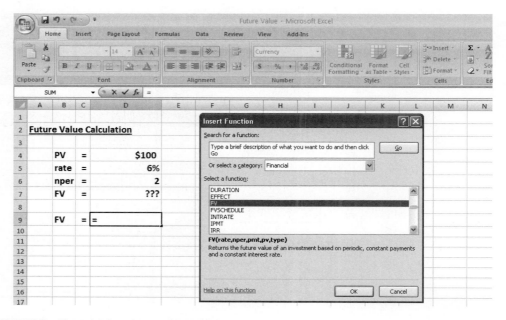

FIGURE 5-3 Financial Category and FV Function

bottom of the Function Arguments window. The solution appears in Cell D9 in Figure 5-5. Excel can be used to solve for other TVM variables as well as the FV. See Appendix 5-B for a detailed discussion.

SKIPPING THE FUNCTION WIZARD   Although it is sometimes helpful to go through the detailed steps as shown, a shortcut may be used. On Figure 5-3, near the bottom of the Insert Function window, the Excel formula for finding the FV appears:

$$FV(rate,nper,pmt,pv,type)$$

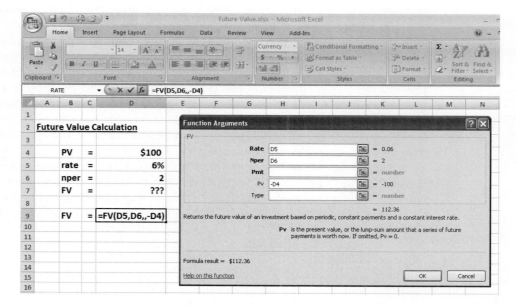

FIGURE 5-4 The Function Arguments Screen

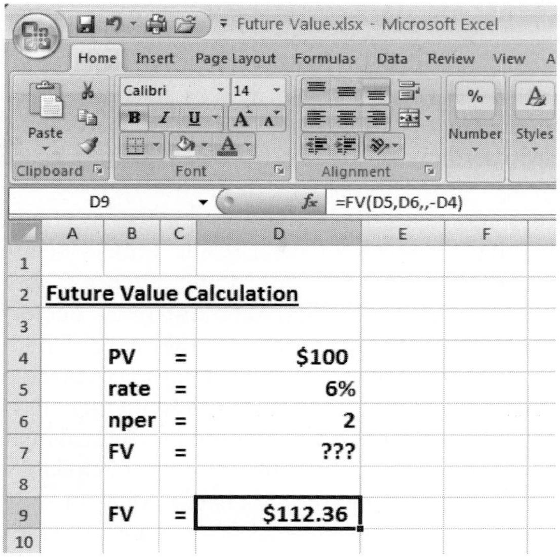

FIGURE 5-5   Solving for Future Value

The future value can be solved by simply entering this formula in a cell, beginning with an equal sign. If this shortcut were used to solve the previous problem, a blank space and extra comma must be left for the *pmt*. The value for the *type* can be omitted. For example, given the cell location of the raw data in the worksheet in Figures 5-1 to 5-5, a *cell reference formula* to solve the above problem would be:

$$= \text{FV}(D5, D6, , -D4)$$

Looking at the formula bar in Figure 5-5, one can see that this is the exact formula that the Function Wizard used to calculate the value for Cell D9. An advantage of a formula that uses the cell references is that it will automatically recalculate the future value if the numeric value in any of the indicated cells is changed. If we were to change the rate in cell D5 from 6% to 8%, a new future value would immediately appear on the worksheet.

Another approach is to show the numeric values for the raw data in the Excel formula, such as:

$$= \text{FV}(6\%, 2, , -100)$$

The advantage of this approach is that it not only will calculate the answer in your Excel spreadsheet, but it can also be communicated to a colleague who can tell exactly what information you have and what you are trying to calculate. Anyone can drop this into their spreadsheet without needing to know the specific cells in which the raw data appear in your spreadsheet. For the remainder of this chapter, TVM Excel problems will be discussed in the form of providing the basic Excel formula for a variable, and the *numeric value formula*, such as:

$$= \text{FV}(rate, nper, pmt, pv, type)$$
$$= \text{FV}(6\%, 2, , -100)$$

Note that if you enter $= \text{FV}(6\%, 2, , -100)$ into an Excel spreadsheet cell, the solution of 112.36 will automatically be calculated.

INVESTMENT ANALYSIS

Investment analysis for the acquisition of capital assets requires careful consideration of the item to be acquired. Alternatives should be examined so that we can be assured that we are making an appropriate selection. Several different analytical approaches can help evaluate alternatives: *net present cost, annualized cost, net present value,* and *internal rate of return.*

In some cases, there may be qualitative benefits from an investment, even though it does not have a solid financial result. Public, health, and not-for-profit organizations may decide that something is worth doing, even if it loses money, because of its benefit to the organizations' clientele. Management must decide whether to invest in a capital asset because of its nonfinancial benefits after considering all factors.

Four general issues should always be considered in evaluation of alternative capital investments. First, the evaluation should include all cash flows. The consideration of all cash inflows and cash outflows is essential to the calculation. Second, the TVM must be considered. Since the flows of the same number of dollars at different points in time are not equally valuable, the analysis should clearly consider not only the amount but also the timing of the cash flows. Third, there should be some consideration of risk. The expected receipt of a cash interest payment in 10 years from a U.S. Treasury bond investment is much less risky than a similar amount expected to be received in 10 years from a current start-up business, which may not even survive for 10 years. There should be a mechanism to incorporate different levels of risk into the calculation. Fourth, there should be a mechanism to rank projects based on the organization's priorities. These issues are addressed below.

Net Present Cost

Many times an organization will find that it must acquire a new piece of equipment and is faced with a choice among several possible alternatives. For example, suppose that Leanna Schwartz, executive director of Meals for the Homeless, is trying to decide between two new industrial-size refrigerators. It has already been decided that the unit currently owned is on its last leg and must be replaced. However, several good units are available. Either of the two models would be acceptable, and Schwartz has decided to choose the less costly option.

The two units under consideration are Model A, which is expensive to acquire but costs less to operate; and Model B, which is less expensive to acquire but costs more to operate:

	Model A Refrigerator	Model B Refrigerator
Purchase Price	$105,000	$ 60,000
Annual Outlay	10,000	20,000
	10,000	20,000
	10,000	20,000
	10,000	20,000
	10,000	20,000
Total Cost	$155,000	$160,000

At first glance, Model A appears less expensive because it only requires a total outlay of $155,000 as opposed to the Model B total cost of $160,000. However, since payments are made over a period of years for each model, we cannot simply add the costs together. Rather, it is necessary to find the PV of each of the future payments. We can add those PVs to the initial outlay to determine the total cost in equivalent dollars today. The total of the initial outlay and the PV of the future payments is called the net present cost (NPC). Whichever project has a lower NPC is less expensive.

To determine the present values, we will need to have an interest rate to use to discount the future payments back to the present. For this example, we will assume a rate of 10 percent. (Later in this chapter, the appropriate choice of rates is discussed.) Since each of the annual payments is identical, they can be treated as an annuity and solved using a calculator:
Model A:

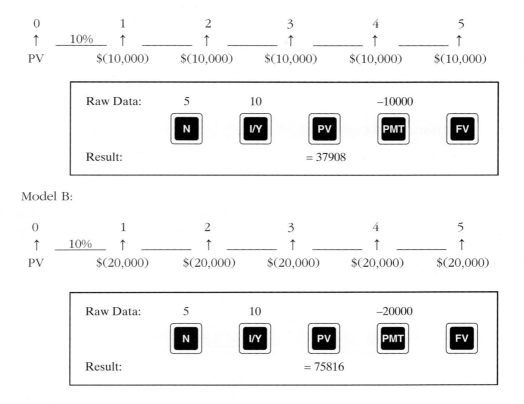

Model B:

Alternatively the same answers can be obtained solving the problem with Excel using the following formulas:

	Model A:	= PV(rate,nper,pmt,fv,type)
		= PV(10%, 5, −10000)
		= $37,908
	Model B:	= PV(rate,nper,pmt,fv,type)
		= PV(10%, 5, −20000)
		= $75,816

The resulting present values for Models A and B tell us what the periodic payments are equivalent to in total today. To find the NPC, we must also consider the initial acquisition price:

$$\text{Model A NPC} = \$105,000 + \$37,908 \qquad \text{Model B NPC} = \$60,000 + \$75,816$$
$$= \$142,908 \qquad\qquad\qquad\qquad = \$135,816$$

Based on this, we see that the NPC of Model B is less than the cost of Model A, even though Model A had initially looked less expensive before the TVM was taken into account.

If we were to acquire and pay for all of the other costs related to Model A, we could pay a lump sum today of $142,908, while Model B would only require a lump sum of $135,816. We are indifferent between paying the NPC and paying the initial acquisition cost followed by the periodic payments. The lump-sum NPC total for Model B is clearly less expensive than the lump-sum NPC for Model A.

This analysis only can assess the financial implications of the two alternatives. If it turned out that Model A was a more reliable unit, Schwartz would have to make a decision weighing the better reliability of Model A against the lower cost of Model B. The preceding example also assumes that the cost of operating each piece of equipment is the same each year. This is likely to be an unrealistic assumption. If the estimates are different each year, then the annuity approach could not be used. The PV for each year would have to be calculated and then added together to get the NPC.

Annualized Cost

The NPC method is very helpful for comparing projects that have identical lifetimes. What if investments aimed at the same ends have different lifetimes? Suppose that Model A has a five-year lifetime, but Model B has only a four-year lifetime, as follows:

	Model A Refrigerator	Model B Refrigerator
Purchase Price	$105,000	$ 60,000
Annual Outlay	10,000	20,000
	10,000	20,000
	10,000	20,000
	10,000	20,000
	10,000	
Total Cost	$155,000	$140,000

One approach would be to try to equalize the lifetimes. We could assume that each time a unit wears out it is replaced. If we repeat that process four times for Model A and five times for Model B, at the end of 20 years the two alternatives will have equal lifetimes (see Table 5-2).

We could then proceed to find the NPC for each of these two 20-year alternatives. However, the uncertainties going forward 20 years are substantial. The purchase prices will likely change, as will the annual operating costs. Our needs might change drastically in 10 years, making the acquisitions in the future unnecessary.

As an alternative to the process of equalizing the lifetimes, we can use an approach called the *annualized cost method*. In that approach one first finds the NPC for each alternative. Then, that cost is translated into a periodic payment for the number of years of the project's lifetime. The project with the lower annualized cost is less expensive on an annual basis in today's dollars.

Consider the refrigerator example. Assume that Model A lasts for five years and Model B lasts for four years. All of the assumptions for Model A are the same as they were originally, so the NPC is still $142,908, as calculated earlier. Model B is different, because it now has only a four-year life:

Model B:

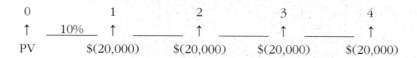

TABLE 5-2 Equalizing Asset Lifetimes

Time Period	Action	Model A Refrigerator	Model B Refrigerator
0	Purchase Models A and B	$105,000	$ 60,000
1	Annual Outlay	10,000	20,000
2	Annual Outlay	10,000	20,000
3	Annual Outlay	10,000	20,000
4	Annual Outlay	10,000	20,000
4	Purchase Model B		60,000
5	Annual Outlay	10,000	20,000
5	Purchase Model A	105,000	
6	Annual Outlay	10,000	20,000
7	Annual Outlay	10,000	20,000
8	Annual Outlay	10,000	20,000
8	Purchase Model B		60,000
9	Annual Outlay	10,000	20,000
10	Annual Outlay	10,000	20,000
10	Purchase Model A	105,000	
11	Annual Outlay	10,000	20,000
12	Annual Outlay	10,000	20,000
12	Purchase Model B		60,000
13	Annual Outlay	10,000	20,000
14	Annual Outlay	10,000	20,000
15	Annual Outlay	10,000	20,000
15	Purchase Model A	105,000	
16	Annual Outlay	10,000	20,000
16	Purchase Model B		60,000
17	Annual Outlay	10,000	20,000
18	Annual Outlay	10,000	20,000
19	Annual Outlay	10,000	20,000
20	Annual Outlay	10,000	20,000
	Total Outlay	$620,000	$700,000

The Excel Spreadsheet Formula to find the PV would be:

$$= PV(rate, nper, pmt, fv, type)$$
$$= PV(10\%, 4, -20000)$$
$$= \$63,397$$

The calculator solution would be:

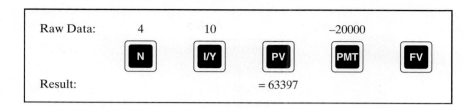

To find the NPC we must also consider the initial acquisition price.

$$\text{Model B NPC} = \$60,000 + \$63,397$$
$$= 123,397$$

Although the $123,397 NPC for Model B is lower than the $142,908 NPC for Model A, we are now comparing apples and oranges. Model B will only last for four years, while Model A will last for five years. We need to account for the fact that we will have to replace it sooner. This is done by treating each NPC as a present value of an annuity and finding the equivalent periodic payment over its lifetime.
Model A:

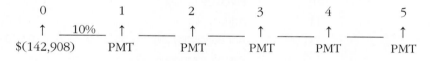

Spreadsheet solution: = PMT(rate,nper,pv,fv,type)
= PMT(10%, 5, −142908)
= $37,699

Calculator solution:

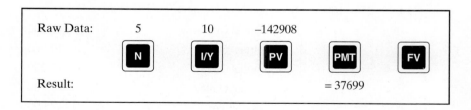

Model B:

0   1   2   3   4
↑ 10%   ↑ ____ ↑ ____ ↑ ____ ↑
$(123,397) PMT   PMT   PMT   PMT

Spreadsheet solution: = PMT(10%, 4, −123397)
= $38,928

Calculator solution:

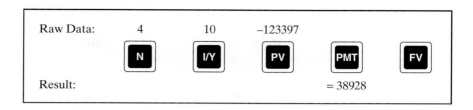

Thus, adjusted for their relative lifetimes, including both the acquisition and annual outlays, Model A is less expensive per year than Model B ($37,699 versus $38,928).[7]

Net Present Value

The NPC and annualized cost methods discussed previously involve assuming that the capital assets would cost money to acquire. However, it does not assume that the capital asset would have a direct effect on revenues or support. Often however, one of the major reasons to acquire a capital asset is to use it to earn more revenues or generate additional financial support. In such cases, we need to consider both the revenues and costs as measured by the present value of their cash inflows and outflows. The *net present value* (NPV) method is one of the most common approaches for making calculations of the present value of inflows and outflows.

The NPV approach calculates the PV of inflows and the PV of outflows and compares them. If the PV of the inflows exceeds the PV of the outflows, then the NPV is positive, and the project is considered to be a good investment from a financial perspective:

$$NPV = PV \text{ Inflows} - PV \text{ Outflows}$$
and if NPV > 0, the project is economically viable.

For example, assume that HOS is contemplating opening a new type of lab. The equipment for the lab will cost $5 million. Each year there will be costs of running the lab and revenues from the lab. As a result of general financial constraints, the hospital only wants to make this investment if it is financially attractive. The hospital's cost of money is 8 percent. In addition, since the hospital feels that often projected revenues are not achieved by new projects, it wants to build in an extra 2 percent margin for safety. It has decided to do the project only if it earns at least 10 percent.

That 10 percent rate is considered to be a *hurdle rate*, or a *required rate of return*. Only if the project can do better than this rate will it be accepted. Therefore, the NPV must be calculated using a 10 percent discount rate. If the project has a positive NPV, that means that it earns more than 10 percent and will be acceptable.

---

[7] In the case of annuities, an alternative annualization approach would be to find the annuity payment equivalent to the initial outlay and add that amount to the annual payments. That will provide an annualized cost. However, that will only work in cases in which the payments after the initial outlay are an annuity.

Assume the following projected cash flows from the project:

Proposed New Investment

(Capital Equipment Has a Four-Year Life)

	Start	Year 1	Year 2	Year 3	Year 4	Total
Cash In		$2,700,000	$2,800,000	$2,900,000	$3,000,000	$11,400,000
Cash Out	$ 5,000,000	1,000,000	1,300,000	1,400,000	1,600,000	10,300,000
Total	$(5,000,000)	$1,700,000	$1,500,000	$1,500,000	$1,400,000	$ 1,100,000

Although we are just assuming these cash flows, it should be noted that estimating future cash flows is often a difficult task that requires a careful budgeting effort. In total, the project shows a $1,100,000 profit. However, that profit does not account for the timing of the cash flows. The hospital will be spending the full $5,000,000 at the start. However, the cash receipts available to repay the cost of the investment and to pay for the cost of capital used are spread out in the future. To determine whether the investment is worthwhile, we will have to find the NPV.

This can be accomplished by finding the PV of each cash inflow and then finding the total PV of the inflows. Then the same procedure can be done for the outflows. The PV of the inflows and the PV of the outflows can be compared to determine the NPV. Alternatively, we can simply find the PV of the net flows for each year. That is, we can take the PV of the $5,000,000 net cash outflow at the start plus the PV of the $1,700,000 net cash inflow from the end of the first year plus the PV of the $1,500,000 net cash inflow from the second year and so on. In Excel this would appear as:

	A	B	C	D	E	F
1						
2		**Start**	**Year 1**	**Year 2**	**Year 3**	**Year 4**
3	**Cash In**		$2,700,000	$2,800,000	$2,900,000	$3,000,000
4	**Cash Out**	$5,000,000	$1,000,000	$1,300,000	$1,400,000	$1,600,000
5	**Total**	($5,000,000)	$1,700,000	$1,500,000	$1,500,000	$1,400,000
6						
7	**Present Value**	($5,000,000)	$1,545,455	$1,239,669	$1,126,972	$956,219
8						
9	**Net Present Value**	($131,685)				
10						

The NPV is the PV of the inflows less the present value of the outflows. If we total the results of the individual present value computations shown in summary form in the above Excel spreadsheet, we find that the NPV is −$131,685. Since the NPV is negative, the investment is earning less than the 10 percent required rate of return. It is therefore not an acceptable project.

Spreadsheets typically have an NPV function to solve this more directly. In Excel the formula to solve an NPV problem is "= NPV(rate, value1, value2, . . .)." The values refer to each of the future values in the problem. For the earlier proposed investment, the $5,000,000 outlay occurs in the present and is not included in the formula. So value 1 would be $1,700,000, value 2 would be $1,500,000, and so on. Once the NPV is found for the future values, however, the initial $5,000,000 outlay needs to be subtracted to find the answer. This can be combined into one formula as follows:

$$= \text{NPV(rate,value1,value2,...)} - \text{Initial Outlay}$$

This can then be solved in Excel as seen below:

	A	B	C	D	E	F
1						
2		**Start**	**Year 1**	**Year 2**	**Year 3**	**Year 4**
3	Cash In		$2,700,000	$2,800,000	$2,900,000	$3,000,000
4	Cash Out	$5,000,000	$1,000,000	$1,300,000	$1,400,000	$1,600,000
5	Total	($5,000,000)	$1,700,000	$1,500,000	$1,500,000	$1,400,000
6						
7	($131,685)					
8						

Formula bar for Cell A7: `=NPV(10%,C5:F5)-B4`

Note the formula for Cell A7, which can be seen on the formula bar above columns C and D. The NPV formula requires the rate, 10%, and the range where the future cash flows are located in the spreadsheet, C5:F5, or Cell C5 to Cell F5. Excel will generate an error message if you enter the individual future cash flow values into the formula rather than providing the cell range in a format such as C5:F5. The initial cash outflow from Cell B4 is then subtracted to finish the NPV calculation.

Internal Rate of Return

The NPV approach indicates whether a project does better than a specific hurdle rate. However, it does not indicate the rate of return that the project actually earns. The *internal rate of return* (IRR) is the rate of return earned by an investment. Many managers are more comfortable ranking projects of different sizes by their rates of return rather than by the NPV. Suppose that we evaluate two projects using a 10 percent hurdle rate. A small project with a 35 percent rate of return might have a lower NPV than a much larger project with a 12 percent rate of return. Both projects have a positive NPV. However, because of the relatively modest magnitude of the smaller project, its exceptional profitability may go unnoticed when compared with another project with a very large NPV. Some managers therefore like to use a method that assesses the project's rate of return, in addition to using the NPV approach. The IRR method can be used to generate that information.

The IRR method is derived from the NPV approach. Assume we start with the following equation:

$$\text{NPV} = \text{PV Inflows} - \text{PV Outflows}$$

Then

if NPV > 0, the project earns more than the discount rate, and

if NPV < 0, the project earns less than the discount rate.

Therefore,

if NPV = 0, the project earns exactly the discount rate.

So, if we want to know the rate of return that a project earns, we simply need to determine the discount rate at which the NPV is equal to zero. And, since

$$NPV = PV\ Inflows - PV\ Outflows$$

then for NPV to be equal to zero,

$$0 = PV\ Inflows - PV\ Outflows$$

or

$$PV\ Outflows = PV\ Inflows.$$

So we need to set the PV of the outflows equal to the PV of the inflows and find the discount rate at which that is true. Suppose we can invest $6,700 today to get a cash flow of $1,000 a year for 10 years (i.e., invest $6,700 to get back a total of $10,000 in the future). What is the IRR for this investment?

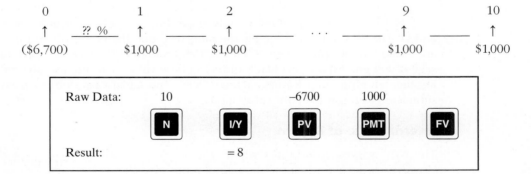

It turns out that the IRR for this investment would be 8 percent.

Note that the preceding problem assumes an annuity. If the cash flows are different each year, it is mathematically harder to determine the IRR. Generally, a computer program such as Excel or a sophisticated calculator is needed to determine the IRR with uneven cash flows. Many handheld calculators would not be adequate.

Suppose, for instance, that the preceding example does not provide payments of $1,000 per year, but rather $1,000 in the first year and then increases by $100 in each subsequent year as follows:

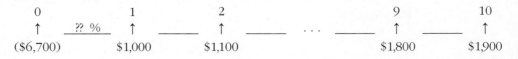

Using Excel, this problem can be solved using the *IRR* function. The Excel formula for internal rate of return is:

$$= IRR(values, guess)$$

The values represent all of the cash inflows and outflows, including the initial time 0 payments or receipts. The guess is the user's best guess of the rate of return. The computer uses this as a starting point as it cycles in on the actual rate. Assume that the user guesses 5%. If a numeric value formula is used, the values must be provided to Excel within curly brackets, so that the spreadsheet program can distinguish the values from the guess, as follows:

$$= IRR(\{-6700, 1000, 1100, 1200, 1300, 1400, 1500, 1600, 1700, 1800, 1900\}, 5\%)$$
$$= 15\%$$

Note that the IRR function also will not work unless there is at least one inflow or positive number and at least one outflow or negative number in the series of values. However, it is generally not necessary to enter a guess value for the rate of return. A step-by-step Excel solution for an IRR problem is provided in Appendix 5-B.

LIMITATIONS OF IRR   Managers should be aware of three important limitations to IRR. First of all, it assumes that cash inflows during the project are reinvested at the same rate that the project earns. Second, sometimes it will cause managers to choose incorrectly from two mutually exclusive projects. Finally, it can create erroneous results if the investment does not have a conventional pattern of cash flows.

Implicit in the NPV technique is an assumption that all money coming from a project during its lifetime is reinvested at the hurdle rate. That is reasonable since the hurdle rate in some way measures the organization's other alternative opportunities. We may want a project to earn at least 10 percent because we have other opportunities that can earn 10 percent.

In contrast, the IRR method assumes that as cash flows are received, they are reinvested at the same rate as the project earns (i.e., the IRR). Suppose that a project has an IRR of 25 percent. Suppose further that this represents an unusually high rate of return for any of the organization's investments. It may be unrealistic to expect to be able to reinvest cash as it is received from the project in additional projects at 25 percent. In effect, then, the IRR method may overstate the true rate that will be earned on the project.

Another problem may arise when one is evaluating two mutually exclusive projects. It is possible that a small project may have a very high rate of return whereas a larger project has a very good, but somewhat smaller, rate of return. For example, suppose that the Millbridge golf course is trying to decide whether to put up a "19th Hole" restaurant and bar on a piece of land or to pave it over for additional parking. Only one piece of land is available on the golf course property to use for any kind of development.

Assume that the parking lot will cost $50,000 and will earn an annual net return of $20,000 per year for 20 years. The IRR for that investment is 39.95 percent. Alternatively, the 19th Hole will cost $500,000 to build and will earn an annual profit of $150,000 for 20 years. This results in an IRR of 29.84 percent. Normally the town and the golf course do not have any investments that earn a higher rate of return than 15 percent.

Both projects are very attractive, but we cannot do both since they both use the same piece of land. Often, when IRR is used to evaluate investments, managers rank the projects in order of IRR, selecting first those with the highest IRR. If that were done in Millbridge, it would be a mistake. Although a 39.95 percent return may appear better than a 29.84 percent return, overall the town would be better off with the 19th Hole. Why? Because if it invests in the parking lot, the town will earn 39.95 percent on an investment of $50,000 but will then invest the remainder of their money at 15 percent. If the managers decide to invest $500,000 for the year, they can put the entire amount into the 19th Hole and earn a 29.84 percent return on the total amount versus investing $50,000 at 39.95 percent and $450,000 at 15 percent.

Consider the following annual returns:

$20,000	for the parking lot (given previously)
71,893	for other projects (PV = $450,000; N = 20; i = 15%; PMT = $71,893)
$91,893	total annual return

versus

$150,000	for the 19th Hole (given previously)

Clearly, the profits are better by investing in the 19th Hole. We would fail to see that if we simply chose the project with the highest IRR first. In contrast, the NPV method gives the correct information. The NPV for the 19th Hole evaluated at a hurdle rate of 15 percent is $438,900, whereas the NPV for the parking lot and other projects is $75,187.

Finally, many investment projects consist of an initial cash outflow followed by a series of cash inflows. This is referred to as a conventional pattern of cash flows. However, it is possible that some of the subsequent cash flows will be negative. In that case, the method can produce multiple answers, and the actual rate of return becomes ambiguous. In such cases, one is better off relying on the NPV technique.

A modified IRR method addresses some of these concerns. The interested reader should consult an advanced text such as several of those listed at the end of this chapter.

Selecting an Appropriate Discount Rate

The rate used for PV calculations is often called the hurdle rate or required rate of return, or simply the *discount rate*. The discount or hurdle or required rate should be based on the organization's cost of capital.

Often not-for-profit organizations receive donations that can be used for capital investments. This complicates the measurement of the cost of capital. For projects that are specifically funded by donations, it may not be necessary to calculate the NPV. However, that involves assuming that all costs are covered by the donation. To the extent that the organization must bear other costs, it should employ TVM techniques with a hurdle rate based on its overall cost of capital.

Selection of an appropriate discount rate for governments to use is difficult. According to Mikesell, "There is . . . no single discount rate that is immediately obvious as the appropriate rate for analysis."[8] The two methods he proposes are the interest rate the government must pay to borrow funds or the rate that the funds could earn if they were employed in the private sector. The problem with the former approach is that the government may be able to borrow money at a substantially lower interest rate than could be earned on money invested in the private sector. This might unduly siphon money out of the private sector. The latter approach (the rate the funds could earn in the private sector) may be more appropriate, but is likely to be much harder to determine.

In practice, there is little consistency in the discount rate used across governments and even within different branches of the same government. Yet despite these difficulties in

---

[8] John Mikesell. *Fiscal Administration: Analysis and Applications for the Public Sector,* 6th ed. Belmont, Ca.: Thomson/Wadsworth, 2003, p. 259.

agreeing on the most appropriate rate for a government to use, there appears to be agreement that taking into account the TVM is clearly appropriate for all types of organizations.

INFLATION   In calculating the TVM, the question often arises regarding how to treat inflation. One approach would be to include the anticipated inflation rate in the discount rate. However, the weakness of that approach is that not all cash inflows and outflows will necessarily be affected by inflation to the same extent. When we hear that the inflation rate in society is a certain percentage, that really represents an average impact of inflation rather than one consistent inflation rate for all things. A preferred method is to try to anticipate the impact of inflation on the various cash inflows and outflows and adjust each individual flow before calculating the PV or FV. In that case, inflation would not be included in the discount rate itself.

For example, suppose that we think that it will cost $1,000 to operate a machine each year, but that does not take into account inflation. Then we may want to adjust the cash flows for the succeeding years to $1,030, and then $1,061, and so on, multiplying the cash flow each year by 103 percent, if we think the cost will rise 3 percent per year due to inflation (be careful to compound the impact of inflation—note that the third-year expected cost is $1,061 rather than $1,060). Other cash inflows and outflows might be expected to rise faster or slower, depending on how inflation affects them.

UNCERTAINTY   There is no way that management can totally predict future cash inflows and outflows in many capital budgeting decisions. Things do not always go as planned. To protect against unexpectedly poor results, many organizations increase their required discount rate. The greater the chance of unexpected negative events, the more the discount rate would be adjusted. For example, in buying a new refrigeration unit, the chances of problems may be small. However, in opening an entire new soup kitchen location, the potential for unexpected problems may be substantially higher. Thus, the hurdle rate is adjusted upward based on the riskiness of the project. The greater the risk, the higher the hurdle rate is raised.

Cost-Benefit Analysis

Cost-benefit analysis (CBA) is another technique widely used by governments for evaluating capital budget decisions. CBA compares the costs and benefits of an action or program. The method takes into account not only private costs and benefits but public ones as well. Cost-benefit analysis has been defined as being an

> analytical technique that compares the social costs and benefits of proposed programs or policy actions. All losses and gains experienced by society are included and measured in dollar terms. The net benefits created by an action are calculated by subtracting the losses incurred by some sectors of society from the gains that accrue to others. Alternative actions are compared, so as to choose one or more that yield the greatest net benefits, or ratio of benefits to costs. The inclusion of all gains and losses to society in cost-benefit analysis distinguishes it from cost-effectiveness analysis, which is a more limited view of costs and benefits.[9]

Many people think cost-benefit analysis is associated with large-scale public projects, such as the building of a dam. However, the technique can be extremely useful even for evaluating small purchases such as a personal computer.

Any organization attempts to determine if the benefits from spending money will exceed the cost. If the benefits do outweigh the costs, it makes sense to spend the money;

---

[9] John L. Mikesell. *Fiscal Administration: Analysis and Applications for the Public Sector,* 4th ed. Fort Worth, Tex.: Harcourt Brace College Publishers, 1995, pp. 559–60.

otherwise it does not. In the case of the government, the benefits and costs must be evaluated broadly to include their full impact on society. In the political arena that government managers find themselves in, the careful measurement of costs and benefits provides the information needed to support a spending decision.

There are several key elements in performing a cost-benefit analysis:

- determining project goals,
- estimating project benefits,
- estimating project costs,
- discounting cost and benefit flows at an appropriate rate, and
- completing the decision analysis.

DETERMINING PROJECT GOALS   To determine the benefits, it is first necessary to understand what the organization hopes the project will accomplish. So identification of goals and objectives is essential. Suppose that Millbridge's town manager is considering buying a new garbage truck. The first question is why he feels that the town would be better off with a new garbage truck. The goals may be few or numerous, depending on the specific situation. Perhaps the old truck breaks down frequently and has high annual repair costs. One goal will be to lower repair costs. Perhaps the old truck is much smaller than newer ones. As a result, it has to make frequent trips to unload. A second goal may be to save labor costs related to the frequent unloading trips. A third goal may relate to reduction of the costs of hauling recyclables. If the new truck is appropriate for multiple uses, it may eliminate the need to pay for an outside service to haul recyclable materials such as paper or bottles.

ESTIMATING PROJECT BENEFITS   Once the goals have been identified, the specific amount of the benefits must be estimated. The benefits should include only the incremental benefits that result from the project. For instance, the manager would not include the benefit to citizens of having their garbage collected, since that will be accomplished (in this example) whether the town uses the old truck or the new truck.[10] However, all additional benefits should be considered, estimated, and included in the cost-benefit calculation.

In the Millbridge example, it is likely that the town manager, Dwight Ives, or one of his assistants will be able to calculate the benefits fairly directly. For example, the town knows how many trips the current truck makes to unload its garbage. Based on the capacity of the new truck, the number of trips the new truck would need to make can be calculated. The estimated number of trips saved can then be calculated. The town can measure how long it takes for the driver to make trips to unload the truck and use that information along with the driver's pay rate to estimate labor savings. This assumes that the driver is an hourly employee and that there really would be reduced labor payments. If the driver is to be paid the same amount no matter how many hours of work are required, then there would be no labor benefit.

The labor savings is one component of the benefits. The town manager will also have to estimate the repair cost savings, the savings from not using an outside service to haul recyclables, and so on. All impacts of the change as well as future circumstances must be considered. For example, if the town is growing in population, it is likely to have more garbage in the future. That could mean the new truck would result in saving even more trips in the future.

However, the estimation of benefits is a potentially difficult process. Many times the benefits cannot be measured by simply evaluating saved costs. In such situations, it is helpful to determine the value of benefits in a private market situation, if possible. If the benefits have a comparable value in the private sector, that can be used as an estimate. However, a private sector comparison is not always available. Suppose that there is a proposal for

---

[10] The example assumes that the old truck is reliable enough to remove garbage on schedule. If collections are occasionally delayed by several days because of the unreliability of the old truck, then the benefit of prompt collection would also need to be measured.

Millbridge to convert a wooded area into a park with a baseball field. Many people will enjoy playing ball on the field. How much is that benefit worth? What would people be willing to pay for the benefit? Mikesell notes that

> When the product or service is of this type . . . a different approach is used. That approach is the *estimation of consumers' surplus*—the difference between the maximum price consumers would willingly pay for given amounts of a commodity and the price that the market demands for the commodity (which would be zero for public services provided at no direct charge). The underlying logic of consumer surplus is relatively simple, although its application is anything but simple: Points along an individual's demand curve for a product or service represent the value the person places on particular amounts of the product in question. . . . Consumer surplus then equals the difference between the maximum price the individual would have paid less the price he or she actually pays multiplied by the number of units purchased.[11]

As part of the cost-benefit analysis, it will be necessary to estimate consumer surplus. An in-depth discussion of demand curves and estimation of consumer surplus is beyond the scope of this book. More complexity is added if the project either is life-saving or may cost lives. The reader is referred to the suggested readings at the end of this chapter for further discussion of these and other advanced cost-benefit issues.

ESTIMATING PROJECT COSTS Projects have costs as well as benefits, and these costs must also be estimated as part of the cost-benefit analysis. In the case of the garbage truck, the primary cost relates to the acquisition of the truck. The truck has a market price, so this estimation is fairly straightforward. But how about the park and baseball field? Certainly we can assign market-based prices to the cost of clearing the woods and preparing the field. However, in cost-benefit analysis it is also critical to consider *opportunity costs*. Opportunity cost refers to the fact that when a decision is made to do something, other alternatives are sacrificed. In the case of converting a wooded area for use as a park and baseball field, Millbridge and its residents will have to sacrifice other possible uses for the land, including preservation of the wooded area. The opportunity cost of the wooded area in its next best use to being a park should be estimated.

Suppose that several houses currently look out on woods and, after the park is made, will look out on a park with lots of people in it. The homeowners might view the ready accessibility of the park to be a benefit. It is possible, however, that since they chose to live near woods, they will be made unhappy by their loss. This is a cost to society and therefore is something that must be included in the analysis. This can be done in the same way as benefits are estimated. While some users of the park will have a consumer surplus, those who prefer the wooded area will have a negative consumer surplus if the project is carried out.

DISCOUNTING COST AND BENEFIT FLOWS Often projects evaluated using CBA require flows of benefits and costs that occur over a period of years. The time value of money techniques discussed earlier in the chapter would have to be applied to these cash flows to find their present value.

COMPLETING THE DECISION ANALYSIS Once all of the relevant costs and benefits of a project have been estimated and adjusted in a discounting process, they can be compared to each other in the form of a ratio. Generally benefits are divided by costs. If the result is greater than 1, it means that the benefits exceed the costs, and the project is desirable. The greater the benefit to cost ratio, the more desirable the project is.

---

[11] Mikesell, pp. 240–41.

Other Techniques of Capital Budgeting

In addition to the techniques for evaluating capital acquisitions that have been discussed previously, there are two other widely known techniques, both of which have serious flaws. Although we do not recommend use of these techniques by themselves, the reader should be aware of their existence and limitations. These two methods are the payback approach and the accounting rate of return (ARR) approach.

The payback approach argues that the sooner we get back our money, the better the project. This is a risk-averse method. Essentially, it focuses on recovery of the initial investment as soon as possible. Then any additional flows are viewed as being profits. The investor is safe at that point, having recovered all the money invested. However, consider the following three projects:

	Investment A ($)	Investment B ($)	Investment C ($)
Start	(100,000)	(100,000)	(100,000)
Year 1	90,000	10,000	80,000
Year 2	10,000	90,000	10,000
Year 3	20,000	20,000	150,000
Year 4	0	0	150,000

The payback technique argues that A and B are equally good and are better than C. In both A and B the $100,000 initial investment is recovered by the end of the second year. In C, the investment is not recovered until sometime during the third year. The objection to the payback method is that it ignores everything that happens after the payback period. It also does not consider the TVM. We would argue that A is better than B because of the TVM. Further, C is better than A or B. For project B, getting $90,000 in the second year instead of the first will result in a lower NPV than that of Project A. Further, the NPV of C is better than A or B because of the large returns in the fourth and fifth years.

Some organizations employ payback together with one of the TVM techniques discussed earlier. They argue that the TVM techniques are good for evaluating profitability, accounting for the timing of cash flows. However, payback adds information about risk. Among differing projects with similar NPVs or IRRs, the one with the shortest payback period involves the least risk. Since the further we project into the future, the greater the uncertainties, employing payback as an additional tool for capital budgeting rather than the primary tool is a potentially useful approach.

The other capital budgeting method not yet discussed is the ARR approach. In this approach, the profits that are expected to be earned from a project are divided by the total investment, as follows:

$$\frac{\text{Profit}}{\text{Investment}} = \text{Return on Investment}$$

For example, suppose that we invest $100,000 today in a project that will have revenues of $50,000 and expenses of $40,000 each year.[12] The project therefore earns annual profits of $10,000 per year for five years. The total profit is $50,000 and the calculation of the accounting rate of return would then be as follows:

$$\frac{\$50,000}{\$100,000} \times 100 = 50\%$$

[12] Assume that each year the expenses include a pro rata (proportional) share of the cost of the capital investment.

This is clearly unrealistic for a number of reasons. First, it is a return for the entire project life. This is sometimes corrected by dividing the return by the years in the project's life, as follows:

$$\frac{50\%}{5} = 10\%$$

However, this still does not resolve the problems related to the failure to account for the TVM. The failure to account for the fact that the investment is made today and the profits are earned in future time periods will typically cause the ARR to be overstated.

These methods do not consider all cash flows, they do not account for the TVM, and they do not rank the projects in terms of their ability to make the organization better off financially. As such, they violate a number of the conditions for a good capital investment analysis tool.

Summary

Assets with lifetimes of more than one year are often referred to as capital assets. The process of planning for their purchase is often referred to as capital budgeting. A capital budget is prepared as a separate document, which becomes part of the organization's master budget.

Capital assets are considered separately from the operating budget, because it is not appropriate to charge the entire cost of a resource that will last more than one year to the operating budget of the year it is acquired. Who could ever justify buying a new building if the entire cost of the building were included as an operating expense in the year it was acquired? Capital items also require special attention because (1) the initial cost is large, making a poor choice costly; (2) the items are generally kept a long time, so the organization often lives with any poor choices for a long time; (3) we can only understand the financial impact if we evaluate the entire lifetime of the assets; and (4) since we often pay for the asset early and receive payments as we use it later, the time value of money must be considered

Consideration of the time value of money requires careful attention to the principles of compound and discount interest. Present values and future values must be determined where appropriate to allow managers to make informed decisions. Often it is necessary to employ TVM techniques such as net present cost, annualized cost, net present value, and internal rate of return when assessing potential capital investments.

Preview

In Chapter 6 we turn our attention to long-term financing. Capital assets are often so costly that they cannot be paid for using just money generated from current operating activities. It is common for the cost of such items, especially buildings or major pieces of equipment, to exceed the cash resources available. Instead, many organizations pay for the purchase of a building or major pieces of equipment by using long-term financing. Long-term financing refers to the various alternatives available to the organization to get the money needed to acquire capital assets. Among the more common alternatives available to public service organizations are fund-raising campaigns, unsecured loans, mortgages, bonds, leases, and equity financing. Long-term financing generally provides the resources to acquire long-term assets and is repaid over a period of years in the future, if it is required to be repaid at all.

Key Terms from This Chapter

accounting rate of return (ARR).   The profitability of an investment calculated by considering the profits it generates, as compared with the amount of money invested.

accumulated depreciation.   Total amount of *depreciation* related to a fixed asset that has been taken over all of the years the organization has owned that asset.

amortization. Allocation of the cost of an intangible asset over its lifetime.

annualized cost method. Approach used to compare *capital assets* with differing lifetimes. The *net present cost* for each alternative is determined and then translated into a periodic payment for each year of the asset's life to find the cost per year, taking into account the time value of money.

annuity. Series of payments or receipts each in the same amount and spaced at even time periods. For example, $127.48 paid monthly for three years.

annuity in advance. An *annuity* with the first payment at the beginning of the first period.

annuity in arrears. An *annuity* with the first payment at the end of the first period.

annuity payments (PMT). See *annuity*.

capital acquisitions. See *capital assets*.

capital assets. Buildings or equipment with useful lives extending beyond the year in which they are purchased or put into service; also referred to as long-term investments, capital items, capital investments, or capital acquisitions.

capital budget. Plan for the acquisition of buildings and equipment that will be used by the organization in one or more years beyond the year of acquisition. Often a minimum dollar cutoff must be exceeded for an item to be included in the capital budget.

capital budgeting. Process of proposing the purchase of *capital assets*, analyzing the proposed purchases for economic or other justification, and encompassing the financial implications of capital items into the master budget.

cash flow. Measure of the amount of cash received or disbursed at a given point in time, as opposed to revenues or income, which frequently are recorded at a time other than when the actual cash receipt or payment occurs.

cell reference formula. An Excel formula that uses the cell addresses where the raw data are located.

compound interest. Method of calculating interest that accrues interest not only on the amount of the original investment but also on the interest that has been earned.

cost of capital. The cost to the organization of its money. Often represented by the interest rate that the organization pays on borrowed money.

cost-benefit analysis. Measurement of the relative costs and benefits associated with a particular project or task.

depreciation. Allocation of a portion of the cost of a *capital asset* into each of the years of the asset's expected useful life.

depreciation expense. Amount of the original cost of a *capital asset* allocated as an expense each year.

discounted cash flow. Method that allows comparisons of amounts of money paid at different points of time by *discounting* all amounts to the present.

discounting. Reverse of compound interest; a process in which interest that could be earned over time is deducted from a future payment to determine how much the future payment is worth at the present time.

discount rate. Interest rate used in discounting.

future value (FV). The amount a present amount of money will grow to be worth at some point in the future.

hurdle rate. See *required rate of return*.

internal rate of return (IRR). *Discounted cash flow* technique that calculates the rate of return earned on a specific project or program.

net present cost. Aggregate *present value* of a series of payments to be made in the future.

net present value (NPV). *Present value* of a series of cash receipts less cash payments.

numeric value formula. An Excel formula that contains the actual raw data values.

opportunity cost. A measure of cost based on the value of the alternatives that are given up to use the resource as the organization has chosen.

ordinary annuity. An *annuity in arrears*.

payback. *Capital budgeting* approach that calculates how many years it takes for a project's cash inflows to equal or exceed its cash outflows.

present value (PV). Value of future receipts or payments *discounted* to the present.

required rate of return. The interest rate that must be achieved for a capital project to be considered financially worthwhile. Also called the *hurdle rate*.

simple interest. Interest that is earned on an investment without any interest being earned on interest that has already been earned in prior periods.

time value of money (TVM). Recognition that money can earn *interest*, and therefore, a given amount of money paid at different points in time has a different value—the further into the future an amount is paid, the less valuable it is.

Questions for Discussion

5-1. Can capital budgets be consolidated into operating budgets to simplify the budget process?

5-2. Do capital budgets have any impact on operating budgets?

5-3. In theory, a capital asset must last at least one year and cost a substantial amount of money. True or false? Explain.

5-4. What are some reasons that capital asset acquisition decisions receive particular attention?

5-5. Wimpy, a character in the Popeye cartoons, offers to "gladly pay you Tuesday for a hamburger today." Why might Burger King find this to be an unattractive offer?

5-6. Explain compounding and discounting.

5-7. What problem would we encounter if we tried to use Table 5-A-2 to solve Exercise 5-14? What can we do to overcome this problem? (This question relates to Appendix 5-A.)

5-8. What is a potential problem with the net present cost method? How can this be overcome?

5-9. What are the limitations of the internal rate of return method?

5-10. What are the problems with the payback method?

Exercises (TVM)

5-11. How much will $8,000 invested at 3 percent simple interest be worth in three years? What will it be worth if the interest rate is 5 percent?

5-12. If you put $20,000 in the bank today to save for college, and leave it for five years, what monthly rate of interest will you have to earn in order to be able to pay a $30,000 tuition bill when you take the money out?

5-13. If you put $1,000 in the bank today and leave it for five years, will you have more money if the bank pays you 5 percent per annum in simple interest or 4.5 percent per year and compounds the interest monthly? Support your answer.

NOTE: For Exercises 5-14 through 5-18:

  A. Solve using the formula for FV or PV.
  B. Solve using a financial calculator.
  C. Solve using a spreadsheet program such as Excel. Indicate the spreadsheet formula showing numeric values rather than cell references. For example, for the value that $100 today could grow to in two years, assuming 10 percent annual compounding, the spreadsheet solution formula would be: "= FV(10%, 2, , 100)". Note that since there is no annuity payment (PMT) in this problem, it is necessary to show the blank between two commas after the number of periods.
  D. Solve using the time value of money tables. See Appendix 5-A. (Optional)

5-14. How much will $20,000 invested today at 3 percent interest be worth in five years if it is compounded annually? Quarterly? See earlier NOTE regarding requirements for Exercises 5-14 through 5-18.

5-15. If we receive $5,000, eight years from now, how much is that equivalent to today, if we believe that we can earn 5 percent on other opportunities? See earlier NOTE regarding requirements for Exercises 5-14 through 5-18.

5-16. If you have $7,500 today, and you could earn 3 percent interest per year, how many years would it be before you would accumulate $9,500 (assume annual compounding)? See earlier NOTE regarding requirements for Exercises 5-14 through 5-18.

5-17. How much must you put into a 4 percent investment annually to have $100,000 eight years from now? Assume all payments are made at the end of each period. See earlier NOTE regarding requirements for Exercises 5-14 through 5-18.

5-18. If you could put $10,000 into a 6 percent investment at the end of each year, how much money could you take out at the end of seven years? See earlier NOTE regarding requirements for Exercises 5-14 through 5-18.

5-19. Paula Morduch is considering purchasing a new van for Meals for the Homeless. She expects to buy the van for $50,000 three years from today. Solve using a calculator or spreadsheet.
  a. If she can invest money at 6 percent compounded quarterly, how much must she invest today? (Note that 6 percent compounded quarterly would call for use of a rate of 1.5 percent per quarterly period.)
  b. Suppose that Morduch believes that Meals for the Homeless can only put aside $35,000 today to buy the new van in three years. However, she thinks that she can invest the money at 12 percent compounded quarterly. Determine if she will have the $50,000 she will need for the new van.
  c. Assuming that Morduch can put aside $37,000 today and needs to have $50,000 available in three

years, what interest rate must be earned? Use quarterly compounding.

d. Assume that Morduch believes that she can only earn 8 percent per year on the money that Meals for the Homeless invests. Assuming monthly compounding, how much must be put aside today to provide $50,000 in three years?

e. Suppose Meals for the Homeless chooses to put aside money each quarter for three years to have $50,000 to buy a van at the end of the three years. Assuming Meals can earn 8 percent compounded quarterly, how much must it put aside each quarter?

f. Morduch is hoping to retire soon. She can put aside $100,000 today. She believes that she can earn 7 percent per year, with monthly compounding, and wants to have $1 million when she retires. How long will that be from now?

Problems

NOTE: For all problems:

A. Solve using a financial calculator.

B. Solve using a spreadsheet program such as Excel. Indicate the basic spreadsheet formula, and show both the numeric value formula and cell reference formula. For example, for the value that $100 today could grow to in two years, assuming 10 percent annual compounding, your solution might appear as shown below:

In the example below, Row 6 shows the basic Excel formula, Row 7 shows a numeric value formula, and Row 8 shows a cell reference formula. C7 is the solution calculated from the B7 formula, and C8 is the solution calculated from the B8 formula. Note that since there is no annuity payment (PMT) in this problem, it is necessary to show the blank between two commas after the number of periods (nper).

	A	B	C
1			
2	PV	($100)	
3	Nper	2	
4	Rate	10%	
5			
6	Excel Formula	= FV(rate, nper, pmt, pv, type)	
7	Numerical Formula Solution	= FV(10%, 2, , −100)	$121.00
8	Cell Reference Formula Solution	= FV(B4, B3, , B2)	$121.00

5-20. Jordan Township has purchased a used snowplow. It must pay the seller $430 at the end of each month for the next three years. If Jordan can borrow at 9 percent annually, what is the effective price paid for the plow, in today's dollars?

5-21. The city museum will have a Picasso exhibit on loan for three years. As part of the conditions of the loan, a specialized alarm and security system must be installed. High Security Company will install a suitable system for a $40,000 initial payment and $3,000 per month in monitoring fees. Tight Security Company will install a suitable system for an $85,000 initial payment and $1,200 per month in monitoring fees. Both security systems would be used for three years. Assuming an annual discount rate of 12 percent with monthly compounding, which contract has the lowest net present cost?

5-22. The City Transit Authority (CTA) is trying to decide between rail cars manufactured by French Corp and Japan Rail Car. The French Corp cars cost more to buy initially but they are expected to last for ten years. The Japan Rail Car cars are cheaper initially but they will wear out in six years. The cash flows related to each of the choices are presented below. If the CTA's cost of capital is 10%, which type of car should the CTA buy? Support your answer.

Year	French Corp	Japan Rail Car
0	($275,000)	($195,000)
1	(10,000)	(15,000)
2	(10,000)	(15,000)
3	(10,000)	(15,000)
4	(10,000)	(15,000)
5	(10,000)	(15,000)
6	(10,000)	(15,000)
7	(10,000)	
8	(10,000)	
9	(10,000)	
10	(10,000)	
Total	($375,000)	($285,000)

5-23. Schallville is considering two contracts to pave Broad Street. The first contractor bid $20,000 for the job and, with maintenance of $1,000 per year, will guarantee the surface for five years. The second contractor bid $14,000 for the same section of road and, with maintenance expenses of $1,500 per year, will guarantee the surface for four years. Assuming a discount rate of 8 percent, which option is the better deal for Schallville? Why?

5-24. The Town of Millbridge has to make a decision on replacing its garbage truck. It has narrowed the choice down to two different models. Model A will initially cost $80,000 and then will cost $5,000 per year to operate for its 20-year life. Model B will initially cost $100,000 and then will cost $2,500 per year to operate for its 30-year life. Use the annualized cost approach to determine which is a better choice. Assume a discount rate of 5 percent per year.

5-25. Smith Good Deeds Society is considering a four-year investment opportunity with the following cash flows:

Year	Cash In	Cash Out
0	0	650
1	140	25
2	140	25
3	140	25
4	340	25

If Smith uses an annual discount rate of 12 percent, should it pursue the investment? Show calculations to support your answer.

5-26. Duncombe Village Golf Course is considering the purchase of new equipment that will cost $1,200,000 if purchased today and will generate the following cash disbursements and receipts. Should Duncombe pursue the investment if the cost of capital is 8 percent? Why?

Year	Cash Receipts	Cash Disbursements	Net Cash Flow
1	1,000,000	500,000	500,000
2	925,000	475,000	450,000
3	800,000	450,000	350,000
4	750,000	430,000	320,000

5-27. The Town of Millbridge has just agreed to pay a pension to the town clerk. The pension will be $25,000 per year for the next 10 years. Dwight Ives, town manager, has decided that the town should put aside enough money today to pay for the entire pension. He has argued that the Town will not receive the clerk's services in the future, so future taxpayers should not have

to pay the pension. How much must be put aside, assuming the Town earns 6 percent compounded annually? Does this funding approach make sense to you?

5-28. Suppose that you were to receive a $20,000 gift upon graduation from your master's degree program, when you turn 31 years old. At the end of each working year for 34 years, you put an additional $2,000 into an IRA. Assuming you earn an annual compounded rate of 10 percent on the gift and the IRA investments, how much would be available when you retire at age 65 years? If you hope to draw money out of that investment at the end of every month for 30 years following retirement, how much could you withdraw each month? Assume that during the years you are retired the money earns an annual rate of 8 percent compounded monthly.

5-29. The Summertime Fun Camp is trying to decide whether it should lease a new handicapped transport van or buy one. The lease would be for four years and calls for the $7,700 annual payments including maintenance and insurance that are shown in the column labeled "Lease" below. As an accommodation to the camp, the leasing company has agreed to accept all payments, except the $2,500 cost of preparing the car for delivery, at the end of the each year of the lease. At the end of the lease, the van would be the property of the leasing company.

If they buy the van, the camp plans to use it for six years. They will pay $31,000 to buy the van, $2,250 each year for maintenance and insurance, and will be able to sell the van for $10,000 at the end of the sixth year. The cash flows associated with owning the van and using it for six years are in the column labeled "Own" below.

The camp was not able to negotiate a six-year lease for the van. If the cost of funds for the camp is 8%, which option should the camp take?

Period	Lease	Own
0	($2,500)	($31,000)
1	(7,700)	(2,250)
2	(7,700)	(2,250)
3	(7,700)	(2,250)
4	(7,700)	(2,250)
5		(2,250)
6		7,750
Total	($33,300)	($34,500)

5-30. The O'Regan Ambulance Paramedics wants to buy a new ambulance for $60,000 that will last for five years. They will pay for the acquisition and maintenance of the ambulance partially from donations and partially from receipts from the town. The local town has agreed to reimburse O'Regan $50 for each run it makes using the new ambulance. They expect to make 200 trips per year with the ambulance. It will cost $1,000 per year to maintain the vehicle. The squad uses a discount rate of 6 percent. How much will the squad need in donations to its capital fund this year to make the purchase a break-even proposition? (Hint: What is the net present value of the costs of buying and operating the ambulance over its lifetime, less the payments that will be received from the Town? Are the payments from the Town sufficient? If not, how much must be raised in donations before the ambulance is purchased?)

5-31. Assume that the Central Park Zoo is considering investing $5,000 today in a popcorn maker. The annual cash profits from the machine will be $800 for each of the seven years of its useful life. What is the IRR on the investment?

5-32. Urban Housing Agency (UHA) is considering contracts with private developers to provide low-income housing at various locations in the city. The startup costs to Urban for each location are $125,000, all of which must be paid to the developers in cash at the beginning. The housing rents would provide UHA net cash flows of $5,000 per month. The contracts last for three years. Urban only invests in projects that earn an annual rate of return of at least 18 percent. What rate of return would Urban earn on the contracts? Should Urban accept the contract? Why?

5-33. Refer to Problem 2-26 at the end of Chapter 2. Assume that the capital acquisitions in that problem were made at the beginning of fiscal year 2010. It is now the end of fiscal year 2012. Prepare a schedule showing those capital assets, their cost, their useful life, the accumulated depreciation at the beginning of 2012, the depreciation expense charged for 2012 (assuming straight-line depreciation and no salvage value), the accumulated depreciation as of the end of the year, and the net book value (cost less accumulated depreciation) as of the end of the 2012 year. Use a spreadsheet program such as Excel. As River Country may dispose of the items at different times, note that it is necessary to track each item separately.

CASE STUDY
Mead Meals on Wheels Center—Part II[13]

Refer to Chapter 4 for the beginning of this case study. You may make whatever assumptions you think are necessary to answer any question. Be sure to state every assumption *explicitly.*

Problem 3

During the year, you analyzed Mead Meals on Wheels Center's (MMWC's) kitchen operations and determined that MMWC could increase the capacity of the kitchen to 10,400 meals per day. You see a chance to increase the number of meals that MMWC can deliver to the elderly as well as a way to increase your weekly revenue. However, expanding the kitchen's capacity will require you to purchase $625,000 worth of equipment. The equipment has a useful life of five years.

Just as you started your analysis of the expansion, a food purveyor from outside the Millbridge city limits responded to MMWC's request for bids and gave the Center a bid that was $.75 per person-week below the quote that was used in your original budget. That is a full $1.25 below the break-even level that you calculated.

The executive director is interested in any idea that will expand service delivery, but she is concerned about being able to pay for the equipment. She tells you that MMWC's cost of capital is 12 percent. She has instructed you to use the new food bid as your cost per person-week for food. She only wants to buy the new equipment if it generates enough additional contribution to pay for itself, taking into account the time value of money.

> *If MMWC buys the equipment to expand their services, will that expansion have a positive financial impact? Support your recommendation and present your findings in a way that the director will understand.* (Hint: You must separate the impact of the change in the cost of food, from the financial impact of the investment.)

---

[13] Mead Meals on Wheels Center and its solution were written by Robert Purtell, Robert F. Wagner Graduate School of Public Service, New York University. Reprinted with permission.

Problem 4

You finish your capital budget analysis just in time to prepare the operating budget for the coming year. The executive director wants you to use the previous year's budget as a starting point. Cold weather and snow in this year's first quarter of operation caused MMWC to exceed the limits of its snowplowing and heating-oil contracts. As a result, MMWC's fixed costs were $2,000 per week above what you had forecasted. To be conservative, the executive director wants next year's budget to reflect these higher first-quarter fixed costs.

In addition, she has decided to accept your recommendation about the kitchen equipment. A local bank has offered to lend MMWC the full purchase price of the equipment and not require the center to repay any principal during the first year of the loan. Interest on the loan would be set at 12 percent per annum. MMWC's normal policy is to assume a 10 percent residual or salvage[14] value on all kitchen equipment and to depreciate it over five years on a straight-line basis.[15]

Incorporating all of the things that have happened during the year as well as your capital budgeting recommendation, prepare a new quarterly operating budget and annual summary (totals) for MMWC for the coming year.

Suggested Readings

Anthony, Robert N., and Leslie Pearlman Breitner. *Essentials of Accounting*, 9th ed. Upper Saddle River, N.J.: Prentice Hall, 2006.

Bierman, Harold, and Seymour Smidt. *The Capital Budgeting Decision: Economic Analysis of Investment Projects*, 8th ed. Upper Saddle River, N.J.: Prentice Hall, 1993.

Boardman, Anthony, David Greenberg, Aidan Vining, and David Weimer. *Cost Benefit Analysis: Concepts and Practice*, 3rd ed. Upper Saddle River, N.J.: Prentice Hall, 2006.

Brigham, Eugene F. and Joel F. Houston. *Fundamentals of Financial Management*, 11th ed. Mason, Ohio: Thomson/South-Western, 2006.

Emery, Douglas R., John D. Finnerty, and John D. Stowe. *Corporate Financial Management*, 3rd ed. Upper Saddle River, N.J.: Prentice Hall, 2007.

Fuguitt, Diana, and Shanton J. Wilcox. *Cost-Benefit Analysis for Public Sector Decision Makers*. Westport, CT: Quorum Books, 1999.

Gramlich, Edward M. *A Guide to Benefit-Cost Analysis*, 2nd ed. Long Grove, Ill.: Waveland Press, 1998.

Horngren, Charles T., Gary L. Sundem, and William O. Stratton, et al. *Introduction to Management Accounting*, 4th ed. Upper Saddle River, N.J.: Prentice Hall, 2002.

Keown, Arthur J., John W. Martin, William D. Petty, and David F. Scott. *Foundations of Finance: The Logic and Practice of Financial Management,* 6th ed. Upper Saddle River, N.J.: Prentice Hall, 2008.

Mishan, E. J., and Euston Quah. *Cost Benefit Analysis,* 5th ed. New York, N.Y.: Routledge, 2007.

Van Horne, James C., and John M. Wachowicz *Fundamentals of Financial Management*, 12th ed. Upper Saddle River, N.J.: Prentice Hall, 2005.

---

[14] The residual or salvage value is the portion of the original cost of a building or piece of equipment that is not consumed while the organization owns it. Salvage or residual is the amount that the organization expects to receive when it sells the equipment or building. When calculating depreciation, only the portion of the item that is consumed can be depreciated. Therefore, the salvage value is subtracted from the cost before depreciation is determined. For example, if you pay $1,200 for a machine that has a five-year life and a $200 salvage value, the depreciation would be $200 per year ($1,200 cost − $200 salvage = $1,000 to be depreciated. $1,000 ÷ 5 years = $200 depreciation per year).

[15] Straight-line depreciation assumes that an equal amount of depreciation is charged each year. Accelerated methods exist that allow for a greater amount of depreciation in earlier years and less depreciation in later years. Accelerated methods for depreciation are discussed in Appendix 10-B.

APPENDIX 5-A

Using Time Value of Money (TVM) Tables

The process of using TVM formulas can become laborious. In an effort to simplify the process, tables commonly referred to as *Present Value* or Time Value of Money tables were introduced. These tables provide the results of the compound or discount interest calculation. The tables appear at the end of this appendix.

TVM tables are prepared using the mathematical formulas discussed in the chapter. For example, suppose that we have $100 today and wish to invest it for 10 years at 10 percent interest, with quarterly compounding. Using the mathematical formulas discussed in the chapter, we can solve this as follows:

$$FV = PV(1+i)^N$$
$$FV = \$100(1+.025)^{40}$$

Before the existence of handheld calculators and personal computers, determining the value of $(1 + .025)^{40}$ would require a tedious calculation by hand. The role of the table is to present the results of the calculation of $(1 + i)^N$ for a variety of different values for both i and N. Users can then look up the values on the table and avoid having to repeat the calculations. Since the formulas to find the PV, and the present and future values of an annuity are even more complex than the formula for finding the FV, having the tables for those calculations is even more beneficial. The future value of $1 table, Table 5-A-1, calculates the value for $(1 + i)$ raised to a power of N. This value from the table is often referred to as a *factor*. The formula for calculating a future value, using Table 5-A-1, would be as follows:

$$FV = PV \times (FV \text{ Factor from FV of \$1 Table, i, N})$$

or

$$FV = PV \times (FVF \text{ from Table 5-A-1, i, N})$$

In words, the future value (FV) is equal to the present value (PV) multiplied by the future value factor (FVF) from the future value of one dollar table,

evaluated at a given interest rate (i) and number of compounding periods (N). The factor is based on $1. By multiplying the factor times the PV, it adjusts the FV for the number of dollars being invested at the present. For example, to find how much $100 would be worth after two years of annual compounding at 6 percent,

$$FV = 100 \times (FVF \text{ from Table 5-A-1, 6\%, 2})$$
$$FV = 100 \times (1.1236) = 112.36$$

To find a factor from Table 5-A-1, look down the left side of the table to find the appropriate number of compounding periods, and then go across the columns to the appropriate interest rate. If compounding more often than once a year, be sure to adjust both i and N. For example, with quarterly compounding,

$$FV = 100 \times (FVF \text{ from Table 5-A-1, 1.5\%, 8})$$
$$FV = 100 \times (1.1265) = 112.65$$

The interest rate is 1.5 percent per quarter, and there are eight quarters in two years. Go to the eighth row for eight compounding periods and across to the third column for 1.5 percent.

Just as there is a table for finding appropriate factors for future values, there is a table of factors for present values, Table 5-A-2. The formula for calculating a present value, using Table 5-A-2, would be as follows:

$$PV = FV \times (PV \text{ factor from PV of \$1 Table, i, N})$$

or

$$PV = FV \times (PVF \text{ from Table 5-A-2, i, N})$$

The PV is the FV discounted back to the present. We find it by taking the future value multiplied by the present value factor (PVF) from Table 5-A-2. In order to remember how to use the tables, it is helpful to keep in mind that to find the PV, we must use the PV table, and to find the FV, we must use the FV table.

Unfortunately, the tables are inherently limited, because they do not have every interest rate. What if we wanted to compound 10 percent monthly? We would need to find 10 percent divided by 12 in the interest rate columns. That would be .83 percent per month. However, there is no column for .83 percent. We could approximate a value based on using the nearest interest rate. For example, we could take a number somewhere between the factors the table gives for .5 percent and 1 percent. This tedious and inexact process can be avoided if a calculator or computer is used to solve the problem.

We can also find PVs and FVs of annuities using Tables 5-A-3 and 5-A-4 at the end of this appendix. The formula for calculating the present value of an annuity, using Table 5-A-4, would be as follows:

$$PVA = PMT \times (PVAF \text{ from PVA \$1 Table, i, N})$$

The present value of an annuity, PVA, equals the periodic annuity payment (PMT) multiplied by a present value annuity factor (PVAF) from the PV of an annuity table (PVA) for \$1, using the interest rate (i) and number of payments (N). Similarly, the FV of an annuity, FVA, can be found using a future value for an annuity (FVA) table. The formula for calculating the future value of an annuity, using Table 5-A-3, would be as follows:

$$FVA = PMT \times (FVAF \text{ from FVA \$1 Table, i, N})$$

Suppose that we expect to receive \$100 per year for the next two years. We could normally invest money at an interest rate of 10 percent compounded annually. What is the PV of those payments?

$$PVA = PMT \times (PVAF \text{ from Table 5-A-4, i, N})$$
$$PVA = \$100 \times (PVAF \text{ from Table 5-A-4, 10\%, 2})$$
$$PVA = \$100 \times 1.7355 = \$173.55$$

That means that receiving two annual payments of \$100 each is worth \$173.55 today, if the interest rate is 10 percent. How much would those two payments of \$100 each be worth at the end of the two years?

$$FVA = PMT \times (FVAF \text{ from Table 5-A-3, i, N})$$
$$FVA = \$100 \times (FVAF \text{ from Table 5-A-3, 10\%, 2})$$
$$FVA = \$100 \times 2.100 = \$210$$

Observe that there is a great deal of flexibility with these approaches. If we know the periodic payment, interest rate, and number of compounding periods, we can find the FV. Or if we know how much we need to have in the future and how many times we can make a specific periodic payment, we can calculate the interest rate that must be earned. Or we could find out how long we would have to keep making payments to reach a certain future value goal. Given three variables, we can generally find the fourth.

The TVM factors that appear in each of the four TVM tables are based on mathematical formulas. The formula used to derive the factors for each table appears in a note at the bottom of the table.

TABLE 5-A-1 Future Value of $1

N	0.5	1	1.5	2	2.5	3	4	5	6	7	8	9	10	12	15
1	1.0050	1.0100	1.0150	1.0200	1.0250	1.0300	1.0400	1.0500	1.0600	1.0700	1.0800	1.0900	1.1000	1.1200	1.1500
2	1.0100	1.0201	1.0302	1.0404	1.0506	1.0609	1.0816	1.1025	1.1236	1.1449	1.1664	1.1881	1.2100	1.2544	1.3225
3	1.0151	1.0303	1.0457	1.0612	1.0769	1.0927	1.1249	1.1576	1.1910	1.2250	1.2597	1.2950	1.3310	1.4049	1.5209
4	1.0202	1.0406	1.0614	1.0824	1.1038	1.1255	1.1699	1.2155	1.2625	1.3108	1.3605	1.4116	1.4641	1.5735	1.7490
5	1.0253	1.0510	1.0773	1.1041	1.1314	1.1593	1.2167	1.2763	1.3382	1.4026	1.4693	1.5386	1.6105	1.7623	2.0114
6	1.0304	1.0615	1.0934	1.1262	1.1597	1.1941	1.2653	1.3401	1.4185	1.5007	1.5869	1.6771	1.7716	1.9738	2.3131
7	1.0355	1.0721	1.1098	1.1487	1.1887	1.2299	1.3159	1.4071	1.5036	1.6058	1.7138	1.8280	1.9487	2.2107	2.6600
8	1.0407	1.0829	1.1265	1.1717	1.2184	1.2668	1.3686	1.4774	1.5938	1.7182	1.8509	1.9926	2.1436	2.4760	3.0590
9	1.0459	1.0937	1.1434	1.1951	1.2489	1.3048	1.4233	1.5513	1.6895	1.8385	1.9990	2.1719	2.3579	2.7731	3.5179
10	1.0511	1.1046	1.1605	1.2190	1.2801	1.3439	1.4802	1.6289	1.7908	1.9672	2.1589	2.3674	2.5937	3.1058	4.0456
11	1.0564	1.1157	1.1779	1.2434	1.3121	1.3842	1.5395	1.7103	1.8983	2.1049	2.3316	2.5804	2.8531	3.4785	4.6524
12	1.0617	1.1268	1.1956	1.2682	1.3449	1.4258	1.6010	1.7959	2.0122	2.2522	2.5182	2.8127	3.1384	3.8960	5.3503
13	1.0670	1.1381	1.2136	1.2936	1.3785	1.4685	1.6651	1.8856	2.1329	2.4098	2.7196	3.0658	3.4523	4.3635	6.1528
14	1.0723	1.1495	1.2318	1.3195	1.4130	1.5126	1.7317	1.9799	2.2609	2.5785	2.9372	3.3417	3.7975	4.8871	7.0757
15	1.0777	1.1610	1.2502	1.3459	1.4483	1.5580	1.8009	2.0789	2.3966	2.7590	3.1722	3.6425	4.1772	5.4736	8.1371
16	1.0831	1.1726	1.2690	1.3728	1.4845	1.6047	1.8730	2.1829	2.5404	2.9522	3.4259	3.9703	4.5950	6.1304	9.3576
17	1.0885	1.1843	1.2880	1.4002	1.5216	1.6528	1.9479	2.2920	2.6928	3.1588	3.7000	4.3276	5.0545	6.8660	10.7613
18	1.0939	1.1961	1.3073	1.4282	1.5597	1.7024	2.0258	2.4066	2.8543	3.3799	3.9960	4.7171	5.5599	7.6900	12.3755
19	1.0994	1.2081	1.3270	1.4568	1.5987	1.7535	2.1068	2.5270	3.0256	3.6165	4.3157	5.1417	6.1159	8.6128	14.2318
20	1.1049	1.2202	1.3469	1.4859	1.6386	1.8061	2.1911	2.6533	3.2071	3.8697	4.6610	5.6044	6.7275	9.6463	16.3665
25	1.1328	1.2824	1.4509	1.6406	1.8539	2.0938	2.6658	3.3864	4.2919	5.4274	6.8485	8.6231	10.8347	17.0001	32.9190
30	1.1614	1.3478	1.5631	1.8114	2.0976	2.4273	3.2434	4.3219	5.7435	7.6123	10.0627	13.2677	17.4494	29.9599	66.2118
35	1.1907	1.4166	1.6839	1.9999	2.3732	2.8139	3.9461	5.5160	7.6861	10.6766	14.7853	20.4140	28.1024	52.7996	133.1755
40	1.2208	1.4889	1.8140	2.2080	2.6851	3.2620	4.8010	7.0400	10.2857	14.9745	21.7245	31.4094	45.2593	93.0510	267.8635
50	1.2832	1.6446	2.1052	2.6916	3.4371	4.3839	7.1067	11.4674	18.4202	29.4570	46.9016	74.3575	117.3909	289.0022	1083.6574

The compounded, or future value of $1 = (1 + i)^N$ where i = the percent interest rate per compounding period and N = the number of compounding periods.

Assumes all payments are made at the end of each period.

TABLE 5-A-2 Present Value of $1

N	0.5	1	1.5	2	2.5	3	4	5	6	7	8	9	10	12	15
1	0.9950	0.9901	0.9852	0.9804	0.9756	0.9709	0.9615	0.9524	0.9434	0.9346	0.9259	0.9174	0.9091	0.8929	0.8696
2	0.9901	0.9803	0.9707	0.9612	0.9518	0.9426	0.9246	0.9070	0.8900	0.8734	0.8573	0.8417	0.8264	0.7972	0.7561
3	0.9851	0.9706	0.9563	0.9423	0.9286	0.9151	0.8890	0.8638	0.8396	0.8163	0.7938	0.7722	0.7513	0.7118	0.6575
4	0.9802	0.9610	0.9422	0.9238	0.9060	0.8885	0.8548	0.8227	0.7921	0.7629	0.7350	0.7084	0.6830	0.6355	0.5718
5	0.9754	0.9515	0.9283	0.9057	0.8839	0.8626	0.8219	0.7835	0.7473	0.7130	0.6806	0.6499	0.6209	0.5674	0.4972
6	0.9705	0.9420	0.9145	0.8880	0.8623	0.8375	0.7903	0.7462	0.7050	0.6663	0.6302	0.5963	0.5645	0.5066	0.4323
7	0.9657	0.9327	0.9010	0.8706	0.8413	0.8131	0.7599	0.7107	0.6651	0.6227	0.5835	0.5470	0.5132	0.4523	0.3759
8	0.9609	0.9235	0.8877	0.8535	0.8207	0.7894	0.7307	0.6768	0.6274	0.5820	0.5403	0.5019	0.4665	0.4039	0.3269
9	0.9561	0.9143	0.8746	0.8368	0.8007	0.7664	0.7026	0.6446	0.5919	0.5439	0.5002	0.4604	0.4241	0.3606	0.2843
10	0.9513	0.9053	0.8617	0.8203	0.7812	0.7441	0.6756	0.6139	0.5584	0.5083	0.4632	0.4224	0.3855	0.3220	0.2472
11	0.9466	0.8963	0.8489	0.8043	0.7621	0.7224	0.6496	0.5847	0.5268	0.4751	0.4289	0.3875	0.3505	0.2875	0.2149
12	0.9419	0.8874	0.8364	0.7885	0.7436	0.7014	0.6246	0.5568	0.4970	0.4440	0.3971	0.3555	0.3186	0.2567	0.1869
13	0.9372	0.8787	0.8240	0.7730	0.7254	0.6810	0.6006	0.5303	0.4688	0.4150	0.3677	0.3262	0.2897	0.2292	0.1625
14	0.9326	0.8700	0.8118	0.7579	0.7077	0.6611	0.5775	0.5051	0.4423	0.3878	0.3405	0.2992	0.2633	0.2046	0.1413
15	0.9279	0.8613	0.7999	0.7430	0.6905	0.6419	0.5553	0.4810	0.4173	0.3624	0.3152	0.2745	0.2394	0.1827	0.1229
16	0.9233	0.8528	0.7880	0.7284	0.6736	0.6232	0.5339	0.4581	0.3936	0.3387	0.2919	0.2519	0.2176	0.1631	0.1069
17	0.9187	0.8444	0.7764	0.7142	0.6572	0.6050	0.5134	0.4363	0.3714	0.3166	0.2703	0.2311	0.1978	0.1456	0.0929
18	0.9141	0.8360	0.7649	0.7002	0.6412	0.5874	0.4936	0.4155	0.3503	0.2959	0.2502	0.2120	0.1799	0.1300	0.0808
19	0.9096	0.8277	0.7536	0.6864	0.6255	0.5703	0.4746	0.3957	0.3305	0.2765	0.2317	0.1945	0.1635	0.1161	0.0703
20	0.9051	0.8195	0.7425	0.6730	0.6103	0.5537	0.4564	0.3769	0.3118	0.2584	0.2145	0.1784	0.1486	0.1037	0.0611
25	0.8828	0.7798	0.6892	0.6095	0.5394	0.4776	0.3751	0.2953	0.2330	0.1842	0.1460	0.1160	0.0923	0.0588	0.0304
30	0.8610	0.7419	0.6398	0.5521	0.4767	0.4120	0.3083	0.2314	0.1741	0.1314	0.0994	0.0754	0.0573	0.0334	0.0151
35	0.8398	0.7059	0.5939	0.5000	0.4214	0.3554	0.2534	0.1813	0.1301	0.0937	0.0676	0.0490	0.0356	0.0189	0.0075
40	0.8191	0.6717	0.5513	0.4529	0.3724	0.3066	0.2083	0.1420	0.0972	0.0668	0.0460	0.0318	0.0221	0.0107	0.0037
50	0.7793	0.6080	0.4750	0.3715	0.2909	0.2281	0.1407	0.0872	0.0543	0.0339	0.0213	0.0134	0.0085	0.0035	0.0009

i

The discounted, or present value of $1 = 1/(1 + i)^N$ where i = the percent interest rate per discounting period and N = the number of compounding periods.
Assumes all payments are made at the end of each period.

TABLE 5-A-3 Future Value of an Annuity of $1

N	0.5	1	1.5	2	2.5	3	4	5	6	7	8	9	10	12	15
1	1.0000	1.0000	1.0000	1.0000	1.0000	1.0000	1.0000	1.0000	1.0000	1.0000	1.0000	1.0000	1.0000	1.0000	1.0000
2	2.0050	2.0100	2.0150	2.0200	2.0250	2.0300	2.0400	2.0500	2.0600	2.0700	2.0800	2.0900	2.1000	2.1200	2.1500
3	3.0150	3.0301	3.0452	3.0604	3.0756	3.0909	3.1216	3.1525	3.1836	3.2149	3.2464	3.2781	3.3100	3.3744	3.4725
4	4.0301	4.0604	4.0909	4.1216	4.1525	4.1836	4.2465	4.3101	4.3746	4.4399	4.5061	4.5731	4.6410	4.7793	4.9934
5	5.0503	5.1010	5.1523	5.2040	5.2563	5.3091	5.4163	5.5256	5.6371	5.7507	5.8666	5.9847	6.1051	6.3528	6.7424
6	6.0755	6.1520	6.2296	6.3081	6.3877	6.4684	6.6330	6.8019	6.9753	7.1533	7.3359	7.5233	7.7156	8.1152	8.7537
7	7.1059	7.2135	7.3230	7.4343	7.5474	7.6625	7.8983	8.1420	8.3938	8.6540	8.9228	9.2004	9.4872	10.0890	11.0668
8	8.1414	8.2857	8.4328	8.5830	8.7361	8.8923	9.2142	9.5491	9.8975	10.2598	10.6366	11.0285	11.4359	12.2997	13.7268
9	9.1821	9.3685	9.5593	9.7546	9.9545	10.1591	10.5828	11.0266	11.4913	11.9780	12.4876	13.0210	13.5795	14.7757	16.7858
10	10.2280	10.4622	10.7027	10.9497	11.2034	11.4639	12.0061	12.5779	13.1808	13.8164	14.4866	15.1929	15.9374	17.5487	20.3037
11	11.2792	11.5668	11.8633	12.1687	12.4835	12.8078	13.4864	14.2068	14.9716	15.7836	16.6455	17.5603	18.5312	20.6546	24.3493
12	12.3356	12.6825	13.0412	13.4121	13.7956	14.1920	15.0258	15.9171	16.8699	17.8885	18.9771	20.1407	21.3843	24.1331	29.0017
13	13.3972	13.8093	14.2368	14.6803	15.1404	15.6178	16.6268	17.7130	18.8821	20.1406	21.4953	22.9534	24.5227	28.0291	34.3519
14	14.4642	14.9474	15.4504	15.9739	16.5190	17.0863	18.2919	19.5986	21.0151	22.5505	24.2149	26.0192	27.9750	32.3926	40.5047
15	15.5365	16.0969	16.6821	17.2934	17.9319	18.5989	20.0236	21.5786	23.2760	25.1290	27.1521	29.3609	31.7725	37.2797	47.5804
16	16.6142	17.2579	17.9324	18.6393	19.3802	20.1569	21.8245	23.6575	25.6725	27.8881	30.3243	33.0034	35.9497	42.7533	55.7175
17	17.6973	18.4304	19.2014	20.0121	20.8647	21.7616	23.6975	25.8404	28.2129	30.8402	33.7502	36.9737	40.5447	48.8837	65.0751
18	18.7858	19.6147	20.4894	21.4123	22.3863	23.4144	25.6454	28.1324	30.9057	33.9990	37.4502	41.3013	45.5992	55.7497	75.8364
19	19.8797	20.8109	21.7967	22.8406	23.9460	25.1169	27.6712	30.5390	33.7600	37.3790	41.4463	46.0185	51.1591	63.4397	88.2118
20	20.9791	22.0190	23.1237	24.2974	25.5447	26.8704	29.7781	33.0660	36.7856	40.9955	45.7620	51.1601	57.2750	72.0524	102.4436
25	26.5591	28.2432	30.0630	32.0303	34.1578	36.4593	41.6459	47.7271	54.8645	63.2490	73.1059	84.7009	98.3471	133.3339	212.7930
30	32.2800	34.7849	37.5387	40.5681	43.9027	47.5754	56.0849	66.4388	79.0582	94.4608	113.2832	136.3075	164.4940	241.3327	434.7451
35	38.1454	41.6603	45.5921	49.9945	54.9282	60.4621	73.6522	90.3203	111.4348	138.2369	172.3168	215.7108	271.0244	431.6635	881.1702
40	44.1588	48.8864	54.2679	60.4020	67.4026	75.4013	95.0255	120.7998	154.7620	199.6351	259.0565	337.8824	442.5926	767.0914	1779.0903
50	56.6452	64.4632	73.6828	84.5794	97.4843	112.7969	152.6671	209.3480	290.3359	406.5289	573.7702	815.0836	1163.9085	2400.0182	7217.7163

The compounded, or future value of an annuity of $1 = $\dfrac{[(1 + i)^N - 1]}{i}$

Note: N = number of compounding periods; i = percent interest rate per compounding period.

Assumes all payments are made at the end of each period.

TABLE 5-A-4 Present Value of an Annuity of $1

i

N	0.5	1	1.5	2	2.5	3	4	5	6	7	8	9	10	12	15
1	0.9950	0.9901	0.9852	0.9804	0.9756	0.9709	0.9615	0.9524	0.9434	0.9346	0.9259	0.9174	0.9091	0.8929	0.8696
2	1.9851	1.9704	1.9559	1.9416	1.9274	1.9135	1.8861	1.8594	1.8334	1.8080	1.7833	1.7591	1.7355	1.6901	1.6257
3	2.9702	2.9410	2.9122	2.8839	2.8560	2.8286	2.7751	2.7232	2.6730	2.6243	2.5771	2.5313	2.4869	2.4018	2.2832
4	3.9505	3.9020	3.8544	3.8077	3.7620	3.7171	3.6299	3.5460	3.4651	3.3872	3.3121	3.2397	3.1699	3.0373	2.8550
5	4.9259	4.8534	4.7826	4.7135	4.6458	4.5797	4.4518	4.3295	4.2124	4.1002	3.9927	3.8897	3.7908	3.6048	3.3522
6	5.8964	5.7955	5.6972	5.6014	5.5081	5.4172	5.2421	5.0757	4.9173	4.7665	4.6229	4.4859	4.3553	4.1114	3.7845
7	6.8621	6.7282	6.5982	6.4720	6.3494	6.2303	6.0021	5.7864	5.5824	5.3893	5.2064	5.0330	4.8684	4.5638	4.1604
8	7.8230	7.6517	7.4859	7.3255	7.1701	7.0197	6.7327	6.4632	6.2098	5.9713	5.7466	5.5348	5.3349	4.9676	4.4873
9	8.7791	8.5660	8.3605	8.1622	7.9709	7.7861	7.4353	7.1078	6.8017	6.5152	6.2469	5.9952	5.7590	5.3282	4.7716
10	9.7304	9.4713	9.2222	8.9826	8.7521	8.5302	8.1109	7.7217	7.3601	7.0236	6.7101	6.4177	6.1446	5.6502	5.0188
11	10.6770	10.3676	10.0711	9.7868	9.5142	9.2526	8.7605	8.3064	7.8869	7.4987	7.1390	6.8052	6.4951	5.9377	5.2337
12	11.6189	11.2551	10.9075	10.5753	10.2578	9.9540	9.3851	8.8633	8.3838	7.9427	7.5361	7.1607	6.8137	6.1944	5.4206
13	12.5562	12.1337	11.7315	11.3484	10.9832	10.6350	9.9856	9.3936	8.8527	8.3577	7.9038	7.4869	7.1034	6.4235	5.5831
14	13.4887	13.0037	12.5434	12.1062	11.6909	11.2961	10.5631	9.8986	9.2950	8.7455	8.2442	7.7862	7.3667	6.6282	5.7245
15	14.4166	13.8651	13.3432	12.8493	12.3814	11.9379	11.1184	10.3797	9.7122	9.1079	8.5595	8.0607	7.6061	6.8109	5.8474
16	15.3399	14.7179	14.1313	13.5777	13.0550	12.5611	11.6523	10.8378	10.1059	9.4466	8.8514	8.3126	7.8237	6.9740	5.9542
17	16.2586	15.5623	14.9076	14.2919	13.7122	13.1661	12.1657	11.2741	10.4773	9.7632	9.1216	8.5436	8.0216	7.1196	6.0472
18	17.1728	16.3983	15.6726	14.9920	14.3534	13.7535	12.6593	11.6896	10.8276	10.0591	9.3719	8.7556	8.2014	7.2497	6.1280
19	18.0824	17.2260	16.4262	15.6785	14.9789	14.3238	13.1339	12.0853	11.1581	10.3356	9.6036	8.9501	8.3649	7.3658	6.1982
20	18.9874	18.0456	17.1686	16.3514	15.5892	14.8775	13.5903	12.4622	11.4699	10.5940	9.8181	9.1285	8.5136	7.4694	6.2593
25	23.4456	22.0232	20.7196	19.5235	18.4244	17.4131	15.6221	14.0939	12.7834	11.6536	10.6748	9.8226	9.0770	7.8431	6.4641
30	27.7941	25.8077	24.0158	22.3965	20.9303	19.6004	17.2920	15.3725	13.7648	12.4090	11.2578	10.2737	9.4269	8.0552	6.5660
35	32.0354	29.4086	27.0756	24.9986	23.1452	21.4872	18.6646	16.3742	14.4982	12.9477	11.6546	10.5668	9.6442	8.1755	6.6166
40	36.1722	32.8347	29.9158	27.3555	25.1028	23.1148	19.7928	17.1591	15.0463	13.3317	11.9246	10.7574	9.7791	8.2438	6.6418
50	44.1428	39.1961	34.9997	31.4236	28.3623	25.7298	21.4822	18.2559	15.7619	13.8007	12.2335	10.9617	9.9148	8.3045	6.6605

The discounted, or present value of an annuity of $1 = \dfrac{1 - [1/(+i)^N]}{i}$

Note: N = number of discounting periods; *i* = percent interest rate per discounting period.

Assumes all payments are made at the end of each period.

APPENDIX 5-B

Using Computer Spreadsheets for Time Value of Money Calculations—Examples

Computer spreadsheet programs such as Microsoft's Excel can be used to solve time value of money (TVM) calculations, as discussed in Chapter 5. The chapter provided a detailed example for finding a future value (FV) using Excel. This appendix provides examples of the specific steps required to find present values (PV), annuity payments (PMT), rates, number of compounding periods (nper), net present value (NPV), and internal rate of return (IRR), using Excel 2007. The procedure may be slightly different for other versions of Excel.[16]

In each case the basic approach is to click on the *fx* function wizard on the formula bar, indicate in the Insert Function window that the category is *Financial*, and select *PV, Rate, Nper, PMT, NPV* or *IRR*, respectively, as the function. As each function is highlighted in the Insert Function window, its Excel formula appears near the bottom of the window. The formulas are:

$$= PV(rate,nper,pmt,fv,type)$$
$$= Rate(nper,pmt,pv,fv,type,guess)$$
$$= Nper(rate,pmt,pv,fv,type)$$
$$= PMT(rate,nper,pv,fv, type)$$
$$= NPV(rate,value1,value2,. . .)$$
$$= IRR(values,guess)$$

PRESENT VALUE

Suppose that we can buy a captial asset that will result in our receiving $15,000, five years from now, and that we believe an appropriate discount rate for this specific piece of equipment is 7 percent. We need to decide the most that we would

FIGURE 5-B-1   Present Value–Data

pay for that asset. What is the PV of that future receipt?

We can start the solution by recording the raw data in an Excel spreadsheet. See Figure 5-B-1. Note that the cursor in this screen is pointing at the function wizard: *fx*. Click on the wizard and the Insert Function window appears. Use the drop-down menu to change the Category to Financial, and scroll down to PV. The result is seen in Figure 5-B-2. Note that we can see in that screen that the formula for the PV is PV(rate, nper, pmt, fv, type). Click OK. Enter the cell references for the Rate, Nper, and Fv. If you want the solution to appear as a positive number, enter a minus sign before the cell reference for the Fv. This will generate Figure 5-B-3. Click OK to solve the problem. The resulting screen would appear as Figure 5-B-4, and the present value is $10,694.79. If we wished to show the formula with numeric values, it would be = PV(7%, 5, , −15000).

RATE

Suppose that we have $10,000 today, could invest it for six years, and need to have $20,000 at

---

[16] The Excel approach used in this chapter is based on Microsoft Excel 2007. Other versions of Excel may differ somewhat in the exact approach, steps, or formulas used, and in the exact appearance of the screen.

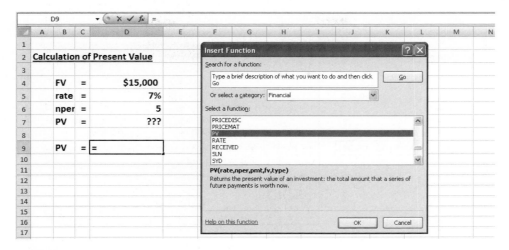

FIGURE 5-B-2 Insert Function Window

FIGURE 5-B-3 Function Arguments Window

the end of that time. What rate would have to be earned? The data setup would be similar to the problem just solved, except that we are looking for the rate rather than the present value. We would click on the function wizard, and in the Insert Function window would select Financial as the category and Rate as the function. The formula appears on the Insert Functions window as Rate(nper, pmt, pv, fv, type, guess). We would then click OK and enter the cell references, as shown in Figure 5-B-5. Note that either the PV or the FV must be a negative number. The rate that must be earned for $10,000 to grow to $20,000 in six years is shown in Figure 5-B-6. The formula for this with numeric

	D9			f_x =PV(D5,D6,,-D4)	
	A	B	C	D	E
1					
2	**Calculation of Present Value**				
3					
4		FV	=	$15,000	
5		rate	=	7%	
6		nper	=	5	
7		PV	=	???	
8					
9		PV	=	$10,694.79	
10					

FIGURE 5-B-4 Present Value Solution

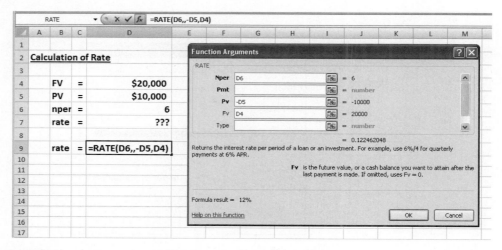

FIGURE 5-B-5 Function Arguments Window for Rate Solution

values would be = Rate(6, , -10000, 20000). We leave a blank between two commas for Pmt as there is no periodic repeating payment in this problem. We do not need to enter any values for type or guess.

NUMBER OF PERIODS

Suppose that we can only earn 9 percent per year. How many years would it be before our $10,000 will grow to become $20,000? After setting up the data, we would click on *fx*, select the Financial category and Nper as the function.

The formula that appears is Nper(rate, pmt, pv, fv, type). Then click OK. The Function Arguments window, showing the cell references, is shown in Figure 5-B-7. After entering the cell references in this window, click OK, and the result is 8.04, or a little bit longer than 8 years. Notice that the result can also be seen at the bottom of the Function Arguments window in Figure 5-B-7. The formula with numeric values would be = Nper(9%, , -10000, 20000).

PERIODIC PAYMENTS (IN ARREARS)

Assume that you can invest money every year for 7 years at 8 percent. If you need $20,000 at the end of the 7 years, how much would you have to put aside each year? Assume you make the payments at the end of each year. After setting up the data, clicking on the function wizard, and selecting the financial category and the PMT function, the formula in the Insert Function window is PMT(rate, nper, pv, fv, type). The Function Arguments window is seen in Figure 5-B-8. After clicking OK we can find that we would have to invest $2,241 each year. We could also see that result at the bottom of the Function Arguments window in Figure 5-B-8. The formula with numeric values would be = PMT(8%, 7, , -20000)

	A	B	C	D	E
1					
2	**Calculation of Rate**				
3					
4		FV	=	$20,000	
5		PV	=	$10,000	
6		nper	=	6	
7		rate	=	???	
8					
9		rate	=	12%	
10					

D9 — f_x =RATE(D6,,-D5,D4)

FIGURE 5-B-6 Rate Solution

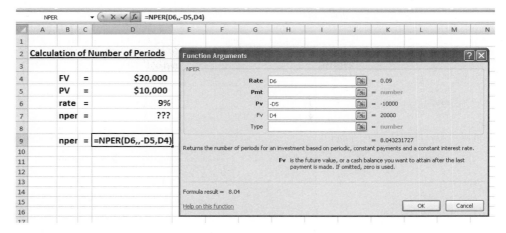

FIGURE 5-B-7   Function Arguments Window for Number of Periods Solution

PERIODIC PAYMENTS (IN ADVANCE)

However, what if we could put aside money at the beginning of each year rather than the end? When payments come at the end of each period, as they do in an *ordinary annuity* or *annuity in arrears* the value for "type" is 0. If we leave it blank, as we have so far, Excel assumes that it has a value of 0. For an annuity in advance we must indicate the "type" as being 1 in the Function Arguments window. Figure 5-B-9 shows how this would appear. If the periodic payments are made at the start of the year, we would only need to put aside $2,075 each year. The formula with numeric values would be = PMT(8%, 7, , −20000, 1).

NET PRESENT VALUE

Suppose that we can invest $1,000 today in a capital asset, and will receive $500, $700, and $800, respectively, at the end of each of the three years of the asset's life. Our discount rate for the project is 6 percent. What is the net present value? After clicking on the function wizard, in the Insert Function window select the Financial category and the NPV function. The formula appears as NPV(rate, value 1, value 2, . . .). After clicking OK, the appropriate cell references can be entered into the Function Arguments window. Note that the initial outlay is *not* one of the values. The intial outlay must be subtracted from the

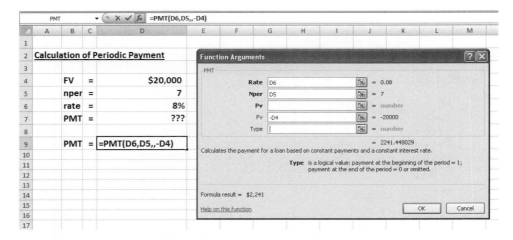

FIGURE 5-B-8   Function Arguments Window for Periodic Payments in Arrears

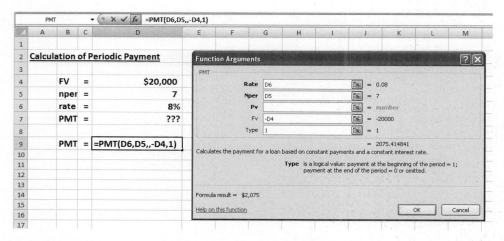

FIGURE 5-B-9 Function Arguments Window for Periodic Payments in Advance

Excel NPV calculation. Figure 5-B-10 shows the problem setup and cell references. The formula result shown at the bottom of the screen is 1766.39. After subtracting the outlay of $1,000, the NPV is $766.39.

INTERNAL RATE OF RETURN

What is the Internal Rate of Return (IRR) of the cash flows described in the NPV section above? After clicking on the function wizard, in the Insert Function window select the Financial category and the IRR function. The formula appears as IRR(values, guess). Provide Excel with the values and an initial guess, such as 15 percent (note that the guess

can generally be left blank if preferred). After clicking OK, the appropriate cell references can be entered into the Function Arguments window. Note that the initial outlay *is* one of the values. In this respect the IRR function works differently than the NPV function. Figure 5-B-11 shows the problem setup and cell references. The formula result shown at the bottom of the screen is 40.42%. This means that the IRR for the capital asset would be approximately 40.4%

CONCLUSION

Each of the major spreadsheet programs handles the TVM process slightly differently. Within any program

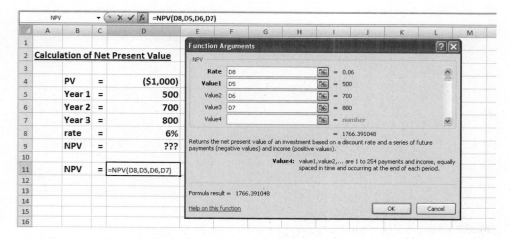

FIGURE 5-B-10 Function Arguments Window for Net Present Value

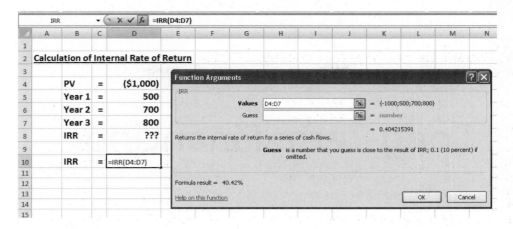

FIGURE 5-B-11   Internal Rate of Return

from one edition to the next, such as from Excel 2002 to Excel 2007, minor changes in the process tend to occur. To some extent the spreadsheet approaches are quirky. For example, not allowing the initial, time zero, outflow to be directly included in the NPV calculation seems odd. Nevertheless, spreadsheets can handle the more complicated numbers found in real world situations with ease, and most organizations now rely almost exclusively on computer spreadsheets for their TVM calculations.

6

Long-Term Financing

The learning objectives of this chapter are to:

- introduce long-term financing and discuss the two main types of long-term financing: equity financing and debt financing;
- explain the nature of retained earnings and its role in long-term financing;
- explain stock issuance and discuss its advantages as a source of long-term financing for for-profit organizations;
- explain how governments can use taxation to generate long-term financing for capital acquisitions;
- discuss the role of contributions in long-term financing;
- define long-term debt;
- explain how mortgages and bonds work, and how debt payments and values can be computed; and
- discuss the advantages and disadvantages of leasing as a source of long-term financing.

INTRODUCTION

Many organizations find that they cannot afford to pay for *capital assets* using just the cash coming from current operating activities. It is common for the cost of such items, especially buildings or major pieces of equipment, to exceed the cash resources available. The various alternatives available to the organization for funding such acquisitions are referred to as long-term financing. Long-term financing provides the resources to acquire long-term assets and is repaid over a period of years, if at all. The two key sources of long-term financing are equity financing and long-term debt.

EQUITY FINANCING

Equity financing refers to money raised for the organization that never has to be repaid. Obviously this has great advantages over debt. When money is borrowed, it places the organization at risk. What if the organization has a bad year and can't meet its required interest or principal payments? The very existence of the organization could be threatened.

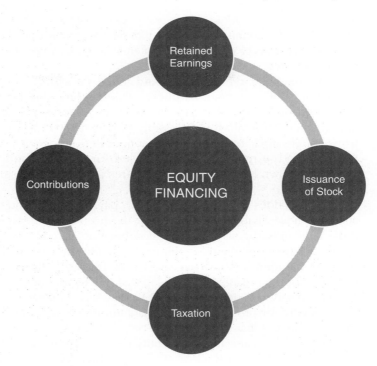

FIGURE 6-1   Sources of equity financing.

If we can find ways to raise money for our long-term needs, without borrowing, that risk can be avoided. The primary sources of equity financing are retained earnings, stock issuance, taxation, and contributions (see Figure 6-1).

Retained Earnings

When an organization earns a surplus or profit, that profit can be retained within the organization or can be distributed to owners. Distributions made to owners of for-profit organizations are called dividends. Not-for-profit organizations do not have owners who are entitled to receive any of the profits that the organization may make.

When profits are retained within the organization, regardless of whether it is a for-profit or not-for-profit organization, those profits can be used to finance capital assets such as buildings and equipment. A great advantage of using retained earnings is that there is no required repayment so there is no risk in using long-term financing from this source.

Issuance of Stock

In the for-profit world, one of the most common sources of long-term financing is the equity markets. Essentially, this means that the organization sells part of itself. The investors who provide money to the organization receive shares of stock in exchange for the money they invest in the company. The stock represents an ownership interest in the organization. The stockholders have "equity" in the company.

For example, suppose that HOS were a for-profit organization. The hospital wishes to build a new building for $100,000,000 but is not anxious to borrow the money. Borrowing money creates risk for the organization. Interest must be paid regularly, and eventually the amount borrowed must be repaid. If interest rates are 8 percent, the hospital would anticipate an annual required interest payment of $8 million per year before repaying any of the borrowed amount (8% × $100 million = $8 million per year of interest). If the hospital has a bad year and cannot pay the interest, a lender might be able to force the organization into bankruptcy.

Alternatively, the hospital could "enter the equity markets" and sell stock. Suppose 10 million shares of stock had been issued earlier, and now the hospital decides to sell 10 million more shares at $10.50 per share. This would generate $105,000,000. Of that amount, the hospital would possibly pay $5,000,000 to the various investment banking firms (often stock brokerage companies) that helped it find buyers for the stock. The remaining $100 million would be used for the new building. The new stockholders would now own half the 20 million shares of outstanding stock and, therefore, half of the organization.

If HOS does well, it may decide to pay dividends, and the new owners will get their share of those dividends. However, if the hospital does poorly, it is not obligated to pay those dividends, the way it would have been obligated to pay interest. And the $100 million does not have to be repaid to the investors. On some occasions, for-profit organizations do repay the amount owners have invested. However, that is relatively unusual. It is more common for the organization to keep that money and use it over time to provide additional goods and services, possibly at a profit. The stockholders then own that profit.

Usually for-profit stockholder organizations take much of their profits and reinvest them in activities that they hope will be profitable. As more and more profits are earned and retained in the organization, the entity becomes more valuable. This should be reflected in a higher value of each share of stock. The stockholders can realize that increased value by selling their stock to other investors at a price higher than they paid to acquire it.

Although there are some for-profit organizations in the public service, that is not the predominant form of organization. Therefore, our discussion is brief, and readers with a greater interest in the for-profit sector are encouraged to explore some of the readings in corporate finance listed at the end of this chapter.

Taxation

Governments can raise long-term financing through taxation. If there is a desire to build a new courthouse, town hall, or school, the government can raise taxes enough to provide the entire desired financing in one year. That money can then be used immediately to pay for the new building or other capital acquisition. Philosophically, there are concerns about inter-generational fairness when such an approach is undertaken. Is it fair to put the entire burden of the cost of a new courthouse on today's taxpayers, when in fact the courthouse will be used for many years? It might be more equitable to borrow the money for the courthouse and to repay it over the years that the citizens will benefit from the courthouse. The repayments can come from taxes each year the courthouse is used. Given the issue of fairness, and also the typical aversion of both citizens and politicians to large tax increases, very large public capital projects are often financed by debt.

Contributions

Another source of long-term financing for many not-for-profit organizations is from donations. Like the other equity financing approaches, a big advantage of donations is that they do not have to be repaid. If the organization can raise a large enough amount of charitable contributions, it can acquire the capital items it wants without having to incur debt. Many not-for-profit organizations solicit donations annually to support operating activities. Those donations are typically unrestricted and can be used for any reasonable purpose related to the organization's mission. So they could be used for routine operations or for capital acquisitions. In addition, when there is a specific financial need to purchase a large capital acquisition, the organization may also undertake a capital campaign to raise money specifically for that acquisition.

CAPITAL CAMPAIGNS   Many not-for-profit organizations have fund-raising drives referred to as capital campaigns, which are aimed at raising money for capital investments. Capital campaigns are often focused on raising money for a specific building or other long-term purpose.

When donors give money specifically under a capital campaign, it is treated as restricted. That means that the money must be held aside and invested in the capital items described during the fund-raising drive. There are generally no repayments of either interest or principal on money that is raised in this fashion.

LONG-TERM DEBT

In contrast to equity financing, debt financing represents money the organization borrows that will be repaid in the future, often with interest. It is referred to as long-term debt if it will be paid back more than one year into the future. Accountants often divide both resources and obligations into *short-term* and *long-term* categories based on whether they relate to the coming year or a period of time beyond the coming year. For example, if the Town of Millbridge were to borrow $1,000,000 to be repaid in equal installments over the next 10 years, that would be considered long-term debt, because it will not all be repaid within one year. The $100,000 portion to be paid in the first year (i.e., one-tenth of the total loan) is referred to as the *current portion of long-term debt*. The primary sources of long-term debt, discussed below, are long-term notes, mortgages, bonds, and capital leases (see Figure 6-2).

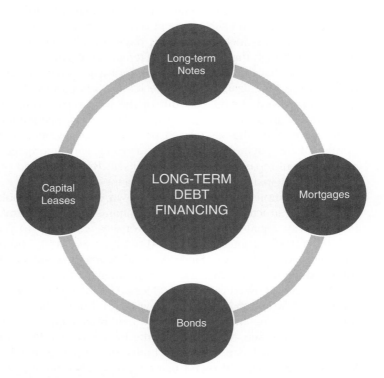

FIGURE 6-2   Sources of long-term debt financing.

Long-Term Notes

One form of long-term debt results when the organization borrows money and signs a note promising repayment. The note indicates the specific terms under which the money has been borrowed, such as the interest rate and timing of payments. Long-term notes are often unsecured loans. This means that the organization as a whole owes the money, but there is no one specific item that the organization pledges as collateral to ensure repayment. Thus, the lender is considered to be an "unsecured" creditor. If the organization has problems making payments to its creditors, this lender will be put in a pool of all the unsecured creditors to share whatever resources are available to repay the organization's various obligations.

In contrast, a lender can ask for *collateral*. Collateral is a specific asset the lender can claim if the borrower fails to make payment of amounts due. For example, if the organization has made an investment buying 10,000 shares of Microsoft stock, it may offer that stock as collateral. By providing the lender with specific valuable collateral, the loan is less risky. Therefore, the lender is more likely to be willing to make the loan and to charge a lower interest rate. In general, the greater the likelihood that a borrower will not be able to repay a loan, the higher the interest rate charged unless there is adequate collateral.

Mortgages

Mortgages are loans secured by a specific asset. The security is generally real estate. This means that land or land and buildings are used as collateral for the loan. Often, the loan is being borrowed to purchase the land and building, but that is not necessarily the case.

There are different possible types of payment arrangements for mortgages. Some do not require any repayment of principal for a number of years, and then a large "balloon" payment is made. It is more common, however, for a mortgage to require equal payments at the end of each month throughout the term of the loan. The equal mortgage payments each include some interest and some principal repayment. However, the amount of interest and principal included in each payment differs from payment to payment. As time goes by, the amount of interest included in each payment falls and the amount of principal repayment rises, even though the total payment remains the same.

Why is that the case? Since each mortgage payment repays part of the loan, after the payment the organization owes the lender less money. Interest is rent on the amount of money borrowed. As the amount of the loan outstanding declines, the required interest payment declines as well. Since the monthly mortgage payment is calculated as a constant annuity payment, the same each period, the repayment portion increases as the interest portion of the payment declines. As a result, early mortgage payments are mostly interest and just small repayments of the loan itself. By the tail end of the mortgage, each payment is mostly principal and only a small amount of interest.

For example, suppose that the Town of Millbridge took out a $500,000 mortgage to build a new structure at the town swimming pool. The terms of the loan were 12 percent interest, with equal annual payments of $88,492.08 for 10 years. The first payment would include $60,000 of interest ($500,000 × 12% = $60,000). The rest of the payment is used to pay back part of the loan. Since the total payment is $88,492.08 and $60,000 of that is interest, the difference, or $28,492.08, is repayment of the original loan. That means that the next year the amount owed is $28,492.08 less. The interest for the second year is calculated based on the $471,507.92 that is still owed at the end of the first year. Table 6-1 is a loan amortization table showing annual interest and loan repayments over the full term of the loan.

As we can see, the balance of the loan is zero at the end of the 10th year. In the early years, the loan balance is large and most of the payment is for interest. Near the end of the loan, the principal still owed has dropped substantially, so the interest portion of each payment is much less and the principal portion correspondingly larger.

TABLE 6-1 Loan Amortization Table

Principal Owed at Beginning of Year	Annual Payment	Interest at 12%	Repayment of Principal	Principal Owed at End of Year
(A)	(B)	(C = A × 12%)	(D = B − C)	(E = A − D)
$500,000.00	$88,492.08	$60,000.00	$28,492.08	$471,507.92
471,507.92	88,492.08	56,580.95	31,911.13	439,596.79
439,596.79	88,492.08	52,751.61	35,740.47	403,856.33
403,856.33	88,492.08	48,462.76	40,029.32	363,827.00
363,827.00	88,492.08	43,659.24	44,832.84	318,994.16
318,994.16	88,492.08	38,279.30	50,212.78	268,781.38
268,781.38	88,492.08	32,253.77	56,238.31	212,543.07
212,543.07	88,492.08	25,505.17	62,986.91	149,556.16
149,556.16	88,492.08	17,946.74	70,545.34	79,010.82
79,010.82	88,492.08	9,481.26	79,010.82	0.00

This leaves one unanswered question: How was the $88,492.08 annual mortgage payment calculated? The payment represents an annuity. We know the PV; that is the $500,000 borrowed at the beginning. We know the number of compounding periods, 10, and the interest rate, 12 percent.

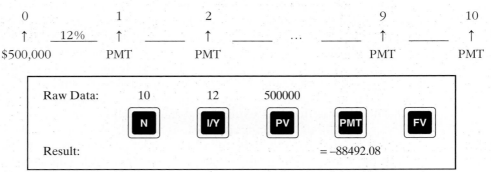

The negative sign indicates that if we borrow and receive money at the start we will have to repay, or pay out, $88,492.08 each year. The Excel Spreadsheet Formula to find the PMT would be:

$$= PMT(rate, nper, pv, fv, type)$$
$$= PMT(12\%, 10, 500000)$$
$$= \$(88,492.08)$$

Bonds

When organizations borrow large amounts of money, they often issue a bond. Bonds are agreements to borrow and repay money with specific *stated, face* or *maturity* values. The stated, face, or maturity value is the amount that will be repaid at the end of the loan period, called the maturity date. Suppose that HOS wishes to borrow $100 million for 20 years to add a new wing. That $100 million is the total maturity value and 20 years from now is the maturity date. Bonds typically pay interest every six months.

Individuals lend a portion of the total amount to the organization in exchange for the organization's promise to repay the loan. That promise is evidenced by a formal document called a bond. For example, we might lend money to the organization in exchange for a $5,000 bond. The organization promises to make regular interest payments and to repay the full $5,000 face value at the maturity date. Although we are lending money to the organization, we often speak of buying and selling bonds. This is because the bond obligation is transferable. After we lend money to the organization, we can wait until the maturity date to get our money back. However, we do not have to. We can sell the bond to someone else. The organization will then pay interest and principal to the person to whom we sold the bond.

WHY ARE BONDS USED?   Organizations issue bonds rather than simply borrow money from a bank for three major reasons: to spread risk, to *dis-intermediate*, and in some cases to save taxes. First, if one lender were to lend a very large amount of money to one borrower, it would take a tremendous risk. No one bank would want to lend $100 million to HOS. The hospital's failure to repay the loan could have a devastating impact on the bank. Lenders would prefer to lend smaller amounts to a larger number of borrowers. Second, lenders such as banks are lending other people's money. People put money in bank accounts, and the bank lends the money to the borrower. The bank acts as an intermediary between the individual and the borrower. If the borrower can eliminate the intermediary (dis-intermediate), it can save that cost. Third, the interest on some bonds is exempt from income taxes.

Cutting the bank out of the lending process can result in a savings of several percent per year. For example, suppose that the bank pays people 4 percent interest on certificate of deposit savings accounts and lends that money to the Town of Millbridge at 8 percent. The 4 percent difference between what the bank charges and what it pays covers all of the bank's costs and profits. If the town borrowed directly from the public by using bonds, it might only have to pay 6 percent. Millbridge will save 2 percent per year and the people will earn 6 percent, which is a higher rate of return on their savings than they get from the bank. The extra 2 percent rewards the person for taking the higher risk by lending to Millbridge, as opposed to putting the money in an insured bank account.

In that case, why not use bonds for all loans? Why would we ever borrow from a bank? The problem is that it is expensive to find individual investors who are willing to lend money to Millbridge. A large sales force is needed, and commissions must be paid. Lawyers are needed to protect the interests of the lender and borrowers. Accountants are needed to track the bond payments. Investment banking firms undertake and coordinate this process.

Bond underwriters sometimes acquire the entire bond issue, and then resell it to their customers. Other times the underwriters just agree to make their best effort to sell the bond, and the issuer bears the risk that the bonds do not sell. The price paid by the underwriter is based either on a negotiation with the issuer, or is the result of a competitive bid. The underwriter will only offer to pay an amount below the price at which it thinks it can sell the bonds. The difference between the underwriter's buying and selling price is referred to as the *spread*. That spread has to be large enough to cover all costs associated with the bond issuance, such as commissions, rent, and profit. Considering the spread as well as fees paid to accountants and lawyers, issuing a bond is costly. It often does not pay to issue a bond if only a relatively small amount of money is borrowed. Instead, taking out a loan from a bank may make more sense in such cases. However, if the borrower can save 2 percent a year for 20, 30, or perhaps 40 years on a large amount of money, this up-front cost may be worthwhile. Would the savings from a lower interest rate offset the high initial costs related to issuing a bond? That is essentially an NPV problem that each potential borrower must solve.

Another factor that makes bonds advantageous is tax treatment. If a state or local government or not-for-profit organization pays interest to the bank on a conventional loan, that interest may be taxable. The bank may have to pay taxes on the profit it makes on the loan.

There are federal laws, however, that allow public service organizations to issue tax-exempt bonds, in some instances.[1] A tax-exempt bond is a bond whose interest is not taxable by the federal and sometimes state and local governments. Such bonds are often referred to as municipal bonds or muni bonds.

From a policy perspective, the government can use tax-exempt status of bonds to raise money for its own use or to help not-for-profit organizations obtain long-term financing for socially desirable projects, such as the construction of a new hospital building. The federal government helps these organizations get long-term financing by making interest on their bonds tax-free.

Suppose a person who lives in Millbridge buys an HOS bond. Assuming the hospital is located in the same state as Millbridge, the person would not pay federal or state income tax on the interest from the HOS bond. This makes the bond relatively more attractive than bonds that are taxable. Since the bond is attractive, investors generally are willing to accept a lower interest rate. That saves the bond issuer additional money.

GOVERNMENT-ISSUED BONDS   Governments borrow money for a variety of purposes, such as to cover deficits, acquire capital assets, or even cover temporary cash shortages within a year. Different levels of government have different borrowing approaches as well. Federal debt occurs to finance the overall operations of the federal government. There is no specific matching of money borrowed with specific investment projects. If the federal government spends more than it receives, it increases the total amount of debt. The federal government issues both short-term debt (e.g., Treasury bills) and long-term debt (Treasury notes).

State and local bonds can best be divided into two categories: general obligation and *revenue bonds*. General obligation bonds are backed by the *full-faith and credit* of the governmental body issuing them. This means that the interest and principal payments are backed by the full taxing power of the government. These bonds can be considered guaranteed, although a government can become bankrupt and default on its debt. In contrast, revenue bonds are backed from the revenues of a specific, limited source. For example, the government may issue revenue bonds to finance the construction of a housing project. The rental revenues from the project may be promised for the repayment of the debt. If the rental revenues turn out to be inadequate, then the bondholders may not be repaid. The full taxing power of the government is not pledged in support of the revenue bonds. Full-faith and credit obligations generally have lower interest rates than revenue bonds because of the government guarantee of payment.

Tax-exempt borrowing has a great advantage. Since the lender usually does not have to pay federal, and often state, tax on the interest earned, such borrowing is substantially less expensive for the borrower. This has led to some controversial practices. For example, Industrial Development Bonds are issued at times by tax-exempt borrowers to borrow money to build facilities that are leased to private organizations. The lease payments pay the debt service. A number of laws have been enacted to control and limit the use of tax-exempt financing that has a primary purpose of benefiting private sector organizations.[2]

---

[1] Interest paid by local and state governments may be taxable to the recipient. This is true regardless of whether the loan takes the form of a bond or other type of obligation. The taxability of the interest depends on the use of the borrowed money. For example, interest on arbitrage bonds issued by state and local governments is taxable. An arbitrage bond is one in which the money is borrowed to be invested at a higher rate. This prevents governments from borrowing at 6 percent on a tax-free bond to invest at 9 percent in a taxable corporate bond. The full listing of uses of borrowed money that are or are not taxable for state and local governments is beyond the scope of this book.

[2] The 1986 Tax Reform Act placed the most severe restrictions to date. For further discussion, see John L. Mikesell. *Fiscal Administration: Analysis and Applications for the Public Sector*, 6th ed. Belmont, Ca.: Thomson/Wadsworth, 2003, pp. 553–554.

COUPON AND ZERO COUPON BONDS At one time, most bonds had interest coupons attached. Every six months the holder of the bond would clip off an interest coupon and exchange it for an interest payment in cash. At that time, bonds were generally unregistered. This means that the borrowing organization did not keep track of whom it owed money. Whoever had the bond could clip the coupons and redeem them for interest. Whoever submitted the bond at the maturity date would be paid the principal amount. These are called *bearer bonds*. Payments were made to whomever had the bond. Bonds are now issued in *registered form*. This means that records are maintained showing who owns the bond. Interest payments can be made without submitting coupons.

Some bonds do not pay interest until the maturity date. These are referred to as *zero coupon bonds*. Even though coupons themselves are outdated, the name zero coupon is meant to reflect that there are no interim interest payments. For example, suppose that we loaned money to the Town of Millbridge in exchange for a 10-year, $10,000 maturity zero coupon bond with an interest rate of 6 percent and semiannual compounding. How much would we lend to Millbridge?

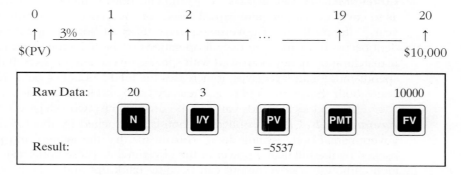

Excel Spreadsheet Formula: = PV(rate, nper, , fv)
= PV(3%, 20, ,10000)
= $(5,537)

You would give Millbridge $5,537 today, and in 10 years they would pay $10,000, which would repay the original loan plus interest. That would be the only payment made by the issuer of the bond. Note that because of the semiannual compounding, there are 20 compound periods at 3 percent each.

TERM VERSUS SERIAL BONDS Another distinction is between *term bonds* and *serial bonds*. Bonds are typically issued in $1,000 increments. Suppose a government wishes to raise $100,000,000 for new construction. It will issue 100,000 bonds at $1,000 each. The 100,000 bonds all together are referred to as a *bond issue*. For a 20-year term bond, the $1,000 principal per bond is repaid at maturity at the end of 20 years for all 100,000 bonds. In contrast, a serial bond has a number of different maturity dates. For example, part of a 20-year serial bond issue might be repaid each year for the last 10 years of the bond's life. Serial bonds are often employed by goverments.

When governments make a large capital investment, they often use a bond to finance the project, rather than raising taxes enough to cover the entire cost in the year of acquisition. If they use a term bond, at the end of the term they will need to have available the full amount that was borrowed. One way to accomplish that is with a *sinking fund*. A sinking fund is a savings account in which money is put aside for a future use. That use might be to acquire a capital item, or else to repay the loan for a capital item that has already been acquired. Each year for the life of the term bond, the government can pay interest to the bondholders and put aside an amount to cover principal into the sinking fund. At the maturity of the bond, the bond principal is repaid from money in the sinking fund. Lenders sometimes require a sinking fund if they are concerned about the possibility that the borrower might default (fail to repay interest and principal). However, since the borrower may earn a lower rate on the sinking fund investment than the interest rate it pays on its outstanding bonds, the sinking fund approach may be more costly than simply repaying the debt.

Serial bonds are used more commonly by governments than term bonds on their own, and in some cases may even be required by law. A serial bond requires payments of principal at set points in time throughout the life of the loan, rather than all at one time. The serial bonds can be used to level the government's total annual payments for interest and principal. In the early years of the bond issue, the government will have large interest payments, because it owes the full amount that it has borrowed. In those years, only a relatively small portion of the principal will typically be repaid. That repayment will lower the interest due in the future years. It is common for the amount repaid periodically to grow as the annual interest cost declines. A 20-year serial bond would have its final payment at the end of the 20th year. However, individual investors could buy a bond with an earlier specific maturity date within the series.

For example, a government borrowing $100,000,000 would still issue 100,000 individual $1,000 bonds as part of the bond issue. However, the bonds would not all have the same maturity dates, or even the same coupon rates. Typically, the bonds with a longer time until maturity will have a higher interest rate than those parts of the serial bond that have a shorter maturity. This is because investors lock up their money for a longer period of time. If interest rates rise in the interim, investors will not be able to benefit from that rise in rates until their bond investment matures. Also, earlier payments lower the lender's risk related to potential default. As a result of these factors, serial bonds may have a lower overall borrowing cost than term loans.

CALL PROVISIONS   Many issuers of bonds are concerned by the long time-frame involved. If a government issues a bond for thirty years when interest rates are high, it would be obligated to pay those high interest rates for the full term of the loan, even if subsequent changes in the economy result in falling interest rates. To deal with this, many bond issuers insert a condition in their bond agreements that allows them to repay the bond early. This is called a *call provision*. When a bond is *called*, it means that the borrower chooses to repay the bond early. Suppose that 10 years have gone by, and the borrowing rate for the government bond issuer has fallen from 8 percent to 4 percent. The government would typically borrow money at 4 percent and use it to call in and pay off the outstanding 8 percent bond.

Although this provides a clear benefit to the borrower, typically bonds that have call provisions have an initial interest rate that is higher than it would be without the call provision. If market interest rates go up, lenders will not benefit from that rise because they have lent money for a long period at a fixed rate. But if market interest rates drop, the bond will be called and they will then only be able to reinvest their money at a lower rate. Therefore, to make up for this unbalanced situation, lenders demand a higher interest rate payment for a bond with a call provision than for one without such a provision.

CALCULATING BOND PAYMENTS AND VALUES   Bonds have a specific *stated interest rate,* such as 10 percent. The organization promises to pay interest at that rate. Therefore, a 10 percent, $5,000 bond with annual interest payments would pay $500 of interest every year until the bond matures. At that point, the organization would make the last interest payment and repay the $5,000 face value. Usually, interest payments on bonds are made semiannually. In that case, this bond would make a payment of $250 every six months until the maturity date.

However, bonds are not always issued or sold at their maturity value. In fact, they are usually transferred for a higher or lower price. This is because interest rates in society fluctuate on a daily basis. Although a 10 percent rate might be appropriate when we are planning to issue a bond, by the time all the legal and administrative details are taken care of, interest rates may have risen or dropped. For example, assume a 20-year, 10 percent bond. What if the bond is about to be issued, but interest rates rise in the general economy? No one will be willing to lend money to get 10 percent if they can get 12 percent elsewhere. The organization must offer to sell (issue) the bonds at a *discount*. (If interest rates have instead decreased, then the organization will be able to charge a *premium* for the bond.)

The actual amount to be paid for a bond is calculated using time value of money (TVM) computations. A bond represents a promise to make periodic interest payments and a repayment of principal. If we know the current interest rate in the marketplace, the number of compounding periods, and the future interest and principal payments, we can find the PV. This calculation, however, is somewhat complex because we have to carefully account for the different payments.

What would Millbridge receive today if it issued a $100 million bond offering at a 10 percent stated interest rate with interest paid semiannually and the principal repaid in 20 years? Assume that interest rates in the general marketplace have risen to 12 percent. First, since the bond pays interest semiannually, there are two compounding periods per year. A 20-year bond would have 40 compounding periods. This number of periods is used to compute the PV of both the interest and the principal payments.

Second, note that the stated interest rate is used to determine the interest payments that will take place over time. A $100 million bond at 10 percent would pay interest of $10 million per year, or $5 million every six months.

Next, we need to find the PV of an annuity of $5 million each period for 40 periods at an interest rate of 6 percent per period, plus the PV of the single future payment of $100 million paid 40 periods from now with an interest rate of 6 percent. Note that the interest rate used for the PV calculations is 6 percent. This is half of the 12 percent market rate. The rate is divided in half because the compounding periods are semiannual. The 12 percent rate is used because that is the current market rate. The value of the bond is determined by the current market rate rather than the stated rate. The stated interest rate only is used to determine the specific amount of the semiannual interest payments.

By taking the PV of the periodic interest payments plus the PV of the future principal payment, we find the value of the bond today at current interest rate conditions. For the Town of Millbridge bond mentioned previously, the future value, FV, is the $100,000,000 maturity payment; the periodic interest payments, PMT, are the semiannual $5,000,000 payments; the number of compounding periods is 40 six-month periods; and the interest rate is the 6 percent semiannual current market rate:

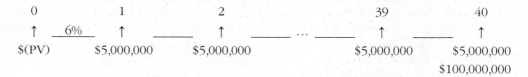

Present value of maturity principal repayment and the periodic interest payments:

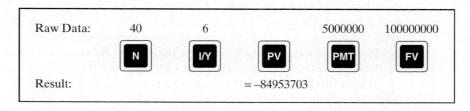

$$\text{Excel Spreadsheet Formula:} = \text{PV (rate, nper, pmt, fv)}$$
$$= \text{PV (6\%, 40, 5000000, 100000000)}$$
$$= \$(84{,}953{,}703)$$

Note that Excel and many financial calculators are able to compute bond values in one calculation. Alternatively, one could find the PV of the interest payments and the PV of the principal repayment and combine them to get the same result. That amount, $84,953,703, is what someone would be willing to pay for the bond. If they pay more, they would be earning less than 12 percent on the money they have invested; if they pay less than this amount, they would be earning more than 12 percent. Notice that the result shows as a negative number. This is because if someone were to buy the bond they would have to pay out $84,953,703 to get it.

Note that this PV calculation says that investors, in total, will pay the Town of Millbridge only about $85 million to get the semiannual payments of $5,000,000 and the lump sum payment at maturity of $100,000,000. Note that the full $100 million will be paid at maturity, even though the town will receive only $85 million now. The bond will have to be issued at a discount because it only pays interest based on a 10 percent rate, whereas the marketplace is currently demanding 12 percent.

Is it fair that Millbridge must repay $100 million even though it only receives about $85 million? Yes! Every six months Millbridge will pay $5 million in interest. However, 6 percent of the $84,953,703 that Millbridge will receive for the bond is $5,097,222. Given the market interest rate, a lender who loans Millbridge $84,953,703 should receive an interest payment of $5,097,222 every six months. Since Millbridge only pays $5 million, it will have to owe the remaining interest to the lender. The extra $97,222 every six months that is not paid currently will accumulate until the maturity date, and it will earn compound interest in the interim. The difference between the $85 million Millbridge receives and the $100 million it pays at maturity is this extra accumulated interest. Altogether, the investors earn exactly 12 percent on the money they have loaned to Millbridge.

Note that the difference in the interest rates in this example are extreme. Interest rates vary by one 100th of a percent. A 10 percent face value bond might be issued when interest rates are 10.03 percent or 10.17 percent. A jump from 10 percent to 12 percent is extreme. Thus, the value of a bond in the real world is not likely to vary nearly as much as in this example at the time of issue. Over time, however, after 5 or 10 years have passed, wider variations in interest rates are common. If the bond is sold by the original lender to a different investor, a new PV calculation is essential to determine a price for the bond that will yield the current market rate.[3] Note that the borrowing organization owes interest and principal to whoever owns the bond. Generally, bond owners may sell the bond whenever they want.

CALCULATING THE INTEREST RATE FOR A SERIAL BOND—NIC AND TIC When bonds are issued, the issuer will want to know the interest rate that must be paid. But computation of this rate is complicated when a serial bond is issued with multiple principal repayment dates, and different coupon rates. Two methods are widely used for computing the interest rate on a serial bond issue: the *Net Interest Cost (NIC)* and *True Interest Cost (TIC)* methods.

---

[3] The change in interest rates can be described in terms of a number of basis points. A basis point is a one-100th of a percent. For example, if the interest rate were to change from 10.03 percent to 10.17 percent, it has risen by .14 percent, or 14 basis points (i.e., .14 × 100). The news media frequently quote interest rate changes by indicating the basis point change.

The NIC gives an average of the yearly debt cost, calculated as a percentage of the principal amount not yet paid. It can be computed as follows:

$$\text{NIC} = \frac{\text{Total Interest (less premium or plus discount)}}{\text{Bond Year Dollars}}$$

Suppose that we were to have a $10,000, five-year serial bond issue today, with principal repayments of $1,000 each year at the end of the first two years, $2,000 at the end of the third year, and $3,000 at the end of the fourth and fifth years. Assume the interest rates are 3 percent, 4 percent, 5 percent, 6 percent, and 7 percent on the five respective maturities, and assume that the bond issue is initially sold at a discount such that the borrower receives $9,900. The interest payments for the five years, respectively, would be:

Par or Principal		Coupon Rate		Years		Interest
$1,000	×	3%	×	1	=	$ 30
1,000	×	4%	×	2	=	80
2,000	×	5%	×	3	=	300
3,000	×	6%	×	4	=	720
3,000	×	7%	×	5	=	1,050
Interest Payments						$2,180
Plus Discount						100
Total Interest						$2,280

Note that the initial discount is considered to be interest. This is because the issuer only received $9,900 when the money was borrowed. However, a total of $10,000 is repaid as the bonds mature. That difference of $100 is additional interest on the $9,900 that was borrowed.

The *bond year dollars* consist of the sum of the amount of money that was outstanding over the years. The first year, the issuer owed $10,000. After the payment at the end of the first year, the issuer only owed $9,000 for the second year, and so on. The sum is found as follows:

$10,000	×	1	=	$10,000
9,000	×	1	=	9,000
8,000	×	1	=	8,000
6,000	×	1	=	6,000
3,000	×	1	=	3,000
Bond Year Dollars				$36,000

Then the NIC is calculated as:

$$\text{NIC} = \frac{\$2,280}{\$36,000} = 6.333\%$$

The TIC approach is somewhat more commonly used because it considers not only the interest payments, but also the timing of the interest. It is more true to the principles of the time value of money, and is therefore more accurate. TIC is solved by setting the amount of money received by the issuer equal to the present value of all the payments made by the issuer over the bond's life, and solving for the interest rate, in a fashion similar to that used to find the IRR. In the case of the above bond, the bond issuer initially received $9,900. In the first year interest must be paid on all bonds in the series, and the principal is repaid on the part of the series with a maturity at the end of the first year. Each subsequent year interest is paid on only the bonds that remain outstanding, and any principal maturing is paid. The payments over the life of the bond series are:

Par or Principal		Coupon Rate		Interest Paid at the End of					Total
				Year 1	Year 2	Year 3	Year 4	Year 5	
$1,000	×	3%	=	$ 30					$ 30
1,000	×	4%	=	40	40				80
2,000	×	5%	=	100	100	100			300
3,000	×	6%	=	180	180	180	180		720
3,000	×	7%	=	210	210	210	210	210	1,050
Interest Payments				$ 560	$ 530	$ 490	$ 390	$ 210	$ 2,180
Principal Payments				1,000	1,000	2,000	3,000	3,000	10,000
Total Payment				$1,560	$1,530	$2,490	$3,390	$3,210	$12,180

Therefore, the TIC is the interest rate that makes:

$$\$9{,}900 = (\text{PV of } \$1{,}560, \text{N} = 1) + (\text{PV of } \$1{,}530, \text{N} = 2) + (\text{PV of } \$2{,}490, \text{N} = 3)$$
$$+ (\text{PV of } \$3{,}390, \text{N} = 4) + (\text{PV of } \$3{,}210, \text{N} = 5)$$

Using a spreadsheet program such as Excel, this can be solved using the IRR function. In Excel, the solution formula would be:

$$= \text{IRR(values, guess)}$$
$$= \text{IRR}(9900, -1560, -1530, -2490, -3390, -3210, 6.3\%)$$
$$= 6.347\%$$

Note that 6.3 percent was used in the formula as an initial guess of the interest rate, because it was the value found using the NIC approach. Although the NIC and TIC seem to give answers that are very close, this difference would be substantial for a large bond offering.

Capital Leases

Sometimes, rather than buying a capital asset and financing the purchase with direct borrowing from a bank or by issuing a bond, organizations will lease capital assets. In the case of long-term, noncancellable contracts to lease buildings or equipment, the organization has made a long-term commitment to make payments in the future. This commitment is treated as a form of long-term financing, and the lease is referred to as a *capital lease*.

In many respects, a capital lease has the same effect as if we bought the asset and paid for it with monthly mortgage payments. A common difference between lease payments and mortgage payments is that often lease payments are made at the beginning of the month before we use the asset, while mortgage payments typically come at the end of each month after we have used the asset. In both cases, each payment contains a portion attributable to paying for the item and a portion that is interest for the outstanding cost of the item. With leases, however, we are paying for the right to use the asset rather than for the asset itself.

To determine the organization's obligation under a capital lease at any point in time, it is necessary to find the PV of the payments that will be made under the lease. There is a temptation simply to multiply the amount of each lease payment by the number of lease payments to calculate the total obligation. However, that approach is incorrect. When lease payments are made, part of each payment is to pay for interest. That interest accrues only with the passage of time. Therefore, at the present time, the appropriate measure of the lease obligation is only the PV of the payments.

Suppose that Meals for the Homeless agrees to lease a piece of equipment for $1,000 per year for 10 years. Assume that this lease calls for payments at the end of each year of use. Also assume that there is an implicit interest rate of 12 percent built into the lease and we treat this as a long-term obligation. How much do we owe?

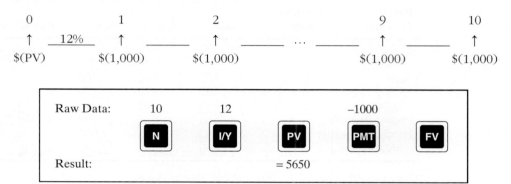

$$\text{Excel Spreadsheet Formula:} = PV(\text{rate, nper, pmt})$$
$$= PV(12\%, 10, -1000)$$
$$= \$5,650$$

The present value of the obligation is $5,650. Effectively, owing lease payments of $1,000 a year for 10 years at 12 percent is the same as if we owed a lump sum of $5,650 today.

Leases often require payments to be made at the beginning of each time period instead of at the end. In the above example, suppose that the 10 payments of $1,000 had to be made at the start of the year rather than at the end. The present value of the lease would not be the same, as each of the payments is occurring one year sooner. When equal payments are made at the end of each period, they are referred to as an *annuity in arrears* or an *ordinary annuity*. When equal payments are made at the beginning of each period they are referred to as an *annuity in advance*.

One way to find the present value of an annuity in advance is to treat it as if it were one year shorter than it is, and then add one full payment to the result (since the present value of the first payment, which is made at the very beginning, is simply the amount of the payment). In this approach, the second payment, which occurs on the first day of the second year, is treated as if it occurred on the last day of the first year, and so on. So you would find the present value for a nine-year annuity in arrears, and then add $1,000 to the resulting value. This procedure is complex and many find it confusing.

Some calculators allow the user to indicate whether they are solving an annuity in advance or in arrears. That significantly simplifies the calculation. Alternatively, annuities in advance can be solved using spreadsheet software programs. When solving using a spreadsheet, this is where the *type* value comes into play. Recall that in Excel, the formula used to solve for the present value is:

$$= PV(\text{rate, nper, pmt, fv, type})$$

Type refers to whether payments are made at the beginning or end of the period. By ignoring it up until this point, we have implicitly indicated that a default value of 0 should be used. A value of zero indicates that payments come at the end of the time period or periods. If the payments come at the beginning of the period or periods, then a value of 1 is used for *type*. The only choices for this element of the spreadsheet formula are 0 or 1. Indicating a value of 1 lets the spreadsheet program know that the payments come at the beginning of the period, and the program then makes automatic adjustments so that the result is computed correctly. For example, for the previous lease, if payments had been due at the beginning of each year, the present value, using Excel, would be calculated as follows:

$$= PV(rate, nper, pmt, fv, type)$$
$$= PV(12\%, 10, -1000, , 1)$$
$$= \$6,328.25$$

A gap separated by commas appears in the formula where the future value would be shown, since there is no future value in this problem. The gap is necessary so that the software program does not interpret the 1 that indicates the *type* of payment (advance or arrears) as being a future value. The value of 1 should be used for the type in Excel spreadsheet for any time value of money computation where payments are made at the beginning of the time period or periods. Its use is not limited to leases or to annuities.

ADVANTAGES OF LEASING   Leasing has a number of advantages. It is more flexible, can save money, can protect us from unexpected events, can provide a higher level of financing, and can have tax advantages. In the case of state and local governments, leases can also help overcome some legal limitations on the total amount of government debt.

Many managers like leasing because it provides flexibility. The term of the lease can be set for limited periods of time. If we expect to need a piece of equipment for only half of its useful life, we will not have to get involved with selling it as we would if we purchased the item. Although a leasing company deals with the purchase and resale of a particular type of equipment all the time, we probably do not. Therefore, the leasing company may be able to sell the used equipment for a better price than we could.

For example, suppose that we could buy a new car for $25,000 and then sell it after three years for $12,000. An auto leasing company might be able to sell the same car for $15,000. The difference of $3,000 can be used, at least partly, to reduce the monthly lease payments. As a result, if we only intend to keep a car for two or three years, it often makes more economic sense to lease it rather than buy it and then sell it.

Also, leasing protects us if we are afraid that the equipment may become obsolete. The lease can be designed so that we have the right to cancel it and replace the equipment with the newer model.

Leases also provide more flexibility in terms of financing. When we buy equipment or buildings, lenders usually require a down payment. This initial payment, typically 20 percent or more, protects the lender. If they have to foreclose on the capital asset because of our failure to make payments, they may not be able to sell it for the full initial purchase price. The down payment provides a margin of safety to protect the lender against losses. In contrast, leasing is similar to purchasing with 100 percent financing, since there is often no initial down payment. This is very helpful if we cannot raise the money for the down payment.

Another factor is related to interest rates. A large leasing company may be able to borrow money at a lower interest rate than a small organization. The leasing company may share some of that savings with the organization leasing the asset.

In certain circumstances, leases may also have tax advantages. This may seem to be a moot point for not-for-profit organizations. However, that is not always the case. Sometimes, it is possible that a for-profit organization can save taxes by purchasing certain items. They can then pass some of that tax savings on to the not-for-profit organization in the form of lower lease payments.

Finally, governments have frequently used leasing as an alternative to buying and owning capital assets. One reason for this is that a lease may enable the government to circumvent legal debt limits. For example, suppose that Millbridge wants to buy new buses to replace its aging mass transit fleet. However, Millbridge can only issue long-term debt, such as a bond, if it obtains voters' approval. Assume that the approval process would require a special election and would be both costly and time-consuming. Several leasing approaches would allow the town to acquire the buses even though the purchase might require tens or even hundreds of millions of dollars of financing beyond the government's legal debt limit.

One approach is for the buses to be leased from either the manufacturer or from a leasing company. However, if the total amount to be financed is very large or the repayment time period is very long, the lease may not be attractive to either the manufacturer or the leasing company. They may consider the risk to be too great. The default by one government could create a huge loss for the leasing company. An advantage that bonds have is that they can spread risk over a large number of bondholders. A bond-like leasing approach is the use of *certificates of participation* (COPs). Each COP is similar to a bond. They can be sold to the public the way that bonds can, and the interest paid to holders of COPs may even be tax-exempt, the way that interest on bonds might be. COPs provide many of the benefits of bonds.

Technically, if the lease commits the governmental body to making annual repayments, it would constitute debt and cause Millbridge to exceed its legal debt limit. Governments often include a clause in COPs or other leases, called a *nonappropriation clause*. This clause states that the lease can be canceled if it is not renewed annually by the legislature. Granof notes that

> the extent to which lease obligations are considered as debt, and thereby subject to debt limitations, has been the object of extensive litigation. . . . The court decisions have often run counter to prevailing accounting and financial wisdom. For example, in some states the courts have keyed their opinions to the nonappropriation clauses, asserting that because the lease payments are subject to annual authorization the leases lack the characteristics of long-term debts.[4]

Although this enables governments to get around debt limits, prudent managers must consider whether such actions are in fact appropriate. In some cases it may clearly make sense. Few would want their local government to hold a special election for approval to finance the purchase of a $2,000 computer system with a three-year useful lifetime. On the other hand, using a lease rather than a bond issuance to finance a long-term $400 million project, specifically to avoid having to seek voter approval, may be inappropriate.

DISADVANTAGES OF LEASING Leasing does tend to be more expensive than purchasing assets. In contrast to the use of bonds to dis-intermediate, or remove an intermediary, leasing adds another intermediary—the leasing company. Therefore, there is one extra layer of profit making. This tends to drive the cost up. Leasing companies also charge a price for some of the advantages that leases offer.

For example, many leases allow us to turn in equipment and replace it if it becomes obsolete. Although the lease agreement may not list a specific charge for this right, it does have a price. Effectively, we are buying an insurance policy against the equipment becoming obsolete. If it does become obsolete, we will collect on the policy. As with any insurance, there is a premium. And the premium will be built into the monthly lease payments. It would be unwise to believe that we are actually "putting one over" on the leasing company by getting protection against obsolescence. The leasing company is aware of the risks it is taking and charges accordingly.

Similarly, by getting 100 percent financing, we are putting the leasing company in a riskier position since there is no down payment. The lessor will charge the lessee an extra

---

[4] Michael H. Granof. *Government and Not-for-Profit Accounting.* New York, N.Y.: John Wiley & Sons, 2001, p. 289.

amount to cover their losses from such risks and also earn a profit for having been willing to take that risk.

There are times when leasing makes good sense. However, we must always consider the basic concept that the leasing company is one extra profit maker added to the process of getting the capital asset to the ultimate user of that asset. Leasing will tend to be more expensive unless there is some explicit benefit from the lease that could not otherwise be obtained. There is nothing wrong with leasing to avoid obsolescence, but we should be aware that we are paying for that peace of mind.

Summary

Assets with lifetimes of more than one year are often referred to as capital assets. Capital assets are often so costly that they cannot be paid for using just money generated from current operating activities. Instead, many organizations pay for the purchase of a building or major pieces of equipment by using long-term financing. Long-term financing refers to the various alternatives available to the organization to get the money needed to acquire capital assets. Long-term financing comes from either equity financing or debt financing. The common types of equity financing are retained earnings, stock issuance, taxes, and contributions. The common types of debt financing are notes, mortgages, bonds, and leasing.

Preview

In Chapters 7 and 8, Part III of this book, the focus shifts from planning to implementation and control of results. An important part of the implementation of plans is careful use of short-term resources and obligations. Chapter 7 considers techniques and approaches designed to maximize the benefit of short-term resources and minimize the cost of short-term obligations. Chapter 8 looks at systems that enable an organization to carry out its plans as closely as possible. Such systems provide the foundation for management control.

Short-term resources, often called current assets, are those resources that are cash or will be either converted to cash or used up within one year. Short-term obligations are those that will have to be paid in cash within one year. Short-term resources, less short-term obligations, are referred to as the organization's working capital. If managers can efficiently control their short-term resources and obligations, they can maximize the resources available to be used to meet the organization's mission. Careful management of short-term resources and obligations can, in some cases, make the difference between ceasing operations and continuing to stay in existence. Chapter 7 considers various approaches to accomplishing the objective of optimizing the management of working capital.

Management control is another element required to achieve the results called for in an organization's plans. It is based in the establishment of a responsibility system that holds managers accountable for their results. For management control to work, the organization must not only assign responsibility, but also motivate its employees to accomplish the organization's goals. It must also measure results and analyze why actual performance differs from expectations. The Chapter 8 exposition on control issues concludes with discussions of ethics and the safeguarding of resources.

Key Terms from This Chapter

bearer bonds. See *unregistered bonds.*

bond. Formal borrowing arrangement in which a transferable certificate represents the debt. The holder of the bond may sell it, in which case the liability is owed to the new owner.

bond issue. The total face value of *bonds* offered by a single borrower, and governed by a set of terms and conditions

bond year dollars. The sum of the amount of money that is outstanding for each year of a *bond* *issue*. If a *term bond issue* is $2,000 for 5 years, then the *bond year dollars* would be $10,000 ($2,000 × 5).

call provision.   An element of a *bond* contract between the *bond* issuer (borrower) and the lender which allows the borrower to repay the bond before its *maturity* date.

capital assets.   Buildings or equipment with useful lives extending beyond the year in which they are purchased or put into service; also referred to as long-term investments, capital items, capital investments, or capital acquisitions.

capital lease.   A form of long-term financing in which a long-term, noncancellable contractual arrangement is made to lease a *capital asset*.

certificates of participation (COPs).   Debt securities similar to bonds that represent participation in a portion of a *capital lease* similar to participation in a bond issuance.

collateral.   A specific asset the lender can claim if the borrower fails to make payment of amounts due.

current portion of long-term debt.   The portion of *long-term* debt that is due for payment during the coming year.

discount.   The amount a lender receives for a *bond* below the *face value* or *maturity value* of the bond. Discounts are the result of market interest rates that are above than the *stated interest rate* for that bond.

dis-intermediate.   Remove an intermediary party. For example, an organization borrows directly from investors to remove the bank from the middle of the transaction.

face value.   See *maturity value*.

full-faith and credit.   Guarantee by a governmental body issuing debt that the obligation's interest and principal payments are backed by the full taxing power of the government.

long-term.   Period of time greater than one year.

long-term financing.   The various alternatives available to the organization to get the money needed to acquire *capital assets*.

maturity.   Due date or end date of a loan arrangement.

maturity value.   The principal amount of a loan to be repaid at the ending date or maturity date of the loan.

mortgage.   Represents a loan that is secured by a specific asset.

net interest cost (NIC).   The yearly debt cost of a *serial bond* issue, calculated as a percentage. This approach does not take the *time value of money* into account. See *true interest cost*.

nonappropriation clause.   A clause governments often include in *leases* that states that the lease can be canceled if it is not renewed annually by the legislature.

ordinary annuity.   An *annuity in arrears*.

premium.   The amount a lender receives for a bond in excess of the *face value* or *maturity value* of the bond. Premiums are the result of market interest rates that are below than the *stated interest rate* for that bond.

registered bonds.   Bonds whose ownership is tracked by the borrower. Taxable interest on registered bonds is reported to the Internal Revenue Service.

revenue bonds.   *Bonds* that are backed from the revenues from a specific, limited source. The full taxing power of the government is not pledged in support of revenue bonds.

serial bonds.   A *bond issue* that has a number of different *maturity* dates, with part of the total *bond issue* being repaid at each of the maturity dates.

short-term.   Period of time of one year or less.

sinking fund.   An account that is used to accumulate money to be used for the eventual repayment of debt, such as a *bond*, or for the future acquisition of a *capital asset*.

spread.   The difference between the underwriter's buying and selling price for a *bond issue*.

stated interest rate.   Bond interest rate that is multiplied by the *maturity value* of the bond to determine annual amount of interest paid.

stated value.   See *maturity value*.

term bonds.   A *bond issue* with one *maturity* date, with all bonds due for repayment on that date.

true interest cost (TIC).   The interest rate cost of a *serial bond* to a *bond* issuer, calculated using *time value of money* methodology.

unregistered bonds.   Bonds for which the borrowing organization does not have a record of whom the borrower is. Often called bearer bonds because interest is paid to the current holder of the bond upon the presentation of a coupon cut off of the bond.

zero coupon bonds. Bonds that do not pay interest until the *maturity* date, when all accumulated *compound interest* and principal is paid.

Questions for Discussion

6-1. What are the various types of long-term debt?
6-2. What is collateral, and why is it used?
6-3. How do mortgages work?

6-4. How do bonds work?
6-5. Summarize the advantages and disadvantages of leasing.

Exercises (TVM)

6-6. Assume that a 5 percent $100,000 bond with semi-annual interest payments and a remaining life of 20 years could be purchased today, when market interest rates are 6 percent. How much would you have to pay to buy the bond?

6-7. You could purchase a zero coupon bond that has a maturity value of $5,000 and earns a current market rate of 5 percent. If the bond matures in 8 years and we assume semiannual compounding, what is the bond worth today?

Problems

Note: For all problems:
  A. Solve using a financial calculator.
  B. Solve using a spreadsheet program such as Excel. Indicate the basic spreadsheet formula, and show

both the numeric value formula and cell reference formula. For example, for the value that $100 today could grow to in two years, assuming 10 percent annual compounding, your solution might appear as:

	A	B	C
1			
2	PV	($100)	
3	Nper	2	
4	Rate	10%	
5			
6	Excel Formula	= FV(rate, nper, pmt, pv, type)	
7	Numerical Formula Solution	= FV(10%, 2, , −100)	$121.00
8	Cell Reference Formula Solution	= FV(B4, B3, , B2)	$121.00

In the above example, Row 6 shows the basic Excel formula, Row 7 shows a numeric value formula, and Row 8 shows a cell reference formula. C7 is the solution calculated from the B7 formula, and C8 is the solution calculated from the B8 formula. Note that since there is no annuity payment (PMT) in this problem, it is necessary to show the blank between two commas after the number of periods (nper).

6-8. Thirdedition City is issuing a 30-year bond with a face value of $5,000,000 and a stated annual interest rate of 6 percent. The city will make interest payments twice a year.

1. Calculate the semi-annual interest payment.
2. Calculate how much Thirdedition City will receive from the bond offering under the following conditions:
   a. Market interest rates remain unchanged at the time of the offering.
   b. Market interest rates decrease to 5.8% at the time of the offering.
6-9. On July 1, 1999, Mountain Sea City issued a 30-year bond with a face (or par) value of $100,000,000 and a stated annual interest rate of 6 percent. Under the terms of the bond offering, the city must make interest

payments twice each year until the final maturity date of the bond on June 30, 2029. At that time, Mountain Sea City will make the final interest payment on the bond and repay the $100,000,000 that it borrowed.

As of July 1, 2009, with exactly 20 years remaining on the life of the bond, interest rates had fallen to 4.6%. What was the value of the bond on June 30, 2009? (Be sure to show all of your work, including the factors you used to determine the value of the bond.)

6-10. Meals for the Homeless borrowed $5,650 to buy kitchen equipment. It used a mortgage arrangement with a bank, agreeing to repay the full amount plus interest at a 12 percent rate in 10 annual installments. How much will it pay the bank each year?

6-11. Meals for the Homeless plans to lease some new equipment. The lease calls for payments of $1,000 per year and is based on eight annual payments and a 9 percent interest rate. As an accommodation to the not-for-profit organization, the bank has agreed to lease payments at the end of each year rather than the beginning, which is more common. What is the present value of the obligation? How much did the bank lose by allowing payments at the end of each year rather than at the beginning?

6-12. Jackson City is selling 10,000 bonds to raise capital for expanding the fire stations in the city. Each bond has a face value of $5,000, an annual coupon rate of 12 percent, a maturity of 15 years, and semiannual interest payments.
  a. The market interest rate on bonds of similar risk is 13 percent at the time the bond is first issued (sold to the market). How much did Jackson City receive for *each* bond when it issued them?
  b. If all the bonds are sold, how much capital will Jackson City have available to expand the fire stations?

6-13. A recent drop in interest rates has caused you to consider selling a $10,000 face value bond that you own. The bond has a 7 percent coupon interest rate, matu-

rity of 20 years, and semiannual interest payments. The bond could be sold today at a price based on a market interest rate of 6 percent. How much could you sell the bond for today?

6-14. New University plans to issue a $100,000 bond. The money is to buy computer projection units for classrooms. The bond matures in 10 years, and it makes semiannual interest payments. The stated interest rate is 8 percent, but rates have risen to 10 percent in the market. How much will the university receive when it issues the bond?

6-15. Assume that HOS could issue a zero coupon bond at an annual interest rate of 4% with semi-annual compounding for 20 years. If HOS receives $2,264.45 for the bond, how much would it have to pay at the maturity date?

6-16. On January 1, 2010, Central City issued a 20-year serial bond to finance improvements to the water distribution system. A total of $80,000,000 face value of bonds were issued with coupon and maturity rates as follows:

December 31, 2014	3.0%	$ 5,000,000
December 31, 2019	3.5%	$ 5,000,000
December 31, 2024	4.0%	$10,000,000
December 31, 2025	4.1%	$10,000,000
December 31, 2026	4.2%	$10,000,000
December 31, 2027	4.3%	$10,000,000
December 31, 2028	4.4%	$15,000,000
December 31, 2029	4.5%	$15,000,000

Cental City received $80,500,000 from the bond issue. Use a spreadsheet program to find the NIC and TIC interest rates for the bond issue. What would the values for NIC and TIC be if the interest rate were 4.2 percent for the bonds with a maturity before 2024 and 5 percent for the bonds with a maturity of 2024 or later? [Note: If you set up your spreadsheet with formulas, you should only have to change the interest rates to get the new NIC and TIC values.]

Suggested Readings

Anthony, Robert N., and Leslie Pearlman Breitner. *Essentials of Accounting*, 9th ed. Upper Saddle River, N.J.: Prentice Hall, 2006.

Bierman, Harold, and Seymour Smidt. *The Capital Budgeting Decision: Economic Analysis of Investment Projects*, 8th ed. Upper Saddle River, N.J.: Prentice Hall, 1993.

Brigham, Eugene F., and Joel F. Houston. *Fundamentals of Financial Management*, 11th ed. Mason, Ohio: Thomson/ South-Western, 2006.

Emery, Douglas R., John D. Finnerty, and John D. Stowe. *Corporate Financial Management*, 3rd ed. Upper Saddle River, N.J.: Prentice Hall, 2007.

Horngren, Charles T., Gary L. Sundem, William O. Stratton, et al. *Introduction to Management Accounting*, 4th ed. Upper Saddle River, N.J.: Prentice Hall, 2008.

Keown, Arthur J., John W. Martin, William D. Petty, and David F. Scott. *Foundations of Finance: The Logic and Practice of Financial Management* 6th ed. Upper Saddle River, N.J.: Prentice Hall, 2008.

Van Horne, James C., and John M. Wachowicz Jr. *Financial Management*, 12th ed. Upper Saddle River, N.J.: Prentice Hall, 2005.

7

Managing Short-Term Resources and Obligations

The learning objectives of this chapter are to:

- define working capital and describe the various elements of working capital management;
- discuss cash management, including short-term cash investment, cash budgets, concentration banking, and maintaining security over cash;
- discuss marketable securities management, including investment objectives, suitable short-term investments, and unsuitable short-term investments;
- discuss liquidity management;
- discuss accounts receivable management, including data collection, credit policies, the billing process, aging of receivables, lock boxes, and electronic payment;
- discuss inventory management, including the distinction between periodic and perpetual inventory, economic order quantity, and just-in-time inventory techniques; and
- discuss management of short-term obligations, including accounts payable, payroll payable, short-term debt, and taxes payable.

INTRODUCTION

In Chapters 7 and 8 the focus shifts from planning to implementation and control of results. An important part of the implementation of plans is careful use of short-term resources and obligations. This chapter considers techniques and approaches designed to maximize the benefit of short-term resources and minimize the cost of short-term obligations. By short-term, we are generally referring to a period of less than one year. Short-term resources, often called short-term assets, *current assets,* or near-term assets, are those resources that are cash or will be either converted to cash or used up within one year. Short-term obligations are those that will have to be paid in cash within one year.

If managers can efficiently control their short-term resources and obligations, they can maximize the resources available to be used to meet the organization's mission. For example, we could leave all of our cash in a non-interest-earning checking account. Alternatively, we might have a procedure that keeps most of our cash in an interest-earning savings account. By being aware of the opportunity to earn interest on idle funds and by setting up a system to take advantage of that, the organization will earn interest. The interest it earns can be used to provide more or better services to its constituency group. Or it can be used to provide financial reserves to improve the long-term survival prospects of the organization.

Careful management of short-term resources and obligations can, in some cases, make the difference between ceasing operations versus continuing to stay in existence.

WORKING CAPITAL MANAGEMENT

Every organization has assets and liabilities. Assets are any resources that the organization has that can help provide goods and services. Liabilities are obligations that the organization owes to other organizations or to individuals. *Working capital* is defined as the organization's current assets less its current liabilities. Current refers to short-term or near-term. Generally, current assets are those that will be used up or will become cash within a year. *Current liabilities* are those obligations that will have to be paid within a year. *Net working capital* is a term often used interchangeably with working capital. Management of current assets and current liabilities to maximize results is called *working capital management*.

Working capital is essential to any organization. At times, it has been compared to "cash register money." Each day when a store opens for business, some money must be in the cash register to make change for the first customer. That customer may not have the exact amount of the purchase. Also, the store will have to pay its suppliers and employees with money from the cash register, even if it has not yet received payment for everything that it has sold. In similar fashion, every organization needs some cash to pay bills and employees. Every organization will owe some money to some of its suppliers and will likely have customers that owe money to it.

Working capital is based on a cycle of inflows and outflows (see Figure 7-1). Cash is initially used to buy supplies. For example, Meals for the Homeless might pay money to acquire food. Then meals are provided to homeless people. Assume that the city has agreed to pay Meals a fixed amount for each meal served to the homeless. Meals must tally how many meals were served and issue a bill to the city. It must then wait to collect from the city. Once the money has been received, the cycle starts over and the organization can use the money to buy more food and to provide more meals.

The cycle, however, may be delicately balanced. If we forget to issue the bill for a week, our receipt of money from the city may be postponed. It is possible that we will have several days or even a week when we cannot provide any meals because we have no cash available to buy food.

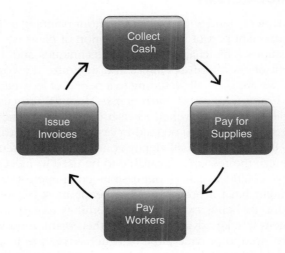

FIGURE 7-1 Working capital cycle.

In performing working capital management, the manager must ensure that the cash on hand is adequate to meet the organization's needs and also to minimize the cost of those resources. To do this, the manager must carefully monitor and control cash inflows and outflows. Cash not immediately needed should be invested, earning a return for the organization. Loans should be approved in advance to provide money when cash shortages are likely to arise.

The organization should not keep excess supplies (inventory). The money spent now to pay for inventory that is not needed until later could be better used by the organization for some other purpose. At a minimum, the money could be invested in the organization's savings account, earning interest.

Sometimes an organization charges for goods and services it provides, but it does not receive cash for those goods or services immediately. We refer to this as providing the goods or services for credit, or on account. The organization records an account receivable when it provides goods or services and payment is not immediately received. Accounts receivable are assets that represent the right to collect the money owed for the purchases that have been made on account. Just as we would not want to buy and pay for supplies too soon because it takes money out of our bank account, we do not want to wait too long to collect money that is owed to us. The sooner we collect all of our receivables, the sooner the organization will have that cash available for its use.

By the same token, short-term obligations, called current liabilities, must also be managed carefully. The organization desires to have sufficient cash to pay its obligations when they are due. However, if the organization pays its bills before they are due, it will lose the interest it could have earned if it had left the cash in its savings account for a little longer rather than paying the obligation.

This chapter focuses on the management of all elements of working capital. The discussion begins with short-term resources. Then we turn our attention to issues related to short-term obligations.

SHORT-TERM RESOURCES

The most essential financial resource is cash. Cash is needed to pay obligations as they come due. Cash is generally defined as both currency on hand and also amounts that can be withdrawn from bank accounts. A second type of short-term resource is *marketable securities*. These investments can be bought and sold in financial markets, such as stock and debt markets. Marketable securities provide managers with an outlet to invest idle resources while maintaining access to the resources when needed. In most organizations, receivables are also important. Receivables often are the largest working capital item. Inventories are often not very sizable in public service organizations. However, they receive a great amount of attention because managers have had difficulty in controlling them. Inventory represents the major supply items that the organization buys and uses to produce its goods or services.

Cash

Organizations should keep some cash on hand or in their bank accounts for three principal reasons: transactions, safety, and investment. First, cash is needed for the normal daily transactions of any activity. For example, cash is needed to pay employees and suppliers. Second, although many activities can be anticipated, managers can never foresee everything that might happen. Experience has shown that it makes sense for organizations to have a safety cushion available for emergencies. A third reason for holding cash is to have it available if an attractive investment opportunity arises. Investment possibilities are not limited to those that earn a profit; they might represent an opportunity to provide a new, valuable service to the organization's clients.

Given the three reasons to hold cash, one might think that the more cash we have, the better. That is not the case. Cash does not directly further the mission of the organization. Imagine if Meals for the Homeless could use two ovens to make 2,000 meals a day. There is a large unmet demand for meals. However, it decides to buy only one oven and keep the rest of the money in the bank. On the one hand, the money in the bank provides a degree of safety. On the other hand, that safety severely reduces the level of services provided.

This is a complex problem. If we fail to have an adequate safety margin to respond to the emergencies that might occur, we may chance putting the organization out of business. However, if we are overly conservative, keeping too great a cash safety margin, we are failing to meet our mission. Managers must find an appropriate cash level that is reasonably safe yet does not unduly restrict the organization's pursuit of its primary mission.

Clearly, managers must be active in the area of cash management. We cannot afford to just have however much cash we have. Managers must project when cash is likely to be received. (Recall the discussion of cash budgeting in Chapter 2.) The cash may come from donations, charges to customers, taxes, or other sources. Regardless of the source, we must anticipate when we will receive the cash. Similarly, the manager must anticipate what cash will be required for payments and when they must be made. The cash excess or shortfall is calculated for each period of time.

For example, if it becomes apparent that there will be an unexpected cash shortfall, the organization has several options. It can try to speed up collections of money that is owed to it. It can try to hold off on payments that it has to make. Or it can arrange for a loan. Banks are more likely to lend to organizations that can anticipate temporary cash needs well in advance, especially if the organization can show when it expects to be able to repay the loan.

Many organizations arrange for credit in advance of a specific need for cash. For example, the Hospital for Ordinary Surgery (HOS) might arrange for a $1 million line of credit at the bank where it does most of its routine financial transactions. The arrangement would typically include repayment terms and interest rates. Interest rates are often tied to some benchmark rate that may vary over time. Thus, if HOS does not need to borrow any of its $1 million credit line for six months and interest rates in general have gone up or down during that six-month period, the interest rate on the amount borrowed will be adjusted based on current rates at the time the money is borrowed. Having a credit line allows the organization to hold lower cash reserves than it might otherwise need.

If we project that we will have more cash than needed, we can invest the surplus in short-term interest-earning investments, plan to use it to repay loans, or plan to use it to expand the services we provide.

SHORT-TERM CASH INVESTMENT Organizations should keep as little money as possible in non-interest-bearing accounts. In fact, even after checks are written, it is possible to earn interest on the money in the interim period until the check is cashed. That period is called the *float*. Many banks have arrangements that allow money to be automatically transferred into a checking account as checks are received for payment. Until then, the money can remain in an interest-bearing account.

Managers should make great efforts to ensure that cash is deposited into interest-bearing accounts as quickly as possible and withdrawn only when actually needed. All organizations should have specific policies that result in cash and checks being processed and deposited promptly.

Although better than non-interest accounts, interest-bearing accounts pay relatively low rates of interest. Managers of public service organizations often have alternatives that allow them to earn a higher rate of return. In a world of no free lunches, however, there is generally a trade-off when one obtains a higher rate of return.

The two most common trade-offs are decreased liquidity and increased risk. Decreased liquidity means that the money is not immediately accessible. Money can be taken out of a checking account immediately with no penalty. If money is put into a higher-yielding investment such as a *certificate of deposit* (CD), there may be a penalty for early withdrawal. CDs generally tie up the organization's money for at least a month. However, they pay interest rates higher than savings accounts. Do you take the risk that you will not need the money for the longer period of time and earn the higher interest rate, or do you keep the money in a checking account so you will have it if an emergency need arises? That is a trade-off that managers must make.

Although CDs may tie up money for a period of time, they are generally safe. Other investments hold promise of even higher rates of return but entail greater risks. For example, cash can be invested in marketable securities such as corporate stocks and bonds. Such investments are subject to market fluctuations. That means that their value might fall.

Another problem with sacrificing liquidity is that there are many unknown future events. Suppose that we invest in a five-year CD at the current market interest rate. Interest rates may rise dramatically in the next year or two. Having money tied up for five years means that the organization will not be able to earn those higher rates. This is another reason that investors often demand a higher rate of return if their money is locked in for a longer period of time.

CASH BUDGETS   Cash budgeting is first introduced in Chapter 2. A *cash budget* is developed with the operating and capital budgets to ensure that they are feasible. One reason departmental operating budgets are rejected is that the cash budget may show that the organization would simply run out of cash if it made all the requested payments.

For example, HOS may want to buy a new $5,000,000 scanner that will last for 10 years. Assume that the scanner will be treated as an expense of $500,000 a year for each of its 10 years. Even if we can charge patients $1,500,000 a year in total for their use of the scanner and make a healthy profit of $1,000,000 each year for 10 years, we must consider where the initial $5,000,000 will come from. Unless we have that much cash or are able to borrow the money to pay for the scanner, we will not be able to buy it.

Pushing this point one step further, even profitable organizations can run out of cash. Profits are often based on *accrual accounting*. Revenues are recorded when they are earned, even if they have not yet been received. It is possible for an organization's cash payments for expenses to precede its receipts from revenues to such an extent that it will run out of money. This is a particular problem for apparently healthy, growing organizations. Their growth, evidence of success, often requires cash investment to expand operations. That cash investment may come well before cash receipts that result from that investment. Careful planning is critical to avoid sudden, unexpected cash shortages.

Cash is of such importance that many organizations prepare a cash budget for each month of the coming year. It is not enough to budget total cash inflows and outflows for the year. We need to know on a more current basis, usually month to month, how much cash will be received and paid.

Cash budgets typically start with the cash balance expected to be on hand at the beginning of the month. The expected cash receipts for the month are added to this. The receipts may be itemized into major categories, such as donations, sales revenue, and investment income, or by source, such as Medicare patient revenue, Medicaid patient revenue, managed care patient revenue, and other patient revenue. The beginning cash balance is combined with the expected receipts to find the expected available cash for the month. Expected payments are subtracted to find the anticipated balance at the end of each month. Surpluses can be invested and are subtracted from the balance. Deficits require borrowing. The amount to be borrowed is added to the balance. The final projected balance for each month becomes the beginning balance for the next month.

The most difficult part of cash budgeting is generally the result of complexities in estimating cash receipts. Although we may be able to predict fairly accurately when we will provide services, receipt of cash payment for those services can depend on a number of factors. HOS may find that different types of payers take different amounts of time to pay for services. For example, an HMO may pay a set amount per member per month, once a month at the beginning of the month, regardless of the amount of services provided to those members. In contrast, it might take Medicare several months before it pays. Similarly, sales taxes for sales made each month may be collected by a municipality during the first week of the following month. Real estate taxes may be collected quarterly. Permit fees might be paid once a year. The timing of when receipts are expected is critical to preparing an accurate cash budget. An accurate cash budget is critical to knowing whether sufficient funds will be available to make payments when they are due.

Combining receipt lags with variations in volume of services from month to month results in a complex cash flow. One cannot simply assume that there will be enough money on hand in any given month to meet the cash needs of that month. That is why cash planning is critical.

CONCENTRATION BANKING   Although many public service organizations deal with more than one bank, they often maintain a significant presence at one or more banks, referred to as *concentration banks*. Arrangements can be made with the concentration bank to *sweep* or transfer money into and out of accounts automatically.

For example, suppose that a state government has many individual agencies that collect money. In many cases, the amount the agencies collect exceeds their current cash needs. This is typically the case with licenses, sales tax payments, income taxes, and so on. The money will often be deposited in separate accounts for each agency, and frequently in multiple accounts earmarked for different purposes within the same agency.

However, the state does not want the collections to sit in these bank accounts for extended periods of time. They often need that cash to make disbursements for various other state purposes that do not directly generate revenues. Therefore, they will arrange with the banks to automatically transfer balances from these feeder accounts to a master account at the concentration bank. There could be daily, weekly, or monthly transfers, depending on the expected balances in the accounts. The transfers could be for the entire balance or just for the balance exceeding a certain amount.

The process can also be reversed with *zero-balance accounts*. In that case, an organization can write checks on an account that has a zero balance. When the checks are presented for payment, the bank keeps a tally of the total amount disbursed. That amount is then automatically transferred from one central account at the concentration bank into the zero-balance account.

This type of automatic transferring of funds back and forth allows the organization to have quick access to its cash resources for payment needs. It also allows it to maintain less cash in total than it would if it had cash balances in many different accounts. The excess cash can be invested in marketable securities to earn interest and may enable the organization to earn a higher yield on investments by purchasing securities in larger denominations.

Nevertheless, sometimes organizations have temporary cash needs in excess of available cash. Often arrangements will be made allowing the organization to overdraw its account. These overdrafts are often referred to as a *line of credit* and are generally treated as loans. Interest is charged. In some cases, banks charge a fee for keeping the money available, even if the organization never borrows against the line of credit. Sometimes arrangements have been made in advance that use the organization's accounts receivable or inventory to secure the overdraft. In other cases, the overdraft is an unsecured loan with no specific assets provided to protect the bank if the organization fails to repay it.

In exchange for credit arrangements, many organizations agree to keep compensating balances in the bank. That is, the organization may always keep a certain amount of money in the bank. It is sometimes curious to see an organization, such as HOS, borrow $200,000 from the bank through a line of credit when it has $500,000 sitting in its concentration checking account. However, HOS may have agreed to maintain a $500,000 minimum balance at all times. If it draws checks that require it to go below the $500,000, it will have to borrow money. On the other hand, the line of credit will typically substantially exceed the required compensating balance and provides a level of cash safety that the organization might not otherwise have.

MAINTAINING SECURITY OVER CASH   Of all the organization's assets, cash requires the greatest care to ensure that it is not misappropriated. Internal control systems to protect resources are discussed in Chapter 8. Cash protection requires a careful set of checks and balances. The specific people who handle cash should be different from those who reconcile cash receipts. Controls should exist for both the organization's receipts and disbursements. All money received should actually enter the organization's records, and no money should be disbursed without proper authorization.

Disbursements should be made by check, if possible. Two independent signatures should be required for checks that are large. All checks should be numbered. Different people should authorize, write, and sign checks. Other principles, discussed in Chapter 8, including bonding, reliable personnel, vacations, and rotation of functions, should be employed if possible.

Marketable Securities

It was noted earlier that one option for cash investment is marketable securities, which are investments that have a ready market for purchase and sale. Unlike a piece of land or a building that might take months or longer to sell, marketable securities can be sold almost immediately and cash from the sale can be received within a few days at most.

There are two major categories of marketable securities: *equity* securities and non-equity instruments. Equity refers to having an ownership interest. Shares of stock are referred to as equity securities. For-profit corporations issue stock in exchange for money. The people who buy the stock become owners of the corporation. The owners of the stock can sell it to other people, transferring their ownership interest in the company to the buyer. If the corporation does very well, the value of each share of stock may rise. Conversely, if the corporation does not do well, the value of the stock may fall.

Obligations such as bonds and notes are referred to either as *debt* instruments or non-equity instruments. The lender is said to buy the debt instrument, and the borrower is said to have sold it. The lender owns the debt instrument, but does not own any part of the company borrowing the money. If the organization that has borrowed money by selling bonds does poorly, it is still obligated to repay the full amount that it has borrowed. The market value of bonds may rise or fall, but the buyer of the bond is reasonably certain to be repaid the face value of the bond at maturity if the borrower remains solvent.

There are two primary reasons that the market price of debt rises or falls. The first relates to changes in the ability of the borrower to eventually be able to repay the debt. If the borrower has financial setbacks that make repayment questionable, the price of the debt will fall. The investors who bought the bond will not be able to sell it for as much as they paid to buy it. The second reason relates to changes in interest rates in general. Suppose that someone issues a bond, borrowing money for 7 percent interest per year. If interest rates for equivalent debt rise to 8 percent in the marketplace, the bond paying 7 percent becomes less attractive, and its price in the market drops. Valuation of bonds is discussed in Chapter 6.

Investing in either stocks or bonds is more risky than leaving cash in a bank account. In general, there is a risk/return trade-off. The riskier the investment, the higher its expected return. Riskier investments must offer the potential for higher returns than less risky alternatives, or else no one would choose those riskier investments.

When investing available cash in either bonds or stocks, the manager must carefully consider whether the expected increase in return is adequate to pay for the extra risk that the organization is taking. The market value of either stocks or bonds can fall dramatically over short periods of time. We can categorize marketable investments as being either suitable for short-term investment of surplus cash or unsuitable, based on the likelihood that purchasers of investments will be able to recover the full amount of their investment plus the expected return when the money is needed.

INVESTING OBJECTIVES Four principal factors must be taken into account when making investments:

- legality,
- risk,
- yield, and
- liquidity.

First, one must ensure that the investment is legal. Many investments are legal for the general public but would not be legal for governmental entities and in some cases not-for-profit organizations. For example, state governments often pass laws restricting the types of investments that these organizations can make. Usually this is done to help ensure that the organizations do not make investments that are overly risky.

Second, different types of investments have different levels of risk. Risk relates to both the safety of the principal amount of the investment and the uncertainty of the rate of return. How great is the chance that some or all of the investment might be lost, or that the rate of return earned will differ from that expected? The investor must carefully consider the risks of the specific investments being considered.

Third, one must consider yield. The yield is the return that one expects to earn from the investment. Generally there is a trade-off between risk and return. As noted earlier, investors are only willing to take greater risk if they earn a higher rate of return.

The fourth factor is liquidity. Liquidity relates to how quickly the investment can be ended and investors can get back their cash when needed or desired. There is usually a trade-off between yield and liquidity. Investors require a higher return to be willing to sacrifice quick access to their money. The factors of risk and liquidity are both considered in determining the yield the investor demands.

In determining what types of investments are suitable for organizations, these four factors should be considered.

SUITABLE SHORT-TERM INVESTMENTS A number of suitable short-term investments are reasonable alternatives to keeping cash on hand in the form of currency or uncashed checks. Cash that is not immediately needed for operations is referred to as idle or surplus cash. Many options are liquid (the money can be retrieved very quickly when needed), safe, and earn interest. Therefore, it is wasteful not to invest idle cash. The two major types of suitable temporary holding areas for idle cash are bank deposits and money market investments.

Suppose that Meals for the Homeless received a foundation grant to allow it to provide additional meals during the coming six months. The foundation gives Meals a check for the full amount. Clearly, the check should not be placed in a drawer until the cash is needed to buy food or pay workers. It might get lost or stolen. It certainly is not earning interest for the organization while it is in the drawer.

Initially the check can be deposited into Meals' bank checking account. This prevents the check from being stolen or accidentally lost or destroyed. However, the checking account generally does not pay any interest. Bank deposits primarily fall into the categories of checking accounts, savings accounts, nonnegotiable CDs, and money market deposit accounts. Checking accounts may offer interest, but if so usually at very low rates. Many checking accounts charge fees, especially if a very low balance is maintained. Some cash can be left in checking accounts to reduce or eliminate fees on the account.

Alternatively, money can be transferred into a bank savings account. A relatively low interest rate will be earned, and the money will be safe, as long as the bank remains financially stable. In addition to the financial stability provided by the bank's own assets, bank accounts are currently insured by the Federal Deposit Insurance Corporation (FDIC) up to $250,000 per depositor per bank. Bank savings accounts are generally safe and liquid but yield low rates of return.

Banks also offer nonnegotiable CDs and money market accounts. Nonnegotiable CDs cannot be sold by the purchaser. They can only be redeemed with their issuer. The depositor puts money into the CD and then gets the money back with interest upon maturity. CDs are generally considered safe, and they pay higher rates of return than regular savings accounts, but they reduce the investor's liquidity. If the depositor needs the money and cashes in the CD before the maturity date, a penalty is generally charged. The penalty is often great enough to reduce the interest rate earned to a lower level than the rate on regular savings accounts.

Money market accounts at banks are bank accounts that have fluctuating interest rates that rise and fall in line with interest rates in the marketplace. We sometimes refer to a *money market*. The money market is the market for short-term marketable securities or the market for short-term debt instruments. Money market bank accounts operate in a manner very similar to money market mutual funds, which are discussed below. However, they have the advantage of being covered by the FDIC insurance mentioned previously.

Money market options exist which compete for cash investments. They often pay a higher interest rate than a bank savings account. One such option is a *treasury bill* (often called *t-bill*). This debt security issued by the U.S. government has maturities ranging from four weeks to one year. All interest on a treasury bill is discounted at the beginning of the investment. Denominations are stated in terms of the maturity value. For example, a one-year "$10,000 treasury bill" might be purchased for $9,600. The buyer of the bill pays $9,600 to buy the bill when it is issued, and receives $10,000 at maturity. This results in a yield of slightly more than 4 percent.[1]

The yield on t-bills depends on current market conditions. Those conditions are influenced by factors such as the anticipated inflation rate and the relative attractiveness of other available investments. If the bill is held until it matures, the federal government guarantees to pay the maturity value. Treasury bills can be purchased directly from the federal government without a fee or through a commercial bank or stockbroker who charges a fee or commission.[2]

Generally, longer-term bills will pay a higher rate than shorter-term bills. Suppose Meals believes it will need the cash to pay suppliers in three months. If a three-month bill currently yields an interest rate of 3.7 percent and a one-year bill yields 4.0 percent, should Meals for the Homeless buy a one-year bill and then sell it after three months?

---

[1] The investor is earning $400 of interest on an investment of $9,600 for one year. This represents an interest rate yield of 4.17 percent. Note that the investor does not invest the full $10,000. That is the amount received at maturity including interest.
[2] One option is to invest by mail or to go directly to a branch of the Federal Reserve Bank. Alternatively, investments can be made through the Treasury Direct system online at http://www.treasurydirect.gov.

That would allow it to earn at a 4 percent rate for the first three months of the investment, rather than the lower 3.7 percent rate. The problem with this approach is that it creates risk. Not only must Meals pay a commission on the sale of the bill after three months, but it must also worry about changes in interest rates over the next three months.

Suppose that interest rates rise sharply. Since individuals can purchase new bills that will yield higher rates, the one-year bill Meals holds becomes relatively less attractive. Its market value (the price it can be sold for) will fall. The entire benefit that Meals hoped to gain by earning the higher rate for three months may be more than offset by the fall in the market value of the bill. In most cases, therefore, it is sensible to try to match the maturity of the bill to when the cash is expected to be needed for the operations of the organization.

Conversely, if you do not expect to need the money for a year and you expect interest rates to rise in the interim, it is not unreasonable to buy a three-month bill and keep reinvesting it at maturity, ideally at increasing rates. However, it is very difficult to predict what will happen in financial markets. That is why it is generally best to match the maturity of your investments to the timing of your need for funds.

Another alternative is money market mutual funds. These investments tend to pay a rate below that of CDs or commercial paper, but competitive with treasury bills and higher than the rate paid by a commercial bank on a money market deposit account. Generally the investor gets one share in the mutual fund for each dollar invested, and the value of the shares remains stable at $1. Interest is earned daily. Money market mutual funds often offer free check-writing privileges, and money can be deposited or withdrawn at any time, generally with no fee or commission. Although the investment has no guarantee, such as a treasury bill, money market funds are generally considered to be reasonably safe investments, and they are very convenient to use.

The next type of money market instrument is a *negotiable certificate of deposit* issued by a U.S. bank. CDs require investors to commit their money for a period of time, such as six months or a year. Banks may pay a higher rate on a large CD than treasury bills pay. A negotiable CD can be sold to someone else, just as a bond can be sold. However, sales commissions will be incurred, and the value of the CD at the time of sale will depend on what has happened to market interest rates and the credit-worthiness of the lender during the time since the investment was initially made.

Another type of money market instrument is *commercial paper*. Commercial paper generally represents a note payable issued by a corporation. Typical maturities are less than one year, and the interest rate is higher than a treasury bill. Although commercial paper is generally issued only by the strongest of organizations, the buyer of the paper is essentially lending money to a corporation. There is a risk, albeit small, that the corporation will not repay the loan.

Repurchase agreements, or *repos,* are another type of short-term investment. They are collateralized by securities. Repos may be for as short a period of time as overnight. The organization with idle cash provides it to the borrower at an agreed-upon interest rate. The interest rate may fluctuate from day to day, and the investment can be ended by either the borrower or lender at any time. Although repos are liquid, they do have a variety of risks, such as the possibility that if the borrower cannot repay the amount invested, the collateral may turn out to be insufficient to cover the full investment.

Commercial paper, negotiable CDs, and repos would only be suitable for organizations that have substantial amounts of cash (perhaps more than $1 million) available for short-term investment. These investments can be quite complicated and should only be used by organizations that employ competent advisors knowledgeable in their intricacies and potential risks.

UNSUITABLE SHORT-TERM INVESTMENTS   There has been growing concern about public service organizations making inappropriate investment choices. What created an environment in which this would be a concern? Granof notes that

> Treasurers and other officials responsible for their organizations' investments have come under considerable pressure to increase their portfolio yields. In part, the demands can be attributed to the need for their organizations to maintain or enhance services in the face of increasing costs. . . . Today, their performance—and consequently, their salary increases and opportunities for advancement—are more likely to be tied to the yields on the portfolios they control. In the face of these incentives it is easy for portfolio managers to ignore a fundamental concept of finance: the greater the returns, the greater the risk.
>
> At the same time, the range of investment "products" offered by Wall Street has increased dramatically. Succumbing to aggressive sales tactics from brokers and dealers, many treasurers purchase securities that they don't understand and that are clearly unsuited to their institutions' investment objectives.[3]

One example of the negative downside to unsuitable investments is the Orange County, California, bankruptcy. The financial problems in Orange County resulted partly from investment in derivatives. *Derivatives* are securities whose value is derived from the value of something else. For example, we could establish a security whose value is the average value of the stock price of five large corporations. Derivatives can be designed to reduce risk by allowing an investor to have the average gain or loss from a large number of securities, without having the expense of investing in all of those securities.

However, derivative securities often allow investors to enter into an investment without paying the full cost of that investment. This concept is called leverage. It offers the potential for much higher returns if the investment performs the way that the investor would like it to. For example, if the prices of the five securities rise, leverage works to the investor's advantage. However, if the investment does not perform as hoped, leverage also amplifies losses. In such cases, investors could lose more than their original investment in the derivative. Often, by investing in a broad portfolio of investments, rather than concentrating in just one investment, risk can be lowered. However, derivatives can also be used for speculation, in which case the risk may be great.

There are many other options for investing idle cash. If the cash is not going to be needed for operating activities in the coming year, some of these investments may be appropriate for some organizations. However, most organizations would deem investments such as U.S. notes and bonds, corporate bonds, state and local government bonds, preferred stock, common stock, and derivatives to be unsuitable for short-term investments.

U.S. notes and bonds are federal government obligations that are similar to treasury bills. However, their maturity period is longer: U.S. notes have maturities of greater than 1 year and not longer than 10 years, and U.S. bonds have maturities greater than 10 years. Also, interest is not discounted, as it is with a t-bill. Instead, the investor pays the face or maturity price to acquire the note or bond. A small part of that amount is often refunded immediately upon issuance of the bond to adjust for the exact market interest rate at the time of issuance. Interest payments are made semiannually, and the face price is repaid at maturity. The obligation is fully backed by the federal government. However, the risk caused by fluctuations in interest rates becomes more severe the longer the time until

---

[3] Michael H. Granof, *Government and Not-for-Profit Accounting: Concepts and Practices.* New York, N.Y.: John Wiley & Sons, 1998, p. 337.

maturity. It would generally be inappropriate to invest cash that might be needed in the coming year to buy notes or bonds that could have substantial fluctuations in value as a result of interest rate changes.

Bonds issued by corporations, state governments, and local governments have the combined risk of interest rate fluctuations, plus the risk that bad news related to the issuer will cause substantial declines in the market value of the bond. Although some bonds may be suitable for long-term investment by some organizations, they are not a good place for investment of money that will be needed during the coming year. Further, governments and not-for-profit organizations would not generally invest in tax-exempt bonds. Such bonds tend to have lower yields (i.e., pay a lower interest rate) because interest earned on them is generally exempt from income taxes. Governments and not-for-profit organizations do not gain any benefit from the tax-exemption on the interest payments that they receive.

Stocks are even more risky. At least in the case of bonds, if the issuer is still financially stable at maturity, the principal amount of the investment will be repaid. With stock, there is risk that even if the company does well, the price of its stock may fall because of general stock market trends. If the company does not do well, the likelihood of financial loss is great.

In many cases governments are prohibited by state law from investing in equity securities. It is common for states to have statutes indicating allowable investments for governments within the state. To further protect public assets, some states even require that financial institutions provide collateral to secure deposits made by governmental units.

States may also have laws regarding appropriate investments by not-for-profit organizations. Prior to making investments, managers should determine whether there are rules or laws in their state governing suitable investments. Regardless of whether it is prohibited by law, the volatility in prices of stocks and bonds makes them unsuitable for short-term investment.

However, it is necessary to distinguish between short-term and long-term investments. Money that will be needed for operating activities should only be invested in bank accounts or money market investments listed in the previous section. However, money that is available for long-term investment may be invested more aggressively. For example, pension funds that will not be paid out for a number of years or a portion of a university's endowment funds should be invested in a diversified portfolio of stocks and bonds. Historically, stocks have provided superior returns over the long term.

Liquidity Management

The above discussion of the management of cash and marketable securities falls under the heading of liquidity management. Optimizing the management of cash and marketable securities requires expertise. Organizations will generally have a manager who is assigned the responsibility for liquidity management. This manager will forecast cash inflows and outflows and develop the organization's cash budget. It is important for the organization to be able to anticipate what its cash balances will be, so that it can determine whether additional funds will need to be raised, or if resources will be available that can be invested to earn a return.

If cash sits idle, the organization misses out on potential earnings. If cash is invested in resources that are too risky, it chances losing critical resources needed for the operation of the organization. Therefore consideration of the risks of various investments is essential. Liquidity managers focus on the management of interest costs (on borrowed money) or returns (on invested money), matching investment risks with returns (not taking on an investment of cash that has more risk than the expected return can justify), and making decisions regarding how to raise money when needed (short-term loans, increased fund-raising appeals, etc.).

Accounts Receivable

Although some organizations collect payment at the same time they provide goods or services, that is not always the case. Sometimes people owe money for goods and services provided to them now and pay at some time in the future. In that case, they are said to be buying the service on account. The amounts they owe are called receivables by the organization that has provided the goods or services. Because we want to keep track of or account for how much is owed to us, the amounts owed are often called *accounts receivable*. More specific terms are sometimes used. Governments tax their constituency so they have taxes receivable. Hospitals charge patients for services provided. Hospital receivables are often called patient accounts receivable. Not-for-profit organizations might also have grants receivable and pledges receivable.

Accounts receivable are collected as a result of a cycle of activities, as follows:

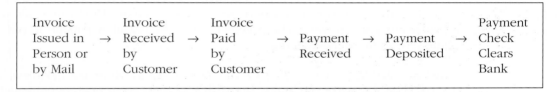

Given the potentially large size of receivables, managers must make an effort to carefully control them. One of the most important issues confronting the manager is how to collect receivables as quickly as possible. This is sometimes referred to as revenue cycle management. The sooner receivables are collected, the sooner the money can earn interest or be used to pay bills or expand services. We are also concerned that some receivables will become *bad debts*. Bad debts are receivables that are never collected. Efforts to collect receivables promptly reduce the likelihood of this happening. Therefore, there should be an attempt to reduce the time required for each step in the accounts receivable cycle shown in the preceding box.

To collect receivables as soon as possible, we must compile the information needed to issue an invoice or bill for goods or services provided. The faster we compile this information and issue the invoice, and the more accurate and complete the invoice, the faster payment can be expected.

An essential feature of accounts receivable management is the development of credit policies. Organizations must decide to whom services will be provided and whom will be charged for the services. In our Meals for the Homeless example, we assume that meals are provided to the homeless and the organization charges a foundation and the city government. In hospitals, care is often provided to patients but billed to managed care or other insurance companies. To collect payment in a timely manner, we must have a system that is set up to bill the right parties and provide them with the information they need in order to verify and pay the bill. For example, a health care insurer may require that we submit the patient's health insurance account number along with specific information about services provided to the patient. Medicare requires the patient's Medicare number and also specific diagnosis information. If we fail to provide that information, we may significantly delay receipt of payment.

Management of accounts receivable does not stop when we issue an accurate, complete invoice. We need to also monitor unpaid receivables. In some cases, we will need to contact those who owe money to find out why they have not paid the amount owed to us. An aging schedule, showing how long our receivables have been outstanding, is a helpful device. In some cases, it may even be necessary to hire a collection agency to try to collect delinquent accounts. When receivables are collected, specific procedures should safeguard the cash until its ultimate deposit in the bank. These issues are discussed next.

EARLY DATA COLLECTION   One aid in receivables management is early collection of data for the billing process. For example, HOS would probably discuss the method and plan for payment when the patient goes through the admission process. By finding out who is responsible for payment (e.g., the patient, an HMO, Medicare) as early as possible, the hospital increases the chances that it will gather the appropriate information and send the bill to the appropriate party. Some health insurers deny payment unless they are notified when treatment begins rather than after the fact. The organization must put systems in place to ensure that the chances of ultimate collection are maximized.

For many public service organizations, clients have limited resources. Although we might like to just give our service for free, that may not be possible. The organization has limited resources as well. By identifying potential payment problems early, reasonable compromises can sometimes be reached. For example, HOS can work with uninsured patients to develop reasonable payment schedules that allow patients to pay what they can afford over an extended period.

CREDIT POLICIES   Credit policies relate to deciding to whom the organization will provide service without receiving immediate cash payment. Many organizations will only provide services to some clients if they pay at the time the service is provided. This is often the case if we feel there is a high risk that we would not be able to collect payment from the person at a later time. One of the more difficult management problems to deal with is whether to exclude someone from an organization's services.

By excluding individuals or organizations from buying our goods or services on account, we take a chance of losing the opportunity to provide some services. The manager must weigh the risk of nonpayment against the potential loss of business. For example, Steve Netzer, the chief operating officer of HOS, feels a need to give credit terms that are as good as the competition. If HOS requires all outpatients to pay at the time service is provided while competing health care providers allow patients to receive services on account, it may lose profitable business.

If certain specific people are rich but are deadbeats with a reputation for not paying bills, there is not much controversy if the organization decides to charge cash on delivery of the services. However, if the organization's clients are poor and unlikely to be able to pay for service, should we give it to them for free or exclude them from service if they cannot pay currently? If we give service for free and cannot recover the cost of the service from some other source, we may threaten the organization's long-term survival.

Frequently public service organizations give away critical services for free to individuals who cannot pay. In some cases, health care organizations are required by law to provide care regardless of ability to pay. HOS will not turn away anyone who is likely to die without immediate care. Part of Netzer's management responsibilities is to find funding sources to pay for that care. However, HOS can refuse to provide elective cosmetic surgery, such as a face lift or nose job, to people who cannot pay.

A difficult problem involves determining where to draw the line. Emergency life-saving care is given. Cosmetic nose jobs are denied. But between these two extremes, what services are given without prepayment to those who are unlikely to make payments later? Some organizations will be more permissive than others for a variety of reasons. For example, one organization may have a better financial position than another and be able to better withstand the losses associated with providing services for free. For those that do limit services provided without payment, refusal to provide service should not be capricious, arbitrary, or discriminatory. Organizations should have explicit, reasoned policies for what services they will or will not provide to people who cannot pay. They should also have clear policies for how they determine ability to pay. And the policies should be applied even-handedly.

ONGOING DATA COLLECTION In many organizations, collection of the full amount due requires a careful ongoing data collection process. If we charge for specific services provided, there is the risk that some charges will be overlooked. The number of units of each type of service provided must be accumulated on an ongoing basis.

THE BILLING PROCESS The activities concentrated around issuing bills are critical. They must be done quickly but also correctly. Something as minor as a missing zip code in the billing address could lead to a payment delay of several months or more. When we have gathered all necessary information and reviewed the information for both completeness and accuracy, a bill should be promptly issued.

Modern technology should be considered in the process. The Internal Revenue Service now encourages that tax returns be filed electronically because it reduces the cost of processing taxes receivable and speeds the collection process. Many large health care payers (including Medicare and Medicaid) will pay health care providers much sooner if they submit their bills electronically rather than on paper. Such approaches should be explored and, if cost-effective, adopted.

Even speeding up collections by two or three days can have a significant impact. For any one bill, it does not seem to matter if there are a few delays. However, when all bills are considered, the impact of prompt billing is significant. For example, suppose that HOS issues $300 million in patient billings on account each year. Also assume that HOS owes money to a bank and pays an annual interest rate of 9 percent on that loan. Earlier receipt of cash means repaying part of the outstanding loan and reducing interest payments. If electronic processing of bills directly to payers means that each bill is collected, on average, just three days sooner than it otherwise would be, the interest savings for the hospital would be over $222,000 a year! ($300 million × 9% = $27 million of interest per year, divided by 365 days = $74,000 of interest per day, or $222,000 for three days.)

In addition to faster collection, electronic billing may prove to be less expensive to process than paper billing. Paperwork requires labor, and labor may be more expensive than computer systems. Electronic billing also allows for quicker communication of problems. If a bill is sent electronically and is rejected electronically, the manager knows that there is a problem right away. The sooner we know that a customer has a problem with an invoice, the greater the likelihood that the organization can still gather any data needed to correct the invoice, and the more likely it is that it will ultimately be paid.

Electronic invoicing is only one way managers can affect collections. Another way to improve the speed of collections is to issue bills more frequently. Rather than mailing out bills monthly, we can invoice weekly or daily. Another approach is to computerize collection of data for inclusion in bills. When managers turn their attention to specifically speeding up the billing process, it is not inconceivable that they might speed their average collections by an entire month. In an organization with $300 million of revenue, a one-month improvement in collections could save several million dollars per year.

AGING OF RECEIVABLES Once bills have been issued, the organization must monitor receivables and follow up on unpaid bills. A useful tool for this process is an accounts receivable *aging schedule,* which shows how long it has been between the current date and the date when uncollected bills were issued. For example, at the end of December, a summary aging schedule for the Town of Millbridge might appear as the example in Table 7-1.

TABLE 7-1 Receivables Aging Schedule

	Township of Millbridge Receivables Aging Schedule As of December 31, 2011				
Payer	1–30 Days	31–60 Days	61–90 Days	>90 Days	Total
By Total Dollars					
Taxes receivable	$ 8,052,342	$ 995,028	$ 702,556	$ 93,050	$ 9,842,976
State grants	3,250,000	475,000	56,000	22,000	3,803,000
Federal grants	861,232	223,637	27,333	2,222	1,114,424
Foundation grants	583,474	389,640	4,500	2,760	980,374
Total	$12,747,048	$2,083,305	$ 790,389	$120,032	$15,740,774
By Percent					
Taxes receivable	81.8%	10.1%	7.1%	1.0%	100.0%
State grants	85.5	12.5	1.5	.6	100.0
Federal grants	77.3	20.1	2.5	.2	100.0
Foundation grants	59.5	39.7	0.5	.3	100.0
Total	81.0%	13.2%	5.0%	.8%	100.0%

In Table 7-1, we notice that 81 percent of the town's receivables have been outstanding for less than one month. Less than 1 percent of its receivables are outstanding for more than 90 days. In the period shortly after invoices are issued, foundations are the slowest to pay, with only 60 percent collected in the first month. In the longer period, taxpayers lag with 7 percent in the 61–90 day period and 1 percent still outstanding after 90 days. Millbridge would want to compare its collection rates with other towns' to see if it is doing comparatively well or poorly.

The aging schedule is a valuable tool because problem areas can be quickly identified. For example, suppose that the state slowed payment of its grants. Dwight Ives, town manager of Millbridge, might immediately detect a decrease in cash receipts. The aging schedule, however, would help him identify exactly why that occurred. He could then contact the state to find out if the slowed payment was the result of some inaction on the part of the town. If the town had failed to file a required form, it could be done immediately. If it turns out that the state had decided to slow down its payments to all towns, then Ives will need to plan on how the town will make up for the delay in cash receipts. Unless it has a surplus of cash on hand, it will need to sell some investments to generate cash, speed up collections from others, slow payments it makes, or plan on a short-term bank loan.

Efforts to collect payment should begin as soon as the invoice is issued. If anything goes beyond the current column (i.e., 1–30 days), there should be a formal procedure, such as the issuance of a reminder statement. If an account exceeds 60 days, there should be procedures such as mailing another statement, often colored pink to get greater attention. The "over-90-day" category in an aging schedule is a particular concern, even though it may be a small part of the total. Amounts in that category probably reflect problems encountered in processing the bills or else an inability or unwillingness to pay. All organizations should have specific follow-up procedures for accounts that fall into this category. These procedures should include not only monthly statements, but also late charges and telephone calls to determine why payment has not been made. The longer a payment goes unpaid, the less likely it will ever be paid.

In some cases, it is necessary to use a collection agency if other efforts have failed and it is believed that the receivable is from someone or some organization that has the financial resources to pay. This is a costly approach, since collection agencies retain as much as half of all amounts that they are successful in collecting.

LOCK BOXES Some organizations have payments sent directly to a *lock box* rather than to the organization itself. Lock boxes are usually post office boxes that are emptied by the bank rather than the organization. The bank opens the envelopes with the payments and deposits them directly to the organization's account.

One advantage of this approach is that the bank will empty the box and deposit the money at least once a day. This gets the money into interest-bearing accounts faster than if it had to go through the organization. This is especially useful in cases in which organizations allow checks to sit around in the business office for days or weeks before they are deposited.

Second, use of a lock box tends to substantially decrease the risk that receipts will be lost or stolen. Not-for-profit organizations, particularly those with limited resources for office staff, are often at risk for theft of receipts. Lock boxes are a fairly simple way to safeguard some of the organization's most at-risk resources.

ELECTRONIC PAYMENT More and more organizations are now starting to both make payments and collect receivables via electronic payment. Most utilities now encourage their clients to allow the utility to directly draw payment for the bill on the due date from the client's bank account by electronic transfer into the utility's bank account. Medicare payments to health care providers are made by electronic transfer, and the federal government is attempting to move all of its payments to such an approach.

Clearly, if your organization can draw money directly from its customer's bank accounts, it can increase the speed of collections and reduce the amount of bad debts. The entire process of collections can be streamlined, often resulting in lower costs to run the office functions of the organization.

Inventory

Inventory represents the major supply items that an organization buys and uses to make its product or services. For example, Meals for the Homeless might purchase cans of food to use when inadequate donations of fresh food are received on a given day; HOS would purchase various pharmaceuticals to give to patients as needed; the Town of Millbridge would buy a mountain of salt to use on roads when it snows. Since many organizations spend substantial amounts to acquire inventory, careful management of that resource is essential.

Inventory management can save money for the organization. A general rule of thumb is that inventory levels should be kept as low as possible. The lower the level of inventory, the less you have paid out to suppliers, and the greater the amount of money kept in your own interest-bearing savings accounts or investments. At the same time, many organizations have uncertainties that require inventory both for current use and as a safety measure.

For example, Meals will keep canned goods in case fresh food donations are low, as noted previously. HOS will keep an extra supply of items that might be needed for emergency situations, even if they arise infrequently; in the case of a hospital, having inventory on hand can be, literally, a question of life or death. Millbridge never knows exactly when it will snow; if it runs out of salt, icy roads can lead to serious traffic accidents and injuries.

However, such critical reasons to maintain safety supplies can lead to lax management and excessive stockpiling of a wide variety of items. Management must develop systems to ensure availability of inventory when needed while keeping overall levels as low as possible.

When possible, storing of inventory should be centralized. If an organization creates separate locations for inventory, convenience rises but so do costs. The more separate storage sites, the greater the amount of each inventory item the organization is likely to have.

The ordering process should also be as centralized as possible. The more decentralized the ordering process, the more time employees spend ordering the same item. Ordering decentralization is also likely to lead to payment of a higher price per unit since the organization is less likely to take advantage of volume discounts.

PERIODIC VERSUS PERPETUAL INVENTORY   When organizations purchase inventory, they must have some way of tracking the amount of inventory that they have used and the amount still on hand. The simplest approach is called *periodic inventory*. In that approach, from time to time, usually once a year, the organization will count each inventory item to see how much is on hand. Presumably all amounts purchased that are not still on hand have been used to provide goods and services. A contrasting approach is called *perpetual inventory*. A perpetual inventory is one in which the organization keeps a record of each use of each type of item. A running balance is maintained so that the organization always knows how much of each item it has on hand.

With a periodic inventory system, it is hard to know when to reorder since you never know exactly how much you have on hand. Many organizations simply order more of an item when they appear to be running low. Since no one wants to run out of anything, there is a tendency to order sooner than actually necessary. With a perpetual inventory system, you always know how much you have on hand so it is easier to decide when it is necessary to order more of any given item.

However, perpetual inventory systems are often expensive since they can be very time-consuming. Employees must record each use of inventory. Historically, perpetual systems have been used primarily for high-cost, or controlled, items. Most states have laws requiring that hospitals use perpetual inventories for narcotics. Automated systems have reduced the cost of using perpetual systems. For example, supermarkets use scanners at checkout counters to keep perpetual inventory. This allows them better ability to restock each item as the amount on hand runs low. Computers and bar codes have become so pervasive that many public service organizations can gain the advantages of perpetual inventory without incurring substantial data costs.

Periodic systems are also flawed in a control sense. When we count inventory once a year, we know how much is no longer on hand. However, we do not know if it was used to provide services, was stolen or broken, or became obsolete and was thrown away. Perpetual systems keep track as each item is removed from inventory, so we tend to have lower losses from theft and more efficient use of inventory in general.

ECONOMIC ORDER QUANTITY   In addition to the cost of paying for inventory when, or shortly after, it is acquired, there are also a variety of other costs related to inventory. We must have physical space to store it, we may need to pay to insure it, and there are costs related to placing an order and having it shipped. A method called the *economic order quantity* (EOQ) considers all of these factors in calculating the inventory level at which additional inventory should be ordered.

The EOQ approach uses mathematics to consider the relative costs of ordering large amounts of inventory infrequently versus ordering small amounts more frequently. The method yields a result that indicates not only the stock level that should be on hand when additional inventory is ordered, but also how much inventory to order at a time.

The more inventory ordered at one time, the sooner we pay for inventory and the greater the costs for things such as inventory storage. These are called *carrying* or *holding costs* of inventory. Conversely, if we keep relatively little inventory on hand to keep carrying costs low, we will have to order inventory more often. That drives *ordering costs* up. EOQ balances these two factors to find the optimal amount to order. The EOQ approach is discussed further in Appendix 7-A at the end of this chapter.

JUST-IN-TIME INVENTORY   One aggressive approach to inventory management is called *just-in-time* (JIT) inventory. This method argues that carrying costs should be driven to an absolute minimum. According to Henke and Spoede,

> In the ideal, the just-in-time (JIT) operating philosophy calls for raw materials and partially processed goods to be delivered precisely at the times—and to the locations—they are needed . . . at exactly the time required to meet customer orders. JIT philosophy seeks to minimize those costs associated with handling and storing inventory that add no value to the product, and to thereby reduce the cost per unit of finished product.[4]

Many would argue that it is unrealistic to believe that many public service organizations will ever be able to count on JIT inventory. What if HOS is about to perform an operation and a critical supply item is not delivered just when it is needed? Given the life-and-death issues faced by some organizations, a pure JIT approach may not be feasible. However, it could represent a philosophy to be adopted to the extent possible and reasonable. Philosophically, the goals of JIT are to reduce warehousing, handling, obsolescence, and interest costs to a minimum.

The application of JIT really centers on how close one can come to the ideal. There invariably will be problems with implementing a JIT system. For any organization, work flow will not necessarily proceed in an orderly manner. There will be peaks and valleys in demand. Some days more people will come to the soup kitchens run by Meals for the Homeless than on other days. An attempt at perfect JIT inventory risks leaving some people unfed to avoid ending the day with some excess food still on hand. If the Town of Millbridge hopes to get its road salt just as the snow starts to fall, it may find that there are shortages and no salt available.

Therefore, public service organizations will probably always need to maintain at least some safety levels of key supply items. However, not all inventory items are critical. It is likely that a careful review of all inventory and supply purchases would indicate that a large percentage of items are not critically time essential.

Movement toward a JIT approach is not costless. The purchase price of inventory units may rise because the organization may lose its quantity discounts. The cost of rush orders may rise if there are more stockouts under the system. An effort should be made to determine the total costs related to inventory without a JIT system and the costs under such a system.

In trying to decide if JIT would be helpful to your organization, note that Henke and Spoede indicate that

> JIT works best in repetitive industries and is not appropriate in a fixed continuous process environment or in plants that produce relatively small quantities of fairly unique products. . . . Job-shop plants, even though they need help controlling inventory and quality, generally cannot benefit from JIT.[5]

---

[4] Emerson O. Henke and Charlene W. Spoede. *Cost Accounting: Managerial Use of Accounting Data*. Boston, Mass.: PWS-KENT Publishing, 1991, pp. 78–79.
[5] Ibid., p. 86.

A job-shop plant is one in which each unit produced is fairly unique. Typically, a job-shop type of organization must have greater protective inventory of every type because of uncertain demand. That protective inventory offsets the benefits of JIT. HOS is very much like a job shop. In contrast, Meals for the Homeless represents more of a repetitive industry. Thus, management must evaluate the nature of their operations and assess whether there is potential benefit from moving to JIT in their specific case.

How does JIT relate to EOQ? The EOQ approach evaluates the trade-off between ordering and carrying costs. JIT argues for reduction of inventory carrying costs. EOQ would indicate that such reduction would increase order costs. JIT contends that by working more closely with suppliers, ordering costs can be controlled. Essentially, then, JIT points out that whereas EOQ accepts the ordering and carrying costs as they are, managers can go further and work to reduce the cost of carrying and ordering inventory.

SHORT-TERM OBLIGATIONS

Working capital management calls on managers to control costs related to both short-term resources and short-term obligations. To this point, this chapter has focused on short-term resources. We now turn our attention to management of short-term obligations, or current liabilities. Careful management of such obligations can save many organizations a substantial amount of money.

Some examples of types of short-term obligations that need management attention are *accounts payable, payroll payable, notes payable,* and *taxes payable.* Accounts payable represent amounts that the organization owes to its suppliers. It is the flip side of accounts receivable. One single transaction will create an account receivable on the records of the organization selling goods or services and an account payable on the records of the organization buying those goods or services. A payroll payable is an amount owed to employees. Notes payable represent an obligation to repay money that has been borrowed. Taxes payable represent not only income, sales, or real estate taxes, which many public service organizations are exempt from, but also payroll taxes that many tax-exempt organizations must pay.

To control the use of organizational resources, managers often delay payment of short-term obligations. This keeps resources in the organization available to earn interest or provide services. Managers also want to avoid unnecessary short-term borrowing, which would cause the organization to have to make interest payments that would not otherwise be necessary.

Accounts Payable

When an organization purchases items without making an immediate cash payment for the full amount due, an account payable arises. Accounts payable are often called *trade credit.* In most cases, there is no interest charge for trade credit, assuming that payment is made when due. For example, Meals for the Homeless might order and receive a shipment of canned goods. Shortly afterward, it receives an invoice from the supplier. The invoice will generally have a due date.

Some suppliers charge interest for payments received after the due date. Others do not. A common practice in many industries is to offer a discount for prompt payment. On an invoice, under a heading called *terms,* there may be an indication such as 2/10 N/30. This would be read as "two 10, net 30." A discount of two 10, net 30 indicates that if payment is received within 10 days of the invoice date, the payer can take a 2 percent discount off the amount of the bill. If payment is not made within 10 days, then the bill is due 30 days from the invoice date, in full.

Although 2 percent is a very common discount for prompt payment, sometimes a 3 percent discount is offered (3/10 N/30), and sometimes only a 1 percent discount is offered (1/10, N/30). Some companies state their terms in relation to the end of the month. Terms of 2/10 EOM (two 10, end of month) would mean that the buyer can take a 2 percent discount for payments received by the company no later than 10 days after the end of the month in which the invoice is issued.

One confusing element of discounts is that the amount to be paid is called "net" if you are paying the full amount. Usually net refers to a number after a subtraction has been made. The reason for this is that many times organizations negotiate a discount from the full price at the time an order is placed. For example, suppose that the regular wholesale price for rice is $2.50 per 50-pound sack. However, Meals successfully negotiated a 20 percent discount off the official, or "list," price. Perhaps this is a volume discount. Alternatively, it may be a discount that the rice company offers to meet a competitor's price. From the seller's viewpoint, $2.50 is the gross price, $2.00 is the net price, and $1.96 is the net price after a discount for prompt payment (the $2.00 negotiated price less the 2 percent discount = $1.96). Thus, 2/10 N/30 means that the buyer can pay $1.96 per sack if the payment is made within 10 days. Otherwise, the net price of $2.00 per sack is due in 30 days.

An important trade credit issue involves whether an organization should take discounts if offered. When a credit discount is offered, it usually pays to take the discount. Although a 2 percent discount might seem small, the organization earns that discount by paying perhaps 20 days sooner than it would otherwise pay the amount due. So the true interest rate is not 2 percent per year but rather 2 percent per 20 days. This generally works out to be a high annual rate. Appendix 7-B at the end of this chapter provides information on how to calculate the impact of credit discounts.

Payroll Payable

Payroll obligations are generally paid soon after they are incurred. Each payroll period, we must pay our employees. At first glance, there does not seem to be much opportunity for management control in this area. However, that perception is incorrect. Two main issues must be considered: the policy regarding the length of the payroll period and the delay between the end of the period and payment of payroll obligations.

Each organization must decide on the length of the payroll period. Employees could be paid daily, weekly, biweekly, monthly, or based on some other time period. Suppose that the Town of Millbridge has historically followed a policy of paying their employees weekly. However, its managers have heard that other towns in the area have transitioned to a monthly payroll period. Why might the other towns have done this?

For one thing, they will only have to write about one-quarter as many checks. This will save a substantial amount of time and effort in the payroll department. More importantly, it pushes off payment of employee earnings. The first week's earnings each month will now be paid three weeks later than otherwise. The second week's earnings will be paid two weeks later, and the third week's earnings will be paid one week later. For an entire year, the interest earned as a result of the deferred payments can be substantial.

A second issue related to the management of payroll relates to the length of the delay from the end of the payroll period until payment. For example, if the payroll period ends each Friday, should payroll be paid that day, or on Monday, or perhaps as late as the next Thursday? To some extent, a delay may be needed to determine the earnings of employees. The longer the delay in payment, the longer the organization retains the money in its interest-bearing account.

With respect to both the frequency of payment and the delay before payment, the potential for savings must be balanced against the relationship the organization has with its staff. Will the change cause financial hardships for the employees? Will the employees feel that they are being treated unfairly? If so, they will often find ways to get back at the organization. Poor morale can turn out to be more costly than the benefits that the organization may have accrued in the form of extra interest.

Short-Term Debt

Public service organizations often have short-term needs for cash. Millbridge may have a temporary cash shortage prior to the due date of real estate taxes. Meals may need cash while it waits to receive money the city owes it for meals it has already provided. The interest on a loan is equal to the amount of the loan multiplied by the annual interest rate multiplied by the fraction of the year that the loan is outstanding, as shown in Equation 7.1:

$$\text{Interest} = \text{Loan Amount} \times \text{Interest Rate per Year} \times \text{Fraction of Year} \qquad \textbf{(7.1)}$$

Typically, organizations obtain short-term debt by borrowing money from banks using *unsecured notes*. In some cases, money can be borrowed from financing and factoring companies, using inventory or accounts receivable as *collateral*. In some cases, an alternative way to obtain short-term debt is through the use of commercial paper.

When a loan is made, the lender sometimes requires some security to guarantee repayment. This is done by providing specific resources that the lender can take if the loan is not repaid. The specific resources offered are called collateral. If the lender does not require any collateral for the loan, it is said to be unsecured. If the borrower fails to repay an unsecured loan, the lender joins with all other creditors in making a general claim on the remaining resources of the organization. This is riskier than having collateral; unsecured loans, therefore, often have higher interest rates to offset the lender's higher risk.

Unsecured loans are generally referred to as notes because a specific document, called a note, gives the details of the loan arrangement, including the agreed-upon interest rate and information about when interest and principal payments will be made. The outstanding balance owed on the note is called the note payable.

For organizations that have limited financial resources, banks may be unwilling to make loans. Another approach for obtaining short-term financing is to borrow money from an organization that specializes in financing and factoring receivables. A factoring arrangement is one in which we sell our receivables. The buyer is called a factor. The right to collect those receivables then belongs to the factor. There is a risk that some of the receivables will never be collected. Therefore, the factor pays less than face value. In most cases, if receivables are factored, the organization receives less than it would have received, but it gets the cash sooner.

Alternatively, a financing arrangement would be one in which money is borrowed with the receivables being used as collateral in case we cannot repay the loan. Often, accounts receivable are used as collateral to back up credit lines. This lowers the cost to the organization, because the interest rate charged is less if there is collateral. Further, since the amount of the credit line available may be a percentage of accounts receivable, it allows the organization to have a sense of the amount that is available for them to borrow at any point in time.

Taxes Payable

Taxes payable seem to be an odd type of obligation for tax-exempt organizations. Many public service organizations qualify for federal tax-exempt status. However, payroll taxes affect many exempt organizations. Federal Insurance Contributions Act (FICA) is a tax that is charged to both employees and the employer to provide Social Security benefits. The employer withholds the employees' portion from their wages along with income taxes and other employee tax obligations. Until these taxes are forwarded to the government, they represent a short-term obligation. As with other short-term obligations, these should not be paid before they are due. However, since there are often penalties in addition to interest for late payment, managers must have a system in place to ensure that taxes are paid on time.

In addition to Social Security taxes, many organizations are liable for a variety of state taxes, such as those related to unemployment funds or disability insurance.

Summary

One element of the implementation of plans is careful control of short-term resources and obligations. This chapter considers techniques and approaches designed to maximize the benefit of short-term resources and minimize the cost of short-term obligations.

The process of controlling short-term resources and obligations is referred to as working capital management. In performing working capital management, the manager must ensure that adequate cash is on hand to meet the organization's needs and also to minimize the cost of having that cash. To do this, the manager must carefully monitor and control cash inflows and outflows. Cash not immediately needed should be invested, earning a return for the organization. The organization should use a cash budget and should employ lock boxes and concentration banking when appropriate.

Excess cash should be invested. A variety of marketable securities may be appropriate for an organization. Such securities can provide a higher yield for the organization while still providing reasonable liquidity and safety of principal.

Efforts must be made to collect accounts receivable as soon as possible. This reduces the rate of bad debts and also allows the collected receivables to start earning interest sooner. Often problems with receivables management stem from inadequate data systems. Data are required to allow invoices to be issued promptly, and then more data are required to track outstanding receivables balances.

Excess supplies (inventory) should not be kept by the organization. The money spent now to pay for inventory that is not needed until later could be better used by the organization for some other purpose. At a minimum, the money could be invested in the organization's savings account, earning interest. The economic order quantity and just-in-time techniques can provide managers with assistance in minimizing the cost of inventory.

Short-term obligations must also be managed carefully. The organization desires to have sufficient cash to pay its obligations when they are due. However, if the organization pays its bills before they are due, it will lose the interest it could have earned if it had left the cash in its savings account for a little longer rather than paying the obligation. Managers should take advantage of opportunities to delay payments, if the delay does not have any negative implications for the organization.

Preview

To achieve the best possible results, an organization's plan needs to be carried out as closely as possible. To ensure that this happens, departments and people must be held accountable for actions and results. Organizations develop systems to enable them to implement their plans successfully. Such systems provide the foundation for management control. They are the topic of Chapter 8.

Management control is based on the assignment of responsibility for the achievement of plans and is one of the important elements of financial management. For management control to work, the organization must not only assign responsibility; it must actually provide motivation for its employees to strive to accomplish the organization's goals.

We must also know how we intend to measure results. Various approaches to performance measurement are discussed in Chapter 8. Following that, the chapter focuses on techniques for variance analysis. If the actual performance differs from expectations, the difference is called a variance. Developing an understanding of why variances have occurred can help the organization avoid undesirable variances in the future.

Chapter 8 concludes with discussions of ethics and the safeguarding of resources. To achieve planned results, it is vital for personnel to be as ethical and error-free as possible. People are fallible. Being aware of this, organizations must try to develop checks and balances to ensure that the risk of losses, as a result of either intent or inefficiency, are minimized.

Key Terms from This Chapter

accounts payable. Amounts owed to suppliers.

accounts receivable. Money owed to the organization or individual in exchange for goods and services provided.

accrual accounting. Accounting system that matches revenues and related expenses in the same fiscal year by recording revenues in the year in which they become earned (whether received or not) and the expenses related to generating those revenues in the same year.

aging schedule. Management report that shows how long a receivable has been outstanding since a bill was issued.

bad debts. Operating expense related to services provided to customers who ultimately do not pay the organization, although they were expected to pay. Amounts that are included in revenues, but never paid, are charged to bad debts.

carrying costs of inventory. Capital costs and out-of-pocket costs related to holding inventory. Capital cost represents the lost interest because money is tied up in inventory. Out-of-pocket costs include such expenses as insurance on the value of inventory, annual inspections, and obsolescence of inventory.

cash budget. Plan for the cash receipts and cash disbursements of the organization.

certificate of deposit (CD). Bank deposit with a fixed maturity term.

collateral. Specific asset pledged to a lender as security for a loan.

commercial paper. Form of short-term borrowing in which the borrower issues a financial security that can be traded by the lender to someone else.

concentration bank. Bank where an organization maintains a significant presence.

current assets. Resources the organization has that either are cash or can be converted to cash within one year or that will be used up within one year; often referred to as short-term or near-term assets.

current liabilities. Those obligations that are expected to be paid within one year.

debt. Liability; an amount owed by one person or organization to another.

derivatives. Securities whose value is derived from the value of something else.

economic order quantity (EOQ). Approach to determine the balance between *ordering costs* and *carrying costs*.

equity. Ownership.

float. The interim period from when a check is written until the check is cashed and clears the bank.

holding costs. See *carrying costs of inventory*.

just-in-time (JIT) inventory. An approach to inventory management that calls for the arrival of inventory just as it is needed, resulting in zero inventory levels.

line of credit. Prearranged loan to be made when and if needed by the organization in an amount up to an agreed upon limit.

lock box. Post-office box that is emptied directly by the bank. The bank removes the receipts and credits them directly to the organization's account.

marketable securities. Investments in liquid debt or equity instruments that the organization intends to sell within one year.

money market. The market for short-term marketable securities or the market for short-term debt instruments.

negotiable certificate of deposit.   Certificate of deposit that can be transferred from one party to another.

net working capital.   Current assets less current liabilities.

notes payable.   Written document representing a loan.

ordering costs.   Costs associated with placing an order for inventory such as clerk time for preparation of a purchase order.

payroll payable.   Amounts owed to employees; also called wages payable.

periodic inventory.   Inventory method under which the organization records only purchases and uses a count of inventory to determine how much has been sold and how much is left on hand.

perpetual inventory.   Inventory method under which the organization keeps a record of each inventory acquisition and sale.

repo.   See *repurchase agreements.*

repurchase agreements.   Short-term investment collateralized by securities. Sometimes called a repo.

sweep.   Arrangements to transfer money into and out of bank accounts automatically.

t-bill.   See *treasury bill.*

taxes payable.   Taxes owed to a local, state, or federal government.

terms.   Refers to payment terms—i.e., when an account payable is due, and what discount is available for early payment.

trade credit.   Accounts payable. These are generally interest free for a period of time.

treasury bill.   A debt security issued by the U.S. government with a maturity of three months to one year.

unsecured notes.   Loans that do not have any collateral.

working capital.   Organization's current assets and current liabilities.

working capital management.   Management of the current assets and current liabilities of the organization.

zero-balance accounts.   Account at a concentration bank that uses a daily sweep to maintain a zero dollar balance; a system in which separate accounts are maintained at a bank for each major source of cash receipt and for major types of payments—at the close of each day, the bank automatically transfers all balances, positive or negative, into one master concentration account and other accounts are kept at a zero balance.

Questions for Discussion

7-1. Define working capital, net working capital, and working capital management.
7-2. Working capital has been compared with "cash register money." Explain.
7-3. What is the role of the manager in working capital management?
7-4. Why does an organization keep cash?
7-5. Should cash on hand and in bank accounts be maximized or minimized?
7-6. Can a profitable organization run out of money?
7-7. For what time periods should cash budgeting be done?
7-8. What are marketable securities? What are the two main types of marketable security?
7-9. What is meant by a "risk/return" trade-off?
7-10. Why is the development of credit policies critical to the organization?
7-11. What are the potential benefits of electronic invoicing?
7-12. What is the purpose of an accounts receivable aging schedule? How should it be used?

7-13. What is a lock box system?
7-14. What are the advantages of careful inventory management?
7-15. What is the difference between periodic and perpetual inventory?
7-16. Can just-in-time work in public service organizations? Why or why not?
7-17. What is the general focus of management of short-term obligations?
7-18. What does "2/10 N/30" mean? Under what conditions should an organization take advantage of "2/10?"
7-19. What are the various types of short-term debt that are available?
7-20. Accounts receivable represent[6]
   a. amounts owed by the organization to outsiders.
   b. amounts owed to the organization by outsiders.
   c. an operating expense.
   d. a possible line item on an operating budget.

---

[6] Questions 7-20 through 7-22 were written by Dwight Denison.

7-21. Short-term debt refers to
  a. money that the organization has just borrowed.
  b. money that must be repaid at some time in the next 12 months.
  c. money that has to be repaid at some time after the next 12 months.
  d. a form of debt that *only* requires the repayment of interest during the coming year.

7-22. An accounts receivable aging schedule shows the _____ and _____ of an organization's accounts receivable that have been outstanding for less than 30 days, 31–60 days, 61–90 days, and so on.

7-23. Working capital management focuses on making sure that an organization has sufficient resources to operate:
  a. in accordance with its mission
  b. over the next year
  c. efficiently
  d. over the expected life of the organization

7-24. Bills that have been sent out by an organization but not yet collected are referred to as _____.

7-25. Amounts that an organization owes to its suppliers, but has not yet paid, are referred to as:
  a. accounts receivable
  b. bad debts
  c. accounts payable
  d. accrued expenses

7-26. An inventory management system that relies primarily on physical counts of inventory is said to be using the _____.
  a. perpetual method
  b. periodic method
  c. warehouse-control method

7-27. Name two tools (techniques) that can be used by an organization to manage its accounts receivable.

7-28. Accounts payable are amounts owed by an organization that have not yet been paid. Name two specific types of accounts payable.

Problems

7-29. Hospitals often have many different customers, not all of whom make their payments on a timely basis. Millbridge Hospital segments its customers into four groups: Medicare, Medicaid, insurance, and self pay. The self pay customers owe Millbridge Hospital $2 million. Insurers owe twice that amount. Medicare and Medicaid owe Millbridge $5 million and $3 million respectively. Half of the Medicare receivable is current, 20 percent was billed more than 30 days but less than 61 days ago, and the balance was billed more than 60 days ago, but less than 91 days. Medicaid's obligation is 30 percent current, 30 percent more than 30 days but less than 61 days, 30 percent more than 60 but less than 91 days, and 10 percent more than 90 days. The insurance receivable is half current and half 31 to 60 days. The self-pay receivables are 25 percent current, 25 percent in the 31 to 60 day category, 25 percent 61 to 90 days, and 25 percent over 90 days. Prepare an accounts receivable aging schedule by total dollars and by percent.

7-30. Meals for the Homeless buys food in bulk. In one recent purchase it bought 3,600 cans of vegetables for twenty cents per can. Payment terms are 1/10 N/30. Meals can earn 7 percent on its idle cash. Should it take the discount, or pay when due? Show calculations. (Appendix 7-B is required to solve this problem.)

7-31. Billings Village is considering shifting its payroll period from twice a month to monthly. Total payroll for the year is $80 million. Billings can earn 6 percent on its invested money. How much would the village save from such a change? Should it shift its payroll period to monthly?

7-32. Meals for the Homeless borrows $28,000 on an unsecured note at 7 percent interest for three months. How much does it pay at the end of the three months?

7-33. Meals for the Homeless buys 30,000 large cans of green beans each year. The cost of each can of beans is $4. The cost to place an order for beans, including the time of the employee placing the order, shipping, and so forth, comes to $20 per order. The out-of-pocket carrying costs (for storage, etc.) are $.30 per can per year. In addition, Meals calculates its interest cost at 5 percent. How many cans should be ordered at a time? How many orders should there be each year? What are the total ordering costs and carrying costs at the EOQ? Contrast the total of the ordering costs and carrying costs at the EOQ to the total of ordering and carrying costs if the cans were all ordered at the beginning of the year. (Appendix 7-A is required to solve this problem.)

CASE STUDY
The Case of the Missing Check

The Millbridge Recreation Department has come under intense scrutiny. First there were concerns because revenues for the year fell short of predictions. Then town residents started complaining to the mayor that the Town had cashed their checks for use of the town pool several months after they were written, and in some cases checks were never cashed.

One irate resident, George Loudly, had complained about a payment he contended that he made for the town pool. The Recreation Department manager, Tenn Uswim, insisted that payment had never been received, and had suggested that perhaps the check was lost in the mail. Loudly countered that he dropped the check off in person. The disagreement had reached an impasse, and the resident had filed formal notice with the Town that he intended to take the floor at the public forum session during the July Town meeting. In response the mayor requested that the recreation manager attend the meeting.

Loudly provided his side of the situation at the July meeting. Then several friends that he brought to the meeting spoke, indicating that their checks were cashed but not until several months after they sent them to the Town. The recreation manager was given an opportunity to respond. Uswim indicated that his policy was to gather checks and have someone run them over to the bank for deposit from time to time. He argued that the money wasn't needed until the pool opened several months after payments were collected, so he didn't see a need to rush checks to the bank. After all, once deposited, he just kept the money in a non-interest-bearing account.

The residents countered that not only was the Town losing the opportunity to earn a return by investing the pool money, but worse, it stood to lose money if payments were misplaced. The recreation manager argued that payment checks could not possibly be lost, because he kept them all safely on top of his desk, usually under a paperweight. He contended that those who claimed their checks weren't cashed obviously never made their payments.

That remark was perhaps not well considered. Loudly felt that the recreation manager was accusing him of lying about having paid his pool fee. Uswim's contention all along was that if Loudly really had paid his fee, he should produce a cancelled check as proof. Loudly contended that he paid in person and the check was just not cashed because of government incompetence. Immediately after Uswim's remark, Loudly insisted on being allowed to immediately search the recreation department office for his check.

The mayor didn't want to give in, but he had known Loudly a long time and respected his honesty. Uswim didn't object, so the meeting moved downstairs to the Rec Office. The town sheriff was asked to conduct a thorough search. Within 10 minutes he had found five checks on the floor under desks and behind file cabinets. The dates on the checks ranged from one week to two years old. One of the checks was George Loudly's payment.

At this point several residents shouted out that they had paid in cash, and how did they know if their cash was deposited or was also lost. The mayor was at a loss for words. He quickly agreed to hire an outside consultant to evaluate the Town's cash management practices. You have just accepted that engagement.

Assignment: Why should the Town hold on to cash? In what form should it hold the cash? What practices and procedures would you suggest that the Town consider to improve their management of short-term resources in general, and cash in particular?

Suggested Readings

Brigham, Eugene F., and Joel F. Houston. *Fundamentals of Financial Management*, 11th ed. Belmont, Ca.: Thomson/South-Western, 2006.

Denison, Dwight V. "Cash Management for State and Local Governments" in Jack Rabin and Bart Hildreth (eds.), *Encyclopedia of Public Administration and Policy*. New York, N.Y.: Marcel Dekker, 2003.

Denison, Dwight V. "How Conservative Are Municipal Investment Practices in Large Cities?" *Municipal Finance Journal*, Vol. 23 (#1 Spring) 2002, pp. 35–51.

Denison, Dwight V., and Colin Chellman. "Double Bottom Line Investment: Responsible Investing in Not-for-Profit Organizations." *Journal for Nonprofit Management*, Vol. 5 (#1 Summer) 2002, pp. 46–65.

Emery, Douglas R., John D. Finnerty, and John D. Stowe. *Corporate Financial Management*, 3rd ed. Upper Saddle River, N.J.: Prentice Hall, 2007.

Finkler, Steven A. *Finance & Accounting for Nonfinancial Managers*, 3rd ed. New York, N.Y.: Aspen Publishers, 2003.

Horngren, Charles T., Gary L. Sundem, William O. Stratton, Jeff Schatzberg, and Dave Burgstahler. *Introduction to Management Accounting*, 4th ed. Upper Saddle River, N.J.: Prentice Hall, 2008.

Keown, Arthur J., John W. Martin, John W. Petty, and David F. Scott. *Foundations of Finance*, 6th ed. Upper Saddle River, N.J.: Prentice Hall, 2008.

Van Horne, James C. *Fundamentals of Financial Management*, 12th ed. Upper Saddle River, N.J.: Prentice Hall, 2005.

Economic Order Quantity

As noted in the chapter, in addition to having to pay for inventory when, or shortly after, it is acquired, there are other costs related to inventory. We must have physical space to store it, we may need to pay to insure it, and there are costs related to placing an order and having it shipped. A method called the *economic order quantity* (EOQ) considers all of these factors in calculating the inventory level at which additional inventory should be ordered.

The more inventory ordered at one time, the sooner we pay for inventory and the greater the costs for things such as inventory storage. These are called *carrying* or *holding costs*. However, if we keep relatively little inventory on hand, to keep carrying costs low, we will have to order inventory more often. That drives *ordering costs* up. EOQ balances these two factors to find the optimal amount to order.

There are two categories of carrying costs: capital cost and out-of-pocket costs. The capital cost is the cost related to having paid for inventory, as opposed to using those resources for alternative uses. At a minimum, this is the forgone interest that could have been earned on the money paid for inventory. Out-of-pocket costs are other costs related to holding inventory, including rent on space where inventory is kept, insurance and taxes on the value of inventory, the cost of annual inventory counts, the losses due to obsolescence and date-related expirations, and the costs of damage, loss, and theft.

Ordering costs include the cost of having an employee spend time placing orders, the shipping and handling charges for the orders, and the cost of correcting errors when orders are placed. The more orders, the more errors.

There is an offsetting dynamic in inventory management. The more orders per year, the less inventory that needs to be on hand at any given time, and therefore the lower the carrying cost. However, the more orders per year, the greater the amount the organization spends on placing orders, shipping and handling costs, and error correction. The total costs of inventory are the sum of the amount paid for inventory, plus the carrying costs, plus the ordering costs:

Total Inventory Cost = Purchase Cost + Carrying Cost + Ordering Cost

The goal of inventory management is to minimize this total without reducing the quality of services the organization provides.

We will use TC to stand for the total inventory cost, P to stand for the purchase cost per unit, CC for the total carrying cost, and OC for the total ordering cost. N will stand for the total number of units of inventory ordered for the year. Therefore,

$$TC = (P \times N) + CC + OC \qquad \textbf{(7.A.1)}$$

We will let C stand for the annual cost to carry one unit of inventory. The annual total carrying cost, CC, is then equal to the carrying cost per unit, C, multiplied by the average number of units on hand. Assume that Q is the number of units of inventory ordered each time an order is placed. On average at any given time we will have $Q \div 2$ units on hand. If we start with Q units and use them until there are 0 units left, on average we will have half of Q units on hand. Carrying costs are determined using the average number of units of inventory on hand. The carrying costs will therefore be as follows:

$$CC = C \times \frac{Q}{2} = \frac{CQ}{2} \qquad \textbf{(7.A.2)}$$

That is, the carrying costs per year (CC) will be equal to the carrying costs of one unit (C), multiplied by the average number of units on hand at any given time, $(Q/2)$.[7]

A formula can also be developed for ordering costs. We will let O stand for the cost of making one order. The total ordering cost, OC, is the cost of

---

[7] This becomes somewhat more complex if a safety stock is kept on hand at all times. In such a case the CC is equal to C multiplied by the sum of $Q \div 2$ plus the safety stock. However, this is not needed for the EOQ calculation. Safety stocks will not affect the economic order quantity, since they are projected to be constantly on hand regardless of the frequency or size of orders.

making an order, O, times the number of orders per year. Recall that the total number of units needed for the year is N and Q is the number of units in each order. Then N/Q is the number of orders placed per year. The ordering costs are as follows:

$$OC = O \times \frac{N}{Q} = \frac{ON}{Q} \qquad \textbf{(7.A.3)}$$

That is, the total cost of placing all orders for the year (OC) is the cost of making one order (O) multiplied by the number of orders per year (N/Q). For instance, suppose that Meals for the Homeless buys 2,000 sacks of rice each year (N = 2,000). If it orders 200 sacks at a time (Q = 200), it would have to make 10 orders per year (N/Q = 2,000/200 = 10).

We now can calculate the purchase cost of the inventory, the carrying costs, and the ordering cost. Suppose that Meals pays $2 per sack for rice. Each time it places an order, it takes a paid clerk about $8.075 worth of time to process the order. The delivery cost is $1 per order. This $9.075 is the only ordering cost. Meals could earn 8 percent interest on their money. Therefore, the capital part of the carrying cost is $.16 per sack per year (8% × $2 price = $.16). Other carrying costs are determined to be $2.84 per sack per year. Therefore the total carrying costs are $3 per sack per year. What is the total cost of inventory, assuming that there are 10 orders per year?

$$TC = (P \times N) + CC + OC \qquad \textbf{(7.A.1)}$$

The first part of the equation to be calculated is the purchase cost of the inventory:

$$P \times N = \$2 \times 2,000 = \$4,000$$

Next, we need to find the carrying cost:

$$CC = C \times \frac{Q}{2} = \frac{CQ}{2} \qquad \textbf{(7.A.2)}$$

$$CC = \frac{\$3 \times 200}{2} = \$300$$

Finally, we need the ordering cost:

$$OC = O \times \frac{N}{Q} = \frac{ON}{Q} \qquad \textbf{(7.A.3)}$$

$$OC = \frac{\$9.075 \times 2,000}{200} = \$90.75$$

So the total costs are as follows:

$$TC = (P \times N) + CC + OC$$
$$TC = \$4,000 + \$300 + \$90.75 = \$4,390.75 \qquad \textbf{(7.A.1)}$$

However, it was arbitrarily decided that there would be 10 orders of 200 sacks each. The EOQ model is designed to determine the optimal number to order at one time. The formula to determine the optimal number to order at one time is as follows:

$$Q^* = \sqrt{\frac{2\,ON}{C}} \qquad \textbf{(7.A.4)}$$

where Q^* is the optimal amount to order each time.

$$Q^* = \sqrt{\frac{2 \times \$9.075 \times 2,000}{\$3}}$$
$$= 110$$

This result differs from the 200 sacks per order that we used earlier. If we use this result, how will it affect total costs? The purchase cost will still be $4,000. However, the carrying costs and ordering costs will change:

$$CC = C \times \frac{Q}{2} = \frac{CQ}{2} \qquad \textbf{(7.A.2)}$$

$$CC = \frac{\$3 \times 110}{2} = \$165$$

Finally, we need the ordering cost:

$$OC = O \times \frac{N}{Q} = \frac{ON}{Q} \qquad \textbf{(7.A.3)}$$

$$OC = \frac{\$9.075 \times 2,000}{110} = \$165$$

So, the total costs are as follows:

$$TC = (P \times N) + CC + OC \qquad \textbf{(7.A.1)}$$
$$TC = \$4,000 + \$165 + \$165 = \$4,330$$

The new total cost of $4,330 represents a cost decrease of $60.75. Relative to the total cost, this may not seem to be a great savings. However, if you put aside the purchase cost of the inventory, the carrying and ordering costs have fallen from $390.75 to $330. This is more than a 15 percent savings. Across all inventory items for an organization, this could amount to a substantial dollar amount of savings.

It is not coincidental that the ordering cost equals the carrying cost. The total cost is minimized at the point where these two costs are exactly the same!

It is important that EOQ calculations only include relevant costs. Carrying and ordering costs that are relevant are those that vary as a result of our EOQ decision. That is, if ordering more or less frequently will affect a cost, it is relevant and should be included in the calculation. For example, ordering less frequently will likely increase capital costs related to interest. It would also likely affect shipping and handling, so these are relevant costs that belong in the calculation. In contrast, the cost of the purchasing department manager will probably not change with the number of orders. Therefore, none of that manager's salary should be included in the ordering costs.

The basic EOQ model, as presented here, involves making a number of assumptions that are often not true. For example, it involves assuming that any number of units can be purchased. In some cases, an item might only be sold in certain quantities, such as hundreds or dozens. Another assumption is that the price per unit does not change if we order differing numbers of units with each order. It is possible that we might get a quantity discount for large orders. Such a discount could offset some of the higher carrying cost related to large orders.

Another assumption is that we will use up our last unit of an item just when the next shipment arrives. A delay in processing, however, could cause inventory to arrive late, and we might run out of certain items. To avoid negative consequences of such stockouts, we might want to keep a safety stock on hand. How large should that safety stock be? That will depend on how long it takes to get more inventory if we start to run out. It also depends on how serious the consequences of running out are. Is it life or death, or merely an inconvenience?

One of the greatest difficulties in employing EOQ is determining the carrying and ordering costs. In most cases, however, at least the major components of such costs—for example, the amount of labor needed to place an order—can be calculated. The purpose of this discussion of EOQ is to familiarize the reader with the basic concept of inventory management. Many more sophisticated issues, such as those noted here, are addressed in more advanced books on managerial accounting, and on operations management. Some of these are included in the list of readings at the end of the chapter.

Inventory models are a part of any efficient management operation that invests dollars in inventory. Public, health, and not-for-profit organizations have often considered their inventories to be of nominal value. However, the costs of ordering and carrying inventory are sometimes surprisingly high, and use of a tool such as EOQ should at least be examined for potential savings.

Key Terms from This Appendix

carrying costs of inventory. Capital costs and out-of pocket costs related to holding inventory. Capital cost represents the lost interest because money is tied up in inventory. Out-of-pocket costs include such expenses as insurance on the value of inventory, annual inspections, and obsolescence of inventory.

economic order quantity (EOQ). Approach to determine the balance between ordering costs

and carrying costs; optimal number of units of inventory to be ordered each time an order is placed.

holding costs. See *carrying costs of inventory.*

ordering costs. Includes those costs associated with an order of inventory such as clerk time for preparation of a purchase order.

stockout costs. Costs incurred when an inventory item is not available but is needed.

APPENDIX 7-B

Credit Terms

An important trade credit issue involves whether an organization should take discounts if offered. When a credit discount is offered, it usually pays to take the discount. A formula can be used to determine the annual interest rate implicit in trade credit discounts:

$$\frac{\text{Implicit}}{\text{interest rate}} = \frac{\text{Discount}}{\text{Discounted price}} \qquad \textbf{(7.B.1)}$$
$$\times \frac{365 \text{ days}}{\text{days sooner}} \times 100\%$$

For example, suppose that HOS purchased $5,000 of pharmaceuticals with payment terms of 2/10 N/30. A 2 percent discount on a $5,000 purchase would be $100. This means that if the discount is taken, only $4,900 would have to be paid. By taking the discount, the hospital must make payment by the 10th day rather than the 30th day. This means that payment is made 20 days sooner than would otherwise be the case:

$$\frac{\text{Implicit}}{\text{interest rate}} = \frac{\$100}{\$4,900} \times \frac{365 \text{ days}}{20 \text{ days}} \times 100\%$$
$$= 37.2\%$$

Although the stated discount rate of 2 percent seems to be rather small, gaining a 2 percent discount off the net price, in exchange for paying just 20 days sooner, represents a high annual rate of return. Suppose that the organization has $4,900 of cash available to pay the bill on the 10th day. For it to make sense not to pay the bill promptly and take the discount, we would have to invest the money for the next 20 days in an investment that would earn at least $100 over that period. Any investment that could give us that return would be earning profits or interest at a rate of at least 37.2 percent per year.

That is, $4,900 × 37.2 percent per year × (20 days/365 days) = $100. That means if we started with $4,900 and earned interest at 37.2 percent per year for a period of 20 days, we would earn $100 in interest. Together with the $4,900 we start with we would have $5,000. If we have projects available to invest in for 20 days that would pay at an annual rate that is even more than 37.2 percent, it would make sense to invest in the projects rather than take the discount. We would earn more than $100 interest for the 20 days and have more than $5,000 at the end of 20 days. We could pay $5,000 and still have something left. But if we can only earn at an annual rate of return less than 37.2 percent for those 20 days, then $4,900 plus interest would be less than the $5,000 needed to pay the full amount due. So we would be better off just taking the discount and paying the $4,900. Since most organizations do not have available investments that are assured of earning such a high rate, it pays to take the discount and pay promptly.

Suppose that we do not have the $4,900 in cash to make the payment on the 10th day. However, a bank is willing to lend us $4,900 at an annual interest rate of 10 percent. Ten percent of $4,900 is $490 per year. Dividing this by 365 days in a year comes to $1.34 per day. We only need to borrow the money for 20 days. Twenty times $1.34 is $26.84. That is the amount of interest we would have to pay the bank for the 20-day loan of $4,900. To save $100, we would have to pay the bank about $27. This is clearly a good deal. So even if you have to borrow money to take the discount, you should, as long as you can borrow at an interest rate of less than 37.2 percent per year.

This assumes, of course, that the invoice will be paid on time if the discount is not taken. Suppose, however, that Meals for the Homeless often pays its bills late. Sometimes it pays after two months, or even three months. Would it make sense to take the discount and pay in 10 days or to wait and pay the bill after 90 days? Paying after 10 days is 80 days earlier than the normal 90 days before making our payment:

$$\text{Implicit interest rate} = \frac{\text{Discount}}{\text{Discounted price}} \quad \textbf{(7.B.1)}$$

$$\times \frac{365 \text{ days}}{\text{days sooner}} \times 100\%$$

$$\text{Implicit interest rate} = \frac{\$100}{\$4,900} \times \frac{365 \text{ days}}{80 \text{ days}} \times 100\%$$

$$= 9.3\%$$

If Meals can earn more than 9.3 percent on its investments, it should wait to pay the bill. If Meals does not have enough money to pay the bill and a bank would charge more than 9.3 percent, then it is better off waiting, assuming its suppliers are willing to wait to receive payment and do not charge interest for late payments. Otherwise, Meals should pay promptly and take the discount.

8

Accountability and Control

The learning objectives of this chapter are to:

- define *management control systems;*
- discuss various measures of performance, including the Balanced Scorecard and triple bottom line performance;
- discuss various approaches for controlling quality;
- explain the role of variance analysis and a variety of techniques for analyzing variances;
- discuss the role of ethics in financial management;
- discuss safeguarding an organization's resources;
- explain the elements of a control system, including the audit trail, reliable personnel, separation of functions, proper authorization, adequate documentation, proper procedures, physical safeguards, bonding, performance audits, and cost-effectiveness analysis;
- discuss the Sarbanes-Oxley Act and its impact on the management of public service organizations; and
- discuss the organization's Form 990.

INTRODUCTION

Planning is an essential element of financial management. Planning is discussed in Chapters 2–6. A good plan is critical if an organization is to do as well as it can. However, to achieve the best possible result, the plan needs to be carried out. To ensure that this happens, departments and individuals must be held accountable for actions and results.

Managers develop control systems to help keep their organizations to their plans, protect resources, motivate employees, evaluate performance, alert management to variations, and take corrective action. Such systems provide the foundation for accountability. Taylor defines *internal control* as

> all actions taken to make an organization run effectively and accomplish its goals, and can be as easy as a supervisory checkoff or as extensive as an automated system used by an agency to track construction of a major project.

Controls even include management's attitude, operating style and integrity, and ethical values. It is how managers communicate with the people they supervise, how they check on staff, how they ensure that their employees do not do the things management does not want them to do. Internal control equals management control and is no longer considered the sole realm of an organization's auditor or accountant.[1]

Management control is based on the assignment of responsibility for the achievement of our plans and is one of the important elements of financial management. However, the organization must not only assign responsibility. It must actually provide motivation for its employees to strive to accomplish the organization's goals.

We must also know how we intend to measure results. This can be done to some extent using simple measures of *inputs* and *outputs*. Inputs are the resources used by the organization to produce its goods or services. Outputs are the goods or services provided. Recently, however, there has been a shift toward trying to better assess the accomplishments of the organization. Various approaches to performance measurement are discussed in this chapter.

After measures of performance have been discussed, techniques for variance analysis are considered. Variances arise if the actual performance differs, or varies, from expectations. Developing an understanding of why variances have occurred can help an organization avoid undesirable variances in the future.

The chapter concludes with discussions of ethics and safeguarding resources. To achieve planned results, it is vital for personnel to be as ethical and error-free as possible. People are fallible. Being aware of this, organizations must try to develop checks and balances to ensure that the risk of losses due to either intent or inefficiency are minimized.

MANAGEMENT CONTROL SYSTEMS

The centerpiece of an organization's attempts to accomplish its plans is its *management control system (MCS)*. An MCS is a set of policies and procedures designed to keep operations going according to plan. Such systems also detect variations from plans and provide managers with information needed to take corrective actions when necessary. Management control systems should:

- provide clear definition of the organization's goals;
- communicate those goals to all employees, along with the action plan to attain those goals;
- report back to managers and other employees on the results the organization has achieved; and
- provide motivation so that managers and other employees have an incentive to achieve the goals of the organization.

Management control systems have often been compared to thermostats. We might set a thermostat for 70 degrees. Our plan is for the temperature to be 70 degrees. It is predetermined, as a budget would be. However, a thermostat does more than just establish the desired temperature. It also monitors the existing temperature in the room. Similarly, an MCS

---

[1] Deirdre A. Taylor. "What Is Internal Control?" in *State and Local Government Program Control and Audit: Handbook for Managers and Auditors.* David R. Hancox and Martin Ives, eds. Austin, Tex.: Sheshunoff Information Services, 1997, pp. 1–2.

assesses the actual *outcomes* for the organization. If the temperature in the room varies from the desired 70 degrees, the thermostat activates the furnace to send heat if it gets too cold or turns off the furnace if it gets too hot. Similarly, the MCS must set in motion actions that are needed if it determines that there are variations from the plan.

Further, MCSs attempt to establish an environment in which it is likely that the organization will come as close to its plans as possible. This means that MCSs are proactive as well as reactive. They are reactive to the extent that they monitor whether something is going wrong. If so, an action is taken to correct the perceived problem. However they are also proactive in that they put in place a set of incentives and controls that help the organization avoid having bad outcomes in the first place.

One proactive aspect of management control is that it should provide managers with a clear way to identify and capitalize on opportunities. Plans cannot possibly anticipate everything that might occur. Organizations need to be flexible enough to respond to unexpected opportunities. However, there must be control. The organization must walk a fine line between allowing everyone to do whatever they want without authorization, using opportunity as an excuse, versus failing to take advantage of truly significant opportunities.

The focus of management control systems is on *responsibility accounting*. Responsibility accounting is the assignment of the responsibility for keeping to the plan and carrying out the elements of the management control system. Such responsibility is generally assigned to managers of cost centers, who take either the "carrot" or the "stick" approach. Some MCSs employ rewards for managers and staff that meet or exceed budgets (the carrot). Others take the approach of doling out punishments if targets are not achieved (the stick). In either case, responsibility accounting should not be primarily focused on assigning blame. The intent is not to have a ready scapegoat when things go wrong.

Rather, the philosophy is that individuals should have a clear understanding of their responsibilities. Given that knowledge, they are likely to act within their ability and the circumstances that surround them in a manner to achieve the best possible outcomes for the organization. Responsibility accounting is oriented toward clearly communicating expectations ahead of time and then tracking results to generate feedback after the fact. The most important reason for the feedback is to improve future outcomes. Thus, the MCS collects retrospective data to allow actions that will enable the organization to avoid repeating its past mistakes.

This is a difficult process. There is a temptation to focus on blame. The MCS has the potential to create severe problems if people are held accountable for things that they either could not control or were unaware they were responsible to control. The common result is low morale and a downward spiral in results, rather than the desired high level of achievement. All activities of organizations are carried out by people. Financial management must be ever aware of the role of people, the incentives that are given to employees (both positive and negative), and the resulting levels of motivation. People make things happen in organizations, not plans or budgets. If we are not mindful of what people are likely to do and why, we are not likely to achieve our hoped-for results.

MEASURES OF PERFORMANCE

The planning process provides goals for the organization. But how will it know if it has achieved its goals? Each organization must decide how to measure its performance. In recent years, there has been growing emphasis on performance measurement. Health care providers have decided measuring the number of patients treated is not adequate. We want better measures of health care improvement. Governments and not-for-profit organizations have all been actively addressing the issue of performance measurement.

There are a number of different ways that a public service organization's performance can be measured. Herzlinger and Nitterhouse note that outcomes can be measured in terms of private benefits to the organization, public benefits to society, effectiveness, efficiency, quality, and quantity.[2]

Organizations compare their planned outcomes with their actual outcomes to see how well they are doing. The organization must guard its viability. This requires taking an internal perspective on whether it is achieving the benefits for the organization that are expected—these are private benefits. At the same time, many public, health, and not-for-profit organizations are also interested in the benefits that they generate for society. If doing public good is a part of the organization's mission, then it is appropriate to compare the expected and actual amounts of public good provided. Often, however, measuring the amount of public good provided is extremely difficult. Proxies are frequently used.

For example, the Hospital for Ordinary Surgery (HOS) cannot easily assess how much its efforts have improved the overall health of its community. Nevertheless, the hospital may choose to measure the number of free health screenings provided or the number of poor patients treated for free to assess (and publicize) the public service being provided. If the organization falls short of its planned goals, it would want to investigate and determine why that had happened.

Organizations also strive to be both effective and efficient. *Effectiveness* relates to whether the organization is accomplishing its desired outcomes. If Meals for the Homeless had hoped to substantially eliminate hunger among the homeless of the city and did in fact accomplish that goal, it could consider itself to be effective. It is working well toward its mission by doing what it set out to do. Effectiveness, however, contrasts with efficiency. *Efficiency* relates to whether the organization uses the minimum needed resources to accomplish its outcomes. Although most organizations strive to be both efficient and effective, an organization can be efficient but not effective or effective but not efficient.

For example, Meals for the Homeless might believe that if it operates carefully, meals should cost $3 each, on average. If it eliminates hunger and provides meals for $3 per meal, then it is operating both efficiently and effectively. If it provides meals at a cost of $4 per meal, it may have been effective in meeting its objective of eliminating hunger but might not have operated in an efficient manner. Resources may have been needlessly used. Conversely, if it keeps costs at $3 per meal but only provides food to one-third of the hungry homeless, it has met the measure of efficiency but has not been as effective as hoped. If the organization falls short in terms of either efficiency or effectiveness targets, it will want to determine by how much and why. That information (or feedback) can be used to help it accomplish its goals both efficiently and effectively in the future.

In addition, organizations will generally have goals in terms of both quality and quantity. Since eliminating hunger is a hard objective to accurately measure, Meals for the Homeless may choose to set a goal, such as 10,000 meals served. Such quantity outcome measures are often easier to measure than true effectiveness. We may not know for sure that we have eliminated hunger, but we know that we provided 10,000 meals, and we infer that this has at least eliminated a fair amount of hunger.

But what do the meals consist of? Is there sufficient protein? Are the meals always a thin vegetable soup, or is there an adequate portion of high-protein items? Organizations will often devise methods to measure not only the quantity of services provided but the quality as well.

---

[2] Regina Herzlinger and Denise Nitterhouse. *Financial Accounting and Managerial Control for Nonprofit Organizations.* Cincinnati, Ohio: Southwestern Publishing, 1994, p. 360.

Herzlinger and Nitterhouse have also noted that there are a number of different approaches for assessing actual outcomes: measuring inputs, measuring process, measuring output, and measuring effects.[3]

Most organizations measure the cost of resources used (*inputs*). This is relatively easy to do but provides only limited information about the activities of the organization. Inputs used tell how much money was spent but not much about what was accomplished. Input usage does not really indicate whether the organization was efficient or effective. Despite this limitation, many organizations do focus a great deal on whether the amount spent was less than or equal to the budgeted amount. This is probably based on a concern about viability. If the organization spends more than budgeted, it may be threatening its viability. If total spending is not controlled and the organization must cease operations, then neither efficiency nor effectiveness will be of much relevance.

An alternative approach to measuring outcomes would be to assess process. For example, HOS could attempt to see how well it has done by measuring how often patient care plans were prepared for its patients and how often there was adherence to those plans. Such measurement does not really tell if patients were made as healthy as possible. However, if the organization has processes that it believes should lead to high quality care, then measurement of whether there was adherence to those processes is helpful. Certainly, the level of adherence to the process tells more about effectiveness than the amount of dollars spent on staff does. HOS may have a goal of getting patients healthy. To do that, it will have to spend a certain amount of money. However, just looking at how much was spent (inputs) does not tell if HOS accomplished its goal. Measuring process is somewhat more likely to tell if the organization is doing what it intended.

Many organizations skip over process measures and focus more on direct proxies for output. For example, the HOS might measure the number of surgeries done; Meals for the Homeless might measure the number of meals provided; and the police department of the Town of Millbridge might measure the number of criminals arrested. Output measures are helpful but inadequate to really tell what the organization has accomplished.

We could measure effects—that is, the impact of what we have done. Schools could assess not only what they pay teachers (input cost), or what process the teachers used (special reading programs), or the number of children taught (output), but also the resulting literacy of the student population. Literacy, after all, might be what we are really trying to achieve. Unfortunately, measuring effects is difficult, and many organizations do not have the ability to make such measurements. Trying to establish causation for the effects is even more difficult. The Governmental Accounting Standards Board has conducted a great deal of research in this area. Starting in 1989, it published a series of Research Reports titled *Service Efforts and Accomplishments Reporting: Its Time Has Come*. The specific subjects of the studies were elementary and secondary education, water and wastewater treatment, mass transit, sanitation collection and disposal, fire department programs, public health, police department programs, and road maintenance.[4]

In the health care sector, the growth of managed care has made the need for performance measurement extremely clear. When health maintenance organization (HMO) members find they cannot get a necessary treatment, they realize that the HMO's monthly premium is not enough information. Report cards have become commonplace in health care, conveying to the public a mix of quality measures (e.g., Are all children in the plan inoculated against major diseases?) and satisfaction measures as well.

---

[3] Ibid., pp. 360–361.
[4] These reports can be ordered directly from GASB on the Web. The GASB homepage can be found at http://www.gasb.org/index.html.

The Balanced Scorecard

During the 1990s Kaplan and Norton developed an approach called the *Balanced Scorecard,* which brings many of these measurement issues together in one systematic approach.[5] The notion of the Balanced Scorecard is that financial measures are just one part of a larger set of measures that are needed to assess organizational performance and control its operations. A Balanced Scorecard is "a carefully selected set of measures derived from an organization's strategy. The measures selected for the Scorecard represent a tool for leaders to use in communicating to employers and external stakeholders the outcomes and performance drivers by which the organization will achieve its mission and strategic objectives."[6]

BALANCED SCORECARD ELEMENTS In the Balanced Scorecard approach, the organization develops a set of *key performance indicators (KPIs)* that management can use to monitor how well the organization is achieving its goals with respect to four critical perspectives:

- financial perspective,
- customer perspective,
- internal business perspective, and
- learning and growth perspective.

By focusing on how well our strategy is working in these four areas, the Balanced Scorecard can assess how well an organization is achieving its goals and objectives.

For example, from a financial perspective, one goal of the Hospital for Ordinary Surgery (HOS) would be for the organization to have financial success as measured by an adequate profit level. One objective to help us attain that profit might be adequate support beyond patient revenues. The KPI that HOS might use to determine if it is achieving the desired support level is the total dollar amount of pledges received. Hospitals traditionally focus monthly on patient revenues, but tend to examine contribution results less frequently. A monthly Balanced Scorecard report would bring donation shortfalls to the attention of top management.

At the same time, a Balanced Scorecard would go beyond financial measures of success and report on things from customer, internal business, and learning and growth perspectives as well. We must determine the things that are important to the customers. HOS's customers will likely consider quality of care to be one of the most important factors. The hospital will develop a KPI such as a measure of patient satisfaction with quality of care received. Although this may not translate into organizational success or failure in the short term, if patients are not satisfied they will tell their friends and it will hurt the organization's patient volume over the long term. Therefore, a Balanced Scorecard can shift the focus from short-term measures toward the requirements for the long-term success of the organization.

The internal business perspective focuses on issues such as whether we are adequately innovative and whether we deliver our service efficiently and effectively. The learning and growth perspective considers factors such as whether we are attracting and retaining competent employees and using continuing education to maintain their expertise. Are our management information systems up to the task of taking us forward into the future?

BALANCED SCORECARDS AND PUBLIC SERVICE ORGANIZATIONS The Balanced Scorecard system was developed for corporate America. Does it make sense in the government, health, and not-for-profit sectors? Yes. If anything, it applies even more directly to these types of

---

[5] Robert Kaplan and David Norton. *Translating Strategy into Action: The Balanced Scorecard.* Boston, Mass.: Harvard Business School Press, 1996.
[6] Paul R. Niven. *Balanced Scorecard Step-by-Step for Government and Nonprofit Agencies*, 2nd ed., Hoboken, N.J.: John Wiley & Sons, 2008, p. 13.

organizations because their mission is not singularly focused on profits. The inherent nature of public service organizations is that their primary purpose for existence is not to make profits. Therefore financial measures of performance are inherently limited in their ability to evaluate how well the organization is doing. A Balanced Scorecard allows a public service organization to develop a strategy to achieve its mission knowing that there will be feedback that will capture performance along a number of dimensions, using KPIs that can be tailored to the nature of the organization and its goals, including nonfinancial goals.

In addition to a heightened focus on mission, public service organizations may also place more importance on the customer perspective than some for-profit organizations do. For some public service organizations their reason for existence is squarely centered on the customer, and it makes sense for the Balanced Scorecard to also have this focus. Nevertheless, the financial element should never be ignored in a Balanced Scorecard. If the finances are not adequate, the organization may cease to exist, and we can't lose sight of that fact.

BALANCED SCORECARD BENEFITS By developing a Balanced Scorecard, managers are forced to consider a broad view of the critical factors for success, define KPIs to measure performance, and collect data that can track how the organization is doing in all of these areas. As such, it results in a stronger strategic planning process and an organization that quickly reacts to issues that may impact success before it is too late to take corrective actions. One of the problems with traditional financial measures of performance is that they often focus too heavily on the past. They report how profitable the organization was last year, not how profitable it will be next year. Balanced Scorecards contain an array of information that provide managers with the ability to look not only backward, but ahead as well.

IMPLEMENTING BALANCED SCORECARDS Conceptually, the process of developing a Balanced Scorecard does not appear to be difficult. But in complex organizations, the detailed efforts needed to create a valuable system that communicates strategies and develops sensible KPIs is not a simple task. Even with a system that can improve management, that doesn't mean measurement will be an easy task. Readers are encouraged to explore this topic further by referring to some of the books listed in the Suggested Readings section listed at the end of this chapter.

Triple Bottom Line Performance

Another approach for measuring performance also got its start in the 1990s. This approach is *triple bottom line accounting*. Triple bottom line argues that organizations should be concerned about, and measure, not only their financial performance, but also their environmental and social performance as well. The concept, developed by John Elkington, argues that organizations have many stakeholders (individuals who are impacted in any way by the actions of the organization) and those stakeholders should all be represented in the performance process.

From a social or people point of view, triple bottom line calls for organizations to consider the interdependencies between the organization and both individuals and society as a whole. Triple bottom line would measure the impacts of the organization's actions on its employees, clients, and others. Essentially such a measurement would consider not only benefits provided to society by the organization, but exploitation or endangerment to stakeholders as a result of the organization's actions. The triple bottom line approach would measure the ills caused by the organization, such as pollution, and also the positives, such as providing health and education services to the poor.

Triple bottom line also focuses on sustainable environmental practices. This means that an objective would be to avoid environmental harm. Further, this would require management of energy use and of waste creation, toxicity, and disposal. Sustainable environmental practices require the organization to consider the impact of its actions throughout the life cycle of its products and services, from their initial manufacture or provision, through their ultimate disposal by the client they were made for or provided to. The organization would measure things such as the extent to which the organization bears part of the costs of the final disposal of the products that it has created. The organization would also measure the extent to which it replenishes the resources it consumes. Examples would be a forestry company planting trees. It has been argued that environmental sustainability may actually be a more profitable course for an organization over the long run. However, that may not always be the case.

The third element of triple bottom line is financial return. However, this should not be viewed as being limited to the profits of the organization. Just as the social and environmental impacts of an organization should be viewed beyond the immediate limits of the organization, so should its profits. In other words, triple bottom line is not traditional profitability plus a focus on social and environmental impacts. All three elements, including profitability, must examine the totality of the lasting impacts of the organization's actions. Such impacts may also create profits (or losses) beyond the organization.

CONTROLLING QUALITY

In addition to having a Balanced Scorecard, an essential element of control is a system to control the quality of services provided. Providing quality services is obviously essential for health care organizations. However, it is something that all public service organizations strive to attain. Historically the traditional approach to achieving a quality result was to inspect finished products for defects, and then fix instances of poor quality. However, in the last several decades better approaches have been developed.

Cost of Quality Report

We can think of the costs related to providing a quality product or service as consisting of four parts:

- prevention,
- appraisal,
- internal failure, and
- external failure.

We spend money to prevent failures from occurring. We spend money on appraisal, examining the finished product or service to see if failures have occurred. If the appraisal finds a defect, the costs of correcting it are considered to be internal failure costs. If the defect is not detected by the appraisal process, and is discovered later by the customer, the costs of correcting it are external failure costs.

For example, suppose that a patient comes into the surgical suite at HOS. First our surgical staff will scrub their hands and put on sterile gloves. Those are prevention costs. We pay the staff while they scrub their hands, so it does cost money. We pay for the gloves. But the goal is to prevent infection. We also will take time during the surgery to be careful not to leave any surgical instruments behind in the patient. Additional prevention cost. At the end of the surgery, the staff count all of the scalpels, forceps, sponges, and other items that might have been accidentally left behind in the patient. The cost of the staff time while we do that is appraisal cost. We are now checking to make sure there were no quality deficiencies. What if we are short one scalpel? We will bring in a portable X-ray machine, take an X-ray, and find the missing scalpel and remove it. That would be an internal failure cost (pun intended). But what if we do an inadequate job of prevention and appraisal? We don't spend the time to be careful about leaving implements behind and we don't count carefully to see if we did. The next day the patient complains about severe back pain, we X-ray the patient and have to have a new operation to remove the scalpel. We also have the costs related to a lawsuit and the negative impact on the hospital's reputation. All of that is external failure cost, because the patient became aware of the failure before we could identify and correct it.

A report can be prepared that shows the costs related to prevention, appraisal, internal failure, and external failure. We can consider the total cost from those four sections of the report to be the total costs related to the level of quality provided. Managers can then consider how they can improve the focus on prevention and appraisal to reduce the costs related to failures. Even if we spend more on prevention and appraisal, we can lower the overall costs by lowering the cost of correcting failures. At the same time we can improve the quality of care provided. A cost of quality report can be valuable for all types of public service organizations.

Total Quality Management

As organizations have focused more on quality, they have sought tools that can help them in this area. Several decades ago Edward Deming introduced America to the Japanese philosophy of Total Quality Management (TQM). The basic approach of TQM is to do things right the first time. That may cost more up-front, but saves a lot of money in terms of correcting mistakes.

America has been considered the land of "ready-fire-aim." We are quick to act, although sometimes it might make more sense to consider things more carefully before acting. In terms of TQM, we want to make our product or service so quickly that we sometimes don't take the care necessary to ensure that we do a first-class job. Philosophically TQM argues that if we spent more time ensuring the product were a good one to begin with, we would save so much money that is spent fixing our mistakes that we could have a better quality result at a lower overall cost. Whether that is always the case is an issue of some debate. However, there is no question that a focus on quality at an early stage in the process can be beneficial.

Six Sigma

More recently the focus in quality control has been on the Six Sigma method. The method relies heavily on measurement of quality failures, because once we know how many failures we have, we can work actively to reduce that number to a lower level. Six Sigma is an approach that strives to reduce the number of defects to fewer than 3.4 defects per million. This methods focuses primarily on defining any process, analyzing the process, and then improving the process so that it is less subject to error.

Quality Control Charts

In order to measure defects or quality failures, a quality control chart can be a helpful tool. On the horizontal axis time is recorded. On the vertical axis either the number of defects or the percentage of the time that a defect occurs is recorded. The organization will establish a maximum defect goal for a particular process. The goal is indicated as a horizontal line. The actual values for defects are then plotted over time. Managers can quickly tell if the process being measured is out of control (defects are above the goal that was set) and needs attention, or if the process is under control (actual values below the goal line).

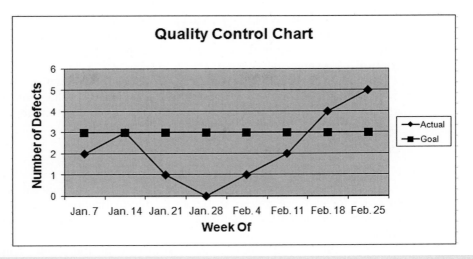

EXHIBIT 8-1

Consider Exhibit 8-1. We can see that the goal is no more than 3 defects or quality failures per week. At the beginning of the year, this process was always at that level or below. However, since January 28 the number of problems has been steadily rising. Not only was the goal for maximum number of defects exceeded in the weeks of February 18 and 25, but the trend is particularly disturbing. A quick glance at this control chart would inform a manager of a need to investigate this process and get its quality back under control.

VARIANCE ANALYSIS

No matter how careful the planning process, actual results often differ from the plan. The difference between the actual results and the planned results represents a *variance,* that is, the amount by which the results vary from the budget. A variance may be the result of less than optimal implementation of the plan, or it may be due to factors beyond the control of the organization. A major element of the control process in any organization relates to analysis of why variances have occurred. If it turns out that a variance is unfavorable and is the result of something that could be controlled better, a *variance analysis* provides the starting point for taking actions to improve future results.

Variances are calculated for three principal reasons. One reason is to aid in preparing the budget for the coming year. By understanding why results were not as expected, the budget process can be improved and be more accurate in future planning. The second reason is to aid in controlling results throughout the current year. By understanding why variances are occurring, actions can be taken to avoid additional unfavorable variances over the coming months. The third reason for variance analysis is to evaluate the performance of units or departments and their managers. By identifying the controllable and noncontrollable elements of variances, one can improve control over the controllable elements, take appropriate actions in response to changes in noncontrollable elements, and better evaluate performance with respect to controllable elements.

Although variance reports are used to evaluate performance, it should be stressed that the main reason for investigating why variances have occurred is not to assign blame; crying over spilt milk is not the primary goal. Rather, the focus is to determine where and how remedial actions can be taken to avoid spilling any more milk in the future.

Variance analysis can help managers locate the cause of inefficiencies and help organizations avoid waste. In addition, variance analysis can also help managers explain why variances have arisen in the occasions when they are due to neither inefficiency nor other controllable events.

Control charts, such as the quality control chart shown in Exhibit 8-1, can be developed to track variances as compared to the budget over time, and help managers quickly identify when variances indicate that some process is out of control.

Understanding Why Variances Happened

Organizations should generally provide each manager with a monthly variance report indicating budgeted expectations, actual results, and the variance for each item in the budget. In order for variance reports to be a valuable managerial tool, managers must be able to determine and understand the causes of the variances. This requires investigating why each substantial variance occurred.

Generally, small variances are assumed to be the result of uncontrollable, random events. A manager would not spend much time investigating a $10 variance. Only variances that are either large in dollar amount or as a percentage of the budgeted amount are investigated. Determination of whether an amount is large enough to warrant investigation requires both skill and judgment, and no easy rules of thumb exist. Many organizations will use institutional history as a guide to determine what size variances should be investigated.

Variance investigation requires the knowledge, judgment, and experience of the manager. Only the person who has supervised a department has enough actual knowledge of that department to effectively determine why it spent more or less than expected. As a result, finance officers often generate variance reports, but each unit or department manager is required to prepare an analysis of why variances occurred in their department. Without such analysis, the reports are not as useful as they might be.

If variances arose as a result of inefficiency (e.g., unduly long lunch breaks), then the process of providing cost-effective services is out of control. By discovering this inefficiency, actions can be taken to eliminate it and to bring the process back under control. In this case, future costs will be lower because of the investigation of the variance.

Although some inefficiencies can be controlled by proper staff supervision, in many cases variances are caused by factors outside of the control of managers. For example, increases in the number of homeless people may cause Meals for the Homeless to provide more meals. This will likely cause its total costs to rise. The cost increase was not the result of inefficiency but rather resulted from the greater-than-expected demand for meals. If the organization decides to provide additional meals because it will help accomplish the organization's mission, it must use care in evaluating the financial impact of that decision. Blaming a manager for increased spending that results from policy decisions outside of his or her control can only result in poor morale and deteriorating future performance.

Nevertheless, even if the cause of a variance is something outside the control of the manager, the variance should be investigated and its cause determined. The impact of such variances on total costs should not be ignored. If the increase in the number of homeless people is likely to persist, then Meals for the Homeless will continue to go over budget. Eventually this may cause the organization to run out of money. This could threaten its continued existence. Decisions will have to be made. Should the organization continue to provide meals to everyone who asks? Should the organization undertake an emergency fund-raising campaign? Can the organization offset the increased food cost by cutting back on some other program? Whether variances are controllable or not, they set into motion a number of actions and decisions that are necessary in order for the organization to achieve its best possible overall result and ensure its continued existence.

Volume increases are not always problematic. Although Meals for the Homeless may have a problem when it unexpectedly serves more meals, many organizations would actually benefit from a volume increase. Suppose, for example, that HOS makes a profit on each surgical procedure. If the number of procedures increases, the resources consumed will likely also increase. It will spend more than the amount that has been budgeted. However, if the additional patients are generating more revenue, then the organization as a whole may benefit from the extra volume. Since some costs are fixed, volume increases that proportionately raise revenues are likely to increase overall profits. Clearly, spending more than the budgeted amount does not always result in a bad outcome for the organization.

Variance Analysis Mechanics

Variance analysis is generally done on a monthly basis. At the end of each month, a report is prepared comparing actual results with the budget. Usually, it takes the financial managers of the organization about one to three weeks to prepare the report for each department.

THE TOTAL VARIANCE The simplest variance analysis approach is to compare the total costs that the entire organization has incurred with the budgeted costs for the entire organization. For example, suppose that HOS had a total budget for September of $8,800,000. The actual costs for the month were $9,200,000; HOS spent $400,000 more than it had budgeted. The difference between the amount budgeted and the amount spent is the hospital-wide *total variance*. This variance will be referred to as an *unfavorable variance,* because the organization spent more than had been budgeted. Accountants use the term *favorable variance* to indicate spending less than expected. The use of the terms *favorable* or *unfavorable* do not carry a connotation of good or bad. There will be times that spending more than budgeted (an unfavorable variance) will actually be good for the organization. If greater volume of profitable customers has caused us to spend more money, an unfavorable variance could be the result of a good event for the organization, because the extra revenues generated will exceed the extra costs. However, when we look at just the costs, we will still call the extra spending an unfavorable variance.

Assuming that HOS begins its year on July 1, the variance could appear in a format somewhat like the following:

This Month			Year-to-Date		
Actual	Budget	Variance	Actual	Budget	Variance
$9,200,000	$8,800,000	$400,000 U	$25,476,000	$25,150,000	$326,000 U

Although most organizations provide year-to-date information, for ease of presentation, the remainder of examples in this chapter will focus on just current month information.

The "U" following the variance refers to the fact that the variance is unfavorable. If the variance were favorable, it would be followed by an "F." An alternative presentation to using U and F would be to use a negative sign for an unfavorable variance and a positive sign for a favorable variance. Sometimes parentheses are used to indicate a negative number. Any systematic approach can be used to indicate favorable versus unfavorable variances. Some organizations show unfavorable variances as negative numbers and favorable as positive, and other organizations do just the reverse. The manager should be cautious to determine whether spending has been more or less than the expected amount.

The objective in doing variance analysis is to determine why the variances arose. Nothing can be done with respect to the goal of controlling costs until the manager knows where the unit or department is deviating from the plan and why. Why has HOS had a $400,000 unfavorable variance for the month of September? Given just this one total variance for the entire organization, the chief executive officer (CEO) has no idea what caused the variance. The CEO does not even know which managers to ask about the variance, since all that is known is a total for the entire organization.

One solution to this problem would be to have organization-wide line-item totals. That is, the total amount budgeted for salaries for the entire organization could be compared with actual total salary costs. The total amount budgeted for supplies could be compared with the actual total amount spent on supplies. The problem with this solution is that there would still be no way to determine what caused the variances. All departments have salaries. A number of departments use supplies. Who should be asked about the variances?

To use budgets for control, it must be possible to assign responsibility for variances to individual managers. Those managers can investigate the causes of the variances and attempt to eliminate them in the future. This leads to the necessity for determining variances by unit or department rather than for the entire organization in total.

DEPARTMENT VARIANCES   The overall HOS variance of $400,000 for the month is really an aggregation of variances from a number of departments. Let us focus on the results for just one department in the hospital, the Department of Radiology Services:

The Hospital for Ordinary Surgery
Department of Radiology Services
September Expense Variance Report

Actual	Budget	Variance
$800,000	$600,000	$200,000 U

Apparently, half of the variance for HOS occurred in the Department of Radiology Services. This provides more information than we had before. Clearly, the director of Radiology must try to find out why this $200,000 variance occurred in the department. It is large in both dollar and percent terms. Unfortunately, this still does not give the Radiology director much to go on. The director simply knows that $200,000 was spent in this department in excess of the amount budgeted.

LINE-ITEM VARIANCES   Is the $200,000 Department of Radiology Services variance the result of unexpectedly high costs for technician salaries? Does it relate to usage of supplies? There is no way to know based on a total variance for a unit or department. More detailed information is needed. In order to have any real chance to control costs, there must be variance information for individual line-items within a unit or department. The Radiology director must know how much of the department total went to salaries and how much to supplies. For example, consider the following:

The Hospital for Ordinary Surgery
Department of Radiology Services
September Expense Variance Report

	Actual	Budget	Variance
Salary	$400,000	$395,000	$ 5,000 U
Supplies	400,000	205,000	195,000 U
Total	$800,000	$600,000	$200,000 U

Now we are starting to get somewhere. By subdividing the total $400,000 hospital-wide variance by department, we were able to find a department, Radiology, that has a substantial variance. By further subdividing the variance by line-item, we have found that there is a very substantial supplies variance and a much more modest salary variance. The Department of Radiology Services manager could now proceed to investigate supplies and try to determine what has caused such a significant variance from the budget.

Even this, however, is a substantial simplification. For example, a real variance report would show the variance for salaries for each class of employees. Essentially, each line in a unit's budget should become a line in the variance report; spending on nurses, technicians, aides, education, publications, office supplies, laundry, and so on would each be examined. As the level of detail becomes greater, it becomes easier to determine which variances are large enough to warrant investigation, and it becomes easier to determine the factors causing the overall variance. Variance reports with detailed line-item results for each unit and department are often available in public service organizations today. This approach of evaluating each line-item for each department is one of the most common approaches for the investigation of variances.

One potential cause of the $195,000 supply variance in the Radiology department mentioned previously is that the manager just did not do a very good job in controlling the use of supplies. Technicians failed to place X-ray film that was not used back in the stockroom, and housekeeping threw the film away. Or perhaps the technicians made a lot of mistakes and often had to take three or four images rather than just one or two. Another possibility is that there were many more patients than anticipated. Of course, if the film is being wasted, we are much more concerned than if we had an increased number of paying patients.

Another possible cause is that the price of X-ray film rose dramatically. X-ray film contains a lot of silver, and if the price of silver rises, the cost of X-ray film rises as well.

The main weaknesses of this traditional type of analysis are that it fails to take into account changes in the volume of services provided, and it does not provide as much direction for the investigation of the causes of variances as possible. Are variances due to prices paid for resources or to the amount of resources used per unit of output? A more sophisticated approach, called flexible budget variance analysis, can overcome these limitations.

Flexible Budget Variance Analysis

Flexible budget variance analysis requires a little more work than the variance analysis approach described previously but can provide managers with substantially more information. Flexible budgets, as discussed earlier in this book, provide budgets for different levels of activity. An organization might approve a budget that assumes one specific activity level but also prepare flexible budgets for different volume levels. The flexible budgets show the expected impacts of volume changes. They recognize the fact that some costs are fixed and some are variable. Thus, a 10 percent volume change would be unlikely to change costs by 10 percent. Flexible budget variance analysis incorporates this concept by recognizing that at least part of the total variance for any line-item is often the result of changes in the level of activity.

The public sector has been slow to adopt this approach. This may reflect a historical lack of emphasis on cost control. As cost control becomes more important to the financial well-being of these organizations, increasing adoption of the technique is likely. Organizations such as hospitals, under intense financial scrutiny, largely adopted this technique in the last decade of the 20th century.

The key concept of flexible budgeting is that the amount of resources consumed will vary with the level of workload actually attained. In other words, the more service an organization provides, the greater its costs will be. It is critical to evaluate whether variances are occurring because we are spending more money to provide the expected level of services or we are spending more money to provide a greater amount of service. The implications of these two alternatives are substantially different.

Suppose that the following was the variance report for Meals for the Homeless:

Meals for the Homeless
Kitchen Department
March Expense Variance Report

	Actual	Budget	Variance
Food	$100,000	$100,000	$0

It looks like Meals came in right on budget. It is probable that the manager would be feeling pretty good about this line-item for March. Suppose, however, that the budget of $100,000 for food was based on an assumption of 33,000 meals served, but there were actually only 20,000 meals. One would expect that the lower volume of meals prepared should have allowed for reduction in food usage and a cost savings as compared with the budget. None of that is apparent from the March Variance Report.

The flexible budget is a restatement of the budget based on the volume actually attained. Basically, the flexible budget shows what a line-item *should* have cost, given the output level that actually occurred. If some costs are variable (see Chapter 4 for a discussion of fixed and variable costs), then increasing volumes should be accompanied by an increase in costs, and decreasing levels of output should be accompanied by a decrease in costs.

In Chapter 3, we note that flexible budgets can be prepared during the planning stage. A flexible budget can give an indication of expected results at a variety of possible volume levels. For variance reporting, however, the flexible budget is prepared after the fact, when the exact volume achieved can be determined.

Using the flexible budget technique, the variance for any line-item can be subdivided to provide the manager with additional information about the cause of the variance. Each line-item variance can be divided into three pieces: a *volume variance,* a *price variance,* and a *quantity variance.*

THE VOLUME VARIANCE   The *volume variance* is defined as the portion of the variance in any line-item that is caused simply by the fact that the output level differed from the budgeted expectation. For example, if the budget calls for the Town of Millbridge to educate 2,000 pupils in its school system but actually 2,200 students enrolled, then it would be expected that it would be necessary to hire more teachers and buy more books. The increased cost of the resources needed for an extra 200 students constitutes a volume variance. Such variances are often outside of the control of the manager. The school superintendent would not likely be considered to be doing a bad job if the quality of the school system attracts more families with school-age children to move into the town.

THE PRICE, OR RATE, VARIANCE   The *price,* or *rate, variance* is the portion of the total variance for any line-item that is caused by spending more per unit of some input resource than had been anticipated. For example, if the average wage rate for kitchen workers at Meals for the Homeless is more per hour than had been expected, a rate variance would result. When the variance is used to measure labor resources, it is generally called a rate variance because the average hourly rate has varied from expectations. When considering the price of supplies, such as the cost of food, it is called a price variance because it is the purchase price that has varied. The terms *price* and *rate* are often used interchangeably in practice.

The price, or rate, variance may or may not be under the control of the manager. Suppose the Purchasing Department at HOS tells the Department of Radiology Services director how much X-ray film is likely to cost per sheet of film. That price is built into the budget. If Purchasing then signs a contract for film at a higher price, the manager of Purchasing should be held accountable to explain the difference.

Note, however, that the extra cost for film will show up on the variance report of the Department of Radiology Services. Supply costs are generally assigned to the department consuming those supplies. The director of Radiology is therefore expected to explain the supply variance. If we can separate the line-item variance into several parts so that we know the part of the variance caused by changes in the price of film as opposed to changes in the amount of film used, we can make better decisions about who should be investigating and determining the cause of the variance.

THE QUANTITY, OR USE, VARIANCE   The third general type of variance under the flexible budgeting approach is the *quantity*, or *use*, *variance*. This is the portion of the overall variance for a particular line-item that results from using more of a resource than was expected for a given output level. For example, suppose that Millbridge spends more than expected on textbooks for the students in its schools. This could occur because there are more students (a volume variance) or because we paid more per textbook (a price variance). However, it could also occur because we used more textbooks per student than we had planned. Several teachers may have added supplementary books during the year that had not been in the original budget. This higher use per student represents a quantity variance.

This variance is often referred to as a *use variance* because it focuses on how much of the resource has been used. In industry, this variance is often called an *efficiency variance*. This is because a favorable variance would imply that each unit of output was produced using less inputs. Most industries can carefully measure the quality of the products they produce. If they can maintain quality at a desired level and make their products using less input, they are functioning with a higher level of efficiency.

For most public, health, and not-for-profit organizations, measuring quality is more difficult. If the schools in Millbridge use fewer textbooks per student, are they operating more efficiently than expected, or are they providing a lower-quality education? It is advisable to use the terms *quantity* or *use variance* rather than *efficiency variance* unless we know that reduced consumption of resources per unit actually is related to changes in efficiency rather than changes in quality.

CALCULATING THE VOLUME, PRICE, AND QUANTITY VARIANCES   Suppose that the Millbridge Township School District expects to spend $32,000 on textbooks for the fall semester, but actually spends $37,800. When the school board questioned the school superintendent about the $5,800 unfavorable variance ($37,800 actual spending less the $32,000 budget), she pointed out that there were more students enrolled, so of course they had to increase spending on textbooks. Is that explanation sufficient?

The school district had expected to have 320 students enrolled, but the actual enrollment was 360 students. It would seem that the superintendent had the explanation correct. However, further examination shows that while the school district had expected to use an average of four books per student at a cost of $25 each, it actually acquired five books per student, with an average cost of $21 each. We can calculate the volume, quantity, and price portions of the total variance to better understand what caused the $5,800 unfavorable variance.

The Original Budget was based on 320 students each consuming four books at a price of $25 per book.

Original Budget:

Budgeted Volume	×	Budgeted Quantity	×	Budgeted Price	
320	×	4	×	$25	= $32,000

However, consider just the change caused by the number of students. Actually, there were 360 students enrolled. We can calculate a Flexible Budget (often called a *Flex Budget*) that uses budgeted information for everything except volume.

Flex Budget:

Actual Volume	×	Budgeted Quantity	×	Budgeted Price	
360	×	4	×	$25	= $36,000

If we compare the difference between the Original Budget and the Flex Budget, we can find the Volume Variance. That is the portion of the total $5,800 unfavorable variance that was in fact due to the number of students.

Original Budget versus Flex Budget:

Budgeted volume × Budgeted Quantity × Budgeted Price
− **Actual volume** × Budgeted Quantity × Budgeted Price

or

320	×	4	×	$25	= $32,000
−360	×	4	×	$25	= 36,000
				Volume Variance	= $ 4,000 U

Note that the only difference between the Original Budget and the Flex Budget is the Budgeted Volume versus the Actual Volume (shown in bold). Both the Original Budget and Flex Budget are calculated using the budgeted quantity and budgeted price information. The superintendent was correct in saying that the higher than expected number of enrolled students caused an unfavorable variance. However, that only explains $4,000 of the total $5,800 unfavorable variance. What else is going on?

The school district expected to buy four books per student. Actually, it purchased five books per student. This gives rise to a Quantity Variance, because we used more books per student than we had planned for in our budget. We can create a *Volume & Quantity Adjusted (VQA) Budget* that indicates what we would have expected to pay for books, if we had known both the actual number of students and actual number of books per student:

VQA Budget:

Actual Volume	×	Actual Quantity	×	Budgeted Price	
360	×	5	×	$25	= $45,000

This budget is similar to the Flex Budget in that it is a mix of budgeted and actual information. The Flex Budget looks at the actual number of students (volume), but uses the budgeted quantity of books per student and the budgeted price per book. The Volume & Quantity Adjusted Budget used the actual number of students, the actual number of books per student, and the budgeted price per book. If we compare those two calculations, we can find the Quantity Variance.

Flex Budget versus VQA Budget:

	Actual Volume	×	**Budgeted Quantity**	×	Budgeted Price	
	− Actual Volume	×	**Actual Quantity**	×	Budgeted Price	

or

	360	×	**4**	×	$25	= $36,000
	−360	×	**5**	×	$25	= 45,000
				Quantity Variance	=	$ 9,000 U

The only element that differs between the Flex Budget and the Volume & Quantity Adjusted Budget is the Budgeted Quantity versus the Actual Quantity (shown in bold). Notice that the combined total of the Volume Variance and the Quantity Variance is $13,000 unfavorable. However the total variance was only $5,800 unfavorable. Something else must be going on.

The school only paid $21 per book, which is $4 per book less than the expected price of $25. The actual amount paid for books was:

Actual:

Actual Volume	×	Actual Quantity	×	Actual Price	
360	×	5	×	$21	= $37,800

We can compare the Volume & Quantity Adjusted Budget to the Actual amount spent to determine the price variance. This variance will show the amount caused by paying a different amount per book than expected.

VQA Budget versus Actual:

	Actual Volume	×	Actual Quantity	×	**Budgeted Price**	
	− Actual Volume	×	Actual Quantity	×	**Actual Price**	

or

	360	×	5	×	**$25**	= $45,000
	−360	×	5	×	**$21**	= 37,000
				Price Variance	=	$ 7,200 F

The only difference between the Volume & Quantity Adjusted Budget and the Actual amount spent is caused by the price. The former uses the budgeted price, while the latter is based on the actual price (shown in bold).

The combined total for the Volume, Quantity, and Price Variances is $5,800 unfavorable ($4,000 U + $9,000 U − $7,200 F = $5,800 U). The total variance is unfavorable, despite a savings of $7,200 that was realized because we were able to purchase books at a lower than expected price. The savings was partially offset by the increased number of students, but part of the reason for the unfavorable total variance is the increased number of books purchased per student. Why did the school district buy more books per student than budgeted?

It is possible that no one was tracking the number of books that teachers were ordering. Meanwhile, the purchasing office did a terrific job negotiating lower prices for books. If that is what happened, we need to acknowledge the fine job done by purchasing, but we also need to improve controls to prevent teachers from ordering books without regard to the budget. Alternatively, it is possible that teachers decided to replace one large, expensive book with several smaller, less expensive, books. If so, we need to consider that the extra cost of buying more books (the $9,000 unfavorable Quantity Variance) was greater than the savings from buying less expensive books (the $7,200 favorable Price Variance). We must investigate to see if the switch in books resulted in an improved outcome that justified the net $1,800 increase in cost above and beyond the $4,000 increase caused by the additional students.

The key is that by subdividing a variance into component parts, we start to get a better sense of what happened. Managers can then investigate the specific Volume, Quantity, and Price variances and decide what management action, if any, is needed to better control operations and keep to the approved budget.

The somewhat technical process of calculating these three types of variances is discussed further in Appendix 8-A at the end of this chapter.

Determination of the Causes of Variances

The volume, price, and quantity variances provide greater direction for the manager. They help to focus the area of investigation. If a line-item variance is caused primarily by the price variance, the manager can explore why prices differed from expectations. If the variance is primarily attributable to volume, we can try to determine what caused the change in volume. However, the analysis cannot tell the manager the ultimate cause of the variance. Managers still have to determine *why* these variances have occurred.

For instance, variance analysis will not tell us why more students have enrolled in Millbridge's schools, why more books have been used, or why we paid less per book. But rather than simply knowing that the cost of books is over budget, we know where to focus our investigation. If we used more books per student, was it done to enhance education or because the school misplaced 100 expensive textbooks over the summer and had to replace them? Were books stolen, or did changes in world history dictate that we buy newer editions, even though the old books were not worn out?

If the organization does not care about the answers to these questions, the variance process can be done primarily by financial managers. However, if the organization wants to use its resources efficiently, it must get answers to questions such as these. Getting these answers requires the experience and judgment of the managers who supervise each area of the organization's activities.

Common internal causes of variances include shifts in quality of service provided, changes in technology used, changes in efficiency, changes in organization policy, or simply budgets based on unrealistic expectations. External causes of variances commonly include price changes for supplies, volume changes, and unexpected shifts in the availability of staff.

Aggregation Problems

In doing variance analysis, the more we aggregate information, the greater the chance that we will misinterpret what has happened. An entire organization may spend nearly the same amount for a given month as it expected. In total, there is nearly no variance. However, that does not mean that there are no problems that need to be investigated.

Some departments might have large favorable variances, and other departments might have large unfavorable variances. Even if these offset each other, the organization would need to investigate these large variances to see why they are occurring. So we cannot rely solely on variances measured for the entire organization; we need variance information department by department.

Even further, it is possible that the total variance for one department might be small. However, there might be one line-item within the department that has a large favorable variance and another that has a large unfavorable variance. For example, salaries may be extremely over budget and supplies extremely under budget. It is not enough to look at the overall spending of the department. We must examine the actual and budgeted results line by line.

However, we cannot rely on information from the total variance for a given line-item, either. Recall that we can subdivide one line-item variance into its volume, price, and quantity subcomponents. For example, for one line-item in one department, it is possible that there might be a favorable volume variance and an unfavorable quantity variance. These variances might offset each other. When we look at the total variance for the line-item, it is small and does not appear to be of consequence. However, when we employ flexible budget variance analysis and consider the price, quantity, and volume variances that make up the total variance for the line-item, we find that there are problems to be investigated.

This could potentially call attention to a serious problem. For instance, suppose that in one department of HOS, the number of patients is falling but staffing has not been reduced. The salary line-item will not show any variance in total. As the volume of work is falling, the volume variance is favorable. But if we do not reduce staffing, we will be consuming more staff time per patient. So there will be an unfavorable quantity variance. If these two variances offset, which is likely, the manager may fail to see the departmental problem. The department is using too much staff time per patient without being aware of it.

Thus, it is essential to calculate price, quantity, and volume variances for every line-item of every department. That way we will have a much better chance of detecting problems at an early stage.

Exception Reporting

For large organizations with numerous departments, we cannot expect either the CEO or the chief financial officer (CFO) to have time to review all variances each month. To cope with this problem, organizations use *exception reports* to list only those variances that are deemed to warrant a manager's attention. Thus, we would calculate all variances, but the CEO might just review a report with a brief listing of the most significant ones. Since variance reports are often prepared on a computer, this process is relatively simple.

The CEO, for example, might review all variances that are greater than $10,000 or more than 20 percent over or under budget. The CFO in turn might review a listing of all variances that are more than $5,000 or 10 percent. The exact cutoffs used can be determined by individual managers. If an organization's director believes in tight, centralized control, the cutoffs will be relatively low. Other managers who prefer to allow the organization to be run on a decentralized basis will want to review only variances that are extremely large.

Although high-level managers will only receive summary exception reports, all variances should be reviewed monthly. Each department head should be examining a listing of all variances for his or her department. If the department is particularly large and a number of managers report to the department director, then the director might look at only an exception report. However, the managers that report to that director would each closely review all variances for their area of the department.

Fixed and Variable Costs

A key element of flexible budget variance analysis is the concept that the flexible budget may differ from the original budget because of a change in volume. However, this assumes that the line-item being evaluated represents a variable cost. If costs are fixed, the amount of resources consumed would not change as a result of a change in activity.

In the case of fixed costs, the original and flexible budgets would be the same, and the volume variance would be zero. Furthermore, in the case of some fixed costs such as rent, it may not be helpful to separate the variance into price and quantity components. Therefore, it may be necessary to evaluate the total variance for the line-item without the aid of subdivision into components for some fixed-cost line-items.

Investigation and Control of Variances

One of the more perplexing aspects of variance analysis is deciding when a variance is large enough to warrant investigation. Should a manager investigate a $100 variance? How about $500? $1,000? How big a variance is too big to tolerate without investigation?

Random, uncontrollable events will cause actual results to vary over and under the budget from month to month. It would be unusual for spending to come out to be exactly the budgeted amount. Therefore, small variances are often ignored.

But how much is small? Unfortunately, there is no general agreement on an answer to this question. Managers must use their skill, judgment, and experience to determine how large a variance represents a potentially important problem that we would need to investigate and that might possibly require corrective action.

Revenue Variances

Up until this point, this chapter has focused on expense variances. Virtually every manager who has budgetary responsibility will need to be able to examine his or her expense variances and determine their causes. Managers may also be called upon to determine why actual revenues differed from budgeted amounts.

Just as with expense variances, it helps little to know the overall variance between the total revenue budgeted for the organization and the actual total revenue. At a minimum, we would want to divide revenues into the various different types of products and services provided. Thus, HOS might want to divide its revenues into those that come from inpatient care and those that come from outpatient treatments. The hospital might want even more detail. For example, it might want to examine revenues for gall bladder surgery, hernia surgery, and heart surgery separately.

The Town of Millbridge might be interested in assessing *revenue variances* related to receipts from the local town real estate taxes separately from variances in the amount of state aid received. Note that revenues and expenses do not necessarily align. For example, we could consider expenses for Millbridge based on salaries and supplies. The revenues, however, are divided by source: real estate taxes versus state aid.

Just as flexible budget variance analysis is useful for examining expense variances, it can be helpful for revenue variances. Suppose that the total revenue HOS received for gall bladder surgery differed from expectations. Why might this have happened? There could be several reasons.

Perhaps there were more gall bladder surgeries than expected, resulting in a volume variance. The hospital would have more revenue from gall bladders than expected because it had more paying patients. The original budget would be the budgeted price per surgery multiplied by the budgeted number of surgeries. In contrast, the flexible budget would be the budgeted price per surgery multiplied by the actual number of surgeries.

Alternatively, the organization may have changed the price it charges for each gall bladder surgery. If the average price for gall bladder surgery is higher or lower than budgeted, that will change the total amount of revenue received for that type of surgery.

There is no quantity variance because there is no comparable concept. The quantity expense variance implies a change in the amount of resource consumed per unit of output. There is no comparable concept on the revenue side. However, it is possible to have a *mix* or *case-mix variance*. Suppose that rather than evaluating the revenue variance for gall bladders, we were interested in looking at the variance related to all surgeries. One possible explanation for a revenue variance would be the mix of patients. There might have been more of the expensive procedures and less of the inexpensive procedures than expected. Thus the total revenue variance for any line-item might be divided into the portion resulting from the volume of patients, the portion resulting from the mix of patients, and the portion resulting from the prices charged.

When we spend more than expected, that is referred to as an unfavorable variance. This makes sense, given that, other things being equal, one thinks of spending more than is budgeted as being unfavorable. The reverse holds true with revenue variances. A higher actual revenue than expected is called a favorable variance, because, other things being equal, one thinks of higher revenues than are budgeted as being favorable. As noted earlier, however, great care is needed in interpreting whether favorable or unfavorable variances are really good or bad for the organization.

Example

For example, suppose that the Hospital for Ordinary Surgery (HOS) had revenue of $339,000 for January, which was below the expected revenue of $350,000. Preliminary investigation has perplexed HOS' managers, as the actual number of surgeries performed was 130, as compared to a budgeted level of 125. Even more disturbing was that revenue fell even though the average revenue per patient had increased for gall bladder surgery, the hospital's most common procedure. Flexible budget analysis can provide additional information about the $11,000 unfavorable revenue variance.

Suppose that HOS performs only two types of surgery: gall bladder and hernia repair. It was expected that 80 percent of the surgeries would be gall bladder and 20 percent would be hernia repair. Assume that HOS expected average revenue for gall bladder cases to be $3,000. There were actually 90 gall bladder patients, and their actual revenue per case averaged $3,100. For hernias, the expected revenue was $2,000 per case, but the actual average revenue was $1,500, and there were 40 cases. This information can be used to calculate volume, mix, and price variances.

The original budget consists of the combined budgeted cost of gall bladder and hernia patients. That could be calculated as follows:

	Budgeted Volume	×	Budgeted Mix	×	Budgeted Price	
Gall Bladders:	125	×	80%	×	$3,000	= $300,000
Hernias:	125	×	20%	×	$2,000	= 50,000
						$350,000

The flexible budget is calculated based on the actual volume and the budgeted mix and price, as follows:

	Actual Volume	×	Budgeted Mix	×	Budgeted Price	
Gall Bladders:	130	×	80%	×	$3,000	= $312,000
Hernias:	130	×	20%	×	$2,000	= 52,000
						$364,000

The volume variance can be calculated by comparing the original and flex budgets as follows:

Original Budget:	$350,000
Flex Budget:	364,000
Volume Variance	= $ 14,000 F

The increase in volume is responsible for a favorable volume variance of $14,000. Note that for revenues, an increase in volume results in a favorable variance.

Next we can create a Volume & Mix Adjusted (VMA) Budget that indicates what we would have expected revenue to be, if we had known both the actual number of patients and the actual mix of patients.

	Actual Volume	×	Actual Mix	×	Budgeted Price	
Gall Bladders:	130	×	(90÷130)	×	$3,000	= $270,000
Hernias:	130	×	(40÷130)	×	$2,000	= 80,000
						$350,000

In calculating the VMA Budget, the actual volume, actual mix, and budgeted price information is used. The actual mix consists of the specific volume for each product or service divided by the total volume. Comparing the Flex Budget to the VMA Budget provides a measure of the variance due to the change in patient mix.

Flex Budget:	$364,000
VMA Budget:	350,000
Mix Variance =	$ 14,000 U

The mix has shifted in a way that lowers revenue. There are now 90 gall bladder patients out of a total of 130 patients. That is 69 percent (90 ÷ 130 × 100% = 69%), which is lower than the expected 80 percent. This means that there is a greater than expected proportion of patients that are the lower revenue hernia patients rather than the higher revenue gall bladder patients.

The last variance to be calculated is the price variance, which compares the VMA Budget to the actual results. The actual revenues are:

	Actual Volume	×	Actual Mix	×	Actual Price	
Gall Bladders:	130	×	(90÷130)	×	$3,100	= $279,000
Hernias:	130	×	(40÷130)	×	$1,500	= 60,000
						$339,000

Comparing the VMA Budget to the actual result,

VMA Budget:	$350,000
Actual:	339,000
Price Variance =	$ 11,000 U

Even though the average revenue per gall bladder case rose, and most cases were gall bladder procedures, the sharp decrease in hernia repair revenue per patient resulted in an unfavorable $11,000 price variance. In fact, the shift toward a greater proportion of hernia patients, combined with the lower than expected revenue per hernia patient, more than offset the favorable $14,000 volume variance. The $14,000 F volume variance less the $14,000 U mix variance less the $11,000 U price variance, results in a total $11,000 U revenue variance. The hospital is unwise to base its revenue expectations simply on overall volume of patients or the price of its most common procedure.

Performance Measures

This discussion largely centers on the evaluation of input variances. We have been attempting to assess, for example, why more money was spent on labor than expected. Variance analysis can also be used to focus the manager's attention on variations in accomplishments. (Recall the discussion of performance measurement earlier in this chapter.)

Perhaps a city government water agency has budgeted a certain allowable level of contaminants in the drinking water. The agency would certainly want to compare the actual levels to the budgeted levels and investigate any significant variations. Similarly, if a school system has budgeted certain levels of performance on standardized tests, part of the routine variance analysis undertaken by the school system should be examination of how much the results differed from expectations and why.

ETHICS

Having a public service mission does not guarantee that all behavior within an organization will be ethical. In late 1997, Congressional hearings disclosed widespread abuses at the Internal Revenue Service (IRS). The IRS was accused of unethical behavior by many taxpayers. Several years earlier top management at United Way was accused of improper spending. Overcharging for services, charging for services that have not been provided, paying bribes or improper referral fees, and similar practices are not new. Certainly, these activities have occurred in some organizations. And, realistically, it is likely that they will continue to occur. However, we must be careful to avoid thinking that such activities are acceptable. "Everyone does it" is just as incorrect a generalization as "no one cheats." Both represent extreme and unrealistic positions.

A survey of most managers in public, health, and not-for-profit organizations would likely show that they strongly support ethical behavior. Yet, due to limited resources, managers of such organizations often come under severe financial pressures. These pressures can lead financial managers to make improper decisions in an effort to help their organizations. Further, there have been instances in which people let the opportunity for personal financial gain cause them to engage in unethical activities, including fraud and embezzlement.

Ethical behavior may be clear-cut in the abstract, but in practice it often becomes hard to draw the line between the clearly acceptable and the clearly unacceptable. Things that are within the letter of the law may not be in the spirit of the law. Things that may be correct in principle may not be legal. This section discusses some of the ethical behavior expectations various financial management organizations have for managers. These expectations are based on a code of ethics designed to help managers deal with some difficult realities that confront them.

A Code of Ethics

Various organizations promulgate codes of ethics for their members. One such organization is the Government Finance Officers Association (GFOA). Another is the Institute for Management Accountants (IMA).[7] The GFOA "is a professional organization of public officials united to enhance and promote the professional management of governmental financial resources by identifying, developing and advancing fiscal strategies, policies and practices for the public benefit."[8] The IMA's membership consists primarily of management accountants. Its members work in the area of financial management within organizations, including both the private and public sectors. Many readers of this text will become managers in areas aside

---

[7] Formerly called the National Accountants Association (NAA).
[8] Government Finance Officers Association (GFOA), Code of Professional Ethics.

from financial management. Nevertheless, it is beneficial to get a perspective on ethics from several of the financial management professional associations.

We first discuss the basic framework of the IMA's code. It can provide useful guidance as one is faced by ethical dilemmas in carrying out management activities. One should not expect a code of ethics to provide specific answers to all ethical issues questions that arise. However, it can provide a foundation of principles upon which to make decisions. The IMA code has four primary elements: competence, confidentiality, integrity, and objectivity.[9] Although the IMA code is discussed here, it is done so only to provide an example. Other associations may have a code that applies more directly to the types of problems and dilemmas faced in different areas.

COMPETENCE The IMA code indicates an expectation that people must be competent in their job; it is unethical to be incompetent. At first, this seems to be very strange indeed. How can it be unethical behavior to not be very good at what you do? After all, you are today what you were when you were hired. The employer knew what it was getting.

However, things change. The IMA code really addresses the need for professionals to maintain their competency over time. To some extent, this means managers must find ways to ensure that their skills are not eroding. It also means that as the field changes a professional has an obligation to keep up-to-date. An individual's knowledge and skills should be constantly developing and improving.

A second part of competence relates to compliance. Ethical behavior requires managers to comply with all laws, regulations, and industry standards. Illegal is unethical. This appears to be one of the easier standards to understand. Unfortunately, ethical dilemmas arise because choices are not always as clear-cut as one might hope: What should one do if one does not agree with a law? What if one feels that the law is foolish or morally wrong? The guidance of the IMA code is that rather than break the law, a professional should employ expert help to find a legal way to achieve the ends he or she believes are morally justified.

The IMA code also calls upon its members to generate reports that are understandable and comprehensive. They should be based on appropriate analysis using dependable information. Many existing non–financial managers in public service organizations, if they knew about this clause, would immediately say that there is not an ethical financial manager in their organization. That reaction, although part in jest, contains enough seriousness to warrant some thought. Many reports in public service organizations are not easily understandable, not comprehensive, or not based on reasoned analysis. Yet, those goals are important enough to the overall success of the organization that the accountants' own code considers it unethical to not at least make an effort to achieve them.

CONFIDENTIALITY A second major section of the IMA code relates to the issue of confidentiality. Information that is confidential must be protected. It is unethical to disclose confidential information unless properly authorized by the organization or legally required to do so. Access to confidential information can sometimes be abused to create personal financial gains. The code specifically prohibits use, or even the appearance of use, of confidential information to make an illegal or unethical gain either for oneself or for others.

INTEGRITY Integrity is a major focus of the code. Ethical behavior bans conflicts of interest, inappropriate influence, bribes, working against the organization, failure to disclose personal skill inadequacies, and failure to disclose important information. Whether conflicts of interest are real or just perceived, they should be avoided. When they do arise, they should be disclosed and actions taken to resolve the conflict.

---

[9] National Association of Accountants, Statements on Management Accounting, New York, N.Y.: June 1, 1983.

Inappropriate influence relates to the fact that one should not do anything to keep another person from acting in an ethical manner. A common example of this is an attempt to suppress a subordinate from disclosing something that might show the manager or organization in an unfavorable light.

Bribes and other payments for influence are clearly attempts to gain undue influence. Accepting any gift, whether monetary or just a favor, should be avoided if it might influence, or even appear to influence, one's actions.

Working against the organization should be a problem we do not have to worry about, if we have developed an adequate MCS, as discussed earlier in this chapter. We should try to motivate everyone to want to work in the interests of the organization. In reality, however, many organizations fail to consider adequately the concerns of their employees. As a result, employees at times feel a desire to get back at the organization for a real or perceived injury that the organization has done to them.

Well, revenge may be sweet, but when carried out against one's employer, it is also considered unethical. Any activities that hinder the organization from attaining its legal and ethical goals are unethical. Conversely, people must guard against the organization influencing them to do things that are not ethical. If an action is inappropriate, it is not unethical to hinder the organization in its attempt to carry out that action. Many federal statutes now protect whistle-blowers.

Ethical behavior requires a person to disclose his or her limitations. Although many believe that professionals should be expert in all technical aspects of a subject, that is clearly an unrealistic expectation. A simple way to make this point is simply to ask skeptical supervisors whether they would want their primary care physician to perform neurosurgery on them. This quickly helps to differentiate the role of the well-trained skilled professional from that of the highly technical specialist. Very few can be specialists in all areas, and it is inappropriate to hold oneself out to be expert in areas that are beyond one's expertise.

The final issue related to integrity involves being the bearer of bad news. Despite the tendency to kill the messenger, the IMA code requires managers to communicate complete, accurate information and honest judgments and opinions, whether they report favorable outcomes or not.

OBJECTIVITY   Information should be communicated in a way that is fair, objective, and relevant. Unfortunately, one person may see fairness in a different way than another person. Therefore, intent is critical. It is inappropriate to present material in a way that is technically accurate but might give the user an incorrect impression. Further, managers should make every attempt to provide the information that is relevant to the decision at hand.

The GFOA Code

The IMA code provides just one perspective on the ethical issues faced by managers. The GFOA code has considerable overlap with the IMA code, but also introduces its own elements as well.

The first two sections of the GFOA code provide an indication of the public service focus of GFOA members. The first section notes that "government finance officers shall demonstrate and be dedicated to the highest ideals of honor and integrity in all public and personal relationships, to merit the respect, trust and confidence of governing officials, other public officials, employees, and of the public."[10] The second section focuses on the responsibility government finance officers have in their role as public officials.

---

[10] GFOA, Op. Cit.

Although those sections differ substantially from the IMA code, there is also substantial similarity. The GFOA code discusses the need for professional development (see "Competence" discussion of the IMA code), integrity (see "Integrity" section of the IMA code), and avoiding conflict of interest (see "Integrity" section of IMA code). Other codes of ethics may add other elements relevant to the primary group to whom the code is directed.

Gray Areas

Formal codes of ethics, such as the IMA's code and that of the GFOA, can be a useful foundation for developing a pattern of ethical behavior. Unfortunately, managers are frequently caught in gray areas. A code cannot anticipate all possible occurrences. Just because something is not explicitly forbidden does not make it ethical. One's own judgment and common sense must be used. However, the principles encompassed by formal codes of ethical behavior can provide managers with at least some guidance when they realize that common sense alone may not provide a clear answer to an ethical issue.

SAFEGUARDING RESOURCES

MCSs, performance measurement, and ethical behavior are three important elements of accountability and control. They are critical elements of internal control. Organizations need to implement systems that will encourage and motivate their employees to achieve their goals. They should find appropriate ways to measure the organization's performance. They should also hire ethical people and create a culture that rewards ethical behavior and clearly condemns unethical behavior. Unfortunately, even if all of these approaches are adopted, there may still be some employees who will try to achieve personal gains at the expense of the organization. To protect the resources of the organization, additional elements of an internal control system are needed.

As the definition of internal control provided early in the chapter indicates, internal control is a broad topic relating to successful implementation of management's plans. Internal control includes actions to ensure efficiency and effectiveness of operations, compliance with all relevant laws, and reliable reporting of financial results.[11] As part of the broad goal of achieving efficiency and effectiveness, internal control works to ensure that assets are safeguarded. This is accomplished through having an appropriate control environment, risk assessment, control activities, communication, and monitoring.[12]

Internal control systems include a set of *accounting controls* and a set of *administrative controls.* Accounting controls are often referred to as preventive, or before-the-fact, controls. Although a primary purpose of accounting controls is to prevent employee misuse of assets (such as embezzlement and fraud), they also attempt to prevent suboptimal use of resources where no wrongful intent is involved. Administrative controls tend to be after-the-fact. They are often referred to as feedback systems. After a loss is incurred, administrative controls help the organization take corrective actions to avoid additional losses in the future. This is done by making adjustments based on observed problems in the past.

For example, a system of budgeted or "standard" costs for each type of patient at HOS would be an accounting control. Having a projection of what it should cost to treat each type of patient provides employees with a target to work toward. This before-the-fact information tends to prevent unlimited spending. In contrast, variance reports compare actual results with expectations, and they are administrative controls.

---

[11] Taylor, pp. 1–17.
[12] Ibid., pp. 1–17.

Accounting and administrative controls are coordinated to minimize avoidable losses. According to the American Institute of Certified Public Accountants (AICPA), control should include four key areas:

1. There should be a system of management authorization, and key activities should not be able to occur without such authorization.
2. Once authorization occurs, financial transactions should be recorded in a manner to allow for preparation of financial statements and to allow for adequate accountability for assets.
3. Access to assets should be limited to those having the authorization of management.
4. Existing assets are compared with assets listed in the organization's records from time to time, and differences are reconciled.[13]

Elements of a Control System

There are a number of elements of an internal control system. One of the most important of these is having an audit trail. Horngren and Foster also discuss the importance of having reliable personnel with clear responsibilities, separation of duties, proper authorization, adequate documents, proper procedures, physical safeguards, bonding, vacations and rotation of duties, independent checks, and cost-benefit analysis.[14] Each of these elements is discussed subsequently.

AUDIT TRAIL   The first element in accounting control is to establish a clear *audit trail*. An audit trail refers to the ability to trace each transaction in an accounting system back to its source. For example, suppose that the Town of Millbridge spent $5,000,000 on public works for the year. That might seem to be an inordinately large amount. Perhaps the budget for public works was only $4,000,000. There must be some way to track backward to see why so much money was spent—25 percent more than budgeted. The $5,000,000 total public works spending should be supported by documents that allow one to trace the spending back to its various components.

For example, within the accounting records of the town, we might find that Millbridge spent $1,000,000 on snow removal, $2,000,000 on garbage collection, and $2,000,000 on road repair. Suppose that the snow removal and garbage collection costs were exactly what we might expect. However, the road repair was double the budget. An audit trail should allow a manager to trace back to see what the $2,000,000 was spent on. The manager might look at a detailed listing of the various major road repair expenditures. These might consist of $100,000 for normal pothole repair, $900,000 for scheduled repaving projects, and $1,000,000 for emergency bridge repair. It turns out that a bridge unexpectedly collapsed. Since the bridge was the only way to connect two major areas of the town, an emergency ordinance was passed authorizing immediate repair, even though the cost was not in the original capital budget.

By having a clear audit trail, we are able to trace back to why expenditures exceeded originally authorized amounts. The existence of the audit trail serves as a preventive device. If an unscrupulous employee knew that we did not have good audit trails, he or she might feel safer in misappropriating money. That employee might assume that we would never be able to backtrack and find where the money went. When people recognize that all spending is carefully documented and that an audit trail will allow the organization to retrace the steps

---

[13] Auditing Standards Executive Committee, American Institute of Certified Public Accountants. *Statement on Auditing Standards No.1—Codification of Auditing Standards and Procedures.* New York, N.Y.: AICPA, 1973, p. 20.
[14] Charles T. Horngren and George Foster. *Cost Accounting: A Managerial Emphasis*, 6th ed. Upper Saddle River, N.J.: Prentice Hall, 1987, pp. 919–22.

in the accounting process back to the source of unusual expenditures, they may be inhibited from inappropriate spending.

The audit trail requires documentation of how financial transactions flow from the initial entry of the transaction to the ultimate summary report. In order for an audit trail to be effective as a tool for control, the trail must be regularly used to identify and examine discrepancies or unusual spending patterns. If employees knew that a trail was kept but investigations never took place utilizing that information, it would not have as strong a preventive influence as if it were used regularly.

Although audit trails are very helpful, they are not adequate by themselves. Clever individuals might still be able to find ways to misappropriate resources. Careless individuals might still make errors that waste resources. Therefore, an internal control system requires additional elements, as discussed in the remaining sections of this chapter.

RELIABLE PERSONNEL   All people, even those who are both well-intentioned and careful, make mistakes. Internal control systems install checks and balances to try to catch and correct such mistakes. Some of these approaches are discussed next. In the end, however, we must rely on fallible people to carry out the elements of the system. The organization must start its internal control system by having a group of employees that are both capable and trustworthy. In addition, employees must be capably supervised.

SEPARATION OF FUNCTIONS   One of the most common elements of an internal control system is separation of functions. For example, the individual at Meals for the Homeless who approves bills for payment should not be the same person who writes checks. And the person who writes checks should not be the same person who signs the checks. In small organizations, it is difficult to accomplish appropriate separation of duties. However, even if there are too few employees to attain total separation, some degree of control is possible. For example, the treasurer from the board of trustees can be the person who signs the checks.

The benefit of such separation is that each person may catch a problem that is missed by another. If a bill is not correct, the person approving payment should catch it. If not, the person writing the check for payment may find the problem. Even if neither of them finds the problem, the person signing the check may raise a question about the payment, which leads to discovery of the problem. This system of separation is also an especially powerful tool for reducing the potential of embezzlement.

If the same person authorizes payments, writes checks, and signs them, that person has the ability to steal money with a minimum likelihood of detection. By separating functions, such activity becomes more likely to be discovered and therefore less likely to occur.

Another example of separation is keeping operations separate from accounting. For example, HOS has a central supply department that stores all of the supply items for the hospital. This department should not be the one responsible for making periodic checks of the amount of supplies on hand (called "taking an inventory"). The members of the department have access to these supply items, and there is the potential of theft. If the same people count the supplies, they can falsify records to hide the theft. If they know that independent individuals from elsewhere in the organization will count the supplies, they know there is a possibility of the theft being discovered.

Note, however, discovery is not a primary goal of the internal control system; prevention is. By letting people know that theft is likely to be discovered, it is discouraged and less likely to occur.

However, any control system can be defeated. Separation of functions will not protect resources if several people collude to steal from the organization. If the person approving payment, the person writing checks, and the person signing checks all agree to steal money and share it, it will be hard for the control system to prevent such actions. That is why having reliable employees is one of the most important elements of a control system.

PROPER AUTHORIZATION   Another control element is to require all spending to be supported by proper authorization. A system of authorization for spending helps the organization to set spending policies and then adhere to them. For example, a policy decision might be that all air travel is done in coach. But the organization may have thousands of employees. What is to stop one of them from buying and using a first-class air ticket and charging the organization for the higher first-class airfare?

Organizations accomplish this by establishing formal authorization mechanisms. Expenditures will only be reimbursed if they have received the proper authorization. This can be stifling if every person has to go through an elaborate process to get authorization to spend any amount on any item. Therefore, some items can qualify for *general authorization*. General authorization is a standing approval of certain spending. Items under a certain dollar limit or for certain purposes may fall under that general authorization. For example, air travel at the coach airfare rate for valid business reasons may fall under general authorization. General authorization may contain limits and prohibitions.

Items that cannot be acquired using general authorization require *specific authorization*. Specific authorization would require an employee to get written permission to override the general authorization policies.

Proper authorization is required for many things in addition to spending. For example, some employees can sign contracts committing the organization to provide specific services. Some employees can represent the organization with respect to legal matters. The ultimate source of authority rests with the board of trustees or directors. The board provides letters of delegation to senior managers, providing them with the authority to undertake a variety of functions on behalf of the organization. These senior managers can, in turn, delegate authority to specific individuals that report to them. In the case of governments, the bounds of authority are often clearly set by law and regulation, in addition to management delegation.

ADEQUATE DOCUMENTATION   The audit trail discussed earlier requires an ability to provide detailed documentation of what was spent and why it was spent. Documents, however, do not have to be on paper. The computer age is pushing us more and more toward electronic record-keeping.

For example, at one time, organizations maintained files with all canceled checks. If a discrepancy arose regarding whether a payment had been made, the organization could find the canceled check in its files and use the check to prove that payment had been made. More and more often, payments are made by electronic transfer rather than by check. In many organizations, for example, very few payroll checks are issued. Instead, payments to employees are deposited directly into the employees' bank accounts.

In light of such dramatic changes, it is essential that organizations carefully think out what documentation will be available to them to allow them to trace back, explain, and prove that transactions have occurred. It is also important to recognize that loss of electronic data (such as the loss or erasure of a computer's hard drive) can be as devastating as a fire that destroys all of an organization's paper records.

PROPER PROCEDURES   Internal control systems rely heavily on standard operating procedures, often in the form of a procedures manual. Doing things "by the book" may seem rigid to some employees, but if we follow clearly documented procedures, we are likely to reduce the number of errors. We will spend less time correcting those errors. Less time spent doing various activities will mean that money is saved.

By the same token, the "book" should be current and relevant. Internal control procedures should be reviewed and updated regularly. New approaches for increasing efficiency and protecting resources should be adopted.

PHYSICAL SAFEGUARDS   Common sense dictates the need for physical safeguards. Cash and blank checks should obviously be kept locked when not in use. Backup copies of computer records should be maintained in a separate location. Controls should be put in place to protect valuable inventory.

BONDING, VACATIONS, AND ROTATION OF DUTIES   If people are in positions where it would be possible for them to steal significant amounts from the organization, it is appropriate to bond them. *Bonding* means that the organization purchases insurance to protect itself against theft by the employee. Often organizations, on the grounds of having carefully hired reliable personnel, fail to bond key employees. Although this does not usually lead to financial loss, in rare cases, it does. Organizations must consider bonding, much as they would consider fire insurance. You do not expect your building to burn down—you may even have a sprinkler system, but just in case of an unexpected catastrophe, you also purchase fire insurance.

Bonding is a good administrative control. Administrative controls work best when combined with accounting controls. What preventive accounting controls go hand in hand with the bonding of employees? One approach is mandated vacations and rotation of staff. Many types of defalcation require constant supervision by the embezzler. If money is being stolen from the accounts receivable cash stream, checks received later are often used to cover the cash that has been taken.

By requiring vacations, we move another employee into each role periodically. That provides an opportunity for discrepancies to be uncovered. Similarly, a formal rotation system establishes that no employee will be doing exactly the same job year after year. If it is well known that all employees must take vacations and that rotation in duties will occur from time to time with little advance notice, these controls can serve not only to discover problems but to prevent them as well.

PERFORMANCE AUDITS   It is important to have an independent check of the organization's activities. The employees of an organization should review and evaluate their internal control systems regularly. We need to attempt to continuously improve. Such improvement can occur in the reliability of controls as well as in reduction of the cost of internal controls. In addition, however, internal auditors should conduct *performance audits,* and outside auditors should review the control system as well.

Performance audits, sometimes called operational audits, include two subcategories: *economy and efficiency audits* and *program audits.* Economy and efficiency audits are reviews that determine if the organization is acquiring, protecting, and using its resources efficiently. Essentially, they check for waste. Program audits check for effectiveness. They determine whether the organization's programs are accomplishing their objectives.

Larger organizations have internal audit departments. These departments work year-round on reviewing the financial and operating systems of the organization. They seek out weaknesses in controls that might allow for theft of resources. They also try to improve systems to reduce the chances that errors will occur in the recording or reporting of financial information. At the same time, internal auditors focus their performance audits on trying to find ways that the organization can better achieve its mission. This will at times require them to evaluate the role and functioning of each unit or department of the organization.

Outside independent auditors also serve a crucial role. Independent auditors have the benefit of experience from reviewing control systems in many different organizations. As a result, these external auditors can often offer suggestions for improvement. From an outsider's perspective, they are also more likely to see flaws in the system that most insiders might not notice.

Independent auditors also perform checks to ensure that the organization reports its financial results in accordance with a set of Generally Accepted Accounting Principles (GAAP). This function and GAAP are discussed further in Chapter 9.

COST-EFFECTIVENESS ANALYSIS Internal control systems can be simple or elaborate. The more careful we are to ensure that the organization's systems catch all potential problems, the more it costs. Systems should be cost-effective. The organization should not spend more on the systems than they are worth. For example, one would not spend $1,000 to prevent someone from possibly stealing $10.

We should also be aware that no matter how careful we are with our control systems, fraud, embezzlements, and some inefficiencies can still take place. Horngren and Foster sum up this issue well:

> No framework for internal control is perfect in the sense that it can prevent some shrewd individual from "beating the system" either by outright embezzlement or by producing inaccurate records. The task is not total prevention of fraud, nor is it implementation of operating perfection; rather the task is designing a cost-effective tool that will help achieve efficient operations and reduce temptation.[15]

The Sarbanes-Oxley Act

A number of scandals from 1998 through 2002 led to a close re-examination of corporate governance and internal control. Perhaps the most notable was the Enron bankruptcy in 2001. However, the AHERF health care system bankruptcy in 1998 and problems at United Way indicate that the not-for-profit and health sectors are not exempt from governance problems. In 2002 the Public Company Accounting Reform and Investor Protection Act, commonly referred to as the Sarbanes-Oxley Act (SOX), was passed. One primary focus of the act is to create more oversight over the public accounting firms that audit organizations. However, the law also creates a greater level of responsibility for managers and board members.

Although most of SOX directly applies only to publicly traded for-profit organizations, there are two elements that apply directly to all organizations, including not-for-profit organizations. These concern whistle-blower protection and general documentation. "SOX requires all organizations, including non-profits, to establish a means to collect, retain, and resolve claims regarding accounting, internal accounting controls, and auditing matters. The system must allow such concerns to be submitted anonymously. SOX provides significant protections to whistle-blowers, and severe penalties to those who retaliate against them."[16] In addition to these whistle-blower provisions, there are also severe sanctions (including up to 10 years in prison) for inadequate internal documentation. Managers must consider a number of factors in setting up a documentation policy, including:

- What documents and records should be preserved and why?
- Are the documents paper-only or are electronic files included? Which ones?
- What about e-mail and instant messaging?

---

[15] Ibid., p. 922.
[16] Peggy M. Jackson and Toni E. Fogarty. *Sarbanes-Oxley for Nonprofits: A Guide to Building Competitive Advantage*. Hoboken, N.J.: John Wiley & Sons, 2005, p. 76.

- What are the expectations about the way in which documents are stored or archived and the ability to retrieve documents?
- How long are you supposed to keep these documents?
- Is there a protocol for disposing of documents once their storage time has elapsed?
- When should you not destroy materials?
- How can you make sure that everyone in the nonprofit—staff and volunteers—understands and adheres to these requirements?
- What will happen if your nonprofit is in violation?"[17]

The answers to these questions will depend on the specific situation of the organization. The managers and board members must work together to make a policy for both whistle-blowing and documentation that is in compliance with the law and is reasonable given the specific situation of the organization. There is also great pressure on not-for-profit organizations to comply with many other provisions of SOX as well. Regulators, insurers, banks, the bond market, and the public are all interested in responsible use of resources by public service organizations. Therefore they are likely to convince not-for-profit organizations to undertake the extra effort that SOX requires.

In addition to the SOX requirements with respect to whistle-blowers and documentation, SOX will typically affect not-for-profit organizations in several principal areas. Jackson and Fogarty note that as a result of SOX, not-for-profit organizations will have to have practices that include:

- a more effective board whose members understand and adhere to their fiduciary obligations and recognize their responsibility in governing the nonprofit;
- higher levels of management and staff accountability;
- effective protocols to ensure that the nonprofit remains in compliance with SOX and nonprofit "industry standards" and addresses future standards;
- better competitive positioning by making known that the nonprofit adheres to the SOX platinum standard in its operating practices;
- greater credibility and ability to recruit high-quality board members and to attract the favorable attention of major donors, foundations, and other funding sources.[18]

There are some specific measures that not-for-profits should undertake as a starting point for implementing SOX provisions. First, the Board of Trustees audit committee will have an enhanced role. Next, key executives of the organization will be required to certify the organization's financial statements. Third, there will be limits on the types of consulting that an organization's auditor can provide to it. Finally, there will be a higher level of manager accountability.

The Board of Trustees' audit committee will have an enhanced role so that it becomes easier to determine if top management is acting inappropriately. The audit committee will retain and supervise the outside auditors so that there is a decreased chance of top management exerting influence over the auditor. Key executives, such as the CEO and CFO, will be excluded from the committee, to reduce their influence over its work, and also so that whistle-blowers will be less inhibited from approaching the committee to report problems. To avoid conflicts of interest, audit committee members will not be allowed to be paid consultants, and audit committees will be required to have some members with financial

---

[17] Ibid., p. 79
[18] Ibid., p. 3

expertise. In the SOX environment, not only are the rules of the Board's audit committee tightened, but the entire expectations about the role of the Board have increased as well. Not-for-profits will have to transition from having Board members who are on the Board solely for their money or their relation to the organization's mission to Board members who prepare for meetings in advance, focus on the finances of the organization, and bring a questioning attitude to Board meetings.

The CEO and CFO of organizations that comply with SOX will have to certify that they have reviewed the annual financial report, that it does not contain any untrue statement of a material fact, and that the statements fairly present the financial condition of the organization. Furthermore, the CEO and CFO will have to certify that internal control systems are in place to ensure awareness of material misinformation, and that any known deficiencies in control, or any known frauds involving key personnel, have been disclosed to both the outside auditors and to the audit committee. As a result of this greater reliance on internal control systems, all organizations, including not-for-profits, are making an effort to upgrade their internal control systems. Managers need to know that they really can rely on their control systems to catch any problems as they arise.

For many not-for-profit organizations, the outside auditor has also served as the primary financial consultant. To try to ensure more independence on the part of the auditor, SOX explicitly lists a number of different types of consulting activities that may not be provided by the accounting firm that is conducting the annual audit of the organization's financial statements. These prohibited areas include bookkeeping, information systems design, appraisal services, actuarial services, internal audit outsourcing, human resources, investment advising, and legal or expert service unrelated to the audit.

Finally, the impact of SOX is to create a higher level of accountability in general for the managers of an organization. Regulations issued in 2003 by the Securities and Exchange Commission, under SOX, require senior managers to certify that they are aware of the internal processes that the organization uses to collect the financial information that is used to prepare the financial statements issued to the public, and of any concerns, issues, or problems that might hamper accurate reporting.

THE FORM 990

Most not-for-profit organizations, exempt from income tax under Internal Revenue Code section 501(a), are required to file an annual information return, the Form 990, usually referred to simply as the organization's 990. Once filed with the Internal Revenue Service, the organization's 990 is a public document and is generally available to the public online from either GuideStar at www.guidestar.org or the National Center for Charitable Statistics at www.nccs.urban.org.

What information is contained in the 990? The form includes information on finances, exempt activities, and governance. The requirements for the form are extensive, asking for information concerning, but not limited to, the organization's mission, program service accomplishments, lobbying and political campaign activities, conflict of interest policy, volunteers, donations, grants, compensation of officers, directors, trustees, key employees, highest compensated employees and independent contractors.

Throughout the 21st century, there has been a growing emphasis on accountability and control. Starting with the 2008 Form 990, substantial revisions were made to data required to complete the 990 in order to enhance the information contained in the reports, providing greater transparency for members of the public scrutinizing the operations of an organization, and a greater ability for the government to ensure compliance with all relevant laws and regulations.

Summary

If an organization is to succeed, it must achieve its plans to the extent possible. Management control systems are used by organizations to motivate their employees to try to achieve those plans. Under management control systems, departments and individual employees are held accountable for their actions and results.

We must also know how we intend to measure results. We can focus on just the revenues and expenses budgeted and the actual revenues and expenses. Or the organization can be more sophisticated and try to assess things such as its efficiency and effectiveness in measuring its overall performance.

Variances arise if actual performance differs, or varies, from expectations. Developing an understanding of why variances have occurred can help the organization avoid undesirable variances in the future.

To keep the organization functioning optimally, it must focus as well on issues related to ethics and the safeguarding of its resources. To achieve planned results, it is vital for personnel to be as ethical and error-free as possible. The elements of a control system are designed to minimize the resource losses that the organization suffers either by intent or by accident.

Preview

Part IV of this book, "Reporting Results," begins in Chapter 9. The focus shifts from implementation and control of plans to the process of recording events, summarizing them, and reporting results. The recording of financial information is done on an ongoing basis throughout the year. The recorded events are summarized and then organized into a reporting form that helps readers understand the current financial status of the organization and how well it has done from a financial standpoint.

These reports help managers to understand the current financial situation of the organization and the financial results of its operations. However, they provide information not only for management of the organization but for outsiders as well. Banks, donors, landlords, vendors, legislators, regulators, unions, bond raters, and others are interested in the performance of public service organizations. Preparation of annual financial reports that will be examined by individuals external to the organization is referred to as financial accounting.

The statement of financial position, commonly referred to as the balance sheet, is the first of the financial statements, and it is the topic of Chapter 9. A balance sheet reports the financial position of the organization at a moment in time—often the end of the fiscal year.

Chapter 10 looks at activity and cash flow statements. Activity statements assess whether the organization has had more or less revenues than expenses or expenditures for the year. Since many organizations use some form of accrual accounting, the operating results reported in the activity statement may differ from the organization's cash flow. Cash flow statements focus on the organization's sources and uses of cash.

There are a variety of special accounting rules for different types of public service organizations. Chapter 11 discusses special financial accounting concerns of not-for-profit and health care organizations. Chapters 12 and 13 consider special financial accounting concerns for governmental organizations.

Key Terms from This Chapter

accounting controls.   Methods and procedures for the authorization of transactions, safeguarding of assets, and accuracy of accounting records.

administrative controls.   The plan of organization (e.g., the formal organization chart indicating who reports to whom) and all methods and procedures that help management plan and control operations.

audit trail.   A set of references that allow a person to trace back through accounting documents to the source of each number used.

balanced scorecard.   A set of measures the organization must focus on to achieve its mission and strategic objectives.

bonding of employees.   Insurance policy protecting the organization against embezzlement and fraud by employees.

case-mix variance. Variance caused because the relative proportions of the amount of each product produced or sold differ from the expected proportions. For example, HOS expected to treat half of its patients as inpatients and half as outpatients, but the actual mix was one-quarter inpatients and three-quarters outpatients.

economy and efficiency audits. Reviews that determine if the organization is acquiring, protecting, and using its resources efficiently.

effectiveness. A measure of the degree to which the organization accomplishes its desired goals.

efficiency. A measure of how close an organization comes to minimizing the amount of resources used to accomplish a result.

efficiency variance. See *quantity variance.*

exception report. A list of only those individual items, such as *variances,* that exceed a specified limit.

favorable variance. Variance in which less was spent than the budgeted amount or more revenues were earned than budgeted.

flexible budget. An operating budget based on varying volume levels.

flexible budget variance. Difference between actual results and the flexible budget.

flexible budget variance analysis. Method of analysis that incorporates the fact that at least part of the total variance for any line item is often the result of changes in the level of activity.

general authorization. A standing approval of spending. Items under a certain dollar limit or for certain purposes may fall under that general authorization.

inputs. Resources used for producing the organization's output (e.g., labor and supplies).

internal control. A system of accounting checks and balances designed to minimize both clerical errors and the possibility of fraud or embezzlement; the process and systems that ensure that decisions made in the organization are appropriate and receive appropriate authorization. Requires a system of *accounting* and *administrative controls.*

key performance indicators (KPI). Measures used in a *balanced scorecard* to assess how well the organization is achieving its goals and objectives.

management control system (MCS). Complete set of policies and procedures designed to keep operations going according to plan.

mix variance. See *case-mix variance.*

outcomes. The results that the organization achieves.

outputs. The number of units of service provided. For example, the number of meals served.

performance audits. Review of the organization's operations, consisting of *economy and efficiency audits* and *program audits.*

price variance. Portion of the total variance for any line-item that is caused by spending a different amount per unit of resource than had been anticipated (e.g., higher or lower salary rates or higher or lower supply prices).

program audits. Reviews of the organization's operations to check for effectiveness. They determine whether the organization's programs are accomplishing their objectives.

quantity variance. Portion of the total variance for any line-item that is caused by using more or less input per unit of output (e.g., patient day) than had been budgeted.

rate variance. Price variance that relates to labor resources. It is typically the hourly rate that has varied from expectations; see also *price variance.*

responsibility accounting. Attempt to measure financial outcomes and assign those outcomes to the person or department responsible for them.

revenue variances. Assessment of how much of the variance between expected and actual revenues results from changes in the total demand in a given geographic region, an organization's share of that total demand, its mix of products or services, and the prices for each class of product or service.

specific authorization. Requirement that a person get written permission to override general authorization policies.

total variance. Sum of the *price, quantity,* or *mix* and *volume variances;* the difference between the actual results and the original budgeted amount.

triple bottom line accounting. Performance measurement approach that includes not only financial performance, but also environmental and social performance.

unfavorable variance. Variance in which more was spent than the budgeted amount or revenues were less than the budgeted amount.

use variance. Another name for the quantity variance; so called because the quantity variance focuses on how much of a resource has been used; see also *quantity variance.*

variance. Difference between the budget and the actual results.

variance analysis. Comparison of actual results as compared with the budget, followed by investigation to determine why the variances occurred.

volume & quantity adjusted budget. A budget that indicates the spending that would have

been anticipated if one had known the actual volume of output and quantity of input that would occur.

volume variance. Amount of the variance in any line-item that is caused simply by the fact that the workload level has changed.

Questions for Discussion

8-1. What is a management control system? What is it compared to in the chapter?

8-2. To what extent is the role of responsibility accounting to assign the blame for poor past performance?

8-3. Do managers tend to motivate their staff by using a "carrot" or a "stick" approach?

8-4. Discuss the four main elements of the Institute of Management Accountants' code of ethics.

8-5. What is an internal control system?

8-6. What are accounting and administrative controls?

8-7. Describe the elements of an internal control system.

8-8. What are some of the principal impacts that the Sarbanes-Oxley Act is likely to have on not-for-profit organizations that decide to follow the provision of the law?

8-9. Which of the following is *not* a component of an internal control system:[19]
    a. adequate documentation
    b. audit trail
    c. separation of duties
    d. none of the above are components of internal control
    e. a, b, and c, are all components of an internal control system

8-10. Why are variances calculated?

8-11. How can outcomes be measured?

8-12. Distinguish between efficiency and effectiveness.

8-13. Why is it that variances are not analyzed by the finance department of the organization?

8-14. If we know that a variance is the result of an uncontrollable price increase for a supply item that we must have, do we need to investigate and make a report regarding the variance? Why or why not?

8-15. Do volume increases that lead to spending increases cause financial problems for organizations?

8-16. What is the essential issue upon which flexible budget variance analysis is based?

8-17. What are the primary variance categories under flexible budget variance analysis? Discuss each.

8-18. What are some common causes of variances?

8-19. What is the aggregation problem in variance reporting?

8-20. What is meant by exception reporting?

8-21. Will all line items have a volume variance?

8-22. Should all variances be investigated?

Problems

8-23. (Control Systems) Pam Crawford is the vice president of the HMO of Millbridge. The organization bills and collects premiums from employers for their employees that are enrolled as members of the HMO. In turn, it receives bills from hospitals and physicians for care they have given to its members. Pam is in charge of optimizing the use of resources and safeguarding the resources of the HMO. She knows that if anything goes wrong (e.g., waste of resources, embezzlement), she will be held responsible.

Therefore, she has called you in as an expert consultant in the area of accountability and control.

Pam has asked you to recommend specific procedures and policies for enhancing the internal controls for the organization. Write a one-page memo to Pam Crawford identifying policies and procedures that she should consider adopting at the HMO of Millbridge.

8-24. Answer the following questions about variance analysis.
    1. Variances are differences between _____ and _____ revenues or expenses.
    2. The three factors involved in variance analysis are: _____, _____, and _____.

[19] This question was written by Dwight Denison.

8-25. Weteachum Elementary school spent $90,000 for textbooks for the Fall 2009 semester. They had expected to have a total enrollment of 400 students who would each have needed 4 books at a cost of $55 each. What is their textbook expense variance? Is it favorable or unfavorable? Why?

8-26. We-Rescue-Dogs Kennel had a labor cost budget of $100,000 for the year. They expected their staff costs related to grooming, feeding, walking, etc. to vary in direct proportion with the number of dogs, based on an hourly rate of $20 for staff, and a need for 10 hours of staff time per dog (before the dogs were adopted). In their budget for the year, they planned on rescuing 500 dogs. It turned out that they rescued 640 dogs for the year. The staff average cost turned out to be just $16 per hour. Staff were paid for a total of 6,000 hours. What is their total labor variance? Was it favorable or unfavorable? Why?

Did the number of dogs rescued result in a favorable or unfavorable volume variance? (You do not have to calculate the flexible variance.)

Did the number of hours of labor actually consumed for each dog cause a favorable or unfavorable variance? (You do not have to calculate the flexible variance.)

8-27. Millbridge Township tries to keep tight control over the costs of the municipal court system. Since the town is small, its courts only operate a few days a week, and they get by largely with part-time workers. Last month it was expected that court stenographers would cost $25,000, but they actually cost $30,000, which is 20% more than the budgeted amount. The municipal judge has argued that the bench heard many more cases than expected, and this caused the increase. The director of the town's budget office feels that a 20% variance is unreasonable. As an analyst for the budget office, you have been asked to explain the variance. Your investigation shows that it was expected that there would be 125 trials, stenographers would be paid $20 per hour, and each trial would take an average of 10 hours. Actually, there were 150 trials, lasting 8 hours each, on average, and stenographers earned $25 per hour. Calculate the volume, quantity, and rate variances, and provide some possible explanations for each.

8-28. The fire department expected to spend $100,000 in April. Actually, it spent $108,680. The department thought it would pay each member of its team of firefighters $25 per hour. However, it paid them each $26 per hour on average. The department expected that the team of firefighters would work a total of 4,000 hours and fight 100 fires. Of course, many hours the firefighters are on duty in the station house between fires. Those hours are considered to be worked and the firefighters are paid for those hours. The actual results were 4,180 hours worked by the team of firefighters and 110 fires fought by the department. What was the total variance? What were the rate (or price), quantity, and volume variances? Which variances were favorable and which were unfavorable? Use either the approach from the chapter or from Appendix 8-A to solve.

8-29. Donate Your Vehicle (DYV) is a charity that receives donations of old cars and converts them into cash to be used for various charitable purposes. DYV budgeted receipt of 300 cars, but actually received one-third more than expected. They sold the cars for $2,700 each, which was 10 percent below the budgeted price. What was the total revenue variance? Was it favorable or unfavorable? What are the two types of subvariances that caused the total variance?

8-30. Assume that you are the nursing administrator for a medical group that expects a severe outbreak of the flu this winter. You hire additional staff to treat patients and administer shots. Your special project budget was for 1,000 hours of part-time nurses' services at $40 per hour, for a total cost of $40,000. It was expected that these nurses would treat 2,000 patients. After the flu season was over, it turned out that the total spent on part-time nurses was $50,000. The nurses worked 1,200 hours and 2,600 patients were treated. Calculate the variances. Was the overall result favorable or unfavorable? Use either the approach from the chapter or from Appendix 8-A to solve.

8-31. Using the information from Problem 8-30, assume that the nursing administrator expected 400 patients for flu shots and 1,600 for flu treatment. The medical group typically charges $50 for a flu shot and $80 for treating a flu patient. Actually, the group had 1,200 patients who received flu shots and 1,400 who had the flu and received treatment. On average, it was able to collect $55 per flu shot and $70 per flu patient. Compute the volume, mix, and price revenue variances. How did things turn out for the group considering just revenues? How did they turn out from a profit perspective? Use either the approach from the chapter or from Appendix 8-A to solve.

8-32. Dr. Eger is a physician who operates on two different types of patients. He has been pressing the Hospital for Ordinary Surgery (HOS) for more operating-room time. HOS is busy and would have to turn away other surgeons if it complies. Eger claims that he has become so efficient lately that the HOS cannot afford to refuse him. As evidence of his improved efficiency, he points out that in August he operated on 18 patients. The total cost of treating the patients was $129,100. In September, he also operated on 18 patients. The total cost of treating the patients was only $127,000. According to Dr. Eger, he has generated a total savings of $2,100.

Your investigation determines that in August, he treated 7 type X patients with an average cost of

$4,300 and 11 type Y patients with an average cost of $9,000. In September he treated 8 type X patients and 10 type Y patients. Costs in September for his patients were $5,000 for type X and $8,700 for type Y. Although the August cost for type X patients had risen, Eger points out that costs for the higher-volume, higher-cost type Y patients had fallen.

Develop a case-mix variance and a cost variance so we can better understand the impact on HOS of the changes in Dr. Eger's practice from August to September. What other information would be of interest in this particular case?

8-33. Joy Becket is the director of Eyeglasses for the Poor (EP). EP receives donations of eyeglasses and recycles them for use by the nearsighted needy around the world. Sometimes the eyeglass frames are expensive designer frames that can be sold to raise operating funds for the organization. Joy is concerned that EP's resources are not adequately safeguarded. This problem is compounded by the fact that there are relatively few employees, so separation of duties is difficult. She does know that if anything goes wrong (e.g., waste of resources, embezzlement), she will be held responsible. Therefore, she has called you in as an expert consultant in the area of accountability and control. She has asked you to recommend specific procedures and policies for enhancing the internal controls for the organization. Write a one-page memo identifying policies and procedures that she should consider adopting.

CASE STUDY
Gore Mountain[20]

Note: You may make whatever assumptions you think are necessary to answer any question. Be sure to state every assumption *explicitly*.

All of the information that you need to answer a given question is provided in the text that immediately precedes the question and the answers to the questions that precede it. Read the entire problem set before you begin. *Make sure you understand the questions before you try to answer them!*

Gore Mountain expects to attract 292,500 skier-days during the coming ski season. A skier-day represents one skier at the mountain for one day. In addition to a $2,000,000 per year subsidy provided by the State, Gore gets its revenue from three sources—lift ticket sales, ski lessons, and food sales in the mountain's lodges. Forty-five percent of the customers come to the mountain on weekends and pay an average of $53.70 to ski. The remaining 55% of the skiers come during the week and pay an average of $46.50 for a lift ticket. On average, 10% of the people who visit Gore take ski lessons. An average person pays $90 for lessons. Management also estimates that each skier spends an average of $4 per day on food.

Gore's central management staff is paid $1,800,000 per year. The remainder of Gore's staff is seasonal and is paid on an hourly basis. The table below shows the number of employees by job title, the number of days they work on average, their hourly wages and the number of hours they work each day. Only ski instructors and patrol costs vary with skier days. Benefits add 30% to direct salary costs for all workers including management. Equipment costs and usage are also shown in the table below. For equipment, number refers to the number of pieces of equipment. In general, equipment costs do not vary with skier days.

Employees	Number	Days Worked	Hours Worked	Hourly Cost
Ski Instructors & Ski Patrol	275	100	7	20.00
Lift Attendants, Maintenance & Grooming	140	130	10	18.00
Kitchen Staff	50	130	8	12.00
Equipment & Fuel Costs	60	130	6	65.00

[20] Gore Mountain Case and its solution were written by Robert Purtell. Used with permission.

Insurance costs are $15,000 per day for each of the 130 days the area is open. Energy costs are $2,240,000 per year regardless of skier volume. Food costs average 40% of total food revenue.

Question 1. Prepare an operating budget for the ski area and show the impact of a 5% reduction in the number of skier days during the 2010–11 season.

The Gore Mountain Kid's Center provides combined day care and ski lessons for children between the ages of 5 and 9 years old. Regardless of the number of children at the Center, the Center employs four full-time child-care/instructors who earn $20 per hour plus a Center manager who earns $30 per hour. The Center provides 6 hours of care per day. Workers are only paid for the hours the children are at the Center. The children are fed lunch and a snack at a cost of $9 per child per day. Gore charges $109 per day per child.

Question 2: How many children have to use the Center for Gore to break even?

Following the lead of the folks at the Jiminy Peak Ski Area in Massachusetts, the New York State Olympic Regional Development Authority is trying to decide if they should install a 1.5 megawatt wind turbine at the top of Gore Mountain. If they do, the ski area will reduce its energy bill by almost 25% or $560,000 per year for the next 15 years. It will cost Gore $4,100,000 to complete the environmental assessments, do the necessary engineering studies, and install the turbine. In addition, the ski area will have to invest $750,000 at the end of the seventh year to overhaul the bearings and replace some time-critical components.

Question 3: If the State uses an 8% cost of capital for its ski areas, should the State install the wind turbine on purely financial grounds?

The snowmaking equipment in the Bear Mountain section of Gore Mountain has been in service for nearly 15 years. It will have to be replaced before next year's ski season. Management has narrowed their decision down to two options: Big-Mouth Snow Guns and the Whisper-Quiet Snow-Making System. The table below shows the acquisition and operating costs for each of the options. The Big Mouth system has a useful life of 15 years while the Whisper-Quiet system is only projected to last for 10 years before it must be taken out of service.

Question 4. Using Gore's 8% cost of capital, which system should the management choose?

Period	Big-Mouth	Whisper Quiet
0	$ 850,000	$ 600,000
1	35,000	50,000
2	35,000	50,000
3	35,000	50,000
4	35,000	50,000
5	35,000	50,000
6	35,000	50,000
7	35,000	50,000
8	35,000	50,000
9	35,000	50,000
10	35,000	50,000
11	35,000	
12	35,000	
13	35,000	
14	35,000	
15	35,000	
Total	$1,375,000	$1,100,000

At the beginning of the 2009–10 ski-season, Gore expected to be able to be open 125 days with an average of 2,250 skiers visiting each day and average lift-ticket revenue of $49.75. At the end of the season, bad weather caused the mountain to only be open for 115 days with an average of 2,400 people per day and an average price per lift ticket of $49.50.

Question 5: Calculate the following variances for the State reimbursement program and indicate whether they were* favorable *or* unfavorable. *Be sure to add up the flexible (partial) variances and check to make sure that sum equals the total variance.

   a. Gore's *total* lift-ticket revenue variance for the 2009–10 ski-season
   b. the portion of the lift-ticket revenue variance that was due to *volume*
   c. the portion of the lift-ticket revenue variance that was due to *quantity*
   d. the portion of the lift-ticket revenue variance that was due to *price*

CASE STUDY
Rutland City Band[21]

You may make whatever assumptions you think are necessary to answer any question. Be sure to state every assumption *explicitly*. All of the information that you need to answer a given question is provided in the text that immediately precedes the question and the answers to the questions that precede it. Read the entire problem set before you begin. *Make sure you understand the questions before you try to answer them!*

   As the volunteer business-manager for the Rutland City Band (City Band), you are responsible for preparing the operating budget for the organization's upcoming summer-concert season. Each year, City Band presents up to 20 weekend performances, depending on weather conditions. The concerts are free to the public but the Band hangs a pot from the bandstand and people leave small donations in it. On average, City Band gets $100 in donations at each of its performances. In addition to donations, the City of Rutland gives the band $3,000 per season plus $125 for each performance.

   City Band also has a small endowment of $100,000 on which it expects to earn 3.5% in the coming fiscal year. City Band's trustees have decided to use that money to pay for operating expenses if they need to.

   City Band pays its conductor $3,000 for the summer season and has an insurance policy to protect it against any loss of equipment or damage to the bandstand. That policy costs the band $500 for the summer plus $25 per performance. New music costs the band $200 per year. Following generally accepted accounting principals, the band recognizes music acquisitions as expenses in the year the music is acquired. In addition, City Band pays music publishers an average of $40 per concert for the rights to perform certain of the pieces in its repertoire.

   The band has an average of 60 musicians at each of its performances. Each musician is paid $5 per performance.

   A. Prepare an operating budget for City Band for the coming fiscal year assuming the band performs on each of its twenty scheduled concert dates.
   B. Prepare a flexible budget showing what would happen if the band could only perform on 80% of its scheduled concert dates.
   C. Calculate City Band's total contribution-margin-per-concert.

Lately, some of City Band's older musicians have been having difficulty climbing the stairs to get up to the bandstand. In addition, there are two disabled musicians who play at all of the

---

[21] Rutland City Band and its solution were written by Robert Purtell. Used with permission.

Band's rehearsals but are reluctant to play at the concerts because of the difficulty they have accessing the bandstand.

City Band's trustees would like to accommodate both groups of musicians. They have gotten an estimate of $10,000 to make the bandstand accessible. You have lined up a 10-year $500-per year grant from the State Office of Disabilities and a five-year $750-per-year grant from the Federal Office of the Ageing to help pay for the modifications to the bandstand. In addition, the local chapter of the Knights of Columbus has offered to donate $1,500 toward the project.

D. If City Band's cost-of-capital is 6%, should it invest in the bandstand modifications based *solely* on the Knight's donation and the proceeds from the grants? Support your answer with the appropriate time-value-of-money calculations.

City Band expected to hold 20 concerts during its 2009 summer-concert-season and pay an average of 60 musicians $5 per concert for their performances. At the end of the summer, the band had only been able to perform 16 times. The other four performances were rained out. Because of the shortened concert-season, the trustees decided to pay the musicians who came to the concerts $6 per performance. On average, 55 musicians were at each performance.

E. Calculate City Band's total musician's stipend expense variance for the season. Indicate whether that variance was favorable or unfavorable. Calculate the portion of that variance that was due to volume. Indicate whether that variance was favorable or unfavorable. Calculate the portion of that variance that was due to quantity. Indicate whether that variance was favorable or unfavorable. Calculate the portion of that variance that was due to the rate paid to the musicians. Indicate whether that variance was favorable or unfavorable.

Hint: Be sure to add up the flexible (partial) variances to make sure that total equals the total variance you calculated directly.

CASE STUDY

Taos Museum of Southwestern Arts and Crafts[22]

The answers to this case are cumulative. **You can *not* skip any section and do the next.**

You may make whatever assumptions you think are necessary to answer any question. Be sure to state every assumption *explicitly.*

All of the information that you need to answer a given question is provided in the text that immediately precedes the question and the answers to the questions that precede it. Read the entire problem set before you begin. *Make sure you understand the questions before you try to answer them!*

The Taos Museum of Southwestern Arts and Crafts (TMSAC) presents rotating exhibits of the works of artists and artisans from the Southwestern United States. Historically, the museum has derived its support from three sources: grants, annual memberships, and visitor revenues. For the 2010 fiscal year, TMSAC knows that it will receive $564,000 in grants from various sources. It also expects 1,255 people to be supporting members of the museum. On average, supporting members give TMSAC $112.75 per year. The museum expects

---

[22] Taos Museum Case and its solution were written by Robert Purtell. Used with permission.

the following mix of visitors during 2010, each paying the amount shown in the right column of the schedule.

Type of Visitor	Percent of Total	Price
Regular	65%	$6.00
Group	15%	$3.00
Senior Citizen	10%	$2.00
Student	10%	$1.00

TMSAC has $985,000 of fixed expenses each year. In addition, the museum spends an average of $.55 per visitor for handouts that describe the exhibits on display. TMSAC estimates that it has variable electric costs of $.15 per visitor. Plus, the museum offers each visitor the option of receiving an audio cassette which describes the featured exhibit of the month. Visitors are allowed to keep the tape as a memento of their visit. Historically, these tapes have cost the museum $1.25 per copy to produce and replicate. On average, 30% of the people visiting the museum have taken advantage of the free tape offer.

Problem 1. The Director of the museum has asked you to tell her the minimum number of visitors that must come to the museum each year in order for TMSAC to break even. Using the information given above, what is TMSAC's break-even visitor volume?

Because of Taos's location in the mountains of New Mexico, the museum tends to have a seasonal pattern to its visitor flow, with proportionally more people visiting TMSAC in the summer than in the winter. In addition, revenue from grants and memberships tend to flow into the museum unevenly throughout the year. The seasonal flow of visitor, grants, and membership revenues is distributed throughout the year as follows:

	Quarter 1	Quarter 2	Quarter 3	Quarter 4
Visitors	15%	25%	45%	15%
Membership Revenue	40%	20%	20%	20%
Grant revenue	25%	50%	10%	15%

Fixed expenses are distributed evenly throughout the year, that is, 25% per quarter. The museum's marketing director forecasts that 80,000 people will visit the museum during fiscal year 2010.

TMSAC's Director of Marketing has convinced the Executive Director that a museum shop can be operated profitably in a small space just off the main entrance. She agrees and the shop is scheduled to open on April 1, 2010, the first day of the second quarter. The Marketing Director estimates that 5% of the people who visit the museum will make purchases from the shop. Based on his experience, he expects the average purchase to be $40. TMSAC's Business Manager estimates that the cost-of-goods-sold will be 65% of the museum-shop's sales revenue. The shop will be staffed by volunteers at no cost to TMSAC.

Problem 2. Using the information above, prepare a budget of revenues, support and expenses for TMSAC for each of the four quarters in fiscal year 2010 and summarize the budget for the full year.

TMSAC has just been approached by the Curator of Special Exhibits at the Smithsonian Museum. The Smithsonian has offered to lend TMSAC a rare collection of 19th-century Navaho crafts. The collection would remain at the museum for a five-year period after which it would be returned to the Navaho nation. To house the exhibit, TMSAC will have to upgrade its environmental and security systems at a one-time cost of $175,000.

Since this may be the last time that this collection will be exhibited in its entirety, the Executive Director is enthusiastic about the impact that it will have on visitor volume and the reputation of the museum. The Marketing Director forecasts that 850 incremental visitors are likely to be drawn to the museum each month that the exhibit is at TMSAC.

The director wants you to tell her if the exhibit is financially self-sufficient or if she will need to get a grant to support it. You know that TMSAC's cost of capital is 9%. You also know the marginal contribution generated by each incremental visitor to the museum from your work on the break-even analysis. Do not count on any gift shop purchases from the incremental visitors.

Problem 3. What do you tell her? Can TMSAC afford to show the exhibit based *solely* on the marginal contribution from incremental visitors? If the exhibit is not financially self-sufficient, how large a grant will TMSAC need to get to meet the projected shortfall? Support your recommendation and present your findings in a way that the director will understand.

Suggested Readings

Arens, Alvin A., Randal J. Elder, and Mark S. Beasley. *Auditing and Assurance Services and ACL Software*, 12th ed. Upper Saddle River, N.J.: Prentice Hall, 2008.

Bowden, Adrian R., Malcolm R. Lane, and Julian H. Martin. *Triple Bottom Line Risk Management: Enhancing Profit, Environmental Performance, and Community Benefits. New York,* N.Y.: John Wiley & Sons, 2001.

Broom, Cheryle A., Marilyn Jackson, Vera Vogelsang-Coombs, and Jody Harris. *Performance Measurement: Concepts and Techniques*, 2nd ed. Center for Accountability and Performance, Washington, D.C.: American Society for Public Administration, 1999.

Elkington, John. *Cannibals with Forks*. Gabriola Island, B.C., Canada: Capstone Publishing Ltd, 1999.

Finkler, Steven A., David R. Ward, and Judith L. Baker. *Essentials of Cost Accounting for Health Care Organizations*. 3rd ed. Sudbury, Mass.: Jones and Bartlett Publishers, 2007.

Finkler, Steven A., Christine T. Kovner, and Cheryl Jones. *Financial Management for Nurse Managers and Executives*, 3rd ed. Philadelphia, Penn.: W.B. Saunders, 2007.

Hannabarger, Charles, Frederick Buchman, and Peter Economy. *Balanced Scorecard Strategy For Dummies*. Hoboken, N.J.: Wiley Publishing, 2008.

Hatry, Harry P., James R. Fountain, Jr., Jonathan M. Sullivan, and Lorraine Kremer, eds. *Service Efforts and Accomplishments Reporting: Its Time Has Come*, GASB Research Report Series. Norwalk, Conn.: Governmental Accounting Standards Board, 1989–1993.

Henriques, Adrian, and Julie Richardson, eds. *The Triple Bottom Line, Does It All Add Up? Assessing the Sustainability of Business and CSR*. London, U.K.: Earthscan Publications Ltd., 2004.

Horngren, Charles T., Gary L. Sundem, William O. Stratton, Jeff Schatzberg, and Dave Burgstahler. *Introduction to Management Accounting*, 14th ed. Upper Saddle River, N.J.: Prentice Hall, 2008.

Horngren, Charles T., Srikant M. Datar, and George Foster. *Cost Accounting: A Managerial Emphasis*, 12th ed. Upper Saddle River, N.J.: Prentice Hall, 2006.

Jackson, Peggy M., and Toni E. Fogarty. *Sarbanes-Oxley for Nonprofits: A Guide to Building Competitive Advantage*. Hoboken, N.J.: John Wiley & Sons, 2005.

Kaplan, Robert, and David Norton. *Translating Strategy into Action: The Balanced Scorecard*. Boston, Mass.: Harvard Business School Press, 1996.

Lander, Guy. *What is Sarbanes-Oxley?* New York, N.Y.: McGraw Hill, 2004.

Marchetti, Anne M. *Sarbanes-Oxley Ongoing Compliance Guide: Key Processes and Summary Checklists*. Hoboken, N.J.: John Wiley & Sons, 2007.

Niven, Paul R. *Balanced Scorecard Step-by-Step for Government and Nonprofit Agencies*, 2nd ed. Hoboken, N.J.: John Wiley & Sons, 2008.

Savitz, Andrew W., and Karl Weber. *The Triple Bottom Line: How Today's Best-Run Companies Are Achieving Economic, Social and Environmental Success—and How You Can Too*. San Francisco, Calif.: Jossey-Bass, 2006.

Stiefel, Leanna, Amy Ellen Schwartz, and Ross Rubenstein. "Measuring School Efficiency Using School-Level Data: Theory and Practice," in Margaret E. Goertz and Allan Odden, eds. *School-Based Financing*. Thousand Oaks, Ca.: Corwin Press, 1999, pp. 40–78.

Taylor, Deirdre A. "What Is Internal Control?" in David R. Hancox and Martin Ives, eds. *State and Local Government Program Control and Audit: Handbook for Managers and Auditors*. Austin, Tex.: Sheshunoff Information Services, 1997.

Welytok, Jill Gilbert. *Sarbanes-Oxley for Dummies*. Hoboken, N.J.: Wiley Publishing, 2008.

A P P E N D I X   8 - A

The Mechanics of Flexible Budget Variance Analysis

The role of this appendix is to provide a somewhat more formalized methodology for the calculation of *flexible budget variances*.

FLEXIBLE BUDGET EXPENSE VARIANCES

The first step in flexible budgeting is to establish the flexible budget for the actual output level. That is, we must determine what we would have expected to spend if we had known in advance the output level that would actually occur. Because of variable costs, we would have budgeted more resources if we knew service levels would be higher and less resources if we knew they were going to be lower. For example, consider an excerpt from the variance report for the Millbridge High School for August.[23]

Town of Millbridge
High School
August Variance Report

	Actual	Budget	Variance
Books	$120,000	$100,000	$20,000 U

The actual spending was $120,000. The budgeted cost was $100,000. Suppose that the budget assumed that there would be 2,000 students, but 2,100 students enrolled. Assuming that the purchase of textbooks would be expected to vary in direct proportion with enrolled students, the budget called for planned spending of $50 per student (i.e., $50 × 2,000 students = $100,000).

For 2,100 students at $50 per student, $105,000 would have been budgeted for supplies. This is the flexible budget. It is the amount the school would have expected to spend had the actual number of students been known. The original budget was $100,000. The flexible budget, which adjusts for the actual volume, is $105,000. The actual amount spent was $120,000:

---

[23] Note that in preparation for the new school year, Millbridge orders most of its books during August of each year. There are many other lines in the variance report, but we will focus on just the line-item for textbooks.

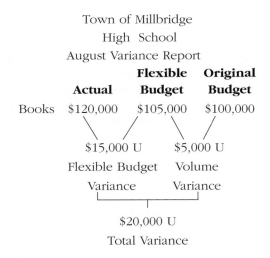

Town of Millbridge
High School
August Variance Report

The difference between the original budget and the actual amount spent is the total variance. This is still $20,000 unfavorable. The $5,000 difference between the original budget and the flexible budget is the volume variance. This volume variance is unfavorable because the flexible budget requires more spending than was expected in the original budget. The increased number of students may be considered to be good or bad, depending on the attitudes of the people in the town. Regardless, from a variance reporting standpoint, the convention is to consider increased spending to be unfavorable. Managers should guard themselves from assuming that unfavorable variances are always bad events.

The difference between the flexible budget and the actual amount spent is referred to as the flexible budget variance. It simply represents all other causes, aside from the volume variance. In this case the flexible budget variance is $15,000. It is unfavorable, since actual spending was $15,000 more than the flexible budget, which is the expected spending for the actual number of students enrolled. If the flexible budget variance and volume variance are combined, we get the total variance for the line-item. Note that if one of these variances was favorable and the other was unfavorable, they would offset each other, like positive and negative numbers.

FLEXIBLE BUDGET NOTATION

At this point in the analysis, we do not know much about the flexible budget variance. It is a combination of the price and quantity variance. We need to be able to calculate each of these two variances. To do this we will introduce some notation. The letter A is used to refer to an actual amount. The letter B is used to refer to a budgeted amount. The letter P stands for a price or rate, and the letter Q stands for a quantity. The letter i is used to stand for an input and the letter o to stand for an output or workload. *Inputs* are resources consumed. These can be labor hours, or units of supplies, or any other resource the organization pays for. *Outputs* are a measure of the volume of goods or service being produced. These can be the number of students or the number of meals or the number of patients.

The notation is combined to form six key variables. Pi stands for the price of the input, such as $20 per textbook. Qo stands for the total quantity of output, such as the number of students. Qi stands for the quantity of input needed to produce one unit of output. For example, we might expect that each year the school will buy, on average, 2.5 textbooks per pupil. The letter B in front of other letters indicates a budgeted amount. The letter A in front of other letters indicates an actual result. The definitions of the notation can be formalized as follows:

BPi: budgeted price per unit of input
BQi: budgeted quantity of input for each unit of output
BQo: budgeted quantity of output
APi: actual price paid per unit of input
AQi: actual quantity of input for each unit of output produced
AQo: actual quantity of output

Suppose that for the Town of Millbridge High School, these six items had the following values:

BPi: $20 per textbook
BQi: 2.5 textbooks per student
BQo: 2,000 students
APi: $22 per textbook
AQi: 2.5974 textbooks per student
AQo: 2,100 students

To calculate the price, quantity, and volume variances, it is necessary to get these six pieces of information. The three budgeted items are generally available from the data that were used in making the original budget. The three actual pieces of information should be available in most organizations. School systems will know the actual number of students, the AQo. Also, if you buy books, you should have a record of how many books were purchased and how much was paid for them.

The actual price paid for each book is not needed. If we know how many books we purchased and how much we paid in total for books, we can divide the total cost for books by the number of books to find the average price paid per book, the APi. Similarly, we do not need to know how many books we acquired for each student. If we know how many books we actually purchased and how many students we actually had, we can divide to find the actual number of books purchased per student, on average, the AQi.

The first step in these data is to calculate the original budget in terms of the notation. The original budget is simply the expected number of new books per student, multiplied by the expected cost per book, multiplied by the expected number of students. Using our notation, this can be shown as follows:

Original Budget

$BQi \times BPi \times BQo$

$2.5 \times \$20 \times 2{,}000$

$\$100{,}000$

That is, BQi, the budgeted quantity of input per unit of output, is 2.5 new books per student; BPi, the budgeted price per book is $20; and BQo, the budgeted quantity of students, is 2,000. The total budgeted amount for textbooks is $100,000.

The next step is to find the flexible budget. Recall that the flexible budget is the amount that one would have expected to spend if the actual number of enrolled students had been known in advance. Therefore, leave the BQi at the budgeted 2.5 books per student, and leave the BPi at the budgeted $20 per book. The only change is from a BQo of 2,000 students to a new AQo of 2,100 students. The flexible budget can be calculated as follows:

Flexible Budget

$BQi \times BPi \times AQo$

$2.5 \times \$20 \times 2{,}100$

$\$105{,}000$

The difference between the original budget and the flexible budget is caused by a difference in the number of students. Other than that, the calculations are the same. The originally budgeted amount of $100,000 can be compared with the flexible budget amount of $105,000 to determine the volume variance of $5,000 U. Since the number of students is higher than expected, cost will be higher than expected. This will give rise to an unfavorable variance. The comparison between the original budget and the flexible budget can be shown as follows:

Flexible Budget   **Original Budget**

$BQi \times BPi \times AQo$ $BQi \times BPi \times BQo$

$2.5 \times \$20 \times 2,100$ $2.5 \times \$20 \times 2,000$

$105,000 $100,000

$5,000 U

Volume Variance

We can also calculate the flexible budget variance that we found earlier, by comparing the flexible budget to the actual spending. The actual amount spent is simply the product of the number of books purchased per student, the cost per book, and the number of students, as follows:

Actual

$AQi \times APi \times AQo$

$2.5974 \times \$22 \times 2,100$

$120,000

Note that to calculate the actual cost, the actual number of books per student, the actual price per book, and the actual number of students is used. Also note that the actual number of books per student is based on the actual number of books acquired in total, divided by the actual number of students. The difference between the flexible budget and the actual amount spent was earlier described as the flexible budget variance:

Actual   **Flexible Budget**

$AQi \times APi \times AQo$ $BQi \times BPi \times AQo$

$2.5974 \times \$22 \times 2,100$ $2.5 \times \$20 \times 2,100$

$120,000 $105,000

$15,000 U

Flexible Budget Variance

The volume variance and the flexible budget variance add up to the total variance for the line-item, as shown earlier. Using our notation, that would appear as follows:

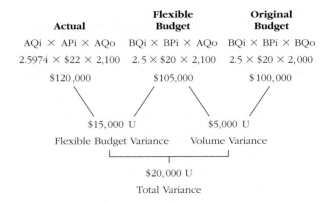

To this point, we have the same information as we had before we started using notation. Now, however, we can go further by determining the price and quantity variances. In order to determine these variances, it is necessary to derive a *subcategory*. This subcategory is simply a device to allow for separation of the flexible budget variance into two pieces: the price variance and the quantity variance. The subcategory is defined as the actual quantity of input per unit of output, multiplied by the budgeted price of the input, times the actual output level. In terms of the notation, the subcategory can be calculated as follows:

Subcategory

$AQi \times BPi \times AQo$

$2.5974 \times \$20 \times 2,100$

$109,091

If the subcategory calculation is compared with the actual costs, the price variance can be determined as follows:

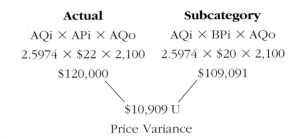

Note that the actual and subcategory calculations both use the AQi and the AQo. The only difference between the two calculations is that the actual uses the APi whereas the subcategory uses the BPi. Since the price is the only element that differs, it must be responsible for the $10,909 difference between the two calculations. This $10,909 variance is because books cost $22 on average, instead of $20 as expected.

To determine the quantity variance, it is only necessary to compare the subcategory with the flexible budget:

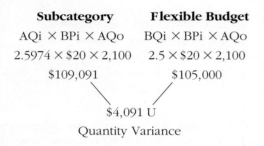

In comparing the subcategory and the flexible budget calculations, we note that both use the BPi and the AQo. However, the subcategory uses AQi, whereas the flexible budget uses BQi. So, the $4,091 difference that is observed is the result of the fact that the number of books purchased per pupil, on average,

differed from the expected number. Thus, we have a quantity difference. Note that this quantity difference has nothing to do with the number of students but rather with the number of books per student.[24]

Reviewing the price and quantity variances, we can look at how they together comprise the flexible budget variance:

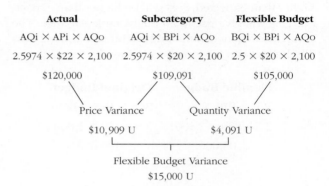

Notice that adding the price variance of $10,909 U and the quantity variance of $4,091 U results in the flexible budget variance. Recall that the flexible budget variance and the volume variance add up to the total variance. Figure 8-A-1 shows that the three individual variances—price, quantity, and volume—add up to the total variance for the line-item.

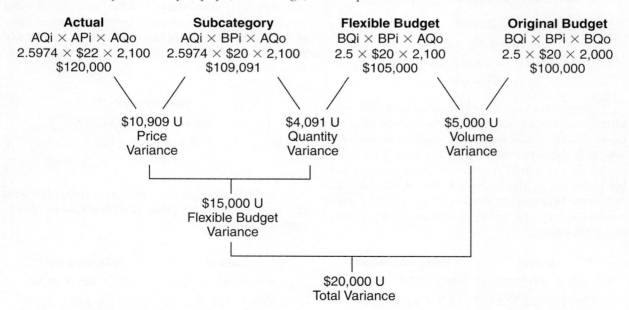

FIGURE 8-A-1 Flexible Budget Variance Analysis Model

[24] In this example we have constructed a subcategory that uses the actual quantity of inputs per unit of output and the budgeted price of inputs. This is an arbitrary convention. We could have instead used the budgeted quantity of inputs per unit of output and the actual price of inputs. We would still generate a price and quantity variance if this switch was made. However, there is an interaction effect of price and quantity, and the answers may vary slightly if the alternative approach is used.

Recall that without flexible budget variance analysis, the total variance for the line-item would be the only piece of information available for analysis. There was an unfavorable variance of $20,000. Without additional information, this variance might be attributed to the increase in the number of students. Using Figure 8-A-1, it is possible to determine that of this total variance, $5,000 was caused by the increase in the number of students. However, $4,091 was caused by an increase in the number of books per student, and $10,909 was caused by either an increase in book prices or perhaps a movement to acquiring different, more expensive books than had been planned. We would certainly want to investigate both the quantity and price variances to determine more specifically why they occurred and whether any remedial action is necessary to avoid cost overruns in the future.

In considering Figure 8-A-1, note that this calculation would need to be done for each line-item for each department. Although that might seem to be a large task in large organizations, it is readily converted to a simple computer spreadsheet program. Thus, the major effort required to calculate price, quantity, and volume variances is to input into the computer the six basic pieces of information needed for each line-item (i.e., BQi, BPi, BQo, AQi, APi, and AQo).

It is also important to realize that the price, quantity, and volume variances are merely components of the total variance for any line-item. In Figure 8-A-1, the total variance is $20,000. Note that if we compare the actual amount spent, $120,000, with the original budget of $100,000 in that figure, the difference is the $20,000 total variance. As we try to understand why that total amount was incurred, the variance has been divided into components. Note that the price variance of $10,909, plus the quantity variance of $4,091 plus the volume variance of $5,000 add up to the total variance.

It sometimes is not obvious whether a variance is favorable or unfavorable. Looking at Figure 8-A-1, an easy rule of thumb is that as one moves from the right side toward the left, larger numbers on the left indicate

unfavorable variances. If the flexible budget amount is larger than the originally budgeted amount, the volume variance is unfavorable. If the subcategory is greater than the flexible budget, the quantity variance is unfavorable. This is true because as one moves from the original budget toward the left, movement is toward the actual result. If the actual result is larger than the original budget, then more was spent than budgeted. Such higher spending indicates an unfavorable variance.

SUMMARY

One of the most important ways that organizations control their operations is by analysis of variances. Comparing actual results with budgeted expectations and analyzing the resulting variances should be done monthly. This can allow for actions to be taken to improve results in future months. Variance analysis also provides information for preparing the coming year's budget and for evaluating department and manager performance.

A valuable approach to variance analysis is based on flexible budgeting. Flexible budget variance analysis establishes an after-the-fact budget—that is, what it would have been expected to cost had the actual output levels been known in advance. Using flexible budgets, it is possible to break down a unit or department's line-item variances into components caused by (1) changes in prices or salary rates from those expected; (2) changes in the amount of input used per unit of output; and (3) changes in the workload volume itself.

Managerial expertise and judgment are still needed to investigate and evaluate the variances once they have been calculated. Ultimately, this technique can make the manager's job easier by segregating the variance into its component parts. This allows the manager to spend more time understanding and explaining why the variance occurred. This information can then be used to make changes in organizational behavior to avoid unfavorable variances during the rest of the year and for improved planning for coming years.

Key Terms from This Appendix

APi.   Actual price paid per unit of input.

AQi.   Actual quantity of input for each unit of output produced.

AQo.   Actual quantity of output.

BPi.   Budgeted price per unit of input.

BQi.   Budgeted quantity of input for each unit of output.

BQo.   Budgeted quantity of output.

subcategory.   The actual quantity of input per unit of output, multiplied by the budgeted price of the input, times the actual output level; a device to allow for separation of the flexible budget variance into two pieces: the price variance and the quantity variance.

9

Taking Stock of Where You Are: The Balance Sheet

The learning objectives of this chapter are to:

- introduce and define *financial accounting* and the *statement of financial position,* or *balance sheet;*
- provide a framework for financial accounting, based on the fundamental equation of accounting;
- introduce the concept of Generally Accepted Accounting Principles (GAAP);
- discuss the entity, monetary denominator, objective evidence, conservatism, going concern, and materiality GAAP;
- explain and discuss the accrual basis of accounting;
- discuss various asset categories, including cash, marketable securities, accounts receivable, inventory, prepaid expenses, fixed assets, and sinking funds;
- discuss various liability categories, including accounts and wages payable, and long-term debt;
- discuss net assets including the subcategories of unrestricted, temporarily restricted, and permanently restricted net assets; and
- discuss the process of recording financial information and generating a balance sheet.

INTRODUCTION

We now turn our attention to the process of recording events, summarizing them, and reporting results. The process of recording financial information is done on an ongoing basis throughout the year. Periodically—monthly, quarterly, or annually—events are summarized. At least annually, the summarized events are then organized into a reporting form that helps managers and outsiders understand the current financial status of the organization and how well it has done from a financial standpoint.

This reporting process can be thought of as the concluding phase of a planning, implementing, controlling, and reporting cycle. The financial management aspects of planning, implementing, and controlling activities are often referred to as *managerial accounting.* Any information generated is primarily for the use of managers in their efforts to optimize the results of the organization. Thus, the focus of the book so far is primarily internal. Our efforts have been to develop tools and techniques that aid managers in managing the organization.

There is also an external side of financial management. Financial reports are prepared by organizations. These reports help managers to understand the current financial situation of the organization and the financial results of its operations. However, they provide information not only for the use of management of the organization but for outsiders as well. Banks, donors, landlords, vendors, legislators, regulators, unions, bond raters, and others are interested in the performance of public service organizations. Preparation of financial reports that will be examined by individuals external to the organization is referred to as *financial accounting*.

For example, a union may want to understand the finances of an organization to determine whether the organization can afford to give its members a raise. A donor may want to examine the finances of a charity to determine whether it puts donated resources to good use. A supplier may want to decide whether it is safe to sell to the organization without immediate payment. A bank may want to examine the finances of an organization before it makes a loan to determine if the organization will be able to repay the loan.

To provide these outside users with information that they can understand and that is somewhat comparable among organizations, a set of accounting conventions is employed. These conventions are called *Generally Accepted Accounting Principles* (GAAP). GAAP are developed by the Financial Accounting Standards Board (FASB) and the Governmental Accounting Standards Board (GASB). A number of these accounting conventions are discussed throughout the remaining chapters of this book.

The FASB (pronounced *faz-B*) establishes the GAAP (pronounced *gap*) that govern the financial reporting of most types of organizations, including health care and not-for-profit organizations. The GASB (pronounced *gaz-B*) establishes the rules followed by state and local government bodies. As a result of the need to comply with rules imposed by FASB or GASB, financial accounting is more rigid in many respects than managerial accounting.[1]

Managerial accounting is primarily prospective in nature. It is the process of preparing plans and implementing and controlling activities to achieve good results in the coming time periods. In contrast, financial accounting is historical. At the end of an accounting period, it looks back to see just how stable the organization is and how well it has actually done.

At least once each year, organizations prepare a set of financial statements that summarize their financial position and the financial results of the organization's activities. The *statement of financial position,* commonly referred to as the *balance sheet,* is the first of the financial statements, and it is the topic of this chapter.

A balance sheet reports the financial position of the organization at a moment in time—often the end of the fiscal year. Chapter 10 looks at activity and cash flow statements. Activity statements assess whether the organization has had more or less revenues than expenses or expenditures for the year. Since many organizations use some form of accrual accounting, the operating results reported in the activity statement may differ from the organization's cash flow. Cash flow statements focus on the organization's sources and uses of cash.

Together, Chapters 9 and 10 provide the essential elements of financial accounting. However, there are a variety of special accounting rules for different types of public service

---

[1] FASB and GASB are private sector organizations that promulgate accounting standards. For corporations that are subject to Securities and Exchange Commission (SEC) jurisdiction, the SEC has the final word if their rules disagree with FASB accounting standards. For state and local governments, state and local law dictate the extent to which the governments must follow GASB standards.

organizations. Chapter 11 discusses special financial accounting concerns of not-for-profit and health care organizations. Chapters 12 and 13 consider special financial accounting concerns for governmental organizations.

THE FRAMEWORK FOR FINANCIAL ACCOUNTING

Exhibit 9-1 presents a hypothetical balance sheet for Meals for the Homeless. For any specific *entity,* this financial document provides a highly summarized view of its financial position at any one particular point in time. An entity is a person, organization, or distinct suborganization. The balance sheet has often been compared to a still photograph. For a specific moment in time, this financial statement provides a great deal of information about the organization. All organizations, whether for-profit or not-for-profit, private or public, use the balance sheet.

Can the organization begin a rapid new expansion of services? Must it severely restrict its services to survive? These and other questions are often asked about an organization. The balance sheet can help address such questions. The balance sheet provides an overview of the financial position of the organization. How much cash does the organization have? What other resources does it have? Does it owe a lot of money to other organizations? Will that money have to be repaid in the near future? The balance sheet is derived from information contained in the *fundamental equation of accounting.*

EXHIBIT 9-1

Meals for the Homeless
Statement of Financial Position
As of December 31, 2011

Assets			Liabilities and Net Assets		
Current Assets			*Liabilities*		
Cash	$	1,000	Current Liabilities		
Marketable securities		3,000	Wages payable	$	2,000
Accounts receivable, net of estimated uncollectibles of $8,000		55,000	Accounts payable		3,000
			Notes payable		5,000
Inventory		2,000	Current portion of mortgage payable		5,000
Prepaid expenses		1,000	Total Current Liabilities	$	15,000
Total Current Assets	$	62,000			
Long-Term Assets			Long-Term Liabilities		
Fixed assets			Mortgage payable		$ 11,000
Property		$ 40,000	Total Long-Term Liabilities		$ 11,000
Equipment, net		35,000	*Total Liabilities*		$ 26,000
Investments		8,000			
Total Long-Term Assets		$ 83,000	*Net Assets*		119,000
Total Assets		$145,000	*Total Liabilities and Net Assets*		$145,000

The Fundamental Equation of Accounting

The framework for financial accounting was developed hundreds of years ago. It is based on an equation, as follows:

$$\textbf{Assets = Liabilities + Owners' Equity}$$

Assets are anything the organization owns of value. *Liabilities* are obligations owed to outsiders. *Owners' equity* represents the share of the organization's assets owned by its owners. By definition, the preceding equation is always in balance. Therefore, once we determine the organization's assets and liabilities, the owners' equity is a residual amount needed to balance the equation. If we know the resources we have (assets) and how much we owe (liabilities), then the amount that would be left over if we used some of our assets to pay off all that we owe is called the owners' equity.[2]

This is similar to the equity a person has in his or her house. If you buy a house for $250,000 and pay for it with $50,000 of your own money and $200,000 borrowed from a bank, the asset (the house) is worth $250,000, the liability to repay the bank (mortgage payable) is $200,000, and your equity in the house is $50,000. People typically use the term *net worth* to refer to their own personal financial net value after subtracting all of their debts from their assets. For individuals, the fundamental equation would appear as follows:

$$\textbf{Assets = Liabilities + Net Worth}$$

or

$$\textbf{Assets - Liabilities = Net Worth}$$

In a for-profit corporation, the owners' equity is called the stockholders' equity. In not-for-profit and governmental organizations, owners' equity is often referred to as the *net assets,* because that it is the result when we subtract (or "net out") liabilities from assets. This term highlights the fact that not-for-profit organizations and governments do not have owners in the same way that for-profit organizations do. We can think of the organization itself or society as the owner of the net assets of such organizations. When considering just one part of their overall finances, not-for-profit organizations and governments sometimes refer to this amount as the *fund balance.* The fundamental equation for these organizations would appear as follows:

$$\textbf{Assets = Liabilities + Net Assets}$$
or
$$\textbf{Assets = Liabilities + Fund Balance}$$

The left-hand side of the fundamental equation lists the organization's valuable resources, or assets. The organization owns those resources. The right-hand side of the fundamental equation represents the sources of or claims against those resources. Outside creditors claim amounts of money that are owed to them. Legally, the first use of the organization's assets is to repay creditors' claims. Anything left after outsiders are paid is owned by the organization and its owners. The entire right side of the equation is sometimes referred

---

[2] Since owners' equity is a residual number once assets and liabilities have been determined, owners' equity will only be a good representation if assets and liabilities have been accurately measured.

to as its *equities*. *Equity* is a word that refers to ownership or source of assets. Both creditors and owners claim ownership or are a source of the assets of the organization.

The fundamental equation of accounting must always remain in balance. When people talk about balancing the books of the organization, they are referring to the fact that this equation must be kept in balance as specific financial events are recorded. If the equation is not in balance after a transaction is recorded, then an error must have occurred in the recording process.

By the same token, the balance sheet, which provides a representation of this equation at a specific point in time, must remain in balance. Generally assets are shown on the left side of the balance sheet, and equities, or liabilities plus net assets, are shown on the right, as in Exhibit 9-1. The totals on both sides must be the same, or in balance. Sometimes assets are shown on the top half of the page and liabilities and net assets are shown on the bottom, as in Exhibit 9-2.

Our three managers, Steve Netzer, Leanna Schwartz, and Dwight Ives, from the hypothetical example introduced in Chapter 1, would each be interested in the detailed elements of the balance sheet. At the end of the year, they will want to know if their plans and the implementation of those plans have left their organizations in a financially acceptable position. As managers, they want a solid understanding of the resources available to them as well as their obligations to outsiders and any restrictions that may exist on their use of the remaining net assets. The information in the financial statements has a critical impact on the actions managers must take for the following year. It also affects many decisions made by outsiders regarding whether to lend money, sell supplies, or make donations to the organization. We now look more closely at what makes up the assets, liabilities, and net assets of the organization.

Assets

We can define an asset as being anything the entity owns of value. Another view is that assets are anything the organization owns as a result of past transactions and events that will better enable it to meet its mission (see Box 9-1). This would include all items that will provide some future benefit or enable the entity to provide services to its clients. The list of assets on the balance sheet reflects the valuable resources owned by the organization.

Some assets are easily identifiable. A respirator owned by the Hospital for Ordinary Surgery (HOS) is a valuable resource that qualifies as an asset. The respirator allows the hospital to treat patients and generate revenues. We would clearly want to include the respirator when we tally up the assets and report them on the balance sheet.

The artwork on the wall in the executive director's office at Meals for the Homeless is also an asset, even though one might view its contribution toward achieving the organizational mission as being much more indirect. To conduct business, and deal with suppliers and possible donors, the executive director must have a presentable office. The painting on the wall contributes to that proper appearance, and it too will appear on the balance sheet as an asset.

BOX 9-1

Note that the definition for assets includes "that will better enable it to meet its mission." It does not say "that are consistent with the mission." What if the Americans Against Lung Cancer Society owned shares of stock in a tobacco company? If the shares can be sold for cash, which can be used by the organization to carry out its mission-related activities, then the stock is an asset, even though owning that particular asset might seem to be contrary to the mission of the organization.

Some assets do not have a physical form or substance. If a taxpayer in Millbridge owes the town real estate taxes, those taxes are classified as an asset referred to as a receivable. The general group of assets called *receivables* refers to amounts of money that other people or organizations owe to the entity, generally because of goods or services that the entity has provided to them. HOS has patient receivables. Because the entity must keep track of or

---

EXHIBIT 9-2

Meals for the Homeless
Statement of Financial Position
As of December 31, 2011

Assets

Current Assets	
Cash	$ 1,000
Marketable securities	3,000
Accounts receivable, net of estimated uncollectibles of $8,000	55,000
Inventory	2,000
Prepaid expenses	1,000
Total Current Assets	$ 62,000
Long-Term Assets	
Fixed assets	
Property	$ 40,000
Equipment, net	35,000
Investments	8,000
Total Long-Term Assets	$ 83,000
Total Assets	$145,000

Liabilities and Net Assets

Liabilities	
Current Liabilities	
Wages payable	$ 2,000
Accounts payable	3,000
Notes payable	5,000
Current portion of mortgage payable	5,000
Total Current Liabilities	$ 15,000
Long-Term Liabilities	
Mortgage payable	$ 11,000
Total Long-Term Liabilities	$ 11,000
Total Liabilities	$ 26,000
Net Assets	119,000
Total Liabilities and Net Assets	$145,000

keep *account* of how much money each patient owes, we often refer to the amounts owed in this manner as *accounts receivable*. Receivables were discussed in Chapter 7.

In the case of the hospital, these accounts receivable or patient receivables represent amounts the hospital expects to collect in exchange for patient care that has been provided. The Town of Millbridge would refer to taxes that are owed to it as taxes receivable. The taxes represent charges the town makes for providing a wide range of services, such as police, fire, transportation, sewers, and so on. Meals for the Homeless may have fulfilled the conditions specified by a foundation for a grant and as a result may have grants receivable. In each case, the receivables represent the money the organization is entitled to collect from someone else. Such receivables are valuable assets that would generally be listed on the balance sheet.

Some assets may be even less tangible than receivables. Meals for the Homeless may pay for an insurance policy to provide fire protection for its building and equipment. The insurance policy does not have physical substance, and if there is never a fire, the policy will expire without any payment to Meals by the insurance company. But the protection that the policy provides is valuable. The policy is referred to as an intangible asset. Accountants often refer to assets as being either *tangible* or *intangible* assets. Both types may appear on the balance sheet.

However, some intangible assets do not show up on the balance sheet. Examples are things such as the entity's good reputation for always paying its bills promptly or the high morale of the entity's employees. Many would argue that these are valuable resources and are assets despite their intangible nature. However, assets are only recorded if they are acquired through a specific exchange transaction, which is generally not the case for morale or reputation.

Sometimes these types of intangibles will show up on the balance sheet if they have been acquired as part of a specific exchange transaction. For example, hospital mergers have become quite common. Suppose that the amount one hospital pays to acquire another hospital exceeds the value of the assets that can be assigned a specific value less the liabilities of the organization. In that case, the excess amount paid is presumed to be the present value (see Chapter 5) of the remaining assets of the organization. This would include various intangibles such as a good reputation, the ability to provide quality services, the skills of the entity's employees, and so on. These intangibles are grouped together and called *goodwill*. Goodwill that has been purchased can be shown on the balance sheet based on the price paid.

We assume that one organization that buys another organization is not stupid. If it pays more than the value of the specific measurable assets, the excess, or goodwill acquired, must be worth the difference. Otherwise, the organization could simply start from scratch rather than buying another organization. Why would a hospital pay $400 million to buy another hospital if it could buy land and build and equip a hospital for $200 million? Therefore, to the extent that the purchase price cannot be assigned to other specific assets, it is assigned to goodwill.[3]

Managers should be aware that their own organization's assets may be more valuable than their balance sheet reflects. There may be intangibles that we know have some value but which were not acquired in an exchange transaction. Without a specific exchange transaction those intangibles will not appear on the balance sheet. Managers should keep such potential "hidden values" in mind.

Liabilities

As organizations work to create goods and provide services, they often incur obligations to other entities. HOS must hire workers and buy clinical supplies. If it buys the supplies and

---

[3] Intangible assets have long created measurement problems. Although accountants have tried to establish rules for when to recognize intangibles such as goodwill on the balance sheet and at what values, debates about appropriate treatment often occur, and the area is murky at best.

has not paid for them, it will owe money to the vendor who sold those supplies to the hospital. If its employees work for the organization and have not been paid, the hospital will owe wages to those individuals. These obligations are referred to as liabilities and will appear on the balance sheet.

The outsiders to whom the organization owes money are called *creditors*. Creditors are entitled to claim a portion of the entity's assets to repay the amounts owed to them. In general, there is no specific one-to-one matching of which asset will be used to pay any specific obligation; all of the assets form a pool of resources available to pay all of the organization's liabilities.

Organizations typically have liabilities that will require payments to suppliers, employees, financial institutions, bondholders, and the government (taxes). Many of these obligations are discussed in Chapter 7. When an organization buys supplies without immediately paying for them, the amount owed is referred to as a payable. In a fashion that parallels accounts receivable, it is important to keep track of how much money an entity owes to each supplier. In trying to keep track of or account of those liabilities, a list of *accounts payable* is created. These accounts payable are shown on the balance sheet along with amounts owed to our employees (wages or salaries payable), amounts owed to the government (taxes payable), and so on.

In some cases, an outsider will only lend money to the entity if there is a pledge of a specific asset that will be given if the obligation is not paid. The asset specified is referred to as *collateral*. For example, if Meals for the Homeless were to buy a new delivery truck, it might need to borrow money to pay for the truck. The truck might be used as collateral for the loan. Although it is Meals' intention to use money to repay the loan, if it falls behind in the payments, the lender can claim (foreclose on) that specific asset, the truck, and sell it to recover the money that had been loaned to Meals. Similarly, the Town of Millbridge can foreclose on property in the town if the owner fails to pay real estate taxes due on that specific property.

Owners' Equity

Generally, a healthy organization will have more assets than liabilities. The difference between the entity's assets and liabilities is referred to as owners' equity, net assets, or fund balance, depending on the type of entity. This is the amount of valuable resources that an organization would have left over if it paid all of its current obligations.

In for-profit organizations, the owners own all of the assets and are obligated to pay all of the liabilities of the organization. For organizations formed as sole proprietorships or partnerships, the owners have unlimited liability. If liabilities exceed assets, the owners are responsible for paying the difference. One of the main reasons that the corporate form of ownership is used is because it may establish limited liability. The owners of a corporation are generally obligated to repay liabilities only to the extent that the corporation has assets. If any assets are left after all liabilities have been paid, they belong to the owners. If there are not enough assets to pay all liabilities, some creditors will not get paid.[4] In the case of a corporation, the residual is referred to as stockholders' equity. The equity is sometimes referred to as the net worth or book value of the organization.

Equity, stockholders' equity, partners' equity, owners' equity, net worth, net assets, and fund balance are all different terms to represent this same concept. However, in not-for-profit organizations, no one owns the organization, although they are often set up as corporations.

---

[4] Who gets paid? This depends on prior agreements and legal issues regarding the priority ranking of different creditors. In some cases, creditors have a legal claim on specific assets that have been used as collateral for specific liabilities.

Since there are no owners of not-for-profits, there are no "residual claimants" of the organization's owners' equity. The net assets of the not-for-profit organization belong to the public. Therefore, we tend to stay away from terms that imply ownership, such as owners' equity. Instead, the term *net assets* is used. The same is true for governments.

Governments and some not-for-profit organizations subdivide their resources into separate groupings called funds. One fund would keep track of routine or general operations of the organization. Another fund might accumulate resources to repay long-term obligations. Yet another fund might be used to track resources being accumulated for a special project or purpose. When the liabilities in each individual fund are subtracted from that fund's assets, the remaining amount, or owners' equity for that fund, is simply called the *fund balance*. When reporting for the entity as a whole, however, state and local governments and not-for-profit organizations use the term net assets.

Note that the various names for owners' equity are not changes in substance, but just semantics. In all cases, owners' equity, net assets, or fund balance represent the residual amount when liabilities are subtracted from assets.

GENERALLY ACCEPTED ACCOUNTING PRINCIPLES

In many instances outsiders want financial information about the organization. They may be unwilling to sell, lend, or donate money to the organization unless they know its finances. In some cases, state regulations call for submission of financial information. Financial information should be relevant, reliable, comparable, and consistent. Relevant information is information that can assist in making decisions. Reliable information is information that can be verified as being accurate. Comparable information allows for meaningful comparisons to be made. Consistent information allows for determining changes and trends over time.

Certified Public Accountants (CPAs) are often called upon to *audit* the financial statements of an organization. Audited financial statements follow rules that are designed to improve the likelihood that the information is relevant, reliable, comparable and consistent. Sometimes this is voluntary on the part of the organization. However, many audits take place because of government laws or regulations that require them. Many lenders will not lend money without receiving audited financial statements. Many state governments require them from organizations that receive payments from the state. Even if there is no requirement that an organization have an audit, it is prudent for the board of trustees to require an audit. Having an outsider review the financial records each year lessens the risk of fraud or embezzlement. It also reduces the likelihood that there are undetected accidental errors in the financial records. This in turn reduces the chance of a crisis resulting from sudden discovery of substantial shortfalls in assets or revenues as compared with management's beliefs and expectations.

CPAs' audits examine financial statements and the underlying financial records on which they are based. Drawing from their examinations, CPAs issue letters giving their opinions as to whether the financial statements are free of *material* (substantial) misstatements and whether they conform to *Generally Accepted Accounting Principles* (GAAP). Although GAAP are called "principles," they might be more accurately described as a set of rules and conventions. They are established by the Financial Accounting Standards Board (FASB) and the Governmental Accounting Standards Board (GASB) to help create some degree of uniformity. This helps people from outside the organization better understand the information contained in the financial statements. It makes the statements from one organization somewhat comparable with the statements from another since they both follow the same set of rules.

One might think that financial statements would be straightforward in any event. Why would we need a set of common rules for something that would logically just follow the standard rules of arithmetic? Actually, recording financial information and reporting financial information are more complicated than one might assume. For instance, suppose that HOS has owned a piece of land for the 120 years since the hospital was founded. In the late 1800s that land was bought by the hospital for $5,000. If we adjusted the cost for the impact of general inflation over all those years, perhaps the land would now be worth $50,000 or $100,000. However, the land is in the center of the city, and some think it is worth $50 million. Others disagree, however. Some feel that the hospital could not receive more than $45 million for the land, others believe it could sell it for $52 million.

When we prepare a balance sheet, what is the value that we should show for the land? We could show any one of the values mentioned. The key, therefore, is to come to some general agreement about the approach to be taken. Different reasonable people might disagree over what approach is best. However, we can all agree to follow one uniform approach.

We consider here a few of the more prominent rules that are part of GAAP. One should bear in mind, however, that this represents a complex field: CPAs take extensive coursework in accounting and finance, take a rigorous state licensing examination, and in most states must also have experience in the field before they can receive their CPA license and designation.

The Entity Concept

As we consider the accounting equation and the balance sheet, we must determine whose assets, liabilities, and owners' equity we are interested in. Are we mostly focused on the financial concerns of Leanna Schwartz? Or are we interested in Meals for the Homeless? Or are we interested in just one particular soup kitchen that is run by Meals for the Homeless? To deal with this question, we must define the *entity* that is of interest to us.

The entity concept requires you to define the person, organization, or part of an organization for which you intend to report financial results. All financial measurements must then use the perspective of that entity. Meals for the Homeless is an entity. We can keep track of the financial resources of that entity. Leanna Schwartz, the executive director of Meals for the Homeless, is also an entity. GAAP requires us to avoid commingling or confusing the financial resources of Schwartz with those of Meals for the Homeless. They are separate and distinct from each other, even though Meals pays a salary to Schwartz.

Consider the following: Suppose that Schwartz works for the month of January and is owed a salary of $6,000 for the month. The legal right to collect that salary is an asset from her perspective. She will call that expected salary "wages receivable" and show it as an asset on her personal balance sheet. In considering her own financial status, she owns something valuable: the right to collect her $6,000 salary. However, when we consider Meals for the Homeless to be the entity, we get a different result. Meals has an obligation to make a payment to Schwartz. Rather than having an asset, from its perspective a liability exists and will appear on the entity's balance sheet. It will keep track of the liability by calling it "wages payable" of $6,000.

Leanna Schwartz and Meals for the Homeless are not the only two possible entities. Meals for the Homeless may have a program specifically for individuals living in shelters that do not have kitchens. At times, various foundations, individuals, and city agencies may be interested in knowing the financial status of just that program. In that case, the program can be viewed as the entity, and all accounting information can be gathered and reported as it relates to just that smaller entity within the larger Meals for the Homeless organization.

Many not-for-profit organizations and all governments use a system called fund accounting for internal accounting purposes, as noted earlier in this chapter. In that system, a number of separate funds are created. Each fund is a separate entity within the larger organization-wide entity. Fund accounting is discussed further in Chapters 11 and 12.

Monetary Denominator

Once we have identified the entity of interest, we can prepare a budget for the entity, track money the entity receives or spends, and prepare reports showing how well the entity has done from a financial perspective. There is a restriction, however, on the way in which we keep track of the entity's events. All events that have a financial element must have a monetary figure attached to them. This is referred to as the *monetary denominator principle*. Even if no cash is involved, we describe an event in terms of amounts of currency. For example, suppose that a philanthropist donates a new kitchen oven to Meals for the Homeless. We will assign a dollar value to the oven.[5]

The reason this convention exists is related to communication. Accounting information is used by individuals within the organization to communicate with each other and is also used by the organization to provide information to a wide variety of users outside of the organization. Without the monetary denominator, such communication would be cumbersome to the point of being noninformative.

Suppose that you were trying to tell someone what assets the organization has. You could try to list each desk, chair, building, book, lamp, and everything else the entity owned. You would of course also describe each item, giving its age, size, condition, and so on. The resulting list of items would likely be hundreds or perhaps thousands of pages long.

The benefit of the monetary denominator is that it allows us to summarize information. Rather than listing each building, we can state that we have buildings that cost $500,000 in total. However, the monetary denominator creates its own problems. Currency values are not necessarily stable over time due to inflation. Stating items in terms of their dollar value allows for substantial aggregation and summarized reporting of values. However, determining the appropriate value to report is not always easy. What is the value of the piece of land that HOS sits on? The land has been owned for 120 years. Over that time, there may have been two prior hospital buildings that were each built and torn down and replaced by a newer one. The land cannot be sold without also selling the hospital. Trying to place a value on the land creates a difficult problem.

Objective Evidence and the Cost Convention

The monetary denominator leads to the next two rules related to the use of *objective evidence* and the *cost convention*. These are sometimes referred to as the objectivity or reliability principle and the *cost* principle. GAAP requires that, whenever possible, values be based on objective rather than subjective evidence. For example, the current value of the land owned by HOS has been estimated (previously) to be either $50 million, $45 million, or $52 million. Those three numbers represent the subjective valuation of three different individuals. The only way to be sure of what the land is worth would be to sell it.

Since the current value of that land is subjective, do we have any objective or reliable evidence that we can use to assign a value to the land? Reliable evidence should be both verifiable and able to be confirmed by an independent party. The land cost $5,000. It is likely that no one believes the cost of that land is a good measure of its current value. However, it is also likely that different people could all agree that $5,000 was in fact the amount spent to acquire the land. The cost convention holds that unless there is some other rule that governs the valuation of an asset, we will show it on the balance sheet at its cost.

Thus the asset that is worth around $45 million or $50 million will be reported as just $5,000 on the balance sheet. Assets make up the left side of the fundamental equation; the

---

[5] In the United States, dollars are used for the monetary denominator. In other countries, the local currency is used.

residual net assets on the right side of this equation are similarly affected by this treatment. We need to know the GAAP conventions to understand the implications of the financial statements and whether the numbers on them are a reasonable representation of the organization's finances.

Notice that this is a result of the monetary convention. We could just describe the piece of land, giving its size and location. However, the monetary convention says that it is too cumbersome to describe individually every asset. So we must report a monetary value. Using a subjective valuation would make it very difficult to interpret the balance sheet. How would we know if the value used was optimistic, neutral, or pessimistic? Subjective approaches also provide management with an undue ability to manipulate the reported information. Thus, the GAAP of using objective evidence pushes us to adopt the cost convention. This results in reporting an objective dollar amount that everyone can agree upon.

Many would also agree that this does not provide very useful information. It can be very misleading to see land on a balance sheet shown at its cost rather than its current value. Accounting systems are not perfect. The lack of relevancy of cost information is something that accountants need to address. One of the prices paid for some degree of uniformity and comparability is a reduction in the relevance of the information provided.

It is important for users of financial statements to understand that assets on balance sheets are not necessarily shown at their current value. In particular, inventory and land are shown at their cost. Buildings and equipment are shown at their cost reduced by an allowance for accumulated depreciation. Depreciation represents the portion of capital assets charged as expenses as the assets are used over time. Depreciation is discussed in Chapter 10. Even if a building rises in value over the period it is owned by the organization, it will be reported on the balance sheet at a net value, which is its cost less all of the depreciation that has been recorded while it has been owned by the organization.

One exception to the cost convention relates to investments in marketable securities. Marketable securities are stocks and bonds that can readily be sold in stock or bond markets. Many newspapers print the closing price of such securities at the end of each business day. This provides a source of objective evidence. Given the ability to assign a current value to these securities based on objective evidence, they generally do not follow the cost convention.

The cost convention has significant managerial implications. For example, when one buys fire insurance, using the balance sheet as a guide for the dollar amount of insurance on the building and equipment may substantially understate the needed insurance to replace those facilities. Buildings are often worth more than the value on the balance sheet.

Conservatism

Another controversial GAAP relates to *conservatism*. This principle requires financial statements to give adequate consideration to the risks faced by the organization. Effectively, this argues for anticipating losses but not gains. According to this philosophy, there is a preference for receiving a good surprise rather than a bad one. It is better to make people aware of poor outcomes that may occur than it is to make them aware of good outcomes that may not occur.

For example, frequently organizations are not able to collect 100 percent of their accounts receivable. Some are never paid and become bad debts. At the time the organization provides goods and services, it records accounts receivable (assuming that it is not paid in cash on the spot).[6] If the full amount of all accounts receivable appeared on the balance

---

[6] This assumes that the organization uses the accrual basis of accounting discussed in Chapter 2.

sheet at the end of the year, it would mislead the reader of that statement. It would overstate the value of the accounts receivable asset since the full amount will probably not all be collected. Therefore, it is necessary to reduce the receivables balance by an estimate of the amount that will not be collected. Accountants would prefer to avoid the use of estimates because they are often not based on objective evidence. However, there are situations in which a good estimate is better than no estimate.

For a long time, the result of the conservatism principle was that if the organization owned shares of stock, it would report the stock investment on its balance sheet at the lower of its cost or market value. If the stock went down in value, perhaps from a $100 purchase price to a $50 current value, we would report it at its lowered value. However, if it went up in value, perhaps from a $100 purchase price to a $200 current value, we would just report it at its $100 cost.

Some believe that the rationale for the principle of conservatism stems from the 1929 stock market crash. Accountants may be trying to prevent an overexuberant interpretation of the information provided; some contend that a key cause of the stock market crash of 1929 was an unduly optimistic picture painted by financial statements of the era. Others argue that conservatism is just a way to protect CPAs from malpractice lawsuits. If a company's stock does very poorly, accountants are often sued by people who bought shares of that stock. Suppose the balance sheet of an organization shows a piece of land with a value of $50 million. What if the land is subsequently sold for $10 million? The company's stock price may plunge, and the CPA may be sued for allowing the organization to report misleading information. In contrast, if the land is reported on the balance sheet at $5,000 and is later sold for $10 million, it is unlikely that any stockholder will sue the accountant if the stock price soars.

Is it really worse to present overly optimistic misleading information than overly pessimistic misleading information? That question cannot be answered definitively here. The principle of conservatism is still used. However, in the case of marketable securities, the principle of lower of cost or market has been abandoned. Marketable securities are generally reported at their fair market value as of the date of the statement of financial position (balance sheet).

The Going Concern Concept

Financial statements are prepared under the assumption that the entity will continue in existence. For example, when Meals for the Homeless prepares its financial statements, including the balance sheet, there is a presumption that the organization is going to continue in business for the foreseeable future. This is referred to as the *going concern principle*.

Why is this important? Suppose that an organization has severe financial difficulties and must declare bankruptcy and cease business. Many of its assets will likely be sold for a substantial discount at a bankruptcy auction. Its balance sheet values may overstate the amount to be obtained in such an auction. Many suppliers would not sell to an organization that was not going to continue in business because there is a higher risk of not being able to collect payment for the supplies delivered. Lenders are less likely to be willing to lend money to an organization that is likely to go out of business.

Therefore, if the results of an audit indicate that there is a serious risk that the organization will not be able to continue in business, the CPA must disclose that fact.

The Principle of Materiality

A *material* error or misstatement is one that is considered to be significant. Many people believe that financial statements are totally accurate. That is generally not the case. Financial statements report a summary of many individual transactions. Most organizations will have thousands, tens of thousands, or even millions of individual financial events that must each be recorded, summarized, and reported in aggregate. It is likely that clerical errors will occur in this process. To ensure that absolutely no errors occur would be extremely expensive, if it is even possible.

CPAs must indicate in their audit report whether in their opinion the financial statements are free of material misstatements. For example, if HOS really has net assets of $150,238,197 but erroneously reported $150,238,917, the auditor would not consider the error to be material. Looking closely at the two numbers, it appears there has been a transposition error: The three last digits were reported as 917 instead of 197, resulting in an overstatement of net assets in the amount of $720. However, that is a very small amount when compared with the total of about $150 million.

How big does an error have to be to be material? That is a difficult question, one that requires experience and knowledge of the specific situation. An error of $10,000 might be material for a small organization but not material for a large one. As a general rule of thumb, accountants focus on whether an error is so large that it would likely affect decisions made by users of the financial statement.

For example, if banks found out that net assets were $720 less than had been reported, would they reconsider making a loan to the hospital? If a supplier found out, would it refuse to sell supplies to the hospital? If the errors are too small to affect the decisions of any users of the financial statement, they are not material.

The Accrual Concept

GAAP requires organizations to report their financial position and results of operations on an *accrual basis* of accounting (discussed in Chapter 2). This means that revenues are recorded in the year that the organization provides goods or services and is legally entitled to receive payment. The revenues are recorded even if payment has not yet been collected by the end of that year. Expenses are recorded in the year that assets have been consumed in the process of providing goods and services. This contrasts sharply with the *cash basis* of accounting, which would record revenue when cash is received and expense when cash is paid.

The rationale for using accrual accounting is that it provides a better measure of how well the organization has done for the year. Suppose that HOS provides a lot of service in the last month of its year. Suppose further that most of its expenses are for supplies and labor. It buys and pays for its supplies before they are used. It pays for most of its labor in the month the employees work. However, the various government and insurance payers delay payment to the hospital for a month or two.

On a cash basis, it might appear that the hospital had a bad year. It would have had expenses for the last month of the year but no revenues. In reality, it did not have a bad year. It will just be collecting the revenues for the last month of the year shortly after the year ends.

Consider another example: Suppose that Middle City provides a subsidy to Meals for the Homeless with monthly payments in advance. On the first day of each month, the city provides a payment to Meals for that month. However, Meals pays its employees on the first day of the following month. It pays its suppliers in the month following purchase. Thus, it would receive city payments for the entire year. However, for the last month of the year, it would not yet have paid its suppliers or employees. On a cash basis, it might appear that a significant surplus had been earned. In reality, one must consider the various resources that have already been consumed but not paid for by the end of the year.

Note that if one used a cash basis, there would be no receivables or payables on the balance sheet of the organization. Since revenues are not recorded until there has been a receipt of cash, the transaction is not recorded at the time the service is provided. The same holds true for the payment of liabilities. No financial event is recorded until the payment is made. In the case of Meals for the Homeless, an outsider might misinterpret the financial position of the organization because he or she would be unaware of all the payments to employees and suppliers that have not yet been made.

To avoid giving misleading information, any financial statements prepared in accordance with GAAP use accrual accounting. That approach gives a much better matching of revenues and expenses (resources earned and used) for the time period covered by the financial statements, often one year.

However, it is important to know how much cash the organization has received and used, where the cash came from, and where it went. Without monitoring the flow of cash, the organization can put itself at financial risk. Some organizations have sold off critical assets to raise cash because of losses from ongoing operations. The overall change in cash may not be significant. However, the implications of such actions are. It is vital to be able to quickly determine whether the organization has a healthy positive flow of cash from its routine operations. If not, then both external and internal users of the financial statements will have cause for concern. Chapter 10 discusses the cash flow statement that provides that information.

INTERNATIONAL FINANCIAL REPORTING STANDARDS

The International Accounting Standards Board (IASB) is the rule-making body that generates International Financial Reporting Standards (IFRS). Until relatively recently, accounting standards varied greatly from country to country. As the world has become a global marketplace, however, there has been a growing need for international consistency in financial reporting. This affects not only global for-profit corporations, but all health care and not-for-profit organizations with branches around the world. Moreover, recent developments may extend IFRS to all non-governmental organizations in the United States.

In 2002 the European Union adopted IFRS as its reporting standard and many other countries soon followed. There are now over 100 countries that either allow or require IFRS for reporting. In the United States, IFRS are being closely examined. The two primary questions being considered are (1) whether U.S. companies should be permitted to prepare their financial statements using IFRS, and (2) whether U.S. companies should be required to prepare their financial statements using IFRS.

There is currently a joint effort by the FASB and IASB to revise both GAAP and IFRS.

In 2002, the aim of the FASB and the IASB was to make their existing financial reporting standards fully compatible with one another. By 2005, the focus shifted from the compatibility of the two reporting standards to that of convergence, with the goal of developing high-quality, common standards over time.[7]

Many aspects of IFRS are not drastically different from GAAP. Issues such as relevance, reliability, and comparability of information are important under both systems. Both systems require the accrual basis of accounting and require balance sheets, income statements, cash flow statements, and notes. However, there are substantial differences. IFRS allow property, plant, and equipment to be revalued to their fair value rather than requiring reporting based

---

[7] Charles Harrell, Joel N. Ephross, Shelton M. Vaughan, and T. John Lin. "United States: IFRS Becoming a Reality: International Financial Reporting Standards, Mondaq Business Briefing, http://www.mondaq.com, July 8, 2008.

on historical cost less depreciation. IFRS does not allow the LIFO inventory method, which is allowed under GAAP (see Chapter 10 for a discussion of LIFO). There are many other more technical differences as well.

The current trend toward convergence is strong. Readers of this book should be aware that this convergence is occurring. It will likely take a number of years for this transition to be completed. Eventually, however, it is probable that most if not all non-governmental organizations will be following a set of IFRS that are significantly different from current GAAP.

FISCAL YEARS

A balance sheet can be prepared to show the organization's financial position at any point in time. Many organizations prepare balance sheets routinely at the end of each month or quarter year. Virtually every organization prepares a balance sheet at the end of its *fiscal year*.

Although individuals usually focus on the calendar year, entities can choose any 12-month period for their financial or fiscal year. Although many public, not-for-profit, and health organizations use a calendar year, a large number do not. An organization that chooses to end its year on June 30 of each year would be said to have a June 30 fiscal year-end. Any time during the period from July 1, 2010, through June 30, 2011, would be said to be part of fiscal year 2011.

The fiscal year-end is chosen to make things easier and less expensive. Often organizations choose the slowest time of the year. For example, hospitals may be busier in the winter, when there are a lot of weather-related illnesses, and slower in the summer. Employees of the hospital will have more time to count inventory items, summarize financial results, and prepare year-end reports when there are fewer patients, fewer bills to be issued, less inventory to count, and so on. So hospitals often end their year on June 30, as do many school districts.

At the end of the fiscal year, many things have to be taken care of by both internal accountants who work for the organization and the external auditor. As noted earlier, many organizations are required to have an annual review of their accounting records by an outside, independent CPA. When this audit takes place, the management of the organization gets tied up answering many time-consuming questions. Often year-end tax returns must be prepared, even by not-for-profit organizations. Other year-end reports, such as Medicare cost reports, are also filed shortly after the fiscal year ends. Therefore, if you can find a time when the accounting functions within the organization are at a slow point, it makes for a good fiscal year-end.

BALANCE SHEET ELEMENTS

We now turn our attention to the components that make up a balance sheet. The basic elements of a balance sheet are shown in Exhibit 9-1, which uses the hypothetical Meals for the Homeless as an example.

The first asset subgroup is *current assets* and the first liability subgroup is *current liabilities*. The words *short-term, near-term,* and current are used interchangeably by accountants and usually refer to a period of time less than or equal to one year. Current assets are those assets that are cash or cash equivalents, or will either become cash or be used up within a year. Cash equivalents are very short-term investments that are readily converted to cash, such as money market deposits or treasury bills. Current liabilities are obligations that must be paid within a year.

Why are current assets and liabilities separated and highlighted by being shown first? These items get prominent attention by being at the top of the balance sheet. This helps the reader quickly determine if the entity likely has enough resources that will become cash in the near future to pay off obligations due in the near future. This becomes a critical diagnostic test of the financial health and stability of the organization.

Current assets include not only cash but also securities, receivables, inventories, and several other items. The primary requirement for classification as a current asset is management's expectation or intention to convert the asset to cash or use it up within a year. Thus, an investment in Microsoft stock would be a current asset only if we expect to sell it in the coming year. Otherwise the stock would be treated as a *long-term* asset.

Long-term (greater than a year) assets are divided into several sections. *Fixed assets* represent the entity's property, plant, and equipment. *Investments* are primarily stocks and bonds purchased with the intent to hold on to them as a long-term investment. Intangibles, when included on the balance sheet, are generally shown as a long-term asset category.

In addition to current liabilities, the firm also typically has obligations that are due more than a year from the balance sheet date. Such liabilities are termed long-term liabilities.

The last section on the balance sheet is the owners' equity. This is reported below liabilities on the balance sheet. As discussed earlier, owners' equity, net assets, fund balance, or stockholders' equity represent the residual amount after liabilities have been subtracted from assets.

ASSETS: A CLOSER LOOK

We now turn our attention to issues regarding the specific components that appear on most balance sheets. Note, however, that this is not a comprehensive listing of all possible asset categories.

Cash

Assets are shown on the balance sheet in the order of liquidity with the most *liquid assets* listed first. Liquidity refers to how close an asset is to being cash. The more quickly an asset can become cash available for spending, the more liquid the asset is. Liquid assets are readily available to pay the organization's obligations. Cash is considered to be the most liquid asset, assuming that it is available for current use. Cash means not only cash on hand, but also checking and savings accounts. Cash is always the first item listed under current assets. And current assets are listed before long-term assets because they are more liquid than long-term assets.

In some cases, the organization has cash in a bank account, but it is being held for some long-term use. For example, we might be legally obligated to put cash aside for repayment of a bond liability when it reaches its maturity. That cash will be shown as a long-term asset because it is not currently available for use.

In Exhibit 9-1, we see that Meals for the Homeless ended the year with $1,000 of cash.

Marketable Securities

The next most liquid class of assets is *marketable securities*. These represent *equity* securities and nonequity instruments that are actively traded in stock and bond markets. Marketable securities are liquid because they can be bought and sold on any business day with settlement of the sale made in cash within a few days.[8]

Stock is referred to as an equity security because when you buy stock you are buying an ownership, or equity, interest in the company. Debt, such as bonds and notes, are

---

[8] Current regulations call for settlement (completion of the exchange) of sales of most stocks and bonds on the second day after the transactions. Sales of treasury securities can often have same-day settlement.

nonequity instruments; they do not infer ownership. If the market value of bonds drops, this has no effect on the holder if the bond is held until maturity when it is repaid.

The current rules for government and not-for-profit organizations require them to report all securities that have readily determinable fair values at their fair value on the balance sheet.[9] In Exhibit 9-1, we see that Meals has $3,000 of marketable securities.

Accounts Receivable

As noted previously, accounts receivable come in a number of varieties. Generally, if we provide goods and services, we use the term *accounts receivable.* Governments have taxes receivable. United Way has pledges receivable. Research organizations have grants receivable. There are an unlimited number of different account names or titles.

Not all accounts receivable are ultimately collected, as noted previously in the discussion of conservatism. The principal risk of allowing people to make purchases on credit, or on account, is that some will never pay the amount they owe you. This creates a significant problem in an accrual accounting system. If we were using cash accounting, we would not record a transaction until the cash was received. At that time, we could record the increase in cash. On an accrual system, we record the increase in accounts receivable at the time the service is provided.

However, this raises the possibility of overstating the receivables asset if not all receivables are ultimately collected. To adjust for this, an estimate is made of the amount of year-end receivables that will not be collected. This adjustment is generally based on historical patterns. One approach to making the estimate is to take a percentage of all sales for the year that are not paid for in cash. This would be based on the percentage of all sales that, based on history, are typically never collected by the organization. Another approach is to take a percentage of outstanding receivables at year-end.

The accounts receivable aging report, discussed in Chapter 7, is particularly valuable for helping managers make an estimate of the amount of receivables that will never be collected. For example, an organization's experience may have shown that 90 percent of all receivables more than 120 days old are never collected, 75 percent of those between 90 and 120 days, 30 percent of those between 60 and 90 days, and 4 percent of all receivables less than 60 days old. These percentages can be multiplied by the balances in each of those age categories to determine how much of the outstanding receivables at year-end are likely to become bad debts.

For Meals for the Homeless, total year-end accounts receivable are $63,000. Of that amount, Meals believes that $8,000 may not be collectible, leaving a net amount expected to be collected of $55,000. The net amount and the estimated uncollectible amount are shown in Exhibit 9-1.

Inventory

The next asset group, in the order of decreasing liquidity, is inventory. This represents supplies that have been acquired to be used in the process of making goods or providing services for sale. For instance, HOS must buy bags of saline solution, pharmaceuticals, and other supplies that will be used for treating patients. Following the cost principle of accounting, inventory is shown on the balance sheet at its cost. There are a number of different approaches to determining the cost of inventory (discussed in Chapter 10). Exhibit 9-1 indicates that Meals for the Homeless had $2,000 of inventory at the end of the year.

---

[9] Investor-owned organizations, such as for-profit hospitals, must report investments in debt securities that the organization intends to hold until maturity based on the cost of the security rather than its fair value.

Prepaid Expenses

Prepaid expenses are assets that represent prepayments. For example, suppose that we paid $100 for a one-year fire insurance policy on the last day of the year. The cash is gone, but the fire insurance will protect us for all of next year. We have not reduced our assets; we have merely exchanged one asset (i.e., cash) for another asset (i.e., fire insurance).

How would that latter asset appear on the balance sheet? It would be listed as a prepaid expense. The title emphasizes the fact that we do not expect this asset to generate cash. We expect it to be consumed over time and become an expense. However, since we paid for it in advance, it is currently an asset.

Short-term prepayments that will be consumed within one year are called prepaid expenses. Longer-term prepayments are referred to as *deferred charges* and appear in the long-term asset section of the balance sheet. For example, if the organization paid for a three-year insurance policy, one-third of the cost would appear on the balance sheet as a prepaid expense and two-thirds would appear as a deferred charge. Meals for the Homeless ended 2011 with $1,000 of prepaid assets.

Fixed Assets

The most prominent of the long-term asset categories for many organizations is fixed assets. This category includes the property (land), plant (buildings), and equipment (including furniture) owned by the organization.

Land is recorded at its cost. Land never gets used up. Therefore, there is no reason to reduce its value on the balance sheet. It may rise or fall in value. However, due to the subjectivity involved in estimating a current value, accountants rely on the objectivity and cost principles and, as a result, record land on the balance sheet at its cost. From Exhibit 9-1, we see that Meals for the Homeless owns land that it paid $40,000 to acquire. We cannot estimate its current market value from the balance sheet.

Plant and equipment are originally recorded at cost when acquired. As time passes, they get used up. They physically decline, requiring more maintenance and eventually replacement. The accrual process requires us to charge an expense in the period that an asset is used to help generate revenue. If a machine is used for five years to generate revenues for the organization, then its cost should be assigned to those five years. This is done through the *depreciation* process.

Suppose that Meals bought a delivery van for $32,000 the previous year. It believes that it can use the van for five years and then sell it for $2,000. The $2,000 is called the salvage value. Since Meals will recover that part of the original cost, it is only using up $30,000 worth of equipment over that time period. This $30,000 can be allocated at a rate of $6,000 per year for each year. The process of allocating a portion of the cost of an asset to each year for a period of years is referred to as taking depreciation. Each year there is a *depreciation expense* of $6,000, and the net value of the equipment is decreased by that amount.[10] Intangible assets, such as patents, are generally *amortized* rather than depreciated. The impact is the same whether we refer to the process as amortization or depreciation. Depreciation expense is part of the activity statement (discussed in Chapter 10).

---

[10] This approach to depreciation is sufficient to assign a part of the cost of the asset to each year that it provides useful service to the organization. However, it is unlikely to provide a good approximation of depreciation from an economic perspective. This issue is discussed further in Chapter 10.

How are plant and equipment shown on the balance sheet? We did not buy the van this year, but we still own it, so it must appear on the balance sheet. However, it is no longer new. We are therefore not allowed to show its full cost, because it has been partly used up. Instead, we report its *net book value*. The net book value is the original cost of the asset less the total amount of depreciation that has been taken for all the years that we have owned it. For example, after Meals owns the van for two years, the *accumulated depreciation* will be $12,000. Suppose that Meals also owns kitchen equipment (e.g., ovens, refrigerators) that cost $21,000. This equipment is expected to last 10 years and have a $1,000 salvage value. We have had the equipment for three years by the end of 2011. The annual depreciation on the kitchen equipment is $2,000. The accumulated depreciation after three years is $6,000:

Kitchen equipment cost	$21,000
Less salvage value	−1,000
Depreciable base	$20,000
Divided by 10-year useful life	÷ 10
Depreciation per year	$ 2,000
Times number of years owned	× 3
Accumulated depreciation	$ 6,000

For Meals as a whole, the net book value, or equipment net of depreciation, or simply the net value of the equipment is as follows:

Van and Kitchen Equipment at Cost $32,000 + $21,000 =	$53,000
Accumulated Depreciation $12,000 + $6,000 =	18,000
Equipment, Net of Depreciation	$35,000

Sometimes land is included in the total. If we are referring to land, buildings, and equipment, the net value of $35,000 would be combined with the land cost of $40,000 and the $75,000 total would be called Property, Plant, and Equipment, Net, or Net Fixed Assets.

The equipment's net value is shown on the balance sheet, as we see in Exhibit 9-1. However, the cost and the accumulated depreciation must also be disclosed. If we do not show that detail on the balance sheet, it must be disclosed in a set of notes that accompany the financial statement. In this case, Meals shows its property and the net value of its equipment. The cost of the equipment and the accumulated depreciation would therefore have to be disclosed in a note.

Why show all three values? They help us understand the size of an organization and how old its facilities are. Compare Meals for the Homeless in City A one year after buying its only van with Feed the Hungry in City B. Which is bigger? Which will have to replace its vans sooner?

	Meals for Homeless City A	Feed the Hungry City B
Net Equipment	$35,000	$30,000

According to this, they certainly seem to be similarly sized organizations. Meals is perhaps a bit larger. However, consider the following more-detailed information provided in the notes that accompany the balance sheet:

	Meals for Homeless City A	Feed the Hungry City B
Equipment at Cost	$53,000	$128,000
Accumulated Depreciation	(18,000)	(98,000)
Equipment, Net	$35,000	$ 30,000

It turns out that Feed the Hungry really has much more equipment than Meals. It is probably a larger organization. It would appear that their equipment is also much older, since there is so much accumulated depreciation, and will need substantial replacement in the near future. Thus, we learn a lot more by looking at the details than we do by just looking at the net value.

Sinking Fund

A *sinking fund* is an account in which money is put aside for some future use. The most common purposes of sinking funds are to accumulate money to be available to repay a bond or to purchase building and equipment replacements in the future. Every year some organizations put into a sinking fund an amount of money equal to the depreciation for the year. That provides a way to accumulate money to replace old facilities. However, in most cases, there are no rules requiring that such savings take place. Meals for the Homeless does not have a sinking fund, although it does have $8,000 of investments (see Exhibit 9-1). Some organizations use investments as a less formal form of sinking fund. The investments can be sold to raise cash that can be used to replace buildings and equipment, or for emergencies or service expansions.

Recording Asset Transactions

For assets to appear on the balance sheet, the financial events that create them must be recorded. Once the events have been recorded, they can be summarized and reported in the financial statements. For assets to be recorded, (1) they must be owned by the entity, (2) they must have a monetary value, and (3) the monetary value must be objectively measurable.

When Meals for the Homeless buys a van, it owns the van, the van has monetary value, and we can measure that value based on what Meals paid. It becomes an asset at the time of purchase. When New York University (NYU) hires a famous professor, it enhances the overall reputation of the university. NYU owns its reputation. The reputation might result in more tuition and contribution revenue to the school, so it has a monetary value. However, the increase in monetary value resulting from hiring the professor cannot be objectively measured. Thus, an asset cannot be recorded because the professor was hired.

LIABILITIES: A CLOSER LOOK

Liabilities are divided on the balance sheet into current (or near-term, or short-term) liabilities and long-term liabilities. *Current liabilities* appear on the balance sheet before *long-term* liabilities. Just as assets are shown in liquidity order, so are liabilities. The sooner the liability is expected to be paid, the higher it appears on the balance sheet. This is done because the organization needs to know how much cash it will need and when it will need it to meet its obligations. Long-term liabilities are those that will not have to be paid until at least one year into the future.

Note that there are many possible types of liabilities. This introduction is not meant to be an all-inclusive listing of the different types of liabilities.

Accounts Payable and Wages Payable

Accounts payable are the flip side of accounts receivable. They represent amounts that the organization owes its suppliers. Most payables have due dates of one month or less. Similarly, amounts owed to employees for wages are generally paid in the very near term. Therefore, both accounts payable and wages payable generally appear quite high on the list of current liabilities.

From Exhibit 9-1, we see that at the end of the year Meals for the Homeless had $2,000 of wages payable and also $3,000 of accounts payable. Meals also had a short-term note payable of $5,000 and $5,000 that represents the current portion of a long-term mortgage. That $5,000 current portion of the long-term mortgage is discussed later.

Long-Term Debt

There are several forms of long-term debt: capital leases, unsecured long-term loans, mortgages, and bonds.

LEASES   There are two major categories of leases: *operating leases* and *capital leases.* A capital lease is one in which the organization is effectively buying an asset but paying for it with monthly lease payments. Capital leases are long-term and noncancellable. An operating lease is any lease that is not a capital lease. Short-term leases (less than one year), or cancellable leases, are treated as operating leases.

When an asset is leased, if the lease is noncancellable and is for a long period of time, or if the lease allows the organization an option to buy the asset at a very low price, accountants feel that the real intent was to have all the benefits of ownership. In that case, the liability under the lease should appear on the balance sheet as a long-term liability. The asset should also appear on the balance sheet as a long-term asset. The lease is referred to as a capital lease, and accountants would say that the lease has been capitalized.[11]

In the case of a capital lease, the organization may ultimately intend to own the asset. But until title transfers, the monthly lease payments are for the right to use the asset rather than for the asset itself. So rather than showing the asset itself on the balance sheet, we show the lease as an asset. For example, a capital lease on a building would not be called a building on the balance sheet. It would be referred to as a *leasehold asset.*

Suppose that Meals for the Homeless did not buy a van but instead signed a five-year noncancellable lease for the van. Since they intended to keep the van for five years anyway, GAAP requires that we show a long-term *leasehold liability* and long-term leasehold asset on the balance sheet.

An operating lease is one that can be canceled or one that does not otherwise meet the conditions for a capital lease. For example, the lease signed on an apartment is generally an operating lease. Operating leases do not appear on the balance sheet as either a liability or asset.

Exhibit 9-1 reveals that Meals for the Homeless does not have any capital leases. We do not know from the balance sheet whether it has operating leases.

---

[11] The exact rules for when a lease must be considered to be a capital lease are technical and are not discussed here. They contain definitions of how long an asset can be leased without being capitalized and how one defines a low optional purchase price.

SECURED AND UNSECURED LONG-TERM LOANS A *mortgage payable* is a long-term loan secured by a specific piece of collateral, usually real estate. An unsecured long-term loan is simply a loan for which no specific collateral is provided. Unsecured loans are riskier than loans with collateral; therefore, they tend to require a higher interest rate. However, they require less processing (appraisal of property and so on) and may be preferable for periods that are more than a year yet still relatively short-range, such as two to five years.

Mortgages are often for longer periods, such as 10 or 30 years. For most mortgages, the amount paid each month is the same, similar to a monthly rent payment on an apartment. However, part of the payment is used to pay interest on the outstanding loan. The rest of the payment is used to pay back part of the loan. That means that the next month the amount owed is less. Therefore, the interest will be less in the subsequent period. Each month a greater portion of the monthly payment is used to pay off the loan. As a result, early in a mortgage, the interest portion of each payment is larger and later in the mortgage, the interest portion of each payment is lower. This is discussed in Chapter 6.

As a review, consider the following example. Suppose that Meals for the Homeless, to buy a delivery van, borrowed money in the form of a mortgage on the van. The loan was for $25,000 with interest at 8 percent and payments of $6,261.41 at the end of each year.

	Beginning Loan Balance	Total Payment	Interest Portion	Repayment Portion	Ending Loan Balance
Year 1	$25,000	$6,261	$2,000	$4,261	$20,739
Year 2	20,739	6,261	1,659	4,602	16,136
Year 3	16,136	6,261	1,291	4,971	11,166
Year 4	11,166	6,261	893	5,368	5,798
Year 5	5,798	6,261	464	5,798	0

At the beginning the balance of the mortgage is $25,000. At the end of Year 1, just prior to the payment, there is still an outstanding balance of $25,000. We have owed $25,000 for the full year. Interest on this amount at 8 percent is $2,000. Therefore, of the $6,261 payment, $2,000 pays the interest for the year, and $4,261 goes toward reducing the balance owed. Since the amount still owed is lower in the second year, the interest is lower. Note that the payment is constant each year, the interest falls each year, and the loan repayment rises.

Although the van costs $32,000, Meals used a down payment of $7,000 of its own money and borrowed just $25,000. It is generally the case that lenders will not give a 100 percent mortgage. If the borrower fails to make all necessary payments, the lender has the right to foreclose on the asset and sell it. As a used asset, it is unlikely to have as much value as when originally purchased. Thus, the down payment serves as protection for the lender.

Although a mortgage is a long-term loan, each year a portion of the principal is repaid. Since that amount is repaid within one year, it must be shown as a current liability. As a result, balance sheets report the portion of the mortgage that will be repaid within one year as a current liability and the portion that will be repaid more than one year in the future as a long-term liability. Meals for the Homeless bought its van at the beginning of the previous year and has owned it for two full years. In Exhibit 9-1, the $16,136 that Meals for the Homeless still owes on the mortgage for the van is shown as $5,000 under current liabilities and $11,000 under long-term liabilities. Meals has chosen to show numbers on its financial statements rounded off to the nearest thousand dollars. Meals really will repay $4,971 of the loan in the coming year. That has been rounded off to the $5,000 shown under current liabilities.

BONDS PAYABLE   *Bonds payable* are loan obligations in which the money generally comes from a large number of lenders, such as individuals. The bonds often can be traded in a manner similar to stocks. Bonds often promise to pay annual or semiannual interest payments plus a lump sum, called the face value, at the maturity point. On the balance sheet, the value shown is the present value of the future cash flows. Recall that in Chapter 6, the value of a bond is determined by taking the present value of the principal payment to be made at maturity plus the present value of the interest payments to be made. That same total present value is reported on the balance sheet. It does not matter if the bond was issued at its face value or at a premium or discount; the present value of the future cash payments is the amount shown on the balance sheet.

Suppose that a bond with a face value of $1,000 has semiannual interest payments of $35 for 30 years and is issued for $900. Although the organization is obligated to pay $1,000 at maturity and will make 60 payments of $35 each over the intervening years, the bond would be shown on the balance sheet at its present value. At the date of issue that would have been $900, since the value of the bond at the time of issue was determined by taking a present value using the current market interest rate for that security.

It seems inadequate to show a liability of just $900 if the organization will have to pay $1,000 at maturity. However, the difference between those numbers represents additional interest. The reason the bond is issued at a discount from its face value is that the semiannual interest payments represent a lower interest rate than is called for by current market conditions. Thus the $100 difference actually represents additional interest to bring the bond's payments up to the market interest rate. Interest is a payment for the use of the money over time. Until we use the money over time, the interest is not due or owed and does not appear as a liability on the balance sheet. So the present value represents the liability for the bond at the balance sheet date.

Recording Liabilities

As noted previously, to prepare a balance sheet in accordance with GAAP, one must first record all financial events. Liabilities may be recorded if (1) they are legally owed, (2) they will have to be paid, and (3) the amount to be paid can be objectively measured. When an organization purchases supplies from a vendor without making payment immediately a liability is recorded because the organization owes the vendor money, will have to pay the vendor, and knows how much it owes.

NET ASSETS OR FUND BALANCE: A CLOSER LOOK

Owners' equity, net assets, or fund balance consists of amounts that have been contributed to the organization and profits or surpluses that have been earned and retained in the organization over time. It represents the ownership of all of the organization's valuable resources or assets that are not needed to pay its liabilities. Generally, lenders are unwilling to provide an organization with loans that equal all assets. They require some owners' equity as a cushion to protect them. If you go bankrupt and sell off all your assets at a loss, they want there to be sufficient assets to repay the amount you owe them.

In Exhibit 9-1, net assets are shown as one summary amount. Current rules require net assets of not-for-profit organizations be subdivided into unrestricted, temporarily restricted, and permanently restricted portions. The first of the three sections, *unrestricted net assets,* are net assets whose use has not been restricted by donors. The second part of net assets are *temporarily restricted* amounts. These represent donated amounts that have restrictions as to when or how they are to be used. The third section is *permanently restricted net assets*. These are amounts that arise when a donation is made that must be maintained in perpetuity. Donations to a permanent endowment would fall into this category. Often income earned on the endowment becomes unrestricted and can be spent by the organization. The three components of net assets are discussed further in Chapter 11.

For-profit organizations have an owners' equity section, which is generally called stockholders' equity and consists of two sections: contributed capital and retained earnings. Contributed capital (sometimes referred to as "paid-in capital") represents the amounts that individuals have paid directly to the firm in exchange for shares of ownership such as common or preferred stock. Retained earnings represent the portion of the profits that the firm has earned over the years that has not been distributed to the owners in the form of dividends. Retained earnings, like all items on the equity side of the balance sheet, represent a source of assets but are not assets themselves.

RECORDING FINANCIAL INFORMATION

The goal of financial accounting is to report financial information that is useful to external users. To prepare such reports, a system is needed to record financial events as they occur. One of the main jobs of the internal accounting systems in any organization, therefore, is to record all events that have a financial impact on the organization. Once the events have been recorded, they can periodically be summarized, and the organization's financial position and the results of operations can be reported. This section looks at the recording process. The next section of this chapter considers how the recorded data are used to develop financial reports and, in particular, the balance sheet.

A financial event is one that affects the fundamental equation of accounting. Recall, for example, that for a not-for-profit organization the equation is as follows:

$$\textbf{Assets} = \textbf{Liabilities} + \textbf{Net Assets}$$

How would financial transactions affect this equation? By causing changes in assets, liabilities, and net assets. The changes in net assets are generally caused by revenues, which increase net assets, or by expenses, which decrease net assets. Revenues, expenses, and other possible causes of changes in the owners' equity or net assets are discussed in Chapter 10. This discussion focuses just on changes in assets and liabilities.

Using Computers to Record Financial Transactions

The process of recording financial information can be quite tedious and subject to many errors. To improve the efficiency and accuracy of the recording process, most organizations use specialized accounting computer software programs. There are many basic, relatively inexpensive, off-the-shelf programs that can be useful for smaller organizations. For example, Intuit's Quickbooks and Sage's Peachtree can meet the basic accounting needs of most organizations and have specialized modules to handle the unique requirements of not-for-profit organizations. Larger organizations often use more specialized programs that have been created to meet specific industry requirements, or even have customized software programmed for their own organization. In this text, however, we are going to focus on understanding the conceptual issues, rather than software applications. The solid foundation for recording financial information provided in this and the next chapter are critical for having an understanding of the process, whether it is carried out manually or using one of the many available accounting software programs.

The General Journal and Journal Entries

The central recording device used by accountants is the *general journal.* A journal is simply a chronological listing of every financial event that affects the organization. The general journal is similar to a diary in that events are listed in the order they occur and as concurrently as possible.

When an event occurs and is entered into the journal, the process is referred to as making a *journal entry.* The general journal is considered to be the book of original entry. This is because no event has been recorded by the organization until it is entered in the general journal.

Each type of asset, liability, revenue, or expense is referred to as an account. We have already discussed accounts receivable and accounts payable. Anything that the organization needs to track or keep account of is referred to as an account. Organizations have a cash account, a buildings account, and so forth.

It is impossible for an event to affect only one account and leave the equation in balance. For example, suppose that not-for-profit HOS buys a piece of equipment for $2,000. What would happen to the equation if we recorded an increase in the equipment account?

ASSETS	=	LIABILITIES	+	NET ASSETS
Equipment				
+$2,000	=	No change on right side.		

The left side of the equation has increased by $2,000, but the right side is unchanged. The equation is no longer balanced. To describe an entire event, it is necessary to record a change to at least two elements in the fundamental equation. In this example, the hospital has purchased a piece of equipment. Assume that HOS has not yet paid for the equipment but expects to pay within 30 days. The organization's liabilities have changed.

ASSETS	=	LIABILITIES	+	NET ASSETS
Equipment		*Accounts Payable*		
+$2,000	=	+$2,000		

The equation is now in balance. The system for recording financial events, more commonly called transactions, is referred to as *double-entry accounting.* The phrase double-entry does not mean that the transaction is recorded twice. It means that both parts of the transaction are recorded, allowing the fundamental equation to remain in balance.

That does not mean that there must be a change on each side of the equation. For example, suppose that HOS buys inventory for $500 and pays cash for it. The equation would change as follows:

ASSETS		=	LIABILITIES	+	NET ASSETS
Cash	*Inventory*				
−$500	+$500	=	No change on right side.		

Clearly, a transaction has occurred, and it has affected two items in the fundamental equation. There was no change on the right side of the equation, but the equation is still balanced because one account on the left side of the equation has increased and another account on the left side has decreased. A journal entry is not limited to changes in just two accounts, either. For example, suppose that HOS only paid $300 when it received the inventory and it owed $200 on account. The transaction would be recorded as follows:

ASSETS		=	LIABILITIES	+	NET ASSETS
Cash	*Inventory*		*Accounts Payable*		
−$300	+$500	=	+$200		

Note that in total there has been a $200 increase on both the left side and right side of the equation. The equation is in balance after the transaction. Double-entry bookkeeping requires at least two items to change when a transaction is recorded. However, it does not limit the number of accounts that can change as part of one transaction.

Debits and Credits

The words *debit* and *credit* are commonly used in the process of recording financial information. In the development of accounting, records were originally only kept to keep track of loan transactions. If money was owed to a person, he or she was considered to be a creditor, and if a person owed money, he or she was considered to be a debtor. Based on the Latin roots for those words, *credit* for creditor and *debit* for debtor became central to the process of recording information.

Today these terms are part of the technical process of bookkeeping. Although they are a useful bookkeeping device, they are primarily a mechanical aid in the process of recording transactions. The bookkeeping use of debits and credits is discussed in Appendix 9-A at the end of this chapter.

Recording Transactions

To get a better understanding of the process of recording financial information, we now consider a series of transactions for HOS for the year 2012. In real life, a hospital would have hundreds of thousands or even millions of transactions. We will consider only a few highly summarized transactions. However, it will provide a better understanding of the process of recording information and allow us to discuss how information is summarized and reported. The example will also be used as a vehicle to review some GAAP.

Exhibit 9-3 presents the balance sheet for HOS as of December 31, 2011. The information on the balance sheet at the end of one year is also the information for the beginning of the next year. Therefore, our fundamental equation of accounting on January 1, 2012, is as follows:

ASSETS	=	LIABILITIES	+	NET ASSETS
$315,000	=	$177,000	+	$138,000

Note that these amounts are taken from Exhibit 9-3. As transactions occur during the year, they change the fundamental equation. As each financial event is recorded, we will keep track of its effect on this equation, and we will record the journal entry. After a journal entry is recorded, journalizing an event into the financial history of the organization, this equation must still be in balance, or some error has been made. At this point, we will only consider transactions that affect the balance sheet. This example is continued at the end of Chapter 10, including transactions that affect other financial statements.

EXHIBIT 9-3

Hospital for Ordinary Surgery
Balance Sheet
As of December 31, 2011

Assets

Current Assets	
Cash	$ 52,000
Accounts receivable	18,000
Inventory	5,000
Total Current Assets	$ 75,000
Fixed Assets	
Plant and equipment, net	240,000
Total Assets	$315,000

Liabilities and Net Assets

Liabilities	
Current Liabilities	
Accounts payable	$ 7,000
Wages payable	30,000
Total Current Liabilities	$ 37,000
Long-Term Liabilities	
Mortgage payable	140,000
Total Liabilities	$177,000
Net Assets	
Unrestricted	$113,000
Temporarily restricted	15,000
Permanently restricted	10,000
Total Net Assets	$138,000
Total Liabilities and Net Assets	$315,000

Consider the following events for HOS during 2012:

1. January 1. HOS purchased a fire insurance policy for $100. A check was mailed to pay for the policy.

The first thing that must be done in recording a journal entry is to determine what has transpired. In this first event, the organization has mailed a check for $100. The movement of cash is a definite indication that a financial event has taken place. The balance in our cash account (an asset) has gone down. The organization now owns an insurance policy, which will provide protection. That represents a valuable asset, called prepaid insurance (P/I). The effect of this transaction on the equation would be as follows:

ASSETS		=	LIABILITIES	+	NET ASSETS
Cash	*Prepaid Insurance*				
−$100	+$100	=	No change on right side.		

Overall, there has been a $100 decrease and a $100 increase, but the total balance on either side of the equation has not changed. However, if we were to prepare a balance sheet at this time, there would be changes. The balance sheet would show less cash and more prepaid insurance.

2. January 23. HOS mails a check to its supplier for $2,000 of the $7,000 it owed it at the end of 2011. (Refer to Exhibit 9-3 for the accounts payable liability at the end of the previous year.)

Cash has again decreased. This time there is a corresponding decrease in the liability accounts payable (A/P).

ASSETS	=	LIABILITIES	+	NET ASSETS
Cash		Accounts Payable		
−$2,000	=	−$2,000		

3. February 9. HOS places an order with a medical supply company to buy a special order X-ray machine. It will cost $50,000, and it will take more than a year to be delivered. HOS signs a contract to buy the machine.

This event does not give rise to a journal entry. From a financial viewpoint, no transaction has occurred. Even though there is a binding contract, HOS has not received anything yet and has not paid anything yet. There has been no exchange, so there is no financial transaction. HOS does not own the machine yet, and it does not have an obligation to pay for it until it does.

However, if the contract is for an amount of money that is considered to be material, then a GAAP referred to as full disclosure requires disclosure of this commitment in the notes that accompany the financial statements. The balance sheet itself, however, does not show an asset or liability related to this contract, and the accounting equation is not affected.

4. May 23. HOS purchases inventory on account for $3,000. When this inventory is used to provide patient care, the hospital will be able to charge $6,000 for it. The inventory has been received, but HOS has not paid for it.

This transaction will affect inventory and accounts payable. HOS has received an asset and owes money for it. The interesting question, however, is whether the inventory is recorded at its cost of $3,000 or resale value of $6,000. Following the cost and conservatism principles of GAAP, the inventory is recorded at its cost. We cannot anticipate the gain on a sale that has not yet taken place.

ASSETS	=	LIABILITIES	+	NET ASSETS
Inventory		Accounts Payable		
+$3,000	=	+$3,000		

5. June 9. Payments are received from insurance companies for patient care provided in 2011. $12,000 of cash is received.

Cash increases as a result of this transaction, and another asset, accounts receivable (A/R), declines.

ASSETS		=	LIABILITIES	+	NET ASSETS
Cash	*Accounts Receivable*				
+$12,000	−$12,000	=	No change on right side.		

The General Ledger and Ledger Entries

From time to time, organizations need to summarize their financial transactions and prepare reports of their financial position and the results of their operations. Although only a few transactions have been discussed previously, most organizations have a huge number of transactions annually. The *general ledger* is a device used to accumulate and summarize the information provided by these transactions.

For example, NYU has more than 20,000 employees. That means that each year close to a million weekly payroll checks are issued. It has more than 40,000 students. That means that a substantial number of tuition payments are received. The university makes rental payments on many buildings each month. Its bookstore buys textbooks for thousands of courses. It buys chalk, computers, and computer LCD projectors. Clearly, the university has well over a million transactions each year. That means more than a million journal entries. Each organization must have a method to summarize the huge amount of data that has been recorded in those journal entries so that it can provide useful information.

Given that financial statements are only a few pages long, we need a way to make the leap from the individual journal entries to the financial statements. This is done by using a device called a general ledger. A ledger is a collection of individual accounts. As noted earlier, anything we want to keep track of separately, or keep account of, is referred to as an account. Every account that might be affected by a journal entry is individually accounted for in a ledger.

For example, every organization wants to know how much cash it has so it establishes a cash account. The same is true for accounts receivable, inventory, accounts payable, wages payable, and so on. As each journal entry is recorded, the corresponding ledger accounts are updated or *posted* for the impact of the journal entry. For example, recall that in transaction 1 for HOS, the journal entry is as follows:

ASSETS		=	LIABILITIES	+	NET ASSETS
Cash	*Prepaid Insurance*				
−$100	+$100	=	No change on right side.		

The posting process consists of going to the ledger account for cash and entering a decrease of $100 and going to the ledger account for prepaid insurance and showing an increase of $100.

Working together, the general journal and general ledger are powerful tools. The general journal provides a complete chronological history of all events that have affected the organization. The general ledger lets us look at any account at any point in time and determine the balance in that account. At one time, all entries into the ledger were done manually in a book that had a separate page for each ledger account. Many organizations have computerized their accounting systems and no longer have a ledger book, per se. Computer programs will automatically update the balance in each ledger account that is affected by a journal entry.

Each ledger account that appears on the balance sheet starts the accounting period with a balance. The balance is simply the balance from the end of the previous period. The journal entries from the current period are used to modify the ledger accounts. Then the balance in each ledger account at the end of an accounting period is simply a sum of the beginning balance plus the impact of all the transactions that have been recorded during the period.

Generating a Balance Sheet

The process of generating a balance sheet is not difficult once all transactions have been journalized (recorded in the form of journal entries) and entered into the ledger accounts. Essentially, one simply needs to take the ending balance in each balance sheet ledger account (as opposed to revenue and expense ledger accounts, which will appear on the activity or operating statement) and place it on the balance sheet.

Exhibit 9-4 presents a transactions worksheet. This worksheet summarizes the five transactions for HOS discussed previously. For each transaction, the worksheet shows the impact of the transaction on the fundamental equation of accounting. It also represents a general journal and general ledger for HOS. The rows represent journal entries. The columns represent ledger accounts.

The first row in Exhibit 9-4 gives the starting balances, taken from Exhibit 9-3. The transaction rows (journal entries) are taken from the analysis of HOS's transactions done previously. The last row provides the ending balance. That row forms the basis for the balance sheet at the end of the period. Each ending account balance from the last row is directly transferred to Exhibit 9-5 to create the balance sheet at the end of the year. For example, the $61,900 from the first column, the cash ledger account, on Exhibit 9-4 is the cash amount shown on the balance sheet, Exhibit 9-5.

In this example, net assets did not change. The changes to net assets are the result of transactions that affect the operating or activity statement (often referred to as the income statement, discussed in Chapter 10). In Chapter 10, the HOS example is expanded with additional transactions that have impacts on both the operating or activity statement and on the balance sheet.

Subsidiary Journals and Ledgers

Many organizations have a set of subsidiary journals and ledgers in addition to the general journal and general ledger. These are used to provide more specific detailed information. For example, suppose HOS provided care to three different patients and sent an invoice to each of them. In each case, the event recorded in the general journal would be an increase in patient receivables and an increase in patient revenues. The general ledger account for patient receivables would increase, and the general ledger account for patient revenues would increase. The patient receivables on the balance sheet would reflect the sum of the journal entries for all three patients.

The organization needs detailed information on each patient as well. Needing to know how much money is owed to it by each of its patients, the organization will maintain a subsidiary accounts receivable journal and set of ledgers. Whereas the main ledger has separate accounts for cash, patient receivables, inventory, buildings, and so on, the subsidiary receivables journal and ledger will have separate accounts for Patient A, Patient B, Patient C, and so on. Subsidiary ledgers and journals are helpful for internal management of the organization. Financial statements, however, can be derived from the general ledger without the subsidiary ledgers.

EXHIBIT 9-4 Transactions Worksheet

| | ASSETS | | | | | = | LIABILITIES AND NET ASSETS | | | | | |
| | | | | | | | Liabilities | | | Net Assets | | |
	Cash	Accounts Receivable	Inventory	Prepaid Insurance	Plant & Equipment		Accounts Payable	Wages Payable	Mortgage Payable	Unrestricted	Temporarily Restricted	Permanently Restricted
Beginning Balance	$52,000	$18,000	$5,000	$ 0	$240,000		$7,000	$30,000	$140,000	$113,000	$15,000	$10,000
Transaction 1	(100)			100								
Transaction 2	(2,000)						(2,000)					
Transaction 3												
Transaction 4			3,000				3,000					
Transaction 5	12,000	(12,000)										
Ending Balance	$61,900	$ 6,000	$8,000	$100	$240,000		$8,000	$30,000	$140,000	$113,000	$15,000	$10,000

EXHIBIT 9-5

Hospital for Ordinary Surgery
Balance Sheet
As of December 31, 2012

Assets

Current Assets	
Cash	$ 61,900
Accounts receivable	6,000
Inventory	8,000
Prepaid insurance	100
Total Current Assets	$ 76,000
Fixed Assets	
Plant and equipment, net	240,000
Total Assets	$316,000

Liabilities and Net Assets

Liabilities	
Current Liabilities	
Accounts payable	$ 8,000
Wages payable	30,000
Total Current Liabilities	$ 38,000
Long-Term Liabilities	
Mortgage payable	140,000
Total Liabilities	$178,000
Net Assets	
Unrestricted	$113,000
Temporarily restricted	15,000
Permanently restricted	10,000
Total Net Assets	$138,000
Total Liabilities and Net Assets	$316,000

Summary

Financial reports are prepared by organizations annually, or more frequently. These financial reports help managers understand the current financial situation of the organization and the financial results of its operations. They provide information not only for management of the organization, but for outsiders as well. Preparation of financial reports that will be examined by individuals external to the organization is referred to as financial accounting. Financial accounting employs a process of recording financial transactions, summarizing all of the information contained in the transactions, and reporting the information in a set of financial statements.

The statement of financial position, commonly referred to as the balance sheet, is the first of the financial statements, and it is the topic of this chapter. A balance sheet reports the financial position of the organization at a moment in time—often the end of the fiscal year. For any specific entity, this financial document provides a highly summarized view of its financial position at any one point in time.

Financial statements are derived from information contained in and changes to the fundamental equation of accounting. That equation states that the assets of the entity equal the liabilities plus the net worth of the entity. All of financial accounting is built around that fundamental equation. In addition, many organizations follow a set of rules or conventions that are referred to as Generally Accepted Accounting Principles (GAAP). These GAAP—such as the entity, monetary denominator, objective evidence, conservatism, going concern, and materiality principles—help to provide structure that makes the financial statements of different organizations understandable and comparable.

Balance sheets provide their reader with information about a variety of different types of assets and liabilities of the entity. Some of the asset categories discussed in this chapter are cash, marketable securities, accounts receivable, inventory, prepaid expenses, and fixed assets. A variety of liability categories are also discussed, including both short-term payables and long-term debt. The residual value of the entity when liabilities are subtracted from assets represents the ownership or equity value of the entity. This may be called net worth, owners' equity, net assets, fund balance, or a variety of other names that convey the equity concept, as appropriate for the specific type of entity.

Preview

The objective of the balance sheet is to report the financial position of the organization at a specific point in time. It has been compared to a still photograph. In this chapter, we focus our attention on the financial position of organizations at a point in time, usually at the end of the fiscal year.

In contrast, in Chapter 10 we examine the activity or operating and cash flow statements. They are designed to show the results of the organization's activities over a period of time. They have been compared to movies, as opposed to still pictures. Rather than a focus on a specific point in time, they attempt to summarize what occurred during a particular accounting period, such as a year.

The activity statement—often referred to by other names, including the income statement, operating statement, statement of revenues and expenses, and statement of revenues and expenditures—compares the entity's revenues and other support to its expenses for a period of time. The cash flow statement looks at where the organization obtained its cash and where it spent cash during that period of time. The focus is not only on how much cash came and went, but also on the specific sources and uses of cash.

Key Terms from This Chapter

accounts payable. Amounts owed to suppliers.

accounts receivable. Money due to the organization for goods and services that have been provided.

accrual basis. An accounting system that records revenues in the year they become earned (whether received or not) and the expenses related to those revenues in the same year.

accumulated depreciation. Cumulative amount of depreciation for a fixed asset that has been taken over the years the organization has owned that asset.

amortization. Allocation of the cost of a long-term asset over its lifetime.

assets. Anything the organization owns of value.

audit. Examination of the financial records of the organization to discover *material* errors, evaluate the internal control system, and determine if financial statements have been prepared in accordance with GAAP.

balance sheet. See statement of financial position.

bond payable. Formal borrowing arrangement in which a transferable certificate represents the debt. The holder of the bond may sell it, in which case the liability is owed to the new owner.

capital lease. A form of long-term financing in which a long-term, noncancellable arrangement is made to lease a capital asset.

cash basis. Accounting system under which revenues are recorded when cash is received and expenses are recorded when cash is paid.

collateral. Specific asset pledged to a lender as security for a loan.

conservatism principle. Financial statements must give adequate consideration to the risks faced by the organization.

cost convention principle. Assets should be valued on financial statements at their cost at the time of acquisition.

credit. Bookkeeping term for an increase in an item on the right side of the fundamental equation of accounting or a decrease in an item on the left side.

creditors. People or organizations to whom the organization owes money.

current. Within one year; *short-term* or *near-term*.

current assets. Resources the organization has that either are cash or can be converted to cash within one year or that will be used up within one year. Current assets are often referred to as *short-term* or *near-term* assets.

current liabilities. Those obligations that are expected to be paid within one year.

debit. Bookkeeping term for an increase in an item on the left side of the fundamental equation of accounting or a decrease in an item on the right side.

deferred charges. Assets that have been paid for and have not yet been used but that will be consumed more than one year from now.

depreciation. Allocation of a portion of the cost of a capital asset into each of the years of the asset's expected useful life.

depreciation expense. Portion of the original cost of a fixed asset allocated as an expense each year.

double-entry accounting. System in which every financial transaction must change at least two accounts in the fundamental equation of accounting to keep the equation in balance.

entity. Specific person, organization, or part of an organization that is the focus of attention.

equities. The right hand side of the balance sheet; i.e., the liabilities and net assets combined.

equity. Ownership, e.g., indicating ownership of a portion of an organization, or the portion of a home owned by the homeowner.

financial accounting. System that records historical financial events, summarizes them, and provides reports of the financial impact of those events.

fiscal year. One-year period defined for financial purposes. It starts at any desired point during the calendar year and finishes one year later.

fixed assets. Those assets that will not be used up or converted to cash within one year; sometimes referred to as long-term or capital assets.

fund balance. One term for the *owners' equity* in a not-for-profit or governmental organization; assets less liabilities.

fundamental equation of accounting. Assets equal liabilities plus net assets.

general journal. First place that financial transactions are entered into the accounting records; chronological listing of all financial transactions.

general ledger. Book of accounts; listing of the balances and all changes in each of the organization's accounts.

Generally Accepted Accounting Principles (GAAP). Set of rules that must be followed for the organization's financial statements to be deemed a fair presentation of the organization's financial position and results of operations.

going concern principle. If there is a significant possibility that an organization will not be able to continue to operate because of financial difficulties, that possibility must be disclosed in the auditor's letter that accompanies a set of audited financial statements.

goodwill. Intangible asset that represents a measure of the value of the organization that goes beyond its specific physical assets.

intangible asset. Asset without physical substance or form.

investments. Primarily stocks and bonds that the organization does not intend to sell within one year.

journal entry. Entry into the general journal or a subsidiary journal.

lease. Agreement providing for the use of an asset in exchange for rental payments.

leasehold asset. The balance sheet title for a capital lease asset.

leasehold liability. The balance sheet title for a capital lease liability.

liabilities. Legal financial obligations the organization has to outsiders.

liquid assets. Cash or other assets that can quickly be converted to cash to meet the short-term liabilities of the organization.

long-term. Period longer than one year.

managerial accounting. Generation of any financial information that can help managers to manage better.

marketable securities. Investments in stocks and bonds that the organization intends to sell within one year.

material. Amount of money great enough so that an error of that size would cause a user of financial statements to make a different decision than would be made if the user had known the correct information.

monetary denominator principle. Resources on the financial statement are stated in terms of an amount of money.

mortgage payable. A loan that is secured by a specific asset.

near-term. Within one year; *current* or *short-term.*

net assets. The equivalent of *owners' equity* in a not-for-profit or governmental organization; assets less liabilities; fund balance.

net book value. The original cost of an asset less the cumulative amount of depreciation that has been taken for all the years that the organization has owned it.

net worth. See *owners' equity.*

objective evidence principle. Assets should be valued on financial statements based on objective rather than subjective information.

operating lease. Lease that is either *short-term* or cancellable.

owners' equity. Residual value after the liabilities of an organization are subtracted from the assets.

This represents the portion of the assets owned by the organization itself or its owners; *net assets* or *fund balance.*

permanently restricted net assets. Net assets that must be maintained in perpetuity due to donor-imposed restrictions.

prepaid expenses. Assets that have been paid for in advance and that generally will be consumed within a year.

post. Update ledger accounts for the impact of a *journal entry.*

receivables. See *accounts receivable.*

short-term. Within one year; current or near-term.

sinking fund. Segregated assets to be used for replacement of plant and equipment or the repayment of a long-term liability such as a bond.

statement of financial position. Report that indicates the financial position of the organization at a specific point in time; often referred to as the balance sheet.

tangible asset. Asset having physical substance or form.

temporarily restricted net assets. Donated amounts that have donor-imposed restrictions as to when or how they are to be used.

unrestricted net assets. Net assets whose use has not been restricted by donors.

Questions for Discussion

9-1. What are assets, liabilities, and owners' equity?
9-2. What are other names for owners' equity?
9-3. What is the connection between the balance sheet and the fundamental equation of accounting?
9-4. Are there any difficulties in measuring assets?
9-5. What are GAAP and how do they relate to CPAs?
9-6. What is the point of the entity concept?
9-7. Explain the monetary denominator concept.
9-8. What are the problems with the objective evidence and cost conventions?
9-9. What major change has occurred regarding the GAAP of *conservatism?*
9-10. Why is it important for the CPA to evaluate the organization based on the going concern GAAP?
9-11. Do CPAs allow errors to exist in audited financial statements?
9-12. Do GAAP have a preference between cash and accrual bases of accounting? Explain.

9-13. What is the primary requirement for classification of an asset as a current asset?
9-14. Why are cash and cash equivalents listed first on a balance sheet?
9-15. What is the difference in the way that bonds are reported by for-profit and not-for-profit organizations?
9-16. Distinguish between the Titanic and a sinking fund.
9-17. Why must financial disclosure include the cost, accumulated depreciation, and net value of fixed assets?
9-18. What requirements must be met to record an asset?
9-19. When can liabilities be recorded?
9-20. What is a journal?
9-21. What is meant by double-entry accounting?
9-22. What are debits and credits?

Problems

9-23. Dall Rose decided to start a new charitable organization, the American Financial Management Student's Association. The transactions for the first month of operations are as follows:
  1. Borrowed $20,000 from a prior financial management student who sympathized with the cause. Dall signed a note promising repayment of the loan in five years.
  2. Purchased the Website address http://www. AFMSA.org for $1,000. They paid cash at the time of purchase.
  3. Purchased 1,000 *Financial Management for Novices* student guides for later resale, at a cost of $5 per guide. They have received the guides, but have not yet paid for them.
  4. Purchased and received office equipment for $4,000. They paid for the equipment when it was received.
  5. Signed a contract with a noted tutor to provide online lessons at a rate of $100 per hour. The contract calls for 200 hours of lessons to be provided, although none has been provided yet.
  Show the impact of these transactions on the fundamental equation of accounting. (Optional: Show journal entries using debits and credits. See Appendix 9-A.)
9-24. Assume that the American Financial Management Student's Association (AFMSA) in Problem 9-23 started the year with a zero balance in all accounts. Record the transactions from Problem 9-23 in a worksheet similar to Exhibit 9-4.
9-25. Use the ending balances from Problem 9-24 to prepare a Balance Sheet.
9-26. Fathers Against Dangerous Drunks (FADD) had the following financial events during the past year:
  1. FADD borrowed $50,000 from the local bank on an unsecured five-year note to buy furniture.
  2. Furniture was purchased for $50,000. Full payment was made.

  3. Received $500,000 from a donor. The donor had pledged the money the prior year, and the donation was treated as revenue in that year.
  4. Purchased and received new brochures that would be used to announce and publicize the foundation's various areas of interest. A check for $10,000 was mailed to the printer as payment in full.
  5. FADD negotiated the purchase of an information system complete with hardware and software for $35,000. They have not yet paid for nor received the system, but they have signed a purchase contract, and expect it to be delivered and installed within the next month.
  6. Paid $700,000 for grants made in the prior year.
  Show the impact of the transactions on the fundamental equation of accounting. (Optional: Show journal entries using debits and credits. See Appendix 9-A.)
9-27. Assume that FADD began the year with the following balances (shown in alphabetical order) in their accounts:

Brochures Inventory	$ 1,000
Cash	270,000
Furniture	0
Grants Payable	700,000
Investments	830,000
Notes Payable	0
Permanently Restricted Net Assets	100,000
Pledges Receivable	500,000
Temporarily Restricted Net Assets	700,000
Unrestricted Net Assets	101,000

Record this information and the transactions from Problem 9-26 in a worksheet similar to Exhibit 9-4.
9-28. Use the ending balances from Problem 9-27 to prepare a balance sheet.

Suggested Readings

Anthony, Robert N., and Leslie Pearlman Breitner. *Core Concepts of Accounting,* 8th ed. Upper Saddle River, N.J.: Prentice Hall, 2003.

Finkler, Steven A. *Finance & Accounting for Nonfinancial Managers,* 3rd ed. New York, N.Y.: Aspen Publishers, 2003.

Granof, Michael H. *Government and Not-for-Profit Accounting: Concepts and Practices,* 3rd ed. New York, N.Y.: John Wiley & Sons, 2004.

Harrison, Walter T., and Charles T. Horngren. *Financial Accounting & Integrated Student CD,* 5th ed. Upper Saddle River, N.J.: Prentice Hall, 2004.

Larkin, Richard E., and Marie DiTommaso. *Wiley Not-for-Profit GAAP 2008: Interpretation and Application of Generally Accepted Accounting Principles for Not-for-Profit Organizations.* New York, N.Y.: John Wiley & Sons, 2008.

Ruppel, Warren. *Wiley GAAP for Governments 2007: Interpretation and Application of Generally Accepted Accounting Principles for State and Local Governments.* New York, N.Y.: John Wiley & Sons, 2007.

Werner, Michael L., and Kumen H. Jones. *Introduction to Financial Accounting: A User Perspective,* 3rd ed. Upper Saddle River, N.J.: Prentice Hall, 2004.

APPENDIX 9-A

The Recording Process: Debits and Credits

The words debit and credit are commonly used in the process of recording financial information. A debit (abbreviated Dr.[12]) represents an increase in an asset or expense. A credit (abbreviated Cr.) represents an increase in a liability or revenue.

To understand the accounting use of debits and credits, we need to make a minor arithmetical transformation in the fundamental accounting equation. The way we have presented the equation, it represents a stock:

$$\text{ASSETS (A)} = \text{LIABILITIES (L)}$$
$$+ \text{NET ASSETS (NA)}$$

By a stock, we mean that the equation tells how much we have of something. The equation indicates the total amount of assets, liabilities, and net assets at a specific point in time. However, to record transactions, we are really focusing more on the flow of resources. That is, we are focusing on what is happening as time passes. Thus, we are interested in the changes in our assets, liabilities, and net assets. We can use the Greek letter Δ (delta) to represent "the change in" some amount.

Thus, the equation now reads:

$$\Delta \text{ ASSETS (A)} = \Delta \text{ LIABILITIES (L)}$$
$$+ \Delta \text{ NET ASSETS (NA)}$$

That is, the change in assets equals the change in liabilities plus the change in net assets. More simply,

$$\Delta A = \Delta L + \Delta NA$$

The two most prominent things that change net assets are revenues, or support, and expenses. When the organization provides goods or services, it earns revenues, or if it receives donations, it has support. Revenue and support increase net assets. We show revenue or support as R. When the organization uses resources to generate revenues, it incurs an expense. Expenses reduce net assets. We show expenses as E. (Revenues and expenses are discussed further in Chapter 10.) We could think of changes to the fundamental equation as being as follows:

$$\Delta A = \Delta L + R - E$$

That is, the change in assets is equal to the change in liabilities plus revenues less expenses for the period. We can somewhat simplify the equation by adding expenses, E, to both sides, to eliminate the need for the negative sign in front of expenses. The resulting equation is

$$\Delta A + E = \Delta L + R$$

A debit is an increase in anything on the left side of this equation. A credit is an increase in anything on the right side of this equation. Conversely, a credit is a decrease in anything on the left side of the equation. A debit is a decrease in anything on the right side of the equation. When an accountant records a journal entry, items that are debited are shown slightly to the left, and credits are shown slightly to the right. This is a convention. For example, when the Hospital for Ordinary Surgery (HOS) purchases a piece of equipment, the journal entry would appear as follows:

	DR.	CR.
Equipment	$2,000	
Accounts Payable		$2,000
Explanation: to record the purchase of equipment.		

Notice that an explanation is placed directly below the journal entry so that if there is a need to refer back to it, the user will be able to understand the transaction that occurred. An accountant looking at the journal immediately knows that HOS now

---

[12] This odd abbreviation is based on the Latin root of the word *debit*. Modern accounting is based on accounting systems developed in Italy more than 500 years ago. Therefore, it is not surprising to find a Latin influence on the language of accounting.

has more equipment, because an asset (on the left) has been debited, and an increase in accounts payable, because the liability (on the right) has been credited.

Based on the definition of debits and credits in the previous paragraph, it turns out that it is impossible to keep the fundamental equation in balance, unless the total of the debits in a journal entry are equal to the total of the credits.

For example, when HOS bought inventory and paid in cash, there was an increase in inventory (debit inventory $500) and a decrease in cash (credit cash $500). The total debits and credits were both $500:

	DR.	CR.
Inventory	$500	
Cash		$500

Explanation: to record purchase of inventory. Paid in full.

When HOS bought inventory and paid only part in cash, there was an increase in inventory (debit inventory $500), a decrease in cash (credit cash $300), and an increase in accounts payable (credit accounts payable $200).

	DR.	CR.
Inventory	$500	
Cash		$300
Accounts Payable		200

Explanation: to record purchase of inventory. Part paid and part on account.

In each transaction, the total of the debits equals the total of the credits. If the debits equal the credits for a transaction, does that ensure that the transaction has been recorded correctly? No. However, if they are not equal, it does mean that an error has been made.

Debits and credits do not have an intuitive basis. The general use of debits and credits in the English language can be quite misleading. Debits are generally viewed as being bad. Credits are generally viewed as being good. This largely comes from the fact that increases in expenses are debits, and increases in revenues are credits. However, the terms cannot be thought of as good and bad

when used in accounting. For example, when an asset such as cash decreases, it is recorded as a credit.

Your intuition based on the use of the word in the English language probably is that cash should increase with a credit. After all, when the bank makes an error and has to make a correction in your favor, it credits your account. When you overdraw your bank account and the bank makes a service charge against your account it debits your account. It would seem to the average person that a credit increases cash and a debit reduces it. Just the reverse is true. How can this be?

It is a result of the entity principle of accounting. Each entity must record all events from its own perspective. When the bank issues a credit memo to your bank account, they are not referring to your having a credit. It is a credit from the bank's perspective. And its managers do not think it is good at all. They issue a credit because they owe you money. Your account is a liability to them. Since liabilities are on the right side of the bank's equation, they increase with a credit. Frankly, when the bank issues a credit memo it is not particularly concerned with the world from your perspective.

If you were to record that bank credit memo on your own personal set of financial records, you would debit cash to show the increase in the item on the left side of your financial records viewed from your perspective. This can be quite confusing. The next time someone says you are a credit to the organization, you will not know if you have just been complimented ("you're just like extra revenue") or insulted ("this person is like a drain on our assets"). One of the misuses of the terms seen by this author is an advice column that had the headline "Make old age an asset, not a debit." Of course, that makes no sense at all, since an increase in an asset is a debit.

There is no doubt that debits and credits are difficult at first. One cannot even think of one as an increase and the other as a decrease. Both are used at times for increases and at times for decreases. We find both debits and credits on the left and both on the right. In fact, watching an accountant and a nonfinancial manager discussing bookkeeping at times can be reminiscent of the classic Abbott and Costello "Who's on First" routine. If the use of debits and credits is ever confusing, simply ask the accountant which accounts are increasing and which are decreasing.

The 2012 journal entries for HOS, used in the example in the chapter, would have the following bookkeeping form:

1. January 1. The HOS purchased a fire insurance policy for $100. A check was mailed to pay for the policy.

DATE		DR.	CR.
1/1/12	Prepaid Insurance	$100	
	Cash		$100

Explanation: to record purchase of fire insurance policy. Paid in full.

2. January 23. HOS mails a check to its supplier for $2,000 of the $7,000 it owed it at the end of last year.

DATE		DR.	CR.
1/23/12	Accounts Payable	$2,000	
	Cash		$2,000

Explanation: to record payment of purchases on account.

3. February 9. HOS places an order with a medical supply company to buy a special order X-ray machine. It will cost $50,000, and it will take over a year to be delivered. HOS signs a contract to buy the machine.

No journal entry.

4. May 23. HOS purchases inventory on account for $3,000. When this inventory is used to provide patient care, the hospital will be able to charge $6,000 for it. The inventory has been received, but HOS has not paid for it.

DATE		DR.	CR.
5/23/12	Inventory	$3,000	
	Accounts Payable		$ 3,000

Explanation: to record purchases on account.

5. June 9. Payments are received from insurance companies for patient care provided last year. $12,000 of cash is received.

DATE		DR.	CR.
6/9/12	Cash	$12,000	
	Accounts Receivable		$12,000

Explanation: receipt of payment from customers.

10

Reporting the Results of Operations: The Activity and Cash Flow Statements

The learning objectives of this chapter are to:

- explain the purpose of the activity statement and statement of cash flows;
- discuss the rules for recording revenue and expense transactions;
- discuss specific aspects of reporting information on activity statements, including reporting by nature versus source or organizational unit, and administrative and general expenses;
- discuss bad debt expense, depreciation expense, and inventory used expense;
- discuss the cash flow statement, providing a derivation of the statement and an example;
- address the issue of interrelationships among the financial statements;
- explain the importance of the notes to the financial statements; and
- provide an example of recording financial transactions, summarizing the transactions, and reporting the summarized information in a set of financial statements.

INTRODUCTION

All organizations can benefit from examining the progress made toward achieving their goals as well as determining the areas in which they are falling short. The purpose of financial statements is to help the user of the statements to assess how well an organization is doing.

The objective of the balance sheet is to report the financial position of the organization at one specific point in time. It has been compared to a still photograph. In Chapter 9, we focused our attention on the financial position of an organization at a point in time, usually at the end of the last day of the fiscal year. The balance sheet provides information about the organization only on a specific day.

In contrast, the *activity statement* and *cash flow statement* are designed to show the results of the organization's activities over a period of time. They have been compared to movies, as opposed to still pictures. Rather than focus on a specific point in time, they attempt to summarize what occurred during a particular accounting period, such as a year.

The activity statement—often referred to by other names, including the income statement, operating statement, profit and loss (P&L) statement,[1] earnings report, statement of revenues and expenses, and statement of revenues and expenditures—compares the entity's *revenues* and other *support* with its *expenses* for a period of time, such as a fiscal year.

The cash flow statement looks at where the organization obtained its cash and where it spent cash during that period of time. The focus is not only on how much cash came and went, but also on the sources and uses of cash.

Balance sheets, activity statements, and cash flow statements can all be prepared for a month, quarter, year, or some other period of time. Statements prepared for periods less than a year are usually referred to as *interim statements*.

This chapter begins with a focus on the activity statement. It starts with a discussion of recording financial events that will appear on the statement and then moves on to a detailed discussion of other issues related to the statement. Next the statement of cash flows is introduced. This is a somewhat complex statement, and the chapter provides a derivation of the statement, as well as an example that discusses the components of the statement. Finally, an overall example shows which transactions are recorded, summarized, and then used to prepare an activity statement, statement of cash flows, and balance sheet.

THE ACTIVITY STATEMENT

Activity statements track the amount and sources of resource inflows and outflows for the organization. Inflows are generated by activities such as sales of goods and services, grants and gifts, taxes and user fees, and investment income. Inflows are classed by nature (e.g., gift, grant, sales revenue), source (e.g., government, foundation, taxpayers, patients), and sometimes by organizational unit (e.g., radiology, lab, pharmacy, or operating room). Outflows are the results of using resources in the process of generating inflows. Examples of outflows are salaries, supplies, and rent. Outflows are classed by nature, often called object of expense (e.g., salary, supplies, rent), function or program (e.g., provide housing, meals, medical care), or organizational unit.

Revenues and support represent the inflows that an organization has received or is entitled to receive. Revenues are generally the result of an exchange for goods or services that the organization has provided. Support represents other money that the organization has received or is entitled to receive in the form of gifts, grants, and other contributions. Taxes and user fees represent common types of government revenues. Various types of governmental revenues are discussed further in Appendix 10-A. Revenues and support result in an inflow of assets to the organization and an increase in owners' equity or net assets.

Expenses are outflows of assets. They represent decreases in owners' equity or net assets resulting from the consumption of assets. Expenses are costs incurred to help generate revenues and support, or to carry out the operating activities of the organization in other ways. Expenses represent recognition of the use of resources in the operation of the organization. For example, the labor of a nurse providing care to a patient is consumed in that process and becomes an expense.

In terms of the fundamental equation of accounting,

$$\text{Assets} = \text{Liabilities} + \text{Net Assets}$$

revenues and support represent events that increase assets on the left and increase net assets (or owners' equity) on the right. Expenses are events that decrease assets on the left or increase liabilities on the right, and decrease net assets on the right.

---

[1] Logically, one ought to say "profit *or* loss statement" or "P *or* L," since the statement will show either a profit (surplus) *or* a loss (deficit). However, "P&L" is the expression commonly used.

The change in net assets (or net income) is simply the difference between revenues and expenses. If revenues and support exceed expenses, the organization has an increase in net assets. A for-profit organization in such an instance would have a positive net income. If expenses exceed revenues and support, the organization has a decrease in net assets, often referred to as a deficit or a loss.

Many organizations in the public service sector avoid use of the words *net income*, or profit, which seem to infer that making profit is the reason for existence of the organization. Instead they use phrases such as surplus or deficit, or excess of revenues over expenses, or simply the change in net assets.

All organizations need to measure their net income, profit, surplus, excess of revenues over expenses, or increase in net assets (or net loss, loss, deficit, excess of expenses over revenues, or decrease in net assets). This allows them to determine whether their asset inflows exceed or fall short of their asset outflows.

The activity statement presents the financial results of operations for a time period. Did revenues fall short of expenses for that period of time? Did revenues just barely cover expenses? Perhaps revenue exceeded expenses by too much. Public service organizations need to have adequate surpluses to sustain, update, and expand the services provided. Failure to earn a profit, or at least break even, can endanger organizations. So an increase in net assets is appropriate. However, since their mission is usually one of public service, many not-for-profit or government organizations do not wish to maximize their profits. For many public service organizations, profits are not the end in themselves, but rather a necessary means if the organization is to be able to accomplish its mission. An excessively large profit could indicate that the organization could provide more services, lower the price it charges for its services, or lower taxes.

The purpose of the activity statement is to provide management with information needed to steer the organization as necessary to best accomplish its objectives. Losses may be acceptable at times. Profits may be deemed to be too high at times. The role of financial accounting is to provide managers and outsiders with information about what the results of operations were. Financial accounting does not pass judgment on whether the results are good or bad. Rather, it provides the information that people can then use to make their own judgments about whether performance has been good or bad, appropriate or inappropriate, and what decisions should be made.

The simplest form of an activity or operating statement appears in Exhibit 10-1. As we can see in that exhibit, expenses are subtracted from revenues to determine the net income, or excess of revenues over expenses, in this case called the increase in net assets.

Recording Financial Events

As noted in Chapter 9, to prepare financial statements in compliance with GAAP, one must record and summarize financial events. This section focuses on recording revenues and expenses under the accrual basis of accounting.

EXHIBIT 10-1

Meals for the Homeless
Activity Statement
For the Year Ending December 31, 2011

Revenues	$196,000
Expenses	191,000
Increase in Net Assets	$ 5,000

Revenues are recorded if two requirements for revenue recognition are met: Revenues must be (1) earned and (2) realized. The first requirement, being earned, is met only if the organization has provided goods or services to the customer. If a legal transfer has occurred, establishing a legal right to collect payment, then the revenues have been earned, and the first requirement is met. To be realized we must be able to objectively measure the amount of money owed, and there must be a reasonable likelihood of eventual collection.

Not-for-profit organizations often receive gifts and pledges of financial support. Support is a subcategory of revenue. The support may be used to provide goods or services to the organization's constituent group. However, there is often no direct connection between the gift and the delivery of goods or services. In the case of such support, the first requirement for recording the support is that all conditions of the gift have been met. In other words, donations are recorded as support even though the gift has not been received and even though no goods or services have actually been provided. An allowance for uncollectible pledges would be needed, since not all pledges are collected.

In contrast, if the organization received a general promise to provide a contribution of an unstated amount, the support could not be recognized because we cannot objectively determine how much will be contributed.

In some cases of support, specific conditions are created. For example, a philanthropist might offer to donate $10 million to a university, if it changes the name of one of its buildings to her name. Since there is a specific amount of money, there is objective evidence of the monetary value. Since the donor is rich, there is reasonable certainty of collection. However, until the building's name is changed, no support is recorded. When the name of the building is changed, all conditions have been met, and at that point the university can record a contribution receivable as an asset, and an increase in support or revenue.

Recording expenses is somewhat complicated by the fact that some types of expenses are *product costs* and others are *period costs*. Product costs are those expenses that are directly connected to providing goods and services. Period costs are those that relate to the passage of time rather than the direct provision of services.

Product costs are treated as expenses based on the *matching* principle. The matching principle of GAAP holds that we should record revenues and the costs of generating those revenues in the same period. For example, if we treat a patient this year and record revenue for that treatment this year, then all the costs of providing that treatment should be recorded this year. If a technician provides service to the patient this year, thereby earning revenue for the organization, but the technician is not paid until next year, the expense related to the technician is recorded this year to match it with the revenues earned from the patient treated. This is in line with the accrual basis of accounting, discussed in earlier chapters.

Period costs are incurred with the passage of time. For example, rent, interest, management salaries, heat, and other costs are incurred largely irrespective of the specific provision of services. These costs are treated as expenses in the time period incurred. For example, rent for administrative office space for the month of December 2011 is recorded as an expense of 2011 regardless of whether that rent is paid in 2011 or 2012.

Another way of thinking about this is that expenses are recorded when assets expire or are used up. They can expire with the passage of time, such as rent on an office for a specific month or year. The passing of time can be considered to be a "using up" or "consumption" of the useful life of an asset. Or they can expire because they are physically used up or consumed specifically in the process of providing goods and services.

Suppose that Meals for the Homeless buys canned food for $1,000. The food has a cost of $1,000. The word "cost" can be ambiguous. "What did the food cost Meals?" The food cost $1,000. However, is the food an asset or an expense? Assets can be thought of as cash or things that will become cash or things that will be consumed in the process of providing the organization's goods and services. Cash is clearly a valuable resource, or an asset.

Receivables will become cash when they are collected, clearly making them valuable resources. Many assets, however, are *unexpired costs*. The cans of food, sitting on the shelf at Meals for the Homeless, are an asset that is an unexpired cost. When the cans have been opened, cooked, and served, the asset has been used up. It has been consumed in the process of providing the organization's services. Accountants would call the food an *expired cost* at that point. An expired cost is an expense. Thus, the amount spent on food was a cost. As long as the cost was unexpired, it was an asset. When the asset was used up it became an expired cost, or an expense.

The Activity Statement: A More Detailed Examination

In Exhibit 10-2, Meals for the Homeless provides a more detailed activity statement than the one used in Exhibit 10-1. Rather than simply showing revenues and expenses in summary form, revenues and expenses are subdivided into major categories. Management has some latitude regarding the amount of detail it provides. For example, it can choose to provide less information about individual types of revenues and expenses than we see in Exhibit 10-2. In that case, less information is provided to competitors. However, less information is also provided to stakeholders[2] and creditors.

In Exhibit 10-2, the bottom line is shown as the Increase/(Decrease) in Net Assets. Notice that for the year ended December 31, 2010, expenses exceeded revenues and support, and the bottom line is shown in parentheses. For the year ended December 31, 2011, revenues and support exceeded expenses, and the change in net assets is a positive number, representing an increase in net assets.

MULTIYEAR PRESENTATION One of the first things to notice in Exhibit 10-2 is that two years' worth of information is provided. This is done for purposes of comparison. Rather than considering how profitable this organization has been for this year in isolation of any other information, providing two—and sometimes three—years' worth of data gives the user of the financial statement a better perspective on the results of operations.

For example, the $5,000 increase in net assets this year is modest. It represents only about two and a half cents of profit from every dollar of revenues and support ($5,000 profit ÷ $196,000 Total Revenue and Support = .0255 or 2.55 cents of profit per dollar of revenue and support). However, by having two years' worth of data we see that the modest increase in net assets is a turnaround from the previous year, when Meals had a $7,000 decrease in net assets. Meals' performance is improving. In light of that prior loss, the current-year increase can be placed within a context that allows the user of the financial statement to make a more reasoned interpretation of the information.

Annual balance sheets and cash flow statements also generally provide two years' worth of information for comparative purposes.

REPORTING IN THOUSANDS Financial statements often round off or truncate numbers. Rounding off would show some digits as zeros. In Exhibit 10-2, the numbers have been rounded off to the nearest thousand. An alternate presentation would be to truncate, or cut off, the three digits on the right completely. In that case, the heading of the financial statement would have to indicate that this has been done. Typical headings would say, "000's omitted" or "in thousands." For very large organizations, data are rounded off or truncated to the nearest hundred thousand or million dollars. For small organizations, financial statements sometimes report figures to the nearest dollar.

---

[2] Stakeholders are any persons who have something at stake with respect to the organization. This covers a wide variety of people, including employees, clients, regulators, vendors, creditors, and others.

EXHIBIT 10-2

Meals for the Homeless
Activity Statement
For the Years Ending December 31, 2011, and December 31, 2010

	2011	2010
Revenues and Support		
Meals		
Client revenue	$ 10,000	$ 8,000
City revenue	20,000	16,000
Shelter Counseling		
Client revenue	1,000	1,000
County revenue	10,000	10,000
Fund-Raising		
Foundation grants	70,000	50,000
Annual ball	12,000	11,000
Telephone solicitation	25,000	28,000
Mail solicitation	48,000	45,000
Total Revenues and Support	$196,000	$169,000
Expenses		
Food	$ 17,000	$ 16,000
Kitchen staff	35,000	33,000
Counseling staff	35,000	34,000
Rent on kitchen locations	15,000	14,000
Administration and general	75,000	65,000
Bad debts	4,000	4,000
Depreciation	10,000	10,000
Total Expenses	$191,000	$176,000
Increase/(Decrease) in Net Assets	$ 5,000	$ (7,000)

The numbers are rounded off or truncated for several reasons. First, it makes the information in the financial statement a bit easier to comprehend. Sometimes presenting data that are too detailed causes the reader to lose the important information content. Second, as noted in Chapter 9's discussion of materiality, it is unlikely that all numbers in the organization's bookkeeping records are exact. If numbers are reported to the nearest dollar, there is an inference of greater accuracy than is really likely to exist. Reported financial information is unlikely to be 100 percent accurate in all respects. Financial statements are intended to be accurate enough to allow them to be used as a reasonable basis for decision making.

REPORTING BY NATURE, SOURCE, AND ORGANIZATIONAL UNIT In Exhibit 10-2, are the revenues shown by their nature, source, or organizational unit? In terms of nature, we know how much of the revenue is earned in exchange for meals provided versus how much of the organization's resources come from responses to fund-raising efforts. In terms of source, we know how much money was received directly from the organization's clients, how much came from the city and county, and how much came from each of the major types of contributors (foundations, event attendees, telephone, and mail). We do not really have information by organizational unit; we do not know revenues or support for one soup kitchen versus another, or about soup kitchens versus delivery by van.

Why is it beneficial to know about revenues by nature, source, and unit? The subcategorizations allow us to go beyond simply knowing whether we are making or losing money.

How good a job are we doing at fund-raising? Are our revenues from meals well-matched with the costs of providing meals? If we start to lose money, what would be the impact of eliminating our shelter counseling services? Are we getting more client revenues per meal from costly van delivery service than from soup kitchens? Are foundation grants falling—do we need to make a greater effort in that area?

Are expenses reported in Exhibit 10-2 by nature, function, or organizational unit? There is a mix of information. We know some expenses by nature. For example, food, kitchen staff, counseling staff, rent, and depreciation are all nature of expense categorizations. In contrast, administration and general tells us the function but not the nature. Is that line made up of salaries, rent, and supplies, and in what proportions? We also know a bit about function from some of the other lines as well. Rather than having one line for staff, we know how much staff was related to meals (kitchen) versus the counseling function. We can also infer that food is for meals. We do not have any information on organizational unit. Another organization might have chosen to provide information by organizational unit. Although there is some latitude in the detail that must be presented, there are a number of rules about how not-for-profit and health organizations must disclose their expense information. (Those rules are discussed in Chapter 11.)

Regardless of the choice made regarding the level of detail to report, the activity statement must at least report revenues and support in a manner to disclose the total amount of revenue and support received. Similarly, total expenses must be shown. In addition to the straightforward expenses such as food, staff, and rent, four types of expenses warrant further discussion: administrative and general, bad debts, depreciation, and inventory used.

ADMINISTRATIVE AND GENERAL EXPENSES The amount of money spent on administrative and general expense for Meals for the Homeless rose this year from $65,000 to $75,000 (see Exhibit 10-2). That represents a 15 percent increase in just one year. What kinds of things are in this category? It will include a wide variety of support services that the organization must have to carry out its mission. There is undoubtedly an executive director; there may be other office staff, such as secretaries, clerks, bookkeepers, and accountants. There may be office rent.

To some, these expenses may seem irrelevant to the mission of the organization. The mission of Meals is to provide food for the homeless. Why should they spend money on such irrelevant overhead costs when it could better be spent providing more meals or counseling the homeless to help them find shelter?

Others would argue that such a philosophy is shortsighted. First, all organizations need some administrative supervision and coordination. Someone has to buy supplies; pay for rent, food, and employees; file employee wage taxes; and do a host of other administrative activities without which the organization could not survive.

Second, from Exhibit 10-2, we know that clients (the homeless) provided Meals with just $11,000 of revenue in 2011 for meals and counseling. Yet Meals spent $17,000 on food alone. The kitchen staff and counseling staff cost another $70,000. Add in rent on the soup kitchen locations, and costs exceed $100,000 without even considering the depreciation on the kitchen equipment (ovens) and delivery van.

How does an organization survive with primary revenue of $11,000 and primary expenses of more than $100,000? For one thing, it has contracts with the city and county for meals and counseling that generate another $30,000. Those contracts were negotiated by administrators, whose salary is within the administrative and general category.

One might argue that at one time administrative costs were needed, but now that the city and county contracts exist, the effort to renew them annually is minor. Note, however, that even with the government contracts, the revenues still fall far short of the direct costs of providing meals and counseling.

Close examination of the activity statement reveals that the revenue from fund-raising is critical to keeping this organization afloat. Foundation grants, the revenue from an annual ball, and telephone and mail solicitations raise approximately $150,000. Without spending money on administrative and general expenses, including fund-raising costs, it is doubtful that this organization could survive.

What about the sharp 15 percent increase in this category? Financial statements often raise more questions than they can answer. Potential red flags, such as the 15 percent increase, warrant management attention. There are a number of possible explanations. For example, city contract revenue and direct client revenue for meals both rose by more than 20 percent. Perhaps more administrative staff was hired to work on increasing revenues from these sources.

Another possibility relates to foundations. Foundation grants were up by 40 percent. Note that the previous year the organization lost money, and this year it made money. Suppose that the organization this year hired a consultant for $10,000 to apply for foundation grants. Meals received $20,000 more from grants in 2011 than in 2010. Perhaps there are even more applications still in the pipeline. Some would argue that spending $10,000 on a consultant to achieve $20,000 of grants is not cost-effective. Half of the grant money went directly to the consultant. Others would argue that Meals had a loss the previous year and a profit this year. Without the consultant and the extra foundation grants, Meals would have lost money again this year, so the investment was worthwhile.

Clearly, organizations will incur overhead costs. These costs do not directly relate to the provision of goods and services. In most cases, however, they do relate directly to the ability of the organization to exist and to be able to provide those goods and services.

BAD DEBT EXPENSE   Bad debts, or uncollectible accounts, arise because not everyone pays us what they owe us. Although we expect each individual client to pay, we also know that some of them probably will not. We just do not know who.

For instance, Meals for the Homeless receives pledges in response to telephone and mail solicitations. Assume that Meals' history has shown that approximately 92 percent of all pledges are ultimately collected. However, there is no way to know in advance which specific pledges will be collected and which will not. It would understate financial support to ignore all pledges, but it would overstate financial results to assume that we would collect 100 percent of the pledges. The solution used is to record 100 percent of the pledges as support (or revenue) and then also record 8 percent as a bad debt expense. This solution complies with the matching principle of GAAP, placing the revenue and the related bad debt expense in the same accounting period.

Recall that in Chapter 9 it was noted that accounts receivable are shown on the balance sheet net of uncollectible accounts (bad debts). The activity statement focuses on what has happened for a period of time. The bad debt expense represents the portion of the revenues earned for that period of time that will probably not be collected. In contrast, the balance sheet looks at a moment in time. Given the amount of receivables owed to us at that moment in time, it indicates the portion of those receivables that will probably not be collected.

The allowance for uncollectible accounts shown on the balance sheet can be a larger number than the bad debt expense on the activity statement. Suppose that Meals gives people at least two full years to pay their pledge before deciding that a specific pledge is uncollectible. At the end of the year, the balance sheet will show all receivables that have not yet been collected. Included in that amount will be all of the amounts related to pledges this year that have not yet been collected and all of the amounts related to pledges made the previous year that have not yet been collected. While the activity statement will show a bad debt expense related to just this year's revenue, the balance sheet will show an allowance for possible uncollectible accounts equal to two years' worth of bad debt expense.

For example, from Exhibit 10-2, we can see that telephone and mail solicitations in 2010 raised $28,000 and $45,000, respectively. Assume that the telephone solicitations were all received as pledges. Also assume that the $45,000 raised by the mail solicitation consisted of $23,000 in immediate cash receipts (checks were mailed to Meals in response to the mail solicitation) and $22,000 in pledges. The total pledges for the year were therefore $50,000 ($28,000 from telephone and $22,000 from mail solicitations). At an anticipated bad debt rate of 8 percent of pledges, the bad debt expense for 2010 would be $4,000. That amount would appear on the 2010 activity statement as an expense called bad debts (see Exhibit 10-2). For 2011, the telephone and mail support was $25,000 and $48,000, respectively (Exhibit 10-2). Assume that the total pledges included in those amounts were again $50,000, and again bad debts expense was calculated at 8 percent of pledges or $4,000.

Suppose that at the end of 2011, Meals had total pledges receivable of $63,000. How could that be? The total pledges to Meals in 2011 were only $50,000. It is possible that some of the pledges that have not been collected by the end of 2011 were made in 2010 or even earlier. The pledges receivable on the balance sheet include all pledges from all years that have not yet been received or specifically declared to be uncollectible. The pledge support on the activity statement, however, includes just support for the current accounting period.

What if the $63,000 of pledges receivable at the end of 2011 represents $45,000 of pledges that were made in 2011 and $18,000 of pledges made in 2010? Each year Meals has charged a $4,000 bad debt expense on the activity statement. From Chapter 9, recall that a financial event must affect at least two accounts. When the bad debt expense goes up by $4,000, another account called the allowance for uncollectible accounts also goes up by $4,000. The allowance for uncollectible accounts (sometimes called the allowance for bad debts) is a *contra asset* account. Contra means going against. The allowance for uncollectibles account is an asset account that always has a negative or zero balance. It offsets, or goes against, the accounts receivable balance. In this case, the accounts receivable are in the form of pledges receivable. Thus, at the end of 2011, the balances related to pledges receivable might be as follows:

Pledges receivable	$63,000
Allowance for uncollectible amounts	−8,000
Pledges receivable, net	$55,000

Note that the balance sheet contains some pledges receivable from two years and also contains the allowance from two years. The balance sheet reports the allowance for uncollectible amounts balance and the pledges or accounts receivable, net balance.

Eventually the organization will decide that a particular pledge will never be collected. At that point the specific pledge is *written off.* This means that receivables are reduced for that one specific pledge. At the same time, the allowance is also reduced. Suppose that on January 10, 2012, Charlie Smith dies without paying a $500 pledge he had made in 2010. Meals decides it will never be able to collect that pledge. On that day, Meals will reduce pledges receivable and will reduce the allowance, resulting in new balances as follows:

Pledges receivable	$62,500
Allowance for uncollectible amounts	−7,500
Pledges receivable, net	$55,000

Note that the net balance of $55,000 has not changed. This is because no asset is consumed when the decision is made to write off an account. But there is a bad debt; Charlie Smith is not paying his pledge. That is true. However, the expense was recorded back in 2010 in the same year as the pledge was recorded as support. That way the revenue and expense were both in the same year, and the matching principle of GAAP was not violated. Lowering the specific pledge receivable and the allowance account allows the net pledges receivable to remain unchanged.[3]

DEPRECIATION EXPENSE   *Depreciation expense* represents the allocation of the cost of a capital asset over its lifetime, charging a share of its cost into each year that the asset is used by the organization. This approach is required by the matching principle. Since we will use a long-term asset to earn revenues over a number of years, it would not make sense in an accrual accounting system to treat the entire cost as an expense in one year. The portion of the asset's cost treated as an expense in a year is called the depreciation expense of that asset for that year.

Ideally, one would want to base the amount of depreciation expense each year on the decline in the value of the item being depreciated. That would make sense from an economic perspective. However, it is difficult in practice to determine how much the value of each capital asset has declined each year. Accountants have developed formulas to allocate the cost of capital assets to the years the asset is expected to provide useful service. However, it should be noted that these formulas are only rough approximations at best. To the extent that they do not accurately estimate the decline in value of the asset, the depreciation expense for the year (on the activity statement) will be inaccurate, and the remaining asset balance (on the balance sheet) will be inaccurate.

The simplest approach to depreciation is to take the initial cost less the expected salvage value (discussed in Chapter 9) and divide that amount over the expected useful life. If Meals for the Homeless buys a delivery van for $32,000 with a $2,000 expected salvage value and a five-year expected life, the annual depreciation would be $6,000:

Cost	$32,000
Less salvage value	−2,000
Depreciable amount	$30,000
Divided by 5-year useful life	÷5
Depreciation expense per year	$ 6,000

This approach, referred to as *straight-line depreciation*, assumes that assets are used up the same amount each year. Are things really used up evenly? In some cases, the value of assets declines more in their early years. This is not a major problem, since the goal of depreciation as used in practice by accountants is not to assign fixed assets a realistic value for the balance sheet. The goal is to allocate the cost of the asset over the asset's useful life.

However, the matching principle would hold that if we use up more of an asset in the early years of its life than in the later years, it would be appropriate to assign more expense to those early years. Suppose that equipment and buildings need more maintenance as they age. If we could charge more depreciation in the early years of an asset's life and less in the later years, the total of the depreciation cost and the maintenance costs would be more stable from year to year. To deal with this problem, there are several alternative methods of depreciation, referred to as *accelerated depreciation*. These accelerated methods charge more depreciation expense in the early years and less in the later years. In total, the

---

[3] In some cases, it is possible for the allowance for uncollectibles at the end of the year to be lower than the bad debt expense for the year. This could happen if some of the specific receivables from the current year are recognized as being uncollectible and are written off before the end of the year.

depreciation taken over an asset's life stays the same. (Accelerated depreciation methods are discussed in Appendix 10-B.)

In addition to any possible improvement in matching, the added benefit of accelerated depreciation is that it makes net income lower in the current time period. For-profit organizations benefit from lower income by having lower income taxes. While the accelerated approaches result in higher depreciation and therefore lower income and lower taxes in early years of the asset's life, just the reverse is true in later years. However, considering the time value of money (see Chapter 5), the present value of the taxes paid is less if lower taxes are paid in the early years and higher taxes in the latter years of the asset's useful life. Also, some not-for-profit organizations are reimbursed for their expenses. They may benefit from accelerated depreciation because the larger expense in the earlier years will result in larger reimbursements in the earlier years. Also, accelerated depreciation will make an organization look poorer in the earlier years of a capital asset's life, and therefore more needful of donations.

INVENTORY USED EXPENSE   As noted in Chapter 9, inventory represents supplies that have been acquired to be used in making goods or providing services. Inventory is recorded as an asset based on its cost. When inventory is used up, it becomes an expired cost and is an expense.[4] This expense is sometimes referred to as supplies expense, inventory expense, or cost of goods sold expense. A problem arises, however, because GAAP allows a choice of how the cost of inventory is measured. The following discussion is provided not only to explain the treatment of inventory on the activity statement and balance sheet, but also to provide an example of a situation in which GAAP allows the organization to make a choice of accounting method. Although GAAP provides some measure of uniformity across organizations, there are a number of instances in which choice is allowed. When this occurs, the financial statements can be significantly affected, and the choice made must be reported in a note that accompanies the financial statements.

The inventory choice relates to an assumption about the flow of inventory. One would normally assume that the organization uses its oldest inventory first. However, during periods of high inflation, the expense reported on the activity statement could substantially understate the economic impact of the use of inventory. For instance, suppose that the Hospital for Ordinary Surgery (HOS) used an expensive medical supply item. At the start of the year, it owns one unit of an item that it paid $50 to acquire. During the year, it purchases a unit for $60. For the coming year, it expects to acquire a unit for $70. It uses one unit during the year. What expense should appear on the activity or operating statement, and what asset value should appear on the balance sheet? (Note that most not-for-profit organizations use the activity statement title for the financial statement that reports revenues and expenses. Health organizations, in contrast, refer to the statement as the operating statement.)

Logically, if it uses its oldest inventory first, the expense on the operating statement will be $50. The balance sheet value of inventory will show the $60 cost of the unit purchased during the year. This is referred to as a FIFO (*first-in, first-out*) approach. However, the operating statement is not reporting the amount that it will cost HOS to replace the inventory it used. HOS will now have to replace that unit of inventory at a higher price.

As an alternative to the FIFO choice, organizations are allowed to assume that their inventory moves on a LIFO (*last-in, first-out*) basis. Under this method one would assume that HOS used the last item it had purchased, at a cost of $60 and held on to the one it had paid $50 to acquire. The operating statement now shows an expense of $60 and the balance sheet shows an asset value of $50. One can see why it is important to disclose the choice

---

[4] Government treatment of inventory may be different; it is discussed in Chapter 12.

made in a note. Two different organizations could have bought and used exactly the same inventory but reported different financial results simply because they chose to make different assumptions about which inventory was used and which was kept.

Note that financial statements report inventory as an asset on the balance sheet and as an expense on the operating statement based on an *assumption* of the order in which inventory is used. An organization can use its oldest inventory first (a FIFO approach) but use the LIFO approach to report on the financial statements. This allows the organization to use its inventory in its usual manner and also have the LIFO benefit of a more accurate operating statement during times of inflation.

Some would even contend that the operating statement should show a $70 expense because that is the anticipated cost to acquire the unit of inventory that will replace the unit used. However, such a replacement cost approach is not allowed.

In some cases, there are specific advantages to reporting inventory consumption on a LIFO basis. If an organization is for-profit, LIFO will lower its taxes during periods of inflation. Why? Because as inventory prices rise, if you assume that you have used the last units purchased, they are likely to be the most expensive. Higher expenses result in lower income and therefore lower taxes.

Why would a not-for-profit organization, exempt from income taxes, use LIFO? In some cases, it may receive payments that reimburse it for the cost of providing services. Suppose that Middle City pays Meals for the Homeless 75 percent of the cost of each meal served. If Meals uses LIFO during an inflationary period, it will report a higher cost per meal and therefore receive higher current reimbursement. This is the same reason that some not-for-profit organizations prefer to use accelerated depreciation.

In addition to the FIFO and LIFO inventory flow assumptions, there are several other allowable, less used, methods. They are discussed in Appendix 10-C, along with a more detailed discussion of inventory valuation calculations.

The Dangers of Estimates

One of the principles of GAAP is that the organization should use objective, verifiable evidence. That is why land is valued on the balance sheet based on its cost rather than some estimate of current market value. Sometimes, however, there is no reasonable alternative to making an estimate. Bad debts are one example. Depreciation is another.

Bad debt expense should be exactly the portion of current revenues that we will be unable to collect. However, we will not know the exact amount for a long time—perhaps several years. So an estimate is made, even though that estimate must be based on a subjective analysis. We try to minimize the subjectivity by basing the estimate on historical experience, the economy, who owes the money, and other factors that might affect ultimate collectability.

Depreciation is also an estimate. We cannot know objectively how the market value of an asset will change from year to year, so accountants use formulas to estimate annual depreciation. Even using those formulas, we cannot be sure how much we will be able to get for the fixed asset when it is sold, so the salvage value used in the calculation is an estimate. Nor can we be sure how long the useful life will be, so that is another estimate. These are subjective best guesses.

One danger with subjectivity is that it opens the door to both honest error and intentional manipulation. Estimates are likely to be imperfect and should be considered carefully, even when they are reasonable. Furthermore, if we want to look poor to encourage donations, we might be tempted to overstate bad debt expense or to underestimate the salvage value for a piece of equipment. Both of those actions would tend to lower the current increase in net assets, making us look poorer now. Conversely, if we planned to borrow a large amount of money in the future, we might want to overstate the increase in net assets to make the organization look more financially solvent to potential lenders. We might underestimate bad debts or overestimate the salvage value of equipment.

The use of a reasonable estimate can improve the information reported in financial statements considerably. Although one should be aware of the danger of information manipulation, this is not meant to say that we would be better off without reasonable estimates. Rather, one should carefully consider information based on estimates, much as one must be careful when interpreting most financial information.

Deferred Revenue

When is revenue not really revenue at all? When it is *deferred revenue*. Deferred revenue is a liability. It is sometimes called unearned revenue. At times, an organization will receive payments for services that have not yet been provided. This is very much like the asset prepaid expenses, except that we have received payment rather than made payment. In fact, it is a mirror image. The prepaid expense on the financial records of one organization will be a deferred revenue on the financial records of the other organization involved. If HOS pays for fire insurance in advance, it will have a prepaid insurance asset and the fire insurance company will have deferred revenue liability in the same amount.

At some future point, the organization with the deferred revenue liability must either provide the services or refund the money. Until then the deferred revenue represents a liability rather than a revenue. When service is provided, the deferred revenue is converted from a liability to a revenue.

For example, suppose that a magazine publisher received $120 for a one-year subscription. At the time the money is received, the publisher has not yet provided its service to its customer. Therefore it must show a liability. However, it never expects to actually pay the customer in cash. It expects the $120 to become revenue when it provides the monthly issues of the magazine. Therefore the liability is called unearned or deferred revenue because the point at which it can be recognized as revenue has been pushed off or deferred to the future.

What if the magazine publisher expects it to cost $60 to fulfill its obligation to provide the monthly issues of the magazine? Should the deferred revenue liability be the $120 that was received or the $60 that it will cost to provide the magazine to the customer? The answer is the full $120. Suppose that for some reason the publisher was unable to provide the magazine. How much would the customer be entitled to as a refund? The $120 paid, or the $60 that it would have cost the publisher? Clearly the customer is entitled to a refund of the $120, so that is the amount of the recorded liability.

Note that many organizations use the term unearned revenue if the liability is short-term and deferred revenue only for long-term liabilities. This parallels the common use of prepaid expense for short-term prepaid assets and deferred charge for those that are long-term.

Earnings per Share

When for-profit corporations issue audited financial statements, in addition to net income, the income statement is required to show the earnings per share of common stock. We can see an example of this in Exhibit 10-3 for Prisons R Us, a fictitious for-profit organization that runs prisons for a growing number of states around the country. Notice that this for-profit organization is likely to call this a statement of net income rather than an activity or operating statement. The excess of revenues over expenses is called net income rather than the increase in net assets. GAAP requires per share profit information because for many individual users of the financial statements, it is more relevant than total net income.

Imagine that a person is trying to decide whether to buy shares of stock in Prisons R Us, or their main competitor, We Lock M Up. Prisons R Us had net income of $200,000 this year. We

EXHIBIT 10-3

Prisons R Us
Statement of Net Income
For the Year Ending March 31, 2012

Revenues	$2,000,000
Less Expenses	1,800,000
Net Income	$ 200,000
Earnings per Share	$ 2.00

Lock M Up had $1,000,000 of income. It might appear that the latter company is much more profitable and therefore a better buy. However, Prisons R Us has 100,000 shares of stock outstanding. Therefore each owner of one share of stock owns $2 of earnings ($200,000 earnings ÷ 100,000 shares = $2). We Lock M Up has 1,000,000 shares of stock outstanding. Therefore, their earnings per share are only $1 ($1,000,000 earnings ÷ 1,000,000 shares = $1). Since owners only own their pro rata (proportional) share of the company and its profits, one can see that the earnings per share information may be more relevant than simply total profits.[5]

Opportunity for Financial Analysis

The activity statement opens a wealth of opportunity for analysis. We noted earlier that foundation grants rose dramatically. Was that a one-shot increase? Can it be sustained in coming years? Will it likely increase even more in coming years? Why did administrative costs rise so steeply this year? What changes from year to year make sense? Which changes do not make sense? What can we conclude from the income statement about the overall results of operations? Activity statements provide information that can be analyzed to better understand the overall financial health of an organization.

For most managers, even more important than being able to generate financial information is development of a critical eye for evaluating financial information. The purpose of becoming comfortable with financial reports such as balance sheets and activity statements is that it allows the manager to examine results and to get an understanding about what is going right and what is going wrong with the organization from a financial perspective. One cannot always get answers from the statements; but if review of the statements allows the manager to ask perceptive questions, the statements can aid enormously in the management of the organization. Chapters 14 and 15 discuss approaches for analysis of the information contained in financial statements.

THE STATEMENT OF CASH FLOWS

The activity statement focuses on the revenues and expenses of the organization. If we used a cash basis of accounting for reporting, the activity statement would provide a wealth of information about the organization's cash. However, most organizations use some form of accrual accounting. They do this to better represent how the organization did for the year by matching the revenues it earned (whether collected or not) to the expenses it incurred (whether paid for or not). Cash, however, is also vitally important.

The statement of cash flows focuses on financial rather than operating aspects of the organization. Where did the money come from, and how was it spent? While the major

---

[5] Note, however, that current earnings per share is just one of many indicators that must be considered in deciding whether to buy shares in a stock. One must consider potential growth in earnings, risk, and many other factors. Consideration of those factors in beyond the scope of this book.

concern of the activity or operating statement may be profitability, the statement of cash flows focuses to a great extent on *viability*. Viability relates to whether the organization is generating and will generate enough cash to meet both short-term and long-term obligations and therefore will be able to continue in existence.

There have been a number of instances of profitable businesses that have fallen into desperate financial crises, at times even leading to bankruptcy. How could this happen? During profitable periods, many organizations expand. Since they are making profits on current services, expanding services should lead to even greater profits.

However, profitability alone does not ensure that such expansion is financially feasible. Expanding the quantity of services offered tends to require additional physical facilities. More employees must be hired and more supplies purchased. What is the problem if all of these additional expenses result in even more additional revenues? The problem relates to delays or lags between paying for expenses and collecting revenues. In many cases, organizations must acquire the resources of production (e.g., buildings, equipment, supplies, employees) and start paying for them before they start collecting revenues for those services. In other words, there may be a profit on an accrual basis, but we have paid more in cash for our expenses this year than the amount of money collected in cash from our revenues. Eventually cash collections should catch up, but by that time we may have failed to pay some obligations when they were due.

This problem is discussed in the planning section of this book. We cannot plan solely based on an accrual-based operating budget. Cash budgets are required as well. Similarly, we cannot judge how well things are turning out based only on a report of actual profitability. We also need to report on what has happened with respect to cash during the period of time being examined. Did we have a net gain in cash or decrease in cash during the time period? Where did we get our cash from and what did we spend our cash on?

Suppose that the Millbridge Blood Bank is having difficulty meeting its obligations as they come due. As a result, during the past year it sold its land for $75,000. That land was purchased by the blood bank a number of years ago for $40,000. The activity statement will include a $35,000 gain from the sale of the land. Even with that gain, however, the organization showed a net income of only $10,000 because of a loss of $25,000 on its other activities. Between the loss of $25,000 on other activities and lags in collection of receivables, at year-end the blood bank's cash balance had increased by just $15,000.

One way to view what has transpired is that the organization made a profit of $10,000 and cash increased by $15,000. Both of those numbers are correct. However, this does not really convey what happened. By themselves, they imply an organization that is both profitable and generating cash surpluses. However, when we examine the sources and uses of cash we learn a different story. Although cash increased by $15,000, the sale of land generated $75,000 of cash. Without that sale, the cash balance would have gone down by $60,000. The organization had only that one piece of land. Can it go on indefinitely selling off its assets to get the cash needed to provide its current services? Probably not. By looking at the sources of cash, we find that, rather than a rosy picture, there are serious financial problems that must be addressed if the organization is to be able to continue providing services.

Consider another example. Suppose that HOS had a cash decrease of $2,000,000 for the year. That might cause great concern. Looking at a detailed statement of cash flows, however, we find that the routine ongoing activities of the organization generated a cash surplus of $3,000,000. Then how did the cash balance decline? The organization is so profitable and generating so much cash that it decided to purchase $5,000,000 of new equipment to expand services offered. It used the full $3,000,000 of cash generated this year and took $2,000,000 of cash out of its bank account. It anticipates that with the new equipment, next year it will generate even more than this year's $3,000,000 increase in cash from ongoing activities.

In this second example, cash fell, but there really is no problem. In the first example, cash rose, but there was nothing to celebrate. In each case, managers could not really interpret the financial situation of the organization without some detailed analysis of the sources and uses of cash.

Cash flow statements are divided into three main categories: cash from operating activities, cash from investing activities, and cash from financing activities. Operating activities are those activities related to accomplishing the organization's primary mission. They include the day-in and day-out operations of the organization. Investing activities are related to buying and selling long-term fixed assets (property, plant, and equipment) and investments such as shares of stock. Financing activities are those related to borrowing and repaying loans.

Derivation of the Cash Flow Statement

The cash flow statement has links to both the activity statement and balance sheet. The first number on the cash flow statement is the change in net assets or net income, taken directly from the activity statement. The ending balance on the cash flow statement is also the cash balance from the balance sheet. In fact, there are additional links as well.

A good way to understand the content of the cash flow statement and also see some of the interdependency among the financial statements is to consider cash flow in terms of the fundamental equation of accounting:

$$\text{Assets} = \text{Liabilities} + \text{Net Assets}$$

As noted in Chapter 9, any changes on the left side of this equation will equal the changes on the right side, so we can consider the organization's financial transactions by considering the following:

$$\Delta \text{ Assets} = \Delta \text{ Liabilities} + \Delta \text{ Net Assets}$$

where the Greek letter delta, Δ, is read as "the change in."

The change in assets must consist of the change in cash and the change in all other assets. Since we want to focus on the causes of the change in cash, we separate the change in assets into the change in cash and change in all other assets, so the equation becomes the following:

$$\Delta \text{ Cash} + \Delta \text{ All Other Assets} = \Delta \text{ Liabilities} + \Delta \text{ Net Assets}$$

To focus clearly on the causes of the change in cash, the changes in all other assets can be subtracted from both sides of the equation, resulting in the following:

$$\Delta \text{ Cash} = \Delta \text{ Liabilities} + \Delta \text{ Net Assets} - \Delta \text{ All Other Assets}$$

Bear in mind that the change in net assets in that equation is generally the organization's revenues less its expenses.[6] Rearranging the equation, we get the following:

$$\Delta \text{ Cash} = \Delta \text{ Net Assets} + \Delta \text{ Liabilities} - \Delta \text{ All Other Assets}$$

---

[6] This is somewhat of an oversimplification. Other factors affect net assets besides revenues and expenses. For example, dividend payments to owners of a for-profit organization reduce net assets. For purposes of this introduction to cash flow statements, however, it is sufficient to note that for the most part, the changes in net assets are made up of revenues and support less expenses.

This equation represents the information in the cash flow statement. The cash flow statement reports all of the changes on the right side of the equation that affect the organization's cash flow, which is isolated on the left side of the equation.

The cash flow statement begins with the organization's change in net assets, or net income, and then lists the changes in liabilities and the changes in all other assets. The changes in liabilities and changes in all other assets appear on the cash flow statement in the section that best represents whether they result from routine operating activities, investing activities, or financing activities. It is easier to derive the various components of the cash flow statement if one thinks of the statement in terms of this equation.

For example, if we borrow money, it increases a liability (the right side of the equation) and increases cash (the left side). If we repay a loan, it reduces the liability and also reduces the cash available. Note that the "all other assets" part of the equation has a negative sign in front of it. If we buy a building, assets go up, but the right side of the equation goes down because of the negative sign in front of Δ All Other Assets. But that makes sense because when one buys a building one uses cash, so both the left side and right sides of this equation decrease.

Each type of financial statement is independent and provides different, valuable information. Yet all of the statements are derived from the same fundamental equation, and all of the statements are interdependent and should be taken together as a whole.

An Example

The cash flow statement for Meals for the Homeless is presented in Exhibit 10-4. As with the activity statement, two years of financial information are presented in the cash flow statement to facilitate analysis of trends that are occurring over time.

CASH FROM OPERATING ACTIVITIES The first section of cash flow statements is cash flows from operating activities. This is considered to be a critical element. The ability of an organization to continue operations over a long time period often depends on whether its normal daily operating activities generate more cash than they consume. An organization that generates more cash than it uses for operations is, ceteris paribus, more financially stable and viable.

A rapidly expanding profitable organization may suffer cash shortfalls as inventories and receivables increase. This need not create a crisis if management is aware of it and plans to handle the cash shortage. The cash flow statement focuses management's attention on the cash shortfall and its causes. It creates a warning flag. With sufficient lead time, other sources of cash, such as long-term debt, may be arranged to avoid a serious problem.

Looking at Exhibit 10-4, the first item in the cash flows from operating activities section is the change in net assets. For 2011, net assets increased by $5,000. That increase in net assets is taken directly from the activity statement, Exhibit 10-2. The net asset change represents revenues less expenses. Often revenues are received in cash and expenses are paid in cash. So the change in net assets may represent a reasonable approximation of cash flow. However, in an accrual system, revenues and expenses are usually not the same as cash flow. Therefore, the change in net assets in the cash flow statement serves only as a first approximation of cash flows. A number of adjustments are needed to convert the change in net assets to cash flow.

The first adjustment made is for expense items that do not consume any cash. In nearly all cash flow statements, the first item listed after change in net assets is depreciation. In 2011, Meals for the Homeless had $10,000 of depreciation. The cash payment to acquire a capital asset would show up as a use of cash in the section of the statement called cash flows from investing activities. This would occur in the year the asset is acquired. In each year

EXHIBIT 10-4

Meals for the Homeless
Statement of Cash Flows
For the Years Ending December 31, 2011, and December 31, 2010

	2011	2010
Cash Flows from Operating Activities		
Change in net assets	$ 5,000	$ (7,000)
Add expenses not requiring cash		
Depreciation	10,000	10,000
Other adjustments		
Add decrease in inventory	2,000	2,000
Add increase in accounts payable	0	1,000
Subtract increase in receivables	(17,000)	(12,000)
Subtract decrease in wages payable	(1,000)	0
Subtract increase in prepaid expenses	(1,000)	0
Net Cash Used for Operating Activities	$ (2,000)	$ (6,000)
Cash Flows from Investing Activities		
Sale of stock investments	$ 4,000	$ 4,000
Purchase of delivery van		(32,000)
Net Cash from Investing Activities	$ 4,000	$(28,000)
Cash Flows from Financing Activities		
Increase in mortgages		$ 25,000
Repayments of mortgages	$ (5,000)	(4,000)
Net Cash from Financing Activities	$ (5,000)	$ 21,000
Net Increase/(Decrease) in Cash	$ (3,000)	$(13,000)
Cash, Beginning of Year	4,000	17,000
Cash, End of Year	$ 1,000	$ 4,000

that we own the asset, a portion is charged as depreciation expense. However, there is no cash receipt or payment related to that annual depreciation charge.

Consider, for example, that Meals for the Homeless purchased a delivery van in 2010. In 2011, no equipment was purchased or paid for. However, the delivery van purchased in 2010 and the kitchen oven equipment purchased in earlier years are being depreciated during 2011. Since Meals used those assets in 2011 to provide meals, it is appropriate to charge some of their original cost as an expense in 2011. However, Meals is not paying cash for them in 2011. They were already paid for in earlier years. Depreciation is only an allocation of cost; it is not a cash payment.

This creates a minor problem. The change in net assets was used as an approximation of cash flow on the first line of the cash flow statement. One would therefore assume that revenues had been received in cash and all expenses paid in cash. However, if there is an expense such as depreciation that is not paid in cash, we must make an adjustment. Since expenses are subtracted to arrive at the change in net assets on the activity statement and since depreciation expense is not paid in cash, we must add depreciation back to changes in net assets to approximate cash flow better.

This creates some confusion. Many people assume that depreciation generates cash since they see depreciation as a positive number on the cash flow statement. It is important to realize that depreciation is not being added because it generates cash. It does not. It is being added to adjust for the fact that it was subtracted to arrive at the change in net assets but did not consume cash.

In addition to depreciation, there are other expense items, such as *amortization*, that reflect a current-year expense but do not consume cash. For example, a patent is not a tangible asset. As such, it cannot be depreciated. Depreciation is just used for tangible assets. But the patent does get used up over a period of time, and its cost is allocated each year as an amortization expense. Meals for the Homeless did not have any amortization for 2010 or 2011.

In addition to expense items that do not use cash, adjustments must be made for a variety of items for which the change in net assets does not capture true cash flow. For example, during 2011, Meals used more inventory than it purchased. We know this from the decrease in inventory on the balance sheet. Exhibit 10-5 repeats Meals for the Homeless's balance sheet from Chapter 9, adding comparative data for 2010 to the 2011 data we saw in Chapter 9.

From the end of 2010 to the end of 2011, inventory declined from $4,000 to $2,000. All of the inventory used this year has been treated as an expense on the activity statement. Therefore, all of the inventory used has been subtracted to arrive at the change in net assets, as if we paid for it with cash. However, part of the inventory used was not purchased and paid for this year. It had been purchased in some prior year. We know that is true because our inventory balance fell from $4,000 to $2,000. Therefore, our expenses overstate how much cash was used to buy inventory this year. To adjust for this, we add the $2,000 decrease in inventory in Exhibit 10-4. We are not adding this because it generates cash. We are adding this because we used less cash to acquire inventory than the activity statement implies.

Think of this complicated issue in another way. We began the year with inventory of $4,000, the balance at the end of the prior year (see Exhibit 10-5). We acquired food inventory

EXHIBIT 10-5

Meals for the Homeless
Statement of Financial Position
As of December 31, 2011, and December 31, 2010

Assets			Liabilities and Net Assets		
	2011	**2010**		**2011**	**2010**
Current Assets			*Liabilities*		
Cash	$ 1,000	$ 4,000	Current Liabilities		
Marketable securities	3,000	3,000	Wages payable	$ 2,000	$ 3,000
Accounts receivable, net			Accounts payable	3,000	3,000
of estimated uncollectibles			Notes payable	5,000	5,000
of $8,000 and $7,000	55,000	38,000	Current portion of		
Inventory (LIFO basis)	2,000	4,000	mortgage payable	4,000	5,000
Prepaid expenses	1,000	0	Total Current Liabilities	$ 14,000	$ 16,000
Total Current Assets	$ 62,000	$ 49,000			
			Long-Term Liabilities		
Long-Term Assets			Mortgage payable	$ 12,000	$ 16,000
Fixed assets			Total Long-Term		
Property	$ 40,000	$ 40,000	Liabilities	$ 12,000	$ 16,000
Equipment, net	35,000	45,000	Total Liabilities	$ 26,000	$ 32,000
Investments	8,000	12,000			
Total Long-Term Assets	$ 83,000	$ 97,000	*Net Assets*	119,000	114,000
Total Assets	$ 145,000	$146,000	*Liabilities and Net Assets*	$145,000	$146,000

during the year. As we buy and pay for food, that uses cash. However, assume that we do not know how much we acquired and paid for. During the year, we had $17,000 of expense related to the use of inventory (see Food line in Exhibit 10-2). As we used the food, it reduces the amount in the inventory account. So a summary of the transactions affecting the food inventory account is as follows:

End of 2010 inventory balance	$ 4,000
Purchase inventory	???
Inventory expense	(17,000)
End of 2011 inventory balance	$ 2,000

It turns out that for this account to be properly balanced we must have purchased $15,000 of food, as follows:

End of 2010 inventory balance	$ 4,000
Purchase inventory	15,000
Inventory expense	(17,000)
End of 2011 inventory balance	$ 2,000

The activity statement assumes that the full $17,000 of food used must have been paid for in cash. However, we see from the preceding calculation that we only purchased $15,000 of food. The activity statement assumes that more cash was used than was actually the case. So we need to add back the difference between the $17,000 and the $15,000. This is equivalent to adding back the decrease in the inventory balance.

In contrast, what if we had purchased more inventory than we had used? Our inventory balance would have increased. Our expense for the use of inventory would show only the inventory used. It would not show the amount paid to acquire inventory that we still owned at the end of the year. It would be necessary to make an adjustment in which we subtracted the year-to-year increase in inventory from the change in net assets. That subtraction would adjust for the fact that we not only paid cash for the inventory we used but also paid cash to acquire more inventory that we still have at the end of the year.

A similar process is undertaken for all items that affect operations. According to the cash flow statement, Exhibit 10-4, Meals must subtract the increase in receivables. Why? Increases in accounts receivable represent revenues that are included in the change in net assets but have not yet been collected. Meals started the year with $38,000 in net receivables (see the 2010 ending balance, Exhibit 10-5). During 2011, revenues were $196,000 (see the activity statement, Exhibit 10-2). At the end of the year, Meals still had outstanding net receivables of $55,000 (Exhibit 10-5):

Beginning accounts receivable	$ 38,000
Increase resulting from revenue	196,000
Collections reducing accounts receivable	???
Ending accounts receivable	$ 55,000

For these receivables accounts to make sense, the organization must have collected $179,000:

Beginning accounts receivable	$ 38,000
Increase resulting from revenue	196,000
Collections reducing accounts receivable	(179,000)
Ending accounts receivable	$ 55,000

However, the cash flow statement starts with the change in net assets. The change in net assets includes the full $196,000 of revenues. Since we only collected $179,000 rather than $196,000, we must subtract the difference, which is the amount accounts receivable has increased.

After looking at inventory and accounts receivable, it becomes apparent that the adjustments in the cash flow from operations include adding decreases in current asset accounts and subtracting increases. Just the reverse is true for current liabilities. This is exactly consistent with the equation derived earlier:

$$\Delta \text{ Cash } = \Delta \text{ Net Assets } + \Delta \text{ Liabilities } - \Delta \text{ All Other Assets}$$

Changes in current assets are part of the change in all other assets in the equation. Increases in current assets are subtracted, for example, because we spend money to acquire those assets, causing both sides of the equation to decline. Notice the negative sign in front of Δ All Other Assets in the equation. Following this equation, Meals must also subtract the decrease in wages payable. If wages payable decline, it is because we have paid employees more than they earned this year. That means that payments to employees exceeded the amount treated as an expense in the activity statement. So a subtraction is required. Looking at the equation, a reduction in a liability reduces both sides of the equation.

Another common adjustment relates to unrealized gains and losses on investments. For example, suppose that an organization owns shares of stock with a value of $30 per share at the beginning of the year. During the year the value of the stock rose, and at the end of the year it is worth $40 per share. On the operating statement, a gain of $10 per share will be shown to reflect this increase in the value of our investments. Since we have not yet sold the stock, this gain is considered to be "unrealized." Although that change has resulted in an increase in net assets, there has been no cash flow. We didn't actually sell the stock, so we didn't receive cash. Therefore, we need an adjustment on the cash flow statement. We will subtract the unrealized gain on investments. Similarly, if there were an unrealized loss on investments, that would have lowered net assets on the operating statement, even though cash is not paid to anyone when an unrealized loss occurs. So unrealized losses are added back in the operating section of the cash flow statement.

These adjustments can be complicated, and they make preparation of a cash flow statement difficult. The vast majority of managers, however, will not have to prepare the statement. So it is more important to focus on interpretation of the numbers. Managers should be able to answer questions such as, "What are the implications of an increase in accounts receivable on the cash generated by operations? Does the increase in accounts receivable imply that we are not making an adequate effort to collect money owed to us? Does the lag in collection of money owed to us affect cash flow to a great enough extent to create a dangerous financial position for the organization?"

Meals for the Homeless has had decreases in cash from operating activities for both 2010 and 2011. The decrease in 2011 was smaller than in 2010, but given Meals' profit in 2011, it might still be considered surprising. The cash decrease in 2011 is not extremely large. And it might be caused by expansion in services and lags in collections of receivables. It does, however, raise a note of caution, and it will be important for managers to keep their eyes on their cash flows during the coming year.

CASH FROM INVESTING ACTIVITIES The second part of the statement of cash flows is cash from investing activities. This section focuses on two very different types of investment activities. First is the purchase and sale of investments not directly related to the production of the organization's good and services. This would include, for example, the purchase and sale of shares of stock. The second type of activity relates to the purchase or sale of the capital assets the organization needs to provide its goods and services, such as buildings and equipment.

In either case, the investing activities section of the cash flow statement shows the total purchase amount for purchases and the total sales amount for sales. If we buy a building for $1,000,000, in the investing activities section of the cash flow statement we would show that we used $1,000,000 of cash. What if we only pay $200,000 in cash when we buy the building, and we borrow the rest from a bank? In the investing activities section of the cash flow statement, we would still show that we used $1,000,000 of cash to purchase the building. Effectively, we have borrowed $800,000 from the bank and paid $1,000,000 for the building. The investing activities section shows the full $1,000,000 payment as a cash use, and the financing activities section of the statement (discussed below) would show that the bank loan provided an $800,000 source of cash for the organization.

When we sell an investment, the investing activities section of the cash flow statement shows the full amount of cash received from the sale. Suppose that we had purchased a piece of equipment for $20,000 three years ago. It had a five-year expected life with no salvage value expected at the end of five years. At a depreciation rate of $4,000 a year, the equipment had a net book value of $8,000 at the end of three years. How would we show this equipment on the cash flow statement if we sold it for $10,000 at the end of the third year? The entire $10,000 that we receive from the sale represents a cash inflow to the organization. We would show that full $10,000 as a source of cash in the investing activities section of the statement. Note, however, that since the item had an $8,000 net book value and it was sold for $10,000, we made a $2,000 profit on the sale. That profit or gain on the sale would be included in the activity or operating statement, because it does increase the organization's net assets. In order to avoid double-counting the cash impact of that profit, the gain on sale of equipment would be subtracted in the operating activities section of the cash flow statement. Similarly, the sale of stocks and other investments should not be reported net of unrealized gains or losses. When investments are sold, the cash from investing activities section of the cash flow statement reports the full cash proceeds of the sale, and the gain or loss is adjusted in the cash from operations section of the statement.

Note that Meals sold $4,000 of stock investments during 2011 (Exhibit 10-4). Given that the proceeds were not reinvested (we can tell from the statement that Meals made no investments in 2011), the money from the sale probably went to cover the cash shortfall from operations. Meals still owns some investments. However, it clearly cannot sell investments indefinitely to provide cash to support operations.

In the prior year, Meals purchased a delivery van. That required a major cash outlay of $32,000. Increases in fixed assets, such as the purchase of the van, require subtractions on the cash flow statement since they represent a use of cash. Decreases in fixed assets, such as the sale of a stock investment, require an addition on the statement because such sales generate cash for the organization. We see that in 2010 there is a $32,000 use of cash to pay for the investment in the delivery van.

CASH FROM FINANCING ACTIVITIES   The third section of the statement is cash flows from financing activities. In 2010, Meals did not have enough cash in the bank to pay the entire cost of the new delivery van. Further, its operations that year consumed $6,000 more of cash than they generated. Therefore, it needed another source of cash to pay for the van. As we can see from the cash flow statement, during 2010 there was a $25,000 mortgage increase. This increase in long-term borrowing provided the source of cash to buy the van.

The van was purchased early in the year, and mortgage repayments were made in both 2011 and 2010. These repayments of money that had been borrowed represent a use of cash. Thus, new loans are additions because they are a source of cash, and repayments or decreases in loans are subtractions because they require payment of cash.

For-profit corporations have another prominent potential source of cash from financing activities. They can sell more shares of ownership in the organization. Issuing stock in exchange for cash represents a source and therefore an addition in this section of the statement.

DISCUSSION   Combining the cash flows from operating, investing, and financing activities yields the net increase or decrease in cash for the year. In 2010, Meal's cash declined by $13,000; in 2011, it declined another $3,000. The change in cash each year is added to the cash balance at the beginning of the year. This tells us how much cash there is at the end of the year. We can see that Meals finished 2010 with $4,000, and 2011 with $1,000. These amounts at the bottom of the cash flow statement (Exhibit 10-4) also appear on the balance sheet (Exhibit 10-5).

In some ways, Meals needs to be more concerned about its cash position than it was a year ago, even though cash declined only $3,000 this year as compared with the $13,000 decline in the previous year. In 2010, Meals made a major equipment purchase. Meals borrowed $25,000 on a mortgage and purchased a van for $32,000, so there was a $7,000 cash drain on the organization to buy the van. In 2011, Meals was profitable and did not make any investment in equipment. Yet, it used $2,000 more cash for operations than it generated from operations, and it finished the year with only $1,000 cash in the bank.

Meals does not, however, have a crisis. With profitability improving, collections from receivables should rise. The cash deficit from operations declined in 2011, and similar improvements in 2012 could yield a positive cash flow from operations. However, Meals did not buy any equipment this year. It would be helpful if it could generate enough of a cash surplus in years when no new equipment investment is made in order to put money aside in savings. Such savings could help provide the down payments for future equipment purchases. It is unlikely that most organizations would be able to finance capital acquisitions without using some accumulated surpluses from prior periods.

INTERRELATIONSHIPS AMONG FINANCIAL STATEMENTS

The balance sheet, activity statement, and cash flow statement are interconnected. The information from each relies to some extent on information from the others. It is important to realize the connectivity of the statements. All three financial statements have their origins in the fundamental equation of accounting discussed in Chapter 9.

The activity statement considers revenues and expenses, both of which change net assets. Suppose that we use up inventory as we provide services during the year. Our asset, inventory, goes down. If we look at the balance sheet at the end of the year, total assets are lower than at the beginning of the year because there is less inventory. However, this cannot possibly tell the whole story, because an equation cannot remain in balance if only one thing changes. A reduction on the left side of the equation leaves the equation unbalanced. When inventory is used up, that lowers the assets owned by the organization or its owners. That creates an expense. Expenses are reductions in net assets, and therefore, reduce the right side of the equation.

Thus, the consumption of inventory causes assets to decline and expenses to rise. This affects the inventory asset reported on the balance sheet and the expense reported on the activity statement. Revenue transactions also affect both the balance sheet and the activity statement. When we charge clients for our services, accounts receivable rise, increasing assets on the balance sheet, and revenues rise, affecting the activity statement. These changes also affect the change in net assets, which is the starting point for the cash flow statement.

NOTES TO FINANCIAL STATEMENTS

The information reported in financial statements is often not enough to tell the entire story. For a variety of reasons, the balance sheet, activity statement, and cash flow statement are inadequate by themselves to give a fair representation of the financial position and results of operations of the organization. GAAP include a principle of full disclosure. This principle requires audited financial statements to contain all information that might be needed by a reasonable user for making decisions.

As a result of that principle, financial statements must be accompanied by a set of explanatory or supplementary notes in order to be deemed a fair representation of the organization's financial position and results of operations. Accounting is not a science. GAAP represent a set of conventions that contain numerous exceptions, choices, and complications. As a result, it is vital that the user of financial statements treats the notes that accompany financial statements as an integral part of the organization's financial report. Notes to financial statements are discussed at length in Chapter 14.

RECORDING AND REPORTING FINANCIAL INFORMATION

In Chapter 9, we introduced the process of using journals and ledgers to record and summarize financial transactions. After transactions are recorded in this manner, financial statements can be developed. We continue that example now, adding transactions that affect the activity or operating statement. Refer back to Chapter 9 for the first five events for HOS in the year 2012. Also refer to Chapter 9 for a discussion of journal entries and posting to ledger accounts. For the reader's convenience, Exhibit 9-3, the balance sheet for the end of the year 2011, appears here as Exhibit 10-6.

In Chapter 9, all of the transactions affected the basic equation by causing changes in one or both sides of the equation:

$$\Delta \text{ Assets } = \Delta \text{ Liabilities } + \Delta \text{ Net Assets}$$

That is, the change in assets equals the change in liabilities plus the change in net assets. However, there were no changes to net assets in the example in Chapter 9. The most common things that change net assets are revenues (or support) and expenses. Therefore, the equation can be shown as follows:

$$\Delta \text{ Assets } = \Delta \text{ Liabilities } + \text{ Revenues } - \text{ Expenses}$$

Continuing with the example from Chapter 9, we pick up with transaction 6:

6. July 17. HOS provides services and charges patients $81,000. Inventory that had cost $4,000 was consumed. The hospital has not yet been paid.

The hospital has both revenues and expenses as a result of this transaction. The revenue side and expense side can be recorded as two separate transactions. First, we have sold patient services in the amount of $81,000. That will increase both accounts receivable and patient revenues. Second, we have consumed some inventory. That will lower inventory by $4,000 and create an expense.

ASSETS	=	LIABILITIES	+	REVENUES	–	EXPENSES
Accounts Receivable +$81,000	=		+	Patient Revenues +$81,000		
Inventory −$4,000	=				–	Supply Expense +$4,000

Notice that although supply expense increased, expenses reduce net assets, so the effect of the expense is to lower the right side of the equation. The journal entries for transaction 6 and the remaining transactions in this example may be found in Appendix 10-D.

EXHIBIT 10-6

Hospital for Ordinary Surgery
Balance Sheet
As of December 31, 2011

Assets

Current Assets	
Cash	$ 52,000
Accounts receivable, net	18,000
Inventory	5,000
Total Current Assets	$ 75,000
Fixed Assets	
Plant and equipment, net	240,000
Total Assets	$315,000

Liabilities & Net Assets

Liabilities	
Current Liabilities	
Accounts payable	$ 7,000
Wages payable	30,000
Total current liabilities	$ 37,000
Long-Term Liabilities	
Mortgage payable	140,000
Total Liabilities	$177,000
Net Assets	
Unrestricted	$113,000
Temporarily restricted	15,000
Permanently restricted	10,000
Total Net Assets	$138,000
Total Liabilities and Net Assets	$315,000

7. August 4. HOS orders $4,000 of additional inventory to replace inventory that had been used up. The inventory has not yet been received and payment has not yet been made.

There will be no journal entry. We need to keep track of the order. However, this order is similar to the X-ray machine ordered in transaction 3 (see Chapter 9). There has been no exchange by either party to the transaction, so no journal entry is recorded.

8. November 28. HOS pays its employees $48,000 of wages. This payment includes all balances outstanding from the previous year plus some payment for work done this year.

Clearly cash decreases by $48,000. Is this all an expense of the current year? No. We owed employees $30,000 for work from the previous year (see wages payable on the Exhibit 10-6 balance sheet from the end of the previous year). Thus, only $18,000 is an expense of the current year. The rest is a reduction of the liability from the start of the year.

ASSETS	=	LIABILITIES	+	REVENUES	–	EXPENSES
Cash		*Wages Payable*				*Labor Expense*
–$48,000	=	–$30,000			–	+$18,000

9. December 10. HOS received $40,000 in payments from customers for services that were provided and billed for at an earlier date.

Cash increases by $40,000 and accounts receivable decrease by that amount as a result of this transaction.

ASSETS		=	LIABILITIES	+	REVENUES	–	EXPENSES
Cash +$40,000	Accounts Receivable –$40,000	=	No change on right side.				

10. December 31. At the end of the year, HOS makes a mortgage payment of $20,000. The payment reduces the mortgage balance by $7,000. The rest of the payment is interest.

Thus, cash is reduced by $20,000, the mortgage payable liability is reduced by $7,000, and there is $13,000 of interest expense.

ASSETS	=	LIABILITIES	+	REVENUES	–	EXPENSES
Cash –$20,000	=	Mortgage Payable –$7,000			–	Interest Expense +$13,000

11. December 31. At the end of the year, HOS makes an adjusting entry for prepaid insurance. Assume that the fire insurance premium paid for two years of coverage.[7]

An adjusting entry is made because something has happened with the passage of time. In this case, half of the prepaid insurance has been used up because one year of the two years on the policy has expired.

Many financial transactions occur at a specific moment in time. Journal entries are recorded as of that date. Some transactions, however, occur over a period of time. One could contend that a small amount of fire insurance protection is used up each day, and a journal entry should be made daily to record that consumption. In practice, however, we do not need to make daily entries for things that occur over time. We just need to make one adjusting entry prior to preparing financial statements.

However, one might wonder why an adjusting entry is made before the item is completely used up. Why not simply wait until the insurance has completely expired? We do not wait because, if we did that, we would be overstating the value of the insurance asset on the balance sheet. We would also be understating the amount of resources used up and, therefore, the expense on the operating statement. Adjusting entries have a goal of placing expenses in the period during which revenues were generated as a result of those expenses.

ASSETS	=	LIABILITIES	+	REVENUES	–	EXPENSES
Prepaid Insurance –$50	=				–	Insurance Expense +$50

12. December 31. HOS owes clinical staff $27,000 at the end of the year. These wages will not be paid until the following year.

This requires an adjusting entry. There is no specific transaction, such as a payment. However, the staff did provide their services to the organization, so there has been an exchange. We must record the obligation to pay for their services.

---

[7] For a two-year insurance premium, the initial entry for transaction 1 in Chapter 9 could have shown an increase of $50 in prepaid insurance and an increase of $50 in deferred insurance charge. In Chapter 9 we simply increased prepaid insurance (the name we would use for a short-term asset) by $100.

ASSETS	=	LIABILITIES	+	REVENUES	−	EXPENSES
		Wages Payable				*Labor Expense*
No change on left side.	=	+$27,000			−	+$27,000

13. December 31. The hospital's building and equipment are now one year older. Depreciation for the year is $18,000.

This adjusting entry transaction increases depreciation expense and reduces the net balance in buildings and equipment. For simplicity, we will directly reduce buildings and equipment. In practice, the original cost of buildings and equipment is maintained, and a separate offsetting contra account is established for accumulated depreciation.

ASSETS	=	LIABILITIES	+	REVENUES	−	EXPENSES
Plant & Equipment, net						*Depreciation Expense*
−$18,000	=				−	+$18,000

These transactions for HOS give a highly consolidated view of the thousands, possibly millions, of transactions that are recorded annually. Not all types of transactions have been considered. However, one can begin to see that there is a systematic approach for recording the financial events that affect an organization.

Summarizing Financial Information

In Chapter 9, we discussed creation of a balance sheet from the information contained in ledger accounts. Now we want to use the ending balance in the ledger accounts to generate both a balance sheet and an operating statement.

Exhibit 10-7 presents the information from which we can prepare a set of financial statements for HOS. This exhibit builds on Exhibit 9-4, adding rows for the transactions from this chapter. All of the journal entries for the year have been recorded, including those from Chapter 9. As in Chapter 9, the first row is the beginning balance, which can be found in Exhibit 10-6. Each transaction is then shown. The last row is the ending balance for each ledger account. Each column presents a ledger account. Note that the total of the ending balances on the asset (left) side of Exhibit 10-7 must equal the total of the ending balances on the liability and net assets (right) side, if the fundamental equation has been kept in balance.

Notice that there are no columns for revenue and expense accounts. These temporary accounts have no balance at the beginning or end of the year. Revenue accounts increase net assets, and expense accounts decrease net assets. At the end of the year, the entire impact of revenues and expenses for the year is to change the unrestricted net assets.

Revenue and expense accounts are temporary accounts because we want the activity or operating statement to reflect just the revenues and expenses for the time period being reported, such as a year. Unlike the balance sheet, which shows the value at any specific point in time, the operating statement's purpose is to show what has occurred for a specific period of time. Once that period of time has passed, the accounts are emptied so they can start over for the next period. Balance sheet accounts are referred to as permanent accounts because their ending balance from one period continues on as the beginning balance for the next period. The complete process from first recording transactions through creating financial statements and finally emptying out the temporary accounts is called the *accounting cycle*. The accounting cycle is discussed in Appendix 10-E.

EXHIBIT 10-7 Transactions Worksheet

| | ASSETS | | | | | = | LIABILITIES AND NET ASSETS | | | | | |
| | | | | | | | Liabilities | | | Net Assets | | |
	Cash	Accounts Receivable	Inventory	Prepaid Insurance	Plant & Equipment, Net		Accounts Payable	Wages Payable	Mortgage Payable	Unrestricted	Temporarily Restricted	Permanently Restricted
Beginning Balance	$52,000	$18,000	$5,000	$0	$240,000	=	$7,000	$30,000	$140,000	$113,000	$15,000	$10,000
Transaction 1	(100)			100								
Transaction 2	(2,000)						(2,000)					
Transaction 3												
Transaction 4			3,000				3,000					
Transaction 5	12,000	(12,000)										
Transaction 6a		81,000								81,000 Patient Revenues		
Transaction 6b			(4,000)							(4,000) Supply Expense		
Transaction 7												
Transaction 8	(48,000)							(30,000)		(18,000) Labor Expense		
Transaction 9	40,000	(40,000)										
Transaction 10	(20,000)								(7,000)	(13,000) Interest Expense		
Transaction 11				(50)						(50) Insurance Expense		
Transaction 12								27,000		(27,000) Labor Expense		
Transaction 13					(18,000)					(18,000) Depreciation Expense		
Ending Balance	$33,900	$47,000	$4,000	$50	$222,000	=	$8,000	$27,000	$133,000	$113,950	$15,000	$10,000

The Operating Statement

Exhibit 10-8 presents the *operating statement* for HOS. The operating statement is a summary of revenues and expenses. This information can be taken directly from Exhibit 10-7.

The preparation of Exhibit 10-8 is straightforward. Each change in the unrestricted net assets column in Exhibit 10-7 is taken and recorded on the operating statement. The order of appearance of the items on the operating statement depends on a number of decisions about how information should be presented. All changes to identical accounts, such as labor expense, are totaled and reported as one item. It is also common practice for some ledger accounts to be combined and reported as one summary amount, such as administrative and general expenses.

In practice, the operating statement is developed by taking the total balance from each revenue and expense ledger account. Each revenue and expense account would have its own detailed account information. Exhibit 10-7 provides all of the ledger account information in one place; it is a very highly summarized document that is used for educational purposes only.

The Cash Flow Statement and the Direct Method

The cash flow statement appears in Exhibit 10-9. This has been developed by taking the $950 increase in unrestricted net assets from the last line of Exhibit 10-8 and using that as the first item in Exhibit 10-9. Then the opening balances from the transactions worksheet, Exhibit 10-7, are compared with the closing balances in that worksheet, and the impact of the change in each account is reflected on the statement of cash flows. The development of a cash flow statement beginning with changes in net assets, or with net income, is referred to as the indirect method. It is indirect because of the use of changes in net assets as the starting point to determine cash flow. An alternative approach, referred to as the direct method, appears in Exhibit 10-10.

The direct method considers each of the transactions that has affected cash and classifies it as being related to operations, investing, or financing. For example, consider Exhibit 10-7. Rather than comparing the beginning and ending balances in each ledger account, the focus of the direct method is the cash ledger account. In the cash column in Exhibit 10-7, Transaction 1 has caused cash to decline by $100. This was as a result of the purchase of

---

EXHIBIT 10-8

The Hospital for Ordinary Surgery
Operating Statement
For the Year Ending December 31, 2012

Revenues	
Patient revenues	$81,000
Total revenues	$81,000
Expenses	
Supplies expense	$ 4,000
Labor expense	45,000
Insurance expense	50
Depreciation expense	18,000
Interest expense	13,000
Total Expenses	$80,050
Increase in Unrestricted Net Assets	$ 950

EXHIBIT 10-9 Cash Flow Statement: Indirect Method

Hospital for Ordinary Surgery
Statement of Cash Flows
For the Year Ending December 31, 2012

Cash Flows from Operating Activities	
Increase in unrestricted net assets	$ 950
Add expenses not requiring cash:	
Depreciation	18,000
Other adjustments:	
Add decrease in inventory	1,000
Add increase in accounts payable	1,000
Subtract increase in accounts receivables	(29,000)
Subtract increase in prepaid insurance	(50)
Subtract decrease in wages payable	(3,000)
Net cash used for operating activities	$ (11,100)
Cash Flows from Investing Activities	
Net cash from investing activities	$ 0
Cash Flows from Financing Activities	
Repayments of mortgages	$ (7,000)
Net cash used for financing activities	$ (7,000)
Net (Decrease) in Cash	$ (18,100)
Cash, Beginning of Year	52,000
Cash, End of Year	$ 33,900

prepaid insurance. Therefore, in the cash flow statement, we would show $100 as a cash use for the purchase of insurance (see Exhibit 10-10).

Continuing down the cash column in Exhibit 10-7, we can determine the other impacts on cash flow. Transaction 2 shows that $2,000 was used to pay suppliers. Transactions 5 and 9 show that a total of $52,000 was received from patients or their insurers. Transaction 8 shows that 48,000 was paid to employees for wages. Transaction 10 shows that $20,000 was paid for the mortgage. However, note that $7,000 of this amount was a repayment of the loan and $13,000 represented interest expense. The payment of interest is considered to be a routine operating expense, shown in the operating portion of the cash flow statement. The repayment of the mortgage loan relates to a financing activity.

In looking at Exhibit 10-10, we can see that the $11,100 cash used for operating activities is exactly the same under the direct method as it is under the indirect approach used in Exhibit 10-9. The totals of each section of the statement and the net change in cash is not affected by which method is used. In fact, many people prefer the direct method. Going down the transactions worksheet and generating the statement from the individual changes to the cash account seems more logical and understandable to many.

GAAP require that either the direct or indirect method be used. However, if the direct method is used, a reconciliation must be provided showing that the result is the same under the direct method as it would be under the indirect method. Note that the reconciliation at the bottom of Exhibit 10-10 is essentially the first section of the cash flow statement shown in Exhibit 10-9. A discussion of the complicated issues behind the GAAP requirement for this reconciliation is beyond the scope of this introductory text. Suffice it to say that since the indirect method is essentially required whenever the direct method is used, few organizations use the direct method; they generally just present the indirect method.

EXHIBIT 10-10 Cash Flow Statement: Direct Method

Hospital for Ordinary Surgery
Statement of Cash Flows
For the Year Ending December 31, 2012

Cash Flows from Operating Activities	
Cash used to purchase insurance	$ (100)
Cash used to pay suppliers	(2,000)
Cash received from patients	52,000
Cash used for payment of wages	(48,000)
Cash used to pay interest	(13,000)
Net cash used for operating activities	$ (11,100)
Cash Flows from Investing Activities	
Net cash from investing activities	$ 0
Cash Flows from Financing Activities	
Repayments of mortgages	$ (7,000)
Net cash used for financing activities	$ (7,000)
Net (Decrease) in Cash	$ (18,100)
Cash, Beginning of Year	52,000
Cash, End of Year	$ 33,900
Reconciliation of increase in unrestricted net assets to net cash	
used for operating activities:	
Increase in unrestricted net assets	$ 950
Add expenses not requiring cash:	
Depreciation	18,000
Other adjustments:	
Add decrease in inventory	1,000
Add increase in accounts payable	1,000
Subtract increase in accounts receivables	(29,000)
Subtract increase in prepaid insurance	(50)
Subtract decrease in wages payable	(3,000)
Net cash used for operating activities	$ (11,100)

The Balance Sheet

Exhibit 10-11 presents the balance sheet as of December 31, 2012. This statement is prepared by using the information from the last (Ending Balance) row from Exhibit 10-7, the transactions worksheet. Notice that the $33,900 cash balance on the balance sheet, Exhibit 10-11, is the same number as the Cash, End of Year amount on the statement of cash flows, Exhibits 10-9 and 10-10. All three statements, the balance sheet, operating statement, and cash flow statement, are interrelated, as noted earlier.

Financial Statement Headings

As one final point, note that financial statement headings indicate the time period covered by the statement. Balance sheets represent a moment in time. They give financial information as of a specific date and will generally read something like "As of June 30, 2012." In contrast, activity, or operating, and cash flow statements give information related to what has happened over a period of time. Often we see annual statements, but it is possible for them to cover a different time period, such as a month. To be clear about the information contained in the report, such statements will indicate the time period covered, such as "For the Month Ending May 31, 2012" or "For the Year Ending June 30, 2012."

EXHIBIT 10-11

Hospital for Ordinary Surgery
Balance Sheet
As of December 31, 2012

Assets

Current Assets
Cash	$ 33,900
Accounts receivable, net	47,000
Inventory	4,000
Prepaid insurance	50
Total current assets	$ 84,950

Fixed Assets
Plant and equipment, net	222,000
Total Assets	$306,950

Liabilities & Net Assets

Liabilities
Current Liabilities:
Acounts payable	$ 8,000
Wages payable	27,000
Total current liabilities	$ 35,000

Long-Term Liabilities:
Mortgage payable	133,000
Total Liabilities	$168,000

Net Assets
Unrestricted	$113,950
Temporarily restricted	15,000
Permanently restricted	10,000
Total Net Assets	$138,950
Total Liabilities and Net Assets	$306,950

Chart of Accounts

A common approach used by organizations when they record transactions is to assign a code number to each account. A *chart of accounts* provides a listing of each account and its assigned code or account number. In most charts of accounts, assets start with a number 1, liabilities with number 2, net assets with number 3, revenues with number 4, and expenses with number 5.

The account number would typically have two digits following that first number, which provide information about the particular type of account. For example, within the asset class of accounts, 01 would usually be assigned to cash. Within the liability class of accounts, 01 would usually be assigned to accounts payable. Thus, if the account number began with 101 it would imply that the account was used to record increases and decreases to the asset cash. If the account number began with 201 it would imply that the account was used for the liability accounts payable. Account numbers in a chart of accounts might have quite a few digits, to be able to accommodate all of the desired information. For example, although 101 indicates the asset cash, we would typically want to know whether we are referring to currency on hand, cash in a checking account, cash in a savings account, and so on. These cash sub-accounts might have numbers 10101, 10102, and 10103.

Why wouldn't the currency, checking, and savings accounts be 1011, 1012, and 1013? Why did we need to allow two digits for the type of account if there are only three different types of cash accounts? There may be another asset account, perhaps account 105, that has more than nine sub-accounts, and therefore needs two digits for its sub-accounts. Even if that is not the case, charts of accounts should be established with the intent to provide flexibility over time. Perhaps as the years go by, the organization will add additional cash accounts as it expands geographically.

When the organization's operating results are reported in its financial statements, accounts are aggregated. For example, the value for cash shown on the balance sheet would be the sum of the account balances for all accounts beginning with the value 101. However, for internal management of the organization, having a detailed chart of accounts provides better control. Managers need to know the details of how much cash is in a drawer in the office, how much in a checking account, and how much in an interest-bearing savings account. The total amount of cash provides inadequate information for effective management.

Account numbers often have a decimal point or dash, with digits on the right as well as the left. The digits on the right can provide information about departments, programs, or projects. This makes it easier to aggregate all of the information that relates to a particular program, function, or responsibility center. As organizations become larger and more complex, so do their charts of accounts. For example, a large university might have accounts with 17 digits, in a format: xxxxx-xx-xxxxx-xxxxx. That account might offer information indicating that the item is an expense for salary spent on a faculty member in the not-for-profit management department of the school of public administration for a specific research project funded by a grant from a specific foundation restricted for that particular purpose. This may seem complicated, but it provides vital information, and is often worth the effort. The university will be able to aggregate all expenses charged to the research project so that it can send an invoice to the foundation. It will be able to generate reports of total salary expenses for the university, and total expenses by school, by department, by project, and so on. Each of these aggregations will generate information that may be compared to budgeted amounts, letting the organization exercise better control over its operations. (See Problem 3-30 at the end of Chapter 3 for an example using a chart of accounts for a state agency.)

STARTING FROM SCRATCH

Most managers take jobs with organizations that already have an existing accounting system. However, in some cases a new organization is being formed, and one must set up an accounting system from scratch. The system should help in the budget process, record transactions, and provide not only financial statements, but also reports that will help managers control operations. Ideally, the organization would have sufficient funds to hire an accounting firm to set up the accounting books for the organization. However, that may not always be the case. Suppose that you had to set up an accounting system on your own.

A good starting point is to establish a chart of accounts, as discussed previously. The key is to establish the typical accounts that will be affected by transactions, often referred to as a general ledger system. (See the Chapter 9 discussion of general ledgers.) It is not critical to list every ledger account at first. As long as the chart has reasonable flexibility, additional accounts may be added as transactions occur that require them. Once a chart of accounts exists, individual transactions may be recorded. Each transaction will not only be recorded as a journal entry, but will also impact on the balance of each individual account. At the end of an accounting period, those balances can be used to prepare financial statements. If need be, this entire process can be done by hand.

However, generally charts of accounts and general ledgers are an integral part of a computerized accounting system for the organization. As accounting transactions are recorded using account numbers from the chart of accounts, the information becomes part of a flexible database. Not only is the transaction recorded, but at the same time the individual ledger accounts are updated. Financial statements and numerous other reports can be generated. Such systems can cost millions of dollars to develop and customize for large organizations.

However, for an organization starting from scratch, much less sophistication is required. Inexpensive accounting programs exist that can get an organization started. Two of the leading providers of business accounting software for small organizations are Peachtree and Quickbooks. Both have accounting programs specifically designed for not-for-profit organizations starting at $500 or less.[8]

What can one expect from a relatively inexpensive accounting system? Look for a program that provides a guided approach to setting up and managing basic accounting tasks. These include setting up a general ledger with a chart of accounts specifically designed for the needs of a not-for-profit organization, recording transactions, printing checks, preparing invoices, generating financial statements, generating reports to aid in preparing the organization's annual Form 990 tax return, and generating reports such as a listing of contributions by donor. Such software should also have some forecasting ability and be able to prepare budgets and a range of other reports.

Also consider future expansion when an accounting system is initially selected. For example, as a not-for-profit organization grows it will need software that can deal with restricted revenues, government grants, endowments, and funding sources that span both programs and fiscal years. At some point it may be necessary to allocate costs to different projects or grants, and so on. Many of the leading programs allow you to upgrade over time, adding more sophisticated not-for-profit modules. For example, QuickBooks sells a Fundware suite, which provides many accounting options for not-for-profit organizations. Some software caters to both not-for-profit and government organizations. For example, AccuFund offers a software program designed around the reporting requirements of both FASB and GASB.[9] It includes modules for municipal governments, including some specifically designed to handle accounting areas such as utility billing, business licenses, and sales tax.

In starting an accounting system for a new organization, it probably also makes sense to hire a payroll service. Many state and federal laws govern payroll. These are often related to withholding taxes for income, Social Security, unemployment, workmen's compensation, and so on. It often makes sense for a small organization to outsource this process, rather than trying to become competent in this complex area. Organizations such as Intuit, ADP, and Paychex offer these services.

Summary

The discussion in this chapter focuses on reporting the results of operations. This is achieved by generating an activity statement and statement of cash flows. Unlike the balance sheet, these statements report on what has happened over a period of time, rather than just disclosing the financial position of the organization at one specific point in time.

The activity statement compares the entity's revenues and other support with its expenses for a period of time, such as a fiscal year. The cash flow statement looks at where the organization obtained its cash and where it spent cash during that period of time. The focus is not only on how much cash came and went, but also on the sources and uses of cash. Together these statements provide the user with a sense of how well the organization has done over the period of time covered by the statements.

---

[8] Peachtree Complete Accounting with Nonprofit Industry Kit, see www.peachtree.com; QuickBooks: Premier Nonprofit Edition, see www.quickbooks.com.
[9] See www.accufund.com.

Preview

Chapters 9 and 10 provide an introduction to financial accounting. The general principles and approaches of financial accounting are broadly applicable to all types of organizations. For-profits and not-for-profits, health, government, automotive, steel, and computer manufacturers all have many common elements in their financial accounting. For example, the fundamental equation of accounting is used across all types of organizations. Most organizations use a statement of financial position (balance sheet), an activity statement (operating statement or income statement), and a cash flow statement.

However, there are also many unique aspects of financial accounting for health, not-for-profit, and government organizations. Chapter 11 considers such unique aspects for not-for-profit and health care organizations. Chapters 12 and 13 consider unique accounting issues for governments.

Key Terms from This Chapter

accelerated depreciation.   Technique that allocates a larger portion of an asset's cost as an expense in the earlier years of its useful lifetime and a smaller portion in the later years.

accounting cycle.   The formal process that starts with the occurrence of financial events and ends with a complete set of financial statements.

activity statement.   Statement that compares the entity's revenues and other support to its expenses for a period of time, such as a year. Often referred to as the income statement, operating statement, profit and loss (P&L) statement, earnings report, statement of revenues and expenses, and statement of revenues and expenditures.

amortization.   Allocation of the cost of a long-term asset over its lifetime.

cash flow statement.   Statement that provides information about the organization's sources and uses of cash.

chart of accounts.   A listing of each account and its assigned code or account number.

contra asset.   An asset that is used to offset or reduce another asset.

deferred revenues.   Items that will become revenue in the future if the organization provides goods or services. They are liabilities until the goods or services are provided.

depreciation expense.   Portion of the original cost of a fixed asset allocated as an expense each year.

expenses.   The costs of services provided; expired cost.

expired cost.   An asset that has been consumed; expense.

first-in, first-out (FIFO).   Method of accounting for inventory that assumes the oldest inventory is always used first.

interim statements.   Financial statements covering a period of time less than one year.

last-in, first-out (LIFO).   Inventory valuation method that accounts for inventory as if the most recent acquisitions are always used prior to inventory acquired at an earlier date.

matching.   For a given unit of service provided, the revenues arising from providing that service and the expenses incurred in providing that service are both recorded in the same fiscal period.

net income.   Revenue less expense; profit.

operating statement.   Compares the entity's revenues and other support with its expenses for a period of time, such as a year. Often referred to as the income statement, activity statement, profit and loss (P&L) statement, earnings report, statement of revenues and expenses, and statement of revenues and expenditures.

period costs.   Costs that are treated as expense in the accounting period that they are incurred, regardless of when the organization's goods or services are sold.

product costs.   Costs that are directly related to the production of goods and services and are recorded as expenses in the period revenue related to those goods and services is recognized.

revenue.   Amounts of money that the organization has received or is entitled to receive in exchange for goods and/or services that it has provided. Also includes *support*.

straight-line depreciation. Technique that allocates an equal portion of the asset's cost as an expense each year.

support. Revenue that consists of contributions or grants.

unexpired cost. Cost of asset that has not yet been used up.

viability. Ability to continue in existence.

write off. Eliminate an asset from the accounting records and record as an expense.

Questions for Discussion

10-1. What are some of the other names for the activity statement?

10-2. Why would public service organizations need to measure income?

10-3. What conditions must be met for revenue to be recorded? Can pledges meet those conditions?

10-4. What is the difference between assets being used up and expiring?

10-5. Why do financial statements often show numbers rounded off rather than exact to the dollar?

10-6. Consider the revenue results from telephone solicitations by Meals for the Homeless in 2011 (see Exhibit 10-2). What do you make of this? What are some possible explanations? What questions do you have?

10-7. Should bad debt expense on the activity statement match up with the allowance for uncollectible accounts on the balance sheet?

10-8. Does the difficulty in determining the current value of an asset create a problem in determining the depreciation expense that should be charged for a year?

10-9. Why would CPAs prefer to avoid estimates in financial reporting?

10-10. Is the cash flow statement a reasonable alternative to the activity or operating statement?

10-11. What are the sections of the cash flow statement? Why is it divided this way?

10-12. Is the information on the balance sheet, activity statement, and cash flow statement independent of one another or connected? Explain.

10-13. Explain the difference between permanent and temporary accounts.

Problems

10-14. The American Natural History Center (ANHC) had the following highly summarized financial events during the current year:

1. Jan. 2 Ordered new equipment with a 10-year life, for $80,000. No payment was made and the equipment has not been delivered.

2. Jan. 14 Received a $100,000 payment on a pledge that had been made three years ago.

3. Feb. 19 Bought $35,000 of books and posters that will be sold in the Center store. Only $20,000 was paid for the inventory on that date, and the balance is owed to the suppliers. ANHC expects to be able to sell the inventory for $60,000.

4. May 15 Paid a $30,000 deposit for the equipment ordered on January 2.

5. July 12 Received the equipment ordered on January 2, and mailed a check for the balance due.

6. Dec. 28 Admission fees for the year were $74,000. They were all collected.

7. Dec. 28 ANHC paid its employees $68,000 of wages. Wage expense for the year is $73,000. The payment included the $2,000 wages payable balance outstanding from the previous year plus some payment for work done this year.

8. Dec. 30 Book and poster sales for the year totaled $53,000. All but $3,000 of that amount has been collected. The entire $6,000 balance in accounts receivable from beginning of the year was also collected. The cost of the books and posters sold was $32,000.

9. Dec. 31 ANHC makes a payment of $134,000 on its long-term note. That amount includes interest expense of $7,000.

10. Dec. 31 The Center building and equipment are now one year older. Depreciation for the year is $60,000.

11. Dec. 31 ANHC estimates that $1,000 of the receivables for book and poster sales made this year will never be collected.

Record these transactions and any other required adjusting entries, by showing either their impact on the fundamental equation of accounting or journal entries.

10-15. Assume that ANHC began the year with the following balances (shown in alphabetical order) in their accounts:

Accounts Payable	$ 2,000
Accounts Receivable	6,000
Buildings and Equipment, Net	550,000
Cash	80,000
Notes Payable	250,000
Permanently Restricted Net Assets	300,000
Pledges Receivable	320,000
Temporarily Restricted Net Assets	30,000
Unrestricted Net Assets	372,000
Wages Payable	2,000

Record this information and the transactions from Problem 10-14 in a worksheet similar to Exhibit 10-7.

10-16. Use the solutions from 10-14 and 10-15 to prepare:
a. An activity statement (operating statement).
b. A comparative statement of financial position (balance sheet).
c. A statement of cash flows.
d. What do you learn from these statements, and what questions do they raise?

10-17. The Hospital for Ordinary Surgery uses pharmaceuticals for its patients. It started the year on January 1, with an inventory of 1,000 doses of an antibiotic drug that cost $17 per dose. On January 2 it purchased another 300 doses for $21 each. From January 3 through June 30 it used 800 doses. On July 1 it bought 500 more doses at $23 each. From July 2 through the end of the year it used 400 doses. What is the inventory value at the end of the year, assuming FIFO? What is the value assuming LIFO?

Suggested Readings

Anthony, Robert N., and Leslie Pearlman Breitner. *Core Concepts of Accounting*, 8th ed. Upper Saddle River, N.J.: Prentice Hall, 2003.

Finkler, Steven A. *Finance & Accounting for Nonfinancial Managers*, 3rd ed. New York, N.Y.: Aspen Publishers, 2003.

Granof, Michael H. *Government and Not-for-Profit Accounting: Concepts and Practices*, 3rd ed. New York, N.Y.: John Wiley & Sons, 2004.

Harrison, Walter T., and Charles T. Horngren. *Financial Accounting & Integrated Student CD*, 5th ed. Upper Saddle River, N.J.: Prentice Hall, 2004.

Larkin, Richard E., and Marie DiTommaso. *Wiley Not-for-Profit GAAP 2008: Interpretation and Application of Generally Accepted Accounting Principles for Not-for-Profit Organizations*. New York, N.Y.: John Wiley & Sons, 2008.

Ruppel, Warren. *Wiley GAAP for Governments 2007: Interpretation and Application of Generally Accepted Accounting Principles for State and Local Governments*. New York, N.Y.: John Wiley & Sons, 2007.

Werner, Michael L., and Kumen H. Jones. *Introduction to Financial Accounting: A User Perspective*, 3rd ed. Upper Saddle River, N.J.: Prentice Hall, 2004.

A P P E N D I X   1 0 - A

Sources of Revenue for Governments

Government revenue comes from a number of different sources. Most government revenue comes from *nonexchange transactions.* This means that they are not the result of the sale of goods and services. Various types of taxes, fines, and fees make up the bulk of nonexchange revenue. In some cases, however, governments do charge for goods or services that they provide, so they typically have some exchange revenue as well.

NONEXCHANGE REVENUES

For-profit businesses typically generate revenues from *exchange transactions.* One party buys goods or services from the other party in exchange for a payment. Not-for-profit organizations often generate some of their revenues this way as well. For example, a hospital provides health care services in exchange for payment. However, governments primarily earn their revenues as a result of *nonexchange transactions.* In a nonexchange revenue transaction a government does not give something that is relatively equal in value in exchange for what it receives.

There are three main categories of nonexchange transactions for governments:

- imposed tax revenues,
- derived tax revenues, and
- grants.

Imposed tax revenues arise when taxes are assessed directly on entities. Examples of imposed tax revenues are property taxes or fines. *Derived tax revenues* are amounts the government earns from taxes on exchange transactions. For example, sales taxes are a form of derived tax revenue. The government is not directly involved in the exchange. It is neither buyer nor seller. However, it earns sales tax revenue as a result of that transaction. Grants include both government-mandated transfers and voluntary gifts to a government. *Government mandated nonexchange transactions* are those in which one government gets revenue from another government, but must use that revenue in a specified way. For example, the federal government gives money to state governments for

Medicaid, but restricts the use of that money to the state's Medicaid program. *Voluntary nonexchange transactions* are unrestricted grants or contributions.

Imposed Tax Revenues

Property taxes fall into a category of taxation that is referred to as *ad valorem taxes.* Ad valorem means "based on value." Most typically property taxes are assessed or levied on buildings and land. Some governments also impose such taxes on inventory and other business items or on cars and other personal property. In some cases property taxes may be imposed on securities and bank deposits. To assess a property tax, the property subject to the tax must be valued at a specific amount. Typically governments will appraise the value of property, and then assign an assessed value based on that appraisal. Generally, the government decides the total amount of revenue to be raised by the tax, then divides that by the total assessed value of all property subject to the tax to determine a rate. That tax rate is then multiplied by the assessed value of a specific piece of property to find the tax due on that property. Tax-exempt organizations are generally exempt from property taxes.

For many governments, fines represent a significant revenue source. We often think of fines as coming from parking and other traffic violations. However, governments may fine individuals and organizations for a wide variety of reasons. For example, construction without a proper permit (that kitchen or bathroom you've recently started to renovate), failure to adhere to fire regulations, restaurant health safety violations, etc., all generate nonexchange revenue for the government. At the same time, fines are used to achieve policy objectives of the government, such as ensuring that restaurants do not create health hazards.

Derived Tax Revenues

Sales and income taxes are both derived tax revenues. They tax either the sale of goods or services, or the income-producing activities of individuals or organizations. The revenue generated by these taxes is much more variable and much less certain than that generated by property taxes, or even fines. For example, the government sets the total amount of revenue to be collected from property taxes before determining the property tax rate. The total amount that will be collected is fairly predictable. Even fines can be forecast with a reasonable amount of certainty. In contrast, sales and income tax revenues are much more dependent on factors such as the economy. A sudden economic downturn can dramatically reduce the tax revenues from these sources.

Another concern related to derived tax revenues is that the government is relying to a greater degree on self-reporting. With derived taxes, the government relies on the taxpayer to accurately report the amount of tax owed. The government must develop ways to ensure that taxpayers report the correct amount of tax. Individuals or businesses might be tempted to underreport the amount of income subject to tax. In fact, they might not file an income tax return at all. Or businesses might underreport sales, and then not submit the full amount of sales taxes that had been collected. A belief that the government is likely to detect and punish taxpayers who fail to report correctly discourages abuse of the system. Therefore, governments need to implement systems to ensure that tax returns are filed, and that the amounts reported are correct.

Grants

Grants are another major source of revenue for many governments and may be classified in a variety of ways:

- restricted grants,
- unrestricted grants,
- contingent grants,
- entitlements,
- shared revenues, or
- payments in lieu of taxes.

It is common for governments to receive grants that have restrictions on them, requiring that the revenue be used for specific purposes. Restricted grants may be either *mandates* or voluntary. For example, a state government might mandate that local governments improve their libraries, and may provide a grant for that purpose. If the grant is in the form of a mandate, the local government must accept the state grant, and must make the required library improvements. Often local governments object to mandates that cost the local government more than the amount of the state grant. However, mandates are a matter of law, and must be accepted.

However, it is much more common for grants to be voluntary. If the government does not want to use the money for the restricted purpose, it does not have to accept the grant if it is voluntary. Unrestricted grants may be used for any desired purpose, and it would be rare for a government to decline such a grant.

Contingent grants are paid to the government only if some requirement is met. For example, a grant to support a public health clinic may be contingent upon the government passing a law that ensures the continued existence of the clinic for at least the next five years.

Entitlements are grants that the government is automatically entitled to receive, typically from a higher-level government, based on a formula. For example, the state government may have a law that requires it to pay local governments a set amount for each day that a student attends school in the local government's school system. In such cases school systems tend to work hard to encourage students not to miss too many days from school for illness or other reasons. This serves to not only support the local education system, but also provide an incentive for the local school system to try to achieve the policy objective of making sure students attend school regularly.

Shared revenues are those that are collected by one government, but shared with other governments based on a set formula. For example, a county may share part of its property tax revenues with municipalities within the county if they agree to maintain country roads within their borders.

Payments in lieu of taxes typically represent payments made in place of property taxes. For example, a not-for-profit university would typically be exempt from property taxes. However, the university uses many local government resources, such as fire and police protection, garbage collection, and so on. To encourage the city to be responsive to its needs, the university may make an agreement to provide an annual payment to the local government in lieu of property taxes.

EXCHANGE REVENUES

Governments do earn some revenues from exchange transactions. For example, if a city operates a golf course, and charges fees for its use, the transaction would be similar to that of a privately owned golf course. However, some government revenues are less clearly exchange transactions. Consider, for example, licenses and permit fees. Some license fees are charged to cover the costs of services related to the license. For example, fishing licenses may cover the cost of stocking lakes with fish. Other license fees may exist primarily as a way to raise general revenues. In such cases they are much more closely related to nonexchange revenue than to exchange revenue.

Another type of exchange revenue that governments earn is related to investments. For example, if a government invests money in an interest-bearing account, the interest that is earned is recorded by the government as revenue. This is exchange revenue because the government receives the interest in exchange for lending its money to another entity for a period of time.

Key Terms from This Appendix

ad valorem tax.   A tax based on value—typically property tax.

derived tax revenues.   Taxes the government earns on *exchange transactions*. For example, sales taxes.

exchange transactions.   A transaction in which the organization provides something that is relatively equal in value to the revenues generated.

government mandated nonexchange transactions.   A situation in which one government receives revenues from another, but must use the revenues in a specified way. For example, the Federal government gives states money that must be used for Medicaid.

imposed tax revenues.   Tax revenues that come from assessments directly on entities. For example property taxes or fines.

mandate.   A requirement by one government for another government to provide services. For example, the Federal government can require a state government to provide social services, even if it does not provide the money needed by the state to provide those services.

nonexchange transactions.   A transaction in which the organization does not provide something that is relatively equal in value to the revenues generated—often the result of taxes, fines, or fees.

voluntary nonexchange transactions. Unrestricted grants or contributions.

APPENDIX 10-B

Accelerated Depreciation Methods

A number of depreciation methods in addition to the straight-line method are described in the chapter. Accelerated depreciation does not imply shortening the asset life for depreciation purposes; rather, the amount of depreciation taken in the early years is increased, and the amount taken in the later years is reduced. The two most common accelerated methods are double-declining balance and sum-of-the-years digits. To describe these methods, we assume that the organization has purchased a new piece of equipment for $2,400. It is expected to have a useful life of six years and a salvage value of $300.

The straight-line method first calculates the depreciable base, which is the cost less the salvage value. In this case, the depreciable base is $2,100 ($2,400 cost – $300 salvage). The base is then allocated equally among the years of the asset's life. For a six-year life, the depreciation would be 1/6 of $2,100 each year, or $350 per year.

The double-declining balance (DDB) method starts with a depreciable base equal to the total asset cost. It ignores the salvage value. The cost is multiplied by double the straight-line rate. In this case, the straight-line rate is 1/6, so DDB uses 2/6. Two-sixths of the $2,400 cost is $800. That is the depreciation for the first year.

At that rate, the asset will be fully depreciated in just three years, and we have said that accelerated methods do not shorten the asset life! Therefore, we need some device to prevent the depreciation from remaining at that high level of $800 per year. This device is the declining balance. Each year we subtract the previous year's depreciation from the existing depreciable base to get a new depreciable base.

In the example, under DDB the depreciable base was $2,400 and the depreciation in the first year is $800. In the second year the depreciable base becomes $1,600 ($2,400 cost – $800 first-year depreciation). In the second year depreciation would be 2/6 of $1,600 or $533. For year 3, we will determine a new base equal to $1,600 less the second year's depreciation of $533. Thus, we have a new base of $1,067, and so on. Note, however, that we cannot take more depreciation during the asset's life than its cost less its salvage value. In this problem, we can take no more than $2,100 of depreciation in total.

Sum-of-the-years digits (SYD) calculates the sum of the digits in the years of the life of the asset. That sum simply consists of adding from 1 to the last year of the asset's life, inclusive. In our example, we would add $1 + 2 + 3 + 4 + 5 + 6$, because the asset has a six-year life. The sum of these digits is 21. The cost less salvage is multiplied by the life of the asset divided by the sum to find depreciation in the first year. Therefore, we would multiply $2,100 (cost less salvage) by 6/21 (the life of the asset divided by the sum). This gives us first-year depreciation of $600.

In each succeeding year, lower the numerator of the fraction by 1; that is, for year 2 the fraction becomes 5/21, and the depreciation would be $500 ($2,100 × 5/21). For year 3 the fraction becomes 4/21 and the depreciation $400, and so on.

Figure 10-B-1 and Exhibit 10-B-1 compare the three methods for this piece of equipment for its entire six-year life. Note that all three methods produce exactly the same total depreciation over the life of the asset.

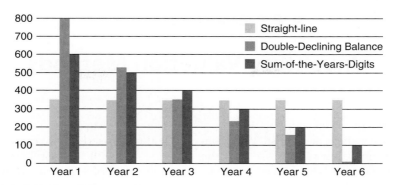

FIGURE 10-B-1 Annual Depreciation Expense

EXHIBIT 10-B-1 Comparison of Depreciation Methods

Year	Straight-Line	Double-Declining Balance	Sum-of-the-Years Digits
1	$ 350	$ 800	$ 600
2	350	533	500
3	350	356	400
4	350	237	300
5	350	161	200
6	350	13	100
Total	$2,100	$2,100	$2,100

APPENDIX 10-C

Inventory Valuation Methods

Following the cost principle of accounting, inventory is shown on the balance sheet at its cost. The problem is trying to determine cost. Suppose that the Hospital for Ordinary Surgery (HOS) has 2,000 units of a drug on hand when the year begins. It had bought those units for $10 each. During the year HOS buys 18,000 more for $12 each. At the end of the year, we count our inventory and find that 2,000 are left. How many did we use? How many are left? What did the leftover ones cost? We can use an equation to calculate the answer to some of these questions:

Beginning					Ending
Inventory	+	Purchases	− Consumption	=	Inventory
2,000	+	18,000	− X	=	2,000
			X	=	18,000

We must have used up 18,000 units. We have 2,000 units left, and they should appear on the balance sheet at their cost. How much did they cost?

This is not a simple question. We started with 2,000 units and bought another 18,000. So we had a total of 20,000 available. We have 2,000 left at year end. Which ones? The units that were in the inventory at the beginning of the year cost $10 each. The ones purchased during the year cost $12 each. So the inventory that is left over may have a cost of $20,000 ($10 per unit × 2,000 units) or $24,000 ($12 per unit × 2,000 units), or something in between.

There are four approaches to tracking inventory flow: first-in first-out (FIFO), last-in first-out (LIFO), weighted average, and specific identification methods. Regardless of which method is used for physical movement of inventory, we may use any of these four approaches for financial statement calculations. However, the organization is required to be consistent from year to year.

The FIFO method is the most widely used for physical flow of inventory. It follows the logical assumption that the oldest inventory (the first in) would always be used first (first out). If we use the FIFO method, then all 2,000 of the units we started with are used up first. Then the first 16,000 of the 18,000 purchased this year are used up. At year-end we are left with the last 2,000 units purchased this year at a cost of $12 each. We would show an inventory value of $24,000 on the balance sheet.

The LIFO method uses the assumption that the last items acquired are the first used. At first this seems illogical. Why would anyone want to use up the newest inventory first? However, some inventory is piled up. When the Town of Millbridge receives a new shipment of salt for melting ice on its roads, the new salt is piled on top of the old salt. When we go to use it, we take from the top of the pile. In that case, LIFO makes intuitive sense for physical flow of inventory. However, LIFO may be used for reporting even if it is not used for the physical flow of inventory.

If the hospital used its drugs under the LIFO method, it would consume this year's purchases first and still have the original 2,000 units on hand at the end of the year. They cost $10 each, so the inventory on the balance sheet would be $20,000.

The weighted-average (WA) method works under the assumption that all of the units get mixed together and we really cannot tell which have been used, so an average approach works best. The classic example would be a gas station. When you buy gas for your car, it is impossible to tell if you are getting gas from the oldest or most recent delivery. It all mixes together inside the underground tanks at the gas station. Using a WA assumption, we spent $20,000 ($10 × 2,000) for the old units and $216,000 ($12 × 18,000) for the new units. The total is $236,000 for 20,000 units, or $11.80 each ($236,000 ÷ 20,000 units). The leftover 2,000 units at year-end cost $23,600 (2,000 × $11.80), and that value would be placed on the balance sheet.

A superior method for tracking physical flow is the specific identification method. Under this more costly method, you would actually track each specific unit. At year-end you would know not only how many units are left, but also which ones. Of course, this is likely to be costly, even under the perpetual inventory system discussed in Chapter 7. It makes sense for high-priced items, such as automobiles, that each have a unique serial number. It generally does not make sense for lower-cost items, such as cartridges for laser printers.

Meals for the Homeless can use the LIFO method, even though it clearly does not want to keep food on hand for long periods of time. Suppose Meals ends each dinner with a piece of cake. One would think that cake should be on a FIFO basis to avoid becoming old and having to be thrown away. When it comes to inventory valuation, however, you can eat your cake and have it too! The organization can actually consume inventory on a FIFO basis but report on its balance sheet under the assumption that it was used on a LIFO basis.

In reading and interpreting a balance sheet, the reader should be aware that the inventory valuation method used can have a dramatic impact on the inventory value reported. For example, if an organization uses LIFO over a long period of time, the inventory reported on the balance sheet may have a cost from purchases made years and years ago, and may substantially understate the true value of the inventory. If the difference in inventory valuation is material, the inventory method used must be disclosed either in the balance sheet or in the notes that accompany an audited financial statement. For example, in Exhibit 10-5 we see that Meals for the Homeless had $2,000 of inventory at the end of 2011, based on the LIFO cost assumption.

A P P E N D I X   1 0 - D

The Recording Process: Debits and Credits

As noted in this chapter,

$$\Delta \text{ ASSETS (A)} = \Delta \text{ LIABILITIES (L)}$$
$$+ \text{ REVENUES (R)} - \text{ EXPENSES (E)}$$

Recall from Appendix 9-A that for bookkeeping purposes expenses are added to both sides of the preceding equation, resulting in the following:

$$\Delta A + \Delta E = \Delta L + \Delta R$$

As noted in Appendix 9-A, increases on the left of this equation are debits (Dr.) and decreases are credits (Cr.). Increases on the right side are credits and decreases are debits. The journal entries for the transactions in this chapter would be as follows:

6. July 17. HOS provides services and charges patients $81,000. During provision of the services inventory that had cost $4,000 was consumed. The hospital has not yet been paid.

DATE		DR.	CR.
7/17/12	Accounts Receivable	$81,000	
	Patient Revenues		$81,000
Explanation: patient care provided on account.			

DATE		DR.	CR.
7/17/12	Supply Expense	$4,000	
	Inventory		$4,000
Explanation: Inventory supplies consumed for patient care.			

7. August 4. HOS orders additional inventory to replace inventory that had been used up. The inventory has not yet been received and payment has not yet been made. There will be no journal entry.
8. November 28. HOS pays its employees $48,000 of wages. This payment includes all balances outstanding from the previous year plus some payment for work done this year.

DATE		DR.	CR.
11/28/12	Labor Expense	$18,000	
	Wages Payable	30,000	
	Cash		$48,000
Explanation: Pay salaries to employees.			

9. December 10. HOS received $40,000 in payments from customers for services that were provided and billed for at an earlier date.

DATE		DR.	CR.
12/10/12	Cash	$40,000	
	Accounts Receivable		$40,000
Explanation: Collect amounts due from patients.			

10. December 31. At the end of the year, HOS makes a mortgage payment of $20,000. The payment reduces the mortgage balance by $7,000. The rest of the payment is interest.

DATE		DR.	CR.
12/31/12	Interest Expense	$13,000	
	Mortgage Payable	7,000	
	Cash		$20,000
Explanation: Mortgage payment.			

11. December 31. At the end of the year, HOS makes an adjusting entry for prepaid insurance. An adjusting entry is made because something has happened with the passage of time. In this case, half of the prepaid insurance has been used up, because one year of the two years on the policy has expired.

DATE		DR.	CR.
12/31/12	Insurance Expense	$50	
	Prepaid Insurance		$50
Explanation: Expiration of prepaid insurance.			

12. December 31. HOS owes clinical staff $27,000 at the end of the year. These wages will not be paid until the following year.

DATE		DR.	CR.
12/31/12	Labor Expense	$27,000	
	Wages Payable		$27,000
Explanation: Accrued wages.			

13. December 31. The hospital's building and equipment are now one year older. Depreciation for the year is $18,000.

DATE		DR.	CR.
12/31/12	Depreciation Expense	$18,000	
	Plant and Equip., net		$18,000
Explanation: Depreciation for year.			

APPENDIX 10-E

The Accounting Cycle

The formal process that starts with the occurrence of financial events and ends with a complete set of financial statements is called the *accounting cycle*. The steps in the accounting cycle are:

- use journal entries to record the individual transactions;
- post the journal entries to the general ledger;
- prepare an unadjusted trial balance when the accounting period ends;
- prepare and post adjusting journal entries;
- prepare an adjusted trial balance;
- prepare the statement of financial position, activity statement, and cash flow statement;
- close temporary accounts; and
- create a post closing trial balance, to prepare for the next accounting period.

Some of these steps have already been discussed in Chapters 9 and 10. This appendix will fill in the gaps in the process.

The first step is to convert individual financial events into journal entries. This process is explained and discussed in Appendix 9-A. Essentially it is a formalized bookkeeping approach to recording individual transactions.

The second step is to post the journal entries to the general ledger. This step is discussed in Chapter 9 in the section headed The General Ledger and Ledger Entries.

The third step in the accounting cycle is to prepare an unadjusted trial balance. This is simply a listing of all of the organization's accounts, together with their ledger balances, before any adjusting journal entries have been made. The primary purpose of the unadjusted trial balance is to quickly see if "the books are in balance" before moving on the adjusting entries. The trial balance shows the debit or credit balance for each account, and then a total of all of the debits and a total of all of the credits. Although the total has no inherent meaning, the total of the debits must equal the total of the credits, or at least one transaction has been recorded incorrectly. This trial balance must be in balance before we can proceed.

The fourth step in the accounting cycle is to prepare adjusting entries. Adjusting entries were first introduced in Chapter 10, with Transaction 11. There are four areas that adjustments are needed at the end of the accounting period. They are for:

- Accrued revenues
- Accrued expenses
- Deferred revenues
- Deferred expenses

Each of these four types of adjustments reflects the fact that something has occurred not as a result of a specific event at a specific point in time, but rather due to the passage of time.

For example, suppose that a very sick patient has been in HOS for a full month. The end of the accounting period arrives, but we are not ready to discharge the patient and issue a bill to the patient or the patient's insurer for the care provided. Since we have provided care to the patient, we need to make a journal entry recording both revenue and account receivable for the care provided up until the end of the accounting period. That is an example of accrued revenue.

Accrued expenses are very similar to accrued revenues. Perhaps HOS's staff have worked to provide care to patients during the last two weeks of the accounting period, but have not yet been paid. We need to calculate the amount that staff is owed for those two weeks and record it as both a labor expense and also as a wages payable liability. Transaction 12 for HOS, discussed in Chapter 10, falls into this category.

A deferred revenue arises if we receive money from a client before we have provided our goods and services. For example, suppose that HOS receives an $18,000 contract to perform research over a 15-month period. At the time the money is received we would record an increase in cash and an increase in deferred revenue, which is a liability account. Suppose that by the end of the accounting period we have completed one-third of the promised research. We can then make an adjusting entry reducing the deferred revenue liability by $6,000 and increasing revenue by that amount.

A deferred expense arises if we pay money to acquire an asset that will expire as time passes. Transaction 11 for HOS presents an adjustment for prepaid insurance which falls into this category. Transaction 13 provides the depreciation adjusting entry, which also falls into this category.

After we have finished recording our adjustments, the fifth step in the accounting cycle is preparation of an adjusted trial balance. All of the information needed to prepare an adjusted trial balance is available in Exhibit 10-7. If we take the total from each column, or ledger account, in Exhibit 10-7, and also separate the revenue and expense accounts out of the unrestricted net assets column in that exhibit, then HOS's adjusted trial balance would appear as shown in Exhibit 10-E-1. Trial balances are usually presented with all accounts listed in alphabetical order. Note that asset and expense accounts typically have debit

balances, which are shown in the left-hand column of numbers in the trial balance. The liability, revenue, and net asset accounts typically have credit balances, which are shown in the right-hand column of numbers. For further discussion of debits and credits as they relate to revenues and expenses, see Appendixes 9-A and 10-D. If the adjusted trial balance total of the debits is not equal to the total of the credits, then we have made an error as we recorded our adjusting entries.

The sixth step in the accounting cycle is to prepare financial statements. In Chapters 9 and 10, Exhibits 9-4 and 10-7 were used to provide the information for creating financial statements. Although these exhibits are useful learning tools, transaction worksheets like these are not prepared in practice. Given the very large number of journal entries and different accounts, a transaction worksheet showing both journal entries and ledger accounts would not be practical. Instead, journal

EXHIBIT 10-E-1		

Hospital for Ordinary Surgery
Adjusted Trial Balance
For the Period Ending December 31, 2012

	Debits	Credits
Accounts Payable		$ 8,000
Accounts Receivable	$ 47,000	
Cash	33,900	
Depreciation Expense	18,000	
Insurance Expense	50	
Interest Expense	13,000	
Inventory	4,000	
Labor Expense	45,000	
Mortgage Payable		133,000
Patient Revenues		81,000
Permanently Restricted Net Assets		10,000
Plant & Equipment, Net	222,000	
Prepaid Insurance	50	
Supply Expense	4,000	
Temporarily Restricted Net Assets		15,000
Unrestricted Net Assets		113,000
Wages Payable		27,000
TOTAL	$387,000	$387,000

entries are recorded in chronological order, and then each entry is posted to the individual ledger accounts affected by that entry. The totals in each ledger account are listed in the adjusted trial balance. It is the numbers appearing on the adjusted trial balance that actually become the source information for preparing the financial statements.

The seventh step in the accounting cycle is to close temporary accounts. Some accounts are permanent, meaning that their balances carry over from year to year. This is true of assets and liabilities. Whatever we own or owe at the end of one year we still own or owe at the beginning of the next year. For example, if HOS ends the year with $33,900 of cash, it will begin the next year with $33,900 of cash. Revenue and expense accounts, however, measure what happens just during the accounting period. The revenue and expense that we record this year relates just to this year. We want to begin next year with zero revenue and zero expense.

Remember, in the fundamental equation of accounting, revenues and expenses are merely the change in net assets for the accounting period. See Appendix 9-A. In fact, in Exhibit 10-7, we simply showed the revenues and expenses in the unrestricted net assets column. The main reason we maintain separate revenue and expense ledger accounts, and show their values separately in the adjusted trial balance, is so we can use that detailed information to prepare the operating or activity statement. Once that statement has been prepared, we want to transfer the balances from the revenue and expense accounts to net assets. This will leave us with zero balances in revenue and expense accounts, so they are all ready to begin the next accounting period, and the net assets account will have been updated for the changes to net assets that occurred during the year as a result of revenue and expenses.

The closing process carries out the transfer of revenue and expenses balances to the unrestricted net assets account. For example, HOS had $81,000 of patient revenue. In the closing process we make a journal entry reducing patient revenue by $81,000, and increasing unrestricted net assets by that amount. From a debit and credit viewpoint, the revenue account has an $81,000 credit balance at the end of the accounting period before we close. We will debit that account by $81,000 and credit unrestricted net assets by $81,000. This will completely eliminate the balance in the revenue account, and will increase the net asset balance by this year's revenue. Similarly, we will empty all of the expense categories as well. Our expense accounts have debit balances. We will credit them to empty them out, and then debit the unrestricted net asset account, decreasing the amount in the unrestricted net asset account. The net impact of this closing process is that our unrestricted net assets after closing will be the beginning balance, plus or minus any profit or loss that we had for the year. And the revenue and expense accounts will all have a zero balance.

The eighth and last step in the closing process is to create a post closing trial balance, to prepare for the next accounting period. The balances in the post closing trial balance will be the beginning ledger balances for all of our ledger accounts for the coming period. Once again, we will check that the total of the debits and credits in the post closing trial balance is the same. If not, we have made an error during the closing process.

11

Unique Aspects of Accounting for Not-for-Profit and Health Care Organizations

The learning objectives of this chapter are to:

- discuss unique rules of financial accounting for not-for-profit and health care organizations;

- explain special rules related to the balance sheet or statement of financial position, the activity or operating statement, and the cash flow statement;

- introduce the statement of functional expenses, explain when it is required, and the role it serves;

- define and describe fund accounting, including the typical types of funds, interfund transactions, and the current use of fund accounting by not-for-profit organizations;

- discuss depreciation rules for not-for-profit and health care organizations;

- discuss special rules related to the recognition and reporting of donated goods and services;

- explain the treatment of investments by not-for-profit and health care organizations on financial statements; and

- discuss tax issues related to not-for-profit organizations.

INTRODUCTION

Chapters 9 and 10 provide an introduction to financial accounting. The general principles of accounting are broadly applied to all types of organizations. For-profits and not-for-profits, health, government, automotive, steel, and computer manufacturers all have many common elements in their financial accounting.

For example, the fundamental equation of accounting is used across all types of organizations. Virtually all organizations use a statement of financial position (balance sheet) and an activity statement (operating or income statement). However, there are also many unique aspects of financial accounting for health, not-for-profit, and government organizations. This chapter considers such unique aspects for not-for-profit and health care organizations. Chapters 12 and 13 consider unique accounting issues for governments.

Generally Accepted Accounting Principles (GAAP) for all nongovernmental organizations are developed through a series of statements issued by the Financial Accounting Standards Board (FASB). In addition to general statements that affect all organizations, specific statements provided by FASB for not-for-profit and health care organizations help clarify presentation of financial information by these organizations. Those statements provide the basis for the discussions of this chapter.

ACCOUNTING FOR NOT-FOR-PROFIT ORGANIZATIONS

Not-for-profit organizations generally have missions that differ substantially from for-profit organizations, and thus it should not be surprising that special reporting rules exist. According to GAAP, a not-for-profit organization is an entity that (1) receives contributions from providers who do not expect an equal return, (2) has goals other than providing goods and services for a profit, and (3) has an absence of ownership interest.[1] The intent of special GAAP for not-for-profit organizations is to provide guidance to "enhance the relevance, understandability, and comparability of financial statements issued by those organizations."[2]

Some special rules apply to the class of not-for-profit organizations that are referred to as *voluntary health and welfare organizations* (VHWOs). VHWOs are those not-for-profit organizations "that provide voluntary services, supported by the public, usually trying to solve health and welfare problems, generally getting revenue from voluntary contributions rather than from the sale of goods or services."[3] The Red Cross is an example of a VHWO. Hospitals do not fall into this category because they generate substantial revenue from the sale of their services.

Prior to the 1990s, there were differing GAAP for a variety of different types of not-for-profit organizations. However, during the 1990s, new rules were issued that provided a much greater degree of uniformity across not-for-profit organizations.[4] Some differences still remain between health and other not-for-profit organizations, and between VHWOs and other not-for-profits. In general, however, there is great consistency in the reporting requirements for most types of not-for-profit organizations.[5]

FINANCIAL STATEMENTS

All not-for-profit organizations must include a statement of financial position (balance sheet), statement of activities (operating or income statement), statement of cash flows, and notes that accompany the statements, whenever they present a set of audited financial statements. VHWOs are also required to present a *statement of functional expenses*.

---

[1] Financial Accounting Standards Board, FAS 117: *Financial Statements of Not-for-Profit Organizations*. Norwalk, Conn.: FASB, 1993, p. 78.

[2] Ibid. Summary.

[3] Ibid. p. 79.

[4] The formal pronouncements and other documents that updated GAAP and created greater uniformity across not-for-profit organizations included: FASB's 1993 Financial Accounting Standards (FAS) 116 and 117, *Accounting for Contributions Received and Contributions Made*, and *Financial Statements of Not-for-Profit Organizations*, respectively; FASB's 1995 FAS 124: *Accounting for Certain Investments Held by Not-for-Profit Organizations*; and in 1996, the American Institute of Certified Public Accountants' (AICPA) audit guide: *AICPA Audit and Accounting Guide for Not-for-Profit Organizations* (The 1996 Guide).

[5] For example, the 1996 Guide covers organizations such as not-for-profit cemeteries, colleges and universities, civic and community organizations, private not-for-profit primary schools, unions, charities, foundations, associations, libraries, museums, performing arts, political parties, political action committees, public radio and television stations, churches, and clubs.

Financial statements should always provide useful, relevant information to individuals outside the organization, such as creditors and vendors; not-for-profit financial statements have the additional purpose of providing adequate information to donors. Thus, although the basic statements are very similar, their presentation has some significant differences.

Statement of Financial Position

The statement of financial position, or balance sheet, first examined in Chapter 9, provides information about the financial position of the organization at a moment in time. Included in the statement is information about liquidity and the organization's ability to meet its obligations.

Not-for-profit organizations are not required to segregate assets into current and long-term or fixed assets on the balance sheet. However, at a minimum, assets should either be shown in order of decreasing liquidity (the most *liquid* assets listed first) or there must be disclosure of relative liquidity in the notes that accompany the financial statements. Exhibit 11-1 presents assets as one group with the most liquid assets listed first.

A second difference with the balance sheet relates to the treatment of restricted assets. Not-for-profit organizations often receive gifts that have strings attached. That is, money is donated, but the use of the money is restricted to certain purposes. Not-for-profits often set up separate funds of money, separate subentities, to better control the use of restricted resources in accordance with the restrictions that exist.

Since this *fund accounting* approach treats restricted amounts as separate entities, a separate set of financial statements is prepared for each entity, or *fund*. The financial statements of one individual fund would not provide financial information for the organization taken as a whole. The fund accounting approach is commonly used as an internal control mechanism. However, GAAP now require audited financial statements of not-for-profit and health care organizations to aggregate all fund information to reflect the organization as a whole. (Fund accounting issues are discussed later in this chapter.) Presenting all of the

---

EXHIBIT 11-1

Meals for the Homeless
Statement of Financial Position
As of December 31, 2011

Assets			Liabilities and Net Assets		
Cash	$	100	Liabilities		
Marketable securities		3,000	Wages payable	$	2,000
Accounts receivable, net			Accounts payable		2,000
of estimated uncollectibles			Notes payable		6,000
of $8,000		55,000	Mortgage payable		16,000
Inventory (LIFO basis)		2,000	Total Liabilities		$ 26,000
Prepaid expenses		1,000			
Property		40,000	Net Assets		
Cash restricted for			Unrestricted		$ 84,100
building acquisition		900	Temporarily restricted (Note 3)		4,900
Equipment, net		35,000	Permanently restricted (Note 4)		30,000
Investments		8,000	Total Net Assets		$119,000
Total Assets		$145,000	Liabilities and Net Assets		$145,000

assets of the organization on one balance sheet gives the user of the financial statements a good understanding of the total resources that are available to the organization.

In general, unrestricted and restricted current assets can be combined on the balance sheet of the not-for-profit organization. Cash for general purposes and cash for current restricted purposes can be reported as one total number on the balance sheet. However, it is important not to give the impression that resources are available for uses for which they are not available. Therefore, if donors have placed restrictions on assets that prevent their use for current operations, they cannot be *commingled* (mixed together) with current assets on the financial statements.

For example, if a donation specifies that the funds be used only for the purchase of a building and the organization does not plan to buy a building in the coming year, then the assets would be shown on the balance sheet near where the organization shows its property, plant, and equipment, and would be labeled something like "cash restricted for building acquisition" (see Exhibit 11-1). A close examination of Exhibit 11-1 informs the user that Meals for the Homeless has $1,000 of cash. However, it is readily apparent from the balance sheet that only $100 of that cash can be used in the coming year.

Restrictions on the use of assets have an impact on the net assets section of the balance sheet as well. The net assets section of the balance sheet must show three different groups of net assets: *permanently restricted, temporarily restricted,* and *unrestricted* (see Exhibit 11-1). Permanently restricted net assets generally arise as the result of endowment gifts. In contrast, temporarily restricted net assets are created when donors give gifts that have temporary restrictions on their use. The temporary restrictions relate either to a specific use for the assets donated, a specific action the organization must undertake, or a specific time when the assets can be used. For example, a donor might indicate that a gift cannot be used until at least five years have passed or can only be used to acquire a new building. All net assets that are neither permanently nor temporarily restricted are unrestricted.

To provide the user of financial statements with a better understanding of the organization's resources, information has to be provided about the specific restrictions. For example, from Exhibit 11-1, we see that Meals for the Homeless has $30,000 of permanently restricted net assets and there is a reference in the exhibit to Note 4. This note would accompany the statement and provide additional information about the nature of the restriction. That $30,000 might be part of the land the organization owns, and it is possible that there are restrictions preventing the organization from ever selling the land. Alternatively, part of the $30,000 might be investments that earn an annual return, which is used to subsidize the cost of providing meals.

Note in Exhibit 11-1, there are $4,900 of temporarily restricted net assets. Can the assets associated with those net assets be identified on the balance sheet? There is $900 of cash restricted for building acquisition. Those are clearly temporarily restricted assets. The remaining $4,000 of temporarily restricted assets are commingled on the balance sheet with the other assets that are either unrestricted or permanently restricted.

Although the assets may be commingled on the balance sheet for financial statement reporting, in practice, restricted assets may be accounted for separately. In some cases, as a result of either law or donor restrictions, organizations may place money in specific individual accounts for specific purposes. This creates a situation in which assets are not *fungible,* or interchangeable.

Suppose that you went out for a night on the town and had $50 in your left pocket and $20 in your right pocket. You have $70 available to spend. It is all your money. You can spend from the left pocket or from the right pocket. You can even move the money around. Put it all in the left pocket or all in the right pocket. Or just move some of the money from one pocket to the other without even counting how much. It would not matter. It is all your money. The money is fungible. It can be interchanged or moved around between the pockets as desired. A good accounting of the money that belongs in each pocket is unnecessary.

In contrast, suppose you left your house with $70 in your left pocket and no money in your right pocket. You proceeded to your church, where you were in charge of selling items at the annual church bazaar. As people paid for the items they purchased, you put all of the receipts in your right pocket. In this case, the money in your pockets is no longer fungible. The money in the left pocket is yours. The money in the right pocket belongs to the church. You do not want to start moving money back and forth between the pockets because it might create confusion. By commingling your money and the church's money, it may become unclear how much is yours and how much belongs to the church. One of the primary roles of fund accounting is to track separately money and other resources that the organization may not or prefers not to commingle.

Note that there is a distinction between donor-imposed restrictions and self-imposed restrictions. Donor restrictions obligate the organization to comply with the restriction. If the restriction is deemed objectionable, then the organization can refuse the donation. For example, it is unlikely that a university would accept an endowment for a chaired professorship if the donor required that he or she be the first recipient of the chair. If the restrictions are agreed to, then the organization must comply with them.

Self-imposed restrictions often arise when the board of trustees or directors decides that money should be segregated and saved for a future purpose, such as building replacement. It is allowable to indicate such board-designated restrictions on assets and net assets. However, only donor-imposed restrictions create permanently or temporarily restricted net assets. Self-imposed restrictions would create a subtotal within the unrestricted net assets category.

For example, suppose that the board of Meals for the Homeless decided that the $8,000 of investments owned by the organization should be used to build a new building at some future time. The board could designate that $8,000 for the specific use. In that case, the net assets portion of the balance sheet would appear as follows:

Net Assets	
Unrestricted	
Board-designated	$ 8,000
Undesignated	76,100
Total unrestricted	$ 84,100
Temporarily restricted (Note 3)	4,900
Permanently restricted (Note 4)	30,000
Total Net Assets	$119,000

Note that the designation has not changed the temporarily or permanently restricted net assets. Total net assets are also unchanged (see Exhibit 11-1). The only impact of the board designation is on the presentation of the unrestricted net assets within the net asset section of the balance sheet. The investments on the balance sheet might show a restricted designation, such as the following:

Investments—designated for building acquisitions	$ 8,000

Not-for-profit health care organizations follow the rules for balance sheets described here. For-profit health care organizations do not refer to equity as net assets. They typically have proprietary, partners', or stockholders' equity. The subdivisions of net assets do not apply to for-profit organizations. This is not typically a problem, as it would be unusual for donors to make gifts to a for-profit organization.

Statement of Activities

The statement of activities (*activity statement*) reports the results of operations over a period of time, as well as some other events that affect the net assets of the organization. It encompasses the information in an income or operating statement but goes further in reporting other changes in net assets. The statement can help users understand how well the organization has done, how viable it is, and how effective its managers are.

The statement includes revenues, expenses, gains, and losses, just as the income statement would for most for-profit organizations. Revenues are shown as increases in unrestricted net assets, except when there are donor-imposed restrictions on the use of the assets received. Expenses are reported as decreases in unrestricted net assets. Contributions are considered to be revenues or gains and are categorized as either a change in unrestricted or restricted net assets depending on whether there are donor-imposed restrictions on their use. Gains and losses on investments and other assets are shown as changes in unrestricted net assets unless there are donor-imposed or legal restrictions.[6]

In any financial report presented to users outside the organization, there is a balance to be achieved in the amount of disclosure. The organization does not want some outsiders, such as competitors, to know too much about its operations. Therefore there is a tendency to try to restrict the amount of information provided. To prevent too much restriction, GAAP require that revenues be reported separately from expenses. That is, one cannot simply provide a net figure of the difference between revenues and expenses. Both revenue information and expense information must be provided. However, some "netting out" is allowed. For example, investment revenues can be reported net of investment expenses, such as stockbroker's commissions.

Not-for-profit organizations have to use a presentation for the activity statement that clearly identifies changes in each category of net assets. For example, see Exhibit 11-2 and 11-3 for two different approaches to providing this information. In Exhibit 11-2, changes that affect unrestricted net assets are shown first, followed by changes in temporarily and then permanently restricted net assets. In Exhibit 11-3, separate columns are used for unrestricted, temporarily restricted, and permanently restricted net assets.

The first section of Exhibit 11-2 shows the changes in unrestricted net assets. This includes all revenue and support that is unrestricted. In the case of Meals for the Homeless (Meals), this includes client revenue, city revenue, county revenue, foundation grants, the annual ball, and contributions. It also includes net assets that have been released from restrictions. In the case of Meals, some donations had restrictions limiting their use for specific purposes (program restrictions), and some were limited as to when they could be used (time restrictions). In Exhibit 11-2, we see that unrestricted net assets increased by $12,000 as a result of the release from restrictions. The first section of the activity statement also includes expenses, since expenses are all treated as decreases in unrestricted net assets.

The next section is changes in temporarily restricted net assets. For Meals, this section includes increases from foundation grants and donations that have restrictions and also decreases as restrictions are met and the donations become unrestricted. Note that the $12,000 decrease in this section (see Exhibit 11-2) exactly offsets the $12,000 increase in the earlier section of the statement. Effectively, net assets have not changed as a result of this reclassification from temporarily restricted to unrestricted. Total net assets increase when a restricted contribution or grant is first received. Notice that the $10,000 foundation grants and the $5,000 in contributions in this section do increase total net assets.

---

[6] FASB, FAS 117, pp. 7–8.

EXHIBIT 11-2

Meals for the Homeless
Activity Statement
For the Year Ending December 31, 2011

Changes in Unrestricted Net Assets:

Revenues and support

Client revenue	$ 11,000
City revenue	20,000
County revenue	10,000
Foundation grants	60,000
Annual ball	12,000
Contributions	65,000
Total revenues and support	$178,000

Net assets released from restrictions:	
Satisfaction of program restrictions	$ 10,000
Expiration of time restrictions	2,000
Total net assets released from restrictions	$ 12,000
Total unrestricted revenues and other support	$190,000

Expenses:	
Meals	$ 67,000
Counseling	35,000
Administration, fund-raising and general	75,000
Bad debts	4,000
Depreciation	10,000
Total Expenses	$191,000
Increase/(Decrease) in Unrestricted Net Assets	$ (1,000)

Changes in Temporarily Restricted Net Assets:	
Foundation grants	$ 10,000
Contributions	5,000
Assets released from restrictions (Note 5)	(12,000)
Increase/(Decrease) in Temporarily Restricted Net Assets	$ 3,000

Changes in Permanently Restricted Net Assets:	
Contributions	$ 3,000
Increase/(Decrease) in Permanently Restricted Net Assets	$ 3,000
Increase in Net Assets	$ 5,000
Net Assets at Beginning of Year	114,000
Net Assets at End of Year	$119,000

The third section of the statement shows changes in permanently restricted net assets. All three categories are then totaled and added to beginning net assets to determine net assets at the end of the year.

The activity statement is meant to capture all changes in net assets. It shows the change in net assets for each of the three net asset subdivisions: permanently restricted, temporarily restricted, and unrestricted. All increases or decreases in temporarily and permanently restricted net assets must be shown.[7]

---

[7] Ibid., p. 7.

EXHIBIT 11-3

Meals for the Homeless
Activity Statement
For the Year Ending December 31, 2011

	Unrestricted	Temporarily Restricted	Permanently Restricted	Total
Revenues and Other Support:				
Client revenue	$ 11,000			$ 11,000
City revenue	20,000			20,000
County revenue	10,000			10,000
Foundation grants	60,000	$ 10,000		70,000
Annual ball	12,000			12,000
Contributions	65,000	5,000	$ 3,000	73,000
Net Assets Released from Restrictions:				
Satisfaction of program restrictions	10,000	(10,000)		
Expiration of time restrictions	2,000	(2,000)		
Total revenues and other support	$190,000	$ 3,000	$ 3,000	$196,000
Expenses:				
Meals	$ 67,000			$ 67,000
Counseling	35,000			35,000
Administration, fund-raising and general	75,000			75,000
Bad debts	4,000			4,000
Depreciation	10,000			10,000
Total expenses	$191,000			$191,000
Change in Net Assets	$ (1,000)	$ 3,000	$ 3,000	$ 5,000
Net Assets at Beginning of Year	85,100	1,900	27,000	114,000
Net Assets at End of Year	$ 84,100	$ 4,900	$30,000	$119,000

For example, suppose that $1,000 was contributed to the organization on July 1, 2011, with the stipulation that $500 could be used any time after December 31, 2012, and another $500 any time after 2013. This transaction would be shown on the activity statement for the year ending December 31, 2011, as a $1,000 increase in contributions under a heading of changes in temporarily restricted net assets. Total net assets would rise by $1,000. This conveys the information that the organization has more resources but also that resources are not currently available for use.

At the end of 2012, half of the money becomes available for any use. The activity statement for the year ending December 31, 2012, would show $500 of net assets released from restrictions under the changes in unrestricted net assets section. It would also show $500 of net assets released from restrictions as a decrease in the changes in temporarily restricted net assets section. These two amounts offset each other. Total net assets are not affected during 2012 by the gift made in 2011.

Since the activity statement provides an explanation for all changes in net assets from one period to the next, it uses terms such as increase in net assets, change in net assets, or change in equity rather than net income. It is a more comprehensive statement than an income statement used by a for-profit organization. It includes the information that for-profits would show in the income statement as well as information that would be contained in a separate statement of changes in owners' equity.

Statement of Functional Expenses

Not only must expenses be shown separately from revenues, but expenses must also be shown in some amount of detail. This provides donors and other outsiders with a sense of where the organization's money is going. Specifically, expenses must be disclosed (either in the activity statement or in the notes) by their functional class. Such disclosure would provide information on expenses for major program services and supporting activities. VHWOs must report information not only by functional class, but also by natural classification such as salaries, rent, depreciation, and so on. The disclosure for VHWOs must be in the form of a matrix in a separate financial statement, called the statement of functional expenses.

The statement of functional expenses' matrix format shows expenses by function and by nature (or expense object—e.g., salary, fringe, supplies), as seen in Exhibit 11-4. Note that the numbers in Exhibits 11-3 and 11-4 cannot be easily compared because of cost allocations made to arrive at Exhibit 11-4. Notice that expenses are divided between program services and support services. What are program services and support services? Program services are the direct areas that result in providing services (or goods) that achieve the organization's mission. For example, providing meals is one program area for Meals for the Homeless. Counseling services is another. The administration of the organization and the fund-raising activities, however, are support services.

Why would the financial statements need to provide information on program services separately from support services? The public is often concerned that not-for-profits spend too much on administrative activities and too little on providing services. There have been instances in which some organizations spent a substantial share of their total resources on fund-raising, more than many believe appropriate. By reporting program activities

---

EXHIBIT 11-4

Meals for the Homeless
Statement of Functional Expenses
For the Year Ending December 31, 2011

| | Program Services | | Support Services | | |
	Meals	Counseling	Management and General	Fund Raising	Total
Expenses					
Salaries and benefits	$35,000	$35,000	$40,000	$17,000	$127,000
Food	17,000				17,000
Supplies and brochures	2,000	1,000	1,000	2,000	6,000
Office expenses	1,000	1,000	1,000	3,000	6,000
Rent	14,000	1,000	2,000	1,000	18,000
Professional fees			3,000		3,000
Bad debts	4,000				4,000
Depreciation	10,000				10,000
Total expenses	$83,000	$38,000	$47,000	$23,000	$191,000

BOX 11-1

Putting Charitable Dollars to Work

It is difficult to make generalizations about how much of an organization's resources should be devoted to programs as opposed to support services. However, in an era when some charities pay telephone solicitors a substantial commission on contributions generated, many users of financial statements are interested in the ratio of spending on program versus support services. Both the National Charities Information Bureau (NCIB) and the American Institute of Philanthropy (AIP) have studied the issue of the appropriate division between program and support services expenses.

separately, financial statement users can quickly determine the share of resources that is actually used in providing services.

Does a high share of spending on program services mean the organization is doing a good job in using its resources? Not necessarily. Meals could be paying too much for food. Or it could inaccurately estimate the number of people who will come for meals—running out of food some days and throwing away a lot of food other days. One might conclude that devoting a large share of overall resources to providing program services is a necessary but not sufficient requirement for efficient management of a not-for-profit organization (see Boxes 11-1 and 11-2).

Providing information about the underlying nature of expenses gives the user additional insight. Where does Meals' program money go? Is it for food? Does the vast majority of its money go for labor? These questions can be answered using the information in Exhibit 11-4. The statement of functional expenses is particularly helpful to the user in gaining insight into the operations of an organization.

Only VHWOs are required to provide a separate statement of functional activities. Why should VHWOs have a different reporting requirement than other not-for-profit organizations? Recall that the current GAAP apply to all not-for-profit organizations, whereas earlier there were a variety of rules for different types of not-for-profits. Traditionally, VHWOs, getting most of their money from gifts rather than from the sale of goods and services, were required to provide this statement. Other not-for-profit organizations covered by other reporting rules were not. When the rules for not-for-profits were standardized, it was difficult to decide whether to eliminate this requirement for VHWOs or to require it for all not-for-profit organizations. The thinking of the FASB on this issue is reported in Box 11-3.

BOX 11-2

What Share of Total Spending Should be for Program Services?

"What ratio is right? The NCIB and the AIP consider a group that spends less than 60 percent of its budget on programs to be inefficient. Among the 300 organizations evaluated by the NCIB last year, the average program ratio was 75 percent. . . . But you cannot look at the ratios alone. Consider too the nature of the group's mission and the demands placed on it. For example, a 'pass through' charity—such as a group that channels money to specialists who conduct medical research—may require little in the way of office space or staff. For such a group, a program ratio of 90 percent or better is appropriate, experts say. An organization like a hospital that provides an extensive network of social services, on the other hand, could still be considered efficient with a ratio below 75 percent."

Source: Consumers Union. "Charitable Giving: How to Make Your Generosity Count," *Consumer Reports*, December 1997, Vol. 62 (No. 12), p. 55.

BOX 11-3

Should the Statement of Functional Expenses Be Required?

"This statement requires that voluntary health and welfare organizations continue to provide a statement that reports expenses by their functional and natural classifications in a matrix format. The Board believes that requirement is appropriate to prevent the loss of information that voluntary health and welfare organizations and users of their financial statements generally have found to be useful. The Board concluded that before extending that requirement to other organizations, further study is necessary to determine whether other cost-beneficial means of reporting information useful in associating expenses with service efforts might be developed."

Source: FASB. *Statement of Financial Accounting Standards No. 117,* p. 25.

Statement of Cash Flows

Not-for-profit organizations are required to provide a statement of cash flows. The statement is similar to that discussed in Chapter 10. However, it is necessary to distinguish between cash that has been received and is available for current operations (i.e., unrestricted resources) versus cash that is restricted and unavailable in the near term. In the "Cash Flows from Operating Activities" section at the top of Exhibit 11-5, note the subtraction of $4,000 of contributions restricted to long-term investments and $3,000 of permanently restricted contributions. These contributions were included in the changes in net assets on the activity statement, which captures all changes in net assets. But they do not provide cash that is available for current operations. Therefore, they are backed out of (subtracted from) the change in net assets to determine cash flows from operating activities. They do, however, generate cash and are shown as a source of cash in the "Cash Flows from Financing Activities" section of the statement.

Exhibit 11-6 provides a summary of the financial statements that are required by GAAP for different types of organizations when presenting an audited set of financial statements. The notes to the statements, required for all types of organizations, are discussed further in Chapter 14.

FUND ACCOUNTING

Not-for-profit and governmental organizations have long used a unique approach to recording and reporting their financial information, referred to as fund accounting. In this approach, the organization's finances are divided into a number of separate entities called funds. A fund

> is an accounting entity with a self-balancing set of accounts for recording assets, liabilities, the fund balance, and changes in the fund balance. Separate accounts are maintained for each fund to ensure that the limitations and restrictions on the use of resources are observed. Though the fund concept involves separate accounting records, it does not entail the physical segregation of resources. Fund accounting is basically a mechanism to assist in exercising control over the purpose of particular resources and amounts of those resources available for use.[8]

---

[8] Vincent M. O'Reilly, Murray B. Hirsch, Philip L. Defliese, and Henry R. Jaenick. *Montgomery's Auditing,* 11th ed. New York, N.Y.: John Wiley & Sons, 1990, p. 791.

EXHIBIT 11-5

Meals for the Homeless
Statement of Cash Flows
For the Year Ending December 31, 2011

Cash Flows from Operating Activities	
Change in net assets	$ 5,000
Add expenses not requiring cash:	
Depreciation	10,000
Other adjustments:	
Add decrease in inventory	2,000
Subtract increase in receivables	(17,000)
Subtract decrease in wages payable	(1,000)
Subtract decrease in accounts payable	(1,000)
Subtract increase in prepaid expenses	(1,000)
Subtract contributions restricted to long-term investments	(4,000)
Subtract permanently restricted contributions	(3,000)
Net cash used for operating activities	$(10,000)
Cash Flows from Investing Activities	
Sale of stock investments	$ 4,000
Net cash from investing activities	$ 4,000
Cash Flows from Financing Activities	
Contributions restricted to endowment	$ 3,000
Contributions restricted to long-term investment	4,000
Increase in Notes Payable	1,000
Repayments of mortgages	$ (5,000)
Net cash from financing activities	$ 3,000
Net Increase/(Decrease) in Cash	$ (3,000)
Cash, Beginning of Year	4,000
Cash, End of Year	$ 1,000

Instead of using the term *net assets* in fund accounting, the owners' equity section of the balance sheet is referred to as *fund balance*. This term refers to the remaining balance in the fund, if all assets were used to pay all liabilities. Since there are no owners of not-for-profits, fund balance is a fairly descriptive term.

Fund accounting is widely used by not-for-profit organizations as an internal control mechanism. Recent GAAP changes have reduced the role of fund accounting for external reporting by not-for-profits. Governments commonly use fund accounting both internally and for reporting. The fundamentals of fund accounting, discussed next, apply to governments as well as not-for-profit organizations.

Fund accounting is a system in which the organization is divided into separate entities, from an accounting perspective. Each organization would have a general unrestricted fund, used to support the general operations of the organization. In addition, there would be a

EXHIBIT 11-6

Summary of Required Financial Statements

General For-Profit Organizations	Health Care Organizations	General Not-for-Profit Organizations	Voluntary Health and Welfare Organizations
Statement of financial position (balance sheet)	Statement of financial position (balance sheet)	Statement of financial position (balance sheet)	Statement of financial position (balance sheet)
Income statement	Operating statement	Statement of activities*	Statement of activities*
Changes in equity	Changes in equity	—*	—*
Statement of cash flows	Statement of cash flows	Statement of cash flows	Statement of cash flows
—	—	—	Statement of functional expenses
Notes	Notes	Notes	Notes

* The Statement of Activities combines the information contained in the Income Statement or Operating Statement and the Statement of Changes in Equity that are provided by for-profit and health care organizations.

variety of other funds for specific restricted purposes such as building replacement, endowment, and research projects.

As noted previously, each fund is a separate accounting entity with its own set of accounting books or records, yet it is also part of the larger organizational entity. Each fund has assets, liabilities, and fund balance. The primary purpose of fund accounting is to ensure that resources are used in compliance with their restrictions.

Suppose that a donor restricts use of a donation to acquisition of a building. The donation would be placed in a building or plant fund. The only expenditures of money from that fund would be to buy buildings. The use of a specific fund for that purpose provides an aid in record keeping of the amount available and the amount used for the specific purpose.

The restrictions used in fund accounting can be even more stringent than those used for reporting. For example, the only resources that are considered restricted for reporting purposes are those for which donors have placed restrictions. Public sector organizations often have a variety of other types of conditions and restrictions with which they must comply. For example, Meals might enter into a contract with a shelter to provide meals to those staying at the shelter. The shelter provides money to Meals and requires Meals to provide an accounting of how the money was used. This is not a donation, so the resources do not qualify as temporarily restricted resources for external reporting purposes. However, by placing the resources in a distinct fund, it is easier to ensure that the resources are used for purposes allowed by the contract.

Types of Funds

Different funds are used depending on the specific types of restrictions faced by the organization. Funds are divided into two main categories: unrestricted and restricted.

Virtually all not-for-profit organizations have an *unrestricted fund*. In hospitals, this might be called the *general fund* or the *operating fund*. Many not-for-profits simply call it the *current unrestricted fund*. This fund is used to account for the day-to-day operations of the organization and all of its resources that are not subject to restrictions.

There is substantially greater variation among the types of restricted funds. *Donor-restricted funds* exist to comply with various requirements donors have placed at the time of the donation. As a result of the differing restrictions, there might be *building replacement funds,* building expansion funds, *endowment funds, custodial funds,* strike funds, and other restricted funds.

Endowment funds are particularly important, since the donated amount must be kept intact, at least for a specified period of time—in some cases forever. Earnings on the principal amount can often be used for operations, and if so, they are transferred to the general unrestricted fund. The fund accounting approach helps to ensure that endowment funds are not inappropriately (accidentally or intentionally) expended.

Custodial funds represent those in which the organization is essentially holding funds for someone else. For example, a foundation might choose to use hospitals to distribute money to poor individuals. The foundation might give $1 million to a hospital to distribute $10 at a time to individuals who appear to need money for food. By tracking the use of the money in a custodial account, we can ensure that the money is used to provide small payments to hungry individuals rather than to buy a new X-ray machine.

Board-designated funds are those that are established to track the use of resources that the board has decided to devote to a specific purpose. Donor restrictions are generally difficult to change. In contrast, if board-designated resources are needed for other purposes, such as to support current operations, the board can remove the restriction, and the resources can be transferred to an unrestricted fund. Although board-designated restricted funds are used for internal purposes, these funds are treated as being unrestricted for external reporting.

Many not-for-profit organizations also categorize their funds between *current restricted funds* and *long-term restricted funds.* Current restricted funds contain resources that are available for general operations within a one-year period but must be used for particular restricted purposes. For example, a foundation might provide a research grant. The project will be done during the coming year, and the money will be used to pay the salary of the researcher doing the project. In contrast, resources that are being accumulated to buy land or buildings, are being held for endowment purposes, or are being accumulated to use in case of a strike would be long-term restricted funds.

Note that there can be funds for resources that would normally fall into any of the three net asset classifications. The general unrestricted fund is an example of unrestricted net assets. A fund established as a result of a contract would also represent resources that would be part of unrestricted net assets. A fund could be set up to track the use of resources for a specific program as required by a donor. That fund represents part of temporarily restricted net assets. Funds set up for endowments represent part of permanently restricted net assets.

It is also possible for the resources from one donor to use funds that fall into each of the three net asset categories. For example, suppose a donor gave $1 million to Millbridge University to be placed in permanent endowment, with a further restriction that half of the earnings can be used for any organizational purpose and half of the earnings can only be used for the law school's program that provides legal aid to the poor. The $1 million goes into an endowment fund, which is part of permanently restricted net assets. Half of the earnings each year go into the law school legal aid fund, which is part of temporarily restricted net assets. And half of the earnings go into the general unrestricted fund, which is part of unrestricted net assets.

The term "restricted" has a narrow definition when applied to external reporting. It relates only to donor-imposed restrictions. Fund accounting uses the term restricted much more broadly. It can refer to resources that are restricted as a result of contracts, board decisions, management decisions, and so on. Often restricted funds are reported on the balance sheet as being unrestricted because they do not meet the narrow reporting definition.

Interfund Transactions

Fund accounting creates accounting entities within an entity, and this creates some unique problems. When you move money from your left pocket to your right pocket, how do you record that event? Essentially there are three types of events that can occur that involve more than one fund in an organization. One is a loan, in which one fund borrows money from another. A second is the sale of services, in which one fund consumes services provided by another fund. The third type of event is a transfer, in which one fund gives resources to another.

Loans between funds are treated the same as a loan from a bank. The borrowing fund has a liability on its balance sheet reflecting the need to repay the loan, and the lending fund has a receivable. These are called "Due to" and "Due from." For example, suppose that the operating fund at the Hospital for Ordinary Surgery (HOS) borrowed $100 from the building fund. This will affect the fundamental equation of accounting for each of the two funds:

Operating Fund

ASSETS	=	LIABILITIES	+	FUND BALANCE
Cash		Due to Building Fund		
+$100	=	+ $100		

Building Fund

ASSETS		=	LIABILITIES	+	FUND BALANCE
Cash	Due from Operating Fund				
−$100	+$100	=	No change on right side.		

The operating fund now has more cash, and it also has a $100 liability in an account called "Due to Building Fund." The building fund has less cash but also has an increase in a receivable account called "Due from Operating Fund."

Sometimes one fund will purchase services from another. Suppose that under the umbrella of HOS, there is also a nursing school, which is operated as a separate fund. The hospital might purchase continuing education services for its nurses from the nursing school. The event would be recorded by both funds just as if the organizations were totally separate. HOS would record the expense the same as if it had used an outside source for the educational program. The nursing school will record the revenue as if it had provided the service to nurses from another hospital.

For example, the hospital sends 10 nurses to the nursing school. Both entities are part of the HOS parent organization. The tuition charge is $10,000 for each nurse. Payment has not been made. The transaction would affect the two funds as follows:

Nursing School Operating Fund

ASSETS	=	LIABILITIES	+	FUND BALANCE
Accounts Receivable				Tuition Revenue
+$100,000	=		+	+$100,000

Hospital Operating Fund

ASSETS	=	LIABILITIES	+	FUND BALANCE
		Accounts Payable		Tuition Expense
No change on left side.	=	+$100,000	−	+$100,000

Notice that the funds use accounts receivable and accounts payable for this transaction. "Due to" and "Due from" account titles are not used for purchase or sale transactions between funds. Also note that tuition revenue increases fund balance and the impact of tuition expense is to decrease fund balance.

A transfer between funds is a permanent movement of resources from one fund to another. The assets and fund balance (net assets) of one fund are reduced, and they are increased for another fund. Some transfers are done at the discretion of management. Other transfers may be mandatory. For example, income from an endowment fund can be transferred to the operating fund for general activities. Or a building can be moved from the building construction fund to the operating fund when its construction is complete. In some cases, there are legal requirements to make transfers, such as transferring enough money to a debt service fund to make loan payments as they come due.

Suppose that the Town of Millbridge transfers $10,000 from the general unrestricted fund to the debt service fund. The transaction would appear as follows:

General Fund

ASSETS	=	LIABILITIES	+	FUND BALANCE
Cash				*Transfer to Debt Service Fund*
−$10,000	=		−	+$10,000

Debt Service Fund

ASSETS	=	LIABILITIES	+	FUND BALANCE
Cash				*Transfer from Operating Fund*
+$10,000	=		+	+$10,000

Note that transfers are neither revenues nor expenses. However, they do directly increase or decrease fund balance. Transfers to another fund decrease fund balance. Transfers from another fund increase fund balance.

Interfund transactions affect each fund as a separate entity. When financial statements are prepared, the entities are all aggregated. Care must be taken at that time to ensure that assets and fund balance are appropriately classified as unrestricted, temporarily restricted, or permanently restricted.

Current Use of Fund Accounting

Prior to the GAAP adopted in the 1990s, most not-for-profit organizations provided a separate balance sheet for each fund or type of fund and an activity statement, which only covered the general unrestricted fund. Contributions made directly to restricted funds bypassed the activity statement completely. As a result, many users felt the financial statements were misleading.

The statements described earlier in this chapter are designed to show the financial position and the results of the organization when taken as a whole. This is believed to provide a better representation of the organization's financial results and status. Donations cannot bypass the activity statement because they must affect unrestricted, temporarily restricted, or permanently restricted net assets.

This does not mean that fund accounting is no longer used by not-for-profit organizations. Many organizations have established their accounting systems around funds and find them to be a useful device for control. In some cases, establishment of separate funds may be required by donors or by law. Fund accounting may be used internally as long as the information from all of the funds is appropriately summarized within the financial statements when an audited set of financials is provided to individuals outside of the organization. Furthermore, information about individual funds, though not required, may be included in audited financial statements as long as the required organization-wide data are provided. Governments still prominently use fund accounting for both internal and reporting purposes, as is discussed in Chapters 12 and 13.

DEPRECIATION

Throughout most of the 20th century, different types of organizations have employed a variety of different approaches for recording fixed assets. Most organizations have recorded buildings and equipment at their cost and then depreciated the assets. However, that approach was far from universally employed.

Many colleges and universities historically recorded buildings at their cost and never adjusted that value upward or downward until the building was sold or torn down. So, some organizations reported certain fixed assets on their balance sheet at their original cost. Other organizations depreciated them and reported the original cost less accumulated depreciation, while others charged the full cost as an expense when acquired and showed no fixed assets on the balance sheet!

Some argue that depreciation is inherent to accrual-based accounting. It provides a sense of the resources that the organization uses each year. Others argue that accounting depreciation does not measure the true change in value of the asset. For example, rather than being used up, buildings sometimes become more valuable over time. Buildings can be seen as being an investment that should not be depreciated. An alternative argument is that since not-for-profits often receive capital assets as gifts, it would overstate costs to depreciate them and include the depreciation expense as a cost.

Although there are differing views on whether depreciation is appropriate, GAAP for not-for-profit organizations now follow one approach. This provides for better comparability across organizations. All not-for-profits are required to depreciate their buildings and equipment and report the cost adjusted for accumulated depreciation when financial statements are prepared in compliance with GAAP. Even fixed assets that have been donated to the organization are subject to this rule. Since there is no payment for such assets, their fair market value is determined at the time of the donation. When they are received, there is an increase in either unrestricted or restricted support equal to the fair value. As they are used, the general rules for depreciation are followed (see Box 11-4).[9] These rules do not, however, apply to governments, as is discussed in the next chapter.

BOX 11-4

Depreciation Requirements for Not-for-Profit Organizations

"Paragraph 149 of FASB Concepts Statement No. 6, *Elements of Financial Statements*, describes depreciation as a 'systematic and rational' process for allocating the cost of using up assets' service potential or economic benefit over the assets' useful economic lives. FASB Statement No. 93, *Recognition of Depreciation by Not-for-Profit Organizations*, requires all not-for-profit organizations to recognize depreciation for all property and equipment except land used as a building site and similar assets and collections. Depreciation should be recognized for contributed property and equipment as well as for plant and equipment acquired in exchange transactions."

Source: American Institute for Certified Public Accountants. *AICPA and Accounting Guide for Not-for-Profit Organizations*. New York, N.Y.: AICPA, 1996, p. 140.

---

[9] American Institute of Certified Public Accountants. *AICPA Audit and Accounting Guide: Not-for-Profit Organizations*. New York, N.Y.: AICPA, 1996, p. 140.

DONATED GOODS AND SERVICES

Not-for-profit organizations differ from for-profits in that many of them receive substantial amounts of gifts or donations. For some VHWOs, donations provide their entire financial support. GAAP provides guidance on recording donations to provide a level of uniformity and comparability across organizations.[10]

Contributions and Promises

Contributions, gifts, or donations are recorded at their fair market value at the time of donation. They are called *support* and are included in the revenue and support section of the activity statement. When the donated resources are used up, they are treated as expenses.

Donations, gifts, or contributions (used synonymously here) are recognized as support in the period the promise to donate is received. Thus, the organization does not actually have to receive cash or other tangible assets to record a contribution. Receipt of a promise is sufficient, as long as there is some proof that there was a promise and there is a likelihood of collection. As with other receivables, an allowance for uncollectible amounts is generally established.

In some cases, a donation is promised only if certain conditions are met. If the organization fails to meet the conditions, the contribution may not be made. Organizations cannot record such donations as revenue until they have met the conditions. For example, suppose that one were to promise a $5 million donation to a university if a building is renamed in the donor's honor. Only after the building is renamed can the donation be recorded as revenue. What if the donor gives the $5 million in cash as soon as the organization agrees to change the building's name? It still would not be recorded as revenue. Cash would increase and so would a liability. This reflects the fact that if the building name is never changed, the money received would have to be returned. The liability in such an instance is called a deferred revenue or deferred support. At the time the building is renamed, the liability will decrease and revenue will increase.

Donors can also place restrictions on the use of their gifts. Only donor-imposed restrictions can create restricted net assets for reporting purposes. See Box 11-5 for a contrast between donor-imposed conditions and restrictions.

Donated Services

Somewhat more controversial is the treatment of donated personal services. For example, how would a social services organization record the services of a volunteer who visits and

---

BOX 11-5

Conditions and Restrictions

Donor *conditions* basically take the form of "I will give you money if you. . . ." The organization cannot record the donation as support because if the organization does not meet the donor's conditions, the donor does not have to make the gift.

Donor *restrictions* basically take the form of "I will give you money that you can only use for. . . ." The organization can record support. The donor is obligated to make the donation, and the organization is obligated to use the donation in accordance with the donor's restrictions.

---

[10] Financial Accounting Standards Board. FAS 116: *Accounting for Contributions Received and Contributions Made.* Norwalk, Conn.: FASB, 1993.

runs errands for housebound individuals? Personal services are recorded as support and expense in the financial records of the organization only if a number of conditions are met. Not-for-profit organizations record contributions of services only if:

> The services received (a) create or enhance nonfinancial assets or (b) require specialized skills, are provided by individuals possessing those skills, and would typically need to be purchased if not provided by donation. Services requiring specialized skills are provided by accountants, architects, carpenters, doctors, electricians, lawyers, nurses, plumbers, teachers, and other professionals and craftsmen. Contributed services that do not meet the above criteria shall not be recognized.[11]

For those services that do fulfill the requirements, the financial statements should include some explanation of the donated services and the program or activities for which they were used. In such an instance, the organization will have support from the donation as well as an expense related to the use of the labor resources.

This is a fairly restrictive rule. The volunteer visiting the housebound would not be recorded. Neither would the volunteer who drives the van for Meals for the Homeless. Delivering meals is an essential part of the mission of Meals. Without the volunteer, a driver would have to be hired. Nevertheless, if the skill is not specialized, the volunteer activity goes unrecorded in the audited financial statements.

This does not mean that an organization cannot track the amount of volunteer work done and report it to the public. It does, however, prevent the organization from treating the volunteer labor as a donation, increasing revenues, and also as an expense, increasing the cost and value of program services provided.

INVESTMENTS

For many years, GAAP required organizations to report their investments at the lower of cost or market value. This meant that if the investment had gone up in value, it was reported at its cost. If it had declined in value, it was reported at its market value, which was less than its cost. However, stock and bond markets provide a specific, measurable market value. In 1995, the rules for reporting investments held by not-for-profit organizations were revised.[12] Under the revised rules, investments in stocks and bonds are reported at their market value, whether that is higher or lower than the cost.

Gains and losses, both realized and unrealized, on investments are shown in the activity statement. A realized gain or loss is one that results from the sale of an asset during the accounting period. It is referred to as being realized because it is locked in. Once the sale has taken place, the amount of the gain or loss can be determined and will not change. An unrealized gain or loss results from the change in the value of an asset that is still owned by the organization. It may change in the future.

For example, suppose the organization buys two shares of Microsoft stock for $100 each. During the year, it sells one share for $110. At the end of the year, it still owns one share that has a current market value of $120. For the share that was sold, there is a realized gain of $10. For the share that is still owned, there is an unrealized gain (sometimes called a "paper gain") of $20. Note that the unrealized gain will change if the value of the Microsoft stock changes before the share of stock is sold. As noted previously, both realized and

---

[11] Ibid., p. 3.
[12] Financial Accounting Standards Board. FAS 124: *Accounting for Certain Investments Held by Not-for-Profit Organizations*. Norwalk, Conn.: FASB, 1995.

unrealized gains or losses are reported on the activity statement. Unless specifically restricted, gains and losses on securities are considered changes in unrestricted net assets.

This rule forces organizations to report increases or decreases in the value of their securities portfolio, even though the securities have not been sold. For example, the bull market of the 1990s increased endowment values substantially for many organizations. Some organizations might prefer not to show those gains. However, they are required to disclose them.

What if an unrealized gain is recorded one year, and the security falls in value the next? Suppose that the Microsoft stock held at a value of $120 at the end of one year has a value of $115 at the end of the following year. Assuming the organization still owns the share, there is a $5 unrealized loss. How can there be a loss? The stock was purchased for $100 and is now worth $115. Since the organization recorded a $20 gain in the first year, it has revalued the stock to its $120 fair value on the balance sheet. If it falls in value from $120 to $115 during the second year, the organization has a $5 loss.

Sometimes endowment fund investments lose money. Endowments are not always invested in bank accounts or treasury bonds. Often part or all of an endowment will be in stocks and bonds that can have fluctuating market values. This creates an interesting situation. The principal amount of a permanent endowment is permanently restricted. Suppose that Millbridge University has been given $100 million of endowment over the years. Suppose further that the endowment is invested in the stock market. Dividends received from the stocks are transferred to the unrestricted general fund.

If the stock market does well and the market value of the investment rises to $110 million, there is a $10 million gain reported on the activity statement. This gain is unrestricted. It does not have to remain as part of the endowment, unless so restricted by the donor or by law.

However, what happens if the stock market declines as it did sharply in 2008 and the value of the endowment investment falls to $60 million? This loss would similarly be recorded in the activity statement as a decrease in unrestricted net assets. The permanently restricted net asset value reported on the balance sheet would not decline. The next year, the stock market might start to recover, and the value of the endowment investment at the end of the second year might rise to $67 million. How is the $7 million dollar increase in value treated? It is an unrestricted gain.

TAXES

Not-for-profit organizations are generally exempt from a variety of taxes including federal and state income taxes, sales tax, and real estate tax. The tax-exempt benefit is substantial, saving some organizations millions of dollars a year. However, if tax-exempt not-for-profit organizations provide services that are not directly related to their charitable mission, they may be subject to tax. Even if they don't offer such services, sometimes they make voluntary payments to government bodies in lieu of taxes. Often this is done to try to counter a growing sentiment against the tax-exempt status of not-for-profit organizations.

The Unrelated Business Tax

Even though a not-for-profit organization may be classified as exempt from tax, it may be liable to pay an unrelated business tax. This tax arises when the organization conducts an activity that tends to compete with for-profit businesses. If a hospital owns a cafeteria inside the hospital building for the convenience of hospital employees and individuals coming to visit patients, that would typically be considered to be part of the hospital's normal activities. The profits of the cafeteria typically would *not* be subject to tax. However, what if the hospital opens an upscale restaurant in one corner of the building, with entrances from the street directly into the restaurant?

If the restaurant attracts customers who come for the restaurant, rather than for some hospital-related business, then the hospital has entered into an unrelated business activity, and the profits from that activity would be subject to income tax. From a public policy perspective we can understand that if the restaurant did not have to pay tax, other tax-paying restaurants that it competes with would feel that they have been placed an at unfair disadvantage. The Unrelated Business Tax is discussed in more detail in Appendix 11-A.

Growing Pressure to Tax Not-for-Profit Organizations

In recent years pressure has been growing to tax not-for-profit organizations. This pressure comes from different areas. Some individuals believe that it is a violation of the constitutional principle of separation of church and state to exempt religious organizations from tax. Others believe that not-for-profit health care organizations compete directly with for-profit health care providers and that tax-exempt status gives them an unfair advantage. Still others believe that not-for-profit organizations promise charitable benefits to society in exchange for their exemption, but never adequately deliver on their part of the bargain.

The tax-exempt treatment for religious organizations has long been a debated issue. Not only do churches, synagogues, mosques, etc., avoid paying income tax on any profits they earn, they also gain a major subsidy by not paying real estate taxes. They enjoy fire and police protection and many other general public services normally paid for by real estate taxes. Further, donors get a tax benefit on their personal income tax returns when they deduct contributions to religious organizations. All of this creates a system of subsidies that some view as being tantamount to state support of organized religion. Nevertheless, at this time, the tax-exemption of religious organizations seems secure.

However, sometimes other things are even more important to not-for-profits than tax exemption. For example, expansion of not-for-profit organizations may conflict with local zoning laws. In those cases the organization will have to obtain zoning variances. Local governments are often extremely concerned by the expansion of not-for-profit organizations because it impacts the tax revenue of the government. Private businesses or home-owners pay real estate tax on their property. If that property is acquired by a not-for-profit organization and used for a charitable purpose, real estate tax is no longer collected on the property. To maintain good relations with the local government and/or to be able to secure necessary variances, it is not uncommon for not-for-profits to make a payment to the government to help defray the various costs of government that are normally covered by real estate tax. Such amounts are generally referred to as "payments in lieu of real estate tax."

Sometimes organizations provide services to the community to avoid having to commit to payments instead of real estate taxes. For example, the University of Massachusetts Memorial Medical Center acquired a piece of property in Worcester, Massachusetts, reducing city revenue by $70,000. In the face of growing pressure to force them to make payments to the city in lieu of the lost taxes, the medical center opened the Worcester Housing Authority Health Clinic to offer health care services to the elderly population in the area.[13]

The last concern is related to ensuring that not-for-profits offer sufficient benefits to society to warrant their tax-exempt status. A team of researchers who developed a benchmark for community benefits argued that, "Estimates of nonprofits' current level of community benefits are compared with the benchmark and show that actual provision appears to fall short"[14] That study focused on hospitals, a likely target for scrutiny because the operations of

---

[13] Anonymous editorial. "UMass Memorial Medical Center Steps Up." *Telegram & Gazette*, Worcester, Mass.: January 6, 2004, p. 6.
[14] Sean Nicolson, Mark V. Pauly, Lawton R. Burns, et al. "Measuring Community Benefits Provided by For-Profit and Nonprofit Hospitals." Health Affairs, Nov/Dec 2000, Vol. 19, Issue 6, p. 168.

not-for-profit hospitals are similar in many ways to those of for-profit hospitals. However, there is a growing belief that many types of not-for-profit organizations benefit far more from their tax-exemption than society benefits from their existence. Pressure may grow on all not-for-profit organizations to justify their tax exemption by demonstrating that they significantly benefit society.

ACCOUNTING FOR HEALTH CARE ORGANIZATIONS

Health care organizations pose an interesting dilemma for the accounting profession. The health care industry consists of both for-profit and not-for-profit organizations. We could have for-profits use rules generally employed by businesses and not-for-profits follow the not-for-profit rules discussed previously. However, comparability is desirable, so it makes sense to have all similar organizations, such as all hospitals, follow the same GAAP. The health care industry therefore follows special rules.[15] These rules apply to for-profit, not-for-profit, and governmental health care organizations.[16]

In many ways, the operations of health organizations are more similar to for-profit businesses than to charities. Often, they receive relatively little from contributions and grants, and most of the money for their assets and operations comes from charges to patients for services provided and from loans. These attributes argue in favor of using reporting rules of for-profit businesses rather than not-for-profit accounting. In many respects, therefore, health care reporting parallels general GAAP. All health care organizations use similar financial reporting except where it is clearly inapplicable.

Financial statements for health care organizations include a balance sheet, statement of operations (income statement), statement of changes in equity (or changes in net assets or fund balance), statement of cash flows, and notes. The statement of operations and statement of changes in equity combine to yield the information contained in the activity statement provided by other not-for-profit organizations. Not-for-profit health care organizations are allowed to combine these two statements into one.

The Statement of Financial Position

Several issues are related to the balance sheet of health care organizations: the disclosure of asset liquidity, the treatment of certain assets and liabilities, and the treatment of net assets.

The balance sheet for health care organizations should show current assets separately from noncurrent assets. This is more restrictive than the rules that other types of not-for-profits must follow. As noted earlier in this chapter, not-for-profits generally are allowed to group all assets in one section, as long as relative liquidity is in some way disclosed. That approach is not allowed for either for-profit or not-for-profit health care organizations.

Many of the customers (patients) of health care organizations do not directly pay their bills. Instead, an insurance organization is responsible for the payment. These payers are referred to as *third-party payers*. Third-party payers include private insurance companies, health maintenance organizations (HMOs), and also government payers. Some third-party payers, Medicare and Medicaid in particular, perform retroactive audits to ensure that their

---

[15] American Institute of Certified Public Accountants. *AICPA Audit and Accounting Guide for Health Care Organizations.* New York, N.Y.: AICPA, 1996.
[16] The GAAP in the *AICPA Audit and Accounting Guide for Health Care Organizations* (Health Guide) cover hospitals, home health, HMOs, nursing homes, rehabilitation facilities, clinics, medical group practices, individual practitioner associations, labs, surgi-centers, and so on. However, the Health Guide does not apply to VHWOs or fund-raising foundations. Governmental health care organizations that use enterprise funds (see Chapter 12) follow this guide (as well as GASB rules) when issuing separate financial statements, as do hospitals that are part of universities and medical schools.

payments have been appropriate. At times the third-party payers find they have overpaid or underpaid. Health care organizations must estimate the likely amount of the future adjustments related to the year just ended and include either a receivable or payable to these payers on the balance sheet.

A number of health care organizations now incur liabilities as a result of actions that take place outside the organization. These present challenges for measurement and reporting. For example, HMOs contract with health care providers who give care to HMO members. Often these contracts call for the HMO to make a payment for care on a discounted fee-for-service basis. *Fee-for-service* means that there is a payment for each unit of care the patient consumes. Physicians will charge for office visits, tests, procedures, and so on.

It is not unusual for treatments to take place near the end of the fiscal year and not be reported immediately to the HMO. This results in a category of liability referred to as *incurred but not recorded* (IBNR). Although the exact amount of the HMO's IBNR liabilities may not be known, they can be substantial. Accounting rules require that the IBNR liability be estimated and reported on the balance sheet, even though the HMO has not yet been invoiced for the services involved.

The reporting of net assets is a concern only for not-for-profit health care organizations. For-profit health care organizations will use traditional owners' equity categories such as stockholders' equity. Not-for-profit health care organizations report net assets in the same way as other not-for-profit organizations. Net assets must be divided into unrestricted, temporarily restricted, and permanently restricted net assets. Also, as with other not-for-profits, information must be provided on the nature of restrictions.

Operating Statement

The basic statement that health care organizations use for reporting their revenues and expenses is the operating statement. This is similar to the income statement used by most for-profit organizations. Health care organizations set prices for their various services. These prices are referred to as "charges." However, many patients or third-party payers do not pay the full amount of the charges for their care. This creates a problem for reporting revenues.

Many third-party payers receive discounts for care. Medicare and Medicaid impose the amounts that they are willing to pay. Blue Cross, HMOs, and some other third-party payers negotiate discounts that are then included in the contracts they make with health care organizations. All of these discounts, those to Medicare and Medicaid as well as those to other payers, are referred to as *contractual allowances*.

Some individuals do not pay for their care because they cannot afford to or because they choose not to. This gives rise to *charity care* and bad debts. Health care organizations must decide if they believe certain patients are too poor to pay for their care. If care is given to such patients for free, it is treated as charity care. No revenue is shown for charity care that is provided. However, the cost of such care is included in the expenses of providing services.

Bad debts are the result of a failure to collect money that is owed to the organization by patients who are not treated as charity care patients. Services provided are treated as patient revenues, shown in the revenue section of the operating statement. An estimate is made of how much of these patient revenues will be uncollectible. That amount is treated as a bad debt expense in the expense section of the operating statement.

It is not uncommon for health care organizations to charge two or three times the average amount collected. HOS might charge $400 million for care, collect $180 million, and have costs of $175 million. The $400 million charge seems to create a high profit margin when compared with the cost. However, since many of the HOS's customers pay much less than the official charge, it must charge a very high amount so that those few customers that pay the full charges generate a modest profit needed to be a viable organization.

Since a large portion of the gross charges consists of an amount that the organization is contractually not entitled to receive, that portion cannot be treated as revenue. To treat it as such would give a misleading view of the true resource inflows of the organization. Therefore, revenue reported on the operating statement is the net amount after removing contractual allowances and charity care.

Although charity care cannot be included in revenues because the organization has no intention of collecting payment for that care, the amount of charity care provided must be disclosed. This is done with a note that explains the amount of care given for free. The measurement of charity care can be in terms of charges, cost, or percentage of total care delivered.

Contributions

The rules concerning the reporting of contributions by not-for-profit health care organizations are the same as for other not-for-profit organizations. Unconditional pledges are recorded as support when the pledge is made. Until cash is received, the pledge appears on the balance sheet as a receivable. Conditional pledges are not recorded until the condition is met. If payment has been received before the condition is met, a liability, deferred support, appears on the balance sheet.

Investments

The treatment of investments is one of the more complicated areas of financial accounting for health care organizations. The approach taken by for-profit (investor-owned) health care organizations differs from that taken by those that are not-for-profit.

INVESTOR-OWNED (FOR-PROFIT) HEALTH CARE ORGANIZATIONS   Investor-owned health care organizations track three classes of securities as follows: *held-to-maturity securities, trading securities,* and *available-for-sale securities.*[17]

Held-to-maturity securities are debt securities that will be held until their maturity date. Debt securities (e.g., bonds) tend to fluctuate in market value. This is the result of changes in interest rates over time as well as changes in the financial status of the borrowing organization. (See Chapter 6 for calculations of bond value as interest rates fluctuate.) Many argue that the fluctuations are irrelevant if the organization expects to hold the bonds until maturity. The value to the holder is based more on the ultimate maturity value than on any interim market swings. Therefore these securities are recorded at their cost.[18]

In contrast, trading securities are debt and equity securities that are bought principally for selling them in the near term. Debt securities represent loans receivable. The holder of the security is entitled to receive interest payments and repayment of principal. Equity securities are those that reflect an ownership interest. In most cases, equity securities refer to shares of stock. Trading securities are reported at fair value, and gains and losses are reported as income whether they are realized (the security has been sold) or unrealized (the organization still owns the security).

---

[17] Financial Accounting Standards Board. FAS 115, *Accounting for Certain Investments in Debt and Equity Securities.* Norwalk, Conn.: FASB, p. 49.

[18] If a held-to-maturity debt security is purchased for more or less than the maturity value, the difference is gradually amortized (allocated over time), and the security is reported at its amortized cost. For example, suppose that the HOS buys a $1 million face value Microsoft bond for $950,000, ten years before its maturity. At the time of purchase, it is recorded on the balance sheet at $950,000. The $50,000 discount from face value is spread out at a rate of $5,000 per year. (Other amortization techniques exist that vary slightly.) Each succeeding year, the bond will appear on the balance sheet at a value $5,000 higher. After holding the bond for one year, it is reported at an amortized cost of $955,000. Note that the held-to-maturity bond would be reported at $955,000 even if market conditions make the fair market value of the bond $925,000 or $975,000. The next year it is reported at $960,000. At maturity, the value of the bond on the balance sheet would be $1 million, and the bond would be given to Microsoft in exchange for $1 million.

Available-for-sale securities are all debt and equity securities that do not qualify as held-to-maturity or trading securities. They are reported at fair value. However, unrealized gains and losses on them are excluded from income and reported as a separate part of equity that does not affect net income for the year.

The distinction between trading securities and available-for-sale securities relates to the role of the securities in the day-to-day operations of the organization. If buying and selling the securities is a regular part of normal operating activities, then the gains and losses are rightfully part of operating income or loss. In contrast, if a security is purchased specifically as a long-term investment, then changes in its value should not affect the results of current-year operations. Since they are not part of operations, their gains and losses would not appropriately be included in annual operating income. However, since investments are generally reported at fair value, the asset value is adjusted, and the impact on equity is also shown.

For both investor-owned and not-for-profit health care organizations, the cash flow statement treats sales and maturities of trading securities as being cash from operating activities. All other cash from investments is recorded as being from investing activities. This reinforces the notion that trading securities are seen as being part of the annual routine operating activities of the organization.

NOT-FOR-PROFIT HEALTH CARE ORGANIZATIONS Not-for-profit health care organizations follow the rules for investments discussed earlier in this chapter for not-for-profit organizations. All debt and equity securities are reported at fair value. Gains and losses are included in changes in net assets. Gains and losses are included in unrestricted net assets unless restricted by donor or law.

Note that all debt securities are shown at fair value, including those that would be considered held-to-maturity by investor-owned health care organizations. The reasoning behind this difference is that fair value gives outside users a better indication of the resources available to the not-for-profit health care organizations to use in providing services related to its mission.

Not-for-profit organizations do not focus on net income to the same extent as investor-owned organizations. The totality of the resources available is of greater importance. Therefore, the distinction of whether to include gains and losses in net income does not exist. What is important is that all gains and losses be included in changes in net assets.

Summary

The general principles of accounting are broadly applied to all types of organizations. However, there are also many unique aspects of financial accounting for health, not-for-profit, and government organizations. This chapter considers unique reporting issues for not-for-profit and health care organizations.

Not-for-profit organization financial statements contain a number of important distinctions from the statements issued by for-profit organizations. For example, donor-imposed restrictions on net assets must be disclosed in the statement of financial position (balance sheet). A statement of functional expenses must be provided for voluntary health and welfare organizations. A specific set of conditions must be met for donated services to be recorded and reported on the financial statements.

Health care organizations must report their revenues net of contractual allowances and charity care. Bad debts must be reported as an expense rather than as a revenue offset. Charity care is not included as a bad debt expense or a revenue offset. The only place it shows up is in the notes that accompany the financial statements.

Despite these unique reporting issues, for the most part not-for-profit and health care organizations do follow the general reporting model that is common to other nongovernmental organizations.

Preview

Just as not-for-profit and health care organizations are subject to some unique reporting requirements, so are state and local governments. Those requirements are discussed in Chapters 12 and 13.

Governments use a wide range of funds for recording their activities. They record many of their financial transactions under a basis of accounting referred to as modified accrual accounting. That basis of accounting differs from both cash and accrual accounting. It has dramatic implications for the way that financial transactions are recorded and reported.

Key Terms from This Chapter

activity statement.   Financial statement that reports the results of operations over a period of time (revenues and expenses), as well as other changes in the net assets of the organization.

available-for-sale securities.   All debt or equity securities that do not qualify as either *held-to-maturity securities* or *trading securities*.

board-designated funds.   Funds that are established to track the use of resources that the board has decided to devote to a specific purpose. If board-designated resources are needed for other purposes, the board can remove the restriction. Treated as being unrestricted for external reporting.

building replacement fund.   Restricted fund whose assets from donors can only be used for replacements of buildings.

charity care.   Care given for free to low-income patients. The provider cannot attempt to collect payment from the patients for charity care, and it is not recorded as revenue, a reduction from revenue, or bad debt.

commingled.   Mixed together.

contractual allowances.   Discounts for health care services given to *third-party payers* based on either contractual agreement between the payer and the provider of care or government regulation or law.

current restricted funds.   Funds that contain resources that are available for general operations within a one-year period but must be used for particular restricted purposes.

current unrestricted fund.   See *operating fund*.

custodial funds.   Funds that contain assets that the organization is holding for someone else.

donor-restricted funds.   General class of funds that must comply with various requirements donors have placed at the time of the donation on how the funds can be used. Examples of such funds include *building replacement funds, endowment funds, custodial funds*, and strike funds.

endowment funds.   Funds on which donors have placed restrictions that prevent the organization from spending the donated amount.

fee-for-service.   System in which there is an additional charge for each additional service provided (as opposed to a prepaid system, in which all services are included in exchange for one flat payment).

fund.   An accounting entity with its own separate set of financial records for recording and reporting assets, liabilities, fund balance (owner's equity), and changes in fund balance.

fund accounting.   System of separate financial records and controls; the assets of the organization are divided into distinct *funds* with separate accounts and a complete separate set of financial records.

fund balance.   The equivalent of *owners' equity* for an individual fund under a *fund accounting* system; assets less liabilities.

fungible.   Interchangeable.

general fund.   See *operating fund*.

held-to-maturity securities.   Investments in debt securities that the organization intends to hold until their maturity.

incurred but not recorded (IBNR).   Liability resulting from health care services that have been provided to patients, for which bills have not yet been received by the third-party payer at the time its financial statements are prepared.

liquid.   Refers to how quickly an asset can be converted to cash. The more quickly an asset can become cash, the more liquid it is.

long-term restricted funds.   Funds that contain resources that have restrictions preventing them from being used for current operations.

net assets. The equivalent of owners' equity in a not-for-profit or governmental organization; assets less liabilities; *fund balance.*

not-for-profit organization. An entity that (1) gets contributions from providers who do not expect an equal return, (2) has goals other than providing goods and services for a profit, and (3) has an absence of ownership interest.[19]

operating fund. Fund used to account for the day-to-day operations of the organization and all of its resources that are not subject to donor restrictions; also called the general fund, unrestricted fund, or current unrestricted fund.

permanently restricted net assets. Net assets that must be maintained in perpetuity due to donor-imposed restrictions.

statement of functional expenses. Detailed statement reporting expenses by functional class (e.g., major groupings of program services and supporting services) and by nature (e.g., salaries, rent, or gas) in a matrix format.

support. Contributions, gifts, or donations. Recorded at fair market value at time of receipt and included in the revenue and support section of the activity statement.

temporarily restricted net assets. Donated amounts that have donor-imposed restrictions as to when or how they are to be used.

third-party payer. Someone or some organization other than the recipient of health care services who pays for those services.

trading securities. Debt and equity securities that are bought principally for the purpose of selling them in the near term.

unrestricted fund. See *operating fund.*

unrestricted net assets. *Net assets* whose use has not been restricted by donors.

voluntary health and welfare organizations (VHWOs). Not-for-profit organizations "that provide voluntary services, supported by the public, usually trying to solve health and welfare problems, generally getting revenue from voluntary contributions rather than from the sale of goods or services."[20]

Questions for Discussion

11-1. How does the accounting industry define a not-for-profit organization and a VHWO?

11-2. How do restrictions affect net assets?

11-3. Do you think that a not-for-profit organization's board can release the restrictions on money in a strike fund and use it for general operations? Does it matter whether we are talking about a strike fund held by a steel workers' union to pay benefits to its members during a strike, versus a fund used by a not-for-profit as a safety reserve in case its workers go on strike?

11-4. Is an activity statement the same as an income statement?

11-5. What type of information must VHWOs provide that is not mandatory for other types of organizations?

11-6. What is a fund?

11-7. What are some common types of funds?

11-8. What are the possible types of interfund transactions? Explain.

11-9. To what extent do not-for-profit organizations have the ability to choose among the following:
   a. using depreciation,
   b. ignoring depreciation,
   c. maintaining building and equipment on the balance sheet at their original cost,
   d. showing such assets at their market value, or
   e. completely charging such assets as expenses in the year acquired?

11-10. Donations in cash are easy to measure. What is the treatment that not-for-profit organizations use for donated goods and services?

11-11. At what value are debt and equity securities shown on the balance sheet of not-for-profit organizations? What is the treatment on the activity statement?

11-12. Distinguish between the way investor-owned and not-for-profit health care organizations treat investments.

11-13. The chapter did not specifically discuss whether health care organizations must depreciate their buildings and equipment. Do you believe that such depreciation is or is not required? Why?

11-14. Please use the following choices to fill in the blanks in the next two questions:
   a. unrestricted
   b. temporarily restricted
   c. permanently restricted

---

[19] FASB. FAS 117: p. 78.
[20] Ibid., p. 79.

1. When Professor Chellman endows an annual lecture series at the Wagner School he stipulates that only the interest income derived from his gift may be used to fund the program. The Wagner School places the gift in its _____ fund.

2. When the Wagner School sets asides a portion of net assets to be used for computer software purchases, the designation is made in the _____ fund.

Problems

11-15. Indicate whether each of the following actions would result in a change in unrestricted, temporarily restricted, or permanently restricted net assets this year.
   a. The organization earns revenues from gift shop sales.
   b. A donor gives cash to the organization, specifying that it cannot be used until the following year.
   c. A donor makes a pledge to the organization for its routine operations, but does not pay the pledge this year.
   d. A donor gives the organization a painting, but makes it promise to only display the painting and never sell it.
   e. The organization earns interest on its permanent endowment.
   f. A foundation gives the organization a $1,000,000 grant to be used for research on homelessness.

11-16. The Unified Path is an umbrella organization that solicits donations to support its many charitable suborganizations. One of these is the Millbridge Family Service (MFS). All transactions for MFS are handled through the MFS special purpose fund. For both the United Path general operating fund and the MFS special purpose fund, show the impact on the fundamental equation of accounting of each of the following events:
   a. Unified Path transfers cash to the MFS bank account for $50,000 for the MFS family counseling program. This is a direct subsidy to MFS. No repayment is required.
   b. Unified Path has a bookkeeping department which assists the suborganizations with their purchase of insurance, supplies, payroll, and other items. This centralized approach is less expensive than if each part of the larger organization had its own bookkeeping staff. Unified Path charges MFS $400 for bookkeeping services for the month. No payment is made at the time.
   c. MFS borrows $20,000 from Unified Path's general fund to meet a current operating shortfall. MFS will repay this loan from money received from charges to its clients within six months.
   Optional: Provide journal entries for the above transactions.

11-17. A not-for-profit's net assets are broken down into three categories.
   1. What are the three categories?
   2. Briefly define or describe the three categories
   3. For each category, give an example of a transaction that would cause a change in net assets.

11-18. Unified Path is lucky to have a broad range of volunteers. For example, just the other day:
   a. A noted celebrity stopped by and made phone calls to raise money for the annual campaign. The calls had to be made, so Unified would have hired someone otherwise.
   b. A pipe burst in the kitchen, and a CPA who was being paid to work on Unified's annual financial report rushed in and repaired the leak for free. It saved Unified from having to call in a plumber.
   c. A carpenter volunteered his services to fix a file cabinet damaged by the CPA while he fixed the leak. The file cabinet needed to be repaired.
   Can any of these activities be recorded as a donation? If so, which?

CASE STUDY
Individual Rehabilitation Services (IRS)[21]

Individual Rehabilitation Services (IRS) is a not-for-profit organization that assists individuals returning to society following a substance abuse conviction. IRS has been greatly successful in its urban efforts. Thus, more resources are needed.

---

[21] Case developed by Ken Milani, Professor, University of Notre Dame. Reprinted with permission.

Late last year, IRS began a restaurant operation, The Golden Kettle, which specializes in soups. Last year's operation was a break-even effort. At the beginning of the year, The Golden Kettle relocated to a mall.

It has been clearly established by the District Director of the Internal Revenue Service (the other IRS) that income generated by The Golden Kettle will be unrelated business income.

Required

Determine the minimum federal income tax liability and the taxes owed at the time of filing based on the following data:

Cash receipts: $160,900 (Sales of $156,100 plus $4,800 donated to IRS by Golden Kettle customers)

Cash Disbursements	
Merchandise purchases	$ 52,000
Wages and related payroll taxes (a)	20,870
Rent—space and equipment (b)	3,600
Property insurance (c)	2,850
Equipment purchases (d)	15,000
Loan payments (e)	1,200
Utilities	1,400
Food license (f)	400
Professional fees (g)	1,900
Repairs and maintenance (R&M) (h)	950
Advertising and promotion (i)	4,000
Taxes (j)	10,000
Telephone	480
Supplies	1,300
Miscellaneous	520
Total	$116,470

Other Information

1. IRS is an accrual-basis, calendar-year taxpayer.

2. Inventory information

	FIFO	LIFO
Beginning Inventory	$12,000	$11,200
Ending Inventory	$14,000	$12,100

3. Explanation of notes:

a. Includes employer's share of FICA.

b. Rent is $250/month. A $350 security deposit was made and the final month's rent was paid in advance on an 18-month lease.

c. Two assets are insured:

Inventory—$150 (a floating figure based on monthly inventory levels). Tangible personal property—$2,700 (a three-year policy that was acquired on July 1 of the current year).

d. Additional equipment not provided by the owner of the facility is required and acquired. Information pertaining to this equipment is shown below:

Description	Class Life	Cost	Current Year Depreciation
Cash register	5-year	$ 5,000	$1,000 (20% × $5,000)
Broaster	7-year	$10,000	$1,430 (14.3% × $10,000)

e. $200 a month to Buckner Bank on a $3,000 loan used to purchase the equipment in (d). Interest expense is $450.

f. $200 is paid on January 1 and July 1 to the city controller who issues a six-month license at those dates.

g. Breakdown of this expense indicates:
   $200—Preparation of prior year's tax return.
   $600—Payment to an architect for her plans, which will be used to build another restaurant in the near future.
   $1,100—Attorney fee in settling a claim brought by a customer who claimed that she was served undercooked food, which led to her illness.

h. The previous customer claim brought about an extensive inspection by the Health Department, which ordered several changes (costing $650) in the operation and fined IRS $300. The $300 is included in the $950 R&M figure. (Note that fines are not deductible on a federal income tax return.)

i. Includes $1,600 of newspaper advertising plus $2,400 paid for a Yellow Pages ad that will appear in next year's telephone directory, which will be distributed in October of next year.

j. Estimated federal income tax payments during the year.

Suggested Readings

American Institute of Certified Public Accountants. *Not-for-Profit Organizations—AICPA Audit and Accounting Guide*. New York, N.Y.: AICPA, 2008.

———. *Health Care Organizations—AICPA Audit and Accounting Guide*. New York, N.Y.: AICPA, 2007.

Financial Accounting Standards Board. Statement of Financial Accounting Standards No. 116. *Financial Statements of Not-for-Profit Organizations*. Norwalk, Conn.: Financial Accounting Standards Board, 1993.

———. Statement of Financial Accounting Standards No. 117. *Accounting for Contributions Received and Contributions Made*. Norwalk, Conn.: Financial Accounting Standards Board, 1993.

———. Statement of Financial Accounting Standards No. 124. *Accounting for Certain Investments Held by Not-for-Profit Organizations*. Norwalk, Conn.: Financial Accounting Standards Board, 1995.

Granof, Michael H. *Government and Not-for-Profit Accounting: Concepts and Practices*, 4th ed. New York, N.Y.: John Wiley & Sons, 2007.

Harrison, Walter T., and Charles T. Horngren. *Financial Accounting & Integrated Student CD*, 7th ed. Upper Saddle River, N.J.: Prentice Hall, 2008.

Larkin, Richard E., and Marie DiTommaso. *Wiley Not-for-Profit GAAP 2008: Interpretation and Application of Generally Accepted Accounting Principles for Not-for-Profit Organizations*. New York, N.Y.: John Wiley & Sons, 2008.

Razek, Joseph R., Martin R. Ives, and Gordon A. Hosch. *Introduction to Government and Non-for-Profit Accounting*, 5th ed. Upper Saddle River, N.J.: Prentice Hall, 2004.

Werner, Michael L., and Kumen H. Jones. *Introduction to Financial Accounting: A User Perspective*, 3rd ed. Upper Saddle River, N.J.: Prentice Hall, 2004.

Wilson, Earl R., and Susan C. Kattelus. *Accounting for Governmental and Nonprofit Entities*, 14th ed. Boston, Mass.: McGraw Hill Irwin, 2006.

APPENDIX   11-A

Taxation of Not-for-Profit Entities

Ken Milani
University of Notre Dame

Albert Einstein felt that "taxes are the most difficult thing to understand." Not-for-profit (NFP) or non-profit organizations (NPO) that have "unrelated business income" will find themselves wrestling with this "most difficult thing to understand" when they report unrelated business income, which the Internal Revenue Code (IRC) defines as follows:

> Gross income derived from any "unrelated trade or business" that is "regularly carried on" less deductions directly connected with the carrying on of such trade or business.

An unrelated trade or business is a venture or operation of the NPO that involves activities constituting a trade or business. Although not substantially related to the NPO's exempt function, the activities display a frequency and continuity similar to the stance taken by a profit-making entity. The manner in which the activities are carried out is also considered in determining whether unrelated business income is being produced by the NPO. For example, the following would not be activities subject to taxation:

- Shuttle bus service operated downtown by Carol Shea College (CSC), an urban university, for the use of CSC faculty, staff, students and visitors. A small annual fee is paid or a daily fee is charged.
- Corned beef and cabbage dinner served annually on St. Patrick's Day as part of the day's festivities by a local parish, St. Casey. The charges ($3.00 per person or $10 per family) are promoted widely in radio, newspaper and Internet advertising. St. Casey sponsors the annual event and is the only recipient of the surplus generated.

On the other hand, the activities listed below would generate unrelated business income.

- Food service operated by Holtz Hospital, an exempt hospital, for its own use plus revenue-

producing activity available to and promoted to other health care organizations in the area which are also exempt. The charges are set at 70 percent of the going market rate.
- Cleaning establishment (i.e., dry cleaning and other laundry) operated by members of a religious organization who are trying to provide employment opportunities for inner-city residents.
- Stengel Signal, a DVD rental service operated as an exempt organization, which is offering wholesome and family-oriented movies to the public.

Use of the activity profits or proceeds to support an NPO will not allow the NPO to escape "the tax man," meaning that the food service profits described above will be taxed no matter how they are used by Holtz Hospital.

GROSS INCOME

Several sources of gross income are available to the NPO. The major categories are described below. Significant contrasts between the treatment of gross income for profit-seeking enterprises and the unrelated business activities of an NPO will be noted throughout.

Gross Profit

Sales of products or merchandise reduced by cost of goods sold and any returns and allowances represent gross profit. The cost of goods sold calculation is based on allowed accounting procedures including first-in first-out (FIFO), last-in first-out (LIFO) and other methods. Standard accounting procedures are used to compute returns and allowances.

Where services are the source of sales or revenue (e.g., DVD rental service), cost of goods sold is not determined while allowances must still be recognized.

The appendix was written by Ken Milani, University of Notre Dame. Used with permission.

Investment Income

Investment income (e.g., dividends, interest, and earnings from annuities) is generally *not* included in the gross income of an NPO. This treatment represents a significant tax break for the NPO since most taxpayers report and pay taxes on investment income.

There are two specific instances when the NPO must include investment income in gross income for tax purposes. The first occurs when the NPO receives investment income from a controlled corporation (i.e., an organization in which the NPO has at least 80 percent control through stock holdings or through representation on a board of directors or trustees). Debt financing, or the acquisition of assets with borrowed funds, triggers the second. This latter topic will be covered later in this effort.

The example below illustrates the investment income provisions as they apply to NPOs.

> Alleluia! Counseling Center (ACC) reports the following cash receipts during the year from a variety of investment vehicles:
>
> $1,200 from Cat & Deere Corporation. This represents a dividend on 800 shares of stock. Cat & Deere has over 2,400,000 shares of stock outstanding.
>
> $6,000 from ACC Resource Center (ARC). This is a dividend on 4,000 shares of stock. ARC has 9,000 shares of stock outstanding.
>
> $8,500 from the ACC Home Visitor Program (AHVP). A dividend paid per a directive from the AHVP Board of Directors. Seven of the eight directors are counselors or administrators at the Alleluia! Counseling Center.
>
> $6,800 from ACC Housing Corporation, a free-standing entity which has 2,900 of its 3,000 corporate shares owned by the Alleluia! Counseling Center. The money represents interest on a loan to the ACC Housing Corporation.

The first two items will not be reported as unrelated business income since the greater than or equal to 80 percent control factor is not present. However, the third and fourth items, $8,500 and $6,800, will be reported on the income tax return of Alleluia! Counseling Center since in both instances it maintains at least 80 percent of the control of the organizations making the payments—87.5 percent of the AHVP and 90 percent of the Housing Corporation.

Royalty Income

The approach of the IRC to royalty income is similar to its stance toward investment income. Royalty income from a controlled organization or generated by debt-financed holdings will be taxed while all other royalty income will not be reported for tax purposes. Consider the following royalties collected by Alleluia! Counseling Center:

> $15,000 from Pinella Publishing, Inc. Royalty income on a book written by a benefactor who instructed Pinella to pay the royalty directly to ACC.
>
> $9,000 from ACC Publications, Inc. Book royalties from an organization that is owned 90 percent by Alleluia! Counseling Center.

Of the $24,000 received, only the $9,000 will be taxed since it came from a controlled organization.

Royalty income received by a profit-seeking entity is fully taxed. Thus, the treatment of royalty income by NPOs is another "tax break" enjoyed by NPOs.

Rent

Another source of income which can qualify for favorable treatment by the income tax law is rent. None of the rent income will be reported for tax purposes if the NPO occupies more than half of the space in a rented facility. Where the rent represents payment for space and the use of tangible personal property (e.g., machinery, equipment, furniture), if less than 10 percent of the rent pertains to the property, none of the rent income will be subject to taxation.

All rental income from the following situations will be included in gross income for tax purposes:

1. More than half the rent is attributable to tangible personal property.
2. Profits from the leased property are the basis for the rent.
3. Personal services, other than routine and ordinary maintenance activities, are rendered as part of the rental.

Only a portion of the rental income will be reported for income tax purposes if the rented property is debt-financed or when the portion of rent allocated to tangible personal property is at least 10 percent but not over 50 percent. Debt-financed situations involve the use of borrowed funds (e.g., mortgages, bonds) to acquire the property. Full treatment of this topic is beyond the scope of this effort. Suffice to say that if any debt remains on a rental property, part of the rent must be reported for federal income tax purposes.

The rent provisions are illustrated by the following example.

> Cubs Care, an exempt organization, reports the following receipts from rentals during the current year:
>
> $24,000—Rent on the Banks Boulevard Apartments. The apartments are furnished and 30 percent of the rent is attributable to the furnishings.
>
> $66,000—Rent on a building-the Carey Circle Building (30%) and machinery and equipment (70%) utilized by the tenant.
>
> $18,000—Rent for use of space in the Cubs Care Convention Center.
>
> $30,000—Rent on the Lee Lane Office Complex. Cubs Care occupies 80 percent of the complex while various nonexempt tenants occupy the remainder.
>
> $19,000—Rent based on 20 percent of the profits generated by the tenant of the Santo Orchards.
>
> $54,000—Rent on the DeRosa Depot which is computed based on the following formula: $2,000 per month plus 3 percent of gross sales.

None of the $18,000, $30,000, or $54,000 rents will be included in gross income for tax purposes because of the type of property involved (in the $18,000 and $54,000 examples) and the exempt organization's use of the facility (in the $30,000 example). All of the $66,000 in the second example (rent for tangible personal property exceeds the 50 percent plateau) and the $10,000 in the Santo Orchards example (rent tied to tenant's profit) will be taxable, while only 30 percent of the $24,000 will be added to gross income since the tangible personal property portion falls between the 10 and 50 percent limits.

Gains

If an NPO disposes of property via a sale, trade, or exchange at a gain, none of the gain will be reported for income tax purposes unless the property is debt-financed. Where debt is involved, the NPO only includes a portion of the gain in its tax computation.

This treatment provides a substantial tax break to an NPO as it sells off surplus land or buildings. When properly planned, all of the gain will go unreported. For example,

> AraDevine Enterprise (ADE), a tax-exempt organization, purchases a building, the Leahy Lane Facility (LLF), using borrowed money. Corporate tenants occupy the LLF. The mortgage is paid in full before the building is sold at a substantial gain. None of the gain on the sale to ADE is reported for income tax purposes.

Other Income

Several other sources of income can be generated by an NPO. Some of these (e.g., advertising, research, partnership agreements) are highly complex arrangements and are beyond the scope of this effort. A competent tax consultant should be engaged when dealing with these rigorous situations.

DEDUCTIONS

To determine "unrelated business taxable income (UBTI)," NPOs are permitted to deduct ordinary operating expenses, special deductions, and a specific deduction. This portion of the chapter will focus on situations that are most pertinent or especially applicable to NPOs that will report UBTI.

Ordinary Operating Expenses

Expenses of an NPO involved in a trade or business are treated similarly to the expenses of a profit-seeking organization. To be deductible in the computation of UBTI, the expense must be incurred in the unrelated trade or business. In many cases, this is easy to determine. For example, wages and salaries of the unrelated unit, equipment and machinery depreciation for assets utilized in the unrelated entity, and other expenses can be readily identified and determined. However, some expenses may have to be allocated between exempt functions and unrelated business functions (e.g., building used for all activities of an NPO, vehicle used for a variety of activities by an NPO).

> Metro Energy and Transportation Solutions (METS), an exempt organization, owns and operates a recycling business, Garbage to Gold

Organization (GGO), which generates unrelated business income. The expenses listed below have been scrutinized and their tax reporting status determined.

$40,000—Administrative assistant's yearly salary. Since this person spends about 30 percent of her time on GGO matters, $12,000 will be deducted in determining UBTI.

$70,000—Machinery depreciation. All of this will be deducted in the UBTI calculation since the machinery is devoted entirely to GGO operations.

$6,000—Delivery vehicle operating costs. 80 percent of the delivery vehicle's usage applies to GGO activities, which means that $4,800 will enter into the UBTI calculation.

$90,000—Salary of the METS Director of Fund-Raising. None of this will be used when determining UBTI since the director of fundraising devotes all of his time to development activities.

Special Deductions

The unrelated business segment of a NPO is a corporate operation. Thus, it is eligible for some special deductions, including a dividends-received deduction and a write-off for charitable contributions. Contributions to charities are fully deductible but a limit of 10 percent of UBTI places a ceiling on the amount that can be written off yearly. Because of it limited applicability within an NPO, dividends received deductions will not be addressed.

Specific Deduction

When calculating unrelated business taxable income (UBTI), the IRC allows each NPO a $1,000 specific deduction. In essence, the first $1,000 of UBTI will not be taxed, as shown below.

Two NPOs report the following information about their unrelated business activities:

	NPO Bear	NPO Bull
Gross income	$300,000	$370,000
Less operating expenses	(240,000)	(368,600)
Special deductions	(3,000)	-0-
Specific deductions	(1,000)	(1,000)
UBTI	$ 56,000	$ 400

TAX LIABILITY

Unrelated business taxable income (UBTI) is the basis for the tax liability of an NPO. The following tax rates applied to UBTI as of January 1, 2008:

Income Tax Rates—Corporations

Taxable Income	Tax Rate (%)
Not over $50,000	15
Over $50,000 but not over $75,000	25
Over $75,000 but not over $100,000	34
Over $100,000 but not over $335,000	39*
Over $335,000 but not over $10,000,000	34
Over $10,000,000 but not over $15,000,000	35
Over $15,000,000 but not over $18,333,333	38**
Over $18,333,333	35

*Five percent of this rate represents a phase-out of the benefits of the lower tax rates on the first $75,000 of taxable income.
** Three percent of this rate represents a phase-out of the benefits of the lower tax rate (34% rather than 35%) on the first $10 million of taxable income.

The above rates are always subject to change. An updated tax service should be consulted for the present rate schedule in effect.

PAYING THE TAX

There are two basic ways of handling the tax liability of an NPO: (1) use credits to reduce the taxes or (2) disburse cash to the Internal Revenue Service. A wide variety of credits are available to the NPO engaged in an unrelated trade or business. These credits (e.g., for targeted jobs, building rehabilitation) will be a direct reduction to the tax liability within specific limits. Since tax credits are a complicated niche within a complex topic, NPOs should seek the assistance of a tax professional when reporting tax credits.

Disbursements to the federal government to satisfy any tax liability remaining after credits may have to occur five times for any taxable year. Four of these payments would be estimated payments made before a tax return is filed. If needed, the fifth and final cash outlay occurs as the return is filed. Estimated tax payments must be made or the NPO may pay a penalty for underpayment of tax. These payments are due on the fifteenth day of the fourth, sixth, ninth, and twelfth months of the NPO's taxable year (e.g., October 15, December 15, March 15, and June 15 for an NPO with a July 1 to June 30 fiscal year). The tax return of the NPO is filed on Form

990-T and is due on the fifteenth day of the third month following the close of the exempt organization's taxable year (e.g., September 15 for an NPO which closes its year on June 30).

CONCLUSION

This appendix has focused on a rigorous subject, the federal income tax provisions that apply to an NPO. Illustrated were the activities and specific elements leading to determination of UBTI. Also covered were the tax rate structure applied to UBTI and ways of handling the tax liability.

Planning is an imperative activity for the NPO. In the area of taxation, planning is critical since taxes can be minimized with proper procedures and practices. Some tax-trimming tips were included. However, a competent tax professional should be consulted due to the complexity of this area, the constant changes to the income tax laws, and the professional's ability to assist the NPO in planning in such as way as to minimize the income taxes that must be paid.

12

Unique Aspects of Accounting for State and Local Governments— Part I: The Recording Process

The learning objectives of this chapter are to:

- define and discuss the *modified accrual basis of accounting*, and contrast it with cash and accrual bases of accounting;
- define the types of funds used by governments, including *governmental, proprietary,* and *fiduciary funds,* and the role of those funds;
- discuss the recording process for government financial transactions;

INTRODUCTION

Governments have a unique accounting approach for recording and reporting their financial events. This chapter focuses on the recording process. In the next chapter we will turn our attention to the unique rules for reporting the financial position and results of operations of governmental organizations.

BASES OF ACCOUNTING

Governments use fund accounting, introduced in Chapter 11. Some funds record data using the traditional accrual basis of accounting. Many of a government's funds, however, record transactions using the modified accrual basis of accounting. The basis of accounting used by an organization determines what is measured by financial statements and when that measurement takes place. It guides organizations as to when to recognize assets, liabilities, revenues, and expenses. Different organizations, and sometimes different funds within the same organization, use different bases of accounting.

Cash Basis of Accounting

The *cash basis* of accounting focuses on inflows and outflows of cash. Under this basis, revenues are recognized and recorded only when cash is received and expenses are recognized only when payments are made. For example, suppose that a city issues tax bills for $1,000. However, only $800 is collected during the year the bills are issued. Another $150 is received 30 days after the year ends. The last $50 is collected three months after the year ends. A government on a cash basis would record only $800 of tax revenue in the year the tax bills are issued, because that is the amount that was collected in cash:

ASSETS	=	LIABILITIES	+	FUND BALANCE
Cash				Tax Revenue
+$800	=			+$800

Under a strict cash basis of accounting, there are no receivables or payables. That does not mean that we would not keep track of who owes how much money. Even under a cash basis of accounting, it is important to maintain some records of the amounts of money an organization owes to others and the amount that is owed to it. However, those amounts do not become part of the financial statements. They would not appear on the balance sheet or activity statement.

Accrual Basis of Accounting

Using the *accrual basis* of accounting, revenue is recorded when it has been earned. If it has not yet been collected in cash, a receivable is recorded for the balance. Using the previous example, the full $1,000 is recorded as revenue in the year the tax bills were issued, even though only $800 was collected in cash. On an accrual basis, the fundamental equation of accounting would be affected as follows:

ASSETS		=	LIABILITIES	+	FUND BALANCE
Cash	Taxes Receivable				Tax Revenue
+$800	+$200	=			+$1,000

Accrual accounting is widely used by both traditional for-profit organizations and by health and not-for-profit organizations. The accrual system is designed to provide a reasonable measurement of the net income or change in net assets of the organization. Under accrual, expenses are recorded in the same time period as the revenue they helped to generate, or in the time period when the resource is used if it cannot be matched directly to revenue. If an organization uses a supply item to provide a service, the cost of the supply item is considered to be an expense at the same time that the revenue for providing that service is recognized. The same holds true for labor and other expenses. Capital resources, such as equipment, are depreciated, and a depreciation expense is charged to each year of the asset's expected useful life.

Modified Accrual Accounting

We now introduce the concept of *modified accrual accounting,* a method widely employed by governments. Under this basis of accounting, the primary focus is on financial resources. Financial resources can be defined as follows:

Cash and other assets that are expected to be transformed into cash in the normal course of operations[1]

Modified accrual places an emphasis on current financial resources. This means that no
accruals are made for items that are not currently due. There are critical differences between
accrual accounting and modified accrual accounting in the areas of revenues, expenditures,
fixed assets, and long-term liabilities.

REVENUES Under modified accrual accounting, revenues are recognized when the organization has a financial resource inflow. This may occur before cash is received. For example, if
taxes are owed to the government and are "measurable and available," they are treated as revenues, even if they have not been collected. Clearly this differs from the cash basis. "Available"
means that they must be collectible in or shortly after the end of the accounting period.

Although this means that we may recognize revenue before we collect cash, it is still a
much more stringent rule for revenue recognition than that followed under accrual accounting. Under accrual we would record a revenue this year if services have been provided this
year, even if we expect to wait three, six, nine, or more months before collection. Under
modified accrual, revenues are only recorded if they are expected to be collected either during the year or within a short period of time after the fiscal year ends.[2]

Therefore, property taxes must be collected during the year or shortly after the end
of the fiscal year to be considered measurable and available. Sixty days or less is the time
period widely used as a measure of availability. Any amounts that will be collected within
60 days of the end of the year are typically considered to be available and are treated as
revenues by most governments.

Using the example discussed previously, of the $1,000 of tax bills issued during the
year, $950 would be considered to be revenue for that year under the modified accrual sys-
tem. This is because $800 was collected during the year, and another $150 was collected
shortly after the year ended. The remaining $50 was not collected until three months after
the end of the year. That $50 would not be considered to be available because it is collect-
ed more than 60 days after the year ends and thus would not be considered revenue in the
year the tax bill was issued. The transaction would be recorded as follows:

ASSETS		=	LIABILITIES	+	FUND BALANCE
Cash	Taxes Receivable		Deferred Revenue		Tax Revenue
+$800	+200	=	+50		+$950

Note that under the cash basis of accounting, $800 of revenue was recorded. Under the
accrual basis of accounting, $1,000 of revenue was recorded. Under the modified accrual
basis, $950 of revenue was recorded. A $50 liability called deferred revenue is also recorded
to offset the $50 portion of taxes receivable that will not be available within 60 days of the
end of the year. In the following year when the $50 is collected, deferred revenue will be
reduced and tax revenue will be increased by this amount. The basis of accounting used can
make a distinct difference in the revenues that a government records for a specific year.

EXPENDITURES Under modified accrual, the term *expenditure* is used instead of *expense*. This
is more than just semantics—the implications of expenses and expenditures are not the same.

---

[1] Michael H. Granof. *Government and Not-for-Profit Accounting: Concepts and Practices*, 2nd ed. New York, N.Y.:
John Wiley & Sons, 2001, p. 163.
[2] GASB Statement Number 38 requires a government to provide disclosure of the time period it uses for resources
to be considered available, in a note that accompanies the financial statements.

Under cash accounting, resources are considered to flow out of the organization and an **expense** is incurred when **cash is paid**. Under accrual accounting, resources flow out of the organization and an **expense** is incurred when a resource **has been consumed** in the process of generating revenue. In modified accrual accounting, however, resources are considered to leave the organization and an **expenditure** occurs as soon as the organization becomes **legally obligated to pay** for a resource and we know that payment will be made from available resources.[3]

In some cases, acquisition and consumption of resources occur simultaneously. For example, this is true for most types of labor. It also tends to be the case for utilities or rent. However, there are times when the acquisition of a resource and the use of the resource may occur at significantly different points in time.

For example, suppose that the Town of Millbridge has purchased a $50,000 supply of fireworks to use at the annual Fourth of July celebration. The first event is placement of an order for the fireworks. The second event is receipt of the fireworks and an invoice from the distributor. The third event is use of the fireworks. Finally, the town pays for the fireworks. Assume the events occur as follows:

May 1	Order fireworks	[Encumbrance]
June 15	Fireworks arrive	[Acquisition]
July 4	Fireworks are used	[Use]
August 15	Payment is made	[Payment]

At the time the fireworks are ordered, May 1, most governments would record an *encumbrance*. Recall from Chapter 2 that an encumbrance is merely a reminder to the government that a certain amount of money has been earmarked for a particular purpose. It lowers the total amount of money available to be used on other spending. At the time that the order is placed, there would not be an expense or expenditure under cash, accrual, or modified accrual bases of accounting.

Event	Cash Basis	Accrual Basis	Modified Accrual Basis
May 1 *Order is placed.*	No transaction is recorded.	No transaction is recorded.	No transaction is recorded.

When the fireworks arrive on June 15, the government, upon receiving them, becomes legally required to pay for them. The payment does not have to be immediate. Nevertheless, under modified accrual accounting, a financial resource outflow, and therefore an expenditure, is recorded at that point. This is true because the payment for the fireworks will be made from currently available resources.

Event	Cash Basis	Accrual Basis	Modified Accrual Basis
June 15 *Fireworks arrive.*	No transaction is recorded.	No transaction is recorded.	*Expenditure is recorded.*

---

[3] Expenditures are decreases in net financial resources, whereas expenses are reductions in overall net assets. Expenditures are generally recognized when resources are acquired, expenses when resources are consumed. Ibid., p. 169.

On July 4, when the fireworks are used, there is a resource outflow under an accrual system of accounting. Accrual accounting is sometimes referred to as *full accrual* or *expense accrual,* to clearly distinguish it from modified accrual. Thus, under full accrual, there is an expense on July 4.

Event	Cash Basis	Accrual Basis	Modified Accrual Basis
July 4 *Fireworks are used.*	No transaction is recorded.	*Expense is recorded.*	No transaction is recorded.

On August 15, when payment is finally made, an expense would be recorded under a cash basis of accounting.

Event	Cash Basis	Accrual Basis	Modified Accrual Basis
August 15 *Payment is made.*	*Expense is recorded.*	No transaction is recorded.	No transaction is recorded.

Suppose that the town ends its fiscal year on June 30. The impact of the transactions is summarized in Exhibit 12-1. Note that the purchase of fireworks never created an asset in the modified accrual system. As soon as a legal obligation to pay arose, an expenditure was recorded, decreasing the fund balance. Thus, acquisitions generally do not generate assets under modified accrual.

Generally, we can say that expenditures are recorded when the government makes cash payments or something happens (such as receiving the fireworks) that obligates it to make cash payments within the current accounting period or shortly afterward. This is consistent with the modified accrual focus on current financial resources. As with revenues, many governments set a 60-day period after the end of the current year as a cutoff. If a transaction this year will result in payments that will be made within 60 days after the end of the year, an expenditure and current liability is recorded. If payment will be made more than 60 days after the end of the accounting period, no transaction is recorded.

EXHIBIT 12-1 Comparison of Fireworks Purchase under Different Bases of Accounting

	Cash	Full Accrual	Modified Accrual
Order fireworks [Encumbrance]	No effect	No effect	No effect
Fireworks arrive [Acquisition]	No effect	Increase accounts payable	Increase accounts payable
		Increase inventory	Decrease fund balance
Fireworks are used [Use]	No effect	Decrease inventory	No effect
		Decrease fund balance	
Payment is made [Payment]	Decrease cash	Decrease cash	Decrease cash
	Decrease fund balance	Decrease accounts payable	Decrease accounts payable

LONG-TERM LIABILITIES   When an organization using the modified accrual method borrows money on a long-term basis, a liability is *not* created in the fund. Rather, the asset cash and fund balance increase as follows:

ASSETS	=	LIABILITIES	+	FUND BALANCE
Cash Increase	=			Other Financing Sources Increase

This approach is controversial. Although we do not technically call the loan a revenue transaction under modified accrual accounting, it has the same impact on fund balance as if it were a revenue. Under a full accrual system, a loan would increase liabilities and have no effect on fund balance or net assets. Some might contend that this is a seriously misleading element of modified accrual accounting. Look at the preceding transaction again. The government has borrowed money to meet its day-to-day operating expenditures but does not record any obligation to repay the money. Instead, fund balance rises; essentially, the government claims ownership of the cash increase.

Recall that governments place heavy emphasis on financial resource flows in the current year. Government funds that use the modified accrual basis of accounting tend to have a short-term focus because of the importance of annual budgets in government. However, the potential for abuse is serious. There could be a failure to charge current-year operations for a variety of costs related to the current year. Since expenditures arise only if they will be paid from available resources, obligations that result from current-year activities, but will not be repaid until well after the end of the year, are not recorded as expenditures or as liabilities. They become expenditures only at some future time when they are paid.

For example, post-retirement health benefits and unused vacation days are current obligations to make future payments. In full accrual systems, they result in long-term liabilities. That is not the case in a modified accrual system. The same is true of other compensated absences, legal judgments and claims, and underfunded pension plans.

Exhibit 12-2 provides a summary of the timing of revenues and expenses or expenditures under modified accrual and accrual bases of accounting. The exhibit also indicates the types of assets and liabilities that exist under each approach. Despite the framework provided in Exhibit 12-2, it must be noted that modified accrual allows for a number of exceptions. For example, materials and supplies (including the fireworks described previously) may be

EXHIBIT 12-2 Summary of Accrual and Modified Accrual Bases of Accounting

	Basis of Accounting	
	Accrual	**Modified Accrual**
Outflow (expense or expenditure)	When resource is used	When resource is acquired, legal obligation to pay exists, and payment will come from available resources
Inflow (revenue)	When resource is earned	When resource is legally owed to the organization and is measurable and available
Assets	Current and long-term assets	Current assets only
Liabilities	Current and long-term liabilities	Current liabilities only

recorded based on either a purchases or consumption method. That is, the expenditure can be recorded when the materials or supplies are received (purchased), as described previously, or when consumed.[4] Prepayments (e.g., fire insurance) can also be recorded as an expenditure using either a purchases or consumption approach.

FIXED ASSETS   Governments want to report adherence to the budget. If the government appropriates money to buy a truck this year and it is acquired, then the reporting should show the use of the money to acquire the truck. Therefore, the acquisition is reported as an expenditure within the governmental funds. No long-term assets exist in governmental funds. Even buildings and infrastructure are recorded as expenditures when acquired and do not create long-term assets under the modified accrual basis of accounting.

The usual modified accrual approach to expenditure recognition—for example, recording the acquisition of a $100 million building as an expenditure as soon as it is acquired—may appear to be very conservative. For example, under such an approach one would never overstate the value of a building on the balance sheet. However, the governmental approach to expenditures also results in some treatments that might be considered to understate governmental consumption of resources and obligations. Consider, for example, treatment of interest on long-term debt. Interest payments due after the year-end are not normally accrued under modified accrual accounting.

Suppose that Millbridge issues a $1 million bond on April 1, with semiannual interest payments. If Millbridge ends its fiscal year on June 30, then the first interest payment is not due until September 30, six months after the bond is issued and three months into the next fiscal year. Under full accrual, the organization would have to recognize that it used the money it received from the bond issuance for three months before the end of the current fiscal year. Therefore, it would accrue three months' worth of interest as an expense. Under modified accrual, it is argued that the payment comes out of the budget appropriations in the following fiscal year. To match reporting with budgets, there is no need to accrue Millbridge's legal obligation to pay the interest. So no expenditure and no accrued interest liability is recorded at year-end. This is certainly not a conservative reporting approach.

To make matters more complicated, there is some inconsistency in the approach taken for different types of expenditures. While there are specific rules that indicate that interest on debt is not accrued, other types of expenses would be accrued. For example, suppose that Millbridge pays professional salaries on the second day of each month for work done the preceding month. In that case, salaries for June, the last month of the fiscal year, are not

---

[4] The consumption method is similar to full accrual in treatment of both the asset and the expenditure. Upon acquisition, the inventory asset and a payable arise, and upon consumption, the inventory declines and an expenditure arises. Under the purchases method, an expenditure is recorded upon purchase as shown previously for the modified accrual method. However, if the value of the inventory is *material,* it must be shown as an asset on the balance sheet even if the purchases method is used. One might argue that this makes little sense. The recognition of an expenditure indicates a decrease in financial resources. However, recording the inventory as an asset would imply that the financial resource still exists. How can inventory be an asset on the balance sheet if an expenditure has already been recorded? The following transaction is recorded:

ASSETS	=	LIABILITIES	+	FUND BALANCE
Inventory				*Inventory Reserve*
Increase	=		+	Increase

The increase in inventory gives the desired result of showing that the inventory still exists. To keep the fundamental equation balanced, an equal amount is recorded in the fund balance and is called an inventory reserve. When the inventory is consumed, it is reduced on the asset side, and the inventory reserve is eliminated.

due and payable until July 2, two days into the next fiscal year. However, unlike interest, salaries would be accrued. The following has been noted:

> Modified accrual accounting, both in theory and practice, is extremely undisciplined. It suffers from the availability of too many options and too many exceptions (both stated and implied) as compared to accrual accounting.[5]

GOVERNMENT FUND ACCOUNTING

Fund accounting is a system that subdivides an organization's accounting records into separate subentities that are tracked and reported separately within the one larger entity. Fund accounting is introduced in Chapter 11. Governments use fund accounting extensively, for both recording transactions and reporting financial information. The *funds* used by governments are generally broken down into three main classifications: *governmental funds, proprietary funds,* and *fiduciary funds.*

Governmental Funds

Governmental funds are the typical funds used to operate most governments. These include the *general funds, special revenue funds, capital projects funds, debt service funds,* and *permanent funds.* Governmental funds record transactions using the modified accrual basis of accounting.

The general fund is similar to the operating fund or unrestricted fund in not-for-profit organizations. This is the fund that is used for the bulk of the day-to-day revenues and expenditures of the government. Money from the general fund can be used for any of the routine, ordinary activities of government. In effect, any resource or obligation, revenue, or expenditure that is not accounted for in another fund will be accounted for in the general fund.

Special revenue funds are used for specific identifiable purposes. These are akin to restricted funds for not-for-profit organizations. As with not-for-profit organization funds, the restrictions may be legal or may be based on management decisions to better control the use of resources. For example, revenue from state gasoline taxes might be earmarked for highway maintenance. All receipts from the tax would go into a special fund, and payments from that fund could only be used for the restricted or specified purpose.

The capital projects fund is used to account for major acquisitions of plant or equipment. Note that money is accumulated in this fund prior to acquisition of the capital assets. Some smaller acquisitions, such as the purchase of cars, may be paid for from the general fund. Usually, the decision of whether to use the capital projects fund depends on the dollar amount and expected life of the equipment. For example, in a large city, the cost of a police car might be low enough, and its life short enough, that it would not be considered to be a major capital acquisition. In such a case, it makes sense to pay for such cars from operating revenues in the general fund.

Note that whether the asset is a car paid for from the general fund or a building paid for from the capital projects fund, under the modified accrual basis of accounting used for governmental funds, no asset is recorded. Instead, cash decreases or a short-term payable increases, and an expenditure is recorded for the full cost of the item.

The debt service fund is used to account for the accumulation of resources to pay principal and interest on long-term debt. In many cases, governments are required to transfer enough money annually into the debt service fund to cover these required payments. Money in the fund is then restricted to making debt service payments.

Permanent funds are similar to endowment funds in not-for-profit organizations. Earnings, but not principal, may be spent from these funds.

---

[5] Martin Ives, personal communication, August 2, 1998.

Proprietary Funds

Proprietary funds are used to account for activities that are run on a business-like basis. For example, these might include hospitals, museums, bridges, or an airport owned by a government. In general, governments do not match specific sources of revenues with specific expenses. Most governments provide police protection but do not have an earmarked tax for that purpose. Governmental funds are typically used to account for such services. In other cases, such as government-owned hospitals or marinas, there may be a desire to match revenues and costs in order to determine whether more is being spent on an activity than it generates. In such cases, proprietary funds are used. Proprietary funds record transactions using the accrual basis of accounting.

Proprietary funds typically get their revenues from a variety of user fees, tolls, and other charges rather than from taxes. The two types of proprietary funds are *internal service funds* and *enterprise funds*.

Many governments own golf courses, other recreational facilities, and other activities that provide services to the public on a business-like basis. In some cases there is a desire for these activities to earn a profit or at least be self-sufficient. When the government is essentially running a business, charging the public for services it consumes, an enterprise fund is established, such as a golf course fund. If the enterprise loses money, that might affect whether the government would want to continue offering the service or would be better off moving to privatize the service. Conversely, some enterprise funds, such as mass transit, are typically tax-subsidized.

Internal service funds are established for elements of government that provide specific services to other government units. For example, a government might have a car pool department. The car pool provides cars to all branches of government as needed. The idea of the car pool is that the city government will need to own fewer cars in total if each branch does not buy its own cars. This is because the cars will be more fully utilized; when one agency does not need a specific car, another agency can be using it.

An internal service fund, such as the car pool fund, charges other branches of the government for the services it provides. In many ways, the car pool becomes an in-house car rental agency for the government. The car pool is run on a business-like basis, and the government can assess whether it is less expensive to maintain the car pool department or to rent cars as needed directly from a private, for-profit car rental company.

Fiduciary Funds

Fiduciary funds are *trust* or *agency funds*. Such funds exist when the government is acting as a trustee or agent. These funds contain resources that the government holds for others. The money in fiduciary funds belongs to the ultimate recipient, not the government holding it. GAAP call for fiduciary funds to use an accrual basis.

Trust funds are established when money is given to the government under the legal terms of a trust. Trusts require that the money be used in a specific manner or for specific purposes. Money for state unemployment compensation payments would be put in such a fund. Pension plans are the most significant trust fund for many governments.

Agency funds are those that account for money the government holds as an agent for some other organization in a temporary, purely custodial capacity. For example, suppose that fire departments are predominantly volunteer not-for-profit organizations throughout a state. Further, a state law requires that each town give the volunteer fire department 3 percent of all real estate taxes collected to be used for equipment and operations. As the town collects its real estate taxes, it will immediately put 3 percent of the money collected in an agency fund, the fire department fund. From time to time, that money will be disbursed to the fire department, which is a separate distinct organization, not part of the town government. By keeping the money in a separate agency fund, it is clear that the money is not available to pay for general government expenses.

RECORDING FINANCIAL INFORMATION

The recording process used by governments is similar to that described in Chapters 9 and 10 for all other organizations. However, there are some differences. First, the use of modified accrual accounting for governmental funds results in some transactions being recorded at different time periods than under accrual accounting, or not at all. For example, there will be no entries for depreciation in the governmental funds. Also, there tends to be a significant number of interfund transactions in government accounting.

Governments report information by function and by object of expenditure. General government, police, and social services are examples of functions. Salaries, supplies, and rent are examples of objects of expenditure. In the example that follows, information is recorded by function only. This is a simplification for purposes of the example. Within each function, governments would normally record expenditures by object of expenditure as well.

We now record transactions (journal entries) for the Town of Millbridge, for the year ending December 31, 2012. In the next chapter, a set of financial statements is generated based on these transactions. Millbridge uses the modified accrual method of accounting for its general, capital projects, and debt service funds. The reader is referred to Chapters 9 and 10 for a discussion of the recording process. Journal entries for the transactions, using debits and credits, are shown in Appendix 12-A.

The financial events for Millbridge are recorded on the worksheet in Exhibit 12-3. That worksheet provides opening account balances as of the beginning of the fiscal year. Consider the following information and events for Millbridge during 2012:

1. Millbridge issues all of its property tax bills on the first day of the year. The total taxes levied are $611,000. Total collections during the year are $600,000. This includes the $25,000 balance from the start of the year and $575,000 from the current year. The remaining uncollected taxes are expected to be collected during the first two months of the following year.

The first step in recording this transaction is to recognize the taxes that have been levied. Part (a) of the transaction is an increase in property tax receivables and property tax revenues of $611,000. The next step is to record collection of taxes. Part (b) of the transaction is the receipt of $600,000 of cash and a reduction of property taxes receivable in the same amount. Note that this transaction affects only the general fund (see Exhibit 12-3, Part A).

General Fund

	ASSETS		=	LIABILITIES	+	FUND BALANCE
	Cash	Property Tax Receivable	=			Property Tax Revenue
1a.		+$611,000	=		+	+$611,000
1b.	+$600,000	−$600,000	=	No changes on right side.		

Note that because the taxes levied this year are all expected to be collected within two months after the completion of the current fiscal year, they are considered to be both measurable and available. Therefore, all of the taxes are considered to be revenue under the modified accrual basis.

2. Millbridge is entitled to payments from the state in the form of aid. Assume that this is unrestricted aid. The $15,000 receivable at the start of the year was collected. In addition, Millbridge was entitled to receive $150,000 of aid for this year. At year-end the state still owed Millbridge $25,000, all of which will be received early in the following year.

EXHIBIT 12-3

Town of Millbridge
Financial Transactions (Journal and Ledger)
Prepared on a Modified Accrual Basis
For the Year Ending December 31, 2012

A. The General Fund

| | Assets | | | = | Liabilities and Fund Balance | | | | Fund Balance |
	Cash	Property Taxes Receivable	State Aid Receivable		Accounts Payable	Due to Debt Service Fund	Due to Capital Projects Fund	Salaries Payable	Fund Balance
Beginning Balance	$ 68,000	$ 25,000	$ 15,000	=	$ 5,000	$ 18,000	$ 70,000	$ 0	$ 15,000
Transaction 1a		611,000							611,000 Property Tax Revenues
Transaction 1b	600,000	(600,000)							
Transaction 2a	15,000		(15,000)						
Transaction 2b			150,000						150,000 State Aid Revenues
Transaction 2c	125,000		(125,000)						
Transaction 3	(580,000)							20,000	(300,000) General Government Expenditures (200,000) Public Safety Expenditures (100,000) Sanitation Expenditures
Transaction 4a	(5,000)				(5,000)				
Transaction 4b	(53,000)				7,000				(40,000) General Government Expenditures (15,000) Public Safety Expenditures (5,000) Sanitation Expenditures
Transaction 5	(97,000)					3,000			(100,000) Transfer to Debt Service Fund
Transaction 6									
Transaction 7	(63,000)						(63,000)		
Transaction 8a									
Transaction 8b									
Transaction 9									
Ending Balance	$ 10,000	$ 36,000	$ 25,000	=	$ 7,000	$ 21,000	$ 7,000	$ 20,000	$ 16,000

EXHIBIT 12-3 continued

B. The Debt Service Fund

	Assets		=	Liabilities and Fund Balance	
	Cash	Due from General Fund		Liabilities	Fund Balance
Beginning Balance	$ 10,000	$18,000		$0	$ 28,000
Transaction 1a					
Transaction 1b					
Transaction 2a					
Transaction 2b					
Transaction 2c					
Transaction 3					
Transaction 4a					
Transaction 4b					
Transaction 5	97,000	3,000			100,000 Transfer from General Fund
Transaction 6	(65,000)				(15,000) Interest Expenditure (50,000) Debt Service—Principal Expenditure
Transaction 7					
Transaction 8a					
Transaction 8b					
Transaction 9					
Ending Balance	$ 42,000	$21,000	=	$0	$ 63,000

C. The Capital Projects Fund

	Assets		=	Liabilities and Fund Balance	
	Cash	Due from General Fund		Liabilities	Fund Balance
Beginning Balance	$ 20,000	$ 70,000		$0	$ 90,000
Transaction 1a					
Transaction 1b					
Transaction 2a					
Transaction 2b					
Transaction 2c					
Transaction 3					
Transaction 4a					
Transaction 4b					
Transaction 5					
Transaction 6					
Transaction 7	63,000	(63,000)			
Transaction 8a	200,000				200,000 Other Sources of Financing—Bond Proceeds
Transaction 8b	(270,000)				(270,000) Capital Outlay Expenditure
Ending Balance	$ 13,000	$ 7,000	=	$0	$ 20,000

Since the state aid will all be received during or shortly after the year, the full amount is recorded as revenue. Of the total $150,000 of aid for the year, $25,000 was still owed, so $125,000 of the aid for the year must have been collected. First, the receipt of $15,000 from the previous year is recorded. Then the full amount of state aid is recorded as revenue. Finally, the impact of the receipt of part of this year's aid is recorded (see Exhibit 12-3, Part A).

General Fund

	ASSETS		=	LIABILITIES	+	FUND BALANCE
	Cash	State Aid Receivable				State Aid Revenue
2a.	+$15,000	−$15,000	=	No change on right side.		
2b.		+$150,000	=			+$150,000
2c.	+$125,000	−$125,000	=	No change on right side.		

3. Town workers earned $600,000 in salaries during the year. General government accounted for $300,000 of that amount, public safety for $200,000, and sanitation $100,000. All but $20,000 of the total amount had been paid by the end of the year.

General Fund

	ASSETS	=	LIABILITIES	+	FUND BALANCE		
	Cash	=	Salaries Payable		Revenues	−	Expenditures
3.	−$580,000	=	+$20,000				− General Government +$300,000
							− Public Safety +$200,000
							− Sanitation +$100,000

The cash payments for salaries must be $580,000 because all but $20,000 of the $600,000 earned was paid. The unpaid portion results in a current salaries payable liability. The expenditures are recorded by function. Governments would also maintain information by object of expenditure, so that it would be known that there were expenditures of $600,000 for salary (see Exhibit 12-3, Part A).

4. Millbridge paid the money it owed to suppliers. It then ordered and received $60,000 of supplies and materials. At the end of the year, $1,000 of these supplies had not yet been used up. Millbridge paid $53,000 to its suppliers for its purchases made during the year. The $60,000 total of supplies received were for general government in the amount of $40,000, for public safety in the amount of $15,000, and for sanitation in the amount of $5,000. The $1,000 of supplies that were not used by the end of the year were for general government activities. Assume there were no supplies on hand at the beginning of the year.

General Fund

	ASSETS	=	LIABILITIES	+	FUND BALANCE		
	Cash	=	Accounts Payable		Revenues	−	Expenditures
4a.	−$ 5,000	=	−$5,000				
4b.	−$53,000	=	+$7,000				
							− General Government +$40,000
							− Public Safety +$15,000
							− Sanitation +$ 5,000

Under modified accrual, the entire $60,000 is an expenditure, even though the town has not fully paid for, nor fully used up, the supplies (see Exhibit 12-3, Part A). This assumes Millbridge uses the purchases method for recording inventory. (Recall that the purchases versus consumption methods for recording inventory are discussed in the "Long-Term Liabilities" subsection of the "Modified Accrual Accounting" section earlier in the chapter.)

5. During the year, Millbridge was legally required to transfer $100,000 to its debt service fund. Only $97,000 of cash was transferred from the General Fund to the Debt Service Fund.

This is the first of the transactions that will affect not only the general fund but also another fund. Since each fund records transactions from its own perspective, we will have mirror image entries:

General Fund

	ASSETS	=	LIABILITIES	+	FUND BALANCE
	Cash		Due to Debt Service Fund		Other Financing Uses
5.					Transfer to Debt Service
	−$97,000	=	+$3,000	−	Fund +$100,000

Debt Service Fund

	ASSETS		=	LIABILITIES	+	FUND BALANCE
	Cash	Due from General Fund				Other Financing Sources
5.						Transfer from General
	+$97,000	+$3,000	=			Fund +$100,000

Note that the full legally required transfer is recorded, even though the full amount of cash was not transferred. The difference is accounted for by recording a payable in the General Fund and a receivable in the Debt Service Fund (see Exhibit 12-3, Parts A and B).

6. Millbridge began the year with $190,000 of long-term obligations related to the purchase of garbage trucks several years ago. The interest and principal due on this debt during the year were $15,000 and $50,000, respectively. These payments were made from the debt service fund. Also assume that when the year began there were $190,000 of capital assets (consisting of the $220,000 cost for garbage trucks less $30,000 of accumulated depreciation). Also, assume that annual depreciation on the garbage trucks is $15,000.

This transaction affects the debt service fund only (see Exhibit 12-3, Part B). Under modified accrual, long-term liabilities, capital assets, and depreciation are not recorded.

Debt Service Fund

	ASSETS	=	LIABILITIES	+		FUND BALANCE	
	Cash				Revenues	− Expenditures	
6.	−$65,000	=				− Interest	+$15,000
						− Debt Service Principal	+$50,000

7. During the year, the general fund repaid $63,000 of its debt to the capital projects fund.

This event affects both the general and capital projects funds (see Exhibit 12-3, Parts A and C).

General Fund

	ASSETS	=	LIABILITIES	+	FUND BALANCE
			Due to Capital		
	Cash	=	Projects Fund		
7.	−$63,000		−$63,000		

Capital Projects Fund

	ASSETS		=	LIABILITIES	+	FUND BALANCE
	Cash	Due from General Fund				
7.	+$63,000	−$63,000	=	No change on right side.		

8. The Town of Millbridge acquired a building to use as a firehouse. It paid $270,000 for the building and issued $200,000 of bonds to help provide the resources to pay for it. The building was paid for in full, and the full proceeds of the bond issue were received.

The acquisition of a building is paid for from the capital projects fund. The building is not recorded as an asset by either the capital projects fund or the general fund. Although the bond interest and principal will be repaid from the debt service fund, the proceeds of the bond issuance flow into the capital projects fund. This inflow is treated as an other source of financing (see Exhibit 12-3, Part C).

Capital Projects Fund

	ASSETS	=	LIABILITIES	+	FUND BALANCE	−	
	Cash				Other Financing Sources		Expenditures
8a.					Bond Proceeds		
	+$200,000	=			+$200,000		
8b.							Capital Outlay
	−$270,000	=				−	+$270,000

Assume that the firehouse was acquired at the very end of the year. Although the government owns it on the last day of the year, it will not use it until the beginning of the next year. Therefore, it would not have any depreciation expense for the year, even under accrual accounting, because it has not been used yet. This information is not needed to record the transaction in the capital projects fund, which uses modified accrual and therefore never records depreciation. However, it will be useful later in preparing a reconciliation of the governmental fund statements to the government-wide statements, which do use accrual and would therefore normally record depreciation.

9. The Town of Millbridge has just concluded a bitter legal dispute regarding a sexual harassment claim against the chief of police. The settlement is for $100,000. However, it will not be paid for three years under the agreed terms.

In this situation, the obligation will not be paid out of current resources because it will not be paid during the year or shortly after it ends. Therefore, it cannot appear as a liability of the general fund and will not be recorded under modified accrual accounting.

Budgetary Accounting

An additional complicating factor in recording financial information for governments is that governments formally record their budgets in the accounting system. A government uses budgetary accounts to record the legally adopted budget. These accounts help keep the government in compliance with legal restrictions. If an approved budget only allows $493,000 to be spent, we want to ensure that spending does not exceed that amount. Budgetary accounts are also used for improved government-wide budgetary control. For example, if revenues are coming in below budgeted expectations, budget directors can instruct agency directors to cut their spending, so that the government avoids a deficit for the year. The government needs to keep budgetary transactions or budgetary entries sepa-rate from the nonbudgetary transactions that record actual revenues and expenditures.

Suppose that a government formally approved a budget with projected revenues of $500,000, expenditures of $493,000, and a surplus for the year of $7,000. At the beginning of the year, the government would record an entry that would increase the following accounts:

Estimated Revenue	$500,000
Appropriations	$493,000
Budgetary Fund Balance	$ 7,000

This government-wide entry covers all of the various agencies of the government. Note that "Appropriations" is used rather than "Expenditures." An appropriation is an amount that the government is authorized to spend. An expenditure represents actual spending. Also, Estimated Revenues represents a budget projection, in contrast with Revenues, which would represent actual amounts. Finally, Budgetary Fund Balance is used to distinguish budgeted from actual changes in the fund balance.

During the year, the government will record transactions for actual events as they occur. For example, suppose that the government expected to collect its revenues evenly throughout the year. Suppose further that during the first half of the year, actual revenues recorded are only $220,000. If the Estimated Revenue account is compared with the total in the Revenue account, managers can determine how much more revenue is still needed to reach the budgeted amount. In this example, halfway through the year:

Estimated Revenue	$500,000
Less: Revenue	220,000
Estimated Revenue Not Yet Received	$280,000

From a control perspective, managers can now immediately see that to meet the budget, revenues in the second half of the year will have to be $280,000, substantially more than half of the budget for the entire year.

Budgetary accounts are particularly helpful in assuring that the government does not spend more than its authorized amount. This is done by using *encumbrances*. To encumber means to impede or hamper an activity. An encumbrance is a bookkeeping device that keeps the government from spending money that has already been committed for some other purpose. When a financial commitment is made, such as placing an order for supplies, a transaction is recorded that increases the balance in an Encumbrance account. The transaction also increases an account called Reserve for Encumbrances. The encumbrance and the reserve accounts offset each other and have no net effect on the fundamental accounting equation.

Before any order is placed, there must always be a check of the Appropriations, Expenditures, and Encumbrances account balances. For example, suppose that included in the $493,000 of total appropriations for the government, was an appropriation of $130,000 for supplies for the Public Safety Department. Assume that early in the year, before there have been any prior orders or expenditures, a manager places an order for $60,000 of supplies. Before actually placing the order, a check reveals that there is still $130,000 available to spend, as follows:

Appropriation	$130,000
Less: Expenditures	0
Less: Encumbrances	0
Amount Available for Spending	$130,000

At the time the order for the supplies is placed, a transaction is recorded which increases encumbrances by $60,000. After the order is placed, but before the supplies have been received, if someone wanted to place another order they would find that the balance available to spend is:

Appropriation	$130,000
Less: Expenditures	0
Less: Encumbrances	60,000
Amount Available for Spending	$ 70,000

When the $60,000 worth of supplies is received, the earlier encumbrance transaction is reversed, and an expenditure transaction is recorded. If someone wanted to place an order at that point, the amount available to spend would be:

Appropriation	$130,000
Less: Expenditures	60,000
Less: Encumbrances	0
Amount Available for Spending	$ 70,000

Notice that the actual receipt of the supplies had no impact on the amount available to spend. It is the same $70,000 that we saw immediately after the order was placed.

The benefit of the encumbrance system is that it prevents the department from spending more than its appropriations. For example, suppose that at this point another order is placed for $50,000 of supplies. We see above that there is $70,000 available to spend, so the order may be placed. The supplies account would be encumbered by the amount of the order, and the new balance available to spend would be $20,000, as follows:

Appropriation	$130,000
Less: Expenditures	60,000
Less: Encumbrances	50,000
Amount Available for Spending	$ 20,000

Since the budget places a legal spending limit on the government, it cannot risk the possibility that someone will simply look at the difference between appropriations and expenditures, and think that there is still $70,000 available to spend. In fact, $50,000 of that amount has already been committed to paying for supplies that we have ordered. On the other hand, we can't record an expenditure for those supplies until they arrive. The encumbrance system solves this problem. If someone now tries to place an order for $35,000 of supplies, the order would not be processed because $35,000 exceeds the $20,000 amount available to spend, often referred to as the unencumbered balance. This approach provides governments with a means to ensure that unauthorized spending in excess of the legally approved budget does not occur.

Summary

There are a number of unique features to accounting for state and local governments. Such governments rely heavily on modified accrual basis accounting, and use a variety of unique funds.

The modified accrual basis of accounting focuses on current financial resources. The implications of this focus are that revenues are only recognized when measurable and available, and expenditures are recorded when a legal obligation to pay for a resource arises. This creates a number of unique reporting results. For example, no long-term assets or liabilities are recorded; major capital acquisitions are treated as expenditures when acquired; and bonds are treated as expenditures when repaid.

Governments record their transactions in three main categories of funds: governmental, proprietary, and fiduciary funds. Governmental funds record transactions using the modified accrual basis of accounting and generally include the general fund, special revenue funds, capital projects funds, debt service funds, and permanent funds. Proprietary funds record transactions on an accrual basis and include enterprise funds and internal service funds. Fiduciary funds also record transactions on an accrual basis. They include trust funds and agency funds.

Preview

This chapter has focused on how governments record financial events. In Chapter 13 we will turn our attention to the special rules concerning how governments report their financial results. This will include discussion of the various financial statements that governments use to report their financial position and the results of their operations.

Key Terms from This Chapter

accrual basis. An accounting system that records revenues in the year in which they become earned (whether received or not) and expenses in the year they are incurred (i.e., resources are consumed).

agency fund. Fund that accounts for money the government holds as an agent for some other organization in a temporary, purely custodial capacity.

capital projects fund. Fund used to account for major acquisitions of plant or equipment.

cash basis. An accounting system that records revenues in the year cash is received and expenses in the year cash is paid.

debt service fund. Fund used to account for the accumulation of resources to pay principal and interest on long-term debt.

encumbrance. Amounts held aside to pay for goods and services that an organization has contracted for but not yet received.

enterprise fund. Fund used to account for government services provided in a business-like fashion, charging the public for services consumed, such as a golf course fund.

expenditure. The equivalent of expenses in a *modified accrual* accounting system. However, expenditures are generally recognized when resources are acquired, while expenses under an accrual system are recognized when resources are consumed.

expense accrual. See *accrual basis*.

fiduciary funds. *Trust* or *agency funds* used to account for resources that the government holds as a trustee or agent.

full accrual. See *accrual basis*.

fund. An accounting entity with its own separate set of financial records for recording and reporting assets, liabilities, fund balance (owners' equity), and changes in fund balances.

fund accounting. System of separate financial records and controls; the assets of the organization are divided into distinct *funds* with separate accounts and a complete separate set of financial records.

fund balance. The equivalent of owners' equity or net assets; assets less liabilities.

general fund. Fund that is used for the routine, ordinary activities of government. The general fund is similar to the operating fund or unrestricted fund in not-for-profit organizations.

governmental fund. Fund used by governments to track the sources, uses, and balances of resources that are not tracked separately in *proprietary* or *fiduciary* funds. Governmental funds include the *general fund, special revenue fund, capital projects fund, debt service fund* and *permanent fund.*

internal service fund. Fund established for elements of government that provide specific services to other government units, such as car pool services.

modified accrual accounting. Accounting basis widely employed by governments for recording

purposes for governmental funds. Under this basis of accounting, the primary focus is on financial resources. Typical financial resources are cash, investments, and receivables.

permanent fund. Fund that cannot be expended, similar to endowment fund.

proprietary fund. Fund that is used to account for the business-type activities of a government.

special revenue fund. Fund used for specific identifiable purposes; similar to restricted fund for not-for-profit organizations.

trust fund. Fund established when money is given to the government under the legal terms of a trust. Trusts require that the money be used in a specific manner or for specific purposes.

Questions for Discussion

12-1. What are the fund categories used by governments? Discuss.

12-2. How does modified accrual accounting differ from cash and accrual accounting?

12-3. What are the benefits of budgetary accounting? What is the difference between appropriations, expenditures, and encumbrances?

Problems

12-4. See Exhibit 12-4 for opening account balances. Record the following financial transactions for Simonsen Village for the fiscal year ending December 31, 2012. Show the impact of the transactions on the fundamental equation of accounting (optional: show journal entries—see Appendix 12-A). Assume that the modified accrual basis is used.

1. Simonsen Village has employees who earned $400,000 for the year. At the end of the year the

salaries payable balance was $10,000. Note that $200,000 of wages related to general government, $140,000 was for education, and $60,000 was for the public works, safety, and sanitation department.

2. Inventory was ordered by Simonsen Village. The entire order was received. The bill for the inventory purchase was $10,000. By the end of the fiscal year, it had used $6,000 of the inventory,

EXHIBIT 12-4 January 1, 2012, Balances

	General Fund	Debt Service Fund	Capital Projects Fund
Cash	$300,000	$ 4,000	
Real estate taxes receivable	20,000		
State grants receivable	10,000		
Due from general fund		16,000	
Salaries payable	90,000		
Due to debt service fund	16,000		
Fund balance/unrestricted net assets	224,000	20,000	

but no payment had been made. The purchases method is used. Each of the three departments had used $2,000 of inventory. The remaining inventory was all earmarked for education.

3. Simonsen Village's major source of funds is from real estate taxes. Total tax bills issued were for $300,000. Total collections were the $20,000 from the previous year's ending balance in taxes receivable and $260,000 of this year's taxes. Eighty percent of the outstanding balance at year-end is expected to be collected early in the next fiscal year.

4. Simonsen Village is entitled to receive unrestricted grants from the state. During the year, grants in the amount of $100,000 were made. The total collections on grants were just $20,000. This $20,000 consisted of $10,000 that the state owed for the previous year and $10,000 for the current year's grant. The state will be paying the balance owed to Simonsen Village within 30 days after the year ends.

5. During the year, Simonsen Village was legally required to transfer $60,000 to its debt service fund. A total of $70,000 of cash was paid to the debt service fund. In years when the full required transfer is not made, the debt service fund has a receivable (Due from General Fund). If more than the required amount is paid, the debt service fund's receivable declines.

6. Simonsen Village acquired a new fire truck early in the year for $200,000. The fire truck is expected to last 10 years and have no salvage value. It was financed by a long-term note for the full amount. Simonsen Village has a capital projects fund.

7. The interest and principal due on Simonsen Village's debt during the year and paid from the debt service fund were $8,000 and $30,000, respectively. The interest covers all long-term borrowing by Simonsen Village. The principal relates to the fire truck purchased during the year.

12-5. Simonsen Village is a relatively new community. At the start of the year, the government had no long-term assets or liabilities. In fact, all of the infrastructure (e.g., roads) in the village are owned by the county or state rather than the town. However, the Village government has the primary responsibility for putting out fires in the village. Transactions 6 and 7 for Simonsen Village, described in Problem 12-4, both relate to the town's new fire truck.

Exhibit 12-4 presents January 1, 2012, balances for Simonsen Village's accounts. These balances at the start of the year were the same on both the modified accrual and accrual bases. (Hint: That may not be the

case at the end of the year.) Show the beginning balances from Exhibit 12-4 and the transactions from Problem 12-4 in a worksheet format similar to Exhibit 12-3. Show ending balances. Make a separate section for each fund.

12-6. Please use the following choices to fill in the blanks below:
a. modified accrual
b. accrual
c. cash

1. Under the _____ method of accounting, expenses are recognized when assets are used up, while under the _____ method, expenditures are recognized when the asset is purchased.

2. The local government's water enterprise fund utilizes the _____ method of accounting because it is run like a business.

12-7. Red City (a local governmental body) sells a building for $1 million in cash to the City Blood Center (a not-for-profit organization).

1. Show the transaction as it would appear on the city's modified accrual transaction sheet. Assume it is a general fund transaction.

2. The city is legally required to transfer all of the proceeds to its capital projects fund for future building purchases. It only pays $800,000 of cash to the capital projects fund. Show the transaction for both the general fund and the capital projects fund.

3. If the city had made a loan repayment of $150,000 ($100,000 interest and $50,000 principal), their expenditure for that transaction would have been:
a. 0
b. 50,000
c. 100,000
d. 150,000

12-8. The South City Golf Course purchased a new golf cart for $18,000 in cash at the beginning of the fiscal year. South City accounts for the golf course using an enterprise fund. They plan on using straight-line depreciation for their capital assets. South City expects the cart to last six years and have no salvage value.

1. At the time of the cart purchase the accountant for South City Golf Course will: (Select the most correct answer.)
a. decrease cash by $18,000 and increase expenses by $18,000.
b. decrease cash by $18,000 and increase equipment assets by $18,000.
c. increase equipment assets by $18,000 and increase net assets by $18,000.
d. NOT record this transaction, as governments do not record long-term assets.

2. At the end of the fiscal year, the accountant for South City Golf Course will: (Select the most correct answer.)
   a. increase accumulated depreciation by $3,000 and increase expenditures by $3,000.
   b. increase accumulated depreciation by $3,000 and increase expenses by $3,000.
   c. increase accumulated depreciation by $18,000 and increase expenses by $18,000.
   d. NOT be required to record journal entries at this time.

12-9. Match the following terms with the most correct statement below.
   a. Debt service fund
   b. Component units
   c. Encumbrance
   d. Proprietary fund
   e. Internal service funds
   f. Special revenue fund
   g. General fund
   h. Trust fund

1. ___ Used to track resources earmarked for a specific purpose.
2. ___ Fund used to track resources available to pay interest and loans.
3. ___ An enterprise or internal service fund.
4. ___ Used to designate funds which are obligated under a legal contract.
5. ___ An entity affiliated with a government but legally separate.
6. ___ Used for routine ordinary activities of government.
7. ___ A type of fiduciary fund.
8. ___ Business-type fund where the services are provided to other units of government.

Suggested Readings

American Institute of Certified Public Accountants. *AICPA Audit and Accounting Guide: State and Local Governments with Conforming Changes as of May 1, 2007.* New York, N.Y.: AICPA, 2007.

Anderson, John E. *Public Finance—Principles and Policy.* New York, N.Y.: Houghton Mifflin Company, 2003.

Freeman, Robert J., Craig D. Shoulders, and Gregory Allison. *Governmental and Non-Profit Accounting*, 8th ed. Upper Saddle River, N.J.: Prentice Hall, 2006.

Granof, Michael H. *Government and Not-for-Profit Accounting: Concepts and Practices*, 4th ed. New York, N.Y.: John Wiley & Sons, 2007.

Hyde, Albert C. *Government Budgeting: Theory, Process, Politics*, 3rd ed. Belmont, Ca.: Wadsworth/Thomson Learning, 2002.

Razek, Joseph R., Martin R. Ives, and Gordon A. Hosch. *Introduction to Government and Non-for-Profit Accounting*, 5th ed. Upper Saddle River, N.J.: Prentice Hall, 2004.

Ruppel, Warren. *Wiley GAAP for Governments 2007: Interpretation and Application of Generally Accepted Accounting Principles for State and Local Governments.* New York, N.Y.: John Wiley & Sons, 2007.

Wilson, Earl R., and Susan C. Kattelus. *Accounting for Governmental and Nonprofit Entities*, 13th ed. Boston, Mass.: McGraw Hill Irwin, 2004.

APPENDIX 12-A

The Recording Process: Debits and Credits

This appendix provides journal entries for the Millbridge transactions described in the chapter. The reader is referred to Chapters 9 and 10 and Appendix 9-A for a discussion of the recording process, including the use of journal entries, ledgers, debits, credits, and the accounting equation in the form: $\Delta A + E = \Delta L + R$, the change in assets plus expenditures equals the change in liabilities plus revenues.

Refer to the detailed transactions information provided in the chapter on pages 459–464.

TRANSACTION 1.

	GENERAL FUND	DR.	CR.
a.	Property Tax Receivables	$611,000	
	Property Tax Revenues		$611,000
	Explanation: to record annual property tax levy.		
b.	Cash	$600,000	
	Property Tax Receivables		$600,000
	Explanation: to record receipt of property taxes.		

TRANSACTION 2.

	GENERAL FUND	DR.	CR.
a.	Cash	$ 15,000	
	State Aid Receivable		$ 15,000
	Explanation: to record receipt of state aid payments.		
b.	State Aid Receivable	$150,000	
	State Aid Revenue		$150,000
	Explanation: to record annual state aid.		
c.	Cash	$125,000	
	State Aid Receivable		$125,000
	Explanation: to record receipt of state aid payments.		

TRANSACTION 3.

GENERAL FUND	DR.	CR.
General Government Expenditure	$300,000	
Public Safety Expenditure	200,000	
Sanitation Expenditure	100,000	
Cash		$580,000
Salaries Payable		20,000
Explanation: to record salary expenditures.		

TRANSACTION 4.

	GENERAL FUND	DR.	CR.
a.	Accounts Payable	$ 5,000	
	Cash		$ 5,000
	Explanation: to record payment to suppliers.		
b.	General Government Expenditure	$40,000	
	Public Safety Expenditure	15,000	
	Sanitation Expenditure	5,000	
	Accounts Payable		$ 7,000
	Cash		53,000
	Explanation: to record acquisition of supplies.		

TRANSACTION 5.

GENERAL FUND	DR.	CR.
Transfer to Debt Service Fund	$100,000	
Cash		$ 97,000
Due to Debt Service Fund		3,000
Explanation: to record transfer.		

DEBT SERVICE FUND	DR.	CR.
Cash	$ 97,000	
Due from General Fund	3,000	
Transfer from General Fund		$100,000
Explanation: to record transfer.		

TRANSACTION 6.

DEBT SERVICE FUND	DR.	CR.
Interest Expenditure	$ 15,000	
Bond Principal Expenditure	50,000	
Cash		$65,000

Explanation: to record payment of debt service.

TRANSACTION 7.

GENERAL FUND	DR.	CR.
Due to Capital Projects Fund	$63,000	
Cash		$63,000

Explanation: to record payment of payable to Capital Projects Fund.

CAPITAL PROJECTS FUND	DR.	CR.
Cash	$63,000	
Due from General Fund		$63,000

Explanation: to record collection of receivable from General Fund.

TRANSACTION 8.

CAPITAL PROJECTS FUND	DR.	CR.
a. Cash	$200,000	
Bond Proceeds—Other Sources of Financing		$200,000

Explanation: to record proceeds of bond issuance.

	DR.	CR.
b. Capital Outlay Expenditure	$270,000	
Cash		$270,000

Explanation: to record acquisition of building.

TRANSACTION 9.

No journal entry.

13

Unique Aspects of Accounting for State and Local Governments—Part II: Reporting Financial Results

The learning objectives of this chapter are to:

- discuss financial reporting objectives for governments;
- define and discuss the governmental reporting components, including *management's discussion and analysis*, the *basic financial statements*, and other *required supplementary information*;
- provide an example of the recording and reporting process for state and local governments; and
- provide a brief discussion of federal government accounting.

INTRODUCTION

Governmental financial reporting standards are developed by an accounting rule-making body, the *Governmental Accounting Standards Board* (GASB, pronounced *gaz-B*). GASB's official pronouncements are considered to be Generally Accepted Accounting Principles (GAAP) for state and local governments.[1]

The rules for reporting financial results that are discussed in this chapter are applicable to public colleges and universities as well as governments. Governments in the United States ultimately answer to the public. The information contained in their financial statements must serve the needs of not only lenders and vendors, but the public and its elected legislators as well.

Many government bodies prepare a *Comprehensive Annual Financial Report* (CAFR). Included as part of that report is a set of audited *basic financial statements* (BFS). There are

---

[1] State and local governments are subject to many laws and regulations that require them to prepare a wide variety of different financial reports for different purposes. Not all state and local governments follow GASB GAAP. "The decision whether or not to follow GASB standards is dictated by state and local laws and customs, and/or by the needs of bondholders and other creditors, the general public, and anyone else to whom governments are accountable" (Dean Mead, GASB, personal communication, December 24, 1999).

specific guidelines as to what statements and information must be included in the audited BFS to be considered a fair presentation in accordance with GAAP.

As part of the government reporting rules, governments report for the entity as a whole. This is accomplished by including two government-wide statements within the BFS. However, unlike not-for-profit reporting, government reporting also requires additional financial statements that report information about the funds that make up the governmental entity.

Also, in addition to the BFS, GAAP require state and local governments to provide a management's discussion and analysis (MD&A) section and other required supplementary information (RSI). One element of the other RSI is a comparison of actual results with authorized budgets.

REPORTING FINANCIAL INFORMATION

The Objectives of Financial Reporting

Governmental financial reporting attempts to help keep the government accountable for its actions. An element of accountability is to ensure that information is provided that is helpful for making not only economic decisions, but also social and political decisions. To have such information, it is critical to be able to compare what actually took place with what was authorized (either directly by the public or by its elected representatives), in the form of an approved budget; to understand the financial condition of the government and the results of its operations; to assess whether finance-related laws and regulations were appropriately complied with; and to understand the effectiveness and efficiency of the government.[2]

In addition, financial reporting by state and local governments should provide information that allows the user to determine if interperiod equity has been achieved. *Interperiod*, or *intergenerational, equity* refers to whether the government has used revenues from the current period to pay for services provided in the current period. If the government were to run a large surplus or deficit, one might argue that interperiod or intergenerational inequity might arise. People may be paying today to provide benefits to future generations or may be creating an unfair debt burden on future generations to pay for benefits that are being received today.

These objectives of financial reporting have guided the process of developing governmental accounting standards. *Governmental funds* are reported using the modified accrual basis of accounting. However, this basis does a better job of demonstrating budget compliance than it does of reporting on interperiod equity. Financial reporting requirements also call for government-wide statements prepared on an accrual basis. Such statements should provide better information for understanding how well a government has achieved interperiod equity. This issue is discussed further in the "Basic Financial Statements" section of the chapter.

Further, government-wide statements prepared on an accrual basis should help users of the financial statement do the following:

- understand the overall finances and operating results of the government,
- assess whether financial results are improving or getting worse,
- understand the cost of services provided to the public,
- understand the sources of money that government uses to pay for its programs,
- understand the government's investment in capital assets, and
- be able to compare the government with other governments.[3]

The Governmental Reporting Components

Figure 13-1 provides an overview of the elements of governmental financial reporting. There are three main sections to a government's financial report. They are the *management's*

[2] Governmental Accounting Standards Board. Concepts Statement No. 1, *Objectives of Financial Reporting*. Norwalk, Conn.: Financial Accounting Foundation, 1987, paragraph 32.
[3] GASB. Statement No. 34, preface.

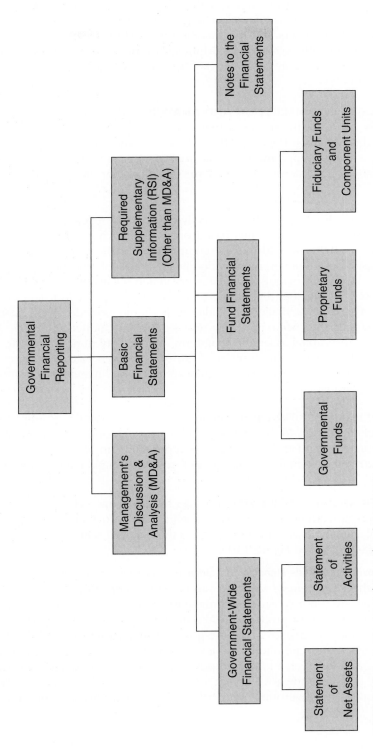

FIGURE 13-1 Governmental Reporting Components

discussion & analysis (MD&A), the *basic financial statements*, and *required supplementary information* (other than the MD&A). In turn, there are three sections to the basic financial statements. They are government-wide financial statements, fund financial statements, and notes to the financial statements. There are two government-wide financial statements: the statement of net assets and the statement of activities. There are three groupings of fund financial statements: governmental funds, proprietary funds, and fiduciary funds and component units (see Figure 13-1). Each of these elements of governmental financial reporting is discussed below.

MANAGEMENT'S DISCUSSION AND ANALYSIS To best achieve the objectives of financial reporting, GASB requires that managers provide a discussion placed before the financial statements. Because MD&A is not a part of the financial statements themselves, it is considered supplementary information. Because it is required, it must accompany the financial statements to have a presentation that complies with GAAP. According to GASB:

> MD&A should provide an objective and easily readable analysis of the government's financial activities based on currently known facts, decisions, or conditions. MD&A should include comparisons of the current year to the prior year based on the government-wide information. It should provide an analysis of the government's overall financial position and results of operations to assist users in assessing whether that financial position has improved or deteriorated as a result of the year's activities. In addition, it should provide an analysis of significant changes that occur in funds and significant budget variances. It should also describe capital asset and long-term debt activity during the year. MD&A should conclude with a description of currently known facts, decisions, or conditions that are expected to have a significant effect on financial position or the results of operations.[4]

To make the MD&A as useful as possible, the inclusion of graphs, charts, and tables is appropriate. It is up to the managers who are preparing the document to include the most relevant information and to be creative in providing an MD&A that achieves the goals of the document rather than following a rigid format that might exclude important information.

BASIC FINANCIAL STATEMENTS The BFS for governmental organizations include two major categories: government-wide financial statements and fund financial statements. The basic financial statements also include notes to the financial statements, as is required for all types of organizations (see Figure 13-1).

Government-Wide Financial Statements There are two government-wide financial statements: the *statement of net assets* and a *statement of activities* (see Figure 13-1). These statements are reported on the accrual basis of accounting, which is the same basis required for health and not-for-profit financial statements that are prepared in accordance with GAAP. They provide information about the government as a whole.

Governments are often complex organizations. There may be housing agencies, school districts, airports, recreational authorities, and so on. These agencies, districts, and authorities may be part of the government, or they may be legally separate entities. But even if they are separate, the government may have financial responsibility for them. When a town, city,

---

[4] Ibid. Summary.

county, or state government issues financial statements, should all commissions, subgovernments, agencies, and authorities be included or excluded? What entities should be included in a government's financial statements?

The key to these questions is the reporting entity. Financial statements can only convey meaningful information if we know what makes up the entity being reported on. Generally, the reporting entity includes the *primary government*, all organizations for which the primary government is financially accountable, and certain other organizations. The primary government is defined as being a state or local governmental body that has a separately elected governing body and is legally and financially separate from other governments.

In preparing government-wide financial statements, the focus is on the primary government. It is shown separately from its *component units*, but information for both the primary government and the component units is provided in the statements. Component units are governmental bodies that are legally separate from the primary government. However, the controlling majority of the component unit's governing body is appointed by the primary government, and there is some close financial relationship between the primary government and the component unit. For instance, the primary government might be obligated to pay any debts of a component unit if it cannot make payment, or the primary government might be able to impose its will on a component unit.

For example, suppose that a city's airport is established as a legally separate entity. However, assume that the city appoints the controlling majority of the airport board and the city is legally obligated for the airport's debt. The airport is reported as a component unit. Clearly, if the debt were substantial, it would be misleading for the city to fail to disclose information about this component unit. See the additional discussion of component units in Box 13-1.

Government-wide statements also provide separate columns to distinguish between activities of the primary government that are governmental versus those that relate to business-type activities. Providing education, police protection, and social services would be considered basic governmental functions. A golf course would generally be considered to be business-type activity because it is usually run like a private business. Prices are set with the intention of at least covering costs. The business is financed primarily or entirely by user fees rather than by taxing the general public.

BOX 13-1

Fund-Raising Organization Component Units

Sometimes fund-raising organizations may be component units of governments. If so, they must be included in the financial statements of the primary government. Such organizations generally must be considered to be component units of the primary government if they generate and hold economic resources that are intended to be used to the direct benefit of a governmental unit.

Public colleges and universities often have fund-raising arms. The same is true of many public health care organizations. These fund-raising organizations may appear at first glance to be separate entities. Until recently they did not always get included in the financial statements of the governmental body. However, under current rules even an organization that is a legally separate, tax-exempt entity must be included as a component unit if the resources it generates are almost entirely for the benefit of the government unit (such as a public university), the government unit has the ability to access or use most of the resources of the entity, and the amount of resources involved are significant to the primary government.

It is beneficial to separate governmental from business-type activities because users of financial reports might have substantially different expectations for the financial results of governmental versus business-type activities. For example, deficits in governmental activities subsidized by profits from business-type activities would almost certainly be considered to be a more acceptable outcome than the reverse.

Statement of net assets. The government-wide statement of net assets is similar to a traditional balance sheet. The owner's equity section is referred to as net assets, the same term that not-for-profit organizations use. Although the statement contains the same information as a balance sheet, the recommended format is the following form of the fundamental equation of accounting[5]:

$$\text{Assets} - \text{Liabilities} = \text{Net Assets}$$

That is, assets would be presented at the top of the statement, and liabilities would be subtracted from assets to arrive at net assets. This helps to emphasize the governmental focus on resources that are available to the government. See Exhibit 13-1 for a sample statement of net assets for the hypothetical Local City.[6]

In the "Assets" section of Exhibit 13-1, there is a heading for capital assets. Included under the heading are land, infrastructure, buildings, property, and equipment. *Infrastructure* assets are stationary assets with extremely long lifetimes, including bridges, tunnels, dams, roads, and similar assets. Such assets last longer than buildings and equipment. Buildings would only be considered infrastructure if they are part of an infrastructure network, such as a building attached to a dam project. In general, governmental capital assets are depreciated in the government-wide statements in a manner similar to that used by other organizations.

As an alternative to depreciation, a modified approach is allowed for reporting some infrastructure. The infrastructure would have to be a network or part of a network, such as a sewer system. To use the modified approach, the government would have to establish a level of condition at which it intends to maintain the infrastructure and document that the infrastructure is being maintained in that level of condition. It would also have to provide an estimate of the annual cost of preserving or maintaining the infrastructure at the condition level specified.[7]

The net assets section of the statement of net assets must be divided into three subcategories: (1) invested in capital assets, net of related debt, (2) restricted, and (3) unrestricted. The first of these subcategories consists of all capital assets, less accumulated depreciation and less the outstanding balance of any debt related to them.

For example, suppose that the Town of Millbridge purchased new buses for $2,000,000, paying one-quarter in cash and borrowing the balance on a 10-year mortgage. At the date of acquisition, the "Assets" section of the statement of net assets would include $2,000,000 for the bus capital asset, the "Liabilities" section would include $1,500,000 for the mortgage liability on the buses, and the "Invested in capital assets" section of net assets would include $500,000, which is the town's equity in the buses. Each year, the balance in

---

[5] The traditional balance sheet format, with the total of assets equal to the total of liabilities plus net assets, is an acceptable alternative for the statement of net assets.

[6] Note that assets and liabilities have been divided into current and noncurrent (long-term) sections in Exhibit 13-1. This approach is referred to as a classified statement of net assets. This approach is permissible but not required (GASB, Statement No. 34, paragraph 31).

[7] One might expect that the government would incur maintenance expense instead of depreciation expense, but that is not explicitly called for by the reporting requirements. See GASB Statement No. 34, paragraphs 22–26, 132–133, 148–166, and 335–342 for further details.

EXHIBIT 13-1 Local City Government-Wide Statement of Net Assets

Local City
Statement of Net Assets
As of December 31, 2012

	Primary Government			Component Units
	Governmental Activities	Business-Type Activities	Total	
Assets				
Current assets:				
Cash and cash equivalents	$ 13,597,899	$ 8,785,821	$ 22,383,720	$ 303,935
Investments	27,365,221	—	27,365,221	7,428,952
Receivables (net)	12,833,132	3,609,615	16,442,747	4,042,290
Internal balances	175,000	(175,000)	—	—
Inventories	322,149	126,674	448,823	83,697
Total current assets	$ 54,293,401	$ 12,347,110	$ 66,640,511	$ 11,858,874
Noncurrent assets:				
Restricted cash and cash equivalents	$ —	$ 1,493,322	$ 1,493,322	$ —
Capital assets (Note 2):				
Land and nondepreciable infrastructure	88,253,120	3,836,119	92,089,239	—
Depreciable infrastructure, net	30,367,241	30,952,214	61,319,455	751,239
Depreciable buildings, property, and equipment, net	51,402,399	116,600,418	168,002,817	36,993,547
Total noncurrent assets	$ 170,022,760	$ 152,882,073	$ 322,904,833	$ 37,744,786
Total assets	$ 224,316,161	$ 165,229,183	$ 389,545,344	$ 49,603,660
Liabilities				
Current liabilities:				
Accounts payable	$ 6,783,310	$ 751,430	$ 7,534,740	$ 1,803,332
Deferred revenue	1,435,599	—	1,435,599	38,911
Current portion of long-term obligations (Note 3)	9,236,000	4,426,286	13,662,286	1,426,639
Total current liabilities	$ 17,454,909	$ 5,177,716	$ 22,632,625	$ 3,268,882
Noncurrent liabilities:				
Noncurrent portion of long-term obligations (Note 3)	83,302,378	74,482,273	157,784,651	27,106,151
Total liabilities	$ 100,757,287	$ 79,659,989	$ 180,417,276	$ 30,375,033
Net Assets				
Invested in capital assets, net of related debt	$ 103,711,386	$ 73,088,574	$ 176,799,960	$ 15,906,392
Restricted for:				
Capital projects	11,705,864	—	11,705,864	492,445
Debt service	3,020,708	1,451,996	4,472,704	—
Community development projects	4,811,043	—	4,811,043	—
Other purposes	3,214,302	—	3,214,302	—
Unrestricted (deficit)	(2,904,429)	11,028,624	8,124,195	2,829,790
Total net assets	$ 123,558,874	$ 85,569,194	$ 209,128,068	$ 19,228,627

Source: Adapted from Dean Michael Mead. "Figure 1: Illustrative Government-wide Statement of Net Assets," *What You Should Know about Your Local Government's Finances: A Guide to Financial Statements.* Norwalk, Conn.: GASB, 2000, pp. 8–9. Reprinted with permission.

this section of net assets would be adjusted for the depreciation on the buses and for the change in the mortgage payable balance.[8]

The second section of net assets is restricted net assets. Net assets are considered restricted for reporting purposes on this statement if restrictions have been imposed by creditors, grantors, donors, law, or regulation.[9]

The last section of net assets, unrestricted net assets, represents the balance in net assets. This would be the amount that does not have to be identified in either of the other two categories. Internal designations of intended use do not constitute restrictions. Thus, if management intends to use some net assets for a particular purpose, they would still be classed as unrestricted net assets unless legislation had been enacted, placing a legal restriction on their use.

Statement of activities. The second government-wide financial statement is the statement of activities. See Exhibit 13-2 for an example of this statement. This statement provides information about the revenues and expenses of the government as a whole, as well as other changes in net assets. Looking at the headings on the left, one can see that the top half of the statement breaks down information by function or program. These functions or programs are divided between the primary government and the component units. Within the primary government, the information is further broken down by type of governmental activity and type of business activity.

In Exhibit 13-2, the first column of numbers shows the expenses related to each activity. Some governments may choose to allocate expenses from some functions to other functions. For example, the general government might process payroll for many of the other parts of the government. To get a better sense of the cost to operate each of those other functions or programs, it might be appropriate to allocate some of the cost of the payroll to them.

If such allocation is done, direct and indirect expenses should be shown in two separate columns. This facilitates comparison of expenses with that of other governments that do not allocate indirect expenses. In Exhibit 13-2, the second column of numbers provides the indirect expense allocations. In this example, some general government direct expenses and all interest expenses are allocated to the other governmental activities. Note that no indirect expenses are allocated to education. The school district may be separate from the rest of the government. For example, it might have its own payroll department. Also note that the total of the second column is zero. The second column is only allocating some of the expenses in the first column *from* some functions *to* other functions. (Cost allocation is discussed in Chapter 4.)

Depreciation is generally treated as a direct expense. It would therefore be included in the expenses of each function. Infrastructure depreciation should be included in the direct expenses of the function that would normally be responsible for the acquisition and maintenance of the infrastructure, such as a public works or transportation department.

In the statement of activities, revenues are either associated directly with functions in the top part of the statement or included in general revenues and other changes in net assets in the bottom part. In Exhibit 13-2, revenues that can be directly associated with

---

[8] That is, depreciation would reduce the net value of the capital asset, reducing net assets, but repayment of the mortgage would offset at least part of the reduction.

[9] If some of the restricted net assets are permanent endowments, then this section of net assets would have to be further subdivided into the *expendable* portion and *nonexpendable fund*. Nonexpendable amounts are those that must be retained permanently.

functions appear in the third, fourth, and fifth columns of numbers, in the top part of the statement. All other revenues would appear in the first two columns of the bottom part of the statement.

Governmental revenues come from four primary sources: (1) taxes, (2) user fees, (3) intergovernmental grants and other outside organizations, and (4) the government itself (e.g., earnings on investments). Taxes are always treated as general revenue, even if their use is limited to a particular program. Therefore, all tax revenue is shown in the bottom part of the statement. User fees are always associated with a particular program and shown in the top part of the statement. Intergovernmental grants and other revenue from outside organizations are treated as general revenue unless they are restricted in use to a particular program. Revenue from the government itself is typically considered general revenue.

The third through fifth columns in the top part of Exhibit 13-2 indicate the revenues related to each activity, under the broad heading of Program Revenues. Under that heading, the three columns indicate the amount of revenue from charges for services, operating grants and contributions, and capital grants and contributions.

The "Charges for Services" column includes user fees. This results from an exchange transaction. An exchange transaction is one in which goods or services are provided in exchange for money or other consideration approximately equal in value to the goods or services. For example, a toll to use a bridge or a charge to use a county ice rink would be a user fee or charge.

The "Grants and Contributions" columns include revenues that do not arise as the result of an exchange and are restricted to use for specific programs. If the grants and contributions are to be spent to pay for operating costs, they would appear in the fourth column of the exhibit ("Operating Grants and Contributions"). If they are intended to pay for capital assets—such as buildings, equipment, land or infrastructure—then they would appear in the fifth column ("Capital Grants and Contributions").

This creates a curious anomaly. Since this statement is prepared on an accrual basis, the expense column does not include the full cost of capital assets. Rather, it includes only one year's worth of depreciation expense. However, the full capital grant is treated as current period revenue. For example, suppose that a state government made a capital grant of $4 million to pay for a town's new police station. Assume that the police station will be depreciated over 40 years. One could reasonably argue that under accrual accounting, only $100,000 (i.e., 1/40) of the capital grant should be treated as revenue each year, because that will match the amount of expense that is included in the town's activity statement. The remainder would be deferred revenue, a liability. The requirement to show the full capital grant as revenue might mislead the financial statement user about the typical annual financial results of the town's police department, which is unlikely to receive a $4 million capital grant each year. Nevertheless, the full grant is recorded as revenue, and only one year's worth of depreciation is recorded as an expense, under GAAP.

In the top part of Exhibit 13-2, the information from the first five columns of numbers is summarized in the remaining four columns. These four columns on the right side of the exhibit indicate whether expenses exceed direct revenues and whether the function is governmental, business-type, or component unit in nature.

The difference between the revenues and expenses is referred to as the net revenue or net expense. The overall heading for these four columns on the right side of the exhibit is "Net (Expense) Revenue and Changes in Net Assets." If expenses are greater than revenues, the net amount is shown in parentheses. Such activities need to draw on the government's general revenues. They are not financially self-sustaining based on their direct revenues. Activities with revenues exceeding expenses are net contributors providing the government with more resources than they consume. The net revenue or expense

EXHIBIT 13-2 Local City Government-Wide Statement of Activities

Local City
Statement of Activities
For the Year Ending December 31, 2012

				Program Revenues	
Functions/Programs	Expenses	Indirect Expenses Allocation	Charges for Services	Operating Grants and Contributions	Capital Grants and Contributions
Primary Government:					
Governmental activities:					
General government	$ 9,571,410	$(5,580,878)	$ 3,146,915	$ 843,617	$ —
Public safety	34,844,749	4,059,873	1,198,855	1,307,693	62,300
Public works	10,128,538	3,264,380	850,000	—	2,252,615
Engineering services	1,299,645	111,618	704,793	—	—
Health and sanitation	6,738,672	558,088	5,612,267	575,000	—
Cemetery	735,866	55,809	212,496	—	—
Culture and recreation	11,532,350	1,858,966	3,995,199	2,450,000	—
Community development	2,994,389	1,740,265	—	—	2,580,000
Education (payment to school district)	21,893,273	—	—	—	—
Interest on long-term debt	6,068,121	(6,068,121)	—	—	—
Total governmental activities	$105,807,013	$ 0	$15,720,525	$ 5,176,310	$4,894,915
Business-type activities:					
Water	$ 3,595,733		$ 4,159,350	$ —	$1,159,909
Sewer	4,912,853		7,170,533	—	486,010
Parking facilities	2,796,283		1,344,087	—	—
Total business-type activities	$ 11,304,869		$12,673,970	$ —	$1,645,919
Total primary government	$117,111,882		$28,394,495	$ 5,176,310	$6,540,834
Component Units:					
Landfill	$ 3,382,157		$ 3,857,858	$ —	$ 11,397
Public school system	31,186,498		705,765	3,937,083	—
Total component units	$ 34,568,655		$ 4,563,623	$ 3,937,083	$ 11,397

General revenues:
  Taxes:
    Property taxes, levied for general purposes
    Property taxes, levied for debt service
     Franchise taxes
     Public service taxes
  Payment from Sample City
  Grants and contributions not restricted to specific programs
  Investment earnings
  Miscellaneous
    Subtotal, excess (deficiency) of revenues over expenses
Special item—gain on sale of park land
Transfers
    Total general revenues, special items, and transfers
Change in net assets
Net assets—beginning
Net assets—ending

Net (Expense) Revenue and Changes in Net Assets

	Primary Government			
Governmental Activities	Business-Type Activities	Total	Component Units
$ —	$ —	$ —	$ —
(36,335,774)	—	(36,335,774)	—
(10,290,303)	—	(10,290,303)	—
(706,470)	—	(706,470)	—
(1,109,493)	—	(1,109,493)	—
(579,179)	—	(579,179)	—
(6,946,117)	—	(6,946,117)	—
(2,154,654)	—	(2,154,654)	—
(21,893,273)	—	(21,893,273)	—
—	—	—	—
$ (80,015,263)	$ —	$ (80,015,263)	$ —
$ —	$ 1,723,526	$ 1,723,526	$ —
—	2,743,690	2,743,690	—
—	(1,452,196)	(1,452,196)	—
$ —	$ 3,015,020	$ 3,015,020	$ —
$(80,015,263)	$ 3,015,020	$ (77,000,203)	$ —
			$ 487,098
			(26,543,650)
			$(26,056,552)
$ 51,693,573	$ —	$ 51,693,573	$ —
4,726,244	—	4,726,244	
4,055,505	—	4,055,505	—
8,969,887	—	8,969,887	—
—	—	—	21,893,273
1,457,820	—	1,457,820	6,461,708
1,958,144	601,349	2,559,493	881,763
884,907	104,925	989,832	22,464
$ (6,269,183)	$ 3,721,294	$ (2,547,889)	$ 3,202,656
2,653,488	—	2,653,488	—
501,409	(501,409)	—	—
$ 76,900,977	$ 204,865	$ 77,105,842	$ 29,259,208
$ (3,114,286)	$ 3,219,885	$ 105,599	$ 3,202,656
126,673,160	82,349,309	209,022,469	16,025,971
$123,558,874	$85,569,194	$209,128,068	$ 19,228,627

Source: Adapted from Dean Michael Mead. "Figure 5: Illustrative Government-wide Statement of Activities," *What You Should Know about Your Local Government's Finances: A Guide to Financial Statements.* Norwalk, Conn.: GASB, 2000, pp. 22–23. Reprinted with permission.

for the governmental activities is shown in the first of these four columns, while the net for the business-type activities is shown in the second. Those two columns are then combined in the third of the four columns to get the totals for the primary government. The net revenue or expense of the component units is shown in the last column in the exhibit (see Exhibit 13-2).

One of the goals of governmental financial reporting is to allow the user to have a sense of which services are funded by general revenues versus which governmental activities are largely self-financing as a result of fees or intergovernmental aid. The format in the top part of Exhibit 13-2 allows the user to quickly get a sense of the extent to which functions are self-financing. In the case of Local City, it is apparent that the governmental activities generate revenues that are only a small portion of their expenses. The total expenses for governmental activities were nearly $106 million (taken from the first column in the exhibit). The net expense of the governmental activities was approximately $80 million (see the "Total governmental activities" row of the sixth column in the exhibit). That $80 million will have to be covered by general revenues, special items, and transfers, or the government will have a deficit from its governmental activities. A large net expense for governmental activities would be typical for most state and local governments.

In contrast, we see that the business-type activities are more than self-sustaining. Local City has three identifiable activities handled on a business-type basis: water, sewer, and parking. From the seventh column of numbers in the exhibit (headed "Business-Type Activities") we see that the water and sewer activities had net revenue; they earned a surplus on a direct revenue and expense basis. Exercise care in interpreting this surplus. We can see from the fifth column of numbers in the activity statement that there were approximately $1.6 million of capital grants and contributions for water and sewer. These were undoubtedly restricted for capital acquisitions and would not be available to pay for operating expenses. The parking facility had nearly $1.5 million more of expenses than revenues. In total, however, the revenues of business-type activities exceeded their costs, even if the capital grants are subtracted. Such information might be of particular interest to some users of the statement. Part of that surplus could be used to help offset the $80 million by which governmental activity costs exceeded revenues.

The bottom part of the statement shows other information about the changes in net assets of the government. The first item listed is general revenues. All taxes are considered to be general revenues. Therefore, even if a portion of the property tax is specifically restricted to be used for education, it is included in the general revenues category, in the bottom part of the statement.[10] Taxes are reported separately by type.

Other government sources of financing—such as endowment contributions, extraordinary items, special items, and transfers between governmental and business-type funds—are also reported in this part of the statement. Intergovernmental grants are a large source of revenue for many governments. If they are restricted for use in a specific program, they would appear in the program revenue columns in the top part of the statement. If they are not restricted, they would appear in the governmental activities column in the bottom part of the statement.

---

[10] Some, including the author of this text, would argue that a tax whose revenue is restricted for education should be shown as revenue in the top half of the statement, on the line for the education function. However, GASB decided to treat them as general revenues, "based on the belief that tax revenues that are raised by the government through its own powers and that are earmarked or restricted for use in a program (as distinct from charges to program customers or applicants for services) should not be regarded as reducing the net cost of the program to be financed from general revenue sources. Rather, it is more meaningful to regard such taxes as one of the sources of general revenues through which the government finances the net cost of the program" (GASB Statement No. 34, paragraph 374).

Extraordinary items are unusual *and* infrequent items. For example, the San Diego city government's costs related to fighting the massive fire in the San Diego area in 2003 would be considered to be an extraordinary item because it was both an unusual and infrequent occurrence.

Special items are unusual *or* infrequent items that are within the control of government. For example, if a government had a large gain on the sale of a building or a piece of land, it would be treated as a special item if such sales are unusual or infrequent, and within the control of the government. In Exhibit 13-2, in the bottom part of the statement, below "General revenues," we see that Local City sold park land, and the profit on the sale was reported as a special item.

Separate reporting of extraordinary and special items is quite beneficial. It allows users of the financial statements to compare usual, recurring revenues and expenses from year to year. It also allows examination of whether the government's ordinary operating activities for a given year are generating an increase or a decrease in net assets. By separating out items that might be considered one-shot revenues, gimmicks, or other atypical changes in net assets, the user potentially avoids being misled.

Similarly, the information from showing transfers as a separate category in the statement of activities is quite valuable. Transfers represent the movement of resources from one fund to another. In Exhibit 13-2, the government's business-type activities transferred $501,409 to the governmental activities. We see this as both an increase in the "Governmental Activities" column and a decrease in the "Business-Type Activities" column. The requirement to report contributions, special items, extraordinary items, and transfers separately from the information in the top part of the statement provides the user with an ability to gain greater insight regarding the financial results of the routine, continuing operations of the government.

From the "Subtotal, excess (deficiency) of revenues over expenses" line near the bottom of Exhibit 13-2, in the "Total" column, we see that even after the inclusion of general revenues, Local City had a decline in net assets of $2,547,889. The modest $105,599 increase in net assets in the "Total" column for the year ending December 31, 2012, resulted only because of a special item. It would appear that the city had to sell park land to avoid having a deficit for the year. The very last line in the Exhibit 13-2 statement of activities for Local City is "Net assets—ending." Note that there are exactly the same amounts as the total net assets in the last line of the Exhibit 13-1 statement of net assets.

Fund Financial Statements The next element of the basic financial statements is a set of fund financial statements (see Figure 13-1). A separate set of fund financial statements is prepared for the *governmental funds, proprietary funds,* and *fiduciary funds.* Fund financial statements are required in addition to government-wide statements. This is somewhat controversial. Some individuals argue that these statements do not provide enough valuable information to be worth requiring. Others argue that the fund financial statements may provide a better ability to determine compliance with finance-related laws, rules, and regulations; find information about the sources and uses of financial resources; and assess the management of short-term resources.

Governmental funds. Recall that governmental funds are the typical funds used to operate most governments. These include the *general fund, special revenue funds, capital projects funds, debt service funds,* and *permanent funds.* A separate set of fund financial statements must be provided for the governmental funds of the primary government. These statements use information recorded on the modified accrual basis of accounting. The required statements are a balance sheet and a statement of revenues, expenditures, and changes in fund balances. See Exhibits 13-3 and 13-4 for examples of governmental

EXHIBIT 13-3

Local City
Balance Sheet—Governmental Funds
As of December 31, 2012

	General	HUD Programs	Community Redevelopment	Route 7 Construction	Other Governmental Funds	Total Governmental Funds
Assets						
Cash and cash equivalents	$3,418,485	$1,236,523	$ —	$ —	$ 5,606,792	$ 10,261,800
Investments	—	—	13,262,695	10,467,037	3,485,252	27,214,984
Receivables, net	3,644,561	2,953,438	353,340	11,000	10,221	6,972,560
Due from other funds	1,370,757	—	—	—	—	1,370,757
Receivables from other governments	—	119,059	—	—	1,596,038	1,715,097
Liens receivable	791,926	3,195,745	—	—	—	3,987,671
Inventories	182,821	—	—	—	—	182,821
Total assets	$9,408,550	$7,504,765	$13,616,035	$10,478,037	$10,698,303	$ 51,705,690
Liabilities and Fund Balances						
Liabilities:						
Accounts payable	$3,408,680	$ 129,975	$ 190,548	$ 1,104,632	$ 1,074,831	$ 5,908,666
Due to other funds	—	25,369	—	—	—	25,369
Payable to other governments	94,074	—	—	—	—	94,074
Deferred revenue	4,250,430	6,273,045	250,000	11,000	—	10,784,475
Total liabilities	$7,753,184	$6,428,389	$ 440,548	$ 1,115,632	$ 1,074,831	$ 16,812,584
Fund balances:						
Reserved for:						
Inventories	$ 182,821	$ —	$ —	$ —	$ —	$ 182,821
Liens receivable	791,926	—	—	—	—	791,926
Encumbrances	40,292	41,034	119,314	5,792,587	1,814,122	7,807,349
Other purposes	—	—	—	—	1,405,300	1,405,300
Unreserved, reported in:						
General fund	640,327	—	—	—	—	640,327
Special revenue funds	—	1,035,342	—	—	1,330,718	2,366,060
Debt service funds	—	—	—	—	3,832,062	3,832,062
Capital projects funds	—	—	13,056,173	3,569,818	1,241,270	17,867,261
Total fund balances	$1,655,366	$1,076,376	$13,175,487	$ 9,362,405	$ 9,623,472	$ 34,893,106
Total liabilities and fund balances	$9,408,550	$7,504,765	$13,616,035	$10,478,037	$10,698,303	

Amounts reported for *governmental activities* in the statement of net assets are different because (see Note 4, also):	
Capital assets used in governmental activities are not financial resources and therefore are not reported in the funds.	161,082,708
Other long-term assets are not available to pay for current-period expenditures and therefore are deferred in the funds.	9,348,876
Internal service funds are used by management to charge the costs of certain activities, such as insurance and telecommunications, to individual funds. The assets and liabilities of the internal service funds are included in governmental activities in the statement of net assets.	2,994,691
Long-term liabilities, including bonds payable, are not due and payable in the current period and therefore are not reported in the funds (see Note 4a).	(84,760,507)
Net assets of governmental activities	$123,558,874

Source: Adapted from Dean Michael Mead. "Figure 6: Illustrative Governmental Funds Balance Sheet," *What You Should Know about Your Local Government's Finances: A Guide to Financial Statements.* Norwalk, Conn.: GASB, 2000, pp. 34–35. Reprinted with permission.

EXHIBIT 13-4

Local City
Statement of Revenues, Expenditures, and Changes in Fund Balances—Governmental Funds
For the Year Ending December 31, 2012

	General	HUD Programs	Community Redevelopment	Route 7 Construction	Other Governmental Funds	Total Governmental Funds
Revenues						
Property taxes	$51,173,436	$ —	$ —	$ —	$ 4,680,192	$ 55,853,628
Franchise taxes	4,055,505	—	—	—	—	4,055,505
Public service taxes	8,969,887	—	—	—	—	8,969,887
Fees and fines	606,946	—	—	—	—	606,946
Licenses and permits	2,287,794	—	—	—	—	2,287,794
Intergovernmental	6,119,938	2,578,191	—	—	2,830,916	11,529,045
Charges for services	11,374,460	—	—	—	30,708	11,405,168
Investment earnings	552,325	87,106	549,489	270,161	364,330	1,823,411
Miscellaneous	881,874	66,176	—	2,939	94	951,083
Total revenues	$86,022,165	$2,731,473	$ 549,489	$ 273,100	$ 7,906,240	$ 97,482,467
Expenditures						
Current:						
General government	$ 8,630,835	$ —	$ 417,814	$ 16,700	$ 121,052	$ 9,186,401
Public safety	33,729,623	—	—	—	—	33,729,623
Public works	4,975,775	—	—	—	3,721,542	8,697,317
Engineering services	1,299,645	—	—	—	—	1,299,645
Health and sanitation	6,070,032	—	—	—	—	6,070,032
Cemetery	706,305	—	—	—	—	706,305
Culture and recreation	11,411,685	—	—	—	—	11,411,685
Community development	—	2,954,389	—	—	—	2,954,389
Education—payment to school district	21,893,273	—	—	—	—	21,893,273
Debt service:						
Principal	—	—	—	—	3,450,000	3,450,000
Interest and other charges	—	—	—	—	5,215,151	5,215,151
Capital outlay	—	—	2,246,671	11,281,769	3,190,209	16,718,649
Total expenditures	$88,717,173	$2,954,389	$ 2,664,485	$ 11,298,469	$15,697,954	$121,332,470
Excess (deficiency) of revenues over expenditures	$ (2,695,008)	$ (222,916)	$ (2,114,996)	$(11,025,369)	$ (7,791,714)	$(23,850,003)
Other Financing Sources (Uses)						
Proceeds of refunding bonds	$ —	$ —	$ —	$ —	$38,045,000	$ 38,045,000
Proceeds of long-term capital-related debt	—	—	17,529,560	—	1,300,000	18,829,560
Payment to bond refunding escrow agent	—	—	—	—	(37,284,144)	(37,284,144)
Transfers in	129,323	—	—	—	5,551,187	5,680,510
Transfers out	(2,163,759)	(348,046)	(2,273,187)	—	(219,076)	(5,004,068)
Total other financing sources and uses	$ (2,034,436)	$ (348,046)	$ 15,256,373	$ —	$ 7,392,967	$ 20,266,858
Special Item						
Proceeds from sale of park land	$ 3,476,488	$ —	$ —	$ —	$ —	$ 3,476,488
Net change in fund balances	$ (1,252,956)	$ (570,962)	$ 13,141,377	$(11,025,369)	$ (398,747)	$ (106,657)
Fund balances—beginning	2,908,322	1,647,338	34,110	20,387,774	10,022,219	34,999,763
Fund balances—ending	$ 1,655,366	$1,076,376	$ 13,175,487	$ 9,362,405	$ 9,623,472	$ 34,893,106

Source: Adapted from Dean Michael Mead. "Figure 7: Illustrative Governmental Funds Statement of Revenues, Expenditures, and Changes in Fund Balances," *What You Should Know about Your Local Government's Finances: A Guide to Financial Statements.* Norwalk, Conn.: GASB, 2000, pp. 38–39. Reprinted with permission.

funds financial statements for hypothetical Local City. Note that *fund balance* is a term that is equivalent to owner's equity or net assets. It is often used when reporting for a fund or funds.

Some funds can be grouped together in these statements. However, *major funds* are reported individually in their own columns. The general fund is always treated as a major fund. It is the fund used for most of the government's routine activities and is essential in every government. In addition, funds that represent a substantial portion of the assets, liabilities, revenues, or expenditures/expenses of their class or type of fund are also considered to be major funds.[11] Governments may also treat any other fund as a major fund, if they believe the extra information would be valuable to users of the BFS.

For example, in Exhibits 13-3 and 13-4, in addition to the general fund there are also individual columns for "HUD Programs," "Community Redevelopment," and "Route 7 Construction," each of which is a major fund. Next comes a summary column for all other governmental funds and a totals column. Requiring disclosure of major funds allows users of the statement to immediately see things such as the money being put aside for the Route 7 construction project.

Notice in Exhibit 13-3, the balance sheet, that fund balances are divided into reserved and unreserved amounts. The reserved portion of fund balances represents amounts that are needed for inventories, encumbrances, and similar purposes. The unreserved portion indicates the amount of fund balance that is unreserved and therefore available for providing services in each of the major classes of governmental funds. Notice, for example, that in Exhibit 13-3 some of the unreserved fund balance is listed as being for the general fund, some for special revenue funds, and some for capital projects funds. Since the balance sheet provides only summary information about the funds, this treatment allows the user to better understand which types of governmental funds have positive or negative fund balances, and their amount.

In contrast to the government-wide financial statements, which are accrual based, the governmental funds statements are prepared on a modified accrual basis. At the bottom of the balance sheet a reconciliation is provided to explain the differences between this statement and the government-wide statement of net assets. In the last column of Exhibit 13-3, "Total Governmental Funds," the total fund balance line shows a balance of $34,893,106. This number is adjusted by the reconciling items at the bottom of the page. For example, Exhibit 13-3 does not include any capital assets, because of their treatment under the modified accrual basis of accounting. This balance sheet does not show any infrastructure, land, buildings, or equipment. The first item in the reconciliation in Exhibit 13-3 is $161,082,708, which is the impact of recording capital assets under the accrual basis. The very last line in the exhibit shows what the fund balance for total governmental funds would have been if the accrual basis had been used. Note that this amount—$123,558,874—is exactly the same as the total net assets for governmental activities in the first column of Exhibit 13-1.

The statement of revenues, expenditures, and changes in fund balances (see Exhibit 13-4) reports revenues by major sources and expenditures in a detailed fashion, at least by function, similar to the government-wide statements. Notice, however, that in this funds statement, both interest and principal payments as well as capital outlays are shown as expenditures. Also, the proceeds from long-term capital-related debt, listed as an other financing source, has the impact of increasing fund balance. This treatment is a result of the use of the modified accrual system for governmental funds financial statements.

---

[11] Specifically, according to GASB Statement No. 37, major funds are those that are at least 10 percent of the revenues, expenditures/expenses, assets, or liabilities of all funds of their type or category (e.g., all governmental funds), and *also* exceed 5 percent of that element (for example, revenues) for all governmental and enterprise funds in aggregate. Enterprise funds are discussed subsequently in the "Proprietary Funds" section.

Expenditures are subtracted from revenues to arrive at a subtotal, the excess (deficiency) of revenues over expenditures. After this subtotal, other financing sources or uses and special items are shown. The other sources or uses section would include proceeds from long-term debt, as noted previously, and also transfers between funds. In Exhibit 13-4, notice that the total of the transfers into governmental funds of $5,680,510 differs from the $5,004,068 total of transfers out of funds. Logically one might expect the transfers between funds to be exactly equal. Keep in mind, however, that this statement reflects only the governmental funds. There are other transfers in the proprietary funds that account for this difference. They are discussed in Appendix 13-A.

The governmental funds financial statements present reconciliations of the fund balances and changes in fund balances to the net assets and changes in net assets, respectively, of the governmental activities in the government-wide statements. As discussed previously, Exhibit 13-3 includes a reconciliation at the bottom of the statement. However, the reconciliations may be shown separately. For example, Exhibit 13-4 does not provide a reconciliation. Instead, Exhibit 13-5 provides a separate reconciliation to explain the differences between the governmental funds statement of revenues, expenditures, and changes in fund balances and the government-wide statement of activities.

From the "Total Governmental Funds" column of Exhibit 13-4, we know that the total net change in fund balances was a decrease of $106,657. This becomes the starting point for Exhibit 13-5. The reconciliation continues with a description of each of the major classes of items that cause the accrual-based government-wide statement of activities to differ from the governmental funds statement. In the case of Local City, the two largest reconciling items are the treatment of capital outlays and bond proceeds. The governmental funds treat capital outlays as expenditures, rather than as capital assets, and treat bond proceeds as a source of fund balance rather than as long-term liabilities. These require adjustments of $14,039,717 and ($16,140,416), respectively, as shown in Exhibit 13-5. All of the adjustments together result in a change in net assets of governmental activities of ($3,114,286). Note that this is the same amount as the change in net assets of governmental activities reported in Exhibit 13-2.

Proprietary funds. Proprietary funds are used to account for activities that are run on a business-like basis. The two types of proprietary funds are *internal service funds* and *enterprise funds.* The fund financial statements that are used for proprietary funds are a statement of net assets,[12] statement of revenues, expenses, and changes in fund net assets, and statement of cash flows. See Exhibits 13-6 through 13-8 for examples of these statements for Local City. Proprietary funds statements are prepared using the accrual basis of accounting and, in most respects, use the accounting approaches of most for-profit industries.[13] There is no need for reconciliations from the proprietary funds statements to the government-wide statements, because the proprietary and government-wide statements are all prepared on an accrual basis of accounting.

Enterprise-type proprietary funds use the major fund reporting approach discussed earlier with respect to governmental funds. Thus, any enterprise fund that is a major fund would be reported separately. Nonmajor enterprise funds may be aggregated and reported in one column. A total is shown for the enterprise funds. To the right of that total, internal service funds are aggregated and reported. Major internal service funds do not have to be segregated. The proprietary fund statement of net assets shown in Exhibit 13-6 reports on two enterprise funds, the Water and Sewer Fund, and the Parking Facilities Fund.

---

[12] The balance sheet format is an acceptable alternative to the statement of net assets for proprietary funds.
[13] It would be inappropriate to say proprietary funds use all for-profit GAAP. For example, the GASB GAAP for pension measurement differs from the FASB approach and applies to both governmental and proprietary funds.

EXHIBIT 13-5	

Local City
Reconciliation of the Statement of Revenues, Expenditures, and Changes in Fund Balances
of Governmental Funds to the Statement of Activities
For the Year Ending December 31, 2012

Net change in fund balances—total governmental funds	$ (106,657)
Amounts reported for *governmental activities* in the statement of activities are different because (see Note 6, also):	
Governmental funds report capital outlays as expenditures. However, in the statement of activities, the cost of those assets is allocated over their estimated useful lives as depreciation expense. This is the amount by which capital outlays exceeded depreciation in the current period.	14,039,717
In the statement of activities, only the gain on the sale of the park land is reported, whereas in the governmental funds, the proceeds from the sale increase financial resources. Thus, the change in net assets differs from the change in fund balance by the cost of the land sold.	(823,000)
Revenues in the statement of activities that do not provide current financial resources are not reported as revenues in the funds.	1,920,630
Bond proceeds provide current financial resources to governmental funds, but issuing debt increases long-term liabilities in the statement of net assets. Repayment of bond principal is an expenditure in the governmental funds, but the repayment reduces long-term liabilities in the statement of net assets. This is the amount by which proceeds exceeded repayments.	(16,140,416)
Some expenses reported in the statement of activities do not require the use of current financial resources and therefore are not reported as expenditures in governmental funds.	(1,245,752)
Internal service funds are used by management to charge the costs of certain activities, such as insurance and telecommunications, to individual funds. The net revenue (expense) of the internal service funds is reported with governmental activities.	(758,808)
Change in net assets of governmental activities	$ (3,114,286)

Source: Adapted from Dean Michael Mead. "Figure 8: Illustrative Reconciliation of Net Changes in Fund Balances to Change in Net Assets," *What You Should Know about Your Local Government's Finances: A Guide to Financial Statements.* Norwalk, Conn.: GASB, 2000, p. 42. Reprinted with permission.

For proprietary funds, the operating results are reported in a statement of revenues, expenses, and changes in fund net assets (see Exhibit 13-7). This statement lists operating revenues and operating expenses before nonoperating items such as interest, transfers, and capital contributions. Transfers are amounts provided by one fund to another. Capital contributions are things such as grants or payments by a developer or a higher-level government.

Why would a developer ever want to give a grant to a government? Suppose that a city-owned boat marina rents dock space only for sailboats. However, the city, under pressure from owners of motorboats, decides to let motorboats dock at the marina as well. It will

EXHIBIT 13-6

Local City
Statement of Net Assets
Proprietary Funds
As of December 31, 2012

	Business-Type Activities—Enterprise Funds			Governmental Activities—
	Water and Sewer	Parking Facilities	Totals	Internal Service Funds (Note 4)
Assets				
Current assets:				
Cash and cash equivalents	$ 8,416,653	$ 369,168	$ 8,785,821	$ 3,336,099
Investments	—	—	—	150,237
Receivables, net	3,564,586	3,535	3,568,121	157,804
Due from other governments	41,494	—	41,494	—
Inventories	126,674	—	126,674	139,328
Total current assets	$ 12,149,407	$ 372,703	$ 12,522,110	$ 3,783,468
Noncurrent assets:				
Restricted cash and cash equivalents	$ —	$ 1,493,322	$ 1,493,322	$ —
Capital assets:				
Land	813,513	3,021,637	3,835,150	—
Distribution and collection systems	39,504,183	—	39,504,183	—
Buildings and equipment	106,135,666	23,029,166	129,164,832	14,721,786
Less accumulated depreciation	(15,328,911)	(5,786,503)	(21,115,414)	(5,781,734)
Total noncurrent assets	$131,124,451	$ 21,757,622	$152,882,073	$ 8,940,052
Total assets	$143,273,858	$ 22,130,325	$165,404,183	$12,723,520
Liabilities				
Current liabilities:				
Accounts payable	$ 447,427	$ 304,003	$ 751,430	$ 780,570
Due to other funds	175,000	—	175,000	1,170,388
Compensated absences	112,850	8,827	121,677	237,690
Claims and judgments	—	—	—	1,687,975
Bonds, notes, and loans payable	3,944,609	360,000	4,304,609	249,306
Total current liabilities	$ 4,679,886	$ 672,830	$ 5,352,716	$ 4,125,929
Noncurrent liabilities:				
Compensated absences	$ 451,399	$ 35,306	$ 486,705	$ —
Claims and judgments	—	—	—	5,602,900
Bonds, notes, and loans payable	54,451,549	19,544,019	73,995,568	—
Total noncurrent liabilities	$ 54,902,948	$ 19,579,325	$ 74,482,273	$ 5,602,900
Total liabilities	$ 59,582,834	$ 20,252,155	$ 79,834,989	$ 9,728,829
Net Assets				
Invested in capital assets, net of related debt	$ 72,728,293	$ 360,281	$ 73,088,574	$ 8,690,746
Restricted for debt service	—	1,451,996	1,451,996	—
Unrestricted	10,962,731	65,893	11,028,624	(5,696,055)
Total net assets	$ 83,691,024	$ 1,878,170	$ 85,569,194	$ 2,994,691

Source: Adapted from Dean Michael Mead. "Figure 9: Illustrative Proprietary Funds Statement of Net Assets," *What You Should Know about Your Local Government's Finances: A Guide to Financial Statements.* Norwalk, Conn.: GASB, 2000, pp. 46–47. Reprinted with permission.

EXHIBIT 13-7

Local City
Statement of Revenues, Expenses, and Changes in Fund Net Assets
Proprietary Funds
For the Year Ending December 31, 2012

	Business-Type Activities—Enterprise Funds			Governmental Activities—Internal Service Funds (Note 5)
	Water and Sewer	Parking Facilities	Totals	
Operating revenues:				
Charges for services	$11,329,883	$ 1,340,261	$ 12,670,144	$ 15,256,164
Miscellaneous	—	3,826	3,826	1,066,761
Total operating revenues	$11,329,883	$ 1,344,087	$ 12,673,970	$ 16,322,925
Operating expenses:				
Personal services	$ 3,400,559	$ 762,348	$ 4,162,907	$ 4,157,156
Contractual services	344,422	96,032	440,454	584,396
Utilities	754,107	100,726	854,833	214,812
Repairs and maintenance	747,315	64,617	811,932	1,960,490
Other supplies and expenses	498,213	17,119	515,332	234,445
Insurance claims and expenses	—	—	—	8,004,286
Depreciation	1,163,140	542,049	1,705,189	1,707,872
Total operating expenses	$ 6,907,756	$ 1,582,891	$ 8,490,647	$ 16,863,457
Operating income (loss)	$ 4,422,127	$ (238,804)	$ 4,183,323	$ (540,532)
Nonoperating revenues (expenses):				
Interest and investment revenue	$ 454,793	$ 146,556	$ 601,349	$ 134,733
Miscellaneous revenue	—	104,925	104,925	20,855
Interest expense	(1,600,830)	(1,166,546)	(2,767,376)	(41,616)
Miscellaneous expense	—	(46,846)	(46,846)	(176,003)
Total nonoperating revenue (expenses)	$ (1,146,037)	$ (961,911)	$ (2,107,948)	$ (62,031)
Income (loss) before contributions and transfers	$ 3,276,090	$ (1,200,715)	$ 2,075,375	$ (602,563)
Capital contributions	1,645,919	—	1,645,919	18,788
Transfers out	(290,000)	(211,409)	(501,409)	(175,033)
Change in net assets	$ 4,632,009	$ (1,412,124)	$ 3,219,885	$ (758,808)
Total net assets—beginning	79,059,015	3,290,294	82,349,309	3,753,499
Total net assets—ending	$83,691,024	$ 1,878,170	$ 85,569,194	$ 2,994,691

Source: Adapted from Dean Michael Mead. "Figure 10: Illustrative Proprietary Funds Statement of Revenues, Expenses, and Changes in Fund Net Assets," *What You Should Know about Your Local Government's Finances: A Guide to Financial Statements.* Norwalk, Conn.: GASB, 2000, pp. 48–49. Reprinted with permission.

be costly to build the additional dock space needed to accommodate the motorboat owners. One way to recover the cost of building the new docks is to allow a gasoline company to contribute the cost of building them in exchange for the right to sell gas from the docks. The government will recover the full cost of construction from the gas company contribution, and will also gain new revenues it charges the motorboat owners for using the docks. The gas company will gain sales of its product.

EXHIBIT 13-8

Local City
Statement of Cash Flows
Proprietary Funds
For the Year Ending December 31, 2012

	Business-Type Activities—Enterprise Funds			Governmental Activities—Internal Service Funds
	Water and Sewer	Parking Facilities	Totals	
Cash Flows from Operating Activities				
Receipts from customers	$11,400,200	$ 1,345,292	$ 12,745,492	$15,326,343
Payments to suppliers	(2,725,349)	(365,137)	(3,090,486)	(2,812,238)
Payments to employees	(3,360,055)	(750,828)	(4,110,883)	(4,209,688)
Internal activity—payments to other funds	(1,296,768)	—	(1,296,768)	—
Claims paid	—	—	—	(8,482,451)
Other receipts (payments)	(2,325,483)	—	(2,325,483)	1,061,118
Net cash provided by operating activities	$ 1,692,545	$ 229,327	$ 1,921,872	$ 883,084
Cash Flows from Noncapital Financing Activities				
Operating subsidies and transfers to other funds	$ (290,000)	$ (211,409)	$ (501,409)	$ (175,033)
Cash Flows from Capital and Related Financing Activities				
Proceeds from capital debt	$ 4,041,322	$ 8,660,778	$ 12,702,100	$ —
Capital contributions	1,645,919	—	1,645,919	—
Purchases of capital assets	(4,194,035)	(144,716)	(4,338,751)	(400,086)
Principal paid on capital debt	(2,178,491)	(8,895,000)	(11,073,491)	(954,137)
Interest paid on capital debt	(1,479,708)	(1,166,546)	(2,646,254)	41,616
Other receipts (payments)	—	19,174	19,174	131,416
Net cash (used) by capital and related financing activities	$ (2,164,993)	$ (1,526,310)	$ (3,691,303)	$(1,264,423)
Cash Flows from Investing Activities				
Proceeds from sales and maturities of investments	$ —	$ —	$ —	$ 15,684
Interest and dividends	454,793	143,747	598,540	129,550
Net cash provided by investing activities	$ 454,793	$ 143,747	$ 598,540	$ 145,234
Net (decrease) in cash and cash equivalents	$ (307,655)	$ (1,364,645)	$ (1,672,300)	$ (411,138)
Balances—beginning of the year	8,724,308	3,227,135	11,951,443	3,747,237
Balances—end of the year	$ 8,416,653	$ 1,862,490	$ 10,279,143	$ 3,336,099
Reconciliation of Operating Income (Loss) to Net Cash Provided (Used) by Operating Activities:				
Operating income (loss)	$ 4,422,127	$ (238,804)	$ 4,183,323	$ (540,532)
Adjustments to reconcile operating income to net cash provided (used) by operating activities:				
Depreciation expense	1,163,140	542,049	1,705,189	1,707,872
Change in assets and liabilities:				
Receivables, net	653,264	1,205	654,469	31,941
Inventories	2,829	—	2,829	39,790
Accounts and other payables	(297,446)	(86,643)	(384,089)	475,212
Accrued expenses	(4,251,369)	11,520	(4,239,849)	(831,199)
Net cash provided by operating activities	$ 1,692,545	$ 229,327	$ 1,921,872	$ 883,084

Source: Adapted from Dean Michael Mead. "Figure 11: Illustrative Proprietary Funds Statement of Cash Flows," *What You Should Know about Your Local Government's Finances: A Guide to Financial Statements.* Norwalk, Conn.: GASB, 2000, pp. 50–51. Reprinted with permission.

Proprietary fund statements also include a statement of cash flows (see Exhibit 13-8). This statement differs from the cash flow statement used in most other types of organizations in several respects. First, it must be presented using the direct method. Second, the categories and their contents are slightly different than those used for the cash flow statement used by for-profit and not-for-profit organizations. The reconciliation at the bottom of the exhibit shows the adjustments that would be needed to convert income to cash flow from operating activities.

The cash flow statement discussed in Chapter 10 has three sections: cash from operating activities, cash from investing activities, and cash from financing activities. As shown in Exhibit 13-8, governments use a different order of presentation and break the information into four categories, as follows: cash flows from operating activities, cash flows from noncapital financing activities, cash flows from capital and related financing activities, and cash flows from investing activities.

The first category, cash flows from operating activities, includes receipts and disbursements related to the operations of the fund. All cash flows that do not belong in one of the other categories are included in this section.

The second category, noncapital financing, relates to borrowing or repaying money for purposes other than to acquire or improve capital assets. Also included in this category are receipts from grants, other funds, and other governments, and some taxes that are not received for either capital or operating purposes. For example, if the general fund transfers money to an enterprise fund to cover an operating deficit, that cash receipt by the enterprise fund would fall into this category.

The third category, capital and related financing activities, is primarily related to acquisition and disposition of capital assets, and borrowing and repaying money related to the acquisition of capital assets. Note that much of this would fall into the investing category for other types of organizations.

The fourth category, cash flows from investing activities, focuses on cash flows related to buying and selling debt and equity instruments (not including the initial issuance of such instruments) as well as lending money and collecting payments on those loans.

Under the GASB approach, interest paid is categorized as a financing activity, and interest received is categorized as an investing activity. This differs from the FASB approach for nongovernmental organizations, which treats interest as an operating activity.

The proprietary funds financial statements, governmental funds financial statements, and the government-wide financials statements are interrelated. Examples of the connections among these statements are provided in Appendix 13-A at the end of this chapter.

Fiduciary funds. The resources in the fiduciary funds are not really resources of the government because they are being held in trust or as agent. These resources are not available for the government to use for the provision of services to the public. Therefore, fiduciary funds are not included in the government-wide financial statements. The fund financial statements that are used for fiduciary funds are the statement of fiduciary net assets and the statement of changes in fiduciary net assets. See Exhibits 13-9 and 13-10 for examples for Local City. Separate columns aggregate the fiduciary funds by type, such as pension or agency funds. These fund financial statements are the only place where fiduciary funds financial information is reported in the BFS. Component units that are fiduciary in nature are not included in the government-wide financial statements. Instead they are included in the fund financial statements of the fiduciary funds.

Notice in the statement of fiduciary net assets (Exhibit 13-9) that the net assets section does not have to be subdivided as is required in the proprietary funds. Also notice that in the statement of fiduciary net assets, the total assets of agency funds always equal their total liabilities. There are no net assets because all of the assets are just being held

EXHIBIT 13-9

Local City
Statement of Fiduciary Net Assets
Fiduciary Funds
As of December 31, 2012

	Employee Retirement Plan	Private-Purpose Trust	Agency Fund
Assets			
Cash and cash equivalents	$ 1,973	$ 1,250	$ 44,889
Receivables:			
Interest and dividends	508,475	760	—
Other receivables	6,826	—	183,161
Total receivables	$ 515,301	$ 760	$183,161
Investments, at fair value:			
U.S. government obligations	$13,056,037	$80,000	$ —
Municipal bonds	6,528,019	—	—
Corporate bonds	16,320,047	—	—
Corporate stocks	26,112,075	—	—
Other investments	3,264,009	—	—
Total investments	$65,280,187	$80,000	$ —
Total assets	$65,797,461	$82,010	$228,050
Liabilities			
Accounts payable	$ —	$ 1,234	$ —
Refunds payable and others	1,358	—	228,050
Total liabilities	$ 1,358	$ 1,234	$228,050
Net Assets			
Held in trust for pension benefits and other purposes	$65,796,103	$80,776	

Source: Adapted from Dean Michael Mead. "Figure 12: Illustrative Statement of Fiduciary Net Assets," *What You Should Know about Your Local Government's Finances: A Guide to Financial Statements.* Norwalk, Conn.: GASB, 2000, p. 56. Reprinted with permission.

temporarily by the government. They will be passed along to other organizations; consequently, there is no net asset balance left over. Logically, because agency funds have no net assets, they are not included in the statement of changes in fiduciary net assets (Exhibit 13-10).

Notes to the Financial Statements In addition to government-wide financial statements and fund financial statements, the basic financial statements of the government should include a set of notes (see Figure 13-1). Notes should disclose all information needed for the financial statements, taken as a whole, to make a fair presentation of the financial position and results of operations of the government. The notes are considered an integral part of the basic financial statements.

GASB Statements 38 and 40 provide considerable discussion of required disclosures that should appear in the notes. These disclosures include areas such as schedules of interfund transfers and balances, detailed information about long-term obligations, detailed information about payables and receivables balances, and the risks related to government deposits and investments.

EXHIBIT 13-10

Local City
Statement of Changes in Fiduciary Net Assets
Fiduciary Funds
For the Year Ending December 31, 2012

	Employee Retirement Plan	Private-Purpose Trust
Additions		
Contributions:		
Employer	$ 2,721,341	$ —
Plan members	1,421,233	—
Total contributions	$ 4,142,574	$ —
Investment earnings:		
Net (decrease) in fair value of investments	$ (272,522)	$ —
Interest	2,460,871	4,560
Dividends	1,445,273	—
Total investment earnings	$ 3,633,622	$ 4,560
Less investment expense	216,428	—
Net investment earnings	$ 3,417,194	$ 4,560
Total additions	$ 7,559,768	$ 4,560
Deductions		
Benefits	$ 2,453,047	$ 3,800
Refunds of contributions	464,691	—
Administrative expenses	87,532	678
Total deductions	$ 3,005,270	$ 4,478
Change in net assets	$ 4,554,498	$ 82
Net assets—beginning of the year	61,241,605	80,694
Net assets—end of the year	$65,796,103	$80,776

Source: Adapted from Dean Michael Mead. "Figure 13: Illustrative Statement of Changes in Fiduciary Net Assets," *What You Should Know about Your Local Government's Finances: A Guide to Financial Statements.* Norwalk, Conn.: GASB, 2000, p. 57. Reprinted with permission.

REQUIRED SUPPLEMENTARY INFORMATION   Governments also present RSI in addition to the basic financial statements (see Figure 13-1). A variety of information geared to different types of users is provided in the RSI. One element of RSI is discussed in an earlier section: MD&A. Another RSI element is a budgetary comparison schedule "for the general fund and for each major special revenue fund that has a legally adopted annual budget."[14] See Exhibit 13-11 for an example of a budgetary comparison schedule for Local City.

For governments, accountability is essential. The *budgetary comparison schedule*, or *statement*, presents the original adopted budget, the final budget, and the actual results. Governments are encouraged to include a column presenting the variance between the final budget and the actual results, and may have a column for the difference between the original

---

[14] Alternatively, the government may provide a budgetary comparison statement, included in the BFS (GASB Statement No. 34, paragraph 130).

budget and the actual budget. The final budget may be the result of numerous changes that have been authorized legally during the year.

For example, consider Exhibit 13-11. The first two columns of numbers provide the original and final budgets. The third column reports on the actual results. The next two columns allow the reader to compare the original budget with the final budget and the final budget with the actual results. One can see that the variance of the original budget from the final budget was substantially greater than the variance of the final budget versus the actual results. The comparison of the final budget versus the actual amounts allows the user to assess legal and budgetary compliance. The comparison of the original budget with the final budget allows the user to assess the competence of the original estimation and the ability of the government and its managers to control its operations.

As discussed earlier, the government uses accrual accounting for government-wide statements and modified accrual for governmental funds financial statements. The cash basis of accounting is also discussed in Chapter 12. The budgetary comparison statements are prepared using the *budgetary basis of accounting*, the basis of accounting that the government uses for its budgets. This varies for different governments. Use of the cash basis for budgeting is not uncommon. A reconciliation must be provided for the differences between the budgetary information and information on a GAAP basis.[15] In Exhibit 13-11, the last two columns provide information to help the user convert from the budgetary basis to GAAP. The next to last column shows differences between the final budget and GAAP, and the last column shows the actual results on a GAAP rather than budgetary basis. At the bottom of the page a summary explanation is given for the differences.

RSI also includes a variety of other schedules and statistical data. The various other elements of RSI are beyond the scope of this book.

The Millbridge Example

The information that was recorded in Chapter 12 for Millbridge is now used to prepare financial statements. Exhibit 12-3 from Chapter 12, which summarizes all of the financial events for Millbridge, is repeated here as Exhibit 13-12, for convenience.

GOVERNMENTAL FUNDS FINANCIAL STATEMENTS   The governmental funds financial statements are reported on a modified accrual basis, so they may be developed directly from the information in Exhibit 13-12, which was recorded on that basis. Exhibits 13-13 and 13-14 present the governmental funds balance sheet and statement of revenues, expenditures, and changes in fund balances. Note that each of the governmental funds is shown in this example because they all meet the criteria for being considered major funds.

The assets and liabilities in Exhibit 13-13 come directly from the ending balances in Exhibit 13-12. For example, the $10,000 of cash in the "General Fund" column comes from the ending balance in the cash column in Exhibit 13-12, Part A. The $42,000 in cash in the "Debt Service Fund" column comes from Exhibit 13-12, Part B. The remainder of the assets and liabilities can be found for all three funds using the ending balances from Exhibit 13-12, Parts A, B, and C.

---

[15] GASB Statement No. 34 does not explicitly indicate if the reconciliation should be from the budgetary basis to an accrual or a modified accrual basis. However, since governmental funds use the modified accrual basis, the comparison would be from the budgetary basis to the modified accrual basis.

EXHIBIT 13-11

Local City
Budgetary Comparison Schedule for the General Fund
For the Year Ending December 31, 2012

| | Budgeted Amounts | | Actual Amounts |
	Original	Final	Budgetary Basis
Revenues			
Property taxes	$ 52,017,833	$51,853,018	$51,173,436
Other taxes—franchise and public service	12,841,209	12,836,024	13,025,392
Fees and fines	718,800	718,800	606,946
Licenses and permits	2,126,600	2,126,600	2,287,794
Intergovernmental	6,905,898	6,571,360	6,119,938
Charges for services	12,392,972	11,202,150	11,374,460
Interest	1,015,945	550,000	552,325
Miscellaneous	3,024,292	1,220,991	881,874
Total revenues	$ 91,043,549	$87,078,943	$86,022,165
Expenditures			
Current:			
General government (including contingencies and miscellaneous)	$ 11,837,534	$ 9,468,155	$ 8,621,500
Public safety	33,050,966	33,983,706	33,799,709
Public works	5,215,630	5,025,848	4,993,187
Engineering services	1,296,275	1,296,990	1,296,990
Health and sanitation	5,756,250	6,174,653	6,174,653
Cemetery	724,500	724,500	706,305
Culture and recreation	11,059,140	11,368,070	11,289,146
Education—payment to school district	22,000,000	22,000,000	21,893,273
Total expenditures	$ 90,940,295	$90,041,922	$88,774,763
Excess (deficiency) of revenues over expenditures [A]	$ 103,254	$ (2,962,979)	$ (2,752,598)
Other Financing Sources (Uses)			
Transfers in	$ 939,525	$ 130,000	$ 129,323
Transfers out	(2,970,256)	(2,163,759)	(2,163,759)
Total other financing sources and uses [B]	$ (2,030,731)	$ (2,033,759)	$ (2,034,436)
Special Item			
Proceeds from sale of park land [C]	$ 1,355,250	$ 3,500,000	$ 3,476,488
Fund balances—beginning [D]	$ 3,528,750	$ 2,742,799	$ 2,742,799
Fund balances—ending [A + B + C + D]	$ 2,956,523	$ 1,246,061	$ 1,432,253

Explanation of differences:

(1) (a) The City budgets for claims and compensated absences only to the extent expected to be paid, rather than on the modified accrual basis. (b) Encumbrances for equipment and supplies ordered but not received are reported in the *year the orders are placed* for budgetary purposes but are reported in the year the equipment and supplies are received for GAAP purposes. (c) Net Increase in fund balance—budget to GAAP

(2) The amount reported as "fund balance" on the budgetary basis of accounting derives from the basis of accounting used in preparing the City's budget. This amount differs from the fund balance reported in the statement of revenues, expenditures, and changes in fund balances because of the cumulative effect of transactions such as those described above.

	Variances		Budget to GAAP Differences Over (Under)	Actual Amounts GAAP Basis
	Original to Final	Final to Actual		
	$ (164,815)	$ (679,582)	$ —	$ 51,173,436
	(5,185)	189,368	—	13,025,392
	—	(111,854)	—	606,946
	—	161,194	—	2,287,794
	(334,538)	(451,422)	—	6,119,938
	(1,190,822)	172,310	—	11,374,460
	(465,945)	2,325	—	552,325
	(1,803,301)	(339,117)	—	881,874
	$ (3,964,606)	$ (1,056,778)	$ —	$ 86,022,165
	$ (2,369,379)	$ (846,655)	$ (9,335) (1)	$ 8,630,835
	932,740	(183,997)	70,086 (1)	33,729,623
	(189,782)	(32,661)	17,412 (1)	4,975,775
	715	—	(2,655) (1)	1,299,645
	418,403	—	104,621 (1)	6,070,032
	—	(18,195)	—	706,305
	308,930	(78,924)	(122,539) (1)	11,411,685
	—	(106,727)	—	21,893,273
	$ (898,373)	$ (1,267,159)	$ 57,590 (1)	$ 88,717,173
	$ (3,066,233)	$ 210,381	$ 57,590	$ (2,695,008)
	$ (809,525)	$ (677)	$ —	$ 129,323
	806,497	—	—	(2,163,759)
	$ (3,028)	$ (677)	$ —	$ (2,034,436)
	$ 2,144,750	$ (23,512)	$ —	$ 3,476,488
	$ (785,951)	$ —	$ 165,523 (2)	$ 2,908,322
	$ (1,710,462)	$ 186,192	$ 223,113	$ 1,655,366
			$ (129,100) (1a)	
			186,690 (1b)	
			$ 57,590 (1c)	

Source: Adapted from Dean Michael Mead. "Figure 16: Illustrative Budgetary Comparison Schedule," *What You Should Know about Your Local Government's Finances: A Guide to Financial Statements.* Norwalk, Conn.: GASB, 2000, pp. 72–73. Reprinted with permission.

EXHIBIT 13-12

Town of Millbridge
Financial Transactions (Journal and Ledger)
Prepared on a Modified Accrual Basis
For the Year Ending December 31, 2012

A. The General Fund

	Assets			=	Liabilities				Fund Balance
	Cash	Property Taxes Receivable	State Aid Receivable		Accounts Payable	Due to Debt Service Fund	Due to Capital Projects Fund	Salaries Payable	Fund Balance
Beginning Balance	$ 68,000	$ 25,000	$ 15,000		$ 5,000	$ 18,000	$ 70,000	$ 0	$ 15,000
Transaction 1a		611,000							611,000 Property Tax Revenues
Transaction 1b	600,000	(600,000)							
Transaction 2a	15,000		(15,000)						
Transaction 2b			150,000						150,000 State Aid Revenues
Transaction 2c	125,000		(125,000)						
Transaction 3	(580,000)							20,000	(300,000) General Government Expenditures (200,000) Public Safety Expenditures (100,000) Sanitation Expenditures
Transaction 4a	(5,000)				(5,000)				
Transaction 4b	(53,000)				7,000				(40,000) General Government Expenditures (15,000) Public Safety Expenditures (5,000) Sanitation Expenditures
Transaction 5	(97,000)					3,000			(100,000) Transfer to Debt Service Fund
Transaction 6									
Transaction 7	(63,000)						(63,000)		
Transaction 8a									
Transaction 8b									
Transaction 9									
Ending Balance	$ 10,000	$ 36,000	$ 25,000	=	$ 7,000	$ 21,000	$ 7,000	$20,000	$ 16,000

Liabilities and Fund Balance

EXHIBIT 13-12 Continued

B. The Debt Service Fund

	Assets		=	Liabilities and Fund Balance	
	Cash	**Due from General Fund**		**Liabilities**	**Fund Balance**
Beginning Balance	$ 10,000	$18,000		$0	$ 28,000
Transaction 1a					
Transaction 1b					
Transaction 2a					
Transaction 2b					
Transaction 2c					
Transaction 3					
Transaction 4a					
Transaction 4b					
Transaction 5	97,000	3,000			100,000 Transfer from General Fund
Transaction 6	(65,000)				(15,000) Interest Expenditure
					(50,000) Debt Service—Principal Expenditure
Transaction 7					
Transaction 8a					
Transaction 8b					
Transaction 9					
Ending Balance	$ 42,000	$21,000	=	$0	$ 63,000

C. The Capital Projects Fund

	Assets		=	Liabilities and Fund Balance	
	Cash	**Due from General Fund**		**Liabilities**	**Fund Balance**
Beginning Balance	$ 20,000	$ 70,000		$0	$ 90,000
Transaction 1a					
Transaction 1b					
Transaction 2a					
Transaction 2b					
Transaction 2c					
Transaction 3					
Transaction 4a					
Transaction 4b					
Transaction 5					
Transaction 6					
Transaction 7	63,000	(63,000)			
Transaction 8a	200,000				200,000 Other Sources of Financing—Bond Proceeds
Transaction 8b	(270,000)				(270,000) Capital Outlay Expenditure
Ending Balance	$ 13,000	$ 7,000	=	$0	$ 20,000

EXHIBIT 13-13 Governmental Funds Balance Sheet

Town of Millbridge
Balance Sheet
Governmental Funds
December 31, 2012

	General Fund	Debt Service Fund	Capital Projects Fund	Total Governmental Funds
Assets				
Cash	$10,000	$42,000	$13,000	$ 65,000
Property taxes receivable, net	36,000	—	—	36,000
State aid receivable	25,000	—	—	25,000
Due from other funds	—	21,000	7,000	28,000
Total assets	$71,000	$63,000	$20,000	$154,000
Liabilities and Fund Balances				
Liabilities:				
Accounts payable	$ 7,000	$ —	$ —	$ 7,000
Salaries payable	20,000	—	—	20,000
Due to debt service fund	21,000	—	—	21,000
Due to capital projects fund	7,000	—	—	7,000
Total liabilities	$55,000	$ —	$ —	$ 55,000
Fund Balances:				
Unreserved	$16,000	$63,000	$20,000	$ 99,000
Total fund balances	$16,000	$63,000	$20,000	$ 99,000
Total liabilities and fund balances	$71,000	$63,000	$20,000	

Reconciliation:

Amounts reported for governmental activities in the statement of net assets (Exhibit 13-16) are different because:

Inventory is treated on a purchases basis in the funds.	1,000
Capital assets used in governmental activities are not financial resources and therefore are not reported in the funds.	445,000
Long-term liabilities are not due and payable in the current period and therefore are not reported in the funds.	(440,000)
Net assets of governmental activities (Exhibit 13-16)	$105,000

Now examine Exhibit 13-14, the statement of revenues, expenditures, and changes in fund balances. The revenues and expenditures also come directly from the changes in the fund balance columns of Exhibit 13-12, Parts A, B, and C.

Reconciliations are required to show the connection between the government-wide statement of net assets and the governmental funds balance sheet, and between the government-wide statement of activities and the governmental funds statement of revenues, expenditures, and changes in fund balances. At the bottom of Exhibit 13-13, we can see that for this example there are three factors that explain the difference between the $99,000 total fund balance as reported on the governmental funds balance sheet and the $105,000 total net assets that will be reported on the government-wide statement of net assets. They are related to inventory, reporting capital assets, and long-term liabilities. These items are discussed subsequently.

EXHIBIT 13-14 Governmental Funds Statement of Revenues, Expenditures, and Changes in Fund Balances

Town of Millbridge
Statement of Revenues, Expenditures, and Changes in Fund Balances
Governmental Funds
For the Year Ending December 31, 2012

	General	Debt Service Fund	Capital Projects Fund	Total Governmental Funds
Revenues				
Property taxes	$ 611,000	$ —	$ —	$ 611,000
Fees	—	—	—	—
Permits	—	—	—	—
Intergovernmental—state aid	150,000	—	—	150,000
Charges for services	—	—	—	—
Investment earnings	—	—	—	—
Total revenues	$ 761,000	$ —	$ —	$ 761,000
Expenditures				
Current:				
General government	$ 340,000	$ —	$ —	$ 340,000
Public safety	215,000	—	—	215,000
Sanitation	105,000	—	—	105,000
Debt service:				
Principal	—	50,000	—	50,000
Interest and other charges	—	15,000	—	15,000
Capital outlay:	—	—	270,000	270,000
Total expenditures	$ 660,000	$ 65,000	$ 270,000	$ 995,000
Excess of Revenues Over Expenditures	$ 101,000	$ (65,000)	$(270,000)	$ (234,000)
Other Financing Sources (Uses)				
Proceeds from long-term capital related debt	$ —	$ —	$ 200,000	$ 200,000
Transfers in	—	100,000	—	100,000
Transfers out	(100,000)	—	—	(100,000)
Total other financing sources and uses	$(100,000)	$100,000	$ 200,000	$ 200,000
Net change in fund balances	$ 1,000	$ 35,000	$ (70,000)	$ (34,000)
Fund balances—beginning	15,000	28,000	90,000	133,000
Fund balances—ending	$ 16,000	$ 63,000	$ 20,000	$ 99,000

Exhibit 13-15 provides a reconciliation of the statement of revenues, expenditures, and changes in fund balances of governmental funds (Exhibit 13-14) to the statement of activities. In this reconciliation we can see that there were four reasons that the changes in fund balances on the governmental funds financial statement will differ from the change in net assets that we will see on the government-wide statement.

These relate to treatment of expenditures for supplies, bond proceeds, capital outlays, and a special item. These reconciling items are discussed subsequently as well.

GOVERNMENT-WIDE FINANCIAL STATEMENTS Exhibits 13-16 and 13-17 present the government-wide statement of net assets and statement of activities. Notice that there are

EXHIBIT 13-15 Reconciliation

Town of Millbridge
Reconciliation of the Statement of Revenues, Expenditures,
and Changes in Fund Balances of Governmental
Funds to the Statement of Activities
For the Year Ending December 31, 2012

Net change in fund balances—total governmental funds (Exhibit 13-14)	$(34,000)
Amounts reported for governmental activities in the statement of activities (Exhibit 13-17) are different because:	
1. Expenditures for supplies that have not been consumed require the use of current financial resources. However, on the statement of net assets they are treated as an inventory asset. This is the amount by which the expenditure for supplies exceeds the expense related to their consumption.	1,000
2. Bond proceeds provide current financial resources to governmental funds, but issuing debt increases long-term liabilities in the statement of net assets. Repayment of bond principal is an expenditure in the governmental funds, but the repayment reduces long-term liabilities in the statement of net assets. This is the amount by which proceeds exceeded repayments.	(150,000)
3. Governmental funds report capital outlays as expenditures. However, in the statement of activities, the cost of those assets is allocated over their estimated useful lives as depreciation expense. This is the amount by which capital outlays exceeded depreciation in the current period.	255,000
4. The special item related to a lawsuit settlement did not require current financial resources. However, in the statement of activities, this is treated as an expense for the current year.	(100,000)
Change in net assets of governmental activities (Exhibit 13-17)	$(28,000)

no amounts in the "Business-Type Activities" columns or in the "Component Units" column because Millbridge has neither business-type activities nor component units. These columns would not have to be shown since there is no information in them.

How are these statements derived? To prepare government-wide statements, the ending balances in the various governmental funds are aggregated. For example, consider the $65,000 of cash in the "Governmental Activities" column (Exhibit 13-16). It is the sum of the ending cash balance of $10,000 from the general fund, $42,000 from the debt service fund, and $13,000 from the capital projects fund. See Exhibit 13-12, Parts A, B, and C, respectively, for those amounts.

All of the other elements of these two statements can similarly be found by looking at the ending balances in Exhibit 13-12, and aggregating amounts for the different funds (as shown in Parts A, B, and C of the exhibit). For example, the Exhibit 13-16 balances for property tax receivables of $36,000 and state aid receivable of $25,000 come directly from the last row of Part A of Exhibit 13-12.

However, some adjustments are required because the government-wide statements are prepared on an accrual basis, while the governmental fund statements are prepared on a modified accrual basis. We can review the individual transactions in Chapter 12 to determine the necessary adjustments.

EXHIBIT 13-16 Government-Wide Statement of Net Assets

Town of Millbridge
Statement of Net Assets
December 31, 2012

	Primary Government			Component Units
	Governmental Activities	Business-Type Activities	Total	
Assets				
Cash	$ 65,000	$ —	$ 65,000	$ —
Property taxes receivable (net)	36,000	—	36,000	—
State aid receivable	25,000	—	25,000	—
Inventories	1,000	—	1,000	—
Capital assets, net	445,000	—	445,000	—
Total assets	$572,000	$ —	$572,000	$ —
Liabilities				
Accounts payable	$ 7,000	$ —	$ 7,000	$ —
Salaries payable	20,000	—	20,000	—
Current portion of long-term obligations	75,000	—	75,000	—
Noncurrent portion of long-term obligations	365,000	—	365,000	—
Total liabilities	$467,000	$ —	$467,000	$ —
Net Assets				
Invested in capital assets, net of related debt	$105,000	$ —	$105,000	$ —
Restricted for:				
Capital projects	20,000	—	20,000	—
Debt service	63,000	—	63,000	—
Unrestricted	(83,000)	—	(83,000)	—
Total net assets	$105,000	$ —	$105,000	$ —

The first two transactions (see pages 459–460) involve revenues. Since all of the revenues are expected to be received early in the next year, there is no adjustment. If some of the taxes or aid was not going to be received until late in the following year, it might not have been considered revenue under modified accrual. In that case, it would be adjusted to be shown as revenue on the accrual-based government-wide statements.

The third transaction (page 462), related to labor, does not require an adjustment because it would have been the same on an accrual basis.

The fourth transaction (pages 462–463) relates to supplies. On an accrual basis, the $1,000 of unused supplies would be shown as an inventory asset. This asset appears in Exhibit 13-16, the government-wide statement of net assets. It does not appear in Exhibit 13-13, the governmental funds balance sheet. This is because all of the supplies were treated as an expenditure under the modified accrual basis of accounting. The first reconciling item at the bottom of Exhibit 13-13 shows this $1,000 difference between the two statements.

EXHIBIT 13-17 Government-Wide Statement of Activities

Town of Millbridge
Statement of Activities
December 31, 2012

| Functions | Expenses | Program Revenues | | | Net (Expense) Revenue and Changes in Net Assets | | | Component Units |
| | | Charges for Services | Operating Grants and Contributions | Capital Grants and Contributions | Primary Government | | | |
					Governmental Activities	Business-Type Activities	Total	
Primary government								
Governmental activities								
General government	$339,000	$ 0	$ 0	$ 0	$(339,000)		$(339,000)	
Public safety	215,000	0	0	0	(215,000)		(215,000)	
Sanitation	120,000	0	0	0	(120,000)		(120,000)	
Interest on long-term debt	15,000	0	0	0	(15,000)		(15,000)	
Total governmental activities	$689,000	$ 0	$ 0	$ 0	$(689,000)		$(689,000)	
Business-type activities								
Total business-type activities	$ 0	$ 0	$ 0	$ 0		$ 0	$ 0	
Total primary government	$689,000	$ 0	$ 0	$ 0	$(689,000)		$(689,000)	
Component units								
None	$ 0	$ 0	$ 0	$ 0				$ 0
General revenues—Property tax					$ 611,000		$ 611,000	
General revenues—State aid					150,000		150,000	
Special items—Lawsuit settlement					(100,000)		(100,000)	
Total general revenues and special items					$ 661,000		$ 661,000	
Change in net assets					$ (28,000)		$ (28,000)	
Net assets—beginning					133,000		133,000	
Net assets—ending					$ 105,000	$	$ 105,000	$

As a result of recording the inventory asset under accrual accounting, the supply expense that was charged to the general government activity should be reduced by $1,000. Therefore, general government total expenditures are reduced from the $340,000 reported on Exhibit 13-14 to an expense of $339,000 shown on Exhibit 13-17. This $1,000 difference is explained in the first reconciling item in Exhibit 13-15.

Transaction 5 (page 463) involves transactions between governmental funds. These transactions have no impact on the government-wide statements, so no adjustment is required. When the governmental funds are combined to prepare the government-wide statements, these items offset each other and are not shown.

In transaction 6 (page 463), the $50,000 principal payment was an expenditure. Under accrual accounting, the principal payment would instead be a decrease in a long-term liability. Note also that for transaction 8 (page 464), the $200,000 of bond proceeds would create a liability under accrual rather than being treated as an increase in fund balance. These two differences [$50,000–$200,000 = $(150,000)] are explained by the second reconciling item in Exhibit 13-15.

From transaction 6 we can also determine that there should be $15,000 of depreciation expense for the garbage trucks under accrual accounting. That will be charged to the sanitation function. As a result of recording this depreciation expense under accrual, the $105,000 sanitation expenditure that appears on Exhibit 13-14 becomes a $120,000 expense on Exhibit 13-17. From transaction 8 we note that there was a $270,000 capital outlay for a firehouse building acquisition. Under accrual accounting, that would create a long-term asset rather than being an expenditure. The impact of recording the $270,000 firehouse capital asset increase, less the $15,000 of depreciation expense on the garbage trucks [$270,000–$15,000 = $255,000], is explained in the third reconciling item in Exhibit 13-15.

Transaction 7 (pages 463–464) does not require any adjustments. The transaction results in offsetting entries within the governmental funds. These entries cancel each other out and do not appear on the government-wide statements.

Transaction 9 (page 464) was not recorded under modified accrual because the payment was not going to be made from currently available funds. However, under accrual accounting, a liability must be recorded. The full $100,000 must be treated as an expense and as a long-term liability.[16] It is tempting to assign the expense to the public safety function (since the alleged harassment took place in the police department). However, if this was a fairly unusual and infrequent type of an expense for Millbridge, it should be segregated as a special item. Otherwise, a user of the financial statements might assume that the typical, ongoing costs of the public safety function are $100,000 per year more than they really are. This expense, which appears as a special item in Exhibit 13-17, does not appear on Exhibit 13-14. It is explained by the fourth reconciling item in Exhibit 13-15.

The preceding discussion provides all the information needed to prepare the government-wide statement of activities (Exhibit 13-17). A few more elements are needed to understand the source of all of the numbers in the statement of net assets (Exhibit 13-16). First we consider the capital assets that appear in Exhibit 13-16 but not in Exhibit 13-13. They are shown in the statement of net assets as being $445,000, net (of accumulated depreciation). In transaction 6 we are told that the beginning balance in capital assets, net, for the year was $190,000. From the same transaction we also know that under accrual accounting this amount must be reduced by $15,000 for depreciation. From transaction 8 we know that it must be increased by $270,000 for the purchase of a new firehouse. The beginning balance,

---

[16] Under GAAP used for organizations other than governments, we would record an expense and liability equal to the present value of the future $100,000 payment. However, GASB does not require use of present value for such liabilities.

less the depreciation, plus the acquisition, totals to $445,000 ($190,000 − $15,000 + $270,000). This amount is explained by the second reconciling item at the bottom of Exhibit 13-13.

Exhibit 13-16 also shows long-term obligations that do not appear on Exhibit 13-13. Transaction 6 gave the opening balance of long-term obligations as $190,000. During the year $50,000 was repaid (transaction 6), lowering the liability to $140,000. However, $200,000 was borrowed (transaction 8), raising the total long-term obligation related to capital assets to $340,000. In addition, the lawsuit settlement (transaction 9) results in another $100,000 long-term liability. The total long-term obligation is therefore $440,000, and that amount is explained in the last reconciliation on the bottom of Exhibit 13-13.

To prepare the statement of net assets (Exhibit 13-16), the government must know how much of its long-term debt is payable in the coming year. Assume that $75,000 must be paid during the coming year as principal payments for the garbage trucks and the firehouse. That amount is the current portion of the long-term liabilities, and the remaining $365,000 is the noncurrent portion.

Finally, we need to understand the derivation of the components of net assets in Exhibit 13-16. The portion of net assets invested in capital assets is simply the $445,000 of capital assets calculated previously, less the $340,000 of long-term obligations related to capital assets (i.e., the total long-term obligation of $440,000 calculated previously, less the $100,000 related to the lawsuit). The resulting amount is $105,000 (i.e., $445,000 − $340,000), as seen in Exhibit 13-16.

Assume that by legal restriction the assets of the debt service fund are restricted to debt service and the assets of the capital projects fund are restricted to specific capital projects. Therefore, the total of the ending balances for the assets in Part B of Exhibit 13-12 less liabilities (there are none in this case) provides the ending restricted fund balance (or net assets) of $63,000 for debt service. Similarly, the total of the assets in Part C of Exhibit 13-12 less liabilities gives the ending restricted net assets of $20,000 for capital projects. These amounts appear under the restricted net assets heading in Exhibit 13-16.

The unrestricted net asset balance is the portion of total net assets that have not been restricted for one of the other purposes listed in the net assets section of the statement. The $71,000 total of the general fund ending asset balances from Exhibit 13-12, Part A, plus the inventory of $1,000 and the capital assets of $445,000 (from the previous adjustments) is $517,000. The $55,000 total of the liability balances from Exhibit 13-12, Part A, and the long-term obligation of $440,000 (from the previous adjustments) equals $495,000. The assets less the liabilities equals the net assets of the general fund, $22,000. Once the net assets of the general fund are found, the $105,000 portion of net assets that is restricted for capital assets must be deducted. This leaves an unrestricted net assets balance of ($83,000).[17] We see this amount in Exhibit 13-16.

We do not have budget information in this example. However, if we did, the government would also prepare a budgetary comparison schedule. A set of notes to the financial statements, MD&A, and other RSI would also be critical parts of the reported information.

Furthermore, this example has only looked at governmental funds. Proprietary and fiduciary funds would also be reported if they existed. However, the fiduciary funds would

---

[17] The assets of the general fund are $10,000 cash plus $36,000 taxes receivable, plus $25,000 aid receivable, plus $1,000 inventory, plus $445,000 capital assets net of accumulated depreciation, for a total of $517,000. The general fund liabilities are $7,000 accounts payable, plus $21,000 due to the debt service fund, plus $7,000 due to the capital projects fund, plus $20,000 salaries payable, plus $440,000 long-term liabilities, for a total of $495,000. The net assets of the general fund are the $517,000 of assets less the $495,000 of liabilities, or $22,000. Since $105,000 of the general fund net assets are invested in capital assets, the unrestricted net assets are the $22,000 total less the $105,000 portion invested in capital assets, or ($83,000).

EXHIBIT 13-18 Key Characteristics of Government Financial Statements

	Government-Wide Financial Statements	Governmental Fund Financial Statements	Proprietary Fund Financial Statements
Accrual	X		X
Modified accrual		X	
Reports buildings and depreciation	X		X
Reports major funds in separate columns		X	X
Reports governmental activities and business-type activities in different columns	X		
Cash flow statement			X
Reports financial results of component units	X		

not be included in the government-wide statements, as discussed earlier. Exhibit 13-18 provides a summary of some key characteristics to keep in mind in preparing government financial statements.

FEDERAL GOVERNMENT ACCOUNTING

This chapter focuses on financial reporting issues for state and local governments. Granof notes that, "Federal accounting historically has been decentralized among the government's various agencies and departments, with each agency and department having its own accounting system and preparing independent reports."[18] However, the federal government has recently adopted the accrual basis of accounting.

Accounting in the federal government is subject to decisions made by three principal bodies: the Treasury, the Office of Management and Budget (OMB), and the Government Accountability Office (GAO), which have varying degrees of jurisdiction over federal government accounting. There is another group, the Federal Accounting Standards Advisory Board (FASAB), which can recommend federal accounting standards. The FASAB has made a number of accounting recommendations in recent years that have been adopted by the Treasury, OMB, and GAO.

Federal government accounting information is used for widely differing purposes, ranging from budget preparation to issues of economic stimulation and wealth redistribution. The FASAB lists the primary objectives of federal financial reporting to be budgetary integrity, operating performance, stewardship, and systems and control.[19]

It appears that progress is being made in terms of creating more uniformity and logic in federal accounting. At least for the foreseeable future, however, individuals working in any specific federal government department or agency will need to become familiar with the particular financial reporting rules and approaches used by that department or agency.

---

[18] Granof, p. 644.
[19] Statement of Federal Financial Accounting. Concepts No. 1, *Objectives of Federal Financial Reporting.* September 1993.

Summary

There are a number of unique features to accounting for state and local governments. Such governments have a complex set of reporting requirements.

Many government bodies prepare a *Comprehensive Annual Financial Report (CAFR)* as required by GAAP. Included as part of that report is a set of audited basic financial statements (BFS). In these statements, governments focus on reporting for the entity as a whole. This is accomplished by the use of government-wide statements prepared on an accrual basis. However, governments also report more detailed fund financial information. In addition to the BFS, GAAP require state and local governments to provide a management's discussion and analysis (MD&A) section and other required supplementary information (RSI). One element of the other RSI is a comparison of actual results with authorized budgets.

Preview

Chapters 14 and 15, Part V of this book, consider how the information from financial statements can be analyzed to gain additional insight into the financial situation of the organization. Chapter 14 focuses on a general framework for financial statement analysis. Chapter 15 focuses on special concerns in the analysis of the financial condition of governments.

There are many potential purposes of financial analysis. Managers must understand the financial situation of the organization to assess its ability to achieve its mission and to improve its results. Donors desire to evaluate organizations to which they are considering making a contribution. Vendors want to understand whether their customers will be able to pay for their purchases. Lenders want to consider the likelihood of an organization being able to repay loans.

For most organizations, the primary focus of financial analysis is on the audited financial statements. The statements themselves are reviewed, the contents of the notes that accompany audited financial statements are carefully considered, and a set of ratios are calculated. Finally, all of the information gathered is brought together and an assessment is made based on the information as a whole. These activities are the subject of Chapter 14.

Government financial condition analysis also requires an understanding of many factors external to the organization. Governmental financial analysis must take into account factors such as debt per capita, tax rates, and citizen income and wealth. The special issues related to evaluating the financial condition of a government are the focus of Chapter 15.

Key Terms from This Chapter

agency fund.   Fund that accounts for money the government holds as an agent for some other organization in a temporary, purely custodial capacity.

basic financial statements (BFS).   Financial statements that must be included in a government annual report to comply with GAAP under GASB Statement No. 34. The required statements are a government-wide *statement of net assets*, a government-wide *statement of activities*, fund financial statements for the governmental, proprietary, and fiduciary funds, and notes to the financial statements.

budgetary basis of accounting.   The basis of accounting (e.g., cash, accrual, modified accrual) that is used in preparing the budget.

budgetary comparison schedule.   See *budgetary comparison statement.*

budgetary comparison statement.   A financial statement that compares the budgeted and actual results for revenues and expenditures.

capital projects fund.   Fund used to account for major acquisitions of plant or equipment.

component units. Governmental bodies that are legally separate from the *primary government*, but for which there is some close financial relationship. For example, the primary government might be obligated to pay any debts of a component unit if it cannot make payment, or the primary government might be able to impose its will on a component unit.

Comprehensive Annual Financial Report (CAFR). Official annual financial report prepared by many governments.

debt service fund. Fund used to account for the accumulation of resources to pay principal and interest on long-term debt.

enterprise fund. Fund used to account for government services provided in a business-like fashion, charging the public for services consumed, such as a golf course fund.

expendable fund. Fund for which all of the money in the fund may be spent, such as an unemployment compensation fund.

fiduciary funds. *Trust* or *agency funds* used to account for resources that the government holds as a trustee or agent.

fund balance. The equivalent of owners' equity or net assets; assets less liabilities.

general fund. Fund that is used for the routine, ordinary activities of government. The general fund is similar to the operating fund or unrestricted fund in not-for-profit organizations.

Governmental Accounting Standards Board (GASB). Authoritative body that develops governmental Generally Accepted Accounting Principles.

governmental fund. Fund used by governments to track the sources, uses, and balances of resources that are not tracked separately in *proprietary* or *fiduciary* funds. Governmental funds include the *general fund, special revenue fund, capital projects fund, debt service fund* and *permanent fund.*

infrastructure. Stationary assets with extremely long lifetimes. This includes bridges, tunnels, dams, roads, and similar assets.

intergenerational equity. See *interperiod equity.*

internal service fund. Fund established for elements of government that provide specific services to other government units, such as car pool services.

interperiod equity. Equity that results from using revenues from the current period to pay for only services provided in the current period. A surplus for this year implies that one is taking resources from the current taxpayers to provide benefits for future taxpayers. A deficit implies that current taxpayers are consuming resources that will have to be paid for by future taxpayers. Thus, a surplus or deficit might be considered to create interperiod inequity.

major funds. The general fund and other important funds and funds that represent a substantial portion of the assets, liabilities, revenues, or expenditures/expenses of their class or type of fund.

management's discussion and analysis (MD&A). An analysis of the government's financial activities prepared by the government and based on currently known facts, decisions, or conditions.

nonexpendable fund. Fund in which only a portion of the money in the fund can be spent.

permanent fund. Fund that cannot be expended, similar to endowment fund.

primary government. A state or local governmental body that has a separately elected governing body and is legally and financially separate from other governments.

proprietary fund. Fund that is used to account for the business-type activities of a government.

required supplementary information (RSI). Information that must be included along with the basic financial statements to present a fair representation of a government's finances in accordance with GAAP.

special revenue fund. Fund used for specific identifiable purposes; similar to restricted fund for not-for-profit organizations.

statement of activities. Statement that provides information about the revenues and expenses of the government as a whole, as well as other changes in net assets.

statement of net assets. Balance sheet presented in a format of assets less liabilities equal net assets.

trust fund. Fund established when money is given to the government under the legal terms of a trust. Trusts require that the money be used in a specific manner or for specific purposes.

Questions for Discussion

13-1. What are the objectives of governmental financial reporting?

13-2. What is a CAFR? Discuss.

13-3. Describe the contents of the MD&A.

13-4. What do BFS contain? Discuss.

13-5. How does one decide what entities to include in the government's BFS?

13-6. What bases of accounting are used in the BFS?

13-7. Will long-term assets appear on the governmental funds balance sheet? Why?

Problem

13-8. For Simonsen Village (see Problems 12-4 and 12-5 from Chapter 12), prepare a government-wide statement of net assets and statement of activities, and a governmental funds balance sheet and statement of revenues, expenditures, and changes in fund balances. Any ending balance in the Debt Service Fund is legally restricted to debt service payments on the firetruck. Also prepare reconciliations for the differences between the governmental and government-wide financial statements. (Hint: The reconciliations require you to determine what would differ under accrual accounting compared with modified accrual.)

Suggested Readings

American Institute of Certified Public Accountants. *AICPA Audit and Accounting Guide: Audits of State and Local Governments with Conforming Changes as of May 1, 2007.* New York, N.Y.: AICPA, 2007.

Anderson, John E. *Public Finance—Principles and Policy.* New York, N.Y.: Houghton Mifflin Company, 2003.

Freeman, Robert J., Craig D. Shoulders, and Gregory Allison *Governmental and Non-Profit Accounting*, 8th ed. Upper Saddle River, N.J.: Prentice Hall, 2006.

Governmental Accounting Standards Board. Statement No. 34. *Basic Financial Statements and Management's Discussion and Analysis—for State and Local Governments.* Norwalk, Conn.: Financial Accounting Foundation, 1999.

Granof, Michael H. *Government and Not-for-Profit Accounting: Concepts and Practices*, 4th ed. New York, N.Y.: John Wiley & Sons, 2007.

Hyde, Albert C. *Government Budgeting: Theory, Process, Politics*, 3rd ed. Belmont, Ca.: Wadsworth/Thomson Learning, 2002.

Mead, Dean Michael. *What You Should Know about Your Local Government's Finances: A Guide to Financial Statements.* Norwalk, Conn.: Governmental Accounting Standards Board, 2000.

——. *What You Should Know about Your School District's Finances: A Guided Tour of Financial Statements.* Norwalk, Conn.: Governmental Accounting Standards Board, 2000.

Razek, Joseph R., Martin R. Ives, and Gordon A. Hosch. *Introduction to Government and Non-for-Profit Accounting*, 5th ed. Upper Saddle River, N.J.: Prentice Hall, 2004.

Ruppel, Warren. *Wiley GAAP for Governments 2007: Interpretation and Application of Generally Accepted Accounting Principles for State and Local Governments.* New York, N.Y.: John Wiley & Sons, 2007.

Wilson, Earl R., and Susan C. Kattelus. *Accounting for Governmental and Nonprofit Entities*, 13th ed. Boston, Mass.: McGraw Hill Irwin, 2004.

APPENDIX 13-A

Interrelationships among Government Financial Statements

The transfers shown in Exhibit 13-7, the statement of revenues, expenses, and changes in fund net assets, provide a good example of some of the interrelationships among the various financial statements. Transfers are amounts provided by one fund to another.

In Exhibit 13-2, the government-wide statement of activities, we see a transfer of $501,409 into the "Governmental Activities" column and out of the "Business-Type Activities" column. In Exhibit 13-7, we see that there is a transfer out of $501,409 in the "Totals" column for the "Business-Type Activities—Enterprise Funds." The activities that the government operates that are accounted for in the enterprise funds have transferred $501,409 to the governmental activities of the government, and this transfer appears on the government-wide statement, Exhibit 13-2.

In Exhibit 13-7 we see that there is also a transfer of $175,033 out of the internal service funds. But that transfer does not show up in Exhibit 13-2. The transfer is not coming from the enterprise funds. Rather, it is being made from proprietary funds that relate to governmental activities. And it is being transferred to the governmental funds that also relate to governmental activities. Since the transfer out and the transfer in both relate to governmental activities, these transfers offset each other and do not appear on the government-wide statement of activities.

Does that mean we cannot trace the $175,033 transfer from the proprietary funds to where it goes? No. Look at Exhibit 13-4, the statement of revenues, expenditures, and changes in fund balances for the governmental funds. The total transfers in are $5,680,510 and the total transfers out are $5,004,068. What accounts for the $676,442 difference between these two numbers? It is exactly the sum of the two transfers out that appear on the proprietary funds statement of revenues, expenses, and changes in fund net assets, Exhibit 13-7!

From this we can surmise that all transfers out on Exhibit 13-4, the full $5,004,068, are transfers from some of the funds that appear in that exhibit to other funds in the exhibit. All of that movement is from governmental funds to governmental funds. Such offsetting amounts would not appear in Exhibit 13-2, which summarizes governmental activities in one column. However, they do appear in the fund financial statements. In addition, $501,409 from the business-type activities and $175,033 from the governmental activities in Exhibit 13-7 are transferred to the governmental funds in Exhibit 13-4. Thus, total transfers in to governmental funds are $5,680,510, as we see in the "Transfers in" line in the last column of Exhibit 13-4.

Notice also that the business-type activities ending total net assets, shown in the last line of Exhibit 13-7, are $85,569,194. This amount also appears in the last row, total net assets, of Exhibit 13-1, the government-wide statement of net assets. What about the internal service funds $2,994,691 ending total net assets from Exhibit 13-7? Where does this number appear in the Exhibit 13-1 government-wide statement of net assets? These net assets relate to governmental activities. Therefore, they must be included in the $123,558,874 governmental activities total net assets in Exhibit 13-1. Looking at the bottom of Exhibit 13-3, the balance sheet for the governmental funds, we see that the internal service fund ending net assets of $2,994,691 has been accounted for as part of the reconciliation at the bottom of the page. The ending net assets from the internal service funds in Exhibit 13-7 are added to the ending fund balance of the governmental funds on Exhibit 13-3 to arrive at the net assets for governmental activities that are reported in Exhibit 13-1. We note from this that the term "governmental activities" is clearly not synonymous with governmental funds. It includes all activity from the governmental funds and also includes governmental activity from the proprietary funds as well.

14

Financial Statement Analysis

The learning objectives of this chapter are to:

- discuss the elements of financial statement analysis, including review of the financial statements, examination of the notes that accompany the financial statements, calculation of ratios, and final assessment;

- explain the parts of a financial statement review, including the audit opinion letter and the individual financial statements;

- explain the importance of examining the notes that accompany the financial statements and discuss the note that focuses on significant accounting policies, as well as other more specific notes;

- define ratio analysis and discuss the role that ratios play in assessing the financial situation of an organization;

- explain the importance of comparing the organization's ratios with its own ratios over time, as well as those of comparable organizations, and the industry as a whole;

- provide cautions in the use of ratio analysis;

- define and explain a number of major classes of ratios and specific individual ratios that are of value in financial statement analysis; and

- discuss the importance of bringing all of the information together to make a final financial assessment of the organization.

INTRODUCTION

Chapters 9 to 13, Part IV of this book, focused on reporting results using financial accounting. The role of financial accounting is to gather, summarize, and report information about the financial history of the organization. The financial statements discussed in the preceding chapters are the vehicle used to communicate the results of operations and the financial position of the entity. The focus of this chapter and the next is on how that information can be analyzed to gain additional insight into the financial situation of the organization. This chapter focuses on a general framework for financial statement analysis. Chapter 15 focuses on special concerns in the analysis of the financial condition of governments.

The two chapters also consider other indirect sources and types of information that may be valuable in understanding the finances of an organization. For example, comparison of the organization's financial results with those of similar organizations can be particularly enlightening. The same is true for comparisons with the organization's industry as a whole.

There are many potential purposes of financial analysis. Managers must understand the financial situation of the organization to assess its ability to achieve its mission. They will want to understand their organization's financial position and results so that they can make decisions that will maintain a satisfactory financial situation or improve an unsatisfactory one. Managers also want to compare the financial performance of their organization with similar organizations to learn if perhaps they could improve their organization's performance.

Donors desire to evaluate organizations to which they are considering making a contribution. Vendors want to understand whether their customers will be able to pay for their purchases. Lenders want to consider the likelihood of an organization being able to repay loans. These represent just a few of the many uses of financial information.

Different users and different uses of information call for different types of information. Some users want an assessment of the likelihood of repayment of a loan due in 20 years. That requires some prediction of long-term *solvency*. Vendors may only be concerned with short-term liquidity: Will the organization be able to make payments next month for its purchases this month? Before investing in an entity, we may wish to know about its profitability. Before making a donation, we may wish to know how much of the money spent by the organization goes to program rather than support services. The goal of financial analysis is to use financial statements and other sources to gather the information needed to answer questions and make decisions.

For most organizations, the primary focus of financial analysis is on the audited financial statements. The statements themselves are reviewed, the contents of the notes that accompany audited financial statements are carefully considered, and a set of ratios are calculated. The notes to financial statements are critical because financial statements alone are often inadequate to convey all important financial information. The Generally Accepted Accounting Principle (GAAP) of *full disclosure* requires that notes be used to convey important financial information that the financial statements do not adequately disclose. *Ratio analysis* compares numbers from financial statements with each other to gain insight from the relationship between the numbers. Finally, all of the information gathered is brought together, and an assessment is made based on the information as a whole.

FINANCIAL STATEMENT REVIEW

A good place to commence a *financial statement analysis* is by carefully and thoroughly reading the financial statements and the accompanying notes. Ratios should then be calculated and comparative data should be obtained if possible. Finally, based on a review of all data, an assessment can be made about the financial status of the organization.

In reviewing the financial statements, three overriding concerns are as follows: (1) Is the organization accomplishing its mission? (2) Is the organization financially stable? and (3) Are the results of operations acceptable? By looking at the financial statements, we are not just looking for numbers; we are also trying to gain an insight as to what has happened to the organization and where it is today. The Certified Public Accountant's (CPA's) opinion letter and management's discussion are other elements of an annual report that should be included in the review process.

Trend information often makes analysis easier and more fruitful. If possible, analysis should use financial statements that show more than one year of information. If such statements are not available, the individual annual financial statements from several preceding years can provide comparable data. In reviewing the statements, changes should be noted. If the changes appear significant in amount, one would want to try to investigate them to determine why they occurred and whether they represent a trend that is likely to continue.

The Audit and the Auditor's Opinion Letter

A *financial audit*, or simply an *audit*, is a detailed examination of the financial statements and financial records of an organization. *Audited financial statements* are financial statements that have been examined by a CPA. The CPA issues an opinion letter, called the *auditor's report*, providing expert opinion about whether the financial statements provide a fair representation of the organization's financial position and the results of its operations. As an outsider, the auditor provides an independent review of the financial statements. The discovery of fraud is an occasional by-product but is not the primary focus of the audit. The primary focus is on whether the financial statements are in compliance with GAAP and are free of material misstatements.

Note that it is the accountant who is certified (by a state licensing board) and not the financial statements, although often people refer to audited financial statements as the "certified financials."

In some cases, the auditor is hired to do something less than an audit. Small organizations, including many not-for-profits, are not required to have an audit by a CPA, which can be quite costly. Sometimes such organizations will employ a CPA to perform a *compilation* or *review of financial statements*. In a compilation engagement, the auditor is hired to develop a set of financial statements. The auditor takes the information that has been recorded by the organization during the year and summarizes that information into a set of financial statements that report the results of operations and the financial position of the organization. In a review engagement, the organization has prepared the financial statements, and the CPA reviews them for form and accuracy. However, in neither a compilation nor a review engagement does the CPA perform the extensive testing of records and detailed review that are part of an audit. The statements compiled or reviewed may not be referred to as audited or certified financials.

One of the major functions of an audit is to review not only specific transactions but also systems. It is too expensive to review every single transaction and find every error that has been made. Instead, auditors use sampling techniques to determine how often errors are occurring and how large they tend to be. If an unacceptable level of errors is occurring, the auditor works with the organization to improve its internal control systems (see Chapter 8). The auditor will send a letter, referred to as the *management* letter, to the organization's management discussing its internal control weaknesses. That letter does not become part of the annual report issued to outsiders.

The management letter, written by the auditor, should not be confused with a separate letter called *management's discussion*, which is written by the organization's management and discusses their assessment of the organization's performance.

In addition to the management letter, the auditor issues an *opinion letter*. This letter follows a standard format, with much of the same wording used for many different organizations. The following auditor's *opinion* letter for The Fresh Air Fund is provided as an example:

Report of Independent Auditors[1]

To the Board of Directors of
    The Fresh Air Fund

We have audited the accompanying statements of financial position of The Fresh Air Fund (the "Fund") as of September 30, 2007 and 2006, and the related statements of activities, functional expenses, and cash flows for the years then ended. These financial statements are the responsibility of the Fund's management. Our responsibility is to express an opinion on these financial statements based on our audits.

---

[1] *Source:* The Fresh Air Fund. *Financial Statements: Years Ended September 30, 2007 and 2006 with Report of the Independent Auditors.* Reprinted with permission of The Fresh Air Fund.

We conducted our audits in accordance with auditing standards generally accepted in the United States of America. Those standards require that we plan and perform the audit to obtain reasonable assurance about whether the financial statements are free of material misstatement. An audit includes examining, on a test basis, evidence supporting the amounts and disclosures in the financial statements. An audit also includes assessing the accounting principles used and significant estimates made by management, as well as evaluating the overall financial statement presentation. We believe that our audits provide a reasonable basis for our opinion.

In our opinion, the financial statements referred to above present fairly, in all material respects, the financial position of The Fresh Air Fund as of September 30, 2007 and 2006, and the changes in its net assets and its cash flows for the years then ended in conformity with accounting principles generally accepted in the United States of America.

Marks Paneth & Shron LLP

January 9, 2008

The first, introductory, paragraph explains what type of job the auditor was hired to do. Sometimes auditors do consulting or tax work, or are hired to perform a compilation or review. The paragraph indicates that in this instance an audit was performed and indicates the specific financial statements that were included in the audit process. For The Fresh Air Fund the CPA firm of Mark Paneth & Shron LLP[2] audited the statements of financial position, as of September 30, 2007 and 2006, and the related statements of activities, functional expenses, and cash flows for the years then ended. Note that since a balance sheet shows the financial position at a moment in time, the letter refers to the statements of financial position as of a particular date, September 30 of each of the years covered by the audit. The other statements provide information on what has happened over a period of time. They are grouped together with an indication that they cover the "years then ended."

The first paragraph of the letter points out that although the auditor can provide an expert opinion, management holds primary responsibility for the contents of the financial statements. In some organizations, the auditors, in practice, provide a substantial amount of help in compiling the financial statements as part of the audit. Nevertheless, managers must remember that if there are later problems with the information contained in the financial statements, it is the organization's management, rather than the auditors, who bear the primary responsibility for their content. Regardless of who actually prepares the statements, managers should assure themselves that they understand their statements and agree with the estimates made and the contents of the statements.

The second, scope, paragraph of the audit letter explains the type of work the auditor did to ensure that the financial statements were in compliance with GAAP. Its purpose is to clarify that not every transaction was examined and that immaterial errors were not necessarily found and corrected. The types and extent of examinations that are undertaken as part of the audit are dictated by generally accepted auditing standards that CPAs follow in carrying out their audit.

The third, opinion, paragraph gives the auditor's opinion on whether the financial statements provide a fair representation of the financial position and results of operations in accordance with GAAP. It is unusual and serious if the statements are not a fair representation (adverse opinion) in the opinion of the auditor. Some auditors condense the information from all three of these paragraphs into one paragraph.

The reader should also carefully examine any additional paragraphs beyond the standard three, or the one condensed paragraph. In the Fresh Air Fund letter, there are no additional

---

[2] LLP stands for Limited Liability Partnership. Generally the partnership business form, unlike corporations, does not limit the liability of its owners. LLP is a legal form of business organization that allows the business to operate as a partnership but provides legal liability protection to its owners.

paragraphs. In other instances, additional paragraphs might call the reader's attention to a particularly important note, such as one regarding a major lawsuit against the organization.

The auditor's letter often appears to be standard and contain nothing out of the ordinary. Nevertheless, it should always be reviewed as one of the first steps. If it does have anything out of the ordinary, it is worth giving it careful attention. Once the audit letter has been reviewed, the next step in financial statement analysis is to thoroughly review the financial statements. We begin with a discussion of the balance sheet.

The Balance Sheet

Exhibit 14-1 provides comparative statements of financial position (balance sheets) for the hypothetical Meals for the Homeless. (Note that this is a new example. The numbers in the Meals for the Homeless Financial Statements in this chapter are not the same as those in Chapters 10 and 11.) *Comparative financial statements* present financial information for more than one fiscal period. Each number on the balance sheet should be examined.

The first section of the balance sheet is current assets. Current assets are the most liquid of the firm's resources. They generally represent resources that will become cash or will be used up within one year. In Exhibit 14-1, one of the first things we notice is that total current assets have increased from $48,100 to $61,100. At the same time, on the liability side of the balance sheet, we see that current liabilities, which will have to be paid in the near

---

EXHIBIT 14-1

Meals for the Homeless
Statements of Financial Position
As of December 31, 2012 and 2011

Assets			Liabilities and Net Assets		
	2012	2011		2012	2011
Current Assets			*Liabilities*		
Cash	$ 100	$ 3,100	Current Liabilities		
Marketable securities	3,000	3,000	Wages payable	$ 2,000	$ 3,000
Accounts receivable, net of			Accounts payable	2,000	3,000
estimated uncollectibles of			Notes payable	6,000	5,000
$8,000 and $7,000	55,000	38,000	Current portion of		
Inventory (LIFO basis)	2,000	4,000	mortgage payable	4,000	5,000
Prepaid expenses	1,000	0	Total Current Liabilities	$ 14,000	$ 16,000
Total Current Assets	$ 61,100	$ 48,100			
			Long-Term Liabilities		
Long-Term Assets			Mortage payable	$ 12,000	$ 16,000
Cash restricted for building and			Total Long-Term Liabilities	$ 12,000	$ 16,000
equipment acquisition	$ 900	$ 900	*Total Liabilities*	$ 26,000	$ 32,000
Fixed assets					
Property	40,000	40,000	*Net Assets*		
Equipment, net	35,000	45,000	Unrestricted	$ 84,100	$ 85,100
Investments	8,000	12,000	Temporarily restricted	4,900	1,900
Total Long-Term Assets	$ 83,900	$ 97,900	Permanently restricted	30,000	27,000
			Total Net Assets	$119,000	$114,000
Total Assets	$145,000	$146,000	*Liabilities and Net Assets*	$145,000	$146,000

The accompanying notes are an integral part of these statements.

term, fell from $16,000 to $14,000. The increase in current assets during a period when there is a decrease in current liabilities, by itself, is a good thing.

It is important, however, to review critically all numbers rather than just summary ones. Although current assets increased, most of the increase is in accounts receivable. In fact, cash has declined from $3,100 to $100. Even though current assets seem adequate overall, one might question whether the $100 is adequate cash on hand to meet obligations as they come due. Furthermore, the increase in accounts receivable is a concern. If this is the result of increased revenues, then it is a positive sign. However, if revenues have not increased substantially, this is more likely to be indicative of problems collecting receivables. In that case, it may be a flag that a problem exists.

All assets that are not current assets fall into the general category of long-term assets. Prominent among the long-term assets are fixed assets, or property, plant, and equipment. Meals' long-term assets have declined from $97,900 to $83,900. The largest element in this decline is a $10,000 reduction in equipment, net of depreciation. This indicates that the equipment of the organization is aging faster than it is being replaced. Depending on the specific circumstances of the organization, this might or might not be cause for concern. For example, if Meals had 10 delivery vans and a goal to replace two each year, the purchases of two new vans would offset the depreciation on the 10 vans. Given inflation, the new vans would cost more than the old ones, and we should see equipment gradually rise on the balance sheet each year. However, if Meals has only one van, it would not be surprising to see equipment, net of accumulated depreciation, decline from year to year until the year that the van is replaced.

We also note that investments declined from $12,000 to $8,000. Perhaps investments were sold to provide cash due to a shortfall from operations. If that is the case, it will show up on the cash flow statement. Alternatively, perhaps the market value of the investments has declined. We can look for more clues in the activity statement. Note that the first review of financial statements is a process that tends to raise more questions than it answers.

Long-term liabilities include any recorded liabilities that are not current liabilities. The only long-term liability for Meals is a mortgage. Note that the part of the mortgage that is due in the coming year is shown as a current liability. Overall, the mortgage for Meals has declined from the end of 2011 to the end of 2012. This is a positive indicator. It would be desirable, however, for the long-term liability reduction to be as great as the reduction in long-term assets. That was not the case for Meals.

The last thing we note in the case of the balance sheet for Meals is that although its total assets are approximately the same in both years and the total liabilities and net assets are approximately the same from 2011 to 2012 year-end, the net assets have increased by $5,000 from $114,000 to $119,000. A healthy, thriving organization generally requires at least a modest increase in net assets over time. In sum, Meals has performed reasonably in this area. The details of the increase will become apparent as we review the other financial statements.

The Activity Statement

The comparative activity statements (sometimes called operating statements, income statements, statements of revenues and expenses, or statements of revenues and expenditures) are shown in Exhibit 14-2. Revenues and support have increased by $9,000 from $169,000 to $178,000. This is a positive sign. However, it is not a large enough increase to explain the $17,000 increase in accounts receivable that was noted when reviewing the balance sheet. This change would therefore warrant further investigation. It is a potential sign of problems with management of the collections process.

Examination of the individual revenue and support items shows that foundation grants are up sharply, by $10,000. However, there is a disturbing decline in contributions to $65,000,

EXHIBIT 14-2

Meals for the Homeless
Activity Statements
For the Years Ending December 31, 2012 and 2011

	2012	2011
Changes in Unrestricted Net Assets		
Revenues and support		
Client revenue	$ 11,000	$ 9,000
City revenue	20,000	16,000
County revenue	10,000	10,000
Foundation grants	60,000	50,000
Annual ball	12,000	11,000
Contributions	65,000	73,000
Total Revenues and Support	$178,000	$169,000
Net assets released from restrictions		
Satisfaction of program restrictions (See Note 5)	$ 10,000	$ 10,000
Expiration of time restrictions (see Note 5)	2,000	1,000
Total Net Assets Released from Restrictions	$ 12,000	$ 11,000
Total Unrestricted Revenues and Other Support	$190,000	$180,000
Expenses		
Meals	$ 67,000	$ 63,000
Counseling	35,000	34,000
Administration, fund-raising and general	75,000	65,000
Bad debts	4,000	4,000
Depreciation	10,000	10,000
Total Expenses	$191,000	$176,000
Increase/(Decrease) in Unrestricted Net Assets	$ (1,000)	$ 4,000
Changes in Temporarily Restricted Net Assets		
Foundation grants	$ 10,000	$ 10,000
Contributions	5,000	2,000
Assets released from restrictions (Note 5)	(12,000)	(11,000)
Increase in Temporarily Restricted Net Assets	$ 3,000	$ 1,000
Changes in Permanently Restricted Net Assets		
Contributions	$ 3,000	$ 2,000
Increase in Permanently Restricted Net Assets	$ 3,000	$ 2,000
Increase in Net Assets	$ 5,000	$ 7,000
Net Assets at Beginning of Year	114,000	107,000
Net Assets at End of Year	$119,000	$114,000

The accompanying notes are an integral part of these statements.

down from $73,000. We would want to investigate and determine if this is a one-year aberration or the beginning of an unfavorable downward trend.

Unrestricted net assets increased by $12,000 during 2012 due to release from restrictions. It is likely that most of this is the result of having spent money in compliance with restrictions. A note is often provided to explain net assets that are released from restrictions.

Although total unrestricted revenues and support have increased by $10,000 from $180,000 to $190,000, expenses have increased at an even faster pace. It is important to compare the organization with itself over time. The total $1,000 decrease in unrestricted net assets in 2012 is not a large amount. However, we note that the previous year there was a

$4,000 increase. The implication is that we are possibly seeing a declining trend developing in the financial results of operations.

Overall, net assets increased by $5,000 in 2012. This is only $2,000 less than the increase the prior year. It is possible that the main change is that more of Meals' contributions are coming with temporary and permanent restrictions. Note that while unrestricted contributions fell by $8,000 (from $73,000 to $65,000), temporarily restricted contributions rose by $3,000 (from $2,000 to $5,000), and permanently restricted contributions rose by $1,000 (from $2,000 to $3,000). While this helps reduce the sting of the reduction in unrestricted net assets, it is not totally reassuring. Restricted donations do restrict the organization's use of resources. They do not provide the organization with the same degree of flexibility in directing resources where management believes they are most needed. Management might decide after reviewing these financial statements that a greater effort is needed to raise additional unrestricted contributions.

The Cash Flow Statement

The cash flow statement focuses on financial rather than operating aspects of the organization. The concern is not with specific revenues and expenses but rather with the general sources and uses of money. The statement provides less information about profitability than the activity statement and more information about viability. It is possible to go long periods without making a profit. However, negative cash flows can create immediate questions regarding continued survival. The cash flow statement can provide some early warning signs when viability problems start to arise.

Sometimes the overall change in cash may seem to be fine, but it turns out that the organization's routine activities lose cash. Long-term assets are sold or money is borrowed to overcome an operating cash deficit. Unless annual cash deficits from operations can be reversed, the survival of the organization is not ensured. In Exhibit 14-3, we see comparative cash flow statements for Meals for the Homeless for 2012 and 2011. Operating activities in 2012 consumed $10,000 more of cash than they generated. This shortfall was partially made up by selling investments for $4,000 and by receiving contributions that are restricted to long-term investments. Overall cash decreased by $3,000.

The cash decline of $3,000 was only half as great as the decline for 2011, when the cash balance fell from $9,100 at the start of the year to $3,100 at the end. However, the implications are much worse. The 2011 cash decline was the result of acquiring a van, which required a $32,000 cash payment. We can see this in the "Cash Flows from Investing Activities" section of the statement. The purchase of the van required an increase in mortgages of only $9,000 (see the "Cash Flows from Financing Activities" section of the statement). Part of the acquisition was paid for by selling investments and part by lowering the cash balance. A substantial portion of the cash for the van, however, was generated by operations. In 2011, there was $15,000 more cash generated from operations than was used for operations. In 2012, the organization sold nearly as much of its stock investments as it did in 2011 but did not acquire any fixed assets. If the trend from 2011 to 2012 is allowed to continue, it will likely have severe consequences for the organization.

When routine operating activities generate a surplus of cash, the organization is more financially stable and viable than if operating activities consume more cash than they generate. There are times when cash deficits from operations cannot be avoided. Growing organizations often have this problem. Receivables and inventory grow faster than collections can keep up. Even when the deficit is the result of healthy growth, however, caution is needed. Rapid expansion will require, at a minimum, careful planning. There must be a determination of how much cash will be needed from sources other than operations. Agreements from banks or other sources must be obtained to ensure that a cash crisis does

EXHIBIT 14-3

Meals for the Homeless
Statements of Cash Flows
For the Years Ending December 31, 2012 and 2011

	2012	2011
Cash Flows from Operating Activities		
Change in net assets	$ 5,000	$ 7,000
Add expenses not requiring cash		
Depreciation	10,000	10,000
Other adjustments		
Add decrease in inventory	2,000	2,000
Subtract increase in receivables	(17,000)	(2,000)
Subtract decrease in wages payable	(1,000)	0
Subtract decrease in accounts payable	(1,000)	(2,000)
Subtract increase in prepaid expenses	(1,000)	0
Subtract contributions restricted to long-term investments	(4,000)	0
Subtract permanently restricted contributions	(3,000)	0
Net Cash Used for Operating Activities	$(10,000)	$ 15,000
Cash Flows from Investing Activities		
Sale of stock investments	$ 4,000	$ 5,000
Purchase of delivery van	0	(32,000)
Net Cash from Investing Activities	$ 4,000	$(27,000)
Cash Flows from Financing Activities		
Contributions restricted to endowment	$ 3,000	$ 0
Increase in notes payable	1,000	3,000
Contributions restricted to long-term investment	4,000	0
Increase in mortgages	0	9,000
Repayments of mortgages	(5,000)	(6,000)
Net Cash from Financing Activities	$ 3,000	$ 6,000
Net Increase/(Decrease) in Cash	$ (3,000)	$ (6,000)
Cash, Beginning of Year	3,100	9,100
Cash, End of Year	$ 100	$ 3,100
Supplemental Cash Flow Information		
Interest paid	$ 1,280	$ 1,600

The accompanying notes are an integral part of these statements.

not occur. It is far easier to obtain financing while one still has cash than it is if one waits until one runs out of cash.

The Statement of Functional Expenses

The comparative statements of functional expenses, shown in Exhibit 14-4 for Meals, provide a great deal of detailed information about the different expenses incurred by the organization. One can see the mix between salaries versus materials and the mix of expenses by type of program. One of the most critical relationships to explore on this statement is the relative program service expense versus the support service expense. For 2012, Meals spent $121,000 on program services ($83,000 for meals plus $38,000 for counseling) while it spent $70,000 on support services ($47,000 for management and

EXHIBIT 14-4

**Meals for the Homeless
Statements of Functional Expenses
For the Years Ending December 31, 2012 and 2011**

	Program Services		Support Services		
	Meals	**Counseling**	**Management and General**	**Fund-Raising**	**Total**
Expenses					
For Year Ending 12/31/12					
Salaries and benefits	$35,000	$35,000	$40,000	$17,000	$127,000
Food	17,000				17,000
Supplies and brochures	2,000	1,000	1,000	2,000	6,000
Office expenses	1,000	1,000	1,000	3,000	6,000
Rent	13,000	1,000	1,720	1,000	16,720
Interest	1,000		280		1,280
Professional fees			3,000		3,000
Bad debts	4,000				4,000
Depreciation	10,000				10,000
Total Expenses	$83,000	$38,000	$47,000	$23,000	$191,000
For Year Ending 12/31/11					
Salaries and benefits	$33,000	$34,000	$36,000	$12,000	$115,000
Food	15,000				15,000
Supplies and brochures	2,000	800	1,000	2,000	5,800
Office expenses	1,000	800	1,000	3,000	5,800
Rent	12,100	1,000	1,700	1,000	15,800
Interest	1,300		300		1,600
Professional fees			3,000		3,000
Bad debts	4,000				4,000
Depreciation	10,000				10,000
Total Expenses	$78,400	$36,600	$43,000	$18,000	$176,000

The accompanying notes are an integral part of these statements.

general plus $23,000 for fund-raising). One must always question whether the support service expenses are too high relative to the program service expenses, which are more directly related to the organization's mission.

The amounts spent on different types of expenses should be carefully considered. Also, changes from one year to the next should be evaluated, especially if the amount of the change is large.

Exhibit 14-5 is the Statement of Functional Expenses for the American Endowment Foundation for the year ended December 31, 2007. Note the extremely high portion of total spending that goes directly for program services ($20,702,979 out of a total of $21,822,344, or 95%). In contrast, the Charity Navigator reported that The Association for Firefighters and Paramedics, for the year ending December 31, 2006, spent $80,530 on program expenses, $239,081 on administrative expenses, and $3,595,480 on fund-raising expenses.[3] That comes out to just 2 percent spent on program services.

---

[3] http://www.charitynavigator.org/index.cfm?bay=search.summary&orgid=8222

EXHIBIT 14-5

American Endowment Foundation
Statement of Functional Expenses
For the Year Ended December 31, 2007

	Program Services	Management and General	Fundraising	Total
Grant expenditures	$ 20,403,417	$ —	$ —	$ 20,403,417
Salaries and benefits	180,239	180,239	185,700	546,178
Investment expenses	—	449,147	—	449,147
Miscellaneous expense	22,139	22,139	22,811	67,089
Employee benefits	19,947	19,947	20,551	60,445
Computer systems	19,777	19,777	20,376	59,930
Development	—	10,878	32,633	43,511
Payroll taxes and fees	12,591	12,591	12,973	38,155
Occupancy	9,635	9,635	9,927	29,197
Travel and education	7,967	7,967	8,209	24,143
Legal fees	7,858	7,858	8,097	23,813
Office supplies and expense	5,561	5,561	5,730	16,852
Telephone	4,858	4,858	5,004	14,720
Accounting services	4,060	4,060	4,182	12,302
Insurance	—	8,237	—	8,237
Life insurance expense	—	8,146	—	8,146
Supplies and postage	2,234	2,234	2,302	6,770
Outside services	1,206	1,206	1,244	3,656
Staff development	840	840	865	2,545
Depreciation	—	2,119	—	2,119
Service charges	585	585	604	1,774
Brochures and publications	65	65	68	198
Total expenses	$ 20,702,979	$ 778,089	$ 341,276	$ 21,822,344

Source: American Endowment Foundation. *Financial Statements for the Years Ended December 31, 2007 and 2006.* May 15, 2008, p. 4. Reprinted with permission of the American Endowment Foundation.

THE NOTES THAT ACCOMPANY FINANCIAL STATEMENTS

Financial statements, in themselves, do not provide a complete picture of the organization's finances. Audited financial statements all refer the reader to the "notes" that follow or accompany the financial statements. In trying to analyze the finances of an organization, the user cannot simply look at total assets and net income. A thorough reading of the statements provides just a start. The notes that accompany the financial statements are an integral part of the annual financial report. In fact, many analysts prefer to review the notes carefully before even beginning to look at the financial statements.

Financial statements do an excellent job of summarizing a very large number of transactions into a usable form. However, they are limited. Throughout this book, we discuss some of the causes of the limitations. Fixed assets are recorded based on their historical cost adjusted for depreciation. Therefore, the balance sheet does not convey the current fair value of the fixed assets. Inventory may be valued on the financial statements based on a last-in, first-out (LIFO) or first-in, first-out (FIFO) cost assumption. Depreciation can be calculated based on a straight-line or accelerated approach.

The notes that accompany financial statements are designed to provide explanations about choices made, methods used, and anything else the reader needs to understand the financial position and results of operations of the organization. They ensure that the financial report presents a "fair representation of financial results in accordance with GAAP." That means that all relevant information that a reasonable person who is knowledgeable of GAAP would need is provided. In many cases, the notes are considerably longer than the financial statements themselves.

To provide a sense of the types of notes that are used and the information they provide, a hypothetical set of notes for Meals for the Homeless is provided in the next section. In addition, examples from real organizations are shown. Notes for Meals are shown in italics, with commentary in normal type. Excerpts of notes from real organizations are shown in boxes.

Significant Accounting Policies

Each organization provides a unique set of notes that apply to its own unique circumstances. However, the notes section generally begins with a statement of accounting policies. This note often has a number of subsections.

NOTE A: SIGNIFICANT ACCOUNTING POLICIES

Meals for the Homeless ("Meals") is subject to the requirements of Statements of Financial Accounting Standard ("SFAS") No. 117—"Financial Statements of Not-for-Profit Organizations." Under SFAS No. 117, Meals is required to report information regarding its financial position and activities according to three classes of net assets: unrestricted, temporarily restricted, and permanently restricted. In addition, Meals is required to present a statement of cash flows and a statement of functional expenses.

Unrestricted net assets represent that part of the net assets that are neither permanently restricted nor temporarily restricted by donor-imposed stipulations. Temporarily restricted net assets represent the part of net assets resulting from contributions and other inflows of assets whose use is limited by donor-imposed stipulations that either expire by passage of time or can be fulfilled and removed by actions of Meals pursuant to those stipulations. Permanently restricted net assets represent the part of Meals' net assets resulting from contributions and other inflows of assets whose use by Meals is limited by donor-imposed stipulations that neither expire by passage of time nor can be fulfilled or otherwise removed by actions of Meals.

When a donor restriction expires or the purpose is accomplished, the restricted net assets are reclassified to unrestricted net assets and reported in the statement of activities as net assets released from restrictions.

The preceding note is fairly standard for not-for-profit organizations. However, it is important to include this note since it indicates critical differences from other types of organizations. The first note for Meals continues with some specific policies:

RECOGNITION OF REVENUES AND EXPENSES

Revenues and expenses are recorded on an accrual basis.

Since some organizations use cash, others use accrual, and others use modified accrual accounting, a note is often included to indicate the basis of accounting. See Box 14-1 for the basis of accounting note for The Fresh Air Fund.

ACCOUNTING FOR CONTRIBUTIONS

All contributions are considered to be available for unrestricted use unless specifically restricted by the donor. Amounts received that are designated for future periods or are restricted by the donor for specific purposes are reported as temporarily restricted or permanently restricted support that increases those net asset classes. Unconditional promises to give that are silent as to the due date are presumed to be time-restricted by the donor until received and are reported as contributions receivable and as temporarily restricted net assets.

This indicates that when a pledge is made, the organization is not free to spend that money until it has been received. Although the pledge may be legally enforceable and one might consider treating it as current period unrestricted resources, this more conservative approach is being taken by the organization. This information is helpful to a user who might be concerned that the organization might get into financial trouble by spending money based on pledges that may never be collected. See Box 14-2 for the contributions note for The American Red Cross.

DONATED MATERIALS, MARKETABLE SECURITIES, AND SERVICES

Donated food and other materials, and marketable securities are reflected as contributions in the accompanying statements at their fair values at date of receipt. Conditional donations are not considered revenue until the conditions have been met.
A substantial number of volunteers donated significant amounts of their time to Meals' food services. SFAS 116 requires that donated services be recognized if the services received (a) create or enhance nonfinancial assets, or (b) require specialized skills, are provided by individuals possessing skills, and would typically need to be purchased if not provided by donation. For the years ended December 31, 2012 and 2011, Meals received $80,000 and $72,000 worth of donated services, respectively, that would otherwise have had to be

BOX 14-1

Basis of Accounting

The accompanying financial statements have been prepared on the accrual basis of accounting.

Source: The Fresh Air Fund. *Financial Statements:* Years ended September 30, 2007 and 2006 with Report of Independent Auditors, January 9, 2008, p. 9.

BOX 14-2

Contributions

Contributions, which include unconditional promises to give (pledges), are recognized as revenues in the period received or promised. Conditional contributions are recorded when the conditions have been met. Contributions are considered to be unrestricted unless specifically restricted by the donor.

The Organization reports contributions in the temporarily or permanently restricted net asset class if they are received with donor stipulations as to their use. When a donor restriction expires, that is, when a stipulated time restriction ends or purpose restriction is accomplished, temporarily restricted net assets are released and reclassified to unrestricted net assets in the consolidated statement of activities. Donor-restricted contributions are initially reported in the temporarily restricted net asset class, even if it is anticipated such restrictions will be met in the current reporting period.

Source: The American National Red Cross. *Consolidated Financial Statements June 30, 2007 (with Independent Auditors' Report Thereon.)* October 16, 2007, p. 9. http://www.redcross.org/pubs/car07/14606D.pdf

purchased. However, these services (related to cooking and serving meals) do not qualify as skilled services. Thus, no amounts have been reflected in the statements for these donated services.

In not-for-profit organizations, a great deal of labor is provided by volunteers. It is important to indicate the extent to which those volunteers' services are recorded as both a contribution and an expense related to providing services. See Box 14-3 for Scholarship America's note related to contributed services.

INVENTORIES

Inventories are stated at cost, not to exceed market value. Cost is calculated using the last-in, first-out method.

By stating that inventory is not valued in excess of market, the organization is telling the user of the financial statements that if inventories have declined in value, they are shown at the lower value. This is referred to as using the lower of cost or market and occurs because of the GAAP of conservatism. Even though we might charge more for the inventory when we use it, we cannot record it above its cost. If it declines in value (e.g., food spoils), we can record a value lower than cost. An important question, however, is how we determine cost. We could use last-in, first-out (LIFO) or first-in first-out (FIFO). This note indicates that Meals uses LIFO. Since different organizations can use different approaches, this note helps the reader to understand this organization and compare it with others. See Box 14-4 for The American Red Cross inventory note. The Red Cross uses the average cost method rather than LIFO or FIFO.

BOX 14-3

Contributed Services

A number of volunteers have made significant donations of their time to program and support functions. The value of this contributed time does not meet the criteria for recognition of contributed services, and accordingly is not reflected in the accompanying financial statements.

Source: Scholarship America, Inc. *Financial Statements and Supplemental Schedules June 30, 2007 and 2006 (With Independent Auditors' Report Thereon).* September 28, 2007, p. 6. http://scholarshipamerica.org/files/ARSA_07_Financials.pdf

BOX 14-4

Supply Inventories

Inventories of supplies purchased for use in program and supporting services are valued using the average cost method. Whole blood and its components are valued at the lower of average cost or market.

Source: The American Red Cross, op. cit., p. 8.

PROPERTY, BUILDINGS, AND EQUIPMENT

Land, buildings, and equipment are recorded at cost, and depreciation over the useful lives of buildings and equipment is charged annually using the straight-line method.

This note distinguishes the organization from organizations that do not depreciate all of their buildings and equipment or that use accelerated depreciation methods. The specific amounts of accumulated depreciation on fixed assets currently owned appear in a note discussed later in this section.

If a user of financial statements is comparing two similar organizations, but one uses straight-line depreciation and another uses accelerated depreciation, one may appear to have higher expenses and lower assets than the other. The user might infer a greater difference between the two organizations than actually exists. By providing information such as this in the notes, the user can make a more meaningful comparison between the organizations. See Box 14-5 for the National Society to Prevent Blindness's property, buildings, and equipment note.

TAX STATUS

Meals is a not-for-profit voluntary organization exempt from income taxes under Section 501(c)(3) of the U.S. Internal Revenue Code.

This note is quite important for users of the financial statements. It indicates to creditors that the organization will not have to pay income taxes, thereby removing a competing creditor. When

BOX 14-5

Land, Building, and Equipment

Land, building, and equipment are stated at cost or, in the case of gifts, fair market value at date of donation, less accumulated depreciation. Building, equipment, and leasehold improvements are depreciated or amortized using the straight-line method over their estimated useful lives, which are as follows:

Buildings	40 years
Equipment	3–10 years
Leasehold improvements	5–10 years

Source: National Society to Prevent Blindness (Doing Business as Prevent Blindness America) and Affiliates, *Combined Financial Statements for the Year Ended March 31, 2007.* September 4, 2007, p. 10.

organizations go bankrupt, the Internal Revenue Service (IRS) is aggressive in collecting amounts owed to it. It also indicates to potential donors that their contributions will be tax-deductible.

ACCOUNTING FOR INVESTMENTS

In accordance with the Statement of Financial Accounting Standards ("SFAS") No. 124, "Accounting for Certain Investments Held by Not-for-Profit Organizations," Meals reports debt and equity securities at their fair value with the related gains and losses included in the statement of activities.

Since investments at one time were reported at lower of cost or market, this is an important policy statement to include. For Meals, Note A concludes with "Use of Estimates."

USE OF ESTIMATES

The preparation of financial statements requires management to make estimates and assumptions that affect the reported amounts of certain assets and liabilities at the date of the financial statements and the reported amounts of revenue and expenses during the period. Actual results could differ.

Many individuals tend to believe that accountants have an ability to be more precise and accurate than is in fact the case. This note's purpose is to point out to the reader that despite the conventions of GAAP, financial statements remain subjective and subject to uncertainty. See Box 14-6 for the Wildlife Conservation Society's note regarding its policy for accounting estimates.

Other Notes

The first note covers a wide range of accounting policies. The remaining notes for the most part focus on a specific issue in somewhat more detail. Where the first note is policy oriented, the remaining notes provide information about specific circumstances or values.

NOTE B: PROGRAM SERVICES

The activities of Meals for the Homeless consist of providing meals and counseling services. The meals are provided in soup kitchens throughout the city. Meals also uses vans to deliver food to shelters. Counseling services are provided to assist clients find both temporary shelter and permanent housing.

In 2012, Meals provided 587 meals per day in its 4 kitchens. In addition an average of 147 meals was delivered each day to shelters. Approximately 1,292

BOX 14-6

Use of Estimates

The preparation of consolidated financial statements in conformity with generally accepted accounting principles requires management to make estimates and judgments that affect the reported amounts of assets and liabilities and disclosures of contingencies at the date of the consolidated financial statements and revenues and expenses recognized during the reporting period. Actual results could differ from those estimates.

Source: Wildlife Conservation Society and Subsidiaries. *Consolidated Financial Statements, June 30, 2007 and 2006 (with Independent Auditor's Report Thereon).* November 19, 2007, p. 8.

individuals are counseled each year. Meals' services are consumed by both individuals and families.

As a result of Meals' programs, a number of individuals have the physical strength to continue work or return to work. Others avoid hospitalization from malnutrition. It is the belief of the organization that without its services, a number of its clients would die each year.

See Box 14-7 for the program services note for The Fresh Air Fund.

NOTE C: MARKETABLE SECURITIES

The market value of Meals investments in marketable securities at December 31[4] was:

	2012	2011
Treasury Bills	$1,000	$1,500
Stocks	2,000	1,500
Total	$3,000	$3,000

It is informative to know the composition of marketable securities and other investments. Treasury bills are very safe investments. High percentages in stock indicate a more risky portfolio. The marketable securities note from the Make-A-Wish Foundation is shown in Box 14-8.

NOTE D: PROPERTY, BUILDINGS, AND EQUIPMENT

As of December 31, the property, buildings, and equipment owned by Meals consisted of the following:

	2012	2011
Land	$ 40,000	$ 40,000
Equipment	70,000	70,000
	$110,000	$110,000
Less Accumulated Depreciation	35,000	25,000
Net Property and Equipment	$ 75,000	$ 85,000

BOX 14-7

Program Services

Fresh Air Camping activities consist of escorting and transporting approximately 3,000 children from their homes in New York City to the Fund's camps in Fishkill, New York. The summer program provides direction, leadership, food, medical care and recreation for two or more weeks at no cost to the children's families. Included within this program is the Fund's Career Awareness Camp, which serves approximately 300 children. The camp program fosters critical career-related qualities such as responsibility, cooperation and leadership. Additionally, the Fund's year-round camping program serves 1,000 disadvantaged teenagers each year.

Source: The Fresh Air Fund. *Financial Statements Years Ended September 30, 2007 and 2006 with Report of Independent Auditors*, p. 8.

---

[4] The value of balance sheet accounts is given as of a specific point in time. Accountants often refer to a value "at" the date, such as "at December 31."

BOX 14-8

Marketable Securities

A summary of investments as of August 31 follows:

	2006	2005
Equity securities	$31,823,423	$29,885,684
Mutual funds	30,109,975	26,269,677
U.S. Government securities	12,340,462	9,258,421
Corporate bonds	10,083,752	9,962,960
Certificates of deposit	9,077,323	8,155,033
Fixed income	7,594,464	5,864,501
Money market funds	2,908,752	2,816,565
Other	749,902	1,492,081
Mortgage backed securities	359,303	567,067
Total investments	105,047,356	94,271,989
Less investments held for long-term purposes	8,543,844	5,054,642
Investments not held for long-term purposes	$96,503,512	$89,217,347

The net unrealized and realized gains on investments for the year ended August 31, 2006 were $2,749,996 and $839,787, respectively. The net unrealized and realized gains on investments for the year ended August 31, 2005 were $4,760,487 and $688,639, respectively.

Source: Make-A-Wish Foundation of America. *2006 Annual Report.* March 5, 2007, pp. 30–31.

From the net amount, we cannot tell how old our equipment is. However, from this note, we can see that we have $70,000 worth of equipment that is about half depreciated. This note therefore gives information that we would not know from looking at the balance sheet. Notice that the information in the notes following Note A provide specific details such as the cost of fixed assets, while Note A and its subparts provide information on the organization's accounting policies. The fixed asset note for Prevent Blindness America is shown in Box 14-9.

NOTE E: PENSION PLAN

Meals has established a defined contribution plan for all eligible employees, effective January 1, 1992. Employees who have completed one year of service and have attained the age of 21 are eligible for participation. Contributions are discretionary and are determined by the Board of Trustees. The contributions are allocated based on an equal percentage of each participant's compensation. No employee contributions are permitted. Participants are fully vested after two years of service. Contributions during 2012 and 2011 were $6,000 and $5,500, respectively.

Pension plans can be extremely complicated. There are two major categories: *defined contribution plans* and *defined benefit plans*. In a defined contribution plan, the amount required to be put aside by the organization is determined each year. That amount is the organization's total obligation to the pension plan. Depending on investment experience, the participants will be able to receive larger or smaller amounts upon retirement. In a defined benefit plan, the organization is required to make specific defined payments to participants upon retirement. The risk or benefit of investment experience falls on the organization rather than the participants. The pension note for St. Jude Children's Research Hospital is shown in Box 14-10.

BOX 14-9

Property, Buildings, and Equipment

Prevent Blindness America's property and equipment consisted of the following as of March 31:

	2007	2006
Land	$ 850,507	$ 850,507
Building	3,229,038	3,218,038
Equipment	3,308,407	3,125,134
Leasehold improvements	359,541	349,790
	7,747,493	7,543,469
Less accumulated depreciation and amortization	3,339,428	3,125,805
	$4,408,065	$4,417,664

Source: National Society to Prevent Blindness (Doing Business as Prevent Blindness America) and Affiliates. *Combined Financial Statements for the Year Ended March 31, 2007.* September 4, 2007, p. 10.

NOTE F: CONTINGENT LIABILITIES

> *There are various lawsuits and threatened actions against Meals, arising out of accidents and other matters, some of which claim substantial amounts of damages. In the opinion of Meals' management, these lawsuits are either without merit or covered by insurance, and will not result in any material adverse effect on the financial position of Meals.*

There are times that organizations have large potential liabilities, called *contingent liabilities,* that are not shown on the balance sheet. For example, the organization might expect to have a large payment as a result of a lawsuit, but the exact amount cannot be

BOX 14-10

Pension Plan

The Hospital sponsors a defined-contribution retirement annuity plan generally covering all employees who have completed one year of service. The plan requires that the Hospital make annual contributions based on participants' salaries. Employee contributions to the plan are not allowed. The Hospital's contributions are 50% vested after two years of service and 100% vested after three years of service. Total contributions to the plan were approximately $12,000,000 and $11,000,000 for the years ended June 30, 2007 and 2006, respectively.

ALSAC sponsors a defined contribution retirement plan generally covering all employees who have completed one year of service. The plan requires that ALSAC make annual contributions based on participants' salaries. Employees can choose to invest their contributions into the options provided through the plan. Employees become 30% vested in the employer contributions after one year of service and completion of one plan year (July to June); 60% after two years of service and completion of two plan years (July to June); 100% after three years of service and completion of three plan years (July to June). ALSAC contributed approximately $2,416,000 and $1,971,000 to the plan during the years ended June 30, 2007 and 2006, respectively.

Source: St. Jude Children's Research Hospital, Inc. American Lebanese Syrian Associated Charities, Inc., *Combined Financial Statements, as of and for the Years Ended June 30, 2007 and 2006, and Independent Auditor's Report,* September 14, 2007, p. 9.

BOX 14-11

Contingencies

From time to time, the national organization and the chapters are involved in litigation and claims arising in the normal course of operations. In the opinion of management based on consultation with legal counsel, losses, if any, from these matters are covered by insurance or are immaterial; therefore, no provision has been made in the accompanying combined financial statements for losses, if any, which might result from the ultimate outcome of these matters.

Source: Make-A-Wish Foundation of America. *2006 Annual Report.* March 5, 2007, p. 33.

determined. Rather than show an approximate amount, the balance sheet would have a reference to the notes. The note would indicate the nature of the liability. The contingencies note of the Make-A-Wish Foundation is shown in Box 14-11.

NOTE G: COMMITMENTS

Although Meals does not own any buildings, it does lease space for its soup kitchens and management offices. Meals has several noncancellable lease agreements that terminate December 31, 2016. Minimum rentals under these leases are as follows:

	Year Ending December 31:
2013	$20,000
2014	21,000
2015	22,000
2016	23,000
Total	$86,000

If Meals owned its own buildings and had borrowed money on a mortgage to finance the buildings, the mortgage would show as a liability on its balance sheet. If it signs a five-year lease on a building, that lease will not show on the balance sheet as a liability. However, the organization is still required to make payments, the same as if it had a mortgage. This note discloses that important commitment to make payments in future years. This information would be quite important to someone contemplating making a loan to Meals and wondering what other payments it is committed to making. Box 14-12 provides the *commitments* note from the Prevent Blindness America annual financial report.

Note that although some leases meet rules that result in treating them as liabilities that show on the balance sheet, many do not. Leases that are noncancellable but do not qualify for treatment as a liability would be reported as commitments, if material in amount.

NOTE H: RESTRICTED NET ASSETS

Temporarily restricted net assets were available for the following purposes at December 31, 2012 and 2011:

	2012	2011
Children's Outreach Program	$4,000	$1,000
Building and Equipment	900	900
	$4,900	$1,900

BOX 14-12

Commitments

Prevent Blindness America occupies certain operating facilities under various operating lease agreements. Substantially all of these leases require that Prevent Blindness America pay real estate taxes, utilities, and maintenance expenses.

At March 31, 2007, the minimum future rental payments due under operating leases with non-cancelable lease terms in excess of one year are as follows:

	Amount
Year ending March 31:	
2008	$ 405,285
2009	300,884
2010	217,010
2011	152,291
2012	142,762
Thereafter	13,404
	$1,231,636

Source: National Society to Prevent Blindness (Doing Business as Prevent Blindness America) and Affiliates. *Combined Financial Statements for the Year Ended March 31, 2007.* September 4, 2007, p. 10.

Temporarily restricted net assets were released from restrictions during 2012 and 2011 by incurring expenses satisfying the restricted purposes. Net releases were as follows:

	2012	2011
Satisfaction of Program Restrictions		
Used to provide meals	$10,000	$ 2,000
Used to acquire delivery van		8,000
Subtotal	$10,000	$10,000
Expiration of Time Restrictions		
Bequest to be used over 10 years	$ 1,000	$ 1,000
2011 donation for use in 2012	1,000	
	$ 2,000	$ 1,000
Total Net Assets Released from Restrictions	$12,000	$11,000

Permanently restricted net assets were restricted as follows:

Invested permanently with income to be used for any organizational purposes:	$30,000	$27,000

The note related to restricted net assets for St. Jude Children's Research Hospital/American Lebanese Syrian Associated Charities in its 2007 annual report is shown in Box 14-13.

NOTE I: INVENTORY

If the FIFO method of inventory had been used, inventories would have been $1,000 and $900 higher at December 31, 2012 and 2011, respectively.

BOX 14-13

Restrictions on Net Assets

Permanently restricted net assets at June 30, 2007 and 2006, were restricted for the following purposes:

	2007	2006
Future needs of the hospital	$594,146,285	$530,674,775
Endowed chairs	95,055,669	75,493,121
Treatment and research	24,797,834	23,600,152
	$713,999,788	$629,768,048

Temporarily restricted net assets of $32,120,742 and $23,569,569 at June 30, 2007 and 2006, respectively, consisted primarily of charitable gift agreements and charitable remainder trust receivables.

Source: St. Jude Children's Research Hospital, Inc. American Lebanese Syrian Associated Charities, Inc., *Combined Financial Statements as of and for the Years Ended June 30, 2007 and 2006, and Independent Auditor's Report,* p. 17.

This note allows a financial statement user to convert income and assets calculated on a LIFO basis to what it would have been if the organization used FIFO, thus making comparison between organizations easier.

Summary of Notes

This section does not provide an inclusive listing of all possible notes. Rather, just a few common notes have been shown to provide the reader with some familiarity and awareness of notes that accompany audited financial statements. Depending on the exact circumstances of different organizations, a wide variety of disclosures are required by GAAP.

Given the wide range of possible ways to report information, it is vital to examine the notes to gain an understanding of which choices were made and the impact of those choices. A good understanding of financial position and results requires more information than the financial statements themselves can convey. What contingent liabilities are there, and are they material in amount? How old are the organization's buildings and equipment?

Not all notes are relevant to all readers. Some items are of more concern to employees than creditors. Some items help donors more than internal managers. Whatever one's purpose in using a financial report, the key is that the financial statements by themselves are incapable of telling the full story. To avoid being misled by the numbers, it is necessary to supplement the information in the statements with the information in the notes that accompany the statements.

RATIO ANALYSIS

Another crucial element in financial analysis is the use of ratios. A ratio is a comparison of one number to another. Ratios help the organization's managers and external users understand the organization's strengths and weaknesses. A better understanding of strengths can allow the organization to build on them. A better understanding of weaknesses can lead to corrective actions.

In financial statement analysis, we compare numbers taken from the financial statements. For instance, if we want to know how much Meals for the Homeless had in current assets compared with its current liabilities at the end of 2012, we would compare its $61,100 in current assets with its $14,000 in current liabilities (Exhibit 14-1). The comparison is done by dividing one number by the other. If we divide $61,100 by $14,000, the result is 4.4. This means that there are 4.4 dollars of current assets for every one dollar of current liabilities. This would be referred to either as a ratio of 4.4 to 1 or simply as a ratio of 4.4. This particular ratio is called the *current ratio.*

Ratios are used because the comparison between two numbers generates information that is more useful than either or both of the numbers separately. If we know that we have $61,100, that does not tell us whether the organization has adequate short-term resources to meet its obligations. Knowing that we have 4.4 dollars of liquid assets for each dollar of short-term obligations tells us much more about the relative safety of the organization.

Ratios are generally computed using computer spreadsheet software programs. However, it is important to think about why each ratio is being computed and the implications of various values for each ratio. Ratio analysis is more of an art than a science and cannot be usefully approached in a mechanical manner.

This chapter provides a number of examples of ratios. However, the discussion is not all inclusive. Each organization can develop its own set of ratios that serve as useful indicators about the health and efficiency of the organization. For example, a key ratio for the health maintenance organization (HMO) industry is the medical loss ratio, which indicates the percentage of total premiums spent on providing medical care as opposed to marketing and administrative costs. New ratios can be created by simply finding a relationship between two numbers that provides useful information.

Making Comparisons

We have calculated the current ratio for Meals as being 4.4. What does that mean? Is 4.4 a very high ratio, or a very low one? We do not want to have too few current assets and risk a financial crisis for nonpayment of obligations. However, it is quite difficult to evaluate a ratio without a standard for comparison. Comparisons are necessary to get a sense of the implications of a ratio. We can compare a ratio with the same ratio for the organization at different points in time, with close competitors, and with the industry. By looking for points of comparison, the organization can determine benchmark standards that it wants to use as targets or goals.

It is often hard for public service organizations to get data from other organizations that are totally comparable. At a minimum, however, any organization can make comparisons of its own data over time. By considering a ratio's value from year to year over a three- to five-year period, trends can be seen unfolding. Gradual changes, either favorable or unfavorable, may be observed, and sudden sharp turnarounds, for better or worse, will be quickly discovered.

In addition to using its own data over time, an organization should make an effort to find a similar organization. Once we determine an organization that is similar, its financial statements should be obtained. Many health care, not-for-profit, and government organizations will provide a copy of their audited financial report upon request. If one cannot be obtained by direct contact, a substantial amount of financial statement information can be obtained from the annual Form 990 tax return that not-for-profits are generally required to file with the IRS. Those tax returns are public documents and must be made available to the public by the organization. Many 990 tax returns may be found online at www.guidestar.org.

A ratio-by-ratio comparison should be undertaken. This can be very helpful in determining why one organization is doing better or worse than another. An analysis of the difference in ratios can provide insight into actions that are required to improve results.

An additional comparative analysis that can be very helpful is comparison with an entire industry. Data for a wide range of for-profit industries are provided by organizations such as

Dun and Bradstreet and RMA, the Risk Management Association. Ingenix publishes an annual almanac of ratios for the hospital industry. Many organizations have trade associations that prepare industry data for their members. Data provided by such organizations and associations often break down ratios by size of organization, geographic region, and other critical elements that differentiate organizations within the industry. Thus, a large, urban, teaching hospital in the South can compare its own ratios with those of all other large, urban, teaching hospitals in the South.

Data are often provided not only for the mean, but also by percentiles. For example, suppose that the average current ratio for the soup kitchen industry is 2. Meals has a ratio of 4.4, which is substantially higher. However, a trade association publication might indicate that 25 percent of all soup kitchens have a current ratio over 5. That would provide a very different implication than if we found that less than 5 percent of all soup kitchens had a current ratio above 3.

Cautions in the Use of Ratios

Although ratios are a powerful analytical tool, they do have certain weaknesses. First, no one ratio is adequate. Ratios must be viewed in context of each other and of the overall financial statement review. Second, ratios are generally drawn from financial statement information, which is subject to many GAAP-imposed limitations. Third, one should not become overly concerned with the precise value of a ratio. Fourth, one cannot assume that we desire to maximize or minimize the value of the ratio. Fifth, one should use common sense. Finally, ratios that are useful for health and not-for-profit organizations will not necessarily be helpful for governments. Each of these issues is discussed here.

Ratio analysis requires a mosaic approach. When you look at a picture made up of individual mosaic tiles, you cannot really learn anything about the picture from one tile. If the tile is blue, it could be sky, water, or almost anything else. Similarly with ratios—a value for a ratio means little by itself. For example, the current ratio may be very high. This would seem to imply robust financial health. However, often a failing organization will sell off its fixed assets in desperation to raise money to pay its creditors. As of the moment the ratio is calculated, current assets may be high. However, ongoing losses may soon wipe out the liquid resources. You must look at the entire picture to get a more realistic understanding of the organization's financial situation.

Ratios are often generated by using numbers from the audited financial statements. However, we know that financial statement data are limited. Fixed assets are reported at historical cost adjusted for depreciation. Some organizations will use straight-line depreciation, while others may use accelerated depreciation. Neither approach will ensure that the balance sheet reflects the market value of the assets. Inventories for some organizations will be reported on a LIFO basis, but others may use a FIFO basis. As a result of these, and similar issues, it cannot be assumed that ratios are perfectly comparable across organizations. This is a serious weakness, given that comparison is one of the major functions of ratio analysis.

Given the inherent weaknesses in financial data and the problem in trying to draw conclusions based on any one or a few ratios, it becomes important to recognize that ratio analysis should be used to develop general impressions about an organization. As noted previously, ratio analysis is an art form rather than a precise science. Different users of ratios may draw different conclusions. It is useful to focus on the gestalt—an overall sense of what we learn about the organization rather than a precise measurement of what each ratio indicates. Thus, it is important to gather information without being overly mesmerized by the level of detail available.

We can calculate ratios to many decimal places. In the current ratio calculated previously for Meals, the true ratio value is 4.36428571428571. Is that a useful number? Do you know more or less about Meals if you use the full number shown here, or if you simply know that Meals has about $4 of current assets for every dollar of current liabilities? In other words, it is important not to become overly concerned with the exactness of the ratio's value. Instead focus on the implications of a ratio of approximately the amount calculated.

When we look at ratios, it would simplify analysis if one knew that a particular ratio should be as low as possible, or as high as possible. However, many times a desirable ratio value is somewhere in between. On the one hand, if a current ratio is too low, it implies the organization may not be able to meet its obligations. That would be a sign of weak financial status. On the other hand, if the ratio is very high, then an unduly large amount of resources are being tied up in current assets. The organization could likely better employ those assets in other ways. This would imply management is not operating the organization efficiently. Unfortunately, this means the analyst has to determine how low is too low and how high is too high. It is like walking a tightrope, trying not to fall on either side.

The use of ratio analysis should always be governed by common sense. One can easily calculate dozens of ratios and quickly suffer from data overload. It is useful to first review the financial statements and notes, and a few representative ratios of each major class. Based on that information, one can identify potential problem areas and then calculate a variety of more detailed ratios for use in a more focused analysis.

Many of the ratios to be calculated in this section of the chapter do not relate directly to governments or must be modified to be used by governments. Specific issues related to using ratios for governments are discussed in Chapter 15.

A final note of caution relates to the specific definitions of ratios. Not everyone calculates ratios using the same definitions. A debt to equity ratio could divide total liabilities by net assets, or just long-term debt by net assets. Although the latter approach is more properly called long-term debt to net assets, confusion can arise. It is always important to define ratios clearly or to determine the exact definitions that have been used. The purpose of the ratio discussion here is not to establish the "correct" ratio definitions, but rather to consider the uses and possibilities of ratio analysis. Ratios can be redefined or invented to meet the needs of the user.

Major Classes of Ratios

Ratios can be grouped in a variety of different ways. This chapter groups them into the following six principal types: (1) common size; (2) liquidity; (3) asset turnover; (4) leverage; (5) coverage; and (6) profitability.

COMMON SIZE RATIOS   A starting point in ratio analysis is the calculation of a set of *common size ratios*. A common size ratio compares all the numbers on a financial statement with one key number. For example, each asset on the balance sheet is compared with total assets. Each item on the activity statement is compared with total revenues.

One of the difficult aspects of comparing different organizations is that they may be substantially different in size. Suppose that Museum A has $100 in cash and Museum B has $500. Does A have too little cash? What if it turns out that Museum A has $1,000 of total assets and Museum B has $5,000 of total assets? Museum B has five times as much cash, but it also has five times as many assets; it is a larger organization. It does not make sense to compare the absolute amount of cash. A common size ratio's purpose is to make the numbers on the financial statement more comparable across organizations.

In the case of the museums, the common size ratio would be cash divided by total assets. We can see that both organizations have one-tenth of their assets in cash:

$$\text{Common Sized Cash} = \frac{\text{Cash}}{\text{Total Assets}} \qquad \begin{array}{c} \underline{\text{Museum A}} \\[4pt] \dfrac{\$100}{\$1,000} = .1 \end{array} \qquad \begin{array}{c} \underline{\text{Museum B}} \\[4pt] \dfrac{\$500}{\$5,000} = .1 \end{array}$$

Relative to the size of the organizations, their cash is similar. If we did this for an entire industry, we would get a sense of what portion of assets are typically held in cash. Common size ratios are usually shown as a percentage. Rather than referring to the cash holdings of the museums as being .1, or one-tenth of total assets, we indicate that their cash is 10 percent. Ratios are converted to percents by multiplying them by 100%:

$$\frac{\$100}{\$1,000} \times 100\% = 10\% \qquad \frac{\$500}{\$5,000} \times 100\% = 10\%$$

The common size ratios for Meals for the Homeless's comparative balance sheets are presented in Exhibit 14-6. A ratio is computed for each individual item by dividing it by total assets and converting the result to a percentage.

Examine the common size ratios for the two years. We can see that total current assets have increased from approximately 33 percent to nearly 43 percent of total assets. The primary reason for this is the change in accounts receivable. This again points out a need to investigate the growth in this area. There has been a considerable decrease in equipment as a percent of assets, which may be cause for some concern.

The common size cash ratio should be neither too high nor too low. Too low a ratio indicates the possibility of inability to pay obligations when due. Too high a ratio indicates surplus cash that could have been used to provide services, reduce high-cost debt, or invest in higher-yielding investments. There is no rule of thumb. Appropriate values differ by industry. We must consider the trend over time and the values at other organizations. For Meals, we note that this ratio has fallen from 2.1 percent to .1 percent in just one year, a cause for some concern.

The accounts receivable common size ratio generally should be relatively low. A high ratio might indicate difficulty collecting money due to the organization. Conversely, too low a ratio might indicate that the organization is unwilling to provide credit to potentially good customers. A rising ratio might not be bad news. It might indicate that total revenues are way up (good news) and that receivables are rising in proportion. Care must be exercised in trying to understand what the number has to say.

The value of common size ratios is greater when they are used to compare the organization with other organizations. However, even if one is only using ratios for internal comparison, it is probably worth the effort to prepare common size ratios. We might note that revenues are changing and so are expenses without common size ratios. However, we can get better insight as to whether the changes are proportional by using ratios.

For example, consider Exhibit 14-7, which displays the common size ratios for Meals' comparative activity statements. Common size ratios for the activity statement are calculated by dividing each individual item by total unrestricted revenues and other support. Thus, each element on the activity statement is assessed as a percentage of unrestricted resource inflows. Note that Exhibit 14-7 not only shows each element as a common size ratio but also has a column for the percent change. This allows the user to not only understand the relationship between each item and the total but also get a better sense for how each item is changing over time.

The percent change is calculated by dividing the change in each item by the base year value. For example, client revenue rose from $9,000 in 2011 to $11,000 in 2012. The change from 2011 to 2012 was $2,000. Dividing that by the 2011 value of $9,000 yields .222. Multiplying that by 100% produces the 22.2 percent change in client revenues from the 2011 to 2012 year.

A good way to begin a financial analysis is to look at the common size ratios of all financial statements to get a sense of the size of each element as a percentage of the total and also to consider each element on a percentage change basis. Combining the two pieces

EXHIBIT 14-6 Common Size Ratios: Balance Sheets

Meals for the Homeless
Statements of Financial Position
As of December 31, 2012 and 2011

Assets

	Percent	2012	Percent	2011
Current Assets				
Cash	.1	$ 100	2.1	$ 3,100
Marketable securities	2.1	3,000	2.1	3,000
Accounts receivable, net of estimated uncollectibles of $8,000 and $7,000	37.9	55,000	26.0	38,000
Inventory (LIFO basis)	1.4	2,000	2.7	4,000
Prepaid expenses	.7	1,000	0.0	0
Total Current Assets	42.1	$ 61,100	32.9	$ 48,100
Long-Term Assets				
Cash restricted for building and equipment acquisition	.6	$ 900	.6	$ 900
Fixed assets				
Property	27.6	40,000	27.4	40,000
Equipment, net	24.1	35,000	30.8	45,000
Investments	5.5	8,000	8.2	12,000
Total Long-Term Assets	57.9	$ 83,900	67.1	$ 97,900
Total Assets	100.0	$145,000	100.0	$146,000

Liabilities and Net Assets

	Percent	2012	Percent	2011
Liabilities				
Current Liabilities				
Wages payable	1.4	$ 2,000	2.1	$ 3,000
Accounts payable	1.4	2,000	2.1	3,000
Notes payable	4.1	6,000	3.4	5,000
Current portion of mortgage payable	2.8	4,000	3.4	5,000
Total Current Liabilities	9.7	$ 14,000	11.0	$ 16,000
Long-term liabilities				
Mortage payable	8.3	$ 12,000	11.0	$ 16,000
Total Long-Term Liabilities	8.3	$ 12,000	11.0	$ 16,000
Total Liabilities	17.9	$ 26,000	21.9	$ 32,000
Net Assets				
Unrestricted	58.0	$ 84,100	58.2	$ 85,000
Temporarily restricted	3.4	4,900	1.3	1,900
Permanently restricted	20.7	30,000	18.5	27,000
Total Net Assets	82.1	$119,000	78.1	$114,000
Liabilities and Net Assets	100.0	$145,000	100.0	$146,000

EXHIBIT 14-7 Common Size Ratios: Activity Statements

Meals for the Homeless
Activity Statements
For the Years Ending December 31, 2012 and 2011

	Percent Change	Percent	2012	Percent	2011
Changes in Unrestricted Net Assets					
Revenues and Support					
Client revenue	22.2	5.8	$ 11,000	5.0	$ 9,000
City revenue	25.0	10.5	20,000	8.9	16,000
County revenue	0.0	5.3	10,000	5.6	10,000
Foundation grants	20.0	31.6	60,000	27.8	50,000
Annual ball	9.1	6.3	12,000	6.1	11,000
Contributions	−11.0	34.2	65,000	40.6	73,000
Total Revenues and Support	5.3	93.7	$178,000	93.9	$169,000
Net Assets Released from Restrictions					
Satisfaction of program restrictions	0.0	5.3	$ 10,000	5.6	$ 10,000
Expiration of time restrictions	100.0	1.1	2,000	.6	1,000
Total Net Assets Released from Restrictions	9.1	6.3	$ 12,000	6.1	$ 11,000
Total Unrestricted Revenues and Other Support	5.6	100.0	$190,000	100.0	$180,000
Expenses					
Meals	6.3	35.3	$ 67,000	35.0	$ 63,000
Counseling	2.9	18.4	35,000	18.9	34,000
Administration, fund raising and general	15.4	39.5	75,000	36.1	65,000
Bad debts	0.0	2.1	4,000	2.2	4,000
Depreciation	0.0	5.3	10,000	5.6	10,000
Total expenses	8.5	100.5	$191,000	97.8	$176,000
Increase in Unrestricted Net Assets	−125.0	−.5	$ (1,000)	2.2	$ 4,000
Changes in Temporarily Restricted Net Assets					
Foundation grants	0.0	5.3	$ 10,000	5.6	$ 10,000
Contributions	150.0	2.6	5,000	1.1	2,000
Assets released from restrictions	9.1	−6.3	(12,000)	−6.1	(11,000)
Increase in Temporarily Restricted Net Assets	200.0	1.6	$ 3,000	.6	$ 1,000
Changes in Permanently Restricted Net Assets					
Contributions	50.0	1.6	$ 3,000	1.1	$ 2,000
Increase in Permanently Restricted Net Assets	50.0	1.6	$ 3,000	1.1	$ 2,000
Increase in Net Assets	−28.6	2.6	$ 5,000	3.9	$ 7,000
Net Assets at Beginning of Year	6.5	60.0	114,000	59.4	107,000
Net Assets at End of Year	4.4	62.6	$119,000	63.3	$114,000

of information (size and change) lets the user see which elements are important and where significant changes have occurred.

Total unrestricted revenues and other support have risen from $180,000 to $190,000. As we can see in the "Percent Change" column in Exhibit 14-7, this is a 5.6 percent increase. Meanwhile, the cost of meals rose $4,000. Is that in line with the total increase in resources? The $4,000 increase was a 6.3 percent rise, not very different from the 5.6 percent increase in resources. We note from the common size ratios that the cost of meals is actually a fairly stable percentage of total revenues in 2012 as compared with 2011, rising from 35.0 percent to 35.3 percent. Administration rose by $10,000, the same dollar amount as total revenues and support. However, administration expenses rose by 15.4 percent, from $65,000 to $75,000, or from 36.1 percent of revenues to 39.5 percent. This is possibly an unfavorable relationship and should definitely be investigated.

Once we have calculated the common size ratios and the percent change ratios, we can use them to compare our organization with itself over time, with specific competitors, and with industrywide statistics.

LIQUIDITY RATIOS   Perhaps the most important focus for any organization must be maintaining financial viability. If the organization cannot remain in business, it cannot provide services to any of its clients. *Liquidity ratios* focus on whether the organization has enough cash and other liquid resources to meet its obligations in the near term. At the same time, we can use liquidity ratios to assess whether the organization is wastefully maintaining too much liquidity. If liquidity is excessive, long-term investments with high relevance to the organization's mission and perhaps high profit potential may be lost.

A manufacturing industry generally has high levels of inventories and receivables. Both of those items result in significant amounts of current assets. An airline, conversely, collects most payments in advance of providing service, so its receivables are low. Its inventory needs are low. One would expect the airline industry to have a very low current ratio. Therefore, one must consider the nature of the organization when determining an appropriate level for the ratio.

The two most common liquidity ratios are the *current* and *quick ratios*. The current ratio compares current assets with current liabilities. Since current assets become cash or are used up within a year and current liabilities are paid within a year, this matchup has relevance for the ability of the organization to meet obligations as they come due.

The quick ratio (sometimes called the *acid test*) is more conservative. It excludes all assets except cash, marketable securities, and receivables in making the comparison with current liabilities. The quick ratio provides a more stringent measure. The rationale behind this calculation is that often current liabilities must be paid off within just a few months. It may take longer than that to use inventory, invoice our customers, and collect payment. Other current assets may be used up rather than becoming cash. Therefore, the acid test compares the current assets that become cash fairly quickly with the current liabilities.

Using numbers from Exhibit 14-1, the two liquidity ratios for Meals for the Homeless can be calculated as follows:

		2012	2011
Current Ratio = $\dfrac{\text{Current Assets}}{\text{Current Liabilities}}$ =		$\dfrac{\$61,100}{\$14,000}$	$\dfrac{\$48,100}{\$16,000}$
	=	4.4 =	3.0
Quick Ratio = $\dfrac{\text{Cash + Marketable Securities + Receivables}}{\text{Current Liabilities}}$ =		$\dfrac{\$100 + \$3,000 + \$55,000}{\$14,000}$	$\dfrac{\$3,100 + \$3,000 + \$38,000}{\$16,000}$
	=	4.2 =	2.8

A widely used rule of thumb across industries is that the current ratio should be about 2.0 and the quick ratio 1.0. However, as noted earlier, rules of thumb should be adjusted to the needs of a particular type of organization. Too low a ratio indicates a possible financial crisis in the near term. Too high a ratio indicates failure to wisely invest resources in higher yielding assets.

Another widely used liquidity ratio is *days of cash on hand.* This measure compares cash and marketable securities with daily operating expenses. This is more stringent yet, its purpose to assess how long the organization could meet its typical daily expenses using just the cash (and near cash assets) on hand. If something happened that cut off our future cash inflows, how long could the organization meet its cash outflows using just the resources on hand?

For instance, in some states until a county passes its budget, towns in that county cannot collect their local real estate taxes. When the county budget process is delayed, towns suddenly have no cash inflow. A town manager would want to know how long the town could go before it would have to borrow money to pay its expenses.

The days of cash on hand ratio is calculated by dividing the cash and cash equivalents by the daily operating expenses that must be paid. Too low is a sign of risk. Too high is a sign of cash lying around rather than being fruitfully invested in plant and equipment to provide resources or services.

This ratio could be particularly helpful in the case of Meals. Accounts receivable have been increasing, and we do not know why. It is possible that we will have trouble collecting those receivables on a timely basis. Days of cash on hand can help us understand the organization's ability to handle a collection crisis. Using numbers from Exhibits 14-1 and 14-2, the days of cash on hand ratio can be calculated:

		2012	2011
Days of Cash on Hand	$= \dfrac{\text{Cash + Marketable Securities}}{(\text{Operating Expenses} - \text{Bad Debts} - \text{Depreciation})/365}$	$= \dfrac{\$100 + \$3,000}{(\$191,000 - \$4,000 - \$10,000) \div 365}$	$\dfrac{\$3,100 + \$3,000}{(\$176,000 - \$4,000 - \$10,000) \div 365}$
		$=$ 6.4 days	$=$ 13.7 days

Bad debts and depreciation are subtracted in the denominator because they do not require a cash outflow. The denominator is divided by 365 to convert annual expenses to daily expenses. Note that the decrease in cash from 2011 to 2012 caused a reduction in this ratio from nearly two weeks to about one week.

ASSET TURNOVER RATIOS   Few government, health, or not-for-profit organizations have money to waste. Therefore, these organizations want to operate in an efficient manner. A set of ratios called *asset turnover ratios* (sometimes called *efficiency ratios*) can help in this area. The ratios in this category are related to *receivables, inventory, fixed assets,* and *total assets.*

Timely collection of receivables is important for all types of organizations. Once receivables are collected, the money received can be used to pay creditors, or it can be invested. This means that once the money is received, either we would be paying less interest, or we would be earning more interest. The receivables turnover ratio is calculated by dividing annual credit sales by accounts receivable. Credit sales are those that result in receivables as opposed to immediate cash payment. The *average collection period* (sometimes called days of sales outstanding or days receivable or average age of receivables) can then be calculated by dividing 365 by the receivables turnover. Sometimes the receivables ratios are calculated using average accounts receivable (the beginning balance plus the ending balance divided by 2).

For Meals, credit sales would probably not include client revenue but would include all other revenues and support.[5] Using data from Exhibits 14-1 and 14-2, we get the following:

		2012	2011
$\dfrac{\text{Receivables}}{\text{Turnover}} = \dfrac{\text{Revenues and Support} - \text{Client Revenue}}{\text{Accounts Receivable}} =$		$\dfrac{\$178{,}000 - \$11{,}000}{\$55{,}000}$	$\dfrac{\$169{,}000 - \$9{,}000}{\$38{,}000}$
	$=$	3.0 $=$	4.2
$\dfrac{\text{Average Collection}}{\text{Period}} = \dfrac{365}{\text{Receivables Turnover}} =$		$\dfrac{365}{3.0}$	$\dfrac{365}{4.2}$
	$=$	121.7 days $=$	86.9 days

In 2011 and 2012, the receivables of Meals only turned over 4.2 and 3.0 times, respectively. This means that the collection of receivables is as if we fully collected and generated receivables 4.2 and 3.0 times in the year. The average collection period presents the same information in a more intuitive fashion. On average, it is taking Meals nearly 122 days to collect a receivable, up from 87 days the prior year. These numbers are both high, indicating that Meals has substantial problems with its collections and that the problems appear to be getting worse. An unfavorable trend over time could indicate lax management in this area. In most industries, a collection period of 30 to 60 days is more normal. Some industries may tend to have a higher average age of receivables, and this is one situation in which the analysis could benefit substantially from industry comparison. The discussion in Box 14-14 raises a potential problem in the calculation of the average collection period.

The same type of ratios calculated for receivables can also be calculated with respect to inventory (with the same type of problem as that discussed in Box 14-14). The inventory turnover ratio is the cost of inventory used divided by the inventory balance (sometimes average inventory is used: beginning + ending inventory ÷ 2). Many for-profit organizations have a line called "Cost of goods sold" on their income statement. That represents the cost of the inventory that has been used during the year. For public service organizations, we have to examine the financial statements and determine which categories are most relevant. In the case of Meals, the appropriate measure of inventory used is food, which is found on the statement of functional expenses, Exhibit 14-4. The ending inventory balance is taken from Exhibit 14-1. We can calculate the ratios as follows:

		2012	2011
$\text{Inventory Turnover} = \dfrac{\text{Cost of Inventory}}{\text{Inventory}} =$		$\dfrac{\$17{,}000}{\$2{,}000}$	$\dfrac{\$15{,}000}{\$4{,}000}$
	$=$	8.5 $=$	3.8
$\text{Days of Inventory on Hand} = \dfrac{365}{\text{Inventory Turnover}} =$		$\dfrac{365}{8.5}$	$\dfrac{365}{3.8}$
	$=$	42.9 days $=$	96.1 days

[5] Client sales would not be included for Meals because all revenues collected from homeless people are likely to be from cash sales rather than sales on account.

BOX 14-14

Stocks and Flows: Apples and Oranges?

The average collection period ratio draws information from both the balance sheet and the activity statement. It is important to bear in mind that the balance sheet represents a stock. It reports the balance in accounts at a specific point in time. In contrast, the activity statement represents a flow, reporting what has occurred over a period of time. This can create problems when ratios are based on information from both statements.

For instance, suppose that the Hospital for Ordinary Surgery (HOS) appears to have a reasonable average collection period ratio of 45 days. That ratio, however, is based on the receivables turnover ratio, which looks at revenues (from the activity statement) for the full year and accounts receivable (from the balance sheet) at the end of the year. This could result in misleading information.

Suppose that the HOS ends its year on August 31, an extremely slow point in its activity. Perhaps November through April represents a very busy period for HOS, and most of its annual revenues are generated during that period. It might take HOS three or four months on average to collect receivables. However, by the end of August, four months after the busy period, receivables are at a very low point. Comparing annual revenues, which include busy and slow periods, with receivables at a particularly low point in the year will overstate the receivables turnover and understate the average collection period.

This is a potential problem wherever ratios are calculated using information from stock and flow statements. One solution is to use average information based on monthly values. For example, if the accounts receivable balance at the end of each month was averaged for the year and that average was used in the calculation, the ratio would be more accurate.

For Meals, the inventory turnover ratio is 8.5 and 3.8 for 2012 and 2011, respectively. That means that inventory turns over only about eight or nine times per year in 2012. That would be considered a slow turnover rate in most industries, let alone one for which the inventory is food. Even with the improvement in 2012 as compared to 2011, food was on hand an average of 43 days (*days of inventory on hand*) before it was consumed. At best, this implies that Meals keeps canned goods on hand for long periods of time. At worst, it may be using food that has passed its safe use expiration date.

By keeping inventory on hand for long periods of time, Meals is using resources inefficiently. It is paying for inventory before it needs to have that inventory. It may also pay for storage costs and will possibly have spoilage costs as well. Meals has a dilemma because it cannot accurately predict when donations of food will arrive and wants to have enough food on hand in case donations are not received (e.g., restaurants may be very busy and have few leftovers). However, the turnover appears to be too low, and management should definitely focus its attention on this problem. Note that a review of the financial statements and the notes did not make us aware of this problem. Ratio analysis is an essential element of financial analysis.

We are also concerned with the efficient use of fixed and total assets. If our organization requires more of these assets than similar organizations, we would like to try to find out why. We are likely to be able to afford to provide more services if we have fewer resources tied up in assets. The fixed asset turnover ratio is calculated by dividing total revenues by net fixed assets. Ratios can be defined in a variety of ways. In the case of Meals, the asset base is supporting all revenues generated. Therefore, it is appropriate to use the total unrestricted revenues and other support as the revenue measure. The net fixed assets in the following calculation are found by subtracting the cash restricted for building acquisitions from the total long-term assets. The total asset turnover ratio is calculated by dividing total revenues by total assets:

			2012	2011
Fixed Asset Turnover	=	$\dfrac{\text{Total Unrestricted Revenues and Support}}{\text{Net Fixed Assets}}$ =	$\dfrac{\$190,000}{\$83,000}$	$\dfrac{\$180,000}{\$97,000}$
		=	2.3 =	1.9
Total Asset Turnover	=	$\dfrac{\text{Total Unrestricted Revenues and Support}}{\text{Total Assets}}$ =	$\dfrac{\$190,000}{\$145,000}$	$\dfrac{\$180,000}{\$146,000}$
		=	1.3 =	1.2

The fixed asset turnover ratio for 2012 indicates that $2.30 of revenue is generated by each dollar invested in fixed assets. The total asset turnover showed $1.30 of revenues for each dollar of total assets. It is difficult to determine whether these ratio levels are appropriate without comparison with other similar organizations.

Note that the fixed asset turnover is good for comparisons that focus primarily on the organization's use of buildings and equipment in generating revenue. In contrast, total assets turnover is more useful if one wants to include management of cash, inventories, and receivables in the comparison over time or between organizations. For example, a museum might have large amounts of fixed assets, making the fixed asset turnover of primary interest, while a hospital might also have major amounts of receivables, making the total asset turnover more relevant.

LEVERAGE AND COVERAGE RATIOS *Leverage* refers to the extent to which an organization supports its activities by using debt. The greater the debt, the riskier the organization becomes. In contrast to the liquidity ratios, whose purpose is to assess short-term risk, the *leverage ratios* provide insight into the ability of the organization to meet its long-term obligations. In particular, we are concerned with whether the organization has incurred obligations to make principal and interest payments in excess of its capacity. While leverage ratios examine the amount borrowed, *coverage ratios* examine the capacity to make payments. These two types of ratios are together referred to as *solvency* ratios.

Debt is a double-edged sword. It often provides organizations with the ability to undertake programs and provide services that they otherwise could not. While some debt may enhance the level of services provided, excessive levels of debt threaten the continued existence of the organization. How much debt is too much? Leverage and coverage ratios are used to help assess whether the organization has a safe level of debt.

Two prominent leverage ratios are the *debt* and *debt to equity ratios*. The debt and debt to equity ratios examine the extent to which the organization uses debt to finance the acquisition of its assets. General rules of thumb are that the debt ratio (debt ÷ total assets) should not exceed .5, and the debt to equity ratio (debt ÷ equity) should not exceed 1. Under those rules of thumb, no more than half of the assets of an organization would be financed with debt. However, the appropriate level will vary from industry to industry, and comparisons are critical.

Some would argue that coverage ratios are even more critical. They examine the organization's capacity to make debt service payments (interest and principal) as they come due. Coverage ratios include *times-interest-earned* and the *cash flow coverage ratios*. The times-interest-earned ratio examines how many times over the organization could pay its interest. For example, if income before considering interest expense was $200 and interest expense was $100, then the organization has earned twice as much as it needed be able to meet its interest payments. Bear in mind that if the organization fails to make required interest payments, it can be forced into bankruptcy by its creditors. The higher the times-interest-earned ratio, the better. The cash flow coverage ratio is more encompassing, considering not only interest payments but all required payments, including required lease payments, interest, and debt repayments.

For Meals for the Homeless, we could calculate the leverage and coverage ratios as follows:

			2012		2011
Debt	=	$\dfrac{\text{Total Debt}}{\text{Total Assets}}$	$\dfrac{\$26,000}{\$145,000}$		$\dfrac{\$32,000}{\$146,000}$
		=	.18 or 18%	=	.22 or 22%
Debt to Equity	=	$\dfrac{\text{Total Debt}}{\text{Total Net Assets}}$	$\dfrac{\$26,000}{\$119,000}$		$\dfrac{\$32,000}{\$114,000}$
		=	.22 or 22%	=	.28 or 28%
Times-Interest-Earned	=	$\dfrac{\text{Income} + \text{Interest Expense}}{\text{Interest Expense}}$	$\dfrac{(\$1,000)+\$1,280}{\$1,280}$		$\dfrac{\$4,000+\$1,600}{\$1,600}$
		=	.2	=	3.5

Debt ratios can be calculated using a range of different definitions for debt. Here we are using total liabilities from Exhibit 14-1. Sometimes the ratio is calculated using just long-term obligations (and is then referred to as long-term debt to equity). The measurement of equity in the debt to equity ratio depends on the type of the organization. It could be stockholders' equity, fund balance, or net assets. For 2012, the debt ratio of .18 and the debt to equity ratio of .22 seem to be at reasonably low levels.

The times-interest-earned ratio provides a number of definitional challenges for not-for-profit organizations. Exactly what is income? We could use the increase in net assets. However, increases in temporarily and permanently restricted net assets are not available for paying current-year interest. Therefore, a more appropriate measure would be the increase in unrestricted net assets.

A second problem arises in trying to locate interest expense on the financial statements. In some cases, interest will be a separate item on the activity statement. Often, however, it is included in another category, such as General and Administration. Cash flow statements generally provide a supplemental line at the bottom indicating the amount of interest paid. It may also show up in the statement of functional expenses. For Meals, interest can be found in both Exhibits 14-3 and 14-4. The 2011 times-interest-earned coverage ratio of 3.5 is low but adequate. By 2012, however, the ratio had fallen to an unacceptably low level, below 1. That means that the organization did not have sufficient increases in unrestricted net assets to even pay the current year's interest.

This problem may be offset somewhat if there is sufficient cash flow. Note that to arrive at the measure of income used in the times-interest-earned ratio, depreciation is subtracted as an expense (see Exhibit 14-2). However, depreciation does not require cash payments. Therefore, the cash flow coverage ratio may provide important additional information. The following cash flow coverage ratio begins with cash from operations taken from the statement of cash flows and adds interest and rent.[6] That total is divided by interest, rent, and debt payments. The numerator is an approximation of the cash available for required payments. The denominator represents the required cash flow payments. Debt

---

[6] An alternative approach starts with income and adds back depreciation as well as interest and rent.

payment information can be taken from the Exhibit 14-3 cash flow statement's "Cash Flows from Financing Activities" section and rent appears on Exhibit 14-4.

		2012	2011

$$\text{Cash Flow Coverage} = \frac{\text{Cash from Operations} + \text{Interest} + \text{Rent}}{\text{Interest} + \text{Rent} + \text{Debt Payments}} = \frac{\$(10,000) + \$1,280 + \$16,720}{\$1,280 + \$16,720 + \$5,000} = \frac{\$15,000 + \$1,600 + \$15,800}{\$1,600 + \$15,800 + \$6,000}$$

$$= .35 \qquad = 1.38$$

For Meals, the 2012 value for the cash flow coverage ratio is .35, or 35 percent of required payments. This represents a potentially serious problem for Meals. Some charities work on extremely tight margins, with cash barely covering expenses each year. This creates the potential for financial crisis at any time. In the case of Meals, we note that without borrowing money or selling investments, the organization would not be able to meet required payments. This situation cannot continue for long periods without creating serious financial crises, possibly leading to cessation of operations.

A problem with the cash flow coverage ratio is that it is retrospective. It involves looking at whether sufficient cash flow was generated to meet payments that were due. At times loans have large payments at maturity. The notes to the financial statements should be carefully examined for future debt principal payment requirements. It is helpful to recalculate the ratio on a pro forma basis. By pro forma, we mean a projected number. Taking into account likely future cash inflows and committed future cash payments, we can get a sense of whether the ratio value is likely to deteriorate even further in coming years.

Note that different industries have different perspectives on what is an acceptable level of debt relative to equity and what level of interest payments can be considered reasonably safe. For an organization with very constant sales and earnings, more debt is relatively safer than for one that has wide swings in activity. Therefore, an arbitrary rule of thumb, such as a debt to equity ratio of .5, is of limited value.

PROFITABILITY RATIOS   All organizations desire to be safe and efficient. But do all organizations want to be profitable? Public service organizations do not provide services primarily to make profits. So why would *profitability ratios* be of concern? Virtually all organizations need to earn a profit to be financially healthy—to be able to replace equipment with newer more costly equipment, acquire new technologies, expand services, and to be able to meet the challenges of the future. At the same time, it might be inappropriate for many not-for-profit organizations to make an excessive profit.

One way to assess profitability is with a performance indicator. GAAP require that health organizations provide a performance indicator that reports the results of operations.

> Because of the importance of the performance indicator, it should be clearly labeled with a descriptive term such as *revenues over expenses, revenues and gains over expenses and losses, earned income,* or *performance earnings.* The notes to the financial statements should include a description of the nature and composition of the performance indicator. Not-for-profit organizations should report the performance indicator in a statement that also presents the total changes in unrestricted net assets.[7]

---

[7] American Institute of Certified Public Accountants. *AICPA Audit and Accounting Guide: Health Care Organizations.* New York: N.Y., AICPA, 1996, p. 101.

Profitability ratios can also help managers and outside users assess whether the organization is making an adequate but not excessive profit. For some types of organizations, a somewhat larger profit might be appropriate. For others, a small surplus might be desirable.

Four of the most common measures of profitability are the *operating margin, total margin, return on assets,* and *return on equity* ratios. The operating margin compares the operating profit (operating revenue less operating expenses) with operating revenue. It assesses the profitability of each dollar of revenues generated by the routine ongoing activities of the organization. For example, if revenues are $100 and operating profits are $3, then operating profits compared with revenues are 3 percent. In other words, the organization earns 3 cents of operating profits for every dollar of revenues generated.

The total margin compares the excess of revenues over expenses with total revenues. That determines the overall profits, including all sources of revenues and expenses, per dollar of revenues. In some cases, organizations will have sources of profits that do not come from its routine operations. For example, gains on investments might fall into that category. The return on assets compares the profit with assets in order to determine the amount of profit earned for each dollar invested in the organization. The return on equity (profits divided by equity) assesses the amount of profit earned on each dollar of equity.

The ratio analysis technique was developed primarily for proprietary organizations. Applying the traditional ratios to health, not-for-profit, and government organizations is a constant challenge because the vocabulary changes, and more substantively, the format of the financial statements changes. Nowhere is this problem more evident than with the profitability ratios.

One might suppose that one could simply look at the amount of net income or increase in unrestricted net assets to assess profitability. However, we can learn more from the relationships developed by the ratios. In an era of inflation, even at low levels, replacing buildings and equipment, and even inventory, will cost more in future years. Knowing that an organization earns $10,000 does not tell us much. Knowing that it earns 3 cents for every dollar of assets tells us that it is accumulating the money needed to replace inventory and facilities at 3 percent annually higher prices than their current cost.

Profit margin ratios are really common size ratios. Both the operating and total margin ratios are comparisons with total revenues. In Exhibit 14-7, note that the increase in unrestricted net assets compared with revenues and support is −.5 percent in 2012 and 2.2 percent in 2011. This is equivalent to the operating margin ratio. The total margin is the overall increase in net assets compared with revenues and support, which was 2.6 percent in 2012 and 3.9 percent in 2011:

		2012	2011
Operating Margin $=$	$\dfrac{\text{Increase in Unrestricted Net Assets}}{\text{Total Unrestricted Revenues and Other Support}} =$	$\dfrac{\$(1,000)}{\$190,000}$	$\dfrac{\$4,000}{\$180,000}$
		$= -.005 \text{ or } -.5\%$	$= .022 \text{ or } 2.2\%$
Total Margin $=$	$\dfrac{\text{Increase in Net Assets}}{\text{Total Unrestricted Revenues and Other Support}} =$	$\dfrac{\$5,000}{\$190,000}$	$\dfrac{\$7,000}{\$180,000}$
		$= .026 \text{ or } 2.6\%$	$= .039 \text{ or } 3.9\%$

We can see from these margin ratios that although Meals is not quite breaking even from operations, when all changes to net assets are taken into account, it is earning a modest 2.6 percent increase in net assets for each dollar of revenues.

Operating and total margins, however, can be misleading. Some organizations, such as supermarkets, earn only a modest 1 percent to 2 percent margin, but they can still be very profitable because their sales are very large. Some industries earn a small margin on large sales, while other industries have lower sales but higher margins. For this reason, some believe that return on assets and return on equity are more useful measures. These ratios are often referred to as return on investment (ROI) ratios.

Return on assets (ROA) is an ROI measure that evaluates the organization's return (net income, surplus, excess of revenues over expenses) relative to the asset base used to generate that income. Consider a for-profit health care organization. If the organization could invest $500 in each of two alternative programs and one program generated twice as much income as the other, it would prefer that program, all other things being equal. Obviously, the benefit to the health of the organization's client base should be considered in making a final decision. The organization that generates more income, relative to the amount of investment, is doing a better job, all other things being equal.

Another profitability measure is the return on equity (ROE). For Meals that would be the *return on net assets* (RONA). If the organization earns a return on total assets that equals or exceeds the inflation rate, it should be able to replace all of its assets over time. However, to the extent that the organization relies on debt, it does not have to earn a profit equal to the inflation rate on its total amount of assets. As long as it earns at least the inflation rate on its equity or net assets, it can keep pace. For example, Meals has $145,000 of total assets. Meals can keep its debt to equity ratio stable at the current level of .22 and still let its total assets grow at the rate of inflation, as long as the profits each year equal the net assets multiplied by the inflation rate.

Consider an example with simpler numbers. XYZ organization begins the year with $1,000 of assets, $400 of liabilities, and $600 of net assets. Inflation is 4 percent and XYZ needs to have assets of $1,040, or 4 percent more assets, next year to support its operations at the same level as this year. Creditors are still willing to finance 40 percent of its assets, but the net assets need to remain at 60 percent of total assets to keep the organization secure. The required 60 percent of $1,040 of assets is $624. In order for the organization to increase its assets by $40 and keep up with inflation, its net assets need to increase by $24. It will be able to borrow the remaining $16 that it needs to expand its total assets by $40. Thus, the organization needs an ROE, or in this case an RONA, of 4 percent. Notice that this necessary $24 increase to net assets requires a profit equal to only 2.4 percent of total of assets ($1,000 × 2.4% = $24 profit), even though the inflation rate is 4 percent.

In the case of Meals for the Homeless, we can calculate the ROA and RONA as follows:

			2012		2011
ROA	$=$	$\dfrac{\text{Increase in Net Assets}}{\text{Total Assets}}$	$= \dfrac{\$5,000}{\$145,000}$		$\dfrac{\$7,000}{\$146,000}$
			$= .034$ or 3.4%	$=$	.048 or 4.8%
RONA	$=$	$\dfrac{\text{Increase in Net Assets}}{\text{Net Assets}}$	$= \dfrac{\$5,000}{\$119,000}$		$\dfrac{\$7,000}{\$114,000}$
			$= .042$ or 4.2%	$=$	.061 or 6.1%

Despite some of the other problems our ratio analysis has disclosed, the ROA and RONA levels of Meals do not appear to be unreasonably low.

OTHER RATIOS   As previously noted, ratio analysis is a field developed primarily to serve for-profit organizations. Managers in public service organizations should be proactive in developing additional useful ratios. For example, the not-for-profit industry in recent years has started to actively report the *program services ratio.* That ratio divides program service expenses by total expenses. Looking at Exhibit 14-4, we see that for Meals the ratio would be as follows:

		2012	2011
Program Services Ratio	$= \dfrac{\text{Program Service Expenses}}{\text{Total Expenses}} =$	$\dfrac{\$83,000 + \$38,000}{\$191,000} =$	$\dfrac{\$78,400 + \$36,600}{\$176,000}$
		$= .63$ or 63%	$.65$ or 65%

This ratio helps the user understand what portion of Meals' spending goes directly into its program services. That does not mean that the money spent on program services is spent efficiently. It only provides some indication of the extent to which Meals spends money on program services (meals and counseling) in contrast to support services (fund-raising and administration).

Care is required in interpreting financial information. Suppose that a comparable charity to Meals in another city spends less on management. Its program services ratio is 80 percent in contrast to Meals' 63 percent. However, with less spending on management, the other charity is unable to recruit as many volunteers to work in its kitchens. With fewer volunteers, it spends much more of its money on kitchen salaries. Its ratio of program services is higher, but it provides fewer meals per dollar of revenue because it does not have enough volunteer kitchen staff. Ratios can be helpful, but they cannot replace a thorough review of all available information. And any one ratio can be very misleading if taken by itself.

ASSESSMENT

At this point in the process of financial statement analysis, one will have completed the following activities:

- review of the financial statements, including the auditor's opinion letter;
- review of the notes that accompany the financial statements; and
- calculation and review of ratios with comparisons with the organization itself over time, the industry and, other specific organizations.

It is necessary next to integrate all of the information and make an assessment about the financial status of the organization being reviewed. Experience plays an important role in seeking out information and assigning appropriate implications to that information. Even the novice can make insightful evaluations, however, by being thorough and inquisitive.

If current liabilities are rising, one must wonder why. Is the organization having trouble with cash flow? If fixed assets are declining, why is that happening? Is the organization unable to replace its facilities as they wear out? Often there are benign answers to our questions. However, the questions must be considered, and the answers carefully reviewed. Only by bringing together all of the available information can the analyst get a clear picture of the overall financial situation of the organization.

Summary

The focus of this chapter is to provide a general framework for financial statement analysis to gain insight into the financial situation of an organization. The basic framework provided is to (1) carefully review the financial statements in detail, including reading the auditor's opinion letter and considering the information in that letter; (2) examine the notes that accompany the financial statements; (3) calculate a series of ratios and compare them with the organization over time, other specific similar organizations, and the industry as a whole; and (4) make a final assessment of the financial situation of the organization, taking all of the available information into account.

Preview

Users of government financial reports are interested in many of the same things as those analyzing other types of organizations. The discussion of financial statement analysis in Chapter 14 is largely applicable to governments as well. However, understanding the financial condition of governments requires additional types of information and, in some cases, modifications to the basic financial statement analysis approach. Governmental financial analysis must take into account factors such as debt per capita, tax rates, and citizen income and wealth. The special issues related to evaluating the financial condition of a government are the focus of Chapter 15.

Key Terms from This Chapter

acid test. See *quick ratio*.

asset turnover ratios. Ratios that examine the efficiency with which the organization uses its resources. Examples are *receivables turnover, average collection period, inventory turnover, days of inventory on hand,* and *fixed asset turnover ratios;* sometimes called efficiency ratios.

audit. Examination of the financial records of the organization to discover material errors, to evaluate the internal control system, and to determine if financial statements have been prepared in accordance with Generally Accepted Accounting Principles (GAAP).

audited financial statements. Financial statements that have been examined by a Certified Public Accountant (CPA) who issues an opinion letter, called the *auditor's report*.

auditor's report. A letter from a CPA providing an expert opinion about whether the financial statements provide a fair representation of the organization's financial position and the results of its operations, in accordance with GAAP.

average collection period. 365 divided by the *receivables turnover ratio;* this *asset turnover ratio* indicates the average number of days from the issuance of an invoice until a receivable is collected. The lower this ratio, the more efficient the organization is, other things being equal.

cash flow coverage ratio. *Coverage ratio* that compares cash from operations with required cash payments such as interest and debt payments to assess the ability of the organization to meet those required cash payments.

commitments. Future obligations the organization has that do not appear on the balance sheet.

common size ratios. Comparison of all the numbers on a financial statement with one key number. For example, each asset on the balance sheet is compared with total assets.

comparative financial statements. Financial statements that present financial information from more than one fiscal period.

compilation of financial statements. Engagement in which the auditor is hired to develop a set of financial statements from information that has been recorded by the organization during the year; the auditor does not perform the extensive testing of records and detailed review that are part of an audit.

contingent liabilities.   Obligations that will exist in the future if certain events occur, such as if the organization loses a lawsuit.

coverage ratios.   Ratios that examine the ability of the organization to make required interest and principal payments on debt; examples are the *times-interest-earned ratio* and *cash flow coverage ratio.*

current ratio.   Current assets divided by current liabilities; this *liquidity ratio* assesses the ability of the organization to meet its current obligations as they come due for payment.

days of cash on hand.   Ratio that compares cash and marketable securities with daily operating expenses to assess the ability of the organization to meet its obligations in the event of a delay in collecting cash owed to the organization.

days of inventory on hand.   365 divided by the inventory turnover ratio; this *asset turnover ratio* assesses how many days supply of inventory is kept on hand. In general, the greater this number, the less efficient the organization is perceived as being.

debt ratio.   Debt divided by assets; this *leverage ratio* assesses the amount of debt relative to the total size of the organization as measured by its assets.

debt to equity ratio.   Debt divided by net assets; this *leverage ratio* considers the relative magnitudes of debt to equity of the organization to assess the risk created by the use of *leverage.*

defined benefit plan.   Pension plan in which the organization is required to make specific defined payments to participants upon retirement. The risk or benefit of investment results falls on the organization rather than the participants.

defined contribution plan.   Pension plan in which the amount required to be put aside by the organization is determined each year. Depending on investment results, the participants will receive larger or smaller amounts upon retirement.

efficiency ratios.   See *asset turnover ratios.*

financial audit.   See *audit.*

financial statement analysis.   Analysis of the profitability and viability of an organization achieved by reviewing financial statements, including their accompanying notes and the *auditor's report,* performing *ratio analysis,* and using comparative data.

fixed asset turnover.   Unrestricted revenues and support divided by fixed assets; this *asset turnover ratio* assesses the number of dollars of revenue and support generated for each dollar invested in fixed assets. The more revenue and support per dollar of fixed assets, the more efficiently the organization is using its investment in fixed assets, other things being equal.

full disclosure.   GAAP that requires that notes convey material financial information that the financial statements do not adequately disclose.

inventory turnover.   The cost of inventory consumed for the entire year divided by the amount of inventory on hand; this *asset turnover ratio* evaluates the relative number of times that the organization's inventory has been consumed and replaced during the year. A higher number is generally indicative of greater efficiency, other things being equal.

leverage.   The use of debt as a source of financing. Increased amounts of debt increase the risk of the organization because of the requirement to make interest payments.

leverage ratios.   Ratios that examine the relative amount of debt the organization has; sometimes referred to as solvency ratios; examples include the *debt ratio* and the *debt to equity ratio.*

liquidity ratios.   Ratios that focus on whether the organization has enough cash and other liquid resources to meet its obligations in the near term.

management letter.   Letter from the auditor to the organization's management discussing its internal control weaknesses.

management's discussion.   Section of an annual report in which the organization's management discusses the organization's performance.

operating margin.   *Profitability ratio* that compares the operating profit (operating revenue less operating expenses) with operating revenue. It assesses the profitability of each dollar of revenues generated by the routine ongoing activities of the organization. For example, if revenues are $100 and operating profits are $3, then operating profits compared with revenues are 3 percent.

opinion letter.   Letter issued by CPA upon completion of an audit, which indicates if financial statements have been prepared in accordance with Generally Accepted Accounting Principles.

profitability ratios.   Ratios that assess the profitability of the organization; examples are the *operating margin* and *total margin ratios.*

program services ratio.   Program service expenses divided by total expenses; this ratio helps the user understand what portion of spending goes directly to program services in contrast to support services.

quick ratio.   Cash, marketable securities, plus receivables divided by current liabilities. This *liquidity ratio* is a more stringent test of the ability to meet current obligations as they come due than the widely used *current ratio*. Sometimes called the acid test.

ratio analysis.   Comparison of one number with another in order to gain insight from the relationship between the numbers.

receivables turnover.   Revenues and support divided by accounts receivable; see also *average collection period.*

return on assets (ROA).   Increase in net assets divided by total assets; *profitability ratio* that measures the rate of return the organization earns on its total assets.

return on equity.   *Profitability ratio* that assesses the amount of profit earned on each dollar of equity.

return on net assets (RONA).   Increase in net assets divided by net assets; profitability ratio that measures the relative increase in net assets.

review of financial statements.   Auditor review for form and accuracy; in a review, the auditor does not perform the extensive testing of records and detailed review that are part of an audit.

solvency.   Ability to meet current and future obligations.

times-interest-earned ratio.   Income before interest expense divided by interest expense; this *coverage ratio* assesses the ability of the organization to make its required annual interest payments.

total asset turnover.   Total unrestricted revenues and support divided by total assets; this *asset turnover ratio* assesses the number of dollars of revenue and support generated for each dollar invested in assets. The more revenue and support per dollar of assets, the more efficiently the organization is using its investment in assets, other things being equal.

total margin ratio.   *Profitability ratio* that compares the excess of revenues over expenses with total revenues to determine the overall profits earned, including all sources of revenues and expenses, per dollar of revenues.

Questions for Discussion

14-1. The primary purpose of an audit is to discover fraud. True or false? Explain.

14-2. Who takes primary responsibility for audited financial statements issued to the public?

14-3. What is covered in the three paragraphs of the typical audit opinion letter?

14-4. In general, what are healthy signs in the cash flow statement?

14-5. Why are financial statements accompanied by notes?

14-6. What are the major classes of ratio analysis? What can we learn from each class?

14-7. What are the major elements of financial statement analysis?

14-8. What types of comparisons should be made with ratios?

14-9. What are some potential problems with ratios?

Problems

14-10. Exhibits 14-8 and 14-9 present the statements of financial position and statements of activities for the Disabled American Veterans (DAV) Charitable Service Trust. For both 2007 and 2006, calculate:
   a. common size ratios for the statements of financial position and statements of activities,
   b. the current ratio,
   c. days of cash on hand,
   d. the debt ratio,
   e. the debt to equity ratio,

   f. the total margin ratio, and
   g. the program services ratio.

14-11. Refer to the 2007 annual report of the American Civil Liberties Union (ACLU) in answering the following questions. The ACLU financial statements are located in the Student Resources Folder of this book's Web site at www.pearsonhighered.com/finkler.[8]

   1. Do the financial statements reflect the activities of the ACLU local affiliates? How do you know?

---

[8] This problem and its solution were written by Drew Franklin. Used with permission.

EXHIBIT 14-8

Disabled American Veterans (DAV)
Charitable Service Trust
Statements of Financial Position
As of December 31, 2007 and 2006

Assets	2007	2006
Cash and Cash Equivalents	$ 1,909,606	$ 1,044,193
Interest and Dividends Receivable	61,244	52,582
Campaigns' Pledges Receivable—Net of allowance for assessment fees and uncollectible pledges of $449,162 in 2007 and $464,486 in 2006	373,788	358,632
Prepaid Expenses and Other	16,244	25,367
Investments	10,944,924	9,653,039
Total	$ 13,305,806	$ 11,133,813
Liabilities and Net Assets		
Liabilities:		
Accounts payable—DAV	$ 201,721	$ 171,550
Accounts payable—other	910	1,017
Annuity payment liability	3,857,262	3,679,148
Total liabilities	4,059,893	3,851,715
Unrestricted Net Assets	9,245,913	7,282,098
Total	$ 13,305,806	$ 11,133,813

Source: http://www.dav.org/cst/documents/cst_annual_report.pdf

2. Did the ACLU receive any endowment type donations during 2007? How do you know?

3. How much did temporarily restricted net assets change during the year ended March 31, 2007? How much of the temporarily restricted net assets became unrestricted in that year?

4. Under the approach used by the ACLU, which of the following would be considered to be cash equivalents?
   a. Checking account
   b. Savings account
   c. Three-month treasury bill
   d. Six-month treasury bill
   e. One-year treasury bill

5. How might you assess the ACLU's short-term liquidity? Is the trend improving or deteriorating? What do you think of the trend?

6. The ACLU had a decrease in net assets for the year ending March 31, 2007. Calculate the total margin for 2007 and 2006. Is the trend improving or deteriorating? Are there any elements in the calculation that might lead you to believe that one year is worse than the other? Explain.

7. Describe how you might measure *Return on Net Assets* to assess the ACLU's profitability. What does this measure reflect in terms of the organization's financial position?

8. Describe the organization's use of financial leverage and its implications on financial position.

9. If you were a fund-raising manager for the organization, and your compensation was somewhat tied to dollars raised, would you rather be focused on new membership or current members?

10. The ACLU reports its program services expenses separately from supporting services expenses. Do generally accepted accounting principles require the organization to make this distinction? Why or why not? Why and for whom might this distinction be informative?

11. Suppose you have a friend who is considering making a donation to the ACLU. She wants to know how much of her money would go directly to the organization's major activities as opposed to paying for administrative expenses. Which ratio would you advise her to use? Calculate the values for 2006 and 2007. Did the

EXHIBIT 14-9

Disabled American Veterans (DAV)
Charitable Service Trust
Statements of Activities
For the Years Ended December 31, 2007 and 2006

	Unrestricted	
	2007	2006
Support and Revenue:		
Contributions—net of assessment fees and provision for uncollectible pledges of $428,587 in 2007 and $433,252 in 2006	$ 4,771,172	$ 2,654,400
Contributions of charitable gift annuities	241,245	178,626
Bequests	2,178,924	32,436,803
Investment income—net	766,580	384,670
Total support and revenue	7,957,921	35,654,499
Expenses:		
Program services	6,053,675	34,754,236
Management and general	85,933	75,499
Fundraising	179,277	168,316
Total expenses	6,318,885	34,998,051
Change in Net Assests before Change in Unrealized Appreciaion of Investments	1,639,036	656,448
Change in Unrealized Appreciaion of Investments	324,779	428,159
Change in Net Assets	1,963,815	1,084,607
Net Assests—Beginning of year	7,282,098	6,197,491
Net Assests—End of year	$ 9,245,913	$ 7,282,098

Source: http://www.dav.org/cst/documents/cst_annual_report.pdf

ratio improve or worsen between 2006 and 2007? Explain.

14-12. Refer to the 2002 annual report of the Make-A-Wish Foundation (Wish), in answering the following questions.[9] The complete report is located in the Student Resources Folder of this book's Web site at www.pearsonhighered.com/finkler.

1. Did the accounting firm of KPMG audit all of the Make-A-Wish Foundation chapters? How do you know?
2. Would you say that the financial statements are free of error, since they have been audited by a CPA?
3. What was the range of the cost of wishes granted in 2002? How do you know?

4. Under the approach used by Wish, which of the following would be considered to be cash equivalents?
   a. Checking account
   b. Savings account
   c. Three-month treasury bill
   d. Six-month treasury bill
   e. One-year treasury bill
5. Is there any difference in the way that Wish treats the donation of land, buildings and equipment from the way it treats the contributions of cash that are restricted for the purchase of land, buildings, and equipment? If so, how, and how do you know? If not, why not?

[9] This is adapted from a final exam prepared by Dwight Dension, Steven Finkler, Robert Purtell, and Edward Roche. Reprinted with permission.

6. Wish records supplies using the FIFO method. Assuming that there has been an average rate of inflation of 2.5 percent in recent years, if Wish used LIFO would they have reported a higher or lower increase in net assets than they did using FIFO?

7. In their notes, Wish indicates that it performs eight functions, listed below. Which of these eight qualify as program services, as opposed to support services?
   a. Wish granting
   b. Chapter support
   c. Program-related support
   d. Committee and board support
   e. Training and development
   f. Public information
   g. Fund-raising
   h. Management and general

8. Wish had a decrease in net assets for the year ending August 31, 2002. Would you say that a sizeable portion of that decrease resulted from stock market losses on Wish's investment portfolio? Explain.

9. Did the amount of land Wish owned increase or decrease during the year ending August 31, 2002? How do you know?

10. How much did permanently restricted net assets change during the year ending August 31, 2002? How much of the temporarily restricted net assets as of August 31, 2002 are restricted for the specific purpose of wish fulfillment?

11. Does Wish include any provision (i.e., liability) for lawsuits in its financial statements? How do you know?

12. What is the Program Services Expense Ratio for Wish for the year ending August 31, 2002?

13. What were fund-raising costs, as a percent of total revenue and other support, for the years ending August 31, 2002 and 2001?

14. a. What percent did Program Service Expenses grow from 2001 to 2002?
    b. What percent did Support Service Expenses grow from 2001 to 2002?
    c. Which is growing at a faster rate, Program Service Expenses or Support Service Expenses?

15. Did Wish meet any donor restrictions during the year ending August 31, 2002, allowing restricted contributions to become unrestricted? If so, how much?

16. What is the unrestricted total margin for the year ending August 31, 2002?

17. From the combined statement of cash flows we see that the change in contributions receivable required a negative adjustment of $710,659 for the year ending August 31, 2002. How would you interpret this adjustment? Explain.

18. Cash used for investing activities was over $9 million. Should we be concerned with this cash decrease? Why or why not?

19. Looking at Wish's assets on the combined statements of financial position, would you consider investments to be short-term or long-term? Why?

20. Assuming that the obligation to international affiliates is short-term, and deferred rent is long-term, what is the current ratio for 2002?

21. What is the ratio of total debt to equity for 2002?

22. Based on your calculation of total margin, current ratio, and debt to equity, in Questions 16, 20, and 21, and your overall review of the financial statements and notes of Wish, how would you categorize their financial position? Circle just one answer.
    a. Weak
    b. Neutral
    c. Strong

23. What is your overall assessment of the finances of Wish?

Case Study Problem

14-13. For the Major Medical Center financial statements on the following pages, complete the following:
   a. Read the auditor's opinion letter. Are any flags raised?
   b. Review the financial statements. Search for unusual items. What things catch your eye on the balance sheet, operating statement, and cash flow statement?
   c. Review the notes. Do any of them raise cause for concern?
   d. Calculate the following ratios: common size, current, quick, days of cash on hand, receivables turnover, average collection period, fixed asset turnover, total asset turnover, debt, debt to equity, times-interest-earned, operating margin, total margin, ROA, and RONA.
   e. What do you think of Major Medical Center's financial status?

CASE STUDY
Major Medical Center[10]

I.N. SINCER AND OLD, CPAs
2650 East 38th Street
New York, New York 10089

Report of Independent Auditors

Board of Trustees
Major Medical Center

We have audited the accompanying statements of financial position of Major Medical Center (the "Medical Center") as of December 31, 2012 and 2011, and the related statements of operations, changes in net assets, and cash flows for the years then ended. These financial statements are the responsibility of the Medical Center's management. Our responsibility is to express an opinion on these financial statements based on our audits.

We conducted our audits in accordance with generally accepted auditing standards. Those standards require that we plan and perform the audit to obtain reasonable assurance about whether the financial statements are free of material misstatement. An audit includes examining, on a test basis, evidence supporting the amounts and disclosures in the financial statements. An audit also includes assessing the accounting principles used and significant estimates made by management, as well as evaluating the overall financial statement presentation. We believe that our audits provide a reasonable basis for our opinion.

In our opinion, the financial statements referred to above present fairly, in all material respects, the financial position of Major Medical Center at December 31, 2012 and 2011, and the results of its operations, changes in net assets, and cash flows for the years then ended, in conformity with generally accepted accounting principles.

April 30, 2013

I.N. SINCER AND OLD, CPAs

---

[10] Major Medical Center and Hospital Support, Inc. are fictional organizations. Any similarity to real organizations is purely coincidental.

Major Medical Center
Statements of Financial Position

	December 31	
	2012	2011
	(In Thousands)	
Assets		
Current Assets		
Cash and cash equivalents	$ 8,065	$ 9,005
Assets limited as to use—compensating balance for letters of credit	1,000	—
Short-term investments	1,387	1,283
Receivables for patient care, net of allowance for doubtful accounts (2012—$27,232; 2011—$31,934)	49,719	47,614
Pledges receivable	1,814	2,205
Inventories, at average cost	1,690	2,326
Due from third-party reimbursement programs	6,539	—
Receivables for government grants	—	467
Other	2,234	3,415
Total Current Assets	72,448	66,315
Assets limited as to use:		
Sinking fund	14,487	13,410
Compensating balance for standby letters of credit	923	—
	15,410	13,410
Long-term investments	1,132	618
Due from affiliates, net	3,417	3,543
Pledges receivable, net of allowance for uncollectible pledges (2012—$2,218; 2011—$4,453)	1,889	1,468
Property, plant, and equipment net	98,555	89,777
Deferred financing costs	1,323	—
Other	2,065	1,043
	$196,239	$176,174
Liabilities and Net Assets		
Current Liabilities		
Current portion of long-term debt	$ 11,608	$ 11,488
Accounts payable and accrued expenses	29,489	25,311
Accrued salaries and related liabilities	25,572	20,096
Due to third-party reimbursement programs, net	—	1,874
Advances on government grants	1,587	—
Total Current Liabilities	68,256	58,769
Long-term debt, less current portion	55,539	47,709
Accrued post-retirement benefits	6,023	6,017
Other noncurrent liabilities	16,445	17,014
Total Liabilities	146,263	129,509
Commitments and contingencies		
Net Assets		
Unrestricted	40,582	38,014
Temporarily restricted	8,262	7,519
Permanently restricted	1,132	1,132
Total Net Assets	49,976	46,665
	$196,239	$176,174

See accompanying notes.

Major Medical Center
Statements of Operations

	Year ended December 31	
	2012	**2011**
	(In Thousands)	
Operating Revenue		
Net patient service revenue	$402,921	$369,512
Other revenue	13,356	13,850
Net assets released from restrictions	4,708	2,863
Total Operating Revenue	420,985	386,225
Operating Expenses		
Salaries and wages	207,141	196,453
Employee benefits	44,456	44,860
Supplies and expenses	137,505	117,838
Depreciation and amortization	22,541	18,856
Research	2,457	2,214
Interest	4,456	5,253
Total Operating Expenses	418,556	385,474
Operating Income	2,429	751
Net assets released from restrictions used for capital acquisitions	139	146
Increase in unrestricted net assets	$ 2,568	$ 897

See accompanying notes.

Major Medical Center
Statements of Changes in Net Assets

	Net Assets		
	Unrestricted	**Temporarily Restricted**	**Permanently Restricted**
	(In Thousands)		
Net Assets at December 31, 2010	$37,117	$ 3,023	$1,132
Increase in unrestricted net assets	897	—	—
Restricted contributions, grants, and other receipts	—	7,253	—
Investment income restricted for specific purposes	—	252	—
Net assets released from restrictions for:			
Operating expenses	—	(2,863)	—
Capital asset acquisitions	—	(146)	—
Change in net assets	897	4,496	—
Net Assets at December 31, 2011	38,014	7,519	1,132
Increase in unrestricted net assets	2,568	—	—
Restricted contributions, grants, and other receipts	—	5,421	—
Investment income restricted for specific purposes	—	169	—
Net assets released from restrictions for:			
Operating expenses	—	(4,708)	—
Capital asset acquisitions	—	(139)	—
Change in net assets	2,568	743	—
Net Assets on December 31, 2012	$40,582	$ 8,262	$1,132

See accompanying notes.

Major Medical Center
Statements of Cash Flows

	Year Ended December 31	
	2012	2011
	(In Thousands)	
Operating Activities		
Operating income	$ 2,429	$ 751
Change in temporarily restricted net assets	743	4,496
	3,172	5,247
Adjustments to reconcile change in net assets to cash provided by operations:		
Depreciation and amortization	22,541	18,856
Investment income earned on assets limited as to use	(774)	(698)
Changes in operating assets and liabilities:		
(Increase) decrease in receivables for patient care	(2,105)	7,589
(Increase) decrease in due from third-party reimbursement programs	(8,413)	4,500
Increase in accounts payable and accrued expenses and accrued salaries and related liabilities	9,654	1,412
Net effect of increases and decreases in other assets and liabilities	2,286	(8,707)
Cash provided by operations	26,361	28,199
Investing Activities		
Acquisitions of property, plant, and equipment, net	(10,043)	(12,998)
Less amounts provided by restricted funds	139	146
Increase in investments	(618)	(70)
Cash used in investing activities	(10,522)	(12,922)
Financing Activities		
Net payment from (to) affiliates	126	(1,773)
Increase in deferred financing costs	(1,323)	
Repayments of long-term debt	(13,326)	(9,510)
Deposits into sinking fund, as required by mortgage loan agreement	(303)	
Increase in compensating balances for standby letters of credit	(1,923)	
(Increase) decrease in pledges receivable	(30)	(3,190)
Cash used in financing activities	(16,779)	(14,473)
Net (decrease) increase in cash and cash equivalents	(940)	804
Cash and cash equivalents at beginning of year	9,005	8,201
Cash and cash equivalents at end of year	$ 8,065	$ 9,005

See accompanying notes.

Notes to Financial Statements

1. Organization and Summary of Significant Accounting Policies

Organization

Major Medical Center (the "Medical Center") is a not-for-profit corporation. The Medical Center provides health care and related services. The accompanying financial statements do not include the accounts of the Research Foundation, a not-for-profit corporation that solicits funds and awards grants to the Medical Center for research purposes, nor for Hospital Support, Inc., which provides certain support services.

Temporarily and Permanently Restricted Net Assets

Temporarily restricted net assets are those whose use by the Medical Center has been limited by donors to a specific time period or purpose. Permanently restricted net assets have been restricted by donors to be maintained by the Medical Center in perpetuity. When a donor restriction expires (i.e., when a stipulated time restriction ends or purpose restriction is accomplished), temporarily restricted net assets are reclassified as unrestricted net assets and reported in the statements of operations as net assets released from restrictions. Donor-restricted contributions whose restrictions are met within the same year as received are reflected as temporarily restricted contributions and net assets released from restrictions in the accompanying financial statements.

Receivables for Patient Care

Patient accounts receivable from third-party programs for which the Medical Center receives payment under reimbursement formulas or negotiated rates are stated at the estimated net amounts receivable from such payors, which are generally less than the established charges of the Medical Center.

Investments

Investments consist of U.S. Treasury bonds and notes, certificates of deposit, and money market funds. Investments are carried at fair value. Amounts classified as long-term investments, consisting primarily of money market funds, represent permanently restricted net assets.

Investment Gains, Losses, and Income

Investment income, which includes real gains and losses, earned on permanently restricted and temporarily restricted funds upon which restrictions have been placed by donors, is added to temporarily restricted funds. All other investment income is reflected in the accompanying statements of operations.

Property, Plant, and Equipment

Property, plant, and equipment purchased are carried at cost, and those acquired by gifts and bequests are carried at appraised or fair market value established at the date of acquisition. Capitalized leases are recorded at the fair market value at the inception of the leases. The carrying amounts of assets and the related accumulated depreciation are removed from the accounts when such assets are disposed of, and any resulting gain or loss is included in operations. Depreciation of assets used in operations is recorded on the straight-line method over the estimated useful lives of the assets. Capitalized leases are amortized over the lease term.

Pledges

Unconditional promises to give cash and other assets are reported at their net present value at the date the promise is received. The gifts are reported as either temporarily or permanently restricted support if they are received with donor stipulations that limit the use of the donated assets. Pledges receivable, discounted at 10 percent, are expected to be paid as follows (in thousands):

Less than one year	$ 1,814
One year to five years	3,145
In excess of five years	962
	5,921
Less allowance for uncollectible pledges receivable	(2,218)
	$ 3,703

Assets Limited as to Use

Assets classified as limited as to use represent assets whose use is restricted for specific purposes under terms of agreements.

Accrued Post-Retirement Benefits

The Medical Center accounts for post-retirement health care and life insurance benefits on the accrual basis of accounting.

Uncompensated Care

As a matter of policy, the Medical Center provides significant amounts of partially or totally uncompensated patient care. For accounting purposes, such uncompensated care is treated either as charity care or bad debt expense. The Medical Center has defined charity care for accounting and disclosure purposes as the difference between its customary charges and the sliding scale rates given to patients in need of financial assistance. Since payment of this difference is not sought, charity care allowances are not reported as revenue. Patients who do not qualify for sliding scale fees and all uninsured inpatients who do not qualify for Medicaid assistance are billed at the Medical Center's full rates. Uncollected balances for these patients are categorized as bad debts. Total uncompensated care for all patient services approximated $22 million and $20 million in 2012 and 2011, respectively.

Use of Estimates

The preparation of financial statements in conformity with generally accepted accounting principles requires management to make estimates and assumptions that affect the reported amount of assets and liabilities and the disclosure of contingent assets and liabilities at the date of the financial statements. Estimates also affect the reported amounts of revenue and expenses during the reporting period. Actual results could differ from these estimates. Management believes that the amounts recorded based on estimates and assumptions are reasonable, and any differences between estimates and actual should not have a material impact on the Medical Center's financial position.

Operating Income

Transactions deemed by management to be ongoing, major, or central to the provision of health care services are reported as operating revenue and expenses, and are included in operating income. Operating income also includes investment income and realized gains and losses from the sale of investments.

Tax Status

The Medical Center is exempt from federal income taxes under Section 501(c)(3) of the Internal Revenue Code. The Medical Center has been classified as an organization that is not a private foundation under Section 509(a)(1). Contributions received by the Medical Center qualify as tax-deductible charitable contributions.

2. Third-Party Reimbursement Programs

The Medical Center has agreements with third-party payers that provide for payments to the Medical Center at amounts different from its established charges. Payment arrangements include prospectively determined rates per discharge, reimbursement of costs, discounted charges, and per diem payments. Patient service revenue is recorded at the Medical Center's established charges when patient services are performed. Adjustments for differences between established charges and payment amounts are deducted directly from receivables for patient care and patient service revenue in the year incurred.

Federal and state regulations provide for certain retrospective adjustments to current and prior years' payment rates based on industrywide and hospital-specific data. The Medical Center has estimated the potential impact of such retrospective adjustments based on information presently available, and adjustments are accrued on an estimated basis in the period the services are rendered and are adjusted in future periods as final settlements are determined. Management believes that amounts recorded in the accompanying financial statements will not be materially affected upon the final settlement of such retrospective adjustments.

Hospitals are reimbursed for Medicare inpatient services under the national prospective payment system ("PPS") and other methodologies of the Medicare program for patient services. Such Medicare payments are based on a blend of national industry and hospital-specific data. The Medicaid program pays rates determined by the state, primarily on a basis of prospectively determined rates per discharge. The Medical Center is paid by non–Medicare/Medicaid payers based on negotiated contract amounts or, if such contracts do not exist, at the Medical Center's established charges. In addition, the state has requested a waiver from the federal government that will allow it to enroll substantially all of its Medicaid participants into Medicaid managed care programs. The ultimate outcome and effect of these changes and proposals on the Medical Center's future operations cannot presently be determined. In 2012, net revenue from the Medicare and Medicaid programs accounted for 44 percent and 23 percent, respectively, of total net patient service revenue.

3. Assets Limited as to Use

A summary of assets limited as to use is as follows at December 31:

	2012	2011
	(In Thousands)	
Sinking Funds:		
Cash and cash equivalents	$ 276	$ 249
U.S. government and agency obligations	14,211	13,161
Total Sinking Funds	14,487	13,410
Collateral for Standby Letters of Credit:		
Cash and cash equivalents	582	—
Corporate bonds	1,341	—
Total Collateral for Standby Letters of Credit	1,923	—
Total Assets Limited as to Use	$16,410	$13,410

4. Property, Plant, and Equipment

A summary of property, plant, and equipment is as follows at December 31:

	2012	2011
	(In Thousands)	
Land	$ 4,980	$ 4,980
Buildings	58,827	58,827
Equipment	164,592	140,707
	228,399	204,514
Less accumulated depreciation	141,502	125,148
	86,897	79,366
Projects in progress	11,658	10,411
	$98,555	$89,777

Approximately $45,673,000 and $45,706,000 of fully depreciated assets are included in buildings and equipment at December 31, 2012 and 2011, respectively. Substantially all property, plant, and equipment is pledged as collateral under various loan agreements.

Capitalized equipment leases, included in property, plant, and equipment, are as follows at December 31:

	2012	2011
	(In Thousands)	
Assets recorded under		
capital leases	$67,434	$51,695
Less accumulated amortization	35,911	27,108
	$31,523	$24,587

5. Long-Term Debt

A summary of long-term debt is as follows at December 31:

	2012	2011
	(In Thousands)	
FHA Section 242 insured		
mortgage loan (a)	$20,865	$ —
FHA Section 241		
mortgage loan (a)	10,941	12,125
2005 mortgage loan (b)	2,216	2,758
1998 insured mortgage loan (a)	—	15,492
Various mortgages, having		
interest rates ranging from 3.5%		
to 10.0%, maturing at various		
dates through 2008	2,020	2,892
Capitalized leases (c)	31,105	25,930
	67,147	59,197
Less current portion	11,608	11,488
	$55,539	$47,709

a. As a condition of these borrowings, the Medical Center is required to establish and maintain a sinking fund. Amounts deposited into the sinking fund, together with investment earnings therein, are available for principal payments and purchases of specified levels of capital assets. Assets on deposit in the sinking fund at December 31, 2012 and 2011, are in compliance with the required amounts.

b. Annual principal payments for all long-term debt, excluding capital leases and required sinking fund balances for the next five years, are as follows:

	Principal Payments	Required Sinking Fund Balance
	(In Thousands)	
2013	$2,789	$15,461
2014	4,688	14,937
2015	4,157	14,162
2016	4,089	13,129
2017	3,746	11,831

c. Future minimum payments, by year and in the aggregate, under capitalized leases consisted of the following at December 31, 2012 (in thousands):

2013	$11,102
2014	9,852
2015	8,204
2016	4,744
2017	1,518
Thereafter	850
Total minimum lease payments	36,270
Less amounts representing interest	(5,165)
Present value of lease payments	$31,105

6. Retirement and Similar Benefits

The Medical Center provides retirement and similar benefits to its union employees through several defined benefit multi-employer pension plans and to its nonunion employees through a noncontributory defined benefit pension plan and tax-deferred annuity plans. Payments to the defined benefit multi-employer union plans are made in accordance with contractual arrangements under which contributions are generally based on gross salaries and are funded on a current basis. The Medical Center contributes amounts to the nonunion plan sufficient to meet the minimum funding requirements set forth in the Employee Retirement Income Security Act of 1974. The Medical Center's pension expense under all existing plans aggregated approximately $10,202,000 and $10,683,000 for the years ended December 31, 2012 and 2011, respectively.

7. Other Post-Retirement Benefits

In addition to the pension plans and the tax-sheltered annuity plans described in Note 6, the Medical Center sponsors a defined benefit health care plan that provides post-retirement medical, dental, and life insurance benefits to certain full-time employees hired prior to July 1, 2004, and who have worked 10 years and attained age 65 while in service with the Medical Center. The plan contains cost-sharing features such as deductibles and coinsurance.

Effective in May 2012, the Medical Center changed the type of the plan from basic hospital plus major medical to a point-of-service plan for nonunion employees. The effects of this change have been reflected in the actuary's calculation for the plan year ended December 31, 2012. At the end of 2012 and 2011, the accrued post-retirement benefit cost was $6,023,000 and $6,017,000, respectively. As of December 31, 2012 and 2011, the plan was unfunded.

8. Government Grants

The Medical Center receives grants from various government agencies. For the contract years ending June 30, 2013, 2014, and 2015, these grant awards are as follows:

Contract Year Ending June 30:	Amount (In Thousands)
2013	$3,791
2014	3,513
2015	3,765

Advances on government grants of $1,587,000 at December 31, 2012, as reflected in the accompanying statement of financial position, represent amounts received from the granting agencies in excess of claims made at that date. The receivable amount of $467,000 at December 31, 2011, represents claims made in excess of advances received from the granting agencies at that date.

9. Professional Liability Insurance

The Medical Center participates in a pooled program with certain other health care facilities (principally medical centers) for professional liability insurance. This participation is with captive insurance companies and, with the other health care facilities, in a pooled layer for additional insurance with commercial insurance companies.

During 2011, the Medical Center had an aggregate deposit of $2,000,000 with two of the captive insurance companies. During 2012, these deposits were replaced with two letters of credit of $1,000,000 each. The deposits were included in other current assets in the accompanying 2011 statement of financial position.

Malpractice claims in excess of insurance coverage have been asserted against the Medical Center by various claimants. The claims are in various stages of processing, and some may ultimately be brought to trial. Medical Center management and counsel are unable to conclude about the ultimate outcome of the actions. There are known incidents occurring through December 31, 2012, that may result in the assertion of additional claims, and other claims may be asserted arising from services provided to patients in the past. It is the opinion of Medical Center management, based on prior experience, that adequate insurance is maintained to cover all significant professional liability losses.

10. Transactions with Affiliates

The amounts due from affiliates in the accompanying statements of financial position at December 31, 2012 and 2011, include a $1,900,000 loan receivable and accrued interest thereon from Hospital Support, Inc. The loan, which does not have specified repayment terms, bears interest at the prime rate, which approximated 7.75 percent at December 31, 2012 and 2011.

11. Temporarily and Permanently Restricted Net Assets

Temporarily restricted net assets are available for the following purposes at December 31:

	2012	2011
	(In Thousands)	
Research and education	$ 817	$2,502
Plant replacement and expansion	7,445	5,017
	$8,262	$7,519

Permanently restricted net assets at both December 31, 2012 and 2011, consist of investments to be held in perpetuity and whose income is restricted as to use.

12. Other Operating Revenue

Other operating revenue consisted of the following for the year ended December 31:

	2012	2011
	(In Thousands)	
Government grant income	$ 1,668	$ 5,053
Real estate rentals	2,838	2,651
Investment income and gains on sale of investments	1,077	1,044
Faculty practice and research overhead	5,703	2,079
Dining room and parking lot income	996	958
Grants and contributions	343	499
Other	731	1,566
	$13,356	$13,850

13. Concentration of Credit Risk

Significant concentrations of patients accounts receivable include 30 percent and 37 percent from government-related programs, 6 percent and 8 percent from Empire Blue Cross and Blue Shield, and 27 percent and 23 percent from Cambridge Health Plans at December 31, 2012 and 2011, respectively.

At December 31, 2012, 95 percent of the Medical Center's cash and cash equivalents balance was held at one financial institution.

14. Fair Value of Financial Instruments

The following methods and assumptions were used by the Medical Center in estimating its fair value disclosures for financial instruments: The carrying amount reported in the statements of financial position for cash and cash equivalents approximates its fair value. Short-term investments consist primarily of government and other debt securities. Fair values are based on quoted market prices. Long-term investments consist primarily of money market funds. Fair values are based on quoted market prices. Assets limited as to use consist primarily of government securities. Fair values are based on quoted market prices. Most of the long-term debt of the Medical Center was refinanced during 2006. The carrying value of the Medical Center's long-term debt at December 31, 2012, approximates its fair value.

15. Contingencies

The Medical Center is a defendant in various legal actions arising out of the normal course of its operations, the final outcome of which cannot presently be determined. The amounts claimed would be material to the financial position of the Medical Center. Medical Center management is of the opinion that ultimate liability, if any, with respect to all of these matters will not have a material adverse effect on the Medical Center's financial position.

Approximately 67 percent of the Medical Center's employees are members of various unions. Of these employees, approximately 70 percent are covered by contracts expiring during 2013.

Suggested Readings

Emery, Douglas R., John D. Finnerty, and John D. Stowe. *Corporate Financial Management*, 3rd ed. Upper Saddle River, N.J.: Prentice Hall, 2007.

Finkler, Steven A. *Finance & Accounting for Nonfinancial Managers*, 3rd ed. New York, N.Y.: Aspen Publishers, 2003.

Fraser, Lyn M., and Aileen Ormiston. *Understanding Financial Statements*, 8th ed. Upper Saddle River, N.J.: Prentice Hall, 2006.

Ingenix St. Anthony. *The 2008 Almanac of Hospital Financial & Operating Indicators*. United States: Ingenix, 2008.

Revsine, Lawrence, Daniel W. Collins, and W. Bruce Johnson. *Financial Reporting & Analysis*, 3rd ed. Upper Saddle River, N.J.: Prentice Hall, 2004.

Werner, Michael L., and Kumen H. Jones. *Introduction to Financial Accounting: A User Perspective*, 3rd ed. Upper Saddle River, N.J.: Prentice Hall, 2004.

15

Financial Condition Analysis

The learning objectives of this chapter are to:

- define and discuss *financial condition analysis*;
- explain how financial condition analysis differs from financial statement analysis; and
- discuss ratios appropriate for financial condition analysis.

INTRODUCTION

Users of government financial reports are interested in many of the same things as those analyzing other types of organizations. The discussion of financial statement analysis in Chapter 14 is largely applicable to governments as well. However, understanding the financial condition of governments requires additional types of information, and in some cases modifications to the financial statement analysis discussed in Chapter 14. Those elements are the focus of this chapter.

There are many potential purposes of financial analysis. As noted in Chapter 14, managers may want to understand their organization's financial position and results of operations so that they can make decisions that will maintain a satisfactory financial situation or improve an unsatisfactory one. Vendors want to understand whether their customers will be able to pay for their purchases. Lenders want to consider the likelihood of an organization being able to repay loans. State governments use financial information for oversight of local governments. The public may want to assess how its tax dollars are being used. These represent just a few of the many uses of financial information.

Financial analysis of governments relies heavily on analysis of *basic financial statements* (BFS) including the notes that accompany them. The notes are particularly useful for finding out about the structure of the organization, the accounting methods used, the assumptions made, and other background information that gives the reader a perspective as the financial statements are reviewed. Also, careful review and analysis of *management's discussion and analysis* (MD&A) and other *required supplementary information* (RSI) is essential. In addition, governmental financial analysis must take into account additional factors such as debt per capita, tax rates, and citizen income and wealth.

Financial condition analysis can be very complex. This chapter serves as a brief introduction to the field and to give the reader a sense of some of the issues and problems related to financial condition analysis. Readers should not expect to be competent to carry out a financial condition analysis on their own based solely on the contents of this chapter.

However, it will provide a foundation for future study and an ability to appreciate some of the difficulties that are inherent in the process.

FINANCIAL CONDITION ANALYSIS

It is easy to believe that charities may experience severe financial difficulties. Just a small drop in donations can upset a delicate balance between available resources and the ability to provide necessary services. With governments, however, it is sometimes harder to see the potential problem. After all, governments can just raise taxes if they need more money, right? Experience has shown, however, that state and local governments have limited ability to raise taxes. The citizens are not wealthy enough to support unlimited tax increases. Nor is such an approach politically feasible.

There have been some bankruptcies and near-bankruptcies of cities and counties. More commonly, economic downturns reduce tax receipts just when the demands for safety net services are rising. Therefore, an analysis of the financial status of a governmental organization is a relevant and appropriate activity for both managers of the government and interested individuals and organizations outside of the government. Such analysis is referred to as *financial condition analysis.*

Berne has defined financial condition as follows:

> The probability that a government will meet both (a) its financial obligations to creditors, consumers, employees, taxpayers, suppliers, constituents, and others as they become due and (b) the service obligations to constituents, both currently and in the future.[1]

Granof and Wardlow note that a government's financial condition is:

> directly dependent upon economic, political, social, and demographic factors within its jurisdiction . . . it is also intertwined with those of other governments that provide financial aid or serve the same constituents.[2]

The *Comprehensive Annual Financial Report* (CAFR) contains much helpful information for financial condition analysis. It contains the BFS, the MD&A, and the RSI. These elements were discussed in Chapter 13. The CAFR contains the auditor's report, which addresses the financial statements' adherence to *Generally Accepted Accounting Principles* (GAAP). CAFRs often also provide information about trends in revenues and expenditures, tax rates, property values, debt, and other variables. Debt per capita and debt to assessed value are solvency ratios that can often be calculated from information in that section of the CAFR.

FINANCIAL STATEMENT ANALYSIS VERSUS FINANCIAL CONDITION ANALYSIS

The primary reason that financial condition differs from financial statement analysis is that there are many external factors that become part of the evaluation of financial health for a governmental body. Economic and demographic factors, such as the wealth and skills of the citizenry, employment rate, and general economy are all critical elements in understanding the financial condition of a government.

---

[1] Robert Berne. *The Relationships Between Financial Reporting and the Measurement of Financial Condition.* Norwalk, Conn.: Government Accounting Standards Board, 1992, p. vii.

[2] Michael H. Granof and Penelope S. Wardlow. *Core Concepts of Government and Not-for-Profit Accounting.* New York, N.Y.: John Wiley & Sons, 2003, p. 362.

The use of fund accounting by governments substantially increases complexity in the analysis of financial health, but it potentially provides valuable additional information. Should ratios be computed based solely on the government-wide financial statements, just on the general fund, or on an aggregate value from several different funds? These questions can only be answered in the context of the question the user is trying to address.

CAFRs must contain a statistical section that provides a wealth of information for financial condition analysis. The *Governmental Accounting Standards Board* (GASB) requires a minimum of 15 statistical tables that must be provided (except for tables that are clearly inappropriate for a particular government). These tables are not audited. However, they provide valuable insight into the government's ability to raise money to meet its financial needs. Exhibit 15-1 lists the required schedules.

The BFS include some statements based on *accrual* and some statements based on *modified accrual.* Also the RSI present the *budgetary comparison schedule* on the *budgetary basis of accounting.* The use of up to three bases of accounting (which occurs if budgets are prepared on a cash basis) in one financial report may create confusion but also presents the user with an array of opportunities. Clearly, the user must be aware of the basis of accounting used for each statement. However, the user can decide whether the focus of a particular analysis can best be addressed with accrual, modified accrual, or possibly cash basis information, and then use that information.

Nevertheless, analysis is cumbersome because of the large number of statements in the BFS, schedules in the RSI, and statistical sections of the CAFR. And governments that are not required to issue a CAFR may decide not to because of the complexity and expense involved in preparing all of the required information.

In performing an analysis, one should take a reasoned approach. For example, if a ratio based on the government-wide financial statements provides adequate information to

EXHIBIT 15-1 CAFR Statistical Tables

Tables Required for Statistical Section of CAFR

1. General Revenues by Source—Previous 10 Fiscal Years
2. Property Tax Levies and Collections—Previous 10 Fiscal Years
3. Special Assessment Billings and Collections—Previous 10 Fiscal Years (if the government is obligated in some manner for related special assessment debt)
4. General Governmental Expenditures by Function—Previous 10 Fiscal Years
5. Assessed and Estimated Actual Value of Taxable Property—Previous 10 Fiscal Years
6. Property Tax Rates—All Overlapping Governments—Previous 10 Fiscal Years
7. Ratio of Net General Bonded Debt to Assessed Value and Net Bonded Debt per Capita—Previous 10 Fiscal Years
8. Computation of Legal Debt Margin
9. Computation of Overlapping Debt
10. Ratio of Annual Debt Service for General Bonded Debt to Total General Expenditures—Previous 10 Fiscal Years
11. Revenue Bond Coverage—Previous 10 Fiscal Years
12. Demographic Statistics
13. Property Value, Construction, and Bank Deposits—Previous 10 Fiscal Years
14. Principal Taxpayers
15. Miscellaneous Statistics

Source: Governmental Accounting Standards Board Codification, Section 2800.103.

answer a question, the fund financial statements would not have to be used. In other cases, the fund financial statements may be more helpful, and the government-wide statements can be ignored.

Although it is important in financial statement analysis, it is even more critical in financial condition analysis to clearly state definitions used (e.g., for ratios) and be consistent in the use of those definitions over time and across organizations.

For financial condition analysis, some ratios need to be modified, others eliminated, and yet others added to create a solid analysis. However, the fundamentals of financial statement analysis still apply. The financial statements should be carefully reviewed. The audit letter should be examined. The notes that accompany the financial statements should be evaluated. Ratios should be calculated. Comparisons should be done both over time and across similar governmental organizations.

Berne indicates the following with respect to financial condition analysis:

> There is considerable agreement over its major components, including the economy and demographics, revenue base, revenues, current and capital expenditures, debt, pensions, internal resources, management capabilities, infrastructure, willingness to raise revenues to provide necessary public services, and idiosyncratic factors. Comparative analysis is the dominant measurement methodology, which includes time series analyses, comparisons with other jurisdictions, and occasionally, comparisons with industry standards.[3]

Granof and Wardlow have compiled a listing of the factors to be considered in a financial condition analysis. They are shown in Exhibit 15-2. How can we obtain this information? Unfortunately, often not easily. At a minimum, a fair degree of creativity in data collection is required, even though some of the data is available from public sources. Netzer notes the following:

> Federal government statistical agencies regularly provide some of the needed data: the U.S. Census Bureau provides annual data on population and retail trade and finances of states and large cities and counties and, every five years, much more extensive and detailed economic and financial data for counties and cities (even small cities); the Bureau of Economic Analysis of the U.S. Department of Commerce provides annual data on personal income and employment by detailed industry for counties; the Bureau of Labor Statistics of the U.S. Department of Labor provides monthly data on employment and the consumer price index; and some other federal agencies, like the Federal Reserve System, provide more specialized economic data. Much of this information can be downloaded from the agencies' Web sites.[4]

Often, however, data are at least several years old before they become available on the Web.

Some state governments regularly publish data on the finances of individual local governments within the state, in printed form, on Web sites, or both. For example, the New York State Comptroller's Office annually publishes its *Special Report on Municipal Affairs*, which provides statistical data on the finances of each local government within that state. However, in some

---

[3] Berne, p. xvi.
[4] Dick Netzer, personal communication, September 11, 1999.

EXHIBIT 15-2 A City's Economic Condition: A Comprehensive Analysis

I. General Approach
  A. Review the current economic, political, and social environment in which the city operates
  B. Identify and assess the impact of key factors likely to affect the city's economic, political, and social environment in the future (e.g., the next five years)
  C. Assess the city's current status as revealed in its comprehensive annual financial report (taking into account the city's reporting practices and policies)
  D. Forecast the city's fiscal status for the next five years taking into account the previously identified environmental changes and the city's likely response to them
II. Current state of, and trends in, the government's operating environment
  A. Population
    1. Age of population
    2. Income level
    3. Educational and skill level
    4. Other relevant demographic factors
  B. Economic environment
    1. Wealth and income of citizenry (e.g., per capita net worth and income)
    2. Major industries (and stability)
    3. Unemployment rates
    4. Value of property per capita
    5. Sales tax base
    6. Elasticity of revenues
  C. Political climate
    1. Formal structure of government
    2. Extent of political competition
    3. Competence of government officials
    4. Overall citizen satisfaction with the expectations of government
    5. "Liberal" or "conservative" citizen view as to role of government
    6. Relations with state government and other local governments (e.g., those of surrounding and overlapping entities)
  D. Social conditions
    1. Crime rates
    2. Other measures of social well-being
III. Changes likely to affect the government's operating environment and its finances
  A. Demographics and geographical boundaries
    1. Impact on infrastructure
      a. Highways and streets
      b. Utilities
    2. Impact on operating revenues
    3. Impact on operating expenses
  B. Nature and scope of government services to be performed
  C. Nature and scope of enterprise activities carried out (e.g., future of electric utility)
  D. Political climate (e.g., pro- or anti-growth; pro- or anti-business)
  E. Form and organization of government (e.g., possibility of single-member election districts)
  F. Political attitudes and intergovernmental relationships
    1. Changing views toward the role of government
    2. Relations with legislature
    3. Extent of state and federal assistance
    4. Additional costs imposed by overlapping governments (e.g., school districts)
  G. Technology (i.e., changes that will affect the government both directly—such as increased use of computers—and indirectly—such as interactive TV and means of transmitting electricity)
  H. Social changes (e.g., changes in family structure resulting in need for more government facilities to provide care for elderly)

(continued)

EXHIBIT 15-2 Continued

    I. Commerce and industry
      1. Major employers (including stability and likelihood of relocating)
      2. Impact on revenues (e.g., property taxes) and expenditures (e.g., infrastructure improvements)
    J. Wealth and income of population
    K. Other economic changes (e.g., those affecting the electric power and health care industries)
  IV. Insight into city's financial position, as revealed by accounting and reporting practices
    A. Overall quality of disclosure
    B. Auditor's opinion
    C. Management's discussion and analysis
    D. GFOA certificate
    E. Key accounting policies
      1. Reporting entity
      2. Number, type, and character of (reason for) funds
      3. Revenue and expenditure or expense recognition
      4. Accounting changes
    F. Budget-related and accounting-related practices
      1. One-shot additions to revenues or reductions in expenditures
      2. Unusual budget-balancing transactions (e.g., certain interfund transfers)
      3. Changes in budget-related practices (such as delaying payments or speeding up tax collections)
      4. Use of off-the-balance-sheet debt (e.g., leases, long-term contracts) and of revenue debt
      5. Use of long-term debt to finance operating expenditures
      6. Increased use of short-term debt to cover temporary cash shortages
   V. Calculating and interpreting financial and economic indicators
    A. Fiscal capacity and effort
      1. Revenues from own sources/median family income
      2. Revenue from own sources/total appraised value of property
      3. Total sales subject to tax/total retail sales
      4. Sales and property tax rates
    B. Trends in fund balance
    C. Trends in mix of revenues and expenditures and reasons for trends
    D. Trends in stability of revenues
      1. Intergovernmental revenues/total operating revenues
      2. Property tax revenues/total operating revenues
      3. Restricted revenues/total operating revenues
      4. One-time revenues/total operating revenues
      5. Uncollected property taxes
    E. Trends in spending patterns
      1. Number of employees per capita
      2. Nondiscretionary expenditures/total expenditures
      3. Percentage breakdown of total expenditures by function
    F. Trends in liquidity
      1. Adequacy of fund balance—unreserved fund balance/operating revenues
      2. Adequacy of working capital—cash, short-term investments, and receivables/current liabilities
    G. Trends in burden of debt
      1. Debt margin
      2. Debt service as a percentage of total general fund and debt service expenditures
      3. Debt per capita
      4. Debt as a percentage of taxable property
      5. Maturity structure

EXHIBIT 15-2 Continued

    H. Trends in pension and other postemployment benefits
        1. Unfunded actuarial accrued liabilities
            a. Funded ratios (pension assets compared to actuarial liabilities)
            b. Unfunded liabilities compared to values of property, annual payroll
        2. Percent of annual pension costs actually contributed
    I. Bond ratings
    J. Trends in amounts of new borrowing
    K. Overlapping debt
    L. Trends in capital expenditures
        1. By type
        2. By geographic area
        3. Reasons behind trends
        4. Commitments and planned expenditures per the capital improvements plan
VI. Fiscal forecasts
    A. Overview of how trends and exogenous variables will affect key fiscal indicators in the next five years (taking into account how city will likely respond to them)
    B. Pro forma financial statements of general and other key funds
VII. Summary and conclusion
    A. Will the city have the financial wherewithal to provide the services expected of it in the future (e.g., the next five years)?
    B. What are the key risks and uncertainties facing the city that might impair its ability to provide these services?
        1. How can the city best manage these risks?
        2. What should be the key concerns of city managers, especially those directly concerned with finances?

Source: Table 14-1, Michael H. Granof and Penelope S. Wardlow. *Core Concepts of Government and Not-for-Profit Accounting*. John Wiley & Sons, 2003, pp. 363–365. This material is used by permission of John Wiley & Sons, Inc.

states, there is a considerable time lag in the provision of such data. Sometimes the state reports use classifications that are not consistent with the categories used in the CAFRs of the local governments, limiting the usefulness of the state government issued data. Comparability with other states is even less reliable.

Some data may be available for large jurisdictions. For smaller jurisdictions (smaller cities, towns, villages), it may not be possible to get much of the desired economic or demographic data at all. When data are obtained, they often do not conform to GAAP.

Nevertheless, analysts should attempt to compare financial data. One approach is to review trends over time for the government being analyzed. For example, a great deal of data can be obtained from the CAFR and tracked over time. This includes not only financial statement data but also information such as that listed in Exhibit 15-1. Another approach is to determine several governments that are as comparable as possible with the government being analyzed and, if available, obtain their CAFR each year and use it for comparison. Such comparisons may still be complicated by differing year-ends, accounting methods, and government structure, but they can provide useful information.

Awareness of community unemployment rates provides some insight into the government's capacity to repay debt. Unemployment information may also indicate a need for the government to spend money on unemployment compensation, income support, job training, and homeless shelters. Assessing economic conditions and understanding outside influences on the government are critical for understanding the context of the government's financial performance. They are not, however, a substitute for a thorough analysis of the financial statements themselves. The financial statements of governmental bodies provide a great deal of information that can be used to assess financial condition.

Governments need to provide services while not outspending their ability to raise resources. Competent management is essential. To the extent the analyst can assess the absolute or relative competence of the management of a government, it should be included in the analysis. Governments are also subject to unique political influences on both the spending side and the taxing side of the equation.

Bowman and Calia argue that it makes sense to employ five tests to evaluate the quality of a government's financial reporting: (1) use of GAAP for financial statements, (2) use of GAAP for budgeting, (3) use of a CAFR format, (4) receipt of an unqualified[5] CPA audit opinion, and (5) timeliness of information (issuance of CAFR within six months of fiscal year-end).[6]

None of those five factors directly relate to the financial status and results of operations of the organization, but they do have a direct bearing on the ability of individuals to assess financial health. For many years, governments employed a wide variety of reporting techniques. Often failure to employ GAAP or delays in reporting information were techniques employed by governments in financial trouble. Compliance with the five factors may give outsiders a level of comfort about the government that could lead to higher bond ratings and lower interest costs on borrowed money.

Use of GAAP does not guarantee that a government will not encounter financial difficulty. Fundamental problems are sometimes treated with temporary patches, such as one-shot revenue enhancements and other gimmicks. For example, a government may sell a fixed asset. One year New Jersey sold a piece of highway to its Turnpike Authority. Although the turnpike did not necessarily want to buy the road, it did want the governor's approval of a rate increase. And the money from the sale allowed the state to balance its budget that year. But such one-shot revenue enhancements do not usually provide long-term solutions to imbalances between receipts and disbursements. Fortunately, under current GASB rules special items such as this must be clearly shown in the financial statements.

So, adherence to the factors cited by Bowman and Calia may not imply financial health, but failure to do so certainly raises red flags that there may be problems with the financial status of the government.

RATIO ANALYSIS

Calculation of ratios presents a challenge in government financial condition analysis. One problem that must be addressed is determination of which information to use in calculating ratios. For example, consider the government-wide statement of net assets presented in Exhibit 15-3. Which column should be used?

One might assume that it would make sense to use the numbers from the "Total" column. However, it is extremely critical to consider why the analysis is being performed. If a user is concerned about potential obligations to pay for debt of the component units, analyses may focus on the information in the "Component Units" column.

If an analysis is being performed to determine the financial health of the enterprise funds, then the focus might be on the "Business-Type Activities" column. However, since proprietary fund financial statements are also prepared on an accrual basis and may provide more detailed information about different business-type activities, the analyst may be less

---

[5] As opposed to a qualified opinion. A qualified opinion expresses some concern that requires particular attention by the reader.

[6] Woods Bowman and Roland Calia. *Evaluating Local Government Financial Health: Executive Summary.* Chicago Ill.: The Civic Federation, 1997, p. 3.

EXHIBIT 15-3 Government-Wide Statement of Net Assets

Jump City
Statement of Net Assets
September 30, 2012

| | Primary Government | | | |
	Government Activities	Business-Type Activities	Total	Component Units
Assets				
Cash and cash equivalents	$ 290,050	$ 234,344	$ 524,394	$ 450,000
Receivables (net)	743,343	25,118	768,461	199,456
Internal balances	85,000	(85,000)	0	—
Inventories	120,872	83,280	204,152	23,958
Capital assets, net	8,750,000	4,326,876	13,076,876	34,345,769
Total Assets	$9,989,265	$4,584,618	$14,573,883	$35,019,183
Liabilities				
Accounts payable	$ 825,443	$ 75,431	$ 900,874	$ 387,158
Deferred revenue	380,000	18,500	398,500	34,946
Noncurrent liabilities				
Due within one year	650,000	70,000	720,000	2,945,639
Due in more than one year	7,300,000	3,600,000	10,900,000	25,145,348
Total Liabilities	$9,155,443	$3,763,931	$12,919,374	$28,513,091
Net Assets				
Invested in capital assets, net of related debt	$ 800,000	$ 656,876	$ 1,456,876	$ 6,148,390
Restricted for:				
Capital projects	15,000	—	15,000	—
Debt service	18,000	—	18,000	—
Unrestricted	822	163,811	164,633	357,702
Total Net Assets	$ 833,822	$ 820,687	$ 1,654,509	$ 6,506,092

likely to use the government-wide statements for that information. An advantage of the proprietary fund financial statements is that they also provide a statement of cash flows.

One problem with using the "Total" column is that governments in distress may not really have access to all of the resources in the "Total" column. The business-type activities may be legally structured in such a way that their resources are dedicated only to their activity. If one is concerned about the ability of the governmental funds to repay long-term debt, the analysis might have to focus on the "Governmental Activities" column of the government-wide statements. The notes that accompany the financial statements provide critical information that can help the analyst to make such decisions based on the specifics of the government being analyzed.

Why not use the governmental fund financial statements for such an analysis? Because the governmental fund financial statements are prepared on a modified accrual basis and include only current financial resources. This may be helpful for liquidity ratios, but not for solvency analysis. In contrast, the government-wide financial statements use accrual accounting and show both current and long-term liabilities. The analyst must carefully consider the question at hand and which statements and which columns in the statements provide the best information to address that question.

Common Size Ratios

Common size ratios should be prepared for all financial statements in a manner similar to that described in Chapter 14. Such analysis should be done for all columns in the statements (i.e., "Governmental Activities," "Business-Type Activities," and so on) unless the analysis is being targeted to some specific questions that require more limited data.

Note that government financial statements generally do not provide information for more than one year, probably due to the amount of information already being displayed on one page. MD&A provides two years of information for some numbers. CAFRs often provide two years of statements. In performing an analysis, an understanding of financial trends is critical, and the analyst should always attempt to obtain information for one or more earlier years as well as the current year.

Liquidity

Liquidity ratios are based on information from the balance sheet or statement of net assets. The statement of net assets in Exhibit 15-3 does not present a segregation of current assets. However, current and quick ratios can still be calculated. Looking at the statement in Exhibit 15-3, it is reasonably clear which items are current and which are long term. For instance, the current ratio using numbers from the "Total" column of that exhibit would be as follows:

$$\text{Current Ratio} = \frac{\text{Cash} + \text{Receivables} + \text{Inventories}}{\substack{\text{Accounts Payable} + \text{Deferred Revenue} \\ + \text{Noncurrent Liabilities} \\ \text{Due Within One Year}}} = \frac{524,394 + 768,461 + 204,152}{900,874 + 398,500 + 720,000}$$

$$= .74$$

What items were excluded from the ratio? The internal balances can be ignored because the governmental and business-type activities offset each other. Clearly, the capital assets are long-term assets and would not be included in the preceding ratio. Similarly, noncurrent liabilities due in more than one year would not be current, so they are not included. Noncurrent liabilities due within one year would be current. What about deferred revenue? That is an account title that could be either short term or long term. However, since there is a heading for noncurrent liabilities, we are reasonably safe in assuming this is a short-term liability. The notes would probably provide information that would be helpful in classifying this item as short term or long term.

What if there had been no heading for noncurrent liabilities, and the notes provided no additional information for classifying the deferred revenue as short or long term? Treatment of deferred revenue as a current liability is a more conservative approach. Consider whether one would rather err on the side of overestimating or underestimating the current ratio. Since this is a ratio designed to indicate if there are adequate short-term resources to cover short-term obligations, it might be a serious error to underestimate obligations in the calculation. Analysts must search for any clues regarding which numbers to include or exclude, and then must consider the ramifications of the decisions. Ratio analysis is often an art, rather than a science.

The governmental fund financial statements are useful for liquidity analysis. Since the governmental fund financial statements are based on current financial resources, there is less guesswork involved in determining what is or is not a current asset or liability.

Consider another problem with using the "Government Activities" column of the government-wide statement of net assets for liquidity ratio analysis. Examine the balance sheet for Robbins Township in Exhibit 15-4. From this exhibit we see that the town is accumulating liquid resources in the New Town Hall Project fund. The government-wide statement of net assets would include all current assets in the "Governmental Activities" column. However, some of those assets might be legally restricted to be used only for the new town hall building. Therefore, the liquid assets in the government-wide statements might overestimate short-term resources available to meet short-term obligations. We might be better off to go directly to the governmental fund financial statements and calculate the current ratio using numbers from the "General Fund" column.

In addition to the current ratio, liquidity is often measured by the acid test ratio. The acid test's purpose is to compare assets that are cash or quickly convertible to cash with current liabilities. The acid test ratio could be calculated for Exhibit 15-4 by dividing the total of the general fund's cash plus investments and receivables by current liabilities.

The truth is that there are no formal rules for financial condition analysis. There is no unique set of indicators that should always be used for performing such an analysis. We do not even have definitive guidance on which columns or even which statements to use.

EXHIBIT 15-4 Governmental Funds Balance Sheet

Robbins Township
Balance Sheet
Governmental Funds
June 30, 2012

	General	New Town Hall Project	Other Governmental Funds	Total Governmental Funds
Assets				
Cash	$ 43,978	$ 5,000	$ 23,965	$ 72,943
Investments	832,190	128,345	67,000	1,027,535
Receivables, net	746,330	—	32,548	778,878
Due from other funds	186,000	50,000	25,000	261,000
Receivables from other governments	458,400	—	72,000	530,400
Total Assets	$2,266,898	$183,345	$220,513	$2,670,756
Liabilities and Fund Balances				
Liabilities				
Accounts payable	$ 28,988	$ —	$ 42,385	$ 71,373
Due to other funds	75,000	—	—	75,000
Payable to other governments	12,000	—	35,089	47,089
Total Liabilities	$ 115,988	$ —	$ 77,474	$ 193,462
Fund Balances				
Reserved for:				
Encumbrances	$ 45,000	$ —	$ —	$ 45,000
Debt service	1,500,000	—	—	1,500,000
Unreserved, reported in:				
General fund	605,910	—	—	605,910
Special revenue fund	—	—	78,344	78,344
Capital projects fund	—	183,345	64,695	248,040
Total Fund Balances	$2,150,910	$183,345	$143,039	$2,477,294
Total Liabilities and Fund Balances	$2,266,898	$183,345	$220,513	$2,670,756

However, it is important that the analyst calculate ratios consistently over time to develop trends and consistently across organizations to develop a basis for comparisons.

Solvency

Do the traditional leverage and coverage ratios, discussed earlier in Chapter 14, provide the information needed to assess governmental solvency? The ratios discussed are debt, debt to equity, times-interest-earned, and cash flow coverage. Debt ratios have been used in government financial condition analysis. However, evaluation of debt ratios is complicated because governments tend to operate with fairly low levels of equity. Their focus is more on current-year receipts and disbursements than on accumulation of ownership of assets.

Solvency analysis focuses on the ability to meet debt payments. Therefore, solvency ratios should be calculated using the government-wide statements and the proprietary fund financial statements rather than the governmental fund financial statements, which do not report long-term assets or liabilities.

There is an important role for coverage ratios in condition analysis. Revenues may be compared with debt service requirements to assess the government's ability to meet required debt payments. In the case of debt service that is paid from only specific revenue sources, those revenues should be segregated and used in the coverage calculations. One might argue that the government's ability to repay debt rests less in its assets and more in its ability to tax and borrow resources to pay obligations as they come due.

Clearly, one of the problems that some governments encounter is a heavy debt load. It should be noted that CAFRs tend to contain very detailed debt information, including amounts of debt, maturity of debt, and timing of required debt service payments.

Often the debt is repaid as it comes due by simply "rolling it over"—that is, old debt is repaid by taking on new debt. This works only so long as lenders are willing to lend to the government. If its financial status becomes weak, lenders may not be willing to make new loans. A reasonable indicator of short-term solvency (the ability to roll over debt) would be the liquidity and amount of net assets as measured on the government-wide statement of net assets.

To focus on longer-term solvency of governments, analysts frequently consider per capita debt, debt as a percentage of full value of property, or debt service expenditures as a percentage of total expenditures or revenues. These are sometimes referred to as debt burden measures. For example, these ratios might be calculated as:

$$\text{Debt Burden} = \frac{\text{Total Long-Term Debt}}{\text{Population}}$$

$$\text{Debt Service Burden} = \frac{\text{Total Debt Service}}{\text{Total Revenues}}$$

The total long-term debt for Jump City would be $10,900,000 (see Exhibit 15-3). By dividing the debt by the population, we find the amount of debt per capita, or per person. This provides a number that makes comparisons with other governments more meaningful than simply the total dollars of debt. Debt service refers to long-term debt principal payments and interest on both short-term and long-term debt. The debt service burden indicates how much of each dollar of the government's revenues are spent on debt service. Ives et al. note that

the greater the portion of an entity's revenues that is consumed by debt service requirements, the less flexibility it has to issue additional debt, to meet operating expenditure needs, and to weather the effects of an economic downturn. Bond rating agencies generally consider a debt service burden of 10 percent to be moderate and a burden of 15 to 20 percent to be high.[7]

Berne and Schramm note that debt burden measures can focus on financial flows or stock. Flows compare the annual debt service with the inflow of resources, such as total revenues or property tax revenues, that are available to pay the debt service. Stock measures would compare outstanding debt with the value of taxable property, personal income, or *fiscal capacity*.[8]

> All governments face political, legal, and economic realities which constrain their efforts to draw resources from their communities. The extent to which the economic base can be tapped by a government within these constraints is the organization's revenue capacity, often referred to as fiscal capacity.[9]

Debt burden measures are tracked over time, compared with a group of comparable governments, and assessed in relation to other debt, financial, and economic factors by municipal bond analysts at organizations such as Moody's Investors Service (Moody's) or Standard and Poor Rating Services (S&P). Unfortunately, these data are not generally available to the public. Independent analysts are put in the difficult position of creating their own data bases.

What debt should be considered in the analysis?

> As a general rule, all government long-term debt except self-supporting long-term debt should be included in the analysis. In most cases the debt to be included in the analysis will be general obligation debt, and the excluded self-supporting debt will be revenue or limited obligation debt. Self-supporting debt is repaid from the revenues of an activity that utilizes the borrowed funds without drawing on the government's tax base or other revenue bases. . . . Similar criteria are used to identify the debt service included in the debt analysis. Debt service includes the principal and interest payments on the long-term debt included above.[10]

Some might argue that self-supporting debt should also be included in the analysis. In many cases, the resources paying for such debt (e.g., in the form of user fees) still come from the local economy. If one believes that fiscal capacity is finite, then the money going to support that debt is no longer available to support other general obligations.

The property tax is one of the primary sources of revenue for local governments. Therefore, a comparison of debt to the market value of property provides a reasonable measure for comparing the debt burden from one locality to another. Such comparisons might be best made from municipality to municipality within one state to minimize external factors that can cause variations in a reasonable ratio level. Many states set limits on municipality debt to property value or limits on property taxing power. In such cases, this debt ratio is particularly important.

---

[7] Martin Ives, Joseph R. Razek, and Gordon A. Hirsch. *Introduction to Governmental and Not-for-Profit Accounting*, 5th ed. Upper Saddle River, N.J.: Pearson/Prentice Hall: 2004, p. 615.
[8] Robert Berne and Richard Schramm. *The Financial Analysis of Governments.* Upper Saddle River, N.J.: Prentice Hall, 1986, p. 380.
[9] Ibid., p. 134.
[10] Ibid., p. 380.

By dividing debt by the population, we can calculate the debt per capita. This is a widely used measure. It does not require an estimate of property values, so it is easier to calculate. However, population per se may not be a good indicator of ability to pay. Comparing the debt to the population's personal income is likely to be a better measure of the ability of the government to raise revenues.

Debt service to annual revenues is one of the more widely used measures of debt burden. However, care should be exercised in using this ratio for comparison, as a number of different measures of revenue may be used in the calculation.

Efficiency

Part of the assessment of the financial condition of a government should include efficiency. Therefore, the asset turnover ratios discussed in Chapter 14 are relevant to some extent. Receivables and inventory turnover ratios both have useful implications for government. Receivables turnover ratios are directly calculable. Governments with relatively long average collection periods are likely overreporting the true value of their receivables or are doing a poor job of managing the collection of receivables. Either of those situations requires specific management attention. Alternatively, it could indicate an inability of the populace to make required tax payments on a timely basis. That also provides important information about the continued financial stability of the entity. Property tax collection information is ordinarily provided in the statistical section of CAFRs. An efficiency ratio commonly calculated for governments is the property tax collection ratio. That ratio is defined as:

$$\frac{\text{Property Tax}}{\text{Collection Rule}} = \frac{\text{Current Year Property Taxes Collected}}{\text{Current Year Property Tax Levy}}$$

The higher the percentage of this year's property taxes that are collected this year, the stronger the financial condition of the government, other things being equal.

Exhibits 15-5 and 15-6 present examples of a government-wide statement of activities and a statement of revenues, expenditures, and changes in fund balances for the governmental funds, respectively. As with other elements of government financial analysis, a considerable amount of care is required in assessing efficiency ratios. While traditional efficiency analysis will likely work well for government-wide or proprietary fund financial statements, it is more complicated when applied to governmental funds. For example, comparisons among governments with different tax calendars might create problems. However, if all municipal governments in one state must use the same fiscal year and the same tax calendar, then the information may be quite useful.

Furthermore, care must be exercised in assessing receivables turnover because some receivables are more within the control of the government than others. For example, the collection of taxes or fees is often subject to management control. In contrast, the collection of grants and reimbursements owed by other governments is much less controllable. This complicates analysis if the user of the financial statements is not able to divide receivables into major categories by source.

Inventory measures would be similarly useful. Is the organization holding excessive amounts of inventory? Does it order too much at a time, or is there a lot of obsolete, useless inventory stored in government warehouses?

Government condition analysis does not lend itself easily to the use of fixed and total asset turnover ratios. These ratios can be calculated. For example, for Jump City, using

EXHIBIT 15-5 Government-Wide Statement of Activities

Jump City
Statement of Activities
September 30, 2012

| Functions | Expenses (A) | Program Revenues | | | Net (Expense) Revenue and Changes in Net Assets | | | |
| | | Charges for Services (B) | Operating Grants and Contributions (C) | Capital Grants and Contributions (D) | Primary Government | | | Component Units (H) |
					Governmental Activities (E)	Business-Type Activities (F)	Total (G)	
Primary Government								
Governmental activities								
Police and fire	$12,735,027	$ 485,554	$384,910	$ 43,448	$(11,821,115)		$(11,821,115)	
Education	34,834,119	—	—	—	(34,834,119)		(34,834,119)	
Sanitation	5,275,923	505,333	—	125,000	(4,645,590)		(4,645,590)	
Total governmental activities	$52,845,069	$ 990,887	$384,910	$168,448	$(51,300,824)		$(51,300,824)	
Business-type activities								
Golf course	$ 3,154,934	$ 4,834,884	$ —	$ —		$1,679,950	$ 1,679,950	
Parking facility	2,694,334	1,834,909	—	250,000		(609,425)	(609,425)	
Total business-type activities	$ 5,849,268	$ 6,669,793	$ —	$250,000		$1,070,525	$ 1,070,525	
Total Primary Government	$58,694,337	$ 7,660,680	$384,910	$418,448	$(51,300,824)	$1,070,525	$(50,230,299)	
Component Units								
Airport	$28,132,639	$27,492,738	$ —	$750,000				$ 110,099
General Revenues—Property Taxes					$ 50,243,270	$ —	$ 50,243,270	$ —
Contributions not Restricted					350,000	—	350,000	—
Special Items—Gain on Sale of Building					482,000	—	482,000	—
Transfers					645,000	(645,000)	0	—
Total General Revenues, Contributions, Special Items, and Transfers					$ 51,720,270	$ (645,000)	$ 51,075,270	$ —
Change in Net Assets					$ 419,446	$ 425,525	$ 844,971	$ 110,099
Net Assets—Beginning					414,376	395,162	809,538	6,395,993
Net Assets—Ending					$ 833,822	$ 820,687	$ 1,654,509	$6,506,092

EXHIBIT 15-6 Governmental Funds Statement of Revenues, Expenditures, and Changes in Fund Balances

Robbins Township
Statement of Revenues, Expenditures, and Changes in Fund Balances
Government Funds
For the Year Ended June 30, 2012

	General	New Town Hall Project	Other Governmental Funds	Total Governmental Funds
Revenues				
Property taxes	$ 8,435,674	$ —	$1,232,476	$ 9,668,150
Fees	1,234,746	—	343,321	1,578,067
Permits	894,035	—	43,984	938,019
Intergovernmental	2,089,994	—	434,598	2,524,592
Charges for services	1,542,959	—	2,324,659	3,867,618
Investment earnings	354,222	—	390,712	744,934
Total Revenues	$14,551,630	$ —	$4,769,750	$19,321,380
Expenditures				
Current				
General government	$ 7,535,980	$ —	$ 340,576	$ 7,876,556
Public safety	3,999,745	—	1,239,435	5,239,180
Sanitation	2,453,909	—	784,445	3,238,354
Debt service				
Principal	250,000	—	2,000,000	2,250,000
Interest and other charges	15,000	—	120,000	135,000
Capital outlay	2,150,000	—	270,395	2,420,395
Total Expenditures	$16,404,634	$ —	$4,754,851	$21,159,485
Excess of Revenues Over Expenditures	$ (1,853,004)	$ —	$ 14,899	$ (1,838,105)
Other Financing Sources (Uses)				
Proceeds from long-term capital related debt	$ 2,000,000	$ —	$ —	$ 2,000,000
Transfers in	200,000	—	10,000	210,000
Transfers out	(85,000)	45,000	(25,000)	(65,000)
Total Other Financing Sources and Uses	$ 2,115,000	$ 45,000	$ (15,000)	$ 2,145,000
Net Change in Fund Balances	$ 261,996	$ 45,000	$ (101)	$ 306,895
Fund Balances—Beginning	2,004,902	138,345	220,614	2,363,861
Fund Balances—Ending	$ 2,266,898	$183,345	$ 220,513	$ 2,670,756

numbers from the "Total" columns in Exhibits 15-3 and 15-5, one measure of these ratios would be the following:

$$\text{Fixed Asset Turnover} = \frac{\text{Total General Revenues, Contributions, Special Items, and Transfers}}{\text{Capital Assets, Net}} = \frac{\$51,075,270}{\$13,076,876}$$
$$= 3.9$$

$$\text{Total Asset Turnover} = \frac{\text{Total General Revenues, Contributions, Special Items, and Transfers}}{\text{Total Assets}} = \frac{\$51,075,270}{\$14,573,883}$$
$$= 3.5$$

However, interpretation is problematic. Does a fixed asset turnover ratio of 3.9 indicate efficient or inefficient use of assets? The general rule regarding asset turnover ratios is that a higher ratio implies greater efficiency. Does one city rent all buildings that it uses to provide social services, while another city owns them?

Even more critical is the fact that charging high taxes and generating large amounts of revenue while providing inadequate infrastructure may result in a high fixed asset turnover ratio. However, that ratio would not necessarily be a sign of efficiency. The fixed asset turnover will not be meaningful unless considered together with RSI infrastructure information, and even then it may turn out to be of limited value.

Analysts might also differ on what to include in these turnover ratios. Some would argue that the assets of the government are used to support all of its functions. Therefore, the revenues directly associated with those functions should be included. The ratio could include not only the total general revenues, contributions, special items, and transfers subtotal from the bottom part of the statement of activities in the numerator, but also the charges for services and operating and capital grant and contribution revenues from the top part of the statement. Others might argue that special items are often unusual and cannot be expected to recur; therefore, they should be excluded from the numerator. These create reasonable alternatives to the ratios as defined previously.

The governmental fund financial statements do not record long-term assets. Therefore, there would not be a parallel set of ratios based on those statements. The proprietary fund financial statements, however, would be subject to all of the financial analyses common to other types of organizations that use accrual accounting. Therefore, asset turnover ratios would often be applied to them.

Profitability and Intergenerational Equity

Profitability ratios are not as prominent in financial condition analysis as they are in financial statement analysis of for-profit organizations. This is largely because profit maximization is not a goal of governments. However, profitability analysis still plays an important role in financial condition analysis.

Although governments may not seek to maximize profits, evaluation of annual surpluses or deficits should be undertaken. To protect itself against a crisis if a deficit occurs, a government should accumulate modest reserves. The exact amount that any specific government should accumulate would depend largely on how severely its revenues and expenses or expenditures vary during good and bad economic times. If a series of large deficits is viewed as being inevitable during economic downturns, then it might be reasonable for the government to run considerable surpluses during economic booms.

Another factor related to profitability analysis relates to intergenerational equity. If a government persistently runs large surpluses, one could argue that it is overtaxing its current citizens. To what end? Eventually, the government will likely spend the surpluses to provide services. However, those services will be provided to future populations, rather than to the individuals who paid for them.

Conversely, if a government runs deficits for a number of years and finances those deficits by issuing long-term debt, what does that imply? It indicates that the current population is not paying the full cost of services currently provided by the government. Eventually, a future population that did not benefit from the services will pay for them. This problem raises considerations about equity between the present and either past or future generations of taxpayers. For this reason, one might argue against large annual surpluses or deficits. Ratios such as the profit margin can be helpful in analysis of the existence or extent of intergenerational equity or inequity.

Risk and Capacity

Financial stability and risk are additional factors that must be considered in evaluating government financial condition. We can assess the extent to which the government relies on steady, dependable resources. We can also consider the government's capacity to increase resources if some expected source falls short.

Bowman and Calia present two ratios that are helpful in this area: the *risk exposure factor* and the *tax leverage factor*.[11] These ratios can be stated as follows:

$$\text{Risk Exposure Factor} = \frac{\text{Investment Revenue} + \text{Intergovernmental Revenue} + \text{Transfers In}}{\text{Own Revenue Sources}}$$

$$\text{Tax Leverage Factor} = \frac{\text{Total Operating Expenditures}}{\text{Own Revenue Sources}}$$

The numerator of the risk exposure factor ratio is intended to capture the revenues that might decline due to factors totally outside of the control of the government. A reduction in interest rates or decline in the stock market could lower the collections from investments. Budget difficulties at the state or federal level could result in declining aid to local governments (intergovernmental revenues and transfers in). The denominator represents the revenue source that the government directly controls. For local governments, that can often be represented by property taxes. In some cases, sales taxes and income taxes and other sources could also be included in the denominator. If outside, uncontrollable sources decline, what impact would that have on the government and its own tax rates?

For example, suppose we start with the following value for the ratio:

$$\text{Risk Exposure Factor} = \frac{\$2,000,000}{\$10,000,000} = .2$$

This would imply that if uncontrollable money (the numerator) fell 10 percent from $2,000,000 to $1,800,000, own source revenues (the denominator) would have to rise 2 percent to make up the difference (i.e., .2 × 10% = 2%). This government does not rely heavily on intergovernment aid and would not suffer greatly if that aid were cut. Alternatively, suppose that the risk exposure ratio were as follows:

$$\text{Risk Exposure Factor} = \frac{\$20,000,000}{\$10,000,000} = 2$$

This would imply that if the numerator fell 10 percent, own revenue sources such as property taxes would have to rise 20 percent to make up the difference (2 × 10% = 20%). This heavy reliance on revenues outside the direct and full control of the government is a further concern because the factors that cause declines in those revenues, such as a weak economy, often make it difficult for local governments to raise tax rates. A government with heavy reliance on such revenues should have surpluses and build reserves in good times that can be used in times of intergovernmental aid decreases, thus avoiding significant local tax increases.

---

[11] Bowman and Calia, p. 5.

The tax leverage factor, defined previously, indicates the amount taxes must increase in response to expenditure increases. For example, if the government spends $30,000,000 a year and has just $10,000,000 of its own revenue sources, then a 1 percent increase in spending, with no other revenue increases, would require a 3 percent increase in the local tax collections:

$$\text{Tax Leverage Factor} = \frac{\text{Total Operating Expenditures}}{\text{Own Revenue Sources}} = \frac{\$30,000,000}{\$10,000,000} = 3$$

That is, if spending goes up 1 percent, or $300,000, there would have to be a 3 percent increase in controllable government revenues ($3 \times 1\% = 3\%$).

In addition to risk factors such as these, the capacity of the region to bear such increases must be considered. Understanding the capacity of the populace to bear tax increases and the capacity of the government to increase debt levels is critical in understanding the financial condition of the government.

Much of the capacity analysis revolves around the demographics of the region. For example, if the population base is very mobile and highly sensitive to tax increases, the government has less stability than it would otherwise. Suppose that the top 10 percent of the population in a state currently provides half of all income taxes. If a state income tax increase causes a substantial number of those individuals to move from the state, the tax increase could actually result in a net decrease in revenues. Governments actually do not have an unlimited ability to increase taxes.

We can, however, start to assess the government's ability to increase its resources by comparing factors such as total population, population growth, employment, tax rates, property values, debt per capita, and average income per capita. A city with a growing population and growing property values, low tax rates, and relatively low debt per capita has room for resource growth. When times are hard, it can borrow money, raise taxes, or both.

But if the population is declining, there are fewer people to tax. Expenditure decreases will be necessary to avoid higher taxes per capita. If property values are declining as well, the tax rate per $100 of property value will have to increase just to keep property tax revenues constant.

A key issue is that we do not really care about the value of any ratio we can already calculate because that is historical information. What we really want to know is "What will be the value of these ratios in the future?" It is necessary to track ratios over time to see trends, compare ratios with that of other organizations, and get a sense of underlying trends in demographics and other factors, because all of this analysis is focused on assessing what is likely to happen in the future.

Other Ratios and Financial Indicators

Many additional ratios could be calculated beyond those discussed here. A handbook published by The International City/County Management Association (ICMA) contains a total of 36 financial indicators.[12] Among the ratios in the ICMA handbook were measures of revenue, expenditure, liquidity, debt structure, and unfunded liabilities. Some of the ratios suggested are:

- Total Revenues/Population
- Total Expenditures/Population
- Operating Expenditures/Total Expenditures
- Total Revenues/Total Expenditures
- Current Liabilities/Operating Revenues
- Unfunded Pension Liability/Net Assessed Value

---

[12] Sanford M. Groves and Maureen G. Valente. *Evaluating Financial Condition: A Handbook for Local Government*, 3rd ed. Washington, D.C: ICMA, 1994.

The ratios suggested in the ICMA handbook may not be an adequate tool for many users. Honadle and Lloyd-Jones note that the ICMA indicators "are much more complicated because much of the information cannot be found in the regular financial statements. When it can be found, it may not be organized in a compatible way."[13]

An auditing firm active in the government area has developed a set of measures called the Performeter™ to evaluate financial condition using the government-wide statements and other information. Exhibit 15-7 summarizes the areas covered by the approach. Exhibit 15-8 provides additional detail about revenue dispersion, one of the areas listed in Exhibit 15-7, for a hypothetical government. The information for this indicator can be gathered from the government-wide statement of activities. In this example, the value for this indicator is 7, which indicates that the government has direct control of somewhere between 50 percent (which would earn a score of 5) and 90 percent (which would earn a score of 10) of its annual revenues.

EXHIBIT 15-7 The Performeter™

The Performeter™ analyzes the following financial performance measures:

- Overall Financial Condition—a measure of the change from the prior period in total net assets of the government as a whole for governmental and business-type activities, excluding any fiduciary activities and net assets.
- Intergenerational Equity—a measure of whether the government lived within its means in the measurement year, or was required to use prior year resources to fund a portion of current year costs, or shifted the funding of some current year costs to future periods.
- Level of Reserves or Deficit—a measure of the adequacy of the amount of the government's total unrestricted net assets or deficit at the measurement date. Reserves are needed to fund cash flow, emergencies, or other unexpected needs.
- Revenue Dispersion—a measure of the exposure to potential financial difficulties resulting from the extent of reliance on revenue sources beyond the direct control of the government to fund the cost of operations.
- Self-Sufficiency—a measure of the extent to which the government's business-type activities are dependent upon subsidies from taxpayer or other general revenues, rather than having the full cost of the activities' operations funded by charges to the users of the service.
- Debt Load—a measure of the extent to which the government had to use current year resources provided for governmental and business-type activities to make payments on long-term debt and the amount of outstanding debt per capita or constituent.
- Financing Margin—a measure of the government's ability to finance future services or capital needs through its ability to levy taxes, raise rates, and/or incur long-term debt considering any legal restrictions on such funding resources.
- Debt-to-Asset Leverage Solvency—a measure of the degree to which the government's total assets has been funded with debt as of the measurement date, indicating the extent of true ownership of government assets.
- Debt Service Coverage Solvency—a measure of the government's ability to meet its long-term financial obligations from net cash generated and available for debt service during the measurement period.
- Liquidity—a measure of the government's ability to meet its current financial obligations (current liabilities) from available cash, cash equivalents, and short-term investments.

Source: http://crawfordcpas.com/html/performeter.html. Reprinted with permission of Crawford & Associates, CPAs.

---

[13] Beth Walter Honadle and Mary Lloyd-Jones. "Analyzing Rural Local Governments' Financial Condition: An Exploratory Application of Three Tools." *Public Budgeting and Finance*, Summer 1998, p. 75.

EXHIBIT 15-8 The Performeter™
A Comprehensive Measurement of a Government's Financial Health and Performance

Performance Measure	Description	Source	Guidelines for Score of 5	Guidelines for Score of 10	Rating (1)	Weight Factor(2)	Weighted Score(3)
Revenue Dispersion	A measure of the exposure to potential financial difficulties resulting from the extent of reliance on revenue sources beyond the direct control of the government to fund the cost of operations. The measure calculates the percentages of individual sources of annual revenue for governmental and business-type activities to the total annual revenue for such activities, excluding special and extraordinary items.	GW—Statement of Activities (Primary Government Only)	Direct control of 50% of annual revenue	Direct control of 90% or more of annual revenue	7	1	7

(1) Scores are based on the professional judgment of the evaluator using the guidelines noted in the above chart. The performance scoring is made on a scale of 1–10 with 10 representing excellent financial health and the highest level of performance, 5 representing satisfactory health and performance, and 1 representing poor financial health and the lowest level of performance. The score is based on ratios calculated and analyzed from the government's audited annual financial report.

(2) The weight factors used in this model are 1 for low weight, 2 for moderate weight, and 3 for high weight.

(3) Overall weighting is calculated by dividing the sum of the weighted individual scores by the maximum possible total score and then multiplying that result times 10.

Abstracted from The Performeter™ with permission of Crawford & Associates, CPAs.

Summary

The discussion of financial statement analysis in Chapter 14 is largely applicable to governments as well. However, as the discussion in this chapter has shown, understanding the financial condition of governments requires additional types of information and, in some cases, modifications to the financial statement analysis discussed in Chapter 14.

Financial analysis of governments relies heavily on analysis of basic financial statements (BFS), including the notes that accompany them. The notes are particularly useful for finding out about the structure of the organization, the accounting methods used, assumptions made, and other background information that gives the reader a perspective as the financial statements are reviewed. Also, careful review and analysis of management's discussion and analysis (MD&A) and other required supplementary information (RSI) is essential. In addition, governmental financial analysis must take into account additional external factors such as debt per capita, tax rates, and citizen income and wealth. The use of ratio analysis is also appropriate.

In the real world, complex scenarios arise. The population might be growing, but property values may be stagnant. There may be high property values but also high debt per capita. In any financial condition analysis, comparison with a relevant group should be made, and strengths and weaknesses should be considered as a whole in making a reasoned assessment about financial condition.

Financial condition analysis often raises questions rather than providing simple answers. Further, the data contained in the financial statements, notes, and ratios might not provide answers to all of the questions raised. It is often necessary to develop specific cost, operations, or other management data.

Financial analysis crosses the line between managerial accounting, discussed in Chapters 1–8, and financial accounting, discussed in Chapters 9–13. Financial analysis, discussed in Chapter 14 and this chapter, takes the financial accounting data that conform to GAAP and analyzes these data to generate useful management information. The analysis is limited only by the availability of data and the creativity of the analyst in using these data.

Key Terms from This Chapter

accrual basis. An accounting system that matches revenues and related expenses in the same fiscal year by recording revenues in the year in which they become earned (whether received or not) and the expenses related to generating those revenues in the same year.

basic financial statements (BFS). Financial statements that must be included in a government annual report to comply with GAAP under GASB Statement No. 34. The required statements are a government-wide statement of net assets; a government-wide statement of activities; fund financial statements for the governmental, proprietary, and fiduciary funds; and notes to the financial statements.

budgetary basis of accounting. The basis of accounting (e.g., cash, accrual, modified accrual) that is used in preparing the budget.

budgetary comparison schedule. A financial schedule that compares the budgeted and actual results for revenues and expenditures. The GASB Statement No. 34 version includes the original budget as well as the final budget.

Comprehensive Annual Financial Report (CAFR). Official annual financial report of a government.

financial condition analysis. An analysis of the financial status of a governmental organization based on a financial statement analysis as well as an evaluation of many external factors that affect the financial condition of the government, such as the wealth of the citizenry, employment rate, and general economy.

fiscal capacity. The extent to which a government can raise money to provide goods and services to its populace, within its economic, legal, and political constraints.

Generally Accepted Accounting Principles (GAAP). Set of rules that must be followed for the organization's financial statements to be deemed a fair presentation of the organization's financial position and results of operations.

Governmental Accounting Standards Board (GASB). Authoritative body that develops GAAP.

management's discussion and analysis (MD&A). An analysis of the government's financial activities based on currently known facts, decisions, or conditions.

modified accrual basis. Accounting basis widely employed by governments for recording purposes for some of their funds. Under this basis of accounting, the primary focus is on financial resources. Typical financial resources are cash, investments, and receivables.

required supplementary information (RSI). Information that must be included along with the *basic financial statements* to present a fair

representation of a government's finances in accordance with GAAP.

risk exposure factor. Investment revenue + intergovernmental revenue + transfers in ÷ own revenue sources; this ratio assesses the relative share of a government's resources that come from sources it does not control, as compared with the share that comes from a tax base it controls.

tax leverage factor. Total operating expenditures ÷ own revenue sources; this ratio assesses the amount taxes must increase in response to expenditure increases. For example, if the government spends $30,000,000 a year and has just $10,000,000 of its own controllable revenue sources, then a 1 percent increase in spending, with no other revenue increases, would require a 3 percent increase in the tax rate.

Questions for Discussion

15-1. What is government financial condition? What is the major source for information about financial condition?

15-2. How does financial condition analysis differ from financial statement analysis?

15-3. How can we obtain information for financial condition analysis?

15-4. How could one assess the quality of a government's financial reporting?

15-5. What general problem must be addressed in doing ratio analysis for governmental financial condition analysis?

15-6. Are liquidity ratios appropriate for financial condition analysis?

15-7. Do traditional solvency ratios adequately address financial condition analysis concerns?

15-8. What are some examples of debt burden measures?

15-9. What are several alternative definitions for the total asset turnover ratios for governments?

Problems[14]

15-10. Using Exhibit 13-1, prepare common size ratios for Local City for its governmental activities.

15-11. Using Exhibit 13-1, calculate current ratios for Local City for governmental activities, business-type activities, total, and component units.

15-12. Using Exhibit 13-1, calculate the solvency ratio of long-term debt to total net assets for the governmental activities.

15-13. Using Exhibit 13-2 for the governmental activities of the primary government, calculate the interest coverage ratio, i.e., change in net assets plus interest ÷ interest.

Case Study Problem

15-14. City of Ponderosa. This case appears starting on the next page. Respond to the four problems raised in the case.

---

[14] These problems require use of the exhibits from Chapter 13.

CASE STUDY
Financial Condition Analysis of City of Ponderosa[15]

Background and Comparative Statistics

The City of Ponderosa, California, is a resort town along the shore of Lake Pristine nestled in the Sierra Mountains. The major industry is tourism, which peaks in the summer as tourists come to swim, boat, and fish the lake or hike and bike the scenic trails. During the winter, tourists are drawn to the local ski resorts, cross-country ski trails, and snowmobile areas. In addition, the tourism industry is helped in that the City of Ponderosa borders the state of Nevada, and a "gaming corridor" of five major casinos and restaurants has emerged just across the state line.

Nearly 80 percent of all jobs in Ponderosa are tied to the tourism industry. Many of the jobs are seasonal, but the tourism industry is diverse enough to provide year-round employment for a large number of residents. The largest employer for the residents is the gaming industry located just across the state line. A regional hospital and the three major ski resorts are the other major employers.

The town lies at an elevation of about 6,223 feet above sea level in the Sierra Mountains. A single state highway provides the main access to Ponderosa. This road winds through a high mountain pass and therefore is frequently impassable during inclement winter weather. However, access to the city improved when the city built a small airport that provides commercial flights to major airline connections in Las Vegas and San Francisco.

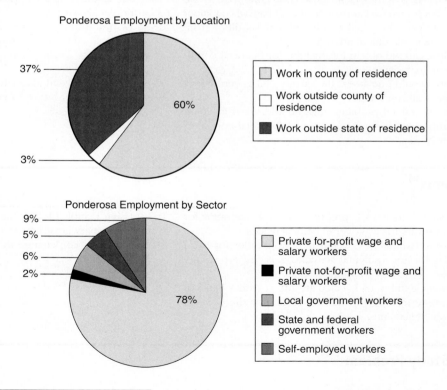

Ponderosa Employment by Location

37%
60%
3%

- Work in county of residence
- Work outside county of residence
- Work outside state of residence

Ponderosa Employment by Sector

9%
5%
6%
2%
78%

- Private for-profit wage and salary workers
- Private not-for-profit wage and salary workers
- Local government workers
- State and federal government workers
- Self-employed workers

---

[15] This case was prepared by Dwight V. Denison, Martin School of Public Policy and Administration at University of Kentucky. The case data are intended only for analysis in context of this case. The city name has been changed and some data have been modified from the original sources. Copyright June 1998, revised January 2000, March 2004, April 2008—All rights reserved. Reprinted with permission. Send comments and suggestions to dwight.denison@uky.edu.

A city council and an appointed city manager govern the City of Ponderosa. The number of permanent residents in the city and encompassing county is about 30,000. The city provides public safety (police and fire), highways and streets, recreation, public improvements, and other administration. Citizens expect public services to be flexible enough to accommodate population increases during the tourism peaks. In addition to the general community services, the city operates a small municipal airport and a local public bus system called LUGE. The community offers all the basic shopping, entertainment, education, and services of most small cities.

The local unified school district is one of the largest in the region, with five elementary schools, one middle school, and two high schools. The district's student population is currently approaching 6,000. In addition, two private schools serve kindergarten through eighth grade. The community college has a growing enrollment of students pursuing degrees in higher education, and new facilities and improvements have begun to attract students from outside the area.

About 34 percent of the residents in Ponderosa are between the ages of 25 and 40 years. The region tends to attract people with a passion for outdoor activities and the environment, many coming to the area to escape metropolitan life. Incorporated in 1965 with a population of less than 10,000, the city has experienced substantial population growth during the recent decade, approaching 30,000 residents. Some residents express concern over the ability of the city to sustain such growth without upsetting the ecological balance of the area.

Ponderosa Census Data Statistics

Total Persons	29,652
Total Families	9,884
Total Households	16,389
Average Persons per Family	3
Total Male	15,336
Total Female	14,316
Race	
White	26,284
Black	255
American Indian, Eskimo, or Aleut	284
Asian or Pacific Islander	1,481
Other Race	1,348

Select Statistics for Ponderosa and Four Cities of Similar Size—Fiscal Year 2009

	Ponderosa	City 1	City 2	City 3	City 4
Population	29,652	29,563	38,961	26,167	27,757
Percent change in population growth over 10 years	61.0%	56.2%	12.3%	8.3%	14.9%
Median income	$ 25,596	$ 22,168	$ 42,019	$ 54,658	$ 21,812
Median housing value	$114,000	$ 71,500	$294,600	$407,500	$ 82,100
School enrollment	5,667	7,677	7,977	4,088	6,973
Retail sales (000)	$282,920	$ 315,613	$569,107	$296,785	$ 358,168
Federal grants	$481,195	$4,305,077	$556,454	$139,443	$3,250,757
Unemployment	6.1%	15.4%	4.0%	2.8%	13.2%
Percent of families below poverty	5.8%	22.1%	3.8%	1.7%	14.6%
Outstanding municipal debt (per capita)	$ 615	$ 549	$ 3,347	$ 2,032	$ 1,059

Per Capita Expenditures in Dollars by Function for FY 2011 with Comparative Data for FY 2010

	FY 2011	FY 2010			
	Ponderosa	City 1	City 2	City 3	City 4
Total expenditures	946	711	550	973	823
Police	167	108	117	140	104
Fire	98	43	66	191	92
Highways	54	80	63	136	68
Sewer	104	206	44	114	56

Per Capita Revenues in Dollars by Source for FY 2011 with Comparative Data for FY 2010

	FY 2011	FY 2010			
	Ponderosa	City 1	City 2	City 3	City 4
Total revenues	803	806	728	928	1,092
Intergovernmental	170	151	117	119	170
Total taxes	532	288	337	478	533
Property taxes	329	147	212	411	344
Charges	91	286	207	207	199

Assignment

The financial officer for Ponderosa is now preparing the management discussion and analysis (MD&A) to go with the basic financial statements (BFS) that follow. She has asked you to put together some information that will aid in that preparation. Use the background material, the financial statements, and notes to the financial statements to answer the following problems to provide information to aid the financial officer in writing the MD&A:

1. Cash solvency refers to the ability of the government to generate enough cash in the short term to meet its current liabilities. Calculate the current ratio for the governmental activities and total primary government. Explain what these ratios suggest about the condition of Ponderosa's cash solvency. Most of the city's cash is invested in financial instruments. What policies are in place to monitor these investments?

2. Long-run solvency refers to the ability of a government to generate revenues sufficient to meet all regular operating costs as well as unusual costs that occur in specific years. These unusual costs might include payments for capital asset replacement and acquisition and pension obligations. Consider how the following questions help assess the long-run solvency of Ponderosa:
   a. For governmental activities and total primary government presented on the statement of net assets and the statement of activities: Calculate debt to total assets ratio, debt to net assets ratio, return on net assets, and times-interest-earned. Do these ratios raise any red flags?
   b. Examine the statement of revenues, expenditures, and changes in fund balances—governmental funds to do the following:
      • Calculate the common size ratios by revenue sources and the revenue per capita for the government funds. Identify the major revenue sources for Ponderosa.

How do these compare with those of the other cities referenced in the background section?

- Calculate and interpret the common size ratios for expenditures. Find the expenditures per capita for the major expenditure items in the governmental funds. How do these compare with those of the other cities referenced in the background section?

c. Examine the statement of activities to determine which government function generates the most program revenue. Which government function is most subsidized by taxes and other general revenues?

3. Budgetary solvency refers to whether a city can generate enough revenues to meet its expenditure obligations and not incur deficits over the normal budgetary period. Review the budgetary comparison schedule for general fund. What do you observe? Comment on the budget solvency of Ponderosa.

4. Consider the financial health of the business activities or enterprise funds.
   a. Calculate and interpret the following ratios for the combined enterprise funds:
      - Liquidity ratios (FY 2010 and 2011): current and quick ratios;
      - Profitability (FY 2010 and 2011): total margin and return on net assets; and
      - Leverage (FY 2010 and 2011): debt ratio, debt to net assets, and times-interest-earned ratio.
   b. What is your assessment of the business activities of the City of Ponderosa? How material are the business activities relative to the primary government activities? In what ways might the business activities be important to the governmental activities of Ponderosa?

5. Considering your analysis in the preceding questions, what are the major strengths and vulnerabilities in the overall financial condition of the City of Ponderosa?

INDEPENDENT AUDITOR'S REPORT

To the City Council of the City of Ponderosa, California

We have audited the financial statements of the City of Ponderosa, California, as of the year ended September 30, 2011. These financial statements are the responsibility of the City's management. Our responsibility is to express an opinion on these financial statements based on our audits.

We conducted our audits in accordance with generally accepted auditing standards and the standards for financial audits contained in Government Auditing Standards. Those standards require that we plan and perform the audits to obtain reasonable assurance as to whether the financial statements are free of material misstatement. An audit includes examining on test basis evidence supporting the amounts and disclosures in the basic financial statements. An audit also includes assessing the accounting principles used and significant estimates made by management, as well as evaluating the overall financial statement presentation. We believe that our audits provide a reasonable basis for our opinion.

In our opinion, the financial statements present fairly in all material respects the financial position of the City of Ponderosa, California, at September 30, 2011, and the results of its operations and cash flows for the year then ended, in conformity with generally accepted accounting principles.

Scrupulous and Germane Associates, Inc.
December 30, 2011

EXHIBIT 15-C-1

City of Ponderosa
Statement of Net Assets
September 30, 2011

	Primary Government		
	Governmental Activities	Business-Type Activities	Total
Assets			
Cash and investments available (Note 3)	$ 6,340,526	$ 37,418	$ 6,377,944
Accounts receivable	1,486,403	136,856	1,623,259
Grants and support receivable	836,962	—	836,962
Internal balances (Note 4B)	159,061	(159,061)	—
Inventory parts and supplies, at cost	256,075	—	256,075
Prepaid expense	1,018	35,931	36,949
Internal advance (Note 4C)	331,215	(331,215)	—
Loans receivable (Note 5)	1,931,687	—	1,931,687
Restricted cash and investments (Note 3)	10,470,997	208,400	10,679,397
Capital assets less accumulated depreciation (Note 6)	129,114,607	10,763,121	139,877,728
Total Assets	150,928,551	10,691,450	161,620,001
Liabilities			
Accounts payable and accrued expenses	1,132,672	8,090	1,140,762
Wages payable	263,566	44,849	308,415
Uninsured losses payable (Note 10B)	857,034	—	857,034
Current portion of long-term liabilities (Note 7)	876,259	50,849	927,108
Deposits	802,629	27,219	829,848
Deferred revenue	2,641,519	17,593	2,659,112
Noncurrent liabilities and debt (Note 7)	65,365,020	2,277,531	67,642,551
Total Liabilities	71,938,699	2,426,131	74,364,830
Net Assets			
Invested in capital assets	62,873,328	9,042,130	71,915,458
Restricted for:			
Capital projects	2,132,547	—	2,132,547
Debt service	8,259,989	—	8,259,989
Low/moderate income housing	307,378	—	307,378
Other purposes	876,971	—	876,971
Unrestricted (deficit)	4,539,639	(776,811)	3,762,828
Total Net Assets	$ 78,989,852	$ 8,265,319	$ 87,255,171

See accompanying notes to financial statements.

EXHIBIT 15-C-2

City of Ponderosa
Statement of Activities
For the Fiscal Year Ended September 30, 2011

Function	Expenses	Program Revenues — Charges for Services	Program Revenues — Operating Grants and Contributions	Program Revenues — Capital Grants and Contributions	Net (Expense) Revenue — Governmental Activities	Net (Expense) Revenue — Business-Type Activities	Net (Expense) Revenue — Total
Primary Government							
Government activities							
Government activities	$ 4,425,146	$ 516,970	$ 392,201	$ 881,248	$ (2,634,727)	$ —	$ (2,634,727)
Public safety	7,859,899		212,574		(7,647,325)	—	(7,647,325)
Public works	3,083,037	322,959	1,299,262	456,392	(1,004,424)	—	(1,004,424)
Recreation	1,691,237	1,002,362	69,134		(619,741)	—	(619,741)
Interest on long-term debt	3,930,419				(3,930,419)	—	(3,930,419)
Total Government Activities	20,989,738	1,842,291	1,973,171	1,337,640	(15,836,636)	—	(15,836,636)
Business-Type Activities							
Airport	1,382,617	375,108	—	(130,943)	—	$(1,138,452)	(1,138,452)
LUGE	1,435,225	840,046	—	452,178	—	(143,001)	(143,001)
Total Business-Type Activities	2,817,842	1,215,154	—	321,235	—	(1,281,453)	(1,281,453)
Total Primary Government	$ 23,807,580	$ 3,057,445	$ 1,973,171	$ 1,658,875	$ (15,836,636)	$(1,281,453)	$(17,118,089)
General Revenues							
Tax and assessments					$ 15,788,535	—	$ 15,788,535
Interest earnings					966,725	—	966,725
Grants and contributions not restricted					1,773,734	—	1,773,734
Other					139,558	—	139,558
Transfers					(339,100)	$ 339,100	—
Total General Revenues and Transfers					18,329,452	339,100	18,668,552
Change in Net Assets					2,492,816	(942,353)	1,550,463
Net Assets—Beginning					76,497,036	9,207,672	85,704,708
Net Assets—Ending					$ 78,989,852	$ 8,265,319	$ 87,255,171

See accompanying notes to financial statements.

EXHIBIT 15-C-3

City of Ponderosa
Balance Sheet—Government Funds
September 30, 2011

	General	Community Redevelopment	Housing Administration	Debt Service	Capital Projects	Other Governmental Funds	Total Governmental Funds
Assets							
Cash and investments available (Note 3)	$2,467,807	$216,762	$ 35,802	$ 422,403	$1,191,508	$2,006,244	$ 6,340,526
Restricted cash and investments (Note 3)	524,265	111,997	—	7,702,188	2,132,547	—	10,470,997
Accounts receivable	635,169	303,987	35,080	—	386,009	126,158	1,486,403
Due from other governments	375,274	—	—	—	427,224	34,464	836,962
Due from other funds (Note 4B)	1,180,052	—	—	800,698	833,405	—	2,814,155
Advance to other funds (Note 4C)	331,215	—	—	—	—	194,029	525,244
Loans receivable (Note 5)	—	—	1,931,687	—	—	—	1,931,687
Prepaids	1,018	—	—	—	—	—	1,018
Parts and supplies, at cost	256,075	—	—	—	—	—	256,075
Total Assets	$ 5,770,875	$632,746	$2,002,569	$8,925,289	$4,970,693	$2,360,895	$24,663,067
Liabilities							
Accounts payable and accrued expenses	$ 355,599	$ 7,549	$ 15,449	$ —	$ 550,106	$ 203,969	$ 1,132,672
Wages payable and compensated absences	232,208	1,070	303	—	—	29,985	263,566
Deferred revenue	958	—	1,931,687	—	708,848	26	2,641,519
Deposits	802,629	—	—	—	—	—	802,629
Uninsured losses payable (Note 10B)	857,034	—	—	—	—	—	857,034
Due to other funds (Note 4B)	—	800,698	—	665,300	1,189,096	—	2,655,094
Advances from other funds (Note 4C)	—	—	—	—	194,029	—	194,029
Total Liabilities	2,248,428	809,317	1,947,439	665,300	2,642,079	233,980	8,546,543

Fund Balance

Reserved for:

Capital projects	—	—	—	—	—	2,132,547	2,132,547
Debt service	—	—	—	8,259,989	—	—	8,259,989
Low/moderate income housing	—	55,130	—	—	252,248	—	307,378
Encumbrances	74,838	—	—	—	19,796	—	94,634
Parts and supplies	256,075	—	—	—	—	—	256,075
Prepaids	1,018	—	—	—	—	—	1,018
Advances to other funds	331,215	—	—	—	194,029	—	525,244
Unreserved, designated in general fund							
Cash reserve	500,000	—	—	—	—	—	500,000
Contingencies/litigation	999,885	—	—	—	—	—	999,885
General liability claims	750,000	—	—	—	—	—	750,000
Worker's compensation claims	510,000	—	—	—	—	—	510,000
Unreserved, undesignated, reported in:							
General funds	99,416	—	—	—	—	—	99,416
Special revenue funds	—	—	(176,571)	—	1,660,842	—	1,484,271
Capital projects	—	—	—	—	—	196,067	196,067
Total Fund Equity	3,522,447	55,130	(176,571)	8,259,989	2,126,915	2,328,614	16,116,524
Total Liabilities and Fund Equity	$ 5,770,875	$ 632,746	$ 2,002,569	$ 8,925,289	$ 2,360,895	$ 4,970,693	$24,663,067

Total fund equity reported for governmental activities in the statement of net assets are different because: — $16,116,524

Capital assets used in governmental activities are not financial resources and therefore are not reported in the funds. — 129,114,607

Long-term liabilities are not due and payable in the current period and therefore are not reported in the funds. — (66,241,279)

Net assets of governmental activities as reported on the statement of net assets: — $78,989,852

See accompanying notes to financial statements.

EXHIBIT 15-C-4

City of Ponderosa
Statement of Revenues, Expenditures, and Changes in Fund Balances
Governmental Funds
For the Fiscal Year Ended September 30, 2011

	General	Community Redevelopment	Housing Administration	Debt Service	Capital Projects	Other Governmental funds	Total Governmental funds
Revenues							
Taxes and assessments	$11,342,525	$3,963,873				$ 482,137	$15,788,535
Intergovernmental	1,773,734		$109,989		$ 1,337,640	1,811,669	5,033,032
Interests and rentals	238,911		19,871	$ 547,495	1,251	159,197	966,725
Licenses and permits	269,542					9,920	279,462
Charges for services	144,692				107,912	1,204,604	1,457,208
Fines, forfeits, and penalties	102,736					2,885	105,621
Other	109,016	5,093	2,000		30,542	44,420	191,071
Total Revenues	13,981,156	3,968,966	131,860	547,495	1,477,345	3,714,832	23,821,654
Expenditures							
Current							
General government	3,340,649	348,276	186,349			266,759	4,142,033
Public safety	7,859,899					—	7,859,899
Public works	2,453,050					629,987	3,083,037
Recreation						1,691,237	1,691,237
Capital outlay	467,093	1,136	442,507		5,318,200	395,759	6,624,695
Debt service							
Principal	62,410			295,000		390,885	748,295
Cost of issuance						—	
Interest and fiscal charges	8,952			3,852,136		69,331	3,930,419
Total Expenditures	14,192,053	349,412	628,856	4,147,136	5,318,200	3,443,958	28,079,615
Excess (Deficiency) of Revenues Over Expenditures	(210,897)	3,619,554	(496,996)	(3,599,641)	(3,840,855)	270,874	(4,257,961)

Other Financing Sources (Uses)							
Proceeds from long-term debt (Note 7)					904,326		904,326
Payment to refunding bond escrow agent (Note 7)					—		—
Operating transfers in (Note 4A)	1,118,956		306,444	3,537,705	3,231,128	1,539,338	9,733,571
Operating transfers (out) (Note 4A)	(1,417,287)	(3,844,853)	(13,561)	(3,160,827)	(23,784)	(1,612,359)	(10,072,671)
Total Other Financing Sources (Uses)	(298,331)	(3,844,853)	292,883	376,878	4,111,670	(73,021)	565,226
Net Change in Fund Balance	(509,228)	(225,299)	(204,113)	(3,222,763)	197,853	270,815	(3,692,735)
Fund Balance, Beginning of Year	4,031,675	48,728	259,243	13,615,299	1,929,062	(74,748)	19,809,259
Fund Balance, End of Year	$ 3,522,447	$ (176,571)	$ 55,130	$10,392,536	4,111,670	$ 196,067	$16,116,524

Net change in fund balances—total governmental funds $ (3,692,735)

Amounts reported for governmental activities in the statement of net assets are different because:

Capital outlays are recorded as expenditures in governmental funds; however, in the statement of activities the cost of these assets are allocated over their estimated useful lives as depreciation expense. This amount is capital outlays less depreciation for the current period. 6,341,582

Bond proceeds provide current financial resources to governmental funds, but debt increases long-term liabilities in the statement of net assets. Repayment of bond principal is an expenditure in governmental funds, but the repayment reduces long-term liabilities in the statement of net assets. This is the amount by which proceeds exceeded repayments. (156,031)

Change in net assets of governmental activities $ 2,492,816

See accompanying notes to financial statements.

EXHIBIT 15-C-5

City of Ponderosa
Budgetary Comparison Schedule for the General Fund
For Fiscal Year Ended September 30, 2011

| | Budget | | | Variance |
	Original	Final	Actual	Final to Actual
Revenues				
Taxes and assessments	$11,060,500	$11,089,914	$11,342,525	$ 252,611
Intergovernmental	1,662,444	1,662,444	1,773,734	111,290
Interest and rentals	340,000	330,500	238,911	(91,589)
Licenses and permits	244,525	244,525	269,542	25,017
Charges for services	145,050	145,050	144,692	(358)
Fines, forfeits, and penalties	76,500	77,000	102,736	25,736
Other	100,000	105,400	109,016	3,616
Total Revenues	13,629,019	13,654,833	13,981,156	326,323
Expenditures				
Current:				
General government	3,026,034	3,026,034	3,340,649	(314,615)
Public safety	8,008,050	8,001,808	7,859,899	141,909
Public works	2,461,345	2,461,345	2,453,050	8,295
Capital outlay	482,211	482,211	467,093	15,118
Principal	63,162	63,162	62,410	752
Interest and fiscal charges	7,783	7,783	8,952	(1,169)
Total Expenditures	14,048,585	14,042,343	14,192,053	(149,710)
Excess (Deficiency) of Revenues				
Over Expenditures	(419,566)	(387,510)	(210,897)	(176,613)
Other Financing Sources (Uses)				
Operating transfers in	1,932,989	1,593,889	1,118,956	(474,933)
Operating transfers (out)	(1,417,287)	(1,417,287)	(1,417,287)	
Total Other Financing Sources (Uses)	515,702	176,602	(298,331)	(474,933)
Net Change in Fund Balance	96,136	(210,908)	(509,228)	(298,320)
Fund Balance—Beginning of Year	4,031,675	4,031,675	4,031,675	—
Fund Balance—End of Year	$ 4,127,811	$ 3,820,767	$ 3,522,447	$(298,320)

Budget adopted on basis consistent with GAAP.

See accompanying notes to financial statements.

EXHIBIT 15-C-6

City of Ponderosa
Statement of Net Assets—Proprietary Funds
September 30, 2011
with Comparative Amounts for the Fiscal Year Ended September 30, 2010

| | Business-Type Activities—Enterprise Funds | | | |
	Airport	LUGE	FY 2011 Total	FY 2010 Total
Assets				
Current Assets:				
Cash and investments available (Note 3)	$ 250	$ 37,168	$ 37,418	$ 73,922
Accounts receivable	45,272	91,584	136,856	86,440
Prepaid expense	—	35,931	35,931	34,942
Total Current Assets	45,522	164,683	210,205	195,304
Noncurrent Assets:				
Restricted cash and investments (Note 3)	208,400	—	208,400	260,051
Fixed assets less accumulated depreciation (Note 6)	8,514,455	2,248,666	10,763,121	11,745,676
Total Noncurrent Assets	8,722,855	2,248,666	10,971,521	12,005,727
Total Assets	8,768,377	2,413,349	11,181,726	12,201,031
Liabilities				
Current Liabilities:				
Accounts payable and accrued expenses	7,954	136	8,090	19,299
Wages payable	39,229	5,620	44,849	43,380
Internal balances (Note 4B)	159,061	—	159,061	111,221
Deposits	26,819	400	27,219	27,806
Current portion of long-term liabilities	50,849	—	50,849	112,970
Total Current Liabilities	283,912	6,156	290,068	314,676
Noncurrent Liabilities:				
Deferred revenue	—	17,593	17,593	19,088
Internal advance (Note 4C)	331,215	—	331,215	331,215
Certificates of Participation (Note 7B)	1,919,745	—	1,919,745	1,983,515
Loan obligations (Note 7B)	357,786	—	357,786	344,865
Total Noncurrent Liabilities	2,608,746	17,593	2,626,339	2,678,683
Total Liabilities	2,892,658	23,749	2,916,407	2,993,359
Net Assets				
Invested in capital assets	6,937,900	2,104,230	9,042,130	9,821,870
Unrestricted (deficit)	(1,062,181)	285,370	(776,811)	(614,198)
Total Net Assets	$5,875,719	$2,389,600	$ 8,265,319	$ 9,207,672

See accompanying notes to financial statements.

EXHIBIT 15-C-7

City of Ponderosa
Statement of Revenues, Expenses, and Changes in Fund Net Assets
Proprietary Funds
For the Fiscal Year Ended September 30, 2011
with Comparative Amounts for the Fiscal Year Ended September 30, 2010

	Business-Type Activities—Enterprise Funds			
	Airport	**LUGE**	**FY 2011 Total**	**FY 2010 Total**
Operating Revenues				
Charges for services	$ 57,417	$ 680,121	$ 737,538	$ 747,570
Rental income	317,691	159,925	477,616	443,597
Total Operating Revenue	375,108	840,046	1,215,154	1,191,167
Operating Expenses				
Personal services	304,521	24,777	329,298	469,263
Contractual services	38,054	1,105,082	1,143,136	1,086,686
Insurance	33,430	—	33,430	48,034
Fuel and supplies	39,896	156,268	196,164	189,571
Utilities	48,242	3,697	51,939	58,149
Depreciation (Note 6)	849,883	143,001	992,884	899,851
Maintenance	42,518	—	42,518	24,161
Other	26,073	2,400	28,473	35,059
Total Operating Expenses	1,382,617	1,435,225	2,817,842	2,810,774
Operating Loss	(1,007,509)	(595,179)	(1,602,688)	(1,619,607)
Nonoperating Revenues (Expenses)				
Grants	10,000	410,147	420,147	539,047
Interest	(142,728)	—	(142,728)	(218,325)
Other	1,785	42,031	43,816	57,871
Net nonoperating revenues (expenses)	(130,943)	452,178	321,235	378,593
Loss before operating transfers	(1,138,452)	(143,001)	(1,281,453)	(1,241,014)
Operating transfers in (Note 4A)	339,100	—	339,100	269,929
Change in Net Assets	(799,352)	(143,001)	(942,353)	(971,085)
Total Net Assets—Beginning	6,675,071	2,532,601	9,207,672	10,178,757
Total Net Assets—Ending	$ 5,875,719	$2,389,600	$ 8,265,319	$ 9,207,672

See accompanying notes to financial statements.

EXHIBIT 15-C-8

City of Ponderosa
Statement of Cash Flows
Proprietary Funds
For Fiscal Year Ended September 30, 2011
with Comparative Amounts for the Fiscal Year Ended September 30, 2010

	Airport	LUGE	FY 2011 Total	FY 2010 Total
Cash Flows from Operating Activities				
Receipts from customers	$ 29,849	$ 655,778	$ 685,627	$ 662,558
Payments to suppliers	(226,755)	(1,279,634)	(1,506,389)	(1,470,635)
Payments to employees	(304,521)	(24,777)	(329,298)	(469,263)
Other receipts	317,104	159,925	477,029	447,069
Net Cash Used by Operating Activities	(184,323)	(488,708)	(673,031)	(830,271)
Cash Flows from Noncapital Financing Activities				
Grants received	10,000	410,147	420,147	538,191
Transfers from other funds	386,940	—	386,940	8,202
Other receipts	1,785	42,057	43,842	57,869
Net Cash Provided by Operating Subsidies and Transfers	398,725	452,204	850,929	604,262
Cash Flows from Capital and Related Financing Activities				
Capital contributions (Note 1C)	36,799	178,806	215,605	962,342
Proceeds from long-term debt				2,458,166
Purchases of capital assets	(47,154)	(178,806)	(225,960)	(2,908,866)
Principal paid on capital debt	(112,970)		(112,970)	(1,662,137)
Interest paid on capital debt	(142,728)		(142,728)	(218,325)
Net Cash (Used) by Capital and Related Financing Activities	(266,053)	—	(266,053)	(1,368,820)
Net Cash Flows	(51,651)	(36,504)	(88,155)	(1,594,829)
Balances Beginning of Year	260,301	73,672	333,973	1,928,802
Balances End of Year	$ 208,650	$ 37,168	$ 245,818	$ 333,973
Reconciliation of Operating Loss to Net Cash Used by Operating Activities				
Operating loss	$(1,007,509)	$ (595,179)	$(1,602,688)	$(1,619,607)
Adjustments to reconcile operating loss to net cash flows provided by operating activities:				
Depreciation	849,883	143,001	992,884	899,851
Change in Assets and Liabilities:				
Receivables	(27,568)	(22,848)	(50,416)	(20,026)
Accounts payable and accrued expenses	1,458	(11,198)	(9,740)	(40,951)
Prepaid expenses		(989)	(989)	11,976
Deferred revenues		(1,495)	(1,495)	(64,986)
Deposits	(587)		(587)	3,472
Net Cash Used by Operating Activities	$ (184,323)	$ (488,708)	$ (673,031)	$ (830,271)

City of Ponderosa Notes to Financial Statements

Note 1. Significant Accounting Policies

A. Reporting Entity

A five-member council elected by City residents governs the City. The City is legally separate and fiscally independent, which means it can issue debt, set and modify budgets and fees, and sue or be sued. These financial statements present the governmental and business-type activities of Ponderosa for which the City is considered to be financially accountable.

B. Fund Accounting

The accounts of the City are organized on the basis of funds, each of which is considered a separate accounting entity. The operations of each fund are accounted for with a separate set of self-balancing accounts that comprise its assets, liabilities, fund equity, revenues, and expenditures or expenses, as appropriate. Government resources are allocated to and accounted for individual funds based upon the purposes for which they are to be spent and the means by which spending activities are controlled. These various funds are grouped as follows, in the basic financial statements:

- Governmental fund types: General Fund is the general operating fund of the City. It is used to account for all financial resources except those required to be accounted for in another fund. Special Revenue Funds are used to account for the proceeds of specific revenue sources (other than major capital projects) that are legally restricted to expenditures for specific purposes. Debt Service Funds are used to account for financial resources to be used for payment of principal and interest on the 2009 Refunding Revenue Bonds and the 2010 Certificates of Participation. Capital Projects Funds are used to account for financial resources to be used for the acquisition or construction of major capital facilities (other than those financed by proprietary fund types).
- Proprietary fund types: Enterprise Funds are used to account for operations (a) that are financed and operated in a manner similar to private business enterprises where the intent of the governing body is that the costs and expenses, including depreciation, of providing goods or services to the general public on a continuing basis be financed or recovered primarily through user charges; or (b) where the governing body has decided that periodic determination of revenues earned, expenses incurred, and/or net income is appropriate for capital maintenance, public policy, management control, accountability, or other purposes.
- Segment information for enterprise funds: The City has two enterprise funds, each of which represents a separate business activity of the City:

Airport: The City owns and operates the Ponderosa Airport, which is used by scheduled commercial carriers and others.

LUGE: Lakefront Unified Ground Express provides transit service in and around the City.

C. Contributed Capital

Contributed capital represents grants and other funds contributed to Enterprise Funds to acquire capital assets, reduced by accumulated depreciation related to such assets. Changes in contributed capital were as follows:

	Airport	LUGE	Total
Balance, September 30, 2010	$7,565,577	$2,040,689	$9,606,266
Capital contributions	36,799	178,806	215,605
Depreciation of contributed assets	(664,475)	(115,265)	(779,740)
Balance, September 30, 2011	$6,937,900	$2,104,230	$9,042,130

D. Basis of Accounting

Basis of accounting refers to when revenues and expenditures or expenses are recognized in the accounts and reported in the basic financial statements. *Basis of accounting* relates to the timing of the measurements made, regardless of the measurement focus applied.

The government-wide statement of net assets and statement of activities are reported using the economic resources measurement focus and the accrual basis of accounting. Revenues, expenses, gains, losses, assets, and liabilities resulting from exchange and exchange-like transactions are recognized when the exchange takes place. Nonexchange transactions are recognized when a government gives or receives value without directly receiving or giving something equal in value in the exchange in accordance with GASB Statement No. 33.

All governmental funds are accounted for using the modified accrual basis of accounting. Their revenues are recognized when they become measurable and available as net current assets.

Those revenues susceptible to accrual are taxes, special assessments, intergovernmental revenues, use of money and property, charges for services, fines and penalties, and license and permit revenues.

Expenditures are generally recognized under the modified accrual basis of accounting when the related fund liability is incurred. An exception to this general rule is principal and interest on general long-term debt, which is recognized when due. Financial resources usually are appropriated in other funds for transfer to a debt service fund in the period in which maturing debt principal and interest must be paid. Such amounts thus are not liabilities of the debt service fund, as their settlement will not require expenditure of existing fund assets.

All proprietary funds are accounted for using the accrual basis of accounting. Their revenues are recognized when they are earned, and their expenses are recognized when they are incurred. The interfund receivables and payables are eliminated to minimize the "grossing-up" effect on assets and liabilities with the governmental and business-type activities columns of the primary government.

The total fund balances reported in the city's governmental funds ($16,116,524) are different from the total net assets ($87,255,171) reported in the statement of net assets because of differences in bases of accounting used to prepare each report. The differences result primarily from the long-term economic focus of the statement of net assets versus the current financial resources focus of the governmental fund balance sheets.

Explanation of Differences Between Governmental Funds Balance Sheet and Statement of Net Assets

	Total Governmental Funds	Long-Term Assets, Liabilities	Enterprise Funds	Reclassifications and Eliminations	Statement of Net Assets Totals
Assets					
Cash and investments available (Note 3)	$ 6,340,526		$ 37,418	$ —	$ 6,377,944
Restricted cash and investments (Note 3)	10,470,997		208,400	—	10,679,397
Receivables, net	1,486,403		136,856	836,962	2,460,221
Due from other governments	836,962		—	(836,962)	—
Due from other funds (Note 4B)	2,814,155		—	(2,814,155)	—
Advance to other funds (Note 4C)	525,244		—	(525,244)	—
Loans receivable (Note 5)	1,931,687		—	—	1,931,687
Prepaids	1,018		35,931	—	36,949
Parts and supplies, at cost	256,075		—	—	256,075
Capital assets less depreciation	—	$129,114,607	10,763,121	—	139,877,728
Total Assets	$24,663,067	$129,114,607	$11,181,726	$(3,339,399)	$161,620,001

(continued)

	Total Governmental Funds	Long-Term Assets, Liabilities	Enterprise Funds	Reclassifications and Eliminations	Statement of Net Assets Totals
Liabilities					
Accounts payable and accrued expenses	$ 1,132,672		$ 8,090	$ —	$ 1,140,762
Wages payable and compensated absences	263,566		44,849	—	308,415
Deferred revenue	2,641,519		17,593	—	2,659,112
Deposits	802,629		27,219	—	829,848
Uninsured losses payable (Note 10B)	857,034		—	—	857,034
Due to other funds (Note 4B)	2,655,094		159,061	(2,814,155)	—
Advances from other funds (Note 4C)	194,029		331,215	(525,244)	—
Long-term liabilities		$ 66,241,279	2,328,380		68,569,659
Total Liabilities	8,546,543	66,241,279	2,916,407	(3,339,399)	74,364,830
Fund Equity					
Total Fund Balances/Net Assets	16,116,524	62,873,328	8,265,319	—	87,255,171
Total Liabilities and Fund Balances/Net Assets	$24,663,067	$129,114,607	$11,181,726	$(3,339,399)	$161,620,001

E. Measurement Focus

The government-wide statements are reported on an economic resources measurement focus, which takes into account both the long-term and current assets and liabilities. The statement of net assets reports all financial and capital resources of the primary government, including business-like activities. Fiduciary activities are not reported in the government-wide statements, as they are not resources available to the primary government.

All governmental funds are accounted for on a spending or financial flows measurement focus, which means that only current assets and current liabilities are generally included on their balance sheets. Their reported fund balance is their net current assets, which is considered only to be a measure of available spendable resources. Governmental fund operating statements present a summary of sources and uses of available spendable resources during a period by presenting increases and decreases in net current assets.

All proprietary fund types are accounted for on an economic resources measurement focus, which means that all assets and all liabilities associated with their activity are included on their statement of net assets. Proprietary fund-type operating statements present increases (revenue) and decreases (expenses) in total net assets.

F. Materials, Parts, and Supplies

Materials, parts, and supplies are held for consumption and are valued at cost on a first-in, first-out basis. General fund supplies are recorded as an expenditure at the time individual supply items are used.

G. Property Tax

The County assesses properties and bills, and collects and distributes property taxes to the City. The County remits the entire amount levied and handles all delinquencies, retaining interest and penalties. Secured and unsecured property taxes are levied on January 1 of the preceding fiscal year.

Secured property tax is due in two installments, on November 1 and March 1, and becomes a lien on those dates. It becomes delinquent on December 10 and April 10, respectively. Unsecured property tax is due on July 1, and becomes delinquent on August 31.

The term "unsecured" refers to taxes on personal property other than real estate, land, and buildings. These taxes are secured by liens on the property being taxed. Property tax revenues are recognized by the City in the fiscal year they are assessed provided they become available as defined previously.

Note 2. Budgets and Budgetary Accounting

A. Budget Process

The City follows these procedures in establishing the budgetary data on a modified accrual basis, reflected in the accompanying financial statements:

- The department heads prepare a budget request based upon the previous year's expenditures and current year estimates for the fiscal year commencing the following October 1.
- The City Manager submits his or her proposed City budget the first week in September each year to the City Council, which make decisions regarding department budgets.
- The budget is legally enacted through passage of an appropriation resolution at the first regular City Council meeting in October.
- The approved budget is placed in the city accounting system and monitored by the Accounting Division of the General Services Department.
- The City Manager is authorized to transfer budgeted amounts between expenditure categories within any department. Revisions that alter the total expenditure of any department above $5,000 must be approved by the City Council.
- Budgets for governmental funds, except the Disaster Relief Special Revenue Fund, are adopted on a basis consistent with generally accepted accounting principles. Budgeted amounts are as originally adopted and as further amended by the City Council.
- Capital projects are primarily "long-term" in nature; however, the budgets are established on a year-by-year basis; and appropriations lapse at the close of the fiscal year to the extent they have not been expended or encumbered.

Encumbrance accounting requires that purchase orders, contracts, and other commitments for the expenditures of monies be recorded in the books in order to reserve that portion of the applicable appropriation. The City's encumbrance accounting is an extension of the formal budgetary process. It reports encumbrances outstanding at year-end as reservations of fund balance, since they are not expenditures. Unencumbered appropriations lapse at year-end.

B. Comparisons with Budget

The following funds incurred expenditures in excess of their budgets in the following amounts as the result of unanticipated expenses. Sufficient resources were available within each fund to finance these excesses.

	Amount of Excess
General Funds	$149,710
Special Revenue Funds	
Community redevelopment	47,184
Snow removal	26,619
Park special activities	11,696
Art programs	13,499
Capital Projects Funds	
Redevelopment	3,909

Note 3. Cash and Investments

The City's dependence on tax receipts, which are seasonal, requires it to maintain significant cash reserves to finance operations during the remainder of the year. The City pools cash from all sources and all funds except Cash and Investments with Fiscal Agents so that it can be invested at the maximum yield, consistent with safety and liquidity, while individual funds can make expenditures at any time.

Cash and investments maturing in three months or less are considered to be liquid assets for purposes of measuring cash flows.

The City invests in individual securities and in investment pools. Individual securities are evidenced by specific identifiable pieces of paper called securities instruments, or by an electronic entry registering the owner in the records of the institution issuing the security, called the book entry system.

Cash and investments comprised the following at September 30, 2011:

	Available for Operations	Restricted	Total Market Value
Securities			
U.S. Treasury bills, bonds, and notes		$ 4,026,440	$ 4,026,440
Mortgage-backed securities	$ 292,606		292,606
Pooled Investments			
California Local Agency Investment Fund	5,160,645	355,811	5,516,456
Mutual funds (U.S. securities)	1,000,000	6,100,318	7,100,318
County treasury		111,997	111,997
Cash Deposits (overdraft)	(75,307)	84,831	9,524
Total cash and investment	$6,377,944	$10,679,397	$17,057,341

A. Cash Deposits

Cash deposits are entirely insured or collateralized by the institution holding the deposit. California law requires banks and savings and loan institutions to pledge government securities with a market value of 110 percent of the deposit or first trust deed mortgage notes with a value of 150 percent of the deposit as collateral for all municipal deposits. This collateral is considered to be held in the City's name and places the City ahead of general creditors of the institution. The City has waived collateral requirements for the portion of deposits covered by federal deposit insurance.

B. Authorized Investments

The City may invest excess funds only in the following securities:

- insured or collateralized certificates of deposit issued by a nationally or state chartered bank or state or federal association;
- prime bankers acceptances with maturities less than 270 days, which are eligible for purchase by the Federal Reserve System and are issued by the top 15 U.S. banks or the top 100 banks in the world;
- securities of the U.S. government or its agencies such as the Federal Home Loan Bank, Federal Farm Credit, and Federal National Mortgage Association;
- repurchase Agreements with maturities not exceeding 30 days purchased through the top 15 U.S. banks;
- prime commercial paper with A1/P1 rating;
- medium-term corporate notes with a maximum maturity of five years issued by corporations doing business in the United States that are rated "A" or its equivalent or better by one of the national rating agencies;

- State of California Local Agency Investment Fund;
- passbook savings account demand deposits;
- domestic money market mutual funds registered with the Federal Securities and Exchange Commission (SEC), rated in the highest rating category by a nationally recognized rating service, or that only invest in the following:
  - — U.S. Government or federal agency securities and repurchase agreements,
  - — Tax-exempt obligations, or
  - — Other instruments as authorized under Section 53601 and 53634 of the California Government Code.

These investments are also subject to other limitations as stated in the City's investment policies.

C. Cash and Investments with Fiscal Agents

The City had $10,043,133 in cash and investments at September 30, 2011, held by fiscal agents, which are pledged for the payment or security of certain bonds or for payment of project expenditures. The California Government Code allows these funds to be invested in accordance with any applicable City ordinance resolution or bond indenture, unless there are specific state statutes governing their investment. All these funds have been invested as permitted under the preceding Code.

The mortgage-backed securities valued at $292,606 are susceptible to custodial credit risk in that the securities are held by the City's agent but are not registered in the City's name.

D. Market Risk and Investment Maturities

The City limits market risk by limiting the types and maturities of its investments and by not borrowing against its investments. Investment yield is ranked after safety and liquidity in making investment decisions. All investments are held to maturity, and maturities are matched to the City's projected cash flow needs. Cash and investments matured as follows at September 30, 2011:

Maturity	2011
Up to one year	$15,413,482
One to five years	1,890,307
Greater than five years	292,606
Total	$17,596,395

Investments with maturities greater than five years represent the City's investments in mortgage-backed securities purchased in 2003.

E. Return on Investments

The City's return on investments comprises only interest income; there were no gains or losses on sales of securities since all were held to maturity. Interest income of $912,614 and $1,407,197 earned during fiscal 2011 and 2010 represented a return of 5.4 percent and 7.8 percent on the City's month-end average investment balances. This income is allocated to funds in which interest is legally required to be allocated and the general fund on the basis of their average month-end cash and investment balances.

Note 4. Interfund Transactions

A. Operating Transfers Between Funds

With Council approval, resources may be transferred from one City fund to another. The purpose of the majority of transfers, called operating transfers, is to reimburse a fund that has made an expenditure on behalf of another fund. Less often, a residual equity transfer may be made to open or close a fund.

Operating transfers between funds during the fiscal year ended September 30, 2011, were as follows:

	Transfers In	Transfers Out
General Fund	$ 1,118,956	$ 1,417,287
Special Reserve Funds	1,845,782	5,470,773
Debt Service Funds	3,537,705	3,160,827
Capital Projects Funds	3,231,128	23,784
Totals for Governmental Funds	9,733,571	10,072,671
Totals for Enterprise Funds	339,100	
Total all Funds	$10,072,671	$10,072,671

B. Current Interfund Balances

Current interfund balances arise in the normal course of business and are expected to be repaid shortly after the end of the fiscal year. At September 30, 2011, current interfund balances were as follows:

	Receivable	Payable
General Fund	$1,180,052	
Special Revenue Funds		
Community Redevelopment		$ 800,698
Debt Service Funds		
Redevelopment	800,698	665,300
Capital Projects Funds		
City	168,105	
Redevelopment	665,300	1,189,096
Enterprise Funds		
Airport		159,061
Total all Funds	$2,814,155	$2,814,155

C. Long-Term Interfund Advances

As of September 30, 2011, the General Fund had advanced $331,215 to the Airport Enterprise Fund, which was used to cover airport cash flow shortages. The advance will be repaid with future Airport operating revenues, but not within the next fiscal year.

As of September 30, 2011, the Low and Moderate Income Housing Special Revenue Fund had advanced $194,026 to the Redevelopment Capital Projects Fund. The advance is expected to be repaid from future Redevelopment Capital Project Fund revenues.

Note 5. Loans Receivable and Deferred Revenue

Housing Rehabilitation and Affordable Housing Loans

The City engages in programs designed to encourage construction or improvement in low- to moderate-income housing or other projects. Under these programs, grants or loans are provided under favorable terms to homeowners or developers who agree to spend these funds in accordance with the City's terms. Although these loans are expected to be repaid in full, their balance has been offset by deferred revenue in the amount of $1,931,713, as they are not expected to be repaid during fiscal year 2012. The balance of the loans receivable arising from these programs at September 30, 2011, was $1,931,687.

Note 6. Capital Assets

General capital assets used for governmental activities include streets and sidewalks, bridges, curbs and gutters, drainage systems, and lighting systems, which have been capitalized. All capital assets are valued at historical cost or estimated historical cost if actual historical cost is not available. Donated capital assets are valued at their estimated fair market value on the date donated. All general capital assets are depreciated except for land, which is reported at cost. Current depreciation of general capital assets is reported as an expense to governmental activities in the statement of activities.

Proprietary fund capital assets are recorded at cost and depreciated over their estimated useful lives. The purpose of depreciation is to spread the cost of proprietary fund capital assets equitably among all customers over the life of these assets, so that each customer's bill includes a pro rata share of the cost of these assets. The amount charged to depreciation expense each year represents that year's pro rata share of the cost of proprietary fund capital assets.

Depreciation of all proprietary fund capital assets is charged as an expense against operations each year, and the total amount of depreciation taken over the years, called accumulated depreciation, is reported on the proprietary funds' statement of net assets as a reduction in the book value of the capital assets.

Depreciation of capital assets in service is provided using the straight-line method, which means the cost of the asset is divided by its expected useful life in years and the result is charged to expense each year until the asset is fully depreciated. The City has assigned the following useful lives to capital assets:

Buildings	15–30 years
Streets and runways	15 years
Vehicles and equipment	3–17 years

Changes in capital assets for the year ended September 30, 2011, were as follows:

	September 30, 2010, Balance	Additions	Retirements	September 30, 2011, Balance
General Capital Assets:				
Land and streets	$108,772,977	$3,545,116	$ 1,578	$112,316,515
Building	10,903,756	55,039	528	10,958,267
Vehicles	5,517,868	667,981	171,531	6,014,318
Furniture and communication equipment	2,949,129	200,737	319,704	2,830,162
Construction in progress	3,378,713	249,992	—	3,628,705
Total General Capital Assets	131,522,443	4,718,865	493,341	135,747,967
Deduct Accumulated Depreciation	(6,350,247)	(283,113)	—	(6,633,360)
Net General Capital Assets	$125,172,196	$4,435,752	$ 493,341	$129,114,607
Enterprise Capital Assets:				
LUGE:				
Buses	$ 1,220,648	$ 2,000	$ —	$ 1,222,648
Transit center buildings	435,247	1,166,196	—	1,601,443
Land	243,797	—	—	243,797
Other equipment	32,683	—	27	32,656
Construction in progress	989,389	176,807	1,166,196	—
Total LUGE Assets	2,921,764	1,345,003	1,166,223	3,100,544
Deduct Accumulated Depreciation	(708,877)	(143,001)		(851,878)
Net LUGE Capital Assets	$ 2,212,887	$1,202,002	$1,166,223	$ 2,248,666

(continued)

	September 30, 2010, Balance	Additions	Retirements	September 30, 2011, Balance
Airport:				
Runways and land	$ 9,423,747	—	—	$ 9,423,747
Terminal building	2,925,848	—	—	2,925,848
Machinery and equipment	2,717,618	$ 35,665	—	2,753,283
Construction in progress	114,086	11,486	$ 1	125,571
Total Airport Assets	15,181,299	47,151	1	15,228,449
Deduct Accumulated Depreciation	(5,864,114)	(849,880)	—	(6,713,994)
Net Airport Capital Assets	9,317,185	(802,729)	1	8,514,455
Enterprise Capital Assets	$ 11,530,072	$ 399,273	$1,166,224	$ 10,763,121

Note 7. Long-Term Liabilities

A. General Long-Term Debt

The City generally incurs long-term debt to finance projects or purchase assets, which will have useful lives equal to or greater than the related debt maturity. The City's debt issues and transactions are summarized as follows and discussed in detail thereafter:

	September 30, 2010, Balance	Additions	Reductions	September 30, 2011, Balance
General Long-Term Debt:				
Refunding Lease Revenue Bonds, 2009 Series A, 4.1%–5.75%, due 2039	$27,150,000			$27,150,000
Refunding Revalue Bonds, 2009 Series B, 4.0%–6.25%, due serially until 10/1/2042	28,555,000		$255,000	28,300,000
Subordinate Bond Anticipation Notes, 2010 Series A, 8% due 10/1/2015	8,295,000			8,295,000
2007 Certificates of Participation, Series B, 3.6%–6.3%, due 2022	665,000		40,000	625,000
State Revolving Fund Loan, 2.8%, due 10/1/2030		$904,326		904,326
Capital lease obligations:				
Vehicle and equipment, 6.5%–8%, due 2014	1,437,126		470,173	966,953
Total	$66,102,126	$904,326	$765,173	$66,241,279
Enterprise Long-Term Debt:				
2009 Certificates of Participation, 4.10%–6.4%, due 11/1/2023	$ 2,040,000		$95,000	$1,945,000
Fuel Farm Loan, adjustable interest due 8/10/2024	401,350		17,970	383,380
Total	$ 2,441,350		$112,970	$ 2,328,380

B. Long-Term Debt Issues

During the 2010–11 fiscal year, the City drew down $904,326 under a State Revolving Fund Loan with the State of California. Proceeds from the loan were used along with grant funds to construct the state line erosion control project. The loan is secured by the project and repayable from Transient Occupancy Taxes of the City. The City may draw up to $1.435 million under the loan.

On November 1, 2009, Ponderosa concurrently issued $27,150,000 principal amount Refunding Lease Revenue Bonds, 2009 Series A, and $28,555,000 principal amount Refunding Revenue Bonds, 2009 Series B. Proceeds from these 2009 Refunding Bonds were used to advance refund the outstanding 2007 Revenue Refunding Bonds, 2007 Series A ("Refunded Bonds"). These proceeds, along with Refunded Bond reserve fund monies, were used to purchase U.S. government securities, which were deposited in an irrevocable trust with an escrow agent to provide for all future debt service payments on the Refunded Bonds. The advance refunding was required to issue the Subordinate Bond Anticipation Notes discussed next.

Interest on the 2009 Series A and B Bonds is payable semiannually on each April 1 and October 1. Principal matures annually each October 1. Principal on the 2009 Series A Bonds maturing on October 1, 2022 and 2029, is subject to mandatory redemption commencing October 1, 2015 and 2023, respectively. Principal on the 2009 Series B Bonds maturing on October 1, 2014, 2024, and 2032 is subject to mandatory redemption commencing October 1, 2011, 2015, and 2025, respectively.

On April 25, 2010, Ponderosa issued the Subordinate Bond Anticipation Notes, 2010 Series A, the proceeds of which are to be used to finance the Ponderosa Redevelopment Agency's costs incurred under the development agreement discussed previously. The Notes may be redeemed prior to maturity on or after October 1, 2012, at par plus accrued interest. The Notes are subordinate to the 2009 Series B Bonds.

The 2009 Series B Bonds and the Notes are repayable from incremental property tax revenues and transient occupancy tax revenues levied and collected by the Agency. Transient occupancy tax revenues levied by the Agency that are not used for debt service on the 2009 Series B Bonds or on the Notes revert to the City and will be used along with other City General Fund resources to repay debt service on the 2009 Series A Bonds.

Under the following certificates of participation (COP) issues, the City makes semiannual payments which are sufficient to pay the principal and interest. The balance of the debt evidenced by the COPs have been included in the City's financial statements, as they are in essence financing arrangements, with ownership of the financed assets reverting to the City at its conclusion.

Certificates of Participation, 2007 Series B: The City issued Certificates of Participation in the original principal amount of $745,000 as part of an Association of Bay Area Governments (ABAG) issue to finance the relocation of a fire station. Principal payments are payable annually on July 1, and interest payments are payable semiannually on January 1 and July 1.

On November 1, 2009, the City issued $2,040,000 principal amount of COPs. Proceeds from these COPs were used to prepay the Airport T-Hangar lease.

During fiscal 2009–10 the City entered into a loan to finance fuel tanks and related facilities, known as the "Fuel Farm," which were constructed at the Airport. The loan bears interest at 6.75 percent until August 7, 2014. The loan agent may reset the interest rate on August 5, 2014 and 2019, based on a formula that uses a U.S. Treasury Index and U.S. Treasury yields.

The Certificates and Fuel Farm Loan are repayable from Airport Enterprise Fund revenues.

C. Debt Service Requirements

Principal and interest payments on all outstanding long-term debt are as follows at September 30, 2011:

	Primary Government Activities			Business Activities			
Year	Principal	Interest	Subtotal	Principal	Interest	Subtotal	Total
2012	$ 876,259	$ 3,462,724	$ 4,338,983	$ 50,849	$ 98,914	$ 149,763	$ 4,488,746
2013	1,369,907	3,416,918	4,786,825	117,968	24,295	154,763	4,941,588
2014	1,432,496	3,345,307	4,777,803	125,432	21,831	159,763	4,937,566

(continued)

	Primary Government Activities			Business Activities			
Year	Principal	Interest	Subtotal	Principal	Interest	Subtotal	Total
2015	1,509,810	3,270,424	4,780,234	138,212	19,051	169,763	4,949,997
2016	9,545,437	3,191,500	12,736,937	146,536	15,727	174,763	12,911,700
2017–21	6,822,630	14,461,491	21,284,121	1,512,333	12,835	1,475,168	22,759,289
2022–26	7,453,688	13,364,252	20,817,940	237,050	5,888	242,938	21,060,878
2027–31	9,662,000	10,878,459	20,540,459	—	—	—	20,540,459
2032–36	12,220,000	7,676,650	19,896,650	—	—	—	19,896,650
2037–41	13,232,594	4,637,225	17,869,819	—	—	—	17,869,819
2042–46	1,072,821	64,369	1,137,190	—	—	—	1,137,190
Total	$65,197,642	$67,769,319	$132,966,961	$2,328,380	$198,541	$2,526,921	$135,493,882

D. Capital Leases

The City has entered into several lease obligations to finance capital assets used in providing primary government services. Lease obligations are currently used to secure computers, police radios, vehicles, trucks, parks equipment, and snow removal equipment. Ownership of all leased property reverts to the City at the end of the lease. The future minimum payments required for the capital leases obligations are:

Year	Payment
2012	$ 531,303
2013	376,788
2014	135,546
Total	$1,043,637

Note 8. Fund Equity

A. Reservations and Designations

Fund equity consists of reserved and unreserved amounts. Reserved fund equity represents that portion of fund balance or retained earnings that has been appropriated for expenditure or is legally segregated for a specific future use. The remaining portion is unreserved.

A portion of unreserved fund balance may be designated to indicate plans for financial resource utilization in a future period such as for general contingencies or capital projects. Such plans are subject to change and may never be actually authorized or result in expenditures.

B. Fund Equity Deficits

The Redevelopment Administration Special Revenue Fund had a deficit of $176,571 at September 30, 2011, which is expected to be eliminated with future tax increment revenues.

The Airport Enterprise Fund had a deficit amounting to $1,062,181 as of September 30, 2011, which is expected to be eliminated with future revenues.

Note 9. Pension Plans

A. Deferred Compensation Plans

City employees may defer a portion of their compensation under a City-sponsored deferred compensation plan created in accordance with Internal Revenue Code Section 457. Under this plan participants are not taxed on the deferred portion of their compensation until it is distributed to them; distributions may be made only at termination, retirement, death, or in an emergency as defined by the Plan.

The Plan is established as a trust managed through contract with the International City Managers' Association (ICMA). As such the assets of the plan are not subject to claims by creditors of the city, and the assets of the plan are not reflected in the city's financial statements.

B. Post-Employment Benefits

The City provides post-retirement health, dental, and vision care benefits for retirees. The benefits vary depending upon the years of service of the retiree. All employees are eligible to participate in the plan upon retirement. At September 30, 2011, 40 retirees participated in this plan at a cost to the City of $90,925 for insurance premiums. The City finances the plan on a pay-as-you-go basis.

C. California Public Employees Retirement System

The City contracts with the California Public Employees Retirement System (PERS), an agent multiple-employer public employee defined benefit retirement plan that acts as a common investment and administrative agent for participating local and state governmental agencies in California.

The City participates in two plans under PERS, the Safety Employees plan and the Miscellaneous Employees plan. All permanent City employees participate in PERS. Benefits vest after five years of service and are payable monthly for life upon retirement. Employees may retire at age 50 years with five years of credited service and receive between 1.426 percent and 2 percent of their average annual salary during their three highest years of employment for each credited service year. Benefits for City employees are established by contract with PERS in accordance with provisions of the Public Employees' Retirement Law.

Benefits increase with age and credited service years up to maximums of between 2.418 percent and 2.7 percent for each credited service year. A credited service year is one year of full-time employment.

Although PERS requires City miscellaneous employees to contribute 7 percent of their annual salary and safety employees to contribute 9 percent of their annual salary, the City's labor contracts require the City to pay all PERS contributions. These benefit provisions and all other requirements are established by state statute and city ordinance. Contributions necessary to fund PERS on an actuarial basis are determined by PERS and its Board of Administration.

D. Funding Status and Progress

The amounts shown in the following table as the "pension benefit obligation" for PERS meet a standardized disclosure measure of the present value of pension benefits, adjusted for the effects of projected salary increases and step-rate benefits estimated to be payable in the future as a result of employee service to date. The measure is intended to help users assess the funding status of pension plans on a going-concern basis, assess progress made in accumulating sufficient assets to pay benefits when due, and make comparisons among employers. The measure is the actuarial present value of credited projected benefits and is independent of the funding method used to determine contributions.

The PERS pension benefit obligation was computed as part of an actuarial valuation performed as of June 30, 2010. Significant actuarial assumptions used in the valuation include (a) a rate of return on the investment of present and future assets of 8.5 percent a year compounded annually; (b) projected salary increases of 4.5 percent a year compounded annually, attributable to inflation; (c) no additional projected salary increases attributable to seniority/merit; and (d) no post-retirement benefit increases.

Total overfunded pension benefit obligation applicable to the City's employees as of June 30, 2010, was as follows:

Pension Benefit Obligation	
Retirees and beneficiaries currently receiving benefits and terminated employees not yet receiving benefits	$17,912,350
Current employees:	
Accumulated employee contributions including allocated investment earnings	12,344,209
Employer-financed vested	12,274,132
Employer-financed nonvested	189,630
Total Pension Benefit Obligation	42,720,321
Net Assets Available for Benefits, at Smoothed Market Value (market value was $55,075,002 at June 30, 2010)	51,285,037
Overfunded Pension Benefit Obligation	$ 8,564,716

E. Actuarially Determined Contribution Requirements and Contributions Made

PERS uses the Entry Age Normal Actuarial Cost Method, which is a projected benefit cost method that takes into account those benefits that are expected to be earned in the future as well as those already accrued. According to this cost method, the normal cost for an employee is the level amount that would fund the projected benefit if it were paid annually from date of employment until retirement. PERS uses a modification of the Entry Age Cost Method in which the employer's total normal cost is expressed as a level percentage of payroll.

The significant actuarial assumptions used to compute the actuarially determined contribution requirement are the same as those used to compute the pension benefit obligation, as previously described.

Contributions to PERS are made in accordance with actuarially determined requirements computed through an actuarial valuation performed as of year-end. Total pension contributions, reduced by PERS surplus used, were as follows for the fiscal year ended September 30, 2011:

	Amount	Percent of Covered Payroll
Covered payroll	$8,302,279	
Total payroll	$9,972,636	
Normal cost contributions	$ 887,622	10.7%
Employee contributions paid by the City	684,642	8.2
Total normal cost	1,572,264	18.9
PERS surplus used	(507,224)	(6.1)
Net PERS contributions	$1,065,040	12.8

F. Trend Information

Trend information gives an indication of the progress made in accumulating sufficient assets to pay benefits when due. PERS systemwide 10-year end information may be found in the California PERS Annual Reports.

For the years ending June 30, 2010, 2009, 2008, 2007, and 2006, net assets available for benefits funded 120 percent, 113 percent, 123 percent, 112 percent, and 107 percent of the pension benefit obligation, and the overfunded pension benefit obligation represented 95 percent, 61 percent, 92 percent, 44 percent, and 27 percent of covered payroll, respectively. For the years ending September 30, 2011, 2010, 2009, 2008, and 2007, the City's PERS contributions, made in accordance with actuarially determined requirements, were 19 percent, 17 percent, 16 percent, 17 percent, and 18 percent respectively, of covered payroll.

Note 10. Risk Management

A. Insurance Coverage

The City is a member of the Public Agency Risk Sharing Authority of California (PARSAC), a joint powers authority that provides annual general liability coverage up to $10,000,000 in the aggregate and workers' compensation insurance coverage up to statutory limits. The City retains the risk for the first $250,000 in both general liability claims and workers' compensation claims.

PARSAC is governed by a board consisting of representatives from member municipalities. The board controls the operations of PARSAC, including selection of management and approval of operating budgets, independent of any influence by member municipalities beyond their representation on the Board.

The City's premiums are based upon the following factors: claims history, total payroll, the City's exposure, the results of an on-site underwriting inspection, total insurable values, and employee classification ratings. Actual surpluses or losses are shared according to a formula developed from overall loss costs and spread to member entities on a percentage basis after a retrospective rating that generally occurs in the third year after the completion of the program year.

B. Liability for Uninsured Claims

The Governmental Accounting Standards Board (GASB) requires municipalities to record their liability for uninsured claims and to reflect the current portion of this liability as an expenditure in their financial statements. As discussed previously, the City has coverage for such claims, but it has retained the risk for the deductible, or uninsured, portion of these claims. The City's liability for uninsured claims is limited to worker's compensation and general liability, and was estimated by management based on prior years' claims experience as follows:

	Worker's Compensation	General Liability	Total
Ending balance, September 30, 2010	$490,000	$25,000	$515,000
Provision for current and prior fiscal year claims and claims incurred but not reported (IBNR)	318,873	381,345	700,218
Claims paid	(318,373)	(39,811)	(358,184)
Ending balance, September 30, 2011	$490,500	$366,534	$857,034

The City has recorded these liabilities as repayable from available expendable resources in the General Fund. In addition to these amounts, the City has also designated $510,000 and $750,000 of general fund balance for worker's compensation future claims and general liability future claims to comply with requirements of PARSAC.

Note 11. Commitments and Contingencies

The City is subject to litigation arising in the normal course of business. In the opinion of the City Attorney, there is no pending litigation that is likely to have a material adverse effect on the financial position of the City.

Note 12. Dependence upon Tourism Industry

Historically, 25 percent of the City's General Fund revenues comes from the collection of transient occupancy taxes, 17 percent is collected from property tax payments, and 15 percent is derived from sales tax collections.

The hotel/motel industry accounts for all the transient occupancy tax collected, in excess of 7 percent of all property taxes collected, and a significant portion of all sales taxes collected. Consequently, a downturn in the tourism industry for the City will result in a substantial reduction in General Fund revenues available to pay all of the City's obligations. In the event of a downturn in the tourism industry, the City may have insufficient revenues in its General Fund to pay all of its obligations.

Suggested Readings

Anderson, John E. *Public Finance—Principles and Policy.* New York, N.Y.: Houghton Mifflin Company, 2003.

Berne, Robert. *The Relationships Between Financial Reporting and the Measurement of Financial Condition.* Norwalk, Conn.: Governmental Accounting Standards Board, 1992.

Berne, Robert, and Richard Schramm. *The Financial Analysis of Governments.* Upper Saddle River, N.J.: Prentice Hall, 1986.

Bowman, Woods, and Roland Calia. *Evaluating Local Government Financial Health.* Chicago, Ill.: The Civic Federation, 1997.

Chase, Bruce W., and Robert H. Phillips. "GASB 34 and Government Financial Condition—An Analytical Toolbox." Government Finance Review, April 2004, pp. 26–31.

Fisher, Ronald. *State and Local Public Finance,* 3rd ed. Florence, KY: South-Western College Publishers, 2007.

Gruber, Jonathan. *Public Finance and Public Policy,* 2nd ed. New York, NY: Worth Publishers, 2008.

International City/County Management Association. *Evaluating Financial Condition: A Handbook for Local Government.* ICMA, 2003.

Razek, Joseph R., Martin R. Ives, and Gordon A. Hosch. *Introduction to Government and Non-for-Profit Accounting,* 5th ed. Upper Saddle River, N.J.: Prentice Hall, 2004.

Revsine, Lawrence, Daniel W. Collins, and W. Bruce Johnson. *Financial Reporting & Analysis,* 2nd ed. Upper Saddle River, N.J.: Prentice Hall, 2002.

Rosen, Harvey S., and Ted Gayer. *Public Finance.* Boston, Mass., McGraw-Hill/Irwin, 2007.

Wilson, Earl R., and Susan C. Kattelus. *Accounting for Governmental and Nonprofit Entities,* 13th ed. Boston, Mass.: McGraw-Hill/Irwin, 2004.

APPENDIX 15-A

Bond Ratings

Bonds are discussed in Chapter 6. When people consider buying a bond, one of the key factors in their decision is whether the bond issuer will be able to make the required debt service (interest and principal) payments. Bond buyers (lenders) are also concerned about whether the interest rate they will earn on the bond is sufficient to reimburse them for the risks they take when they buy the bond. Bond ratings are a system of providing information about the financial stability of bond issuers, and therefore about the risk of buying a bond. The more financially stable the borrower, the better the rating, and the lower the interest rate the borrower must pay to attract lenders. The financial condition analysis principles discussed in Chapter 15 are critical to assessing a government and assigning a rating to its bonds.

FACTORS AFFECTING INTEREST RATES

A number of factors influence bond interest rates: general economic conditions, the duration of the loan, and the financial condition of the borrower. Interest rates on a bond issue are also influenced by other factors, such as whether the bond has call provisions, and if so what they are, whether there is bond insurance or not, whether tax or other revenue streams are pledged to repayment versus just the general credit of the borrower, and many other technical factors that are beyond the scope of this book.

When the economy is booming, interest rates tend to be high, since there are many potential borrowers competing for money. Businesses want to borrow money to finance major expansions. When the economy is in recession, few businesses are borrowing money to expand their businesses. The lower demand for loans, combined with federal monetary policy intended to stimulate the economy, tends to result in lower interest rates during recessions.

The longer the duration of a bond, generally the higher the interest rate it commands. There are several reasons for this higher rate. First, investors sacrifice liquidity when they buy a bond, and the longer the term of the bond, the riskier it is for them. They may need cash at a time when interest rates

have risen and the value of the bond has fallen. That might cause them to have to sell the bonds at a loss. Next, the longer the duration, the harder it is to accurately anticipate inflation rates over the life of the loan. Unexpectedly high inflation may raise overall interest rates, and therefore lower the present value of the future principal payment. Investors may demand a premium to cover that risk. Finally, some argue that it is partly a case of supply and demand. More people have money available to lend for short periods than for long periods. Therefore the price (interest rate) for a long-term loan will be higher.

Another key factor in determining interest rates is the credit-worthiness of the borrower. Lenders want some assurance that they will be repaid. The greater the chance that the borrower will not be able to repay, the higher the interest rate demanded by the lender to reward them for taking the risk. The elements of financial condition that were discussed in Chapter 15 are critical to how likely a government is to be able to pay its debt service. But how are individual lenders supposed to assess the likelihood that a borrower will be able to make its required debt service payments? Do they each have to perform an assessment of a government's financial condition? No. "Bond rating" organizations perform analyses and convey their assessments to the public via ratings that they assign to bond issues.

RATING ORGANIZATIONS

Three major organizations rate bonds: Moody's Investors Services, Standard & Poor's, and Fitch Ratings. These private firms issue a credit-worthiness report in exchange for a fee paid by the issuer. Part of the report is a letter rating for the bond issue. Moody's uses a scale of Aaa, Aa, A, Baa, and so forth, with Aaa being the best possible rating. Standard & Poor's and Fitch use a similar scale of AAA, AA, A, BBB, and so forth. A rating of Aaa or AAA ("triple A") is the best rating issued. It is generally indicative of either an organization that is financially extremely strong or a bond issuance for which the issuer has purchased insurance.

Four major organizations insure tax-exempt bonds: MBIA, AMBAC, Financial Guaranty Insurance Corporation (FGIC), and Financial Security Assurance (FSA). The insurance guarantees payment of principal and interest if the bond issuer defaults. Bond issuers pay a premium to acquire such insurance. Since the insurance company guarantees payment, the bond issue gets a rating based on the financial strength of the insurer. Although the premiums are costly, the issuer will typically have a better bond rating with the insurance. A better rating means the bond is less risky. Therefore, the interest rate demanded by investors is lower. Whether the cost of insuring a bond issue is justified by the savings in interest cost must be decided on a case-by-case basis.

A government will seek insurance if the combined cost of interest and insurance is lower than the cost of interest alone without insurance. In some cases, a government will not be able to issue a bond without insurance. Bond insurance has increased the liquidity of the municipal bond market, raising credit-worthiness to the highest levels for many different types of bonds.

Rating agencies base their ratings on a number of factors, generally broken down into four categories: financial operations, debt profile, economic indicators, and managerial ability. First is a financial analysis of the issuer. Such analysis will focus on issues such as existing outstanding debt, the revenue base, current tax levels (for governments), and many other factors related directly to the finances of the issuer. In addition the general economy is evaluated. A city with a healthy economy and growing population base might receive a better credit rating than one with urban blight and declining population and industry. The quality of the issuer's management is also considered. Issues specifically related to the bond, such as its maturity, are also considered.

Some issuers receive poor ratings. Typically a rating below BBB is not considered to be good enough to be *investment grade.* That means that the bonds, often called *junk bonds* or *high-yield bonds,* are speculative investments. Many organizations have rules that prevent them from acquiring bonds that are not considered investment grade. As a result, the demand for such bonds tends to be limited. Such bonds have to pay substantially higher interest rates in order to attract investors.

GUARANTEES AND LETTERS OF CREDIT

As noted, sometimes credit ratings are enhanced by the presence of bond insurance. Bond ratings may also be improved if state guarantees or bank *letters of credit* support the bond issuance.

A state guarantee exists if the state officially takes on the burden of making required bond payments if there would otherwise be a default. For example, a housing authority might issue bonds that would normally be *revenue bonds,* paid off by tenants' rents or homeowners' mortgage payments. Therefore, if the authority's revenues fall short, it might not be able to make required bond payments. The state might have a fund from which it guarantees to make up any shortfall in the housing authority revenues. This would raise the bond rating, although not to a triple A level, unless the state has a triple A level itself. Another common form of state enhancement is the moral obligation, in which the state obligates itself to provide funds in the event of a revenue shortfall. Moral obligations can take many forms and consequently vary in the level of actual credit enhancement they provide.

Another potential way of improving a bond rating is to secure a letter of credit (LOC) from a bank. Such a letter is a guarantee from the bank to make agreed-upon payments. LOCs are often used by issuers who have issued variable rate debt, to offset the exposure posed by fluctuating interest rates. This tends to be a limited way to improve bond ratings because bonds may be issued for longer time periods and larger amounts of money than a bank will be willing to secure with a LOC.

Key Terms from This Appendix

high yield bonds.   See *junk bonds.*

investment grade.   A bond with a rating high enough (usually above BBB) that it is not considered to be a speculative investment. Many organizations have rules that prevent them from acquiring bonds that are not considered to be investment grade.

junk bonds.   A bond that has a rating below that required to be *investment grade.* Such bonds are considered to be speculative investments and generally must pay a higher interest rate to attract investors.

letter of credit (LOC).   A guarantee from a bank to make agreed upon payments.

revenue bonds.   Bonds that are backed only by the revenues from a specific, limited source. The full taxing power of the government is not pledged in support of revenue bonds.

INDEX